DEATH
OF A
GUNFIGHTER

DEATH
OF A
GUNFIGHTER

The Quest for Jack Slade,
the West's Most Elusive Legend

Dan Rottenberg

WESTHOLME
Yardley

Frontispiece: A pair of Colt 1851 Navy revolvers, the type of gun carried by Jack Slade.

First Westholme Paperback 2010
© 2008 Dan Rottenberg

Maps © 2008 Westholme Publishing, LLC
Maps by Tracy Dungan

Westholme Publishing, LLC

Eight Harvey Avenue

Yardley, Pennsylvania 19067

Visit our Web site at www.westholmepublishing.com

For additional background material related to this book, including a Slade genealogy and profiles of the principal characters, visit www.deathofagunfighter.com

First Printing: April 2010

10 9 8 7 6 5 4 3 2 1

ISBN: 978-1-59416-112-4

Printed in United States of America

To the memory of my mother

Lenore G. Rottenberg

who taught me to look at the big picture in every situation

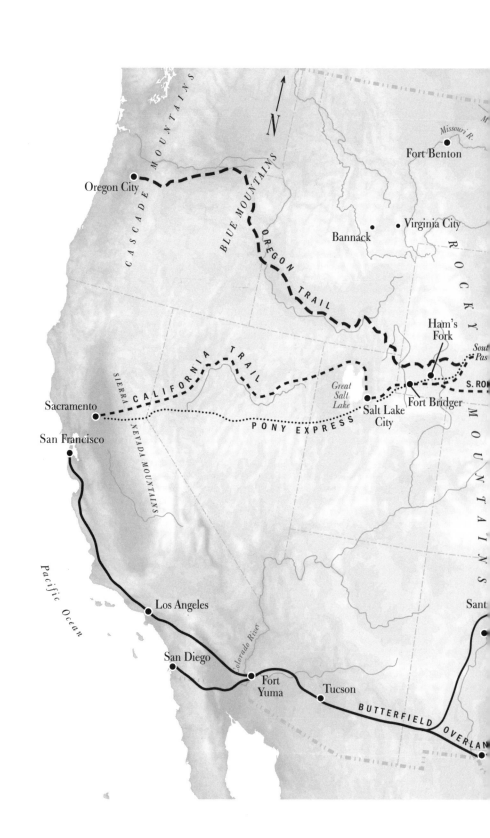

The World of Joseph Alfred Slade
1831 - 1864

Missouri River

0   250   500

Miles

lpin

N

Missouri River

orseshoe
Station
Fort Laramie

Julesburg

Fort Kearny

CENTRAL OVERLAND

PONY EXPRESS

LEAVENWORTH AND PIKE'S PEAK EXPRESS CO.

Blue R.

St. Joseph

Leavenworth

Atchison

Kansas City

St. Louis

Carlyle

Bent's Fort

SANTA FE TRAIL

CIMARRON CROSSING

Dodge City

Arkansas River

Fort Scott

Fort Smith

We cross the prairie as of old
Our fathers crossed the sea,
To make the West as they the East
The homestead of the free!

—*John Greenleaf Whittier, "The Kansas Emigrants," 1854*

We are very much like the classicists in our dependence upon a few sources of doubtful merit.

—*Western historian J. W. Smurr, Montana, 1958*

CONTENTS

✳

PREFACE

I first encountered Joseph Alfred "Jack" Slade in 1951 in the pages of *The Pony Express*, a children's book by Samuel Hopkins Adams. I was nine years old at the time and found myself instinctively drawn to this unstable roughneck who, when handed a seemingly impossible assignment, fulfilled it beyond anyone's wildest expectations, only to be destroyed by the weight of the burden. On the naïve presumption that I was the first person to feel such a kinship with Slade, I resolved to write a novel about him. Eventually I discovered that the historical Slade was far more extraordinary than anything my imagination could have conjured up. And so a childhood curiosity about Slade has blossomed into a lifelong quest to find and understand him.

As a wagonmaster and stagecoach mail superintendent in the 1850s and 1860s, Slade organized mobs of unruly men and animals into efficient teams capable of defying floods, droughts, blizzards, outlaws, and hostile Indians. In a land devoid of courts and law enforcement (present-day Nebraska, Colorado, and Wyoming), he functioned as a benevolent prairie feudal lord, almost single-handedly protecting settlers, emigrants, stagecoach passengers, and the U.S. Mail. By maintaining order along the roughest division of the Central Overland stagecoach line on the eve of the Civil War, Slade enabled the government in Washington to maintain contact with the Pacific at a time when California with all its riches threatened to secede from the Union. He helped launch the fabled Pony Express, and once the war began, Slade's presence enabled the gold and silver of the West to flow to the East Coast banks that financed the Union cause.

Famous Western figures like Wild Bill Hickok, Wyatt Earp, Bat Masterson, and Buffalo Bill Cody owed their exaggerated reputations largely to the promotional talents of Eastern journalists, dime novelists, and carnival publicists. Slade, by contrast, was the genuine article: He remained on the job for four years at a time when other would-be Western heroes burned out within months. His exploits, such as having shot and killed a man "in cold blood" years before gunfights became a hallmark of the West, can truly be said to have inspired the myth of the gunslinger.

Yet this same gifted and courageous leader, a man once known across the Great Plains as "the law west of Kearny," ultimately degenerated into a brawling drunk incapable of managing himself, much less wagon trains and stagecoach lines. In the process Slade lost not only his life but his reputation as well. His name, as one acquaintance put it, "became synonymous for all that is infamous and cruel in human character."[1] In this respect Slade makes a most unlikely hero. He held no strong political convictions (if anything, as the son of a slaveholding former Virginian, his sympathies probably lay with the South). He shared all the harsh frontier prejudices against Indians and the French, and no doubt against blacks as well. He was an alcoholic who became a dangerous bully when drunk. Yet at a critical moment when the future of the Union was in peril, this manifestly flawed individual rose to the occasion.

Slade's enigmatic life seems a natural subject for historical investigation. Yet three obstacles have caused most historians to keep their distance.

One reason is the paucity of reliable documentary material by Slade or about him. "No character in the history of the West more deserves a book than Jack Slade," the Western historian Raymond Settle once observed in a private letter. "But in my opinion no book on him, true to history, will ever be written. There are too many gaps in his life, too many unknowns."[2] In addition, despite abundant evidence that Slade could read and write, he left no written personal record. The only surviving statements from Slade's own hand or mouth are two prosaic affidavits about operations of the Central Overland stage line, which he provided to Congressional investigating committees in 1859 and

1862. For his thoughts or motives we must rely on the uncertain recollections of others.

The second difficulty in exploring Slade's history is the abundance of *fictitious* material he inspired. Slade was a man about whom a great deal was written and spoken, much of it false. Mark Twain's sensationalized portrait of Slade in *Roughing It* misled historians for generations after its publication in 1872. Slade himself encouraged many legends of his terrifying deeds, as a means of enhancing his effectiveness as a one-man peacekeeping force. Many writers, confronted with the challenge of sifting the facts about Slade from the fiction, have thrown up their hands and embraced what some of them call "the higher truth of good fiction." And consequently the Slade of history has long been overshadowed by the Slade of Western fantasy.

The third barrier to a full understanding of Slade is the complexity of his character. He resists neat categorization: he was neither a lawman nor an outlaw, nor a cowboy nor a farmer. He was both a gentleman and a terror. He could not even be labeled a good man or a bad one. In his last years he was more than a bit of both. There was simply nobody quite like Slade in the history of the West.

As a consequence, most Western historians have left Slade and his legacy in the hands of yarn-spinners and folklorists. So while Hickok (known in his prime as "the Slade of western Kansas"),[3] Cody, and the rest became household names even into the twenty-first century, Slade was forgotten by all but a handful of Western scholars.

Still, almost from the moment of Slade's death, a small but dedicated assortment of writers, Western history buffs and amateur detectives have scoured cowboy memoirs, pioneer letters, courthouse records, cemeteries, and archives in the hope of answering such tantalizing questions as: Was Slade a sadistic killer? Or did he cultivate that reputation as a means of maintaining order along his Central Overland division? Or both? Did Slade leave his home in Carlyle, Illinois, as a fugitive from the law? Precisely what was he doing during the "missing" eleven years between his discharge from the Army in 1848 and his reappearance as a superintendent of the Central Overland stage line in 1859? Where did his wife, the dashing horsewoman Maria Virginia Slade, come from, how did they meet, and what became of her after his death? Was Slade ever an outlaw? Above all, what caused Slade, at the height of his power and prestige, to deteriorate into a helpless drunk?

In each generation since his death a new band of Slade devotees has arisen to tackle these questions. This group includes a former chief justice of the Montana Supreme Court, Llewellyn L. Callaway, whose father knew Slade and who later wrote a monograph on Slade. In the 1920s the author Arthur Chapman interviewed surviving Pony Express riders for their memories of Slade. In the 1950s, Dean DuComb, a former title clerk in Clinton County, Illinois, where Slade was born, unearthed information about Slade's origins. In the 1960s Dabney Otis Collins, a Denver advertising salesman, pursued Slade through cemeteries and censuses and found documentary clues to Slade's previously unknown whereabouts in the 1850s. Collins's writings in turn inspired a Montana probate judge named John B. McClernan to locate Slade's probate papers in the courthouse attic in Virginia City, Montana, as well as Slade's military records at the National Archives. (McClernan's subsequent book, self-published in 1978, exemplifies the esoteric nature of Slade scholarship: its thirteen pages of text are followed by forty-nine pages of notes and appendices.) In the 1980s a legal editor in Indiana named Richard Patterson delved into Mark Twain's papers and found convincing evidence that Twain's depiction of Slade in *Roughing It* had little factual basis. In the 1990s Roy O'Dell of Cambridge, England, traced Slade's genealogy back to eighteenth-century Britain. In the 2000s a retired Wyoming academic named Lawrence Silvey contributed a monograph about the mysterious origins and the equally mysterious demise of Slade's wife.

Slade aficionados built on the efforts of their predecessors, but none has previously assembled the pieces into a work that would tell his story in the context of his era. This book is the first full-length treatment of Slade's life and times. My purpose is not merely to reconstruct a fascinating true story, but to provide future researchers with the tools to pick up where I have left off. I believe we have barely begun to scratch the surface of Joseph Alfred Slade and the West he inhabited.

PART I

*

Prospects

CARAVAN OF EMIGRANTS FOR CALIFORNIA.
(Crossing the Great American Desert in Nebraska.)

A wagon train of emigrants bound for California, engraved around 1850. The emigrants' customary westward route took on many names—the Oregon Trail, the Emigrant Trail, the Mormon Trail, and the Overland Trail—but as far as the Rocky Mountains, it was essentially the same. Here Jack Slade first made his name as a wagonmaster. (*Library of Congress*)

Chapter 1

THE MAN AND
HIS MOMENT

∗

If you cross the Union Pacific tracks and the South Platte River from Julesburg and head west along the River Road, you will soon find yourself alone. No motorist stumbles accidentally upon this gravel strip, which extends only some 10 miles and leads nowhere. Nor will you encounter much traffic anywhere else in this remote northeast corner of Colorado: Sedgwick County contains fewer than 2,800 inhabitants, most of them clustered in Julesburg, the county seat. In the congested East, a town as small as Julesburg might not even appear on a state map; but here it is the largest community for 25 miles in any direction.

I have come to this desolate road on a historical detective quest. My quarry has been dead for nearly a century and a half, but even in death he has eluded a long line of distinguished authors and Western devotees, just as in life he eluded his friends and foes alike—everyone, in fact, but his worst enemy: himself. I have pursued his trail for half a century on a mission to sift the truth of my character's life from his legend. Where Mark Twain, Zane Grey, and the late Montana Chief Justice Llewellyn Link Callaway have tried and failed, I am determined to succeed.

My guide is Lee Kizer, a dapper octogenarian Julesburg barber and real estate developer as well as the town's former mayor, who in the process of cutting hair for local old-timers over more than half a century inevitably evolved into a history buff. "All of them would talk," he says. "I'm just sorry I didn't write any of it down." Of course, Kizer reminds me, oral recollections delivered from a barber chair pose a unique challenge to any seeker of truth: "People always tell negative stories—never nice ones. It's still that way today."[1]

A mile or two west of Julesburg Kizer indicates a steep bank sweeping down from the South Platte River on our right. "This is Devil's Dive," he says. "The hill was so steep here that the stagecoaches had to slow down to climb it. The passengers would get out and walk. That's when the outlaws would swoop down from the river and hold them up." But Devil's Dive is not what has brought me here, so we continue on.

A bit farther ahead, some 5 miles west of Julesburg, we reach a seemingly nondescript stretch that separates the River Road from the South Platte River to the north. Two historical markers stand next to each other along the roadside. Here Kizer instructs me to pull over. "This is the place," he says.

At first glance it's difficult to conceive that anything of consequence ever happened here. The weeds and brush offer no hint that on this barren spot, near the bank of a largely dried-out river, the future of the Union's connection to California and indeed its ultimate survival once hung in the balance. For several minutes I search hopefully for some evidence of what transpired here in the fall of 1859. And upon close inspection I find it.

Indented in the ground are sets of parallel grooves, pointing north toward the river—tracks permanently imprinted upon the soil a century and a half earlier by the cumulative weight of thousands of covered wagons headed west. Homesteaders seeking fertile valleys in Oregon, Mormons seeking sanctuary in Utah, prospectors seeking gold in California, freighters hauling goods from the East—all of their wagons forded the river here because it was the shallowest point along the great east-west waterway called the Platte River.

The earliest explorers, on foot and in pack trains, had hugged the shoreline of this river and its western forks—the North Platte and South Platte—as they made their way west. Over the next century and a half these same Platte rivers provided the routes followed successively by stagecoaches, telegraph lines, railroads, highways, and, most recently, Interstates.

But the Platte and its tributaries were not navigable channels; they were shallow, treacherous, meandering streams—"a mile wide and an inch deep," as pioneers described them. When heavy snowmelt in the Rocky Mountains scoured the encroaching vegetation on these riverbanks, it produced quicksand and gravel on the river bottom, so that sometimes eighteen yoke of oxen were required to drag a single wagon across.[2] Thus in the 1840s and 1850s the great challenge for westbound emigrants lay in the continuing search for a river crossing. At this so-called Upper California Crossing the South Platte was only a half-mile wide and no deeper than four feet;[3] and after its discovery in 1858 it was not uncommon for emigrant trains of a hundred wagons or more to wait patiently here along the riverbank—often for hours, sometimes for days—for their turn to splash across the South Platte. These tracks imprinted in the ground are their calling cards.

In those days the South Platte reached to the very point where Kizer and I now stand; but today, its water level having been depleted by runoff from suburban sprawl around Denver, some 200 miles upstream, the South Platte is barely visible in the distance. Nevertheless, Kizer reminds me, "There are still several wagons buried in there—they got stuck in the quicksand."

Even before the first wagon trains passed through, this crossing had been used by fur trappers, hunters, and settlers attracted by the Platte Valley's abundance of buffalo, antelope, beaver, and wild horses. And long before these first white explorers knew of this site, hunting parties of the Sioux and especially the Cheyenne tribes used it as a crossing as well as a campground.

Still another new westbound multitude—prospectors, some 100,000 of them—lumbered through this spot after gold was discovered near Pike's Peak in 1858. These emigrants didn't cross the South Platte; instead they continued along the river's south bank toward the new mining hamlet of Denver City. But whatever the emigrants' destination—California, Oregon, the Great Salt Lake, or Denver—they all passed along this now virtually forgotten River Road. Today its official name is Sedgwick County Road 28; but once it bore the names of the great westbound routes that have captivated American imaginations ever since: the Oregon Trail, the Emigrant Trail, the Mormon Trail, the Overland Trail, and the Pony Express.

In the afternoon sun, I notice another hint of modern civilization's first presence here: a shiny reflection beneath the bushes. My close inspection reveals the source of the glare. Glass bottles, dozens of them, perhaps hundreds—far more than the current population of Sedgwick County could possibly generate—are strewn every few yards. These are not the sleek Coke or Absolut vodka bottles of an affluent, consumer-oriented twenty-first-century society, but narrow, greenish, unmarked containers, each one only eight inches long, its glass so thick that little space exists for any liquid inside. This is the "two-bit glass" that was filled with a vile combination of whiskey and as much water as a nineteenth-century saloonkeeper could get away with, to be foisted upon exhausted travelers for twenty-five cents and then discarded onto the prairie. These containers provide an enduring reminder of the combustible prime ingredients of frontier life: liquor, guns, boredom, and an excess of boisterous young single males preoccupied with proving their toughness and unrestrained by law enforcement or religion or the domesticating influence of women.[4]

One such saloon did a brisk trade here as early as 1858. Its proprietor, a French-Canadian trapper and Indian trader known along the Platte mostly as "Old Jules," first opened a ranch and an adobe trading post here to barter goods with the Sioux and Cheyenne hunters when they camped nearby. Although Jules was well-known to the Indians and white men alike who passed through, his surname remains a mystery to this day, mangled then and now into at least a half-dozen variations. (His widow, many years later, said the name was Beni or Benoit, but even she wasn't certain.) As westward freight traffic increased, Old Jules added a blacksmith shop, a warehouse, a stable, and a billiard saloon. When the first stagecoaches came through in 1859, he put up a large boardinghouse where passengers could sleep overnight. By then the stagecoach station and stables—long, one-story structures built of hewed cedar logs—were said to be the largest buildings along the 350-mile stretch between Fort Kearny in Nebraska Territory and Denver.

At first this cluster was called Jules Ranch or Jules Trading Post and finally Julesburg—not to be confused with the present-day town of Julesburg located 5 miles to the east. By the time this original Julesburg was burned down in 1865 by a raiding party of some 1,500 Cheyenne Indians, the village comprised a dozen buildings housing some fifty permanent residents. But from the first it was a nasty little place: a rendezvous for robbers, horse thieves, gamblers, and hard-boiled adventurers, by reputation the toughest town between the Missouri River and the Rocky Mountains.

When the newborn Jones & Russell stagecoach line to Denver acquired the failing Hockaday & Co. line to Salt Lake City in May 1859, Julesburg logically became the critical point where the two west-bound lines diverged, and Old Jules seemed the logical choice to man-age the company's station there. Old Jules lost no time in demonstrat-ing that he was the wrong man for the job—a petty hustler who per-ceived his new position only as an opportunity to enrich himself. From his first day, horses and other valuable company property began to dis-appear, often to be speedily returned for a reward arranged through Jules's kindly offices. Hay purchased by the company would unac-countably catch fire, and a ranchman offering hay for sale would, through Jules's intervention, make a lucrative sale to the company. Under these conditions Jones & Russell was hard put to keep its coaches on schedule and, more important, to fulfill its government contract to transport the U.S. Mail—the company's primary source of revenue.

Partly as a result of this mischief, by October 1859 Jones & Russell was out of business, its mail contract taken over by the newly organ-ized Central Overland California & Pike's Peak Express Company. The irrepressible frontier entrepreneur William H. Russell, who remained as president of the reorganized company, was deeply in debt and, in his desperation, concocted an audacious gamble to recoup his partnership's losses by winning a larger mail contract from the U.S. Post Office.

By the late 1850s the gold rush had transformed California into the richest state in the Union, if not the world, and nearly 400,000 people

had flocked there from all over the globe.[5] Yet it took three weeks for a
letter to reach California from the East Coast. William Russell proposed to supplement the Central Overland's heavy stagecoaches with
a unique mail system of lightweight couriers on horseback, provided
with fresh mounts at relay stations located every 10 or so miles
between St. Joseph, Missouri, and Sacramento. Such a "Pony
Express," he theorized, could reduce the cross-country delivery time
from three weeks to as few as eight days. In the process it would win
his stage line a much more lucrative U.S. Mail contract.

The scheme was critical not only to his company's survival but also
possibly to the nation's as well. At this very moment, decades of ten-
sion over slavery between America's northern and southern states
were coming to a violent head. A southern postmaster general was promoting the much longer southern "ox-bow" mail route to California,
at the expense of the more direct northern route operated by Russell's
Central Overland.[6] California had entered the Union as a free state in
1850, but it was filled with southern sympathizers and its loyalty to the
Union couldn't be taken for granted. Without a fast and reliable northern line of communication, it was conceivable that, as the North and
South moved apart, California would cast its lot with the South, or the
Pacific states might break off and form an independent federation of
their own.

Without California's gold wealth, the Union might be doomed. Yet
the Union's sole northern link with California in the fall of 1859 was
William Russell's struggling Central Overland line. And that line's viability depended largely on finding someone to clean up its most trou-
bled division. In effect that meant cleaning up Julesburg, which meant
confronting its de facto ruler, Old Jules himself.

The line's new superintendent, a dashing and rambunctious
Virginian named Benjamin Franklin Ficklin, concluded that Old Jules
must be replaced and probably driven away altogether, if not killed
outright. But Jules would not quietly quit the hamlet he had created
and now ruled. The closest government authority of any sort resided
nearly 175 miles to the northwest at Fort Laramie, but the soldiers stationed there exercised no police powers. Their sole task was to pacify
hostile Indian tribes, not to arrest civilian bandits and horse thieves.

In this society devoid of courts or sheriffs, Ficklin needed an enforcer. Such a position would require someone who was fearless, audacious, incorruptible, perhaps a bit crazy. Yet this same post also required someone capable of supervising stations, maintaining horses and supplies, meeting schedules and budgets, and hiring and managing coach drivers and stationkeepers. Who on earth would accept such a job?

Ficklin thought he knew such a man. Joseph Alfred Slade had fought in the Mexican War and captained freight trains along the Emigrant Trail. He had driven stagecoaches and supervised stagecoach lines. He liked to be called "Captain," supposedly in deference to his army rank. Slade's origins were murky, and in each new phase of his life he had compounded the confusion by assuming a variety of nicknames: "Alf," "Joe," "Jim," "Cap," and just plain "Slade" (although the name later used by Western writers—"Jack Slade"—didn't surface in print until 1871, years after his death).[7] He was something of a wild man, and word of mouth had amplified his fierce reputation wherever freighting men camped between the Missouri River and the Pacific.

It was said that Slade had fled his hometown in Illinois after killing a man with a rock during a fight. In the Mexican War, it was said, he had once killed nine men while on a reconnaissance mission. He was said to have participated in the storming of Chapultepec, the mountain fortress that guarded Mexico City. It was said that he had lived among Indians—or, conversely, that he had fought Indians and sliced off his victims' ears as souvenirs. It was said that he was a dead shot with either hand, and that he had killed men for sport. It was said that he was ferocious when drunk, and that he could take the fight out of most men just by looking at them. All told, it was said that Slade had killed twenty-six men. It was said that Slade was the most feared man west of the Mississippi, and that his hell-raising wife Virginia—a tall, striking, dark-haired former dance-hall girl, adept with both guns and horses— was feared more than he was.

But was any of this true? In a land without courts or newspapers, who could have tabulated and verified Slade's alleged twenty-six killings, other than Slade himself? And what could a potential employer like Ficklin make of another very contradictory set of Slade legends? For it was also said that Slade was educated, polite, soft-spoken, clean-shaven, rigorously honest, generous, even charming. It was said that Slade's father had served in the U.S. Congress, and that his stepfather had been the U.S. marshal for Kansas Territory during its guerrilla war over slavery barely two years earlier. According to some, Slade was descended from English gentry, and his family still engaged in the daily English practice of pausing for afternoon tea. It was said that Slade was devoted to his wife like few husbands in the West.

For all Slade's storied longevity on the frontier, the man Ficklin had chosen to drive the outlaw gangs from Julesburg was actually not yet twenty-nine years old. For all his oversized reputation, this Slade stood less than five-foot-eight with his boots on, hardly a physical match for the hulking Old Jules. Slade's build was not lean but husky; he weighed about 160 pounds. His hair was reddish rather than black or brown. Of Slade's physical characteristics, only his dark, piercing eyes could be described as intimidating. His preferred sobriquet of "Captain" actually derived from the wagon trains, not from the army (where he had never risen above the rank of private). And he had never come anywhere near the storming of Chapultepec.

Was it possible that the fearsome J. A. Slade was merely a figment of campfire imaginations? Or was Slade so inherently violent that the Central Overland would find him impossible to control? Was Slade a gentleman or a desperado?

At this urgent moment Ficklin couldn't afford the luxury of further investigation. In Slade's fearsome reputation Ficklin perceived an asset. Only the roughest fugitives and adventurers were attracted to overland freighting. In this trade, where disagreements were commonly settled with fist, knife, or pistol, only a boss with a touch of wildness could survive as long as Slade had lasted. Out there beyond the reach of lawyers and journalists, perception trumped reality. If Slade was *perceived* as a tough man, other tough men would respect him accordingly.

And so in the fall of 1859 Joseph Alfred Slade became superintendent of the Central Overland's Sweetwater Division, covering nearly 500 miles from Julesburg west toward the Rockies, the most dangerous section of the company's 1,200-mile route between the Missouri River and Salt Lake City. Now it was only a matter of time before Slade encountered the inevitable challenge uttered wherever boastful young men gathered in freighting trains, saloons, and mining camps throughout the West: Are you really as tough as you claim? And how will you prove it?

My journey to that South Platte riverbank sought to answer a larger question: Who, ultimately, was this Joseph Alfred Slade who had been summoned to save the Union's tenuous northern link to California at this critical moment? And what strange combination of human events had conspired to entrust this awesome task to such an unlikely hero?

Chapter 2

THE ROPEMAKER

∗

J oseph Alfred Slade's grandfather Charles Slade appears to have been the younger son of an English mercantile family.[1] He and his wife, Mary, were probably in their early thirties, with four or five children all under the age of ten, when they left England in the late 1790s to settle in Alexandria, Virginia.[2] At the time the mid-Atlantic states were the leading destination for many immigrants from English cities;[3] the Slades probably chose Alexandria because of their apparent relationship with the family of John Carlyle, one of early Alexandria's leading citizens.[4]

John Carlyle himself was a classic prototype of the eighteenth-century immigrant to America. As the second son of a landed Scottish family, he was deprived of an inheritance and consequently had been apprenticed to an English merchant firm. Released from his apprenticeship when he turned twenty-one in 1741, Carlyle emigrated to Virginia as the American representative of the English merchant William Hicks. Here Carlyle hoped to make "a fortune sufficient . . . to live independent."[5]

Alexandria, where he settled, had been founded by Scottish merchants who staked their future business hopes on the town's port on the south bank of the Potomac River, "with water sufficiently deep to launch a vessel of any rate or magnitude."[6] Alexandria soon became northern Virginia's most important port, shipping flour and tobacco to the West Indies, England and other parts of Europe. Having constructed a wharf along Alexandria's waterfront, John Carlyle compounded his success as an importer and exporter by marrying Sarah Fairfax, the daughter of one of colonial Virginia's leading families. Sarah's father, William Fairfax, was the business agent for his English cousin Thomas Lord Fairfax, who lived in England but owned more than five million acres of land in Virginia, comprising nearly one-quarter of the commonwealth. William Fairfax had also been a member and sometime president of Virginia's governing council. Sarah's brother George, in his capacity as a land surveyor, was an early associate and friend of America's future first president George Washington; and Sarah's sister Anne was married to Washington's brother Lawrence.[7] In 1753 John Carlyle settled his family in an elegant stone mansion whose prominent location (facing the river and the newly erected Fairfax County Courthouse) announced his position as the town's leading citizen.

But by the time Charles Slade and his family arrived, perhaps about 1798, John Carlyle had been dead for nearly twenty years, leaving only a single heir to survive into the nineteenth century. His in-laws, the Fairfaxes, remained an important presence in Alexandria, but much of their vast Virginia land holdings had been confiscated during the Revolution because of the family's loyalist sympathies.[8] Whatever connections the Slade family had with the Carlyles in England had landed them, for better or worse, in the soon to be created District of Columbia at the very heart of the new nation they had just adopted.

The available records suggest that Charles Slade flourished in Alexandria as a nail manufacturer and hardware merchant, selling everything from cut nails to anvils to cooking stoves.[9] The federal census of 1800 found the newly arrived Charles and his wife presiding over a household of ten people, including six children, a laborer, and one slave.[10] In August 1805 Charles (and presumably his family, now expanded to at least seven children) occupied a two-story frame double dwelling with a separate kitchen, smokehouse, washhouse, and stable. Charles also owned a three-story brick dwelling nearby. Both lots were still owned by Charles ten years later.

In 1809 Charles entered into a partnership in the rope-making business with one Thomas Grimshaw, offering "a general assortment of cordage and ship chandlery" at their shop on the Merchant's Wharf. After Grimshaw withdrew about a year later, Charles brought his fifteen-year-old third surviving son, also named Charles, into the business in 1812 and renamed it Charles Slade & Son.[11]

A clue to Charles's status within the community is suggested in the fact that both of his houses stood barely one block from the John Carlyle house, now occupied by Carlyle's sole surviving heir, his daughter Sarah Carlyle Herbert. Three of Charles's children eventually married children of the Episcopal minister and author Mason L. Weems, an early friend of George Washington and author of the first *Life of Washington* (in which Parson Weems created the legend of Washington and the cherry tree).[12]

All of this evidence, fragmentary as it may be, suggests that within a few years of his arrival Charles Slade had established himself as a civic figure in Alexandria. Though he may not have attained the wealth and prominence of the Carlyle and Fairfax families, he had achieved the sort of respectable level of comfort and stability that he and his wife had hoped to find when they left England.

Yet his younger sons confronted much the same dismal future prospects in Alexandria that Charles had suffered in England. Charles Slade was no longer bound by England's laws of primogeniture, but with seven children—including four sons who grew to adulthood—he was bound by a need to keep his properties intact. In a will he made out in December 1810, Charles left his property equally to his wife and children but designated his two eldest surviving sons, Richard and Henry, as his executors; and by the time Charles died in 1820 the two brothers had taken over their father's businesses.[13] Under the terms of Charles's will of 1810, his fifteen-year-old slave George was to be set free by 1822, along with "any other person of color that I may hereafter hold" who reached the age of twenty-seven. Charles's third son, Charles Jr., and his younger siblings would need to fend for themselves.

Like his older brothers, young Charles was born in England, probably about 1797.[14] In his youth he received a serviceable education in common schools, then worked for his father as a ropemaker. By the time Charles Jr., came of age, the best he could look forward to was a life spent down by the Potomac waterfront fashioning riggings for Alexandria's thriving shipbuilding industry.[15] For such modest opportunities in America, previous generations had voluntarily bound themselves to years of indentured servitude. But now a new phenomenon, observed only in America, and only since the Revolution—the law of rising expectations—had seized young Charles and his generation.

As families along the rapidly populating Eastern seaboard ran out of land, their younger male children—crowded out of their inheritances by an excess of siblings—turned their eyes westward. Why should any American—even an eldest son—settle for a modest lot in his father's town and a small voice in that community when vast acres—where he could create his own domain—were available for the taking farther west? Ever since George Rogers Clark had captured Kaskaskia from the British in 1778, tales had drifted eastward of "the American Bottom," an incredibly fertile section of the Mississippi River basin in what by 1809 had become the Territory of Illinois. Why should any Virginia farmer content himself with tobacco-stained land when more productive soil beckoned across the Alleghenies?

By the time young Charles Slade came of age in the wake of the War of 1812, the scales for people in his situation had tipped heavily in favor of moving west. His oldest brother Richard and two partners opened a hardware store in 1815, but the following March one partner withdrew, and the partnership dissolved altogether a few months later.[16] The younger Slade brothers confronted much the same unappetizing set of choices that younger siblings in their teens and twenties had faced in England: they could learn a trade, join the army, or go to sea. In America the big difference lay in the land opportunities along the frontier, waiting to be exploited.[17]

The Slade brothers actually enjoyed another option, for the Fairfax family was eager to keep them nearby in Alexandria and had offered them as much land as they wanted if they would settle and develop it. But the pressure of a growing population along the eastern seaboard was beginning to deplete Virginia's soil, so the Fairfax land no longer seemed so attractive. The Slade brothers apparently preferred a new start.[18]

Even given the temptations of the West, why would anyone leave the paved streets, frame houses, and relative security of a civilized East Coast community for the mud, isolation and danger of the unknown wilderness? In an age when antibiotics were unknown, the supposed dangers of the frontier paled beside the dangers to the human immune system. Yellow fever had driven the U.S. government out of Philadelphia in the 1790s before running its course just as inexplicably as it had arrived. Cholera, the nineteenth century's most horrible disease, struck cities and rural villages alike, seaports as well as inland farm communities, whites as well as Indians, London and Paris as well as Alexandria and New York. Yet as long as the cause of these diseases remained unknown, their arrival and departure seemed a matter of fate, bad luck or divine disfavor.[19] When the Slade brothers began their westward trek in 1816 they had no way of knowing that cholera was also beginning its westward journey from the far side of the globe. But like most of their contemporaries they understood instinctively that the risks of the unknown frontier were no greater than the risks of unknown bacilli. A man concerned about his health and longevity might as well take his chances on the Illinois frontier as anywhere else.

Thus in the spring of 1816, the brothers Charles, Richard and Thomas Slade bid their parents farewell, loaded an extensive stock of goods into wagons, and joined the exodus to the fertile "American Bottom." Young Charles Slade, the future father of the Central Overland superintendent Joseph Alfred Slade, financed the trip by borrowing funds from his older brother Henry (and possibly also from the Fairfax and Carlyle families).[20] Richard, the oldest brother, apparently went along on the journey to look after his younger brothers but had no intention of staying in Illinois; the genuine emigrants were Charles, then about nineteen, and his younger brother Thomas, then fifteen. They harbored a vague intention of establishing themselves as merchants in an area where general merchandise was inaccessible.[21] In Alexandria young Charles had been a ropemaker with limited prospects; in his new destination he would marshal his hitherto untapped reservoir of social, agricultural, and entrepreneurial skills to carve his own community out of the wilderness.

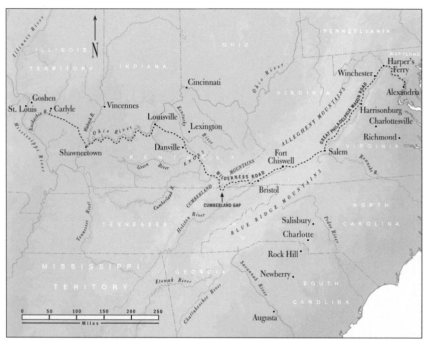

The Slade brothers' route from Alexandria, Virginia, to the future site of Carlyle, Illinois, in 1816 began along the Wilderness Road, America's primary avenue of westward migration since 1775.

The price inherent in the journey was huge: young Charles would never see his parents again.[22] But the potential opportunities seemed limitless, and in Charles Slade's case they exceeded all expectations, including his own. The next time the former Alexandria ropemaker returned to the District of Columbia, he would do so as a U.S. Congressman from the infant state of Illinois.

Chapter 3

THE PROMOTER

*

Wof 1816, they were hardly alone. Each year the roads to the
west were crowded from early spring to late fall with the sons of
Eastern families that had run out of land. In many of the nation's new
territories, Congress had offered undeveloped public land at two dollars an acre to anyone willing to settle there.[1] But the best land along
the rivers and highways was already taken. The roundabout westward
route followed by the three Slade brothers in the spring of 1816 was
dictated largely by existing roads, by the direction of other emigrants
with whom they traveled for mutual protection, and by their lack of a
clear idea as to their final destination. Because they had a wagon
loaded with goods and were riding their own horses, river travel was
not an option.[2] So the Slade brothers followed a familiar route blazed
by Daniel Boone more than forty years earlier.

From Alexandria they traveled northwest along the Potomac some
seventy miles to Harper's Ferry, Virginia, where they followed a road
leading some 250 miles southwest to Fort Chiswell in the Shenandoah
Valley. Here two heavily traveled roads—one from Harper's Ferry, the
other from Richmond in the east—converged to form the main branch
of the Wilderness Road, America's primary avenue of westward migration since 1775. This took them southwest for another two hundred
miles to the Cumberland Gap, the pass through the central

Appalachians where the southwestern corner of Virginia met the borders of Kentucky and Tennessee. From here the Slade brothers probably continued along the Wilderness Road to Louisville, then followed the south bank of the Ohio River for nearly 200 more miles—until, sometime in the early summer of 1816, they reached the western end of Kentucky, where a ferry large enough to carry the Conestoga wagons of new settlers transported them across the Ohio River to the settlement of Shawneetown in southern Illinois Territory. Here the Slades found a bustling Ohio River port town of some three hundred souls, where the French had exported salt from the nearby Saline Springs to the east for 150 years.

From Shawneetown the Slade brothers followed the Goshen Road as it meandered northwestward about 150 miles toward the Goshen settlement along the Mississippi River above Fort Cahokia, somewhat north of St. Louis. Like the Wilderness Road through the Appalachians, the Goshen Road had begun as hardly more than a collection of vague parallel paths cut by migrating buffalo herds. Indians searching for game learned to follow these routes as their easiest way through the tall, thick prairie grasses, which sometimes grew as high as seven feet.[3] By default, these trails became the primary east-west route for anyone traveling across Illinois Territory, and in about 1808 the Goshen Road had been widened to accommodate wagons heading from the salt works at Shawneetown on the Ohio to the Mississippi River.

For several days the Slades followed the Goshen Road as it made its serpentine way through virgin forests and broad prairies teeming with wildlife. Eventually the Slades passed through a settlement called Walnut Hill, just a few miles from what subsequently became the southern Illinois railroad junction of Centralia. Some 20 miles to the west, and still 50 miles east of Goshen, the Goshen Road reached a picturesque stream that the English called the Kaskaskia River, and that everyone colloquially called "the Okaw." This "river of many moods," as one observer described it, had once carried the war drum and many canoes for the Ottawa Indian chief Pontiac and, as recently as 1812, for the Potawatomi chieftain Metea. When the Slades arrived it was still being used by war messengers for the Sauk chief Black Hawk.[4]

The Slades, it is said, were captivated by the river's romantic beauty, by the richness of the soil through which it passed, and by the site's commercial potential as the point where the Goshen Road crossed another westward road, from Fort Vincennes in Indiana to St. Louis, some 50 miles to the west. A mail route had been operating along this road since 1805.[5] A natural ford, formed from the hard river bottom, made it easier to cross the river at this place on horseback or by wagon.[6]

On this spot—almost 1,000 miles from the Slades' previous home in Alexandria—dwelled a single white settler: a man named John Hill, who had arrived in 1811 or 1812 at the ford on the river's west bank.[7] Here he built a rudimentary pole cabin and established a flatboat ferry across the river, charging a toll to the travelers who used it.[8] In April 1815 Hill had filed the first claim for land in the records of what was then St. Clair County, for 160 acres.[9]

Hill had also built a crude blockhouse, some fifteen feet square, of large logs, which became known as Hill's Fort because it served not only as his home but also as a refuge for travelers seeking shelter from hostile Indians.[10] In theory the federal government had purchased the Indians' lands in Illinois in exchange for their agreement to move west of the Mississippi; but what seemed a reasonable transaction to the government seemed inexplicable to many Indians, who remained unwilling to abandon their familiar haunts and resentful of the whites who sought to displace them.

Despite these dangers, or perhaps oblivious to them, the Slade brothers chose this spot to pursue their destiny. Charles Slade acquired Hill's property and also entered claims to vast tracts of the surrounding land—289 acres in November 1816, and an additional 448 acres in July 1817, all at the Congressionally mandated price of two dollars per acre—and vigorously set to work to improve it.[11]

What became of Hill is lost to posterity;[12] from this point forward the story of this land becomes inseparable from the story of the middle brother, Charles Slade, Jr., who would be the father of Joseph Alfred Slade.

The frontier did not suit everyone, even within the Slade family. By 1818 Charles's older brother Richard had returned to Alexandria, where he operated a hardware store, married one of Parson Weems's daughters, and contemplated a permanent move to Europe.[13] But Charles himself remained, convinced that the raw materials of his dreams existed right there on the west bank of the Kaskaskia River.

Most people on the frontier—and indeed some 70 percent of all Americans at that time—made their living from farming,[14] and the Slades initially did the same. But the revolutionary McCormick reaping machine was still fifteen years in the future and "the meager profits of agriculture gained by the primitive methods of farming at that day," wrote a historian in 1903, "failed to satisfy Mr. Slade." As new emigrants settled nearby, Charles sought other economic outlets for his energies. Within a year of his arrival, Charles and a man named Hubbard bought a stock of goods and built a store not far from Hill's Fort, becoming the first merchants in that part of Illinois. As their clientele expanded in numbers and needs, Hubbard & Slade expanded its stock and became a flourishing business.[15] In 1818, when Illinois became the twentieth state in the union, Charles and another friend named Thomas F. Herbert hired a surveyor and laid out the streets and lots of a new town, which Charles named Carlyle in honor of his grandmother's family.[16] (The street where the Hubbard & Slade store stood was named Fairfax Street, presumably after John Carlyle's equally prominent in-laws in Alexandria.)[17]

The notion of a town in this forested wilderness was audacious on its face. Town dwellers were regarded, at best, as middlemen serving the farmers' needs and at worst as parasites draining the real wealth produced by farmers. So the challenge confronting Charles Slade and the town's other promoters, as a Carlyle writer noted in 1855, was: "How, then, could a country prosper when the farmers had to support a town-loafing population . . . when the farmer scarce outnumbered the townsmen?"[18]

Nevertheless, the presence of a town symbolized prosperity, so the idea appealed to the wishful thinking of settlers and speculators alike. And in any case, Charles Slade had little choice if he hoped to recover the $2,000 or so that he had invested in his land. Charles leaped to the task with alacrity, peddling lots by painting majestic but imaginary visions of grand business blocks, brownstone fronts, and palatial homes, all arranged to stunning architectural effect among the dramatic elevations and depressions skirting the western bank of the Kaskaskia.

"He soon created the impression that Carlyle was destined to become at no distant day the leading city in this part of Illinois," a local history noted in 1881. "Hence his lots found ready sale, and at extravagant prices. The spirit of speculation seemed to be contagious. The people of the surrounding country under the prevailing excitement were led to invest all their surplus money in these town lots. The town grew like a western mining village."[19] One abstract from 1819 indicates that a lot sold for $500—an extraordinary amount for a place where Charles and his brothers had paid just two dollars an acre only three years earlier.[20]

Among the earliest arrivals in 1818 was an enterprising middle-aged Virginian named John Kain, who had moved his wife, Mary Darke Kain, and five children to Ohio a few years earlier and had subsequently moved them farther west to Illinois. Mary Darke, then forty-eight, was descended from an English family that had arrived in Bucks County, Pennsylvania, in the late seventeenth century and moved to western Virginia in 1741; the Darkes were said to be "large people, kind-hearted and obliging, possessing a fiery but quickly controlled temper."[21] At Carlyle, Kain bought several hundred acres near the Slades, opened a hotel, and shortly became one of the new town's most substantial citizens.[22] The following June, Charles Slade married Kain's nineteen-year-old daughter Mary.[23] In much the same way that John Carlyle's marriage to Sarah Fairfax had established him as Alexandria's leading citizen, Charles Slade's marriage to Mary Kain—followed soon thereafter by the birth of a son William in 1820, another son named Charles Richard in 1822, and a daughter named Mary in 1824—reinforced Charles's position as Carlyle's first citizen.[24] But the burden of developing the town—and thus justifying the exorbitant prices his neighbors had paid for their lots—rested largely on the shoulders of this consummate civic booster.

Immediately Charles set about constructing the basic building blocks of the future metropolis his mind envisioned. His first order of business was the establishment of a post office—the town's first formal recognition by the outside world—which was granted in March 1819. Charles's partner Thomas Herbert served as its first postmaster; when Herbert withdrew from the job two years later, Charles assumed the position himself for at least the next seven years.[25] The post office was housed in the Hubbard & Slade store, which also functioned, by default, as Carlyle's first town hall.

Although Charles held no other public office at this point, he was a visible presence in the first session of the Illinois General Assembly in 1819, lobbying there successfully for permission to build (with his partner Thomas Herbert) a mill-dam across the Kaskaskia River, to charter (with his father-in-law John Kain) a state bank at Carlyle, and to create a school called Washington Academy, to which Charles, Herbert, and Kain were appointed as trustees.[26] At the same time, Charles hatched and promoted a scheme to move the state capital from Kaskaskia to Carlyle, pressing his case by offering land in Carlyle as a gift to the state.[27] His efforts very nearly paid off: Carlyle came within a single vote of the winning community, Vandalia.[28]

Undeterred by this defeat—and more sensitive to the close relationship between land development and politics—Charles sought and won election to the state legislature in 1820.[29] Here Charles pursued a new strategy: If Carlyle couldn't become the state capital, he could make it a county seat.[30] As settlers increased, the Illinois legislature carved new smaller counties out of the original larger ones.[31] At Charles Slade's urging, in 1824 one such new county—named for DeWitt Clinton, New York State's canal-building governor—was created out of parts of Washington, Bond, and Fayette counties.[32]

Charles immediately took it upon himself to ensure Carlyle's designation as the new county seat. In July 1825 he and his wife, Mary, donated twenty acres—on land conveniently adjoining their own—to Clinton County for a courthouse, on the condition that the county seat would remain permanently in Carlyle.[33] Until the courthouse was built, the newly chartered county conducted its business in the Hubbard & Slade store, paying Charles an annual rent of $15 for the privilege. During that time Charles himself served as clerk of the circuit court, in addition to his postmaster duties.[34]

Carlyle's designation as county seat augured well for its future prospects; so did the establishment, in 1820, of a stagecoach service between Vincennes and St. Louis, which used Carlyle as a way station.[35] Yet much of its growth up to the mid-1820s existed only in Charles Slade's fertile imagination. The first state census in 1825 found just fifteen households in Carlyle proper (two of them accounted for by Charles Slade and his brother Thomas, by now twenty-four years old) and 169 more households in the surrounding county.[36] By this time Charles Slade's original merchant partner Hubbard had departed, and Thomas Herbert, who had laid out Carlyle with Charles in 1818, was dead.[37] Yet as early as 1820 Charles moved his wife and their three small children out of John Hill's fort and into a new two-story frame house on East Fairfax Street—the largest residence in the county, with rooms that boasted the finest quality walnut lumber.[38] In this Carlyle equivalent of a mansion, the county's elite often gathered for social functions.[39]

At that time, mail from the East arrived sporadically, carried by a horseback rider who forded the Kaskaskia River at the shallow point near Hill's fort.[40] To encourage a regular mail route and stimulate trade along the Goshen Road, in 1823 Charles persuaded the state legislature to authorize him to build a wooden toll bridge across the Kaskaskia River.[41] Charles opened the bridge—actually more of a mud bridge supported by logs—in 1825, replacing the ferry that he and his brothers had acquired from John Hill.

Three years later, presumably as the result of Charles's prodding as postmaster, the U.S. Post Office opened a regular mail route between Vincennes, Indiana, and St. Louis along the Goshen Road through Carlyle.[42] If by this time anyone doubted Charles Slade's status as a mover and shaker, the state census of 1825 provided a bizarre confirmation. It found 1,106 people living in Clinton County, of whom 220 were white male adults qualified to vote. Of those 220, only one man owned slaves—five of them, to be exact. Charles Slade was not only Clinton County's largest landholder; he was also its only slaveholder.[43]

Charles Slade's slaveholding status was no minor matter for an aspiring Illinois politician. In 1824 the Illinois legislature approved a referendum calling for a constitutional convention whose unstated aim

Charles Slade's house in Carlyle, Illinois, was the largest in the town he founded in 1818. At first it doubled as the local courthouse and post office. Joseph Alfred Slade was born here in 1831. (*Denver Public Library*)

would be the legalization of slavery, but the voters rejected the proposal that same year. In the process they fortuitously spared Charles Slade the necessity to confront the issue when he returned to the legislature in 1826, after a four-year absence. Charles appears to have kept his slaves, declining to follow the example of the state's then-governor, Edward Coles, who had freed his own slaves on coming to Illinois (not to mention the example of Charles's own father in Alexandria, who had freed his only slave upon his death in 1820).[44]

It was not the slavery issue that carried Charles Slade to political prominence but an entirely new and equally potent political force. General Andrew Jackson, the hero of the battle of New Orleans in 1814 and the invasion of Spanish Florida in 1818, was elected president in 1828. In many respects Charles Slade exemplified the Jacksonian ideal: the hard-working, self-reliant small-town Western yeoman making a fresh start far from the ossified East. During his term in the Illinois legislature from 1826 to 1828 Charles became a loyal and dependable supporter of Jackson's presidential ambitions.

Jackson returned the favor in 1829 by appointing Charles as U.S. marshal for Illinois.[45] This office was primarily concerned with routine tasks like serving federal court papers and enforcing the relatively few federal laws, but its prestige was disproportionately huge. As Charles was the sole U.S. marshal for the entire state, he and his deputies became in effect the public face of the U.S. government in Illinois over the next four years.

That same year Charles built a gristmill on the Kaskaskia River, near his toll bridge—the first mill of any pretensions in the region.[46] As such it represented, as Charles no doubt perceived, an economic magnet for an aspiring frontier town, for it converted farmers' produce into potential food for the benefit of anyone who lived nearby. When his mud bridge across the Kaskaskia burned down in 1830, Charles resumed the ferry and ford that he and his brothers had operated before the bridge was built.[47] And when his new mill burned down in 1831, Charles immediately replaced it with a larger mill, a three-stone affair employing eight men and capable of producing seventy-five barrels of flour daily.[48]

In retrospect, all of Charles Slade's roles—as merchant, miller, land promoter, toll bridge operator, and public official—together convey the sense of a man trying to breathe life into his community by sheer personal determination. What is remarkable is the extent to which Charles succeeded. A traveler from Virginia whose stagecoach passed through Carlyle in the early 1830s described a seemingly vibrant town of great promise, "situated on the Kaskaskia river which is large enough for small steamboats to navigate it nearly one half of the year." Elbowing his way into a store—presumably Charles Slade's store—opposite the hotel on a Saturday, the traveler "found the store filled with as many sorts of people as there was a variety of wares on the shelves, and there was, for an inland town, an excellent apportionment."[49]

It was in this promising village, within its largest and most luxurious home, that Joseph Alfred Slade was born to Charles and Mary Slade on January 22, 1831.[50] Alfred, as he was known, was the first child born to his parents in the more than six years since his sister Mary was born in 1824. Alfred was his parents' fourth child, and one more sister—Maria Virginia—would follow a year later. It is tempting to imagine that Charles, as a third son himself, may have felt some special affinity toward his own third son. But Alfred's arrival was probably overshadowed by an even more exciting prospect in his father's life.

Following the 1830 federal census, which reported that the population of Illinois had nearly quadrupled since statehood, to 157,445, the state became entitled to three seats (not one) in the U.S. House of Representatives. Less than a month after Alfred Slade was born, the Illinois legislature divided the state into three Congressional districts. The First Congressional District's boundaries largely coincided with the area where Charles Slade was well known and well liked, and he already held a statewide office as U.S. marshal for Illinois. Consequently he decided to run for Congress.

That election of 1832, when Jackson ran for a second term, was something of a watershed in American politics. That summer two potential crises—one medical, one financial—confronted the country. A second Asian cholera pandemic from India arrived in Britain in the autumn of 1831 and in America the following year, with devastating results in both countries. It surfaced in New York City in the summer of 1832 and by August had spread to Brooklyn and Philadelphia.[51] This intestinal disease killed half the people it struck, with terrifying swiftness. A man or woman could feel hearty at breakfast, complain of queasy bowels at noontime dinner, and be dead by supper. Cholera's physical devastation was compounded by the full horror of consciousness: Until the very last stages, the victim remained aware of what was happening. Yet the world's most prominent physicians and public officials seemed helpless to map the disease or assist anyone who lived in its path.[52]

At the same time, Jackson's foes in Congress passed a bill renewing the charter of the Second Bank of the United States, even though the Philadelphia bank's charter wasn't due to expire until 1836. Jackson promptly vetoed the bill. Since the Second Bank generally exerted a stabilizing influence on banking conditions and currency rates from one state to another, Jackson's veto amounted to what the Second Bank's president, Nicholas Biddle, called a "manifesto of anarchy." Nevertheless, Congress sustained Jackson's veto on July 13. The issue of where to deposit the government's funds would be left to the next Congress.

Only a month before the election, Charles Slade had eagerly cast himself, for better or worse, in Jackson's camp.[53] Among his formidable competitors for the First District seat was the Kaskaskia lawyer Sidney Breese, the former U.S. district attorney for Illinois. Charles Dunn, a former state legislator who had twice been elected clerk of the Illinois House of Representatives, was next to announce. Then came the virtual father of Illinois himself: Ninian Edwards. As appointed governor of Illinois Territory from 1809 to 1818, Edwards had guided it into statehood, served a term as U.S. Senator, and then won statewide election as governor in his own right in 1826. Against this competition Charles Slade and one other candidate, Henry L. Webb, seemed minor entries in a five-man field. But when the votes were counted following the election, Charles Slade had won.[54]

It was an inauspicious moment to enter Congress, for a new crisis threatened to tear the nation apart. In November 1832, South Carolina reacted to a high-tariff act of Congress by declaring the federal tariff laws null and void within the state and threatening to secede if the federal government tried to collect duties at the port of Charleston.

On the fourth of March 1833, as Andrew Jackson was inaugurated for a second term, Charles Slade formally resigned as U.S. marshal and assumed his new title as a U.S. Congressman. But he did not actually take his seat until the first Monday of December, when the first session of the Twenty-third Congress began.[55] By this time South Carolina had backed off from its confrontation with Jackson and rescinded its nullification ordinance, lifting Jackson to new levels of national popularity.[56]

Under normal conditions a freshman Congressman like Charles Slade could have expected to take his seat quietly in the House and defer to his more illustrious and experienced colleagues, like former President John Quincy Adams and the orator Edward Everett, both of Massachusetts; the House Speaker James K. Polk of Tennessee; and the colorful Tennessee frontiersman Colonel Davy Crockett. But this was a Congress dominated by newcomers. The redistricting required by the 1830 federal census had expanded the House of

Representatives from 213 members to 240. The crises over the Second Bank and South Carolina's nullification ordinance, together with the upheavals within Jackson's own party, had brought the defeat of large numbers of incumbents. Consequently, of the 240 men who took their seats in the House that December, 136 were freshmen like Charles Slade. Although a majority of the House was aligned behind Jackson, in the Senate such giants as Henry Clay, John C. Calhoun, and Daniel Webster stood united at the head of an opposition that seized the initiative in the fight over the Second Bank.[57]

Charles Slade seems to have made no speeches in that first session, but the available evidence suggests that he was faithful in his attendance, attentive to his duties, and zealous in his support of Jackson. "All his votes were against the bank and in favor of the people," noted one Washington observer.[58] Still, Charles was "entirely free from the rancor of party," if we are to believe one account, "and had the charity, if not the good sense, to believe that political infallibility was not peculiar to any set of men."[59] As a member of the House Committee on Roads and Canals, Charles proposed, not surprisingly, bills to improve navigation on the Kaskaskia River and to survey a national road across Illinois to the Mississippi River, on the not unreasonable contention that the Goshen Road had become an important national highway.[60] By the time Congress adjourned on June 30, 1834, the forces of the Second Bank had been stymied and Charles Slade had filed his candidacy for reelection that fall.[61]

After the session, Charles lingered in Washington for a few days, attending to Congressional business and visiting his relatives and friends in the District of Columbia, most of whom he hadn't seen in eighteen years. By this time both his parents were gone, but Charles's oldest brother Henry, who had inherited the family's businesses in Alexandria, was living in Washington with his wife and at least one child. Charles Slade's older brother Richard, who had left Illinois shortly after the three brothers settled there, lived in Alexandria too, a widower operating a hardware store.[62] Charles's younger sister Mary Slade English was also in Alexandria, and two younger sisters, Maria Catherine Heath and Ascenath Weems, were married and living in Virginia as well, in Richmond and nearby Dumfries, respectively.[63]

When Charles started back for Illinois early in July, he found that a traveler's available options had expanded vastly since his covered wagon journey along the narrow and indirect trails of 1816. Through one conveyance or another, a traveler like Charles Slade, who had taken months to reach the banks of the Kaskaskia River in 1816, could now reasonably expect to arrive home in ten days or less. But at Cincinnati, on the Ohio River—about three hundred miles from Carlyle—Charles was suddenly attacked by a mysterious sickness that delayed him briefly. He soon rallied, however, and hastened homeward.

His coach had crossed almost the entire width of the state of Indiana when he suffered a relapse that made it impossible for him to travel farther. This time there could be no mystery about what had befallen him. In a roadside tavern at the crossroads village of Wheatland, some twelve miles east of Vincennes and the Illinois state line, a physician was hastily summoned and all possible care was administered. But in the face of this illness nothing could be done, even for a man of Charles Slade's determination, other than to make his last moments comfortable. On July 11, 1834, less than twenty-four hours after Charles arrived at Wheatland, the Asiatic cholera claimed its latest victim.[64]

His remains were quickly buried in a makeshift grave whose marker and location were soon lost. Seemingly in an instant, the driving force behind Clinton County had vanished. Now Charles Slade's family and his community would have to fend for themselves.

Chapter 4

THE WIDOW'S QUANDARY

*

When her husband died in July 1834, Mary Slade was a month short of her thirty-fifth birthday. As Charles Slade's wife, she had presided over the relatively privileged household of a first lady in a frontier community. The 1830 U.S. census suggests that six servants (perhaps including Charles's five slaves) were living with Charles, Mary, and their three children in Carlyle's largest house.[1] But as his widow, she was suddenly reduced to the lesser rank of a single mother in a society where law and custom alike required women to depend on the protection of men.

Charles had left Mary a small collection of businesses she was incapable of operating, and whose value depended almost entirely on her husband's acumen and charisma. He had also left her with a continuing piece of litigation between Charles and his brothers in Alexandria over how much his older brother Henry had advanced Charles for his Illinois adventures and consequently how much Charles owed his siblings from his share of the estate of their father, dead since 1820.[2] Since most of Charles's wealth was tied up in his land and his businesses, Mary was left with a variety of debts she was unable to pay.

Mary's father, the Carlyle innkeeper and banker John Kain, had died the previous year at an advanced age, and her mother had expired several years before that. With the birth of her son Joseph Alfred in 1831 and her daughter Maria Virginia in 1832, as well as the sale or

liberation of Charles Slade's slaves around the time of his death, Mary
Slade now had five children, all under the age of fifteen, to raise by herself, apparently without any household servants[3]—an overwhelming
task, as the law itself recognized. As a widowed mother of minors without male protection, Mary was technically not entitled to retain legal
custody of her own children.

Some attempt to resolve this quandary may have occurred a few
months after Charles Slade's death, when his older brother Richard
arrived from Alexandria and took up residence in Mary's home.[4]
Richard, unlike Charles, had returned to Alexandria soon after the
three Slade brothers had acquired John Hill's fort and ferry along the
Kaskaskia; there he had married Susana Weems in 1820, only to lose
her (and their baby) to childbirth the following year. So now two powerful incentives—potentially lucrative properties, plus a sister-in-law in
need of his help—propelled Richard to return to the place he had
abandoned nearly twenty years earlier.

When Charles Slade died, two of his brothers were living in or
around Alexandria: Henry, who had taken over their father's
Alexandria properties; and William, the youngest. Their brother
Thomas, one of the three brothers who first came to Illinois, remained
in Carlyle with his wife Caroline and two small children. But Thomas
died in May 1835, at the age of thirty-four—probably of the same
cholera that had killed his brother Charles the previous year.[5] (Indeed,
some evidence suggests that Thomas and his family moved back to
Washington in the early 1830s, and it is possible that Richard returned
to Carlyle in 1834 with Thomas and his family; it's also possible that
their primary motivation for this journey was not so much to assist
their sister-in-law Mary Slade as to escape the cholera epidemic then
ravaging America's eastern cities.)[6]

One can speculate that Richard Slade contemplated marriage to
Mary Slade. Certainly such a union would have provided benefits to
both partners: for Mary, legal and financial protection; for Richard—a
childless widower in his early forties—instant family, property, social
position and a set of heirs unencumbered (because Richard and Mary
were already in-laws) by the complications of new family relationships.
But such speculation was rendered moot in September 1835 when,

five months after Thomas Slade's death, Richard Slade too expired, most likely of cholera as well, at the age of forty-one.[7] Within the space of fourteen months and nearly 1,000 miles, the great pandemic of the nineteenth century had wiped out all three of the brothers who had settled the area that became Carlyle, Illinois.

With Richard's death, Mary Dark Slade, as she now called herself (using her original middle name rather than her maiden name), was forced to apply to the Clinton County Court for appointment as legal guardian of her own children. This request was readily granted in August 1836—although not, we may imagine, without some embarrassment to a woman of such local prominence.[8] But Mary Slade's financial predicament remained; and its solution—a marriageable man willing to assume responsibility for five children not his own—seemed unlikely in a village that, even by 1836, still numbered only twenty-three households, including Mary's own and that of her sister-in-law Caroline Slade.[9]

Mary's desperation was compounded by a nationwide financial panic set in motion by Charles Slade's patron and political leader, Andrew Jackson.[10] Within ten weeks of Jackson's departure from office following his second term in March 1837, credit had virtually vanished from the United States as a result of the ex-president's closing of the Bank of the United States. Thousands of banks and businesses from New Orleans to Boston closed their doors; some parts of the country were reduced to the primitive process of bartering goods and services; and even the U.S. government (whose own resources had evaporated as well) was forced to print currency to pay its clerks. The entire country was gripped by its first major economic depression, the Panic of 1837.[11]

We can imagine Mary Slade's elation when the apparent answer to her prayers serendipitously turned up in Carlyle in the person of Elias Smith Dennis. This ambitous striver was born in 1812 in Newburgh, in upstate New York, and had grown up on Long Island. For reasons lost to posterity, he migrated to Carlyle in 1836. Local folklore there as well as the recollections of some of his descendants suggest that here was a man every bit as motivated and charismatic as Charles Slade. (A photo taken during the Civil War suggests a ruggedly handsome man with curls reminiscent of General George Custer in his prime.) For a short time after his arrival Dennis taught school in Carlyle.[12]

To this newcomer, Mary Slade seemed a providential catch. Marriage to her would instantly bring Dennis property and social position, not to mention a substantial home beyond the dreams of a footloose young man still in his mid-twenties. When they were married in February 1838, Elias Dennis was only twenty-five and Mary was thirty-eight; indeed, Elias was barely seven years older than his oldest stepson, William Slade.

Within three years of their wedding Elias Dennis assumed the first of several of Charles Slade's former public offices, serving as clerk of Clinton County Circuit Court beginning in 1841, then winning election to the Illinois House of Representatives in 1842 and the State Senate in 1846. In the meantime Elias and Mary had brought into the world a son of their own, named Elias Dennis, Jr., born in 1840. In 1843 Elias also shepherded his stepson Charles Richard Slade into an advantageous marriage with Eloise Breese, eldest daughter of the newly appointed U.S. Senator Sidney Breese—the same Sidney Breese whom the late Charles Slade had defeated for Congress in 1832—who in 1835 had relocated to Carlyle with his large family to become a circuit judge.[13] With these stepping-stones Elias solidified his place in the family as well as his family's place in the community. Whether it improved his family's financial condition is another question: in 1843 Mary was forced to sell twenty-five lots adjacent to the courthouse for only $81.50 to satisfy her first husband's debts.[14]

Later generations of Western historians have theorized that young Alf Slade's lack of a strong father figure turned him into a juvenile delinquent. One biographical account describes Alf as "a rather wild youth" who "finally departed for the 'wild and woolly West'"[15]—a kind of *ex post facto* reasoning, akin to concluding that people who live in high-crime neighborhoods must be criminals themselves. A 1953 movie portrayed Alf as a good boy transformed into a hardened killer after seeing his father gunned down in cold blood.[16]

Yet for Alfred Slade, the loss of his father was nothing compared to the trauma suffered by his mother. Even before his death Charles Slade had often spent long periods away from home, either serving in his

capacity as U.S. marshal or lobbying state legislators in Vandalia.
Alfred was not yet three when he
last saw his father, and he was seven
when his mother remarried. To
Alfred and his younger sister Maria
Virginia, Elias was the only father
they had ever known, and he
appears to have been a conscien-
tious parent.

Nevertheless, throughout his
adult life and ever after, Alfred was
shadowed by a totally spurious
story that he had committed his
first murder as a mere adolescent in
Carlyle. "At age thirteen, Slade displayed an ungovernable temper and
killed a man by striking him with a

Elias S. Dennis, shown here about 1862,
was an ambitous new arrival from New
York when he married the widowed Mary
Slade in 1838. She was 12 years his senior, but both of them perceived advantages
in their match. (*National Archives*)

stone," the Wyoming historian G. C. Coutant related in 1899, in the
first published account of this alleged crime. "The man had interfered
with some boys with whom young Slade was playing."[17]

Yet there is no evidence that such a killing ever took place.[18]
Nothing in the historical record suggests that as a boy Alfred Slade was
anything other than what a more scrupulous biographer has called "a
quiet, well-behaved, inoffensive youth."[19] Unlike his two older brothers, Alfred doubtless benefited from attendance at Carlyle's first
schoolhouse, which doubled as a church on Sundays. (Unlike many
figures of the early West, Alf Slade unquestionably knew how to read
and write.)[20] He probably spent time at his stepfather's mill or at the
Hubbard & Slade store, which by 1840 was being operated by his oldest brother, William. If Alfred Slade subsequently developed into a
hard case, most likely the catalyst was neither his father's death nor his
hometown nor his stepfather but the next chapter in his life, courtesy
of the U.S. government.

Chapter 5

HOTBED OF EVIL

*

It took six years for the U.S. to recover from the Panic of 1837, and
in the western states the effects lingered even longer. Indiana gave
up all attempts to pay interest on its state debt as early as 1840. In
Illinois, money and jobs were scarce, and most people were still bartering for goods and services.[1] "Every attempt at commercial or industrial enterprise had failed," one historian noted; "farmers could not sell
their crops at paying rates; with boundless force in heart and brain the
young man could find nothing worth while to do."[2] Along the western
frontier, from Illinois and Missouri down through Arkansas and
Louisiana, "are great numbers of bold and restless spirits," wrote the
American Review, "men gathered out of all the orderly and civilized
portions of society as its most turbulent members, and ready for any
enterprise that can minister to their reckless manner of life and love of
danger and of change."[3]

Alfred Slade was one of thousands of impatient young men who
waited for some excuse to cast off their plows and their chores and
unleash their pent-up energies in some grand adventure. In the spring
of 1846, they got their wish. When Andrew Jackson's protégé James
K. Polk took office in March 1845 he was the youngest president in
U.S. history, an enthusiastic and vigorous man of forty-nine, eager to
deliver on his campaign promises to bring Texas and Oregon into the
Union. As it happened, Texas was annexed to the Union three days

before Polk took office. But this triumph further whetted the insatiable national appetite for more territory.

Although (or perhaps because) Polk was not a military man like some of his predecessors, he felt no qualms about using force to achieve that goal. When the Mexican government informed the United States that it regarded the annexation of its former province of Texas as an act of war, Polk responded by dispatching troops under General Zachary Taylor to Louisiana, ostensibly to protect Texas from any Mexican military threat.[4] Over the next year Polk's diplomats offered to pay Mexico for a disputed 150-mile strip of land between the Nueces River and the Rio Grande del Norte in southern Texas, but Mexico declined. In late February 1846 Polk ordered Taylor to cross the Nueces and advance to the southern edge of the disputed zone along the Rio Grande, a move that Mexico strongly protested. Finally, late in April 1846, a force of Mexican cavalry crossed to the northern side of the Rio Grande and overwhelmed a small American patrol near Point Isabel, killing eleven American soldiers and wounding six.[5]

That attack provided Polk with the justification he needed for going to war. Mexico, he told Congress in his war message of May 11, "has passed the boundary of the United States, has invaded our territory and shed American blood upon the American soil."[6] Polk had successfully maneuvered a weaker nation, as well as his own, into a war of his choosing.

Polk perceived a war against Mexico as a brief and simple affair. But to many military observers, the U.S. Army seemed utterly unprepared for this war. American soldiers had never fought before on foreign soil. No body of American troops had ever crossed the Great Plains. Nor did the United States possess much of an army to speak of: at the beginning of 1846 Congress had authorized an army of just 8,613 soldiers and officers, but illness and desertion had created nearly 3,300 vacancies.[7] Since the Battle of Waterloo in 1815, the world had enjoyed a remarkable thirty-year era of peace as well as pacifism, to such an extent that when a young Connecticut tinkerer named Samuel Colt invented a remarkable pistol capable of firing six bullets in succession from a revolving chamber, he elicited no interest from the army and was forced to close his factory for lack of customers in 1842.[8] On the day Polk delivered his war message, Congress was engaged in a debate over whether to close the U.S. Military Academy at West Point.[9]

Polk's message quashed that debate and also discarded sixty years of national military policy. Congress, suddenly desperate for troops, now passed a war budget of $10 million.[10] Samuel Colt took an order from the War Department for a thousand revolvers and soon was operating the greatest arms factory in the world.

The war would be fought not by career soldiers—for few such soldiers existed—but almost entirely by volunteers. Polk issued an immediate call for 20,000 volunteers from the "Western and Southern states," on the theory that these states were most threatened by their proximity to the Mexican enemy. Volunteers were asked to enlist for just twelve months, in keeping with the widespread belief that the war would end soon.[11]

Illinois needed three thousand men to fill its quota. At a rally in Springfield (where the state capital had moved in 1839), General John Hardin of nearby Jacksonville drummed up potential volunteers. "Let us not say Taylor and his brave men can whip Mexico without our aid," he told a receptive crowd. "This is not the language of brave men. Let us have a hand in whipping her."[12]

It was the sort of rhetoric geared to a youth like Alfred Slade, then working at his stepfather's mill in Carlyle. But Alfred at fifteen and a half was still two and a half years below the army's minimum enlistment age.[13] His two older brothers, on the other hand, were well above enlistment age but no longer footloose. William was twenty-six and managing the family store. Charles Richard, known like Alfred by his middle name, was twenty-four, married to Senator Sidney Breese's daughter Eloise, the father of a newborn son, and ensconced in his father's old position as clerk of the Clinton County Court. Whether either brother contemplated Governor Thomas Ford's call for volunteers is unknown, but in any case their services seemed unnecessary. Within ten days of the governor's call, 8,370 eager Illinois recruits had stepped forward, of whom only 3,720 were accepted.[14]

In its first phase the war fulfilled its promoters' rosy expectations. In late June the Army of the West under General Stephen W. Kearny left Fort Leavenworth on the Missouri River, heading west along the Santa Fe Trail, and by the end of August had occupied Santa Fe without a struggle. Taylor, meanwhile, invaded northern Mexico itself, captured the important city of Monterrey, and defeated a major Mexican force at the battle of Buena Vista in February 1847.

But now the war effort bogged down. Taylor failed to pursue the Mexican armies he had defeated. In Santa Fe, a well-organized civilian rebellion in January 1847 succeeded in assassinating the military governor, Charles Bent, and several other officials. That March a seaborne army led by General Winfield Scott captured the key seaport of Veracruz and headed inland toward Mexico City, but by April, Scott's force had halted in the face of continued Mexican resistance.

The one-year enlistments of all those volunteers who comprised the bulk of U.S. forces in Mexico were due to expire at the end of May. With no end of the war in sight, the government had no legal way to keep these volunteers in the service—and almost all of them, having had their fill of war, chose to return home.[15]

Now Secretary of War William L. Marcy issued a call for a new batch of six thousand volunteers to serve not for one year, but for "the duration of the war." Illinois, which in 1846 had produced four regiments—nearly four thousand men—was now allotted only a single new regiment.[16] But recruiting this second batch would be a much tougher sell: instead of experiencing the glory of battle, these volunteers would be required to occupy and guard hostile territory won by their predecessors—for how long, no one could say.

The government appealed to young men's more selfish motives by promising volunteers the same bounties, land warrants, and pensions previously offered only to regular army recruits. Volunteers who completed twelve months of service were promised 160 acres of land or $100 in land script.[17]

In Carlyle, Illinois, a forty-two-year-old carpenter named Thomas Bond—nephew of the first Illinois state governor, Shadrach Bond—drummed up recruits from Carlyle and the surrounding Clinton County.[18] Ultimately Illinois provided not its assigned single new regiment but two.[19] So it came to pass that all three sons of the late Charles Slade joined the war effort that spring of 1847. William, the eldest, received a political commission as a second lieutenant in the regular army.[20] On May 4, 1847, Alfred, then only sixteen, enlisted with his brother Richard and about 115 of their neighbors in a Clinton County company of the Illinois Foot Volunteers.[21] On the enlistment form Alfred gave his age as eighteen—embroidering his resumé for the first time, but certainly not the last.[22]

In many eastern states, militia officers were appointed by the governor or the state legislature, or the volunteers elected their company commanders, who in turn appointed the regimental field officers. But in Illinois, Indiana, Mississippi, Tennessee, Alabama, and Arkansas—states most firmly rooted in the frontier democratic tradition of "citizen soldiers"—every man was entitled to vote not only for his company commander but for his regimental commander as well.[23] In theory this meant that the lowliest seven-dollar-a-month private like Alfred Slade felt a sense of responsibility for the success of his outfit. But in practice this policy often meant that soldiers like Alfred and his colleagues would be led into war by inexperienced officers who had commanded troops only on militia days and possessed only the barest technical skill to lead their men.[24] Thomas Bond, whom the Carlyle recruits elected as their captain, was later described as "a man of many eccentricities, the most peculiar of which was that he entertained for almost every man with whom he came in contact . . . either the warmest friendship or the most intense hatred."[25] This man was to be Alfred Slade's primary role model for his next fifteen formative months.

As soon as the full company was enrolled, its recruits set off on a fifty-five-mile march to the regimental rendezvous point: Alton, Illinois, just below the confluence of the Missouri and Mississippi Rivers. From the start, the march took on a festive air. The recruits had gone but a few miles when they stopped for midday dinner at the home of a Clinton County farmer named Rodgers. "While the company were seated enjoying their bountiful meal," the host's son, John Rodgers, later recalled, the captain prevailed upon a neighbor youth "to volunteer and go along with them; who after a few parting words for friends and relatives, took leave with the noble band of volunteers, the westward bound for the battlefields beyond the Rio Grande."[26]

The company arrived in Alton on May 19, and three days later Alfred and his comrades were mustered into the service as soldiers of Company A in the replacement First Regiment of Illinois Foot Volunteers. A few days' delay ensued while the men of Company A awaited the arrival of the nine other newly recruited companies from more distant Illinois towns, including one from faraway Chicago.[27] When the regiment was finally assembled on June 8, Edward W. B. Newby of Brown County, east of Springfield—later characterized as "a non-professional soldier with a corresponding lack of interest in red-tape reports"—was elected colonel and commanding officer.[28] In the subsequent organization, Newby appointed Alfred Slade's brother Richard as regimental quartermaster sergeant—perhaps by virtue of Richard's status as Clinton County clerk, or his political connections, or both.[29] Company A's sojourn in Alton—from May 19 until the company departed a month later by steamboat for Fort Leavenworth— appears to have constituted the only training camp these citizen-soldiers would receive.[30]

Alfred Slade had never before left his home state, but here on the Missouri River the steamboat took him and his comrades across the entire width of the state of Missouri, depositing them five days later at Fort Leavenworth in what was then unorganized territory attached to Missouri for judicial purposes.[31] This fort had been established in 1827 and had to be supplied entirely by river.[32]

By the end of June 1847, as the men camped in tents on a broad field called the West End, the last of the regiment's ten companies arrived at Fort Leavenworth, bringing the regiment's total strength to more than a thousand men. Here they joined two regiments of Missouri volunteers, one mounted and one infantry. These combined forces hurriedly prepared for their arduous trek west on the Santa Fe Trail to relieve the occupying force there—900 miles across an uninhabited expanse of mostly dry land, with no navigable rivers and barely any agriculture.[33] One reason for the hurry was a measles epidemic at Fort Leavenworth, which killed about a dozen Illinois men.[34] On July Fourth, the newly gathered regiment participated in a general parade, heard the reading of the Declaration of Independence, and listened to an address by the fort's chaplain; and on July 9, the first Illinois companies moved out.[35]

As Kearny's army had discovered when covering the same ground a year earlier, the army had given little forethought to the condition of roads, the availability of water, or the transportation of supplies.[36] Because of limited water, firewood, and forage along the route, a military unit of this size—about 2,250 men, as well as horses, mules, supply wagons, and other equipment—was forced to break up into detachments to escort wagon trains transporting commissary, quartermaster, and other supplies.[37] Captain Bond's Company A from Clinton County appears to have acted as a guard to a large herd of beef cattle intended to feed the occupying army in New Mexico.[38]

For twenty-seven days, men unaccustomed to outdoor living or sleeping on the ground marched along a route that afforded no protection from the intense midday summer sun, nor from the cold nights, nor from severe thunderstorms. Exhausted from marching in daytime heat, exposed to severe weather swings, and subjected to contaminated food and water in unsanitary camps, the weakened members of the First Illinois began succumbing to measles—then a serious disease—as well as amoebic dysentery, diarrhea, and yellow fever long before the regiment reached Santa Fe. Three days after the Illinois force and the wagons crossed the Kansas River by ferry on July 10, a private named John W. Collins was buried; on July 20 another private named Aaron J. Campbell was buried; and on August 5 a third casualty named Private Robert Easley was buried at a place called Pawnee Fork.[39]

Colonel Newby, meanwhile, had temporarily stayed behind; his departure from Fort Leavenworth (with three remaining Illinois companies) was delayed until July 20 while he wrestled with logistical problems: Who would escort future wagon trains to Santa Fe? How would official dispatches be carried there? But when the assistant quartermaster asked him to remain to arrange an escort for another herd of beef cattle, Newby refused to delay any longer, citing the advanced season and the ill health of his men.[40]

The woes of the First Illinois en route to Santa Fe reflected a larger problem of the war effort that the army had never before encountered: the need to continuously supply thousands of troops in garrisons at least 800 miles from the nearest supply depot at Fort Leavenworth. Kearny's Army of the West in 1846 had been supplied by a system of army-operated wagon trains, but the whole operation had been plagued by inexperience. For one thing, many of the drivers were greenhorns; for another, no military escorts were provided to the small trains of twenty-five to thirty military wagons, so that Indians drove off many oxen, robbed the trains, and killed some of the teamsters.[41] Civilian traders and their wagons had traversed this route effectively for a generation, for a reason that seems obvious in retrospect: The traders' trains were manned by experienced drivers; they combined their trains to achieve safety in numbers; they elected able captains; and they guarded their animals carefully.[42]

Eventually the War Department would try awarding contracts to civilian freighters for transporting military supplies to Santa Fe; as early as 1846, in fact, a private freighter named Ben Holladay had secured a contract to supply Kearny's army with wagons, mules, bacon, and flour.[43] But for the moment, the army continued to rely on its own soldiers to drive its wagon trains. A muster roll for Company A, dated August 31, 1847, notes that Private Joseph A. Slade was "on extra daily duty since July 11 as a teamster."[44] In this manner Alfred Slade first learned the trade that would prove critical to the opening of western North America and would bring him into the service of Ben Holladay himself. But their paths would not cross for another fifteen years.

W hen the First Illinois contingents arrived in Santa Fe in late August and September, the actual fighting in the Mexican War was about to reach its climax hundreds of miles to the south.[45] Scott's army, advancing westward from Veracruz, routed a Mexican force at Molino del Rey on September 8, thereby clearing the road to Mexico City. Five days later Scott's army stormed Chapultepec, the fortress protecting the Mexican capital, and the following day the Americans occupied Mexico City itself.

The military phase of the war was over; Alfred Slade and his comrades from Clinton County, like the thousands of recruits who had signed up "for the duration of the war," would never see a shot fired in anger. But until a peace treaty was signed, the messy (and, in fact, far more dangerous) business of occupation remained.

Upon his arrival, Colonel Newby concluded that his force—in tandem with existing units of reenlisted men already there—was greater than needed for the occupation of Santa Fe. In October he divided his regiment into two battalions, dispatching one to El Paso while keeping the other—including Clinton County's Company A—in Santa Fe.[46] Those who remained soon discovered that the capital of the province of New Mexico was no Xanadu.

Without the adrenaline rush of battle, life in an occupying army was deadeningly dull. "All is hubbub and confusion here," wrote a Santa Fe correspondent of the *New York Courier and Enquirer* on August 13, about the time the First Illinois arrived. "Discharged volunteers are leaving, drunk, and volunteers not discharged, are remaining, drunk."[47]

The same New Mexicans who a generation earlier had welcomed American traders to Santa Fe with open arms now greeted the occupying army with contempt bordering on outright hostility, and the Americans responded in kind. In the wake of Governor Bent's assassination in January 1847, six conspirators had been condemned to death by civil courts in Santa Fe, and more than two dozen others—some of whom were most likely innocent—had been tried by army court-martial and hanged.[48] By the time the First Illinois volunteers arrived in August 1847 the revolt had been stamped out, but so had any trace of the idyllic quality of New Mexico life as well as the Americans' last idealistic illusions concerning their presence there. All that remained was the smoldering resentment of local citizens.

American soldiers perceived Mexicans as belonging to another race, and one with a parasitic religion, to boot.[49] In Santa Fe, American volunteers who longed for a fight but never saw battle inevitably began taking out their aggressions on the local population. An English observer called the soldiers in the streets of Santa Fe "the dirtiest, rowdiest crew I have ever seen collected together" and added: "Crowds of volunteers filled the streets, brawling and boasting but never fighting. Mexicans, wrapped in *serapes*, scowled upon them as they passed.... Every other house was a grocery, as they call a gin or whiskey shop, continually disgorging reeling, drunken men, and everywhere filth and dirt reigned triumphant."[50]

To the army's regular commanders, the problem lay not with American soldiers as such but with Washington's almost total reliance on *volunteer* soldiers across all its Mexican fronts. General Zachary Taylor, whose regulars had started the war along the Rio Grande, was the loudest of these critics. Each time the War Department wrote to urge that he curb the excesses committed by the volunteers under his command, Taylor wrote a lengthy reply attacking the government's policy of sending unmanageable and untrained boys to wage war in a foreign country.[51]

In Santa Fe, Colonel Newby's recourses were limited. He posted a public notice deploring drunkenness among his troops; he ordered that no liquor could be sold without permission from the company commander; and he ordered that no "fandango, ball or dance" could be held without obtaining a permit (at a cost of five dollars).[52] Beyond these gestures the army's only disciplinary tools were whipping, "bucking and gagging," and other forms of corporal punishment, which merely exacerbated the rebelliousness of volunteers who viewed such treatment as demeaning for freeborn men.[53]

"An inactive army," a disgusted quartermaster's wife concluded, is "a perfect hotbed of evil."[54] It was also, for all its idleness, a hotbed of death. Disease—mostly due to unsanitary conditions—killed seven times as many Americans in Mexico as battle did.[55] And volunteers were especially vulnerable. Ignorant of even the basic rudiments of camp life, frequently living in filth and squalor, they suffered a much higher rate of disease and debilitations than regular army soldiers. "They cannot take care of themselves," one regular officer remarked of the volunteers. "The hospitals are crowded with them, they die like sheep."[56] Robert E. Lee, then a captain on Winfield Scott's headquarters staff, summed up the army's Mexican nightmare a few years later. "My experience has taught me," he told a fellow officer in 1856, "to recommend no young man to enter the service."[57]

Alfred Slade at this point was a very young man indeed—perhaps the youngest in his regiment. He was also smaller than most of his comrades: his discharge paper described him as "five feet, six inches high."[58] He spoke in a high-pitched voice. On this evidence alone he seems a likely target for the older and larger bullies of his regiment.

Whether Alfred himself became a troublemaker or remained merely an observer in this charnel house is unknown, but it's safe to suggest that a youth not fully grown would be deeply scarred by such an experience.

His most likely protection was his older brother, the quartermaster sergeant Richard Slade; but that protection vanished on February 9, 1848, less than three weeks after Alfred turned seventeen, when Richard, not yet twenty-six years old, died of an unspecified disease. "Keenly alive to all the higher impulses that actuate the human breast," wrote his superior officer to the bereaved Mary Slade Dennis in Carlyle, "noble, kind and generous in the extreme, he has left a void in the regiment which can never be filled."[59] This formulaic wording constituted the standard condolence message in a place where it was routine for soldiers to die not gallantly in battle but pathetically of disease. Yet in one sense it was astute, for Richard's death no doubt left a significant void in his brother Alfred's life.

Nor was Alfred permitted any time to mourn. The very day Richard died, Company A and one other company were removed to Albuquerque, 60 miles south of Santa Fe.[60] From that point on, Alfred's primary survival skill lay in his own ability, presumably self-taught, to project an image of toughness toward civilians and his fellow soldiers alike.

During its year in New Mexico the First Illinois never lost a single soldier in battle. But the regiment had lost more than one-tenth of its men to disease.[61] Alfred was lucky to have survived; and as a teamster he had acquired a valuable skill. But he had not emerged unscathed. Years later, on the plains, he was routinely described as ten years older than his real age.

The war officially ended in February 1848 with a peace treaty signed by U.S. and Mexican representatives at the Mexico City suburb of Guadalupe Hidalgo. Mexico acknowledged America's claims in Texas and ceded to the United States its provinces of New Mexico and California, which included all or parts of the future states of Arizona, Nevada, Utah, Colorado, and Wyoming. In exchange, the United States agreed to pay $15 million for these lands—roughly what Polk had offered Mexico before the war—and to assume responsibility for

Construction on Fort Marcy, Santa Fe, New Mexico, was begun in 1846 and finished in 1847 while Alfred Slade was part of the occupation force. This was the first U.S. military fortification in the Southwest. (*Library of Congress*)

any claims made by U.S. citizens against Mexico. Now the United States spanned the continent for the first time and encompassed an area roughly equivalent to all of Europe. Mexico, for its part, was well compensated for the former Spanish territories in which it had never shown much interest.[62]

Polk's war, which had added so much new territory to the U.S., had also inadvertently produced a class of young men so hardened as to be ideally suited to taming that wild new territory. Alfred Slade, as one of the war's youngest surviving volunteers, had likely been hardened more than most.

The First Illinois Regiment left New Mexico toward the end of June 1848. By mid-September the Illinois contingents began arriving at Fort Leavenworth; by October 10, the last had arrived back at Alton; and on October 16 Alfred Slade and his fellows from Company A were officially mustered out of the service of the United States. The men of the regiment had not been paid since June, so upon their discharge they probably received three months' back pay plus the three months' severance mandated by Congress.[63] In Alfred Slade's case the pay package would have come to forty-two dollars—a substantial nest egg for a young man living at home with no other expenses.

True to his campaign promise of 1844, James K. Polk declined to stand for reelection in 1848, and despite his successful prosecution of the war with Mexico, his party failed to retain the presidency. Polk's successor was his most despised Whig opponent: General Zachary Taylor, who had so stubbornly resisted Polk's direction during the war. In March 1849, as the two political rivals rode uncomfortably together in a carriage down Pennsylvania Avenue to the Capitol for Taylor's inauguration, Polk attempted to make conversation by inquiring about Taylor's plans for California. Taylor replied, Polk wrote with dismay in his diary that night, "that California and Oregon were too distant to become members of the Union, and that it would be better for them to be an independent government. He said that our people would inhabit them, and repeated that it would be better for them to form an independent government for themselves. These are alarming opinions to be entertained by the President of the U.S."[64]

In light of his successor's lack of interest in shepherding America's new territories into the Union, that task would be left to others, and much sooner than either Polk or Taylor anticipated. On a clear, cold California morning in January 1848—nine days before the Treaty of Guadalupe Hidalgo was signed—the foreman in charge of building John Sutter's sawmill in the Sacramento Valley was taking his customary morning walk along the millrace when his eye was caught by "a glimpse of something shining in the bottom of the ditch."[65] James Marshall had stumbled upon a greater source of gold than the entire world had produced over the previous 350 years.[66] Virtually overnight the old American dream of the Puritans, of Benjamin Franklin's Poor Richard, of Thomas Jefferson's yeoman farmer—the dream of prosperity accumulated through hard work and patience—would be replaced by the old dream of the Spanish conquistadors: the dream of instant wealth, won by sheer audacity and luck.

Back home in Carlyle, Alfred's stepfather, Elias Dennis, was serving as a state senator and had also taken over the county clerk's job vacated when Alfred's brother Richard went off to war. Although Alfred was still only seventeen, almost immediately upon his return he set about making plans to head for the gold fields of California. To finance the trip, Alfred needed to cash in his veteran's land bounty. The reverse side of his honorable discharge paper contained a printed "Oath of Identity" form for use by a veteran in claiming his military bounty land. Alfred filled out and signed this form on October 31— just two weeks after he returned home—and had it acknowledged by the local justice of the peace three days later.[67] Both forms were then sent to the appropriate authorities in Washington with a request for Alfred's land warrant. When no reply was received over the next three months, Alfred turned for help to his politically connected stepfather, who in turn sent a note to his friend Robert Smith, the district's U.S. Congressman.[68]

> Carlyle, Illinois
> February 16, 1849
> My dear friend,
> In behalf of Alfred Slade, my stepson, I write you soliciting your aid in getting his Land Warrant. Slade was with the Volunteers from this county in New Mexico. At an early day after his return home he made application for his Warrant. He is disposed to go to California and if possible wishes to get it previous to his departure which will be sometime in the month of April. If you can be of any service to him in procuring it at an early day you will not only confer a particular favor to him but add another to the many obligations I am already due you for the kind favors already conferred.
> Your friend,
> Elias S. Dennis[69]

Congressman Smith appears to have wasted no time in forwarding the necessary document to young Alfred. Land Warrant No. 50654 was issued to Joseph A. Slade on March 14, 1849.[70] There is no evidence that young Slade ever claimed his land, and certainly not in California, which in its earliest days as a U.S. territory and state did not honor federal land warrants.[71] More likely Alfred sold the warrant, as most Mexican War veterans did.[72] With that stake—perhaps $100 or so—plus his $42 army severance package, he had the funds to finance a trip westward. The way was now clear for Alfred to join the hordes of other young male Americans heading for California. Like his father and grandfather before him—all losers in the inheritance lottery—he was destined to seek his fortune far from home.

PART II

*

Possibilities

In the absence of navigable rivers and manufacturing plants west of Missouri, freight wagons became essential to the viability of western settlements like Salt Lake City and Denver. In this photograph, probably from the 1850s, a team of eight mules pulls a wagon load. As the freighting industry grew more sophisticated, mules were replaced by oxen and simple wagons were replaced by larger and more sophisticated "prairie schooner" models, so called because they were shaped like boats. (*Library of Congress*)

Chapter 6

THE WAGONMASTER

*

"The tide of emigrants westward increases, and almost hourly wagon after wagon, some drawn by oxen and some by mules, roll past." So scribbled William G. Johnston, formerly of St. Louis, on April 17, 1849, as he waited impatiently in the little frontier town of Independence, Missouri, for his wagon train to depart. More than a month earlier, Johnston and his party had steamed up the Missouri River from St. Louis in just four days, only to be holed up in Independence ever since while their guide made the necessary preparations. "We had yet to purchase mules and numerous things needed on the plains," Johnston noted, "and time would be required for the grass to grow upon which the animals must subsist. . . . Our guide, Jim Stewart, tells us to be in no haste. He says the parties starting this early are making woeful mistakes and that when once we take up the line of march, he will engage to pass every mother's son of them."[1]

On just such a caravan, at just such a time and place, eighteen-year-old Alfred Slade most likely joined the nearly 50,000 "Forty-Niners" stampeding to the California gold fields that spring from all over the world.[2] The California gold rush of 1849 dramatically altered the balance between the Pacific coast and the states back east. Within two years of James Marshall's discovery, more than 100,000 fortune-seekers had flocked to California from all over the world, by one reckoning the most astonishing mass movement of people since the Crusades.[3]

By 1852 California had attracted nearly a quarter of a million people; by the late 1850s its population approached 380,000—greater than four of the six established states of New England.[4]

Many Forty-Niners were driven by the prospect of finding instant wealth on the banks of the Sacramento River; others, like Alfred Slade, were simply young and adventurous men who lacked any compelling reason to stay home.[5] But even older, propertied men found the allure of California hard to resist. Alf Slade's brother William, as the family's eldest male, was tending to the family's mill and store in Carlyle with his stepfather Elias Dennis. Nevertheless, on May 9 William and two dozen other Illinois men joined a California-bound wagon train from Independence that included twenty passenger carriages "fitted up with springs, and almost every other convenience," according to a newspaper report.[6]

The gold strike that drew the Forty-Niners to California was no mirage. During the year 1848—while Alfred Slade was still serving in the army at Santa Fe and word of the find had barely seeped back to the East—some 6,000 would-be miners had made their way to the Sacramento Valley and extracted some $10 million worth of gold. The amount more than doubled with each succeeding year until, in 1852, miners were extracting about $80 million in gold from creeks in the Sacramento Valley. All told, between 1848 and 1856 California produced more than $500 million in gold, amounts unparalleled in human history.[7]

The migrants pushing west were neither the richest nor the poorest of Americans. The rich had no reason to go, and the poor couldn't afford to. Several independent stagecoach lines offered passage to California, but the cost was about seven cents a mile, or $140 from the Missouri River—more money than many Americans earned in a year.[8] For a family seeking to move permanently, the cost of a wagon, supplies, and housing would have required an investment of at least $500, and more likely two or three times that amount.[9] Alfred Slade had perhaps $200 when he set out. If, as seems likely, he joined a wagon train in some working capacity, those funds would have sufficed to take him to California. How he would survive once he got there was another question.

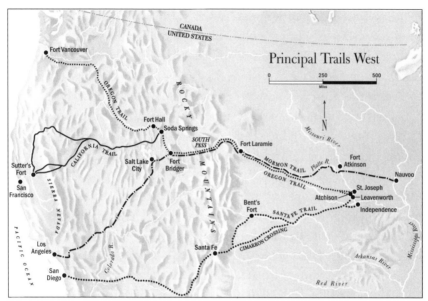

The central routes to the American West Coast and Utah all met at South Pass.

Only a few routes to California were available to the gold-seekers, and all of them took months. The most comfortable route from America's populous East Coast—via clipper ship around Cape Horn at the southernmost tip of South America and then up the West Coast—was expensive and took about five months.[10] Or Easterners could sail part way down the Atlantic to the Gulf of Mexico and Panama, there to forage their way across the isthmus before boarding another ship on the Pacific side—a journey that took only about two months but subjected travelers to deadly mosquito-infested jungle terrain. Americans from the Mississippi Valley, like the Slade brothers, enjoyed the option of steaming south on the Mississippi River to New Orleans and proceeding from there to Panama by sailing ship.

But for most migrants from the upper Mississippi Valley, the trip westward, like the diarist William Johnston's, began on a steamship headed west along the Missouri River to a jumping-off point, usually Independence, St. Joseph, or Westport (later Kansas City) in Missouri. In these towns that spring of '49 and for several springs thereafter, thousands of wagons would gather to await the departure of their wagon trains—often so many wagons that it would take days just to clear up the congestion involved in getting all the wagons on the road. The wagon trains usually hired a guide—generally a mountain man who knew the route well—and elected leaders from among their ranks who would make decisions throughout the trip.

These thousands of wagons all converged upon a single route. The Emigrant Trail—like the Wilderness Trail and the Goshen Road that Charles Slade had followed a generation earlier through Virginia, Kentucky, and Illinois—was the main highway for anyone making the 2,000-mile journey from western Missouri to California. By 1849 it benefited from decades of discoveries and four years of especially heavy use. The original overland route followed by Meriwether Lewis and William Clark in 1804 had been impassable by wagon, so Lewis and Clark had traveled mostly by boat on the Missouri, the only navigable river route west. The mountain men who had followed Lewis and Clark had discovered more accessible passes through the Rockies for foot travel or packhorse but still found nothing suitable for a wagon.

Then in 1826 the explorer Jedidiah Smith came upon the South Pass, a gently sloping gap 20 miles wide through the Rocky Mountains at what was then the border between the U.S. and Britain's Oregon Territory. When Smith arrived in California that year, the Mexican settlers there were astonished, and Mexican officials were apprehensive. They feared, presciently, that a deluge of American settlers would overwhelm their sparsely populated province. One glimpse of the South Pass was often all it took to dismantle the barriers between east and west in a traveler's mind.

"The passage through these mountains," wrote the missionary Samuel Parker of his crossing in August 1835, "is in a valley so gradual in the ascent and descent that I should not have known that we were passing them had it not been that as we advanced the atmosphere gradually became cooler. At length we saw the perpetual snows upon our right hand . . . elevated many thousand feet above us. . . . Probably the time may not be very far distant when trips may be made across the continent as they have been made to Niagara Falls to see Nature's wonders."[11]

Since the early 1840s, emigrant wagons had followed the Oregon Trail from the Missouri River at Independence, then trundled along the Platte River across the Great Plains before cresting the Continental Divide at the South Pass.[12] The Forty-Niners followed much the same route to California, forking south off the Oregon Trail to what became known as the California Trail through the Great Basin and across the Sierra Nevada mountains.[13]

A rare photograph of a Mormon wagon train making its way to Salt Lake City along the Mormon Trail. (*Denver Public Library*)

A third deviation, known as the Mormon Trail, took emigrants from South Pass to Salt Lake City. It was after crossing that pass in July 1847 that Brigham Young and some 15,000 Mormon followers, fleeing religious persecution in the States, departed from the Oregon Trail by heading due west instead of northwest to settle at the Great Salt Lake, in an arid canyon seemingly cut off from the rest of the world—a location, Young presumed, unlikely to be coveted by anyone else. Yet the Mormon community he established at Salt Lake City soon became a critical stopping place for all travelers, if only by virtue of its status as the only sizable town along this two-thousand-mile route between the Missouri River and the Pacific. With a population of 11,000 as early as 1850, Salt Lake City was an urban oasis of order, safety, commerce, industry, family life, communal values, fresh food, shade—all the trappings of civilization customarily associated only with the older cities back in the States, even if the Mormons themselves persisted in rejecting and insulting the religious beliefs of mainstream Christian Americans.[14]

Mormons were happy to trade provisions for coveted household furnishings: the fine paintings, modern cooking stoves, pianos and other objects that emigrants had concluded were too heavy to transport any farther.[15] Eventually non-Mormon merchants found it worth their while to settle in Salt Lake City, and Mormons found it worth *their* while to tolerate their presence.

The Mormons' need to maintain contact with their missionary organizations in the States and Europe provided the impetus for America's first Western mail service.[16] The demands of a large, isolated city gave rise to the first commercial freighting and passenger stagecoach lines. The Mormons could be vilified, ridiculed, appeased, or attacked; but they could not be ignored. And all westbound emigrants—whether to California, Oregon, or Salt Lake—found themselves sharing the same Overland Route at least as far west as South Pass.

William G. Johnston's California-bound wagon train did not pull out of Independence until the morning of April 28, 1849; by June 21 they were in the Rockies, struggling "up a ravine, narrow and precipitous," through which coursed a stream that "had washed out the earth and left bare rocks and boulders which clogged our way over which mules and wagon wheels had to be pulled or lifted constantly."[17] Two days later they arrived in Salt Lake City, where "both men and mules were to enjoy two days of relaxation from our recent severe toils," but where, while observing the Mormons' worship service, "I found the heat so unendurable that I felt obliged to withdraw to camp where under an awning I found some comfort." On July 24 they reached California, "the first train with wagons to enter California." It had taken them eighty days to travel 1,974 miles.[18]

These adventurers soon discovered that the land they had struggled to reach was no paradise but a chaotic world of unkempt young men just like themselves, dressed in flannel shirts and heavy boots, with no plan or desire other than to hurry on to the mines, strike it rich, and return home. Cholera and other diseases infested the mining camps, where sanitation was primitive. San Francisco was a human gutter much like Santa Fe during its military occupation barely a year earlier, only now it was miners rather than soldiers who were preyed upon by gamblers and prostitutes while whiskey destroyed their immune systems.

"Only young healthy people are fit to travel to California," one recent arrival in San Francisco remarked in 1852.[19] The Forty-Niners did consist overwhelmingly of young men: In the 1850 U.S. Census,

92 percent of California's population was male. Yet within six months of arrival, one in five Forty-Niners was dead. "The number of deaths is beyond all calculation," wrote Jerusha Merrill of San Francisco in October 1849. "Many have no friends to put them under the turf. . . . I warn all against the gaming house and the grog shop."[20] So many died there that life insurance companies refused to write new policies for Californians or charged additional premiums for migrants already covered.[21]

Most of the surviving Forty-Niners returned to their homes in the States within a year or two, having failed to find the fortune they sought but grateful to escape with their lives.[22] Alfred Slade's previous experience in Santa Fe probably prepared him for California better than most Forty-Niners, who typically came from respectable families, sufficiently comfortable to afford such a journey. His Santa Fe memories may have prompted his early departure from California. It is also possible that his less adventurous older brother William's purpose in traveling to California in May 1849 was to fetch young Alfred—who was still only eighteen—home to Illinois.[23] Whatever the explanation, by 1850 Alfred was back home in Carlyle, where that fall's U.S. Census reported him working with his stepfather at the family mill and living at home with his mother, stepfather, older brother William, younger sister Virginia, his half-brother Elias Dennis, Jr., his sister Mary Doyle's two-year-old daughter, and two German servants: a fifty-year-old woman and her seventeen-year-old daughter.[24]

To be sure, by the time the census taker arrived at the Dennis home on Fairfax Street, Alfred may have been in transit again—listed by his family as living in Carlyle for want of another location. What is certain is that some time in 1850, most likely in the spring or summer, Alfred Slade departed once again for the West, this time in the company of several young friends and Mexican War comrades from Carlyle, including their former Company A captain Thomas Bond.[25] Bond was an exception to the rule about footloose young California-bound adventurers: at this point he was forty-five with a wife and two children back home.[26]

The Carlyle party kept no journals and left no written record of their journey; the sole clue to their route and destination appeared in an obscure reference within a Clinton County history published in 1881—specifically, in a paid biographical entry (presumably approved by the subject) of Alfred's traveling companion Joseph W. Maddux: "He remained in the county at work upon the farm until 1850, when he made several trips north into Minnesota and, in company with Captain Bond, Alf Slade, and others, traveled by the Overland route to Oregon."[27]

How Slade and his companions financed this journey, we do not know. He and his companions no doubt pooled their resources, and, based on what we know of Slade's subsequent life as a teamster with an entrepreneurial bent, most likely they worked their way west. Indeed, that was precisely the method chosen by a much younger Clinton County farm boy named Dwight Fisk, who may well have followed Slade's footsteps west in the spring of 1853, when he was only fourteen. (Fisk subsequently wound up working for Slade on the Central Overland stage line.)

But did Alf Slade reach California on this, his second journey west? The Carlyle contingent headed west just as the first economic depression hit the gold country, and it continued through 1852.[28] So Alfred may have left California early, if he reached there at all.[29] The Joseph W. Maddux biography says only that the group from Carlyle "traveled by the Overland route to Oregon." Maddux himself, according to the entry, remained on the Pacific coast five years, spending "two years in mining in northern California, and the remaining three in mercantile business"; it does not specify when, or whether, Maddux and his comrades ever reached Oregon.[30] The entry leaves open the possibility that Alf Slade and the others, like most gold rush migrants, may have parted company once they reached California. Men customarily traveled west in groups for self-protection, but "after arriving at the scenes of the gold fields, such organization was forgotten," the nineteenth-century author Emerson Hough noted; "even the parties that had banded together in the Eastern states as partners rarely kept together for a month after reaching the region where luck, hazard and opportunity, inextricably blended, appealed to each man to act for himself and with small reference to others."[31]

One hint of Alfred Slade's separation from his Carlyle chums lies in the fact that, once he reached the Far West, Joseph Alfred Slade ceased to use his childhood name of Alfred. Now, as he moved from one place to another, he operated under a shifting variety of sobriquets—"Joe," "Jim," even "Charley." These nicknames may have been designed to obscure earlier chapters of his life; more likely they were designed to reinforce his standing among the social outcasts and fugitive criminals with whom he often worked. "Those were the days," Hough explained in 1908, "when it was not polite to ask a man what his name had been back in the States."[32] In subsequent years men often called Slade "Jack" behind his back, but apparently never to his face. When he signed his name, he used only his initials: "J. A. Slade." In any case, by the late 1850s he was sufficiently well-known along the Overland Trail that a single name sufficed: "Slade."[33]

Slade's own whereabouts through most of the 1850s have baffled historians. He worked as a freighter and stagecoach driver but did not remain long in any one place or job. In both capacities he was constantly on the move between the Missouri River and the Rockies, if not California. He may have briefly driven a stagecoach for Wells Fargo, the express company launched in California in 1852.[34] Some unverified accounts say he lived among Indians;[35] another report from the 1850s has him living in St. Louis.[36] In the late summer of 1853 Slade seems to have materialized as far east as Virginia, designating power of attorney to his stepfather to dispose of the residue of the family's estate there.[37] In September 1853 a Carlyle neighbor won a judgment against Slade for a debt of $194.93, which in Slade's absence resulted in his forfeiting his interest in his father's Illinois real estate—which tells us at the very least that Slade was not then in Carlyle.[38] In November 1854 Slade's stepfather, Elias Dennis, contacted him by stagecoach mail at Leavenworth, in the newly created Kansas Territory—then a principal jumping-off point for military freight trains—concerning Charles Slade's estate (Alfred and two siblings divided $1,000 equally among them).[39] He may have worked from time to time as a self-employed contract freighter.[40]

At a time when most overland travelers required months to reach California and many never returned, Slade's mobility was unusual but hardly unique. Slade did not find his calling in a stationary activity like gold mining. Gold was the lure that enticed people to the far West, but transportation and communications were the devices that kept them there. Horses, mules, oxen, and wagons were in Slade's blood, at least since he had first handled them in the army as a sixteen-year-old. In this open land the most essential tool was not the axe—which his father had used to clear forests in Illinois—nor the gold miner's pan, but the wheel: the necessary device for transporting freight across vast empty distances. An entire new industry, demanding as well as lucrative, required his services.

The California gold rush also created a new challenge for the U.S. Army. Before the Mexican War the regular peacetime army had been limited to a few thousand men charged with guarding the nation's borders.[41] But now a larger army was needed to protect the hundreds of thousands of California-bound emigrants from Indian tribes, many of them fiercely hostile, along the way. To the Plains Indians the early white traders had been reciprocal trading partners, and the Oregon emigrants of the 1840s had seemed a minor nuisance. But now the Indians fiercely resented the endless gold rush wagon trains, whose oxen, mules, and horses ate all the grass and fouled the streams while white hunters shot the buffalo, driving the herds from the trail.[42] These Indian grievances were surely justified, but that was not the army's concern; its mission was to protect travelers by keeping these tribes quiescent. To that end, the War Department began building permanent military posts in the West, manned by year-round garrisons.

The first of these, Fort Kearny, was established in 1848 along the Platte River, some 200 miles west of Omaha in what later became Nebraska Territory. The following year, another 300 miles farther west, at the confluence of the North Platte and Laramie rivers in what later became Wyoming, the army took over a former fur trading post called Fort Laramie and turned it into the largest and most important military post in the West. By that time seven similar Western army posts were operating, with 987 troops; a decade later there were sixteen.[43]

In the fertile Western states like Illinois and Missouri, the establishment of an army post was usually followed by the arrival of farmers and traders capable of supplying the necessary food and goods to the garrison. But these barren regions in the "Great American Desert" seemed incapable of supporting soldiers or civilians. Moreover, no goods were manufactured west of the Missouri; everything used there had to be shipped from the East. The manufacturing states east of the Mississippi routinely moved goods along navigable rivers, barge canals, and, increasingly, railroads; yet none of these conveyances existed west of the Mississippi. In that whole western expanse, only the Missouri River could be used by steamboats for any great distance, and the Missouri was hazardous as well as indirect. From St. Louis its path meandered 3,175 miles far to the northwest, so that even steamers capable of braving its unpredictable shallows to its distant headwaters at Fort Benton still found themselves at least 1,000 miles north of California or New Mexico or Salt Lake.[44] In effect only one means existed for moving bulk supplies and heavy machinery across the Great American Desert: the freight wagon.

So to meet the needs of soldiers, emigrants, and settlements alike, a large industry sprang up.[45] Every morning and afternoon for nearly half a century, the cry of "Stretch out! Stretch out!" echoed along the Overland and Santa Fe trails. With this command, large trains of heavy freight wagons, drawn by mules or oxen, uncoiled from their defensive circular corrals and took up single-file lines toward their distant westbound destinations. These slow-moving wagons carried the lifeblood of struggling young towns, mining camps, and army posts: food, clothing, furniture, even fine china.[46]

As cumbersome as a wagon train may have seemed to an outsider, freighting was a surprisingly easy business to enter. Any man who could raise the price of a wagon, a few head of oxen, and enough food for a few months could set himself up as a freighter. With luck, he could recoup his original investment in a single trip. Western merchants were happy to pay ten dollars and more per hundred pounds, and each wagon could carry a five-thousand-pound load. (One mercantile house in Salt Lake City paid $150,000 for hauling in 1865.)[47] In some cases the cost of shipping an item exceeded the value of the item itself. In one joke widely circulated through the Rockies, a pioneer woman complained about the high price of a paper of sewing needles. "But madam," the peddler replied, "the freight!"[48]

As the freighters established themselves through the 1850s, their dependable presence emboldened emigrants to settle along their routes. Instead of making the hard trip all the way to California, settlers now followed the freight wagons and staked out ranches and communities across Kansas Territory, along the Platte River and its forks, and from there out into the Rocky Mountains. Large sections of the so-called Great American Desert, these settlers discovered upon closer inspection, were regions of unsurpassed fertility, well adapted to raising cattle and growing grains and fruits.[49] Although the freighters never conceived of themselves as colonizers, they inadvertently became the driving force behind the populating of the empty spaces between Missouri and California.

At first St. Louis was the eastern terminus of these freighting operations, but as steamboat captains pushed their vessels farther up the lower reaches of the Missouri River, new jumping-off points sprang up to the west. The village of Franklin in central Missouri constituted such a terminus when William Becknell left there in the first successful trading expedition to Santa Fe in 1821. By the early 1850s new Missouri River ports like Independence, Westport, and St. Joseph—each a little closer to the Pacific but still accessible to Missouri River steamers—had sprung up as gateways to the west. With the creation of Kansas and Nebraska territories in 1854, groups of Missouri speculators crossed into Kansas and established two new port towns, Leavenworth and Atchison.

All these Missouri River towns competed fiercely with each other for freight business, yet the main distinction between them lay in their location: Leavenworth stood some 25 miles farther west along the Overland route than Independence and Westport, and it was just 3 miles south of Fort Leavenworth, the army's main depot in the West.[50] Atchison as late as 1859 had just a few hundred residents and only four brick buildings downtown, but it stood some 25 miles closer to California than Leavenworth and enjoyed access to the best wagon road leading directly west.[51] Such differences might save a wagon train a day or two of travel.

Freighter wagons photographed with oxen teams in Colorado territory in 1862. Oxen were preferred by teamsters to pull their freight wagons for a number of reasons, including their great strength and endurance, and the fact that Indians would not steal them. (*Denver Public Library*)

These ports quickly settled into a pattern that lasted as long as the freighting industry itself. Every year in late February or early March, parties of men were sent out onto the plains to round up the oxen that had wintered there, some hundreds of miles to the west. The horse was unsuitable for pulling heavy freight loads because it couldn't sustain its strength over long periods on a diet of nothing but buffalo grass; mules were better adapted to heavy work but expensive and vulnerable to theft; but oxen were strong, inexpensive, and—as one early Santa Fe trader discovered in 1851—served three useful purposes: "1st, drawing the wagons; 2nd, the Indians will not steal them as they would horses and mules; and 3rdly, in case of necessity part of the oxen will answer for provisions."[52]

As soon as enough grass was available, the animals were brought in and wagons were prepared, each outfitted with a toolbox and assorted hardwood for repairs along the trail. Early in April the first trains were loaded and rolled out. For the next six months, life in these towns was hectic, as loaded trains rolled out and empty trains returned to load up and move out again. In Atchison it was common to see loaded ox trains a mile long on Commercial Street, stretching from the levee out to Harmony Garden in the town's western suburbs.[53] By early December the freighters were ready to quit for the season and send their stock out to winter range.[54]

The wagons used in high plains freighting were usually manufactured in Pittsburgh or St. Louis and then shipped by steamer to these Missouri River embarkation ports, where their parts were assembled on the levee.[55] The original Conestoga wagons used for hauling freight in the eastern U.S. were so large—about twenty-three feet long—that it was impossible for animal teams to pull them through the Oregon Trail's treacherous mountain passes. West of the Missouri the most popular wagon was about half that size and called a "prairie schooner" because of its boatlike appearance and sloping floor (higher at both ends), design elements deliberately intended to prevent the wagon's load from shifting on upgrades and downgrades.[56]

Men who worked at freighting fell into four categories: the entrepreneurs raised the capital and ran the business; the wagonmasters supervised the day-to-day operations of the trains; the teamsters—bullwhackers, muleskinners, herders, and cooks—manned the trains; and the clerks staffed the headquarters offices. Slade worked his way up from teamster to wagonmaster and eventually became probably the most celebrated freighter on the plains.

O f the dozens of freighting operators that arose in the 1850s, the most impressive was a partnership headed by a consummately exuberant entrepreneur named William H. Russell. Although this pint-sized promoter was widely hailed as the "Napoleon of the West," Russell was actually born in Vermont, rarely ventured farther west than Leavenworth, and functioned most comfortably among Washington politicians and New York bankers. Russell's aristocratic English genes had endowed him with the firm but deluded conviction that he could do no wrong, and his experienced partners rarely objected to his visionary schemes.[57]

Russell's parents brought him to western Missouri in the late 1820s, when he was in his teens. There he started as a clerk for retail merchants in several towns along what was then the frontier. He

enhanced his social status by marrying a local preacher's daughter, and
graduated to a partnership in a successful general store in Lexington,
Missouri. By 1848 Russell had
made enough money to build himself a twenty-room mansion in
Lexington.[58]

His partner in that store was in
many respects the perfect complement to Russell's dynamism and
charm. William B. Waddell was
phlegmatic, stoical, cautious, stingy,
and incapable of reaching decisions
without ponderous deliberation.[59]
He had been born in 1807 in
Kentucky and had worked in the
lead mines of Galena, Illinois, and a
dry goods store in St. Louis. In

The impetuous visionary William H.
Russell jumped from freighting to stagecoaching to mail servce, sinking deeper
into debt with each new grandiose venture.

1829 Waddell returned to Kentucky, married, and settled down to
farm, but farming didn't suit him. He opened a dry goods store in
Kentucky, then moved his family in 1835 to Lexington, Missouri,
where he opened another dry goods store on the Missouri riverfront
and subsequently took on William Russell as a partner.

But the hyperactive Russell couldn't be confined to a single business venture. After the Mexican War, Russell sought to capitalize on
the opportunities in military contracting by joining in a partnership
with James Brown of Independence, Missouri, to carry freight for the
War Department between Fort Leavenworth and Santa Fe. Their first
train in 1849 succeeded, but a year later Russell impulsively took a
chance on transporting a load of freight to Santa Fe in midwinter. Not
only did he lose his gamble with the weather, but his partner Brown
died of typhoid fever en route, and the partnership was forced to ask
Congress for relief of $39,800 in losses on the trip.[60]

In 1854 a new and far greater freighting opportunity arose that
exceeded the resources of any single entrepreneur. By this time the

army had so many Western military posts that the tedious and time-consuming process of contracting dozens of small freighters to supply individual forts no longer made sense. The freighters were unhappy with this short-term system as well, because it forced them to assemble the necessary wagons, oxen, and teamsters on short notice, and then to disband the operation when the train returned, since there was no certainty of receiving another contract the following year.[61] To address these problems, in 1854 Quartermaster General Thomas Jesup dropped the system of individual contracts in favor of a single two-year contract to supply most army posts in the West and Southwest from a single depot at Fort Leavenworth. This new arrangement would elevate the winning contractor from a speculative venture into a solid business enterprise. But at that point no enterprise of such size and capability existed.

The quartermaster at Fort Leavenworth, eager to find the most qualified combination of men to fulfill the contract, probably brought Russell and Waddell together with Alexander Majors, an imposing man with an equally imposing long beard who was the most successful freighter of the day. Unlike Russell and Waddell, Majors was a genuine frontiersman, born in Kentucky in 1814 and brought by covered wagon at age five to the western frontier of Missouri, where he grew up. After marrying at age twenty, Majors produced a large family of mostly daughters, and his success as a farmer was limited by his lack of sons to work his land. To supplement his income, Majors turned to freighting.

It was a business he came to know and love intimately, performing every task from driving oxen in searing summer heat and numbing winter cold to cooking under the stars over a campfire heated by burning cow chips. In 1847 Majors successfully took a wagonload of cheap merchandise to Indians living on the Potawatomi Reservation in what later became Kansas Territory. After the Mexican War, Majors became one of the first Missouri traders to freight supplies to Santa Fe. He started out with six wagons, freighting goods for other merchants. On his first expedition, he set a record of ninety-two days for a round trip, making a profit of $650 per wagonload. The following year, Majors set out with twenty wagons and netted $13,000; and in 1851, Majors left

The freighter Alexander Majors, left, ran a tight outfit, hiring only reliable and trustworthty teamsters. He required them to treat animals with kindness, avoid profanity, stay sober, and behave like gentlemen. The cautious and phlegmatic William B. Waddell, right, ran the Russell, Majors & Waddell office from Leavenworth City, Kansas.

Fort Leavenworth with a train of twenty-five wagons, three hundred oxen, and thirty teamsters. Two years later, he took a train of private merchandise to Santa Fe, returned, and then transported a train of military freight to Fort Union, making $28,000 in profit for his services that year.[62]

Majors ran a tight outfit, hiring only reliable and trustworthy teamsters, whom he required to sign a pledge to treat animals with kindness, avoid profanity, stay sober, and behave like gentlemen. He invested carefully in land to provide pasture for his oxen, and he rested his oxen and men from Saturday afternoon to Monday morning, conducting worship services for his men on Sunday. He equipped each man, as he reminded his teamsters in his customary speech to departing wagon trains, with "one copy of the Holy Bible to defend himself against moral contaminations, and also a pair of Colt's revolvers and a gun to defend yourselves against warlike Indians."[63] His last words to teamsters as they departed were, "Now, young gentlemen, in time of peril remember your fathers and mothers who raised you, and the God who sustains you."[64] When the wagons began to roll. Majors invariably rode on horseback from train to train, carrying his mess kit and blanket attached to his saddle, sitting cross-legged on the ground to share meals with his teamsters, and sleeping on the ground beneath a wagon like everyone else.[65]

His moral standards were of course impossible to enforce—as one of his teamsters remarked, humans might conceivably communicate with each other without using profanity, but how else could they communicate with their animals? Yet there was no disputing his superior results: without forming any partnerships, by 1854, Majors had 100 wagons, 1,200 oxen, and 120 employees, and was considered by many one of the foremost freighters west of the Missouri.[66]

To successfully compete for the army's two-year Western freighting contract, Russell, Waddell, and Majors pooled $60,000 of their capital in December 1854 and formed the largest freighting partnership then in existence. The three men divided their responsibilities according to each individual's talents and temperament: Waddell supervised the firm's headquarters office in Leavenworth City, 3 miles south of Fort Leavenworth; Russell cultivated customers and government contacts in Washington, Philadelphia, and New York; and Majors managed the freighting operations.[67]

Three months later, the War Department awarded their firm a two-year contract to transport supplies to the posts west of the Missouri River. It granted Russell, Majors & Waddell, as the firm was styled, a virtual monopoly on all contracted military freighting in that part of the country.[68] To support their operation, early in 1855 the three partners purchased more than fifty lots in the new town of Leavenworth City, where they constructed warehouses, offices, a blacksmith shop, a wagon-repair shop, extensive corrals, a lumberyard and sawmill, and a packing plant to supply meat for their trains.[69] Within two years of its birth in late 1854 this partnership was doing $2 million worth of business a year and was considered perhaps the most formidable private organization in the West. Its drivers, wrote a government wagonmaster, consistently possessed "unusual courage, perseverance, good judgment, and business ability" and were "remarkable in the management of men."[70]

Did Slade lead military wagon supply trains for this partnership, whose path crossed with his own in a different capacity just a few years later? No hard evidence exists, but circumstantial evidence has tempted many observers to suggest that Slade may have worked for Russell, Majors & Waddell. Slade had a background in military freighting, and by the late 1850s he was well known along the Overland route as a freighting captain.[71] Slade's family contacted him at Leavenworth City in late November 1854, where one can presume he was involved in launching or (more likely, given the lateness of the season) bringing home one of the two military freight trains dispatched that year from Fort Leavenworth: one to Albuquerque, the other to Fort Fillmore in southern New Mexico and then to nearby El Paso.[72] The firm of Russell, Majors & Waddell did not yet exist (it was formed at the end of 1854). But those three partners had been operating separately out of Fort Leavenworth, and it's possible one of them may have made use of Slade at some point.[73]

The earliest firsthand evidence that Slade functioned as either a teamster or a wagonmaster survives in an account of an 1858 freighting expedition led by Slade, provided half a century later by a novice bullwhacker named Hugo Koch. But Koch's description of Slade's knowledge of the terrain, his confidence, and the esteem in which he was held leaves little doubt that Slade had been freighting for years before.

On his first day in camp, Koch was told by Slade's assistant that his name was "outlandish" for a freight train and therefore Koch would henceforth be called "Fred" instead of "Hugo"—and since the crew already included three or four Freds, Koch would be known as "Dutch Fred."[74] Other exercises of power by Slade were more serious. A day west of Marysville, Kansas—then the westernmost outpost of civilization—a wagon overturned due to its driver's neglect. Koch described what happened next.

> We were driving along until about noon when Slade sent for me. I found the boys had righted an upset wagon and had just finished loading. It was Lazy Bill's, and Slade discharged him on the spot, and his big whip with a four-foot stick and a sixteen-foot lash was given to me.

"Now Fred, the boys will help you up the hill from the creek bed, then you will drive this team." That was all Slade said.[75]

Another incident, a day after the train left Fort Kearny in Nebraska Territory, demonstrated Slade's courage and shrewdness in the face of adversity. As Koch recalled,

we saw ahead a black line of something on either side of the road. Slade soon stopped the train and the dark lines proved to be about three hundred Indians who wanted to collect internal revenue for permission to traverse their domain. Slade pulled his gun and told them to go about their business hunting buffalo, and then told Brigham [the assistant wagonmaster], who drove the lead team, to go on, and he [Slade] remained there until the train had passed and we were not further molested that day. . . .

A few days later we saw many Indians in the distance on the hill and all about us. We made an early camp, and Brigham went to all three messes and urged the men to clean and reload their guns, as he felt sure we would be attacked by Indians before daybreak. Some of the boys had shotguns and some rifles. Brigham had a rifle and he cleaned and loaded it and was ready for the skirmish. He cautioned all the boys to sleep on their guns and have ammunition ready. . . .

The next day the Indians killed a buffalo, and as Slade saw the hunt to the south of us and apprehended a stampede should the bunch cross the road, he stopped Brigham and the train. We could see them coming. The Indians had singled out and separated one animal and drove it full of arrows. Not more than 50 feet in front of the first wagon and not more than that distance from the road the animal fell and the Indians butchered it in less than no time. Slade traded some sugar, coffee and bacon for meat and we feasted for several days on buffalo hump.[76]

The teamsters, in whose ranks Slade got his start, constituted a rare breed among American workingmen. Teamsters and bullwhackers ranked among America's best-paid unskilled laborers: in the late 1850s some teamsters made forty dollars a month plus board, at a time when a typical Michigan farm worker made eight dollars.[77] But few men went into freighting for the money. The work was irregular, and no dollar amount could compensate for long monotonous weeks spent toiling across baking plains or snow-filled passes. Because most freight trains crossed the plains in summertime, insects were a constant harassment. Prairie hailstorms could rip wagon covers to shreds and stampede the animals. If a freight train didn't make its destination by early fall, blizzards often took their toll on men and animals alike.

William Henry Jackson's self-portrait as a bullwhacker upon arrival in Salt Lake City in 1866. (*Denver Public Library*)

Most teamsters signed up for the adventure, or to escape something. Some were lonely men attracted by the camaraderie of the trail, where every teamster took his turn at cooking, herding, and guarding the stock overnight.[78] But lonely or gregarious, they were rough men performing rough work that involved far more than handling bulls. The twelve-ox team trundled heavy freight wagons at just two or three miles per hour, but Indian warriors inflamed by intrusions on their land could kick their ponies to bursts of twenty miles per hour.[79]

When teamsters weren't fighting Indians they often fought among themselves. "Men fought with fist, knife, pistol, at the drop of a hat, and even without that formality," one account reports. "The passing of the lie, flinging the unpardonable epithet, called for action."[80] In this environment, the coolheaded man with a true eye, quick on the trigger, exercised a natural authority over his peers.

By most accounts, Slade from his earliest days as a teamster fit this description. Few of the posturing roughnecks who worked as teamsters had survived a war, as he had. If the greatest challenge on the trail was boredom—well, Slade had already survived the monotony of daily drills and roll calls in the army that occupied Santa Fe. His skill with a revolver, rifle, and sawed-off shotgun—he was a "walking arsenal," by one account—enhanced his status, as did his willingness to use them.[81] "As a marksman with a Colt's navy revolver," wrote his colleague Frank Root, "no one on the Plains could surpass Slade, and few could equal him."[82]

The outlaw Polk Wells claimed that, as an eleven-year-old runaway, he was taught to shoot by Slade. As Wells described the encounter in his memoirs (written in prison), Slade noticed young Wells shooting prairie dogs and complimented him on his marksmanship; then "Slade drew his pistol and showed me how to shoot without taking aim."

> This mode of handling firearms is similar to throwing a stone from the hand. The eye, of course, plays [a] part, but the elevation and range, or direction of the muzzle of the gun, is wholly the work of the mind. I readily saw the advantages of this style of shooting and adopted it in preference to that of taking sight, or as Slade termed it, "Hoosier shooting."[83]

Whether or not such an encounter took place—and there is reason to suspect that Wells concocted the incident out of whole cloth—the story does reflect the high esteem in which Slade's marksmanship was held.[84]

Above all, Slade exuded a sense of strength and confidence that attracted other less secure men to follow his lead. What the U.S. Supreme Court Justice Catron had once written of Andrew Jackson's "hardy industry" and "sleepless energy few could equal" applied to Slade as well: "The way a thing should be done struck him plainly. . . . His awful will stood alone, and was made the will of all he commanded."[85] Slade's quick temper—presumably inherited from the Darke branch of his mother's family—was legendary, but as the Montana historian Llewellyn Callaway noted, "He possessed the unusual faculty of being abnormally cool in anger or when laboring under excitement."[86]

The wagonmaster, or "train boss," was the kingpin of the whole freighting operation and the key to its success. He alone shouldered the ultimate responsibility for $18,000 to $30,000 worth of wagons, livestock, and accessories, as well as $25,000 to $250,000 worth of goods, all of which belonged to someone else. For that reason wagonmasters were selected with great care and compensated accordingly: usually $100 to $150 per month, plus board.[87] Nine out of ten wagonmasters were former teamsters promoted from the ranks, like Slade. By the very nature of his job, a wagonmaster had to be strong, brave, tireless, and skilled at exacting obedience to his commands. He needed a loud voice capable of carrying for a mile on the plains. Beyond that, writes Henry Pickering Walker, author of the definitive work *The Wagonmasters*,

> He had to be a farrier able to shoe oxen and mules and a wheelwright able to repair wagons with the simplest tools. He had to know how to get wagons out of bog holes, up and down steep hills, and across rivers. He had to know where water and grass were to be found for the noon halt and the night camp. He was expected to be a physician to his men and a veterinarian to his animals. He had to be a hunter to provide fresh game as a relief from the usual sowbelly. He had to have the magical ability to be everywhere at the same time—riding out a mile or so ahead, scouting for campsites or bad places in the road, watching out for Indians. . . . or looking up and down the lines of wagons stretched over a mile or more of prairie. . . . Above all, the wagonmaster was expected to know how to get the best out of both animals and men.[88]

Long before a train hit the trail, the wagonmaster was responsible for assembling the oxen and hiring a crew. The loading of wagons was usually supervised by the wagonmaster as well, since the task required tremendous ingenuity at combining a broad variety of articles, from tea and sugar to ready-made clothes and casks of whiskey to stoves and sheet iron. The load had to be distributed so as to keep the center of gravity as low as possible and centered in the wagon while protecting fragile items like mirrors and showcases.[89]

It was on the freighting trains that Slade developed a fierce hatred of horse thieves—a characteristic he shared with most frontiersmen.

On the plains, the element most essential to survival was not a man's gun but his horse, for a man set afoot in a wilderness infested with hostile Indians was likely as good as dead. In the first makeshift miners' courts, the theft of a horse was considered the most serious offense.[90] "Horse stealing in those days was the greatest crime a man could commit," the frontiersman George Beatty recalled. "Murder didn't amount to anything."[91]

Aside from the wagonmaster, the scattered army forts represented the only other legal authority on the plains. Occasionally the officers there were called on to resolve disputes between wagonmasters and their men. If, for example, a driver quit over unfair treatment and the wagonmaster refused to pay his wages due, the case might be referred to the post commander, acting as a justice of the peace. If the commander found in the driver's favor and the wagonmaster refused to pay the wages, the wagonmaster was confined to the guardhouse. If the teamster was in the wrong, he was held in the guardhouse for ten days—until the train was well on its way and presumably beyond his vengeful reach—and then was turned loose to shift for himself.[92]

A wagonmaster had to guard constantly against pilfering of the train's cargo by his own men, and sometimes a wagonmaster paid for his disciplinary efforts with his life. In 1859 a train crew was returning from Denver with a single wagon. The wagonmaster announced that the wagon was reserved for the cook and the rations and no one else could ride in it. When a teamster was found in the wagon and the wagonmaster tried to drag him out, the teamster drew a knife and killed the boss. When the crew returned to its home base in Nebraska Territory, the teamster was turned over to the local authorities, who promptly released him, pleading lack of jurisdiction, because the murder had taken place on the open plains.[93]

After four months or more spent plodding beside oxen and wagons, the end of the trail released the crew from their oxen, their wagons and each other, and the towns at either end were only too happy to help them celebrate. In one contemporaneous description of a "hurdy-gurdy" house, a place where men could socialize with women, the reader was invited to picture a large room, furnished with a bar at one end—where champagne at $12 (in gold) per bottle, and "drinks" at twenty-five to fifty cents, are wholesaled (correctly speaking)—and divided, at the end of this bar, by a railing running from side to side. The outer enclosure is densely crowded. . . . with men in every variety of garb that can be seen on the continent. Beyond the barrier sit the dancing women, called "hurdy-gurdies," sometimes dressed in uniform, but, more generally, habited according to the dictates of individual caprice, in the finest clothes that money can buy, and which are fashioned in the most attractive styles that fancy can suggest. On one side is a raised orchestra. The music suddenly strikes up, and the summons, "Take your partners for the next dance," is promptly answered by some of the male spectators, who paying a dollar in gold for a ticket, approach the ladies' bench, and—in style polite, or otherwise, according to antecedents—invite one of the ladies to dance.[94]

In such dance halls and gambling parlors, as the teamster George Beehrer put it, freighting crews "squandered not only their money, but also their souls." Within three days of his train's arrival in Salt Lake in September 1858, Beehrer wrote, three of his train comrades were dead: one stabbed in a feud over a barmaid, one shot at a gaming table, and one murdered in a saloon brawl.[95]

Fights over women were common because there were so few of them. In 1849 the frontier was said to number fifty men for every woman.[96] The so-called fair sex, reasoned George Napheys, author of a popular advice book for women, was "unfitted for the hardships of pioneer life."[97] The monotony of the Great Plains, with its flat and depressing landscape and constant, debilitating wind, was unleavened by the comforting presence of other women. "This country is all right for men and dogs," went a popular frontier aphorism, "but it's hell on women and horses."

Adult women in the early West fell almost entirely into two groups: wives reluctantly following their husbands, and prostitutes servicing the needs of all those lonely single men. These needs were not necessarily sexual, for in this grindingly masculine world, a woman's companionship was often valued as much as her body. Some miners paid an ounce of gold (worth $16) just to have a prostitute sit beside them at a bar or a gaming table.[98] "Often a miner would be found sitting in the cabin of a 'painted' lady while she mended his socks and sewed buttons on his shirt," the writer Anne Seagraves has noted.[99] A young California miner spent $150 on new clothing and traveled more than 100 miles just to see a French woman who was dealing "twenty-one" in a gambling hall. "She's got a voice like music," he wrote in his diary, "and just her speaking to me in that way put me all in a flutter."[100]

The mere presence of a woman often exerted a moderating influence on male behavior. "Many's the miner who'd never wash his face or comb his hair, if it wasn't for thinkin' of the sportin' girls he might meet in the saloons," one Montana miner admitted.[101]

With few exceptions, the only women in mining camps were prostitutes, and their presence was so rare there that they were accorded the respect usually reserved for "respectable" women.[102] They also commanded exorbitant prices. Such was the gender imbalance during the gold rush that miners paid anywhere from $200 to $400 for a night of sex in San Francisco. This demand helped drive up the supply: By 1853 San Francisco had an estimated two thousand prostitutes.[103]

But prostitutes alone could never address the great irony of the early West: The frontier may have been no place for a woman, but without women it ultimately proved no place for a man either. As David Courtwright has noted, women were the everyday healers of the nineteenth century: the practical companions adept at nursing, sanitation, and nutrition. Primitive farms proved incomplete and untenable without women to cook and wash and nurture. The absence of women ensured that illness claimed more lives than it would have in a society dominated by families rather than young single men.[104] Men who had gone west to escape feminine restraints ultimately yearned for those restraints. "Gone to Find a Wife," read the sign tacked to many a miner's abandoned cabin. "Lucky Miners House But No Wife," read another where gold had been struck.[105]

Without the restraining influence of women, almost all men drank on the frontier. Some handled it better than others. Whenever a wagon train captained by Slade disbanded, the Missouri River port towns like

Atchison and Leavenworth witnessed the first evidence of his greatest flaw: his inability to hold his liquor.

"Liquor seemed to change Slade into a demon," one of Slade's colleagues observed.[106] Years later a driver named Thomas J. Ranahan, known as "Irish Tommy," described one of Slade's binges that Ranahan had witnessed at Westport: "A negro deckhand had done some slight thing that displeased Slade. Slade, who was drunk, took after the offender. Slade's face was so terrifying that the deckhand jumped over the rail, into the river, and swam to safety."[107]

It was probably in a hurdy-gurdy house in one of these Missouri River towns, perhaps about 1857—perhaps even during one of his binges—that Slade met his match. Until that moment his character had been molded primarily by his stepfather, by his military service in Santa Fe, and by the freighting cycle on the Plains. Now those influences would be supplanted by a woman every bit as captivating, feisty, and combative as Slade himself. From that point forward, his story would be her story as well, for better or worse.

Chapter 7

THE GATHERING STORM

*

The woman who became Slade's wife was his equal in many respects, not the least of which was the lasting impression—favorable or not—that she left on everyone she encountered.

"Her figure was queenly, and her movements the perfection of grace," rhapsodized Nathaniel Langford, who knew Maria Virginia Slade later in Idaho Territory. "Her countenance was lit up by a pair of burning black eyes, and her hair, black as the raven's wing, fell in rich curls over her shoulders. She was of powerful organization, and having passed her life upon the borders, knew how to use the rifle and revolver, and could perform as many dextrous feats in the saddle as the boldest hunter that roamed the plains."[1]

If the accounts of impressionable Western writers are to be believed, this versatile woman was "an expert seamstress, horse-woman, dancer, good shot, excellent cook."[2] Small wonder, then, that Virginia Slade, as she was known, tended to intimidate men and women alike.

"Mrs. Slade," Margaret Gilbert, the wife of a Slade friend, recalled years later, "could ride and shoot as well as any man. . . . Get her in overalls, as she dressed a lot, and she would have been taken for a man."[3]

But whether she wore overalls or an evening gown, what impressed most people about Virginia was less her striking appearance than her rambunctious and belligerent nature. "A remarkably strong personality," reported a bullwhacker named Thomas Bishop.[4] "Mrs. Slade would fight at the drop of a hat and was grittier than he was, by long odds," the Colorado pioneer Frank Bartholf recalled.[5] After meeting Virginia, a cross-country traveler named Fitz Hugh Ludlow reflected, "Not only is Mrs. Slade one of the finest pistol-shots in the West (without any allowance for her sex), but a woman of long memory, and in reckless courage the perfect match and compeer of her late husband."[6] George Beatty, an army corporal enlisted by Slade to assist him in catching horse thieves, once recounted a scene in Slade's home when Beatty waited for Slade to write out an order: "His wife walked across the room gowned in a black silk dress. My! What a swell she cut! The thought came to me: Here is another Lady Macbeth."[7]

If Virginia Slade was an intimidating figure, she was probably well suited as a companion to Slade himself. "Mrs. Slade was not altogether a lovely character, often interfering in her husband's business," the bullwhacker Hugo Koch told the historian G. C. Coutant, "and many of the difficulties he had with people originated with her. . . . His wife always possessed great influence over him, even when he was drunk."[8] Wrote the historian Charles Lilley, a son of Colorado pioneers who had known Slade: "There was one person of whom he stood in real and deadly fear—and that was none other than Mrs. Slade, who is said to have had a temper that outmatched his."[9]

Where Maria Virginia Slade came from, what her maiden name was, or how she met Slade are all questions shrouded in mystery. In some accounts she came from Texas; in others, from Georgia.[10] (The dearth of background information has led one researcher to theorize that the woman known as Slade's wife was actually his younger sister, coincidentally also named Maria Virginia, posing as his wife for her own self-protection out West.)[11] The most trustworthy source suggests that she was born in Missouri, probably in the early 1830s, and was raised in the 1840s in or near the newly created Missouri town of Carthage, in the southwest corner of that state.[12] Some Western writers have concluded that Virginia's maiden name was "Dale" because Slade named a Colorado stagecoach station "Virginia Dale" in her honor; but the question of whether that "Dale" referred to Virginia's surname or the valley in which the station was located remains unresolved to this day.[13]

Virginia's contemporaries conjectured that she had been a dance-hall girl or a prostitute before she met Slade. "Some said she had been a hurdy-gurdy girl, others a gambling woman, but all agreed she had once been a lady of negotiable virtue," wrote Anne Seagraves in *Soiled Doves*, a book about prostitutes in the West.[14] This is hardly a definitive assertion, but since many unmarried women on the frontier were prostitutes or dance-hall girls, it's not unreasonable. An attractive single woman would have served little other purpose on the frontier, and Virginia did demonstrate her proficiency as both a dancer and a card player later in her marriage to Slade.[15]

The most popular account claims that Slade met Virginia in a gambling house where she ran a game of faro (then called "bucking the tiger"). According to this story, Slade got into a shooting scrape, whereupon Virginia pulled her guns, ordered everyone out of the place, and cared for the wounded Slade until he recovered.[16] This romantic fable sounds like something lifted from a bad dime novel—the sort of yarn that bored frontiersmen would spin and embellish over a campfire to relieve the tedium of their dreary days. Yet the story does reflect the impulsive and combative natures of both Slade and Virginia.

If this incident took place, it established the pattern for their future relationship. On the frontier a single woman needed a male protector, but with the Slades, the gender roles sometimes were reversed: Slade, the protector of teamsters and bullwhackers, often relied on his wife to pull him out of scrapes. This "far-famed feminine fire-eater," as one Montana paper called Virginia, waged unceasing warfare against Slade's drinking habit and those who abetted it.[17]

If only by virtue of their scarce numbers, frontier women enjoyed their pick of men. Why, then, would an attractive and strong-willed woman like Virginia have cast her lot with a man like Slade? The answer probably lies in the same qualities that drew men to Slade. In a world of swaggering and posturing young males, Slade's confidence and his polite manner set him apart from most frontier men. "When sober [he] was one of the most charming acquaintances that could be imagined," Slade's successor on the Central Overland, Robert Spotswood, once observed. "He was well-educated, a good conversationalist, quiet and unassuming, and would be taken for a law-abiding citizen in any community."[18] The government attorney John Clampitt, writing twenty-five years after Slade's death, recalled him as "withal an honest, kind-hearted, intelligent man, noted for his strong friendships and generous qualities and the power of attracting the favorable notice of even strangers."[19]

Only when he was drunk did Slade become what one historian called "domineering, quarrelsome and dangerous."[20] Once he had sobered up, Slade invariably demonstrated genuine remorse for his misbehavior—an emotion rarely seen in a time and place where most men considered displays of sorrow and regret as signs of weakness.

Slade's previous experience with women was probably limited to Indians. One account of such

Slade's wife, Maria Virginia, is variously described as "queenly," "a big woman," and "another Lady Macbeth," with long dark curls that fell to her shoulders. No certain photo of her has surfaced. This image comes closest: Three copies of it were found in an archive belonging to Charles Bovey of Virginia City, Montana, each marked "Mrs. Slade" on the back. But some historians have questioned its authenticity. If it is Mrs. Slade, she was probably an embittered widow by the time this photograph was taken. (*Timothy Gordon*)

relationships, while not necessarily accurate, deserves at least serious consideration. Susan Bordeaux Bettelyoun, daughter of a French-American fur trader and a Lakota Indian mother, was born in 1857 at Fort Laramie on the Overland Trail and grew up not far from Slade's subsequent headquarters at Horseshoe Creek. In her memoirs—recorded in the 1930s, when she was nearly eighty—Bettelyoun wrote that "Slade had a white wife in Denver, but he also had an Indian woman. . . .in fact, he had been living with Indian women whom he bought in different places, but there were never any offspring from any of them. The last was a Sioux woman who was related to my mother."[21]

Whatever their previous sexual histories, at this point Slade and Virginia became devoted companions. Whether or not she had been a dance-hall girl or prostitute before, from this moment Virginia assumed the persona of Mrs. Slade. Together these two strong personalities cut a formidable figure wherever they ventured. Whether Virginia exerted a matronly restraining influence on Slade or kindled his reckless instincts—that is another question.

To trace Slade's whereabouts through most of the 1850s, it will help to follow the paths of three men he subsequently worked for. William H. Russell, John M. Hockaday, and Benjamin Holladay all operated on the frontier but were not frontiersmen per se. They belonged instead to an adventurous breed of frontier capitalists for whom the money mattered less than the excitement of the game. They were pure entrepreneurs, in the sense that they moved easily from one business to another—from freighting, say, to stagecoaching, to mail and telegraph service—wherever they perceived opportunity (unlike Russell's freighting partner Alexander Majors, who remained a "pure" freighter throughout his career and felt uncomfortable in any other role). They were also political animals whose adrenaline thrived on the power that coursed through Congress and the White House.

These bold men appeared cautious and calculating only in contrast to a man of pure action like Slade, who rarely seems to have reflected on the broader implications of his deeds or their long-run consequences. And so Slade would become the instrument for other men's visions.

William Russell's impetuous nature was restrained, at least for a while, by his partnership with the experienced freighter Alexander Majors and the cautious bookkeeper William Waddell. Another freight operator who hired Slade was less fortunate in his choice of partner.

John M. Hockaday—a peripatetic adventurer like Russell, but a generation younger—was one of several Western merchants who got into freighting in order to provision their retail stores and subsequently branched out into transporting goods for other customers as well. Hockaday may have been born in Virginia about 1830 but grew up in

Independence, Missouri. As a young man he qualified himself for the law and also may have attended West Point before dropping out. He entered the retail trade between Missouri, Salt Lake City, and California in 1850 before taking up a business residence at Salt Lake in 1852, when he was about twenty-two.

Over the next year or so Hockaday seems to have functioned as a surveyor, as an aide to the U.S. Indian Agency, and as an intermediary between the Mormons and "gentiles" whom the Mormons were trying to drive off their lands, including the mountain man Jim Bridger, proprietor of Fort Bridger, a trading post northeast of Salt Lake City.[22] In the mid-1850s Hockaday dabbled in a short-lived mail and passenger stagecoach service between Independence and Salt Lake City, in partnership with a politically connected promoter named William Magraw. By the later 1850s Hockaday had hedged his bets by opening a tannery in Salt Lake City. With another political figure—David H. Burr, surveyor general of Utah Territory from 1855 to about 1858— Hockaday also opened a large dry goods emporium in Salt Lake City. Although Burr was a generation older than Hockaday (he was born in 1803), their store was styled Hockaday & Burr. It was to supply this store that Hockaday opened a warehouse in Atchison, 25 miles up the Missouri River from Leavenworth, and launched his freight operation between Atchison and Salt Lake.[23]

These activities suggest a bright, ambitious, and energetic young man juggling many opportunities, relying heavily on personal connections and hedging his bets without focusing much attention on any single operation.[24] Given the unpredictable nature of freighting, stage coaching, and mail service at that time, Hockaday was astute not to put all his eggs in one basket and to seek stability in government contracts (as the partnership of Russell, Majors & Waddell was doing). But once having ventured into these risky businesses, Hockaday had to keep his hand in them, if only to salvage his investments and maintain his connections. Within a few years Hockaday would find himself competing with Russell, Majors & Waddell in an entirely different business, with Slade caught in the middle.

The freighter Ben Holladay was every bit as ambitious and ener-getic as William Russell and John Hockaday, but Holladay was shrewder and more calculating. His Holladay ancestors had arrived in Virginia from Scotland in 1620, but after two centuries the family had little to show for its time in America. Holladay and his six siblings were raised on a humble farm in Kentucky with little formal education. The family moved in the early 1830s to Weston, Missouri, just across the Missouri River from Fort Leavenworth. Like many another young man in a booming frontier town, Ben tried his hand briefly at many busi-nesses, jumping at each new opportunity. After taking a job as a store clerk in Weston in 1838, when he was nineteen, Holladay opened a dram shop—that is, a liquor store—the following year. Six months later he was operating a tavern, and by the age of twenty-one he owned a small hotel. In the 1840s Holladay worked as a postmaster, a drug-gist, proprietor of a general merchandise store, and owner of a packing plant prompted by its ideal location: Its ice-cold springs provided refrigeration, and a stream carried the plant's waste into the Missouri River.

But Holladay's ambitions couldn't long be contained in any town, no matter how fast it grew. As a seventeen-year-old in 1836 he had made a trip to Santa Fe as a stock tender in a freight train, where he developed the idea of using wider wheels on the freight wagons to increase their ability to navigate in sand and mud.[25] The Mexican War turned his attention, like that of Russell and Majors, to freighting again. In 1846 Holladay won a contract to supply General Stephen Kearny with wagons, mules, bacon, and flour for his march from Fort Leavenworth to Santa Fe. Holladay's prompt delivery of the shipment in good order won him repeat business from the army, and his profits were sometimes as high as 200 percent.

When the war ended and the government no longer needed its wag-ons and oxen, Holladay used his profits to buy the surplus goods and stock at low prices and set himself up as a commercial freighter. In 1849 he gambled his entire Mexican War fortune on a wagon train to Salt Lake, consisting of fifty wagons loaded with $70,000 worth of merchandise. A single Indian attack, bad storm, or hostile Mormon reaction would have put him out of business; but the train negotiated

A freight stop along the Oregon Trail photographed in the 1850s. This image captures a typical scene that would have been familiar to Ben Holladay, Jack Slade, and other western freighters. (*Library of Congress*)

South Pass without mishap. Holladay had also taken the astute precaution of carrying a letter from the Mexican War hero General Alexander Doniphan, reminding Brigham Young of Holladay's friendly treatment of Mormons during the war. At Salt Lake, Young received Holladay, blessed him, and vouched for him in his sermon the following Sunday: "Brother Holladay has a large stock of goods for sale and can be trusted as an honorable dealer."[26]

Flush with this success, Holladay sent a second wagon train to Salt Lake the following year, carrying $150,000 worth of goods. This time he and his partner opened a store in Salt Lake City, and Holladay traded some of his goods for a herd of cattle, which he then drove from Utah to California. Despite the perils of this trip, his herd reached the Sacramento Valley safely. Here Holladay fattened his cattle on the rich grass and waited for the price of beef to rise. Although he later admitted that he almost lost his nerve, Holladay resisted the temptation to sell his herd too soon. Eventually a beef shortage brought the wealthy Panama Steamship Company to his corral, paying thirty cents a pound on the hoof for cattle he had bought at six dollars a head. The success of this clever dickering was even more satisfying to Holladay than the profits he derived, and after this coup he continued in the cattle business. At the same time, he used some of his profits to buy up large tracts of land back home in Weston for a mill as well as a pretentious brick mansion on a high hill.

But Holladay never gave up freighting. Beginning in 1851, like Russell he transported stores for the army from Fort Leavenworth to Fort Kearny and Fort Laramie. Like Alexander Majors, Holladay loved the uncertainties, the dangers, and the camaraderie of the wagon trains as much as he loved the profits. Eventually his freighting operation embraced 15,000 men on his payroll, 20,000 wagons, and 150,000 draft animals—a capacity for hauling 100 million pounds of freight.[27] But Holladay never grew so attached to freighting that he couldn't quit it if a better opportunity came along.[28]

These entrepreneurs operated at a time when corporations and other large institutions hardly existed. Most businesses were partnerships or sole proprietorships—flimsy entities that might last a few years at most. To hedge their risks, all three of these men counted heavily on the relative stability of government contracts. Like most other Americans in the spring of 1857, these three freighting operators failed to perceive that the U.S. government was an increasingly thin reed on which to grasp for security.

Washington was struggling desperately to prevent its states and territories from breaking apart over the issue of extending slavery into the new western territories and states. The great irony of the 1850s was that slaves had nothing to do with the opening of the West—and everything to do with it.

Toussaint Louverture's successful slave revolt against the French in Haiti had convinced Napoleon in 1803 to abandon the New World and sell France's vast Louisiana Territory to the United States. The high birth rates of North American slaves had prompted their masters to seek new lands in the West where they could put their surplus labor to work.[29] The crisis over Missouri's admission to the Union as a slave state, culminating in the Missouri Compromise of 1820, had shattered the illusions of northerners and southerners alike that they could avoid a confrontation over slavery. A similar crisis over California's admission as a free state had turned the confrontation violent. The Compromise of 1850, by resurrecting the Fugitive Slave Act, sanctioned the capture of escaped slaves and consequently provoked the retaliatory violence of John Brown and other abolitionists.

In the late 1840s the strong-willed and manipulative President James K. Polk had been driven to an early grave by his inability to control hordes of office-seekers; but by March 1857 the government was in far more serious jeopardy, and "Grandma Buchanan," as the new president's associates called him behind his back, was incapable of controlling even his own cabinet members, many of them southerners determined to undermine the Union. Like his predecessor Franklin Pierce and Senator Stephen Douglas of Illinois, James Buchanan was a northern "Peace Democrat" who believed that slavery was morally wrong but that Congress couldn't legally interfere with it.

Just two days after Buchanan took office, the Supreme Court delivered its decision in the case of Dred Scott, a Missouri slave who had sued for his freedom. The Court ruled that slaves were private property; that under the Constitution, the federal government could not deprive a citizen of his property based on where he lived; and that consequently the Missouri Compromise of 1820 was unconstitutional because it excluded slavery from the northern half of the Louisiana Purchase. President Buchanan had hoped the Court's decision would put the slavery issue to rest. Instead, the intense public reaction accelerated the chain of events that made civil war inevitable. The government's very survival now seemed in jeopardy.

Nevertheless, in February 1857, when Russell, Majors & Waddell's two-year freighting contract with the U.S. Army expired, the three partners readily signed a new one-year extension committing them to transport up to five million pounds of military supplies.[30] That same spring, John Hockaday wangled an appointment from Buchanan as U.S. attorney for Utah Territory,[31] and his partner Magraw finagled an important contracting job from Buchanan.

Ben Holladay, meanwhile, seeing his freighting in decline, tried to move into the stagecoach business in 1856 when he submitted a bid to carry the U.S. Mail between Independence and Salt Lake City for $45,000 per year. But he was beaten by a $23,000 low bid submitted by the Mormon contractor Hiram Kimball. After this failure Holladay bided his time and awaited new opportunities to invest the small fortune he had accumulated in freighting. In retrospect, his rejection by Washington and his willingness to retire briefly to the sidelines may have been a blessing in disguise.[32] Ben Holladay had perceived something that William Russell and John Hockaday were beginning to realize as well: at a moment when Congress was preoccupied with preventing the Union from unraveling, a frontier entrepreneur might find greater opportunities in carrying the U.S. Mail than in transporting freight.

A s early as the 1840s President Polk had acknowledged that mail service between the East and California was "indispensable for the diffusion of information, and for the binding together [of] the different portions of our extended Confederacy."[33] This hunger for mail was almost palpable in the early 1850s. When the monthly steamer arrived from Panama bearing mail from the East, a cannon was fired on San Francisco's Telegraph Hill, followed by bedlam throughout the city.[34]

The physician William S. McCollumn, writing in 1850, described men waiting in line for days; men paying other men to stand in line for them; miners paying with gold dust to buy places in line from other men; men who expected no mail but stood in line anyway, to sell their position to someone else; men sleeping overnight in blanket rolls, all to hold their place in the hope of news from home.[35]

Pressure from homesick Californians eventually led Congress to increase the steamship mail service frequency to twice a month. But it still took a month to deliver a letter by ship from New York to San Francisco. Some entrepreneurs began tinkering with the idea of delivering mail to California by mule or stagecoach along the Overland route followed by the emigrants. Since the Mormons had settled Salt Lake City in 1847, the Mormon capital's mail had been carried to California on muleback and to the Missouri River by a few covered wagons pulled by mule teams (and occasionally on the backs of men through narrow mountain passes).[36] The first of the private express firms, Wells Fargo, conducted a thriving business carrying mail in stagecoaches within California beginning in 1852. But conveying mail across the continent was too costly for any one operator to undertake without a federal subsidy and without breaking the route into shorter segments.[37]

In 1850 the government contracted with Samuel Woodson, a lawyer in Independence, Missouri, to serve the route between his frontier outpost and Salt Lake City once a month for $19,500 per year.[38] The following year Absalom Woodward and George Chorpenning contracted with the Post Office to provide mail service along the remaining segment, between Salt Lake City and California, monthly for a mere $14,000 per annum.[39] The contracts specified thirty-day service each way on each segment, so that theoretically a letter could be delivered from Independence to San Francisco in sixty days. But harsh weather conditions and periodic Indian raids meant that the 750-mile trip on the Western segment took not the contracted thirty days but fifty-four; and on one trip Woodward himself was killed by Shoshone Indians. Some carriers along this primitive route were known to turn back and send the mail by sea, having concluded that mail from California could reach Salt Lake faster by steamship through New Orleans and up the Mississippi River and then by Woodson's Missouri-to Salt Lake mule service.[40]

But Woodson's service on the eastern leg was no better, and in 1854 his mail contract was revoked and a new four-year contract bestowed upon William Magraw, also of Independence. Magraw possessed no real qualifications for the job—he was the western representative for a Philadelphia mercantile firm—but he did enjoy excellent connections in the Buchanan administration.[41] To make the mail service viable, Magraw soon took on the peripatetic but only slightly more experienced John Hockaday as his silent partner.[42] Between Magraw's connections and Hockaday's energy they appeared to make a good team. That same summer of 1854, Hockaday and his cousin Isaac Hockaday launched a monthly passenger stagecoach service to be operated in conjunction with Magraw's mail route.[43]

The mail contract gave Magraw and Hockaday only $14,400 for once-a-month service, and the government got what it paid for. This primitive operation used two light mule wagons—one to carry Magraw's mailbags, the other for the Hockadays' passengers—and had only six stations along the 1,200-mile route; on most nights, passengers were required to camp out on the plains.[44] William Russell's partner Alexander Majors, who traveled on one of these Hockaday stages from St. Joseph to Salt Lake, later recalled, "They had a few stages, light cheap vehicles, and but a few mules and no stations along the route. They traveled the same teams for several hundred miles before changing, stopping every few hours and turning them loose to graze, and then hitching them up again and going along. . . . It was twenty-one days . . . traveling at short intervals day and night."[45]

This service was only a few months old when its November run was ambushed by Sioux Indians, who killed all but one passenger and made off with $1,070 in gold coin. That disaster prompted Isaac Hockaday to withdraw from the passenger business, but John Hockaday stayed with it and assumed a larger role in the enterprise.

Magraw's mail contract was annulled by the Post Office Department in 1856 in response to complaints of slow service and tampering with the mail—which may have been valid, because neither Magraw nor Hockaday was devoting his full attention to it. The loss of the contract forced Magraw out of business and ended John Hockaday's passenger service as well.[46] But the two partners, undaunted, soon perceived another opportunity for government business. That same year, through the urging of General William T. Sherman, Congress commissioned the building of a military road along the Overland Trail from Omaha to Fort Kearny in Nebraska Territory and then from Fort Kearny to South Pass.[47] Its prime purpose was to facilitate the westward movement of troops and military supplies, but as a side benefit, Sherman presciently anticipated, "a stage will use the wagon road as soon as the wants of the people demand."[48]

Sherman's road did usher in the age of stagecoaches and the promise of faster and more reliable mail—and with that, perhaps, the prospect of a federal mail contract worth taking such a risk. But it would take tough and adventurous men like J. A. Slade to navigate the many remaining dangers of overland travel.

Chapter 8

THE CALIFORNIA MAIL

*

A s a method of moving people from one place to another, the horse-drawn stagecoach had been ubiquitous in other parts of the world for centuries. Even after the invention of steamboats and railroads, stagecoaches were needed to take people everywhere that rivers and train tracks didn't reach. Since 1830 the Abbott-Downing Company of Concord, New Hampshire, had manufactured its elegant, hand-tooled Concord mail coach for customers throughout the Eastern states as well as in Britain, Europe, South America, South Africa, and Australia.[1]

The need in the West seemed plain enough. Some 350,000 travelers passed through Fort Laramie between 1841 and 1866.[2] But in America's Western territories, stagecoach travel wasn't physically feasible until Sherman's military road provided the necessary smooth and durable surface. At a time when no railroads existed west of the Missouri River, Sherman's road tempted freight operators like William Russell and John Hockaday to branch out into operating stagecoaches—the first "public" conveyances capable of carrying individual travelers over the vast expanses between the steamboat landings and the railheads. Slade would play a key role in both men's plans.

Stagecoaches, pulled by six horses (for speed) or by mules (for endurance), traveled much faster than wagons pulled by an equal number of oxen. A coach could cover about 110 miles in a twenty-two-hour day, compared to only about 15 miles for a loaded freight wagon.[3]

The coaches were more comfortable, too. The Concord mail coach, the top of the line, was famous for its elegant design, its hand-tooled workmanship, and its suspension of heavy leather springs. Its models could seat six, nine, or twelve passengers inside; it could also accommodate as many as a dozen additional passengers on the coach's flat roof in what the Concord catalogue called "relative comfort."

The optimal heavy load, unfortunately, usually meant an inhuman experience that squeezed nine passengers together for at least six days and nights between the Missouri River and the Rockies.[4] Several days' intense jolting invariably left passengers complaining about aches and sore flesh.

Sleep inside a stagecoach was almost impossible. At a sudden lurch, passengers dozing in corners or curled up on the middle seat would fall in a heap, untangle themselves, and doze off again. The alternative was to borrow hay from a station, spread it on the top of the coach and cover it with blankets for a bed. Especially in warm weather, such a fresh-air bed was heaven compared to the cramped interior. But the outdoor sleeper was required to tie ropes around his body and fasten them to the railings to avoid being jolted onto the prairie as he slept.[5]

When stagecoaches rattled across narrow, hazardous canyons at high speeds, seasoned passengers learned to avert their eyes as the coach tipped toward the edge of a precipice. Indians and outlaws were a constant hazard, and so was the weather. On the plains, a heavy hailstorm could frighten the horses or mules into running away. When sudden rains swelled the streams, the horses often had to swim across while the coaches—built to maintain an even balance—floated behind. Blizzards periodically prevented the coaches from moving at all.

The "swing" stations—where horses were changed, ideally every 12 to 15 miles—were monotonous square, one-story log structures of one to three rooms. The "home" stations, where the division agent lived, were usually two or three times larger and provided with sheds, outbuildings, and other conveniences.[6] Passengers who failed to pack their own food were at the mercy of whatever meals the station might provide (for an additional charge, usually fifty cents to two dollars), although sometimes the menu was surprisingly varied.[7] "Eating sta-

An overland mail stagecoach along the Butterfield route, photographed around 1859. (*Wells Fargo Archives*)

tions," spaced at roughly 20-mile intervals, furnished such staples as fried bacon and ham, as well as buffalo, elk, and antelope steaks in season.

Paying passengers quickly discovered that they were all second-class patrons next to the stagecoach's most valued customer: the U.S. Mail. Although coaches actually carried little letter mail due to the high cost of postage, Congress in 1825 had authorized the free exchange of newspapers among publishers.[8] This meant that frequently the "publication mail" was so heavy and bulky that it was stacked on the floor of a coach, and the passengers had to arrange themselves among the mail sacks as best they could.[9] Nor could passengers ever be quite sure when they might be transferred from the relative luxury of the Concord coach pulled by horses to a "celerity wagon" pulled by mules. This lightweight vehicle, known as a "mud wagon" beyond the stage company's front office, was easy on the animals and quite comfortable—but only for the mails.[10]

Frank Root, the journalist-turned-stagecoach driver, insisted that stage company officials were keenly sensitive to their passengers' anxieties. "For that reason," he wrote, "it was the aim of the stage officials to employ none but careful, experienced men," presumably like Root himself.[11]

But in fact the stage companies largely drew their drivers and station agents from the same pool of roughnecks who worked for the freight operators: drifters from California, deserters from the army, fugitives from the law, or rogues fleeing from organized society.[12] The division agent who supervised a stretch of perhaps 250 miles, like the wagonmaster on a freight train, was a tough man charged with controlling equally tough men. But where a wagonmaster dealt only with freight, animals, and his fellow teamsters, a stagecoach superintendent had to train his drivers to handle more sensitive cargo: human passengers (some of them female) and of course letters. Mark Twain observed, with his customary hyperbolic flourish, that the division agent "was a very, very great man in his division: a kind of Grand Mogul, a Sultan of the Indies, in whose presence common men were modest of speech and manner, and in the glare of whose greatness even the dazzling stage-driver dwindled to a penny dip."[13]

Even more daunting than riding a stagecoach was operating a stagecoach line. An overland freighter could put his oxen out to pasture every night under the open sky, but a stagecoach line needed stations at frequent intervals to change horses or mules and to rest and feed passengers. Even with an exorbitant fare of $75 from Atchison to Denver or $150 from Atchison to Salt Lake, at most a dozen paying passengers could be squeezed inside a coach, plus a few more on the roof, for a week-long trip.[14] After a coach company finished paying $40 to $100 per month to its drivers, $40 to $50 to its stock tenders, $75 to its carpenters, $100 to $125 to its harness makers and blacksmiths, $100 to its station agents, $100 to $125 to its division agents, and $3,000 to $5,000 per year to its superintendent—not to mention the cost of coaches, horses, stations, equipment, and food for all those employees and animals—a profit margin on passenger operations alone was unlikely.[15] Only a government mail subsidy could make the operation financially viable. But the appropriate balance between passenger service and a government subsidy was learned only through trial and error. And in any case, William Russell and John Hockaday were not the sort of men to conduct a rigorous profit-and-loss analysis before plunging into a new venture.

When William Magraw lost his Utah mail contract to a Mormon company in 1856, the cancellation caused John Hockaday's related stagecoach line to close down as well.[16] But Magraw refused to acknowledge that his own poor service was at least partly to blame. Magraw and the Hockadays assumed that the Mormons who succeeded them were pulling strings in Washington just as they had (when in fact the Mormons had gone out of their way to antagonize Washington). From Independence, Missouri, Magraw and the Hockadays launched a letter-writing campaign to President Franklin Pierce, insisting that in Utah—as Magraw informed his "personal and political friend" the president—"there is left no vestige of law and order, no protection for life or property."[17]

These letters continued after Pierce left office. Another partner of John Hockaday, the Utah Surveyor General David Burr, wrote the newly installed President Buchanan that he had fled Utah for his life in February 1857. "These people," Burr wrote of the Mormons, "repudiate the authority of the United States in this country, and are in open rebellion against the government."[18] These and similar letters sent to Buchanan and Eastern newspapers were intemperate and often false, but they contained a germ of truth. Although the Mormons ostensibly desired only to be left alone, they had set up their own church-state as well as their own court system, which systematically harassed and defied the Utah territorial court system so as to reduce it to virtual paralysis. John Hockaday, as one of the few gentile merchants in Salt Lake City as well as an outspoken critic of the Mormons' treatment of women, was caught in this maelstrom, especially after he became U.S. attorney for Utah Territory.[19]

By the spring of 1857 Magraw seems to have seized on the idea of military intervention in Utah as the ideal means of avenging himself on the Mormon community there—a notion he promoted in a pseudonymous letter published in the *National Intelligencer* in Washington.[20]

To placate Magraw, two days after his letter appeared the Department of the Interior authorized him to organize a party of one hundred men to lay out a new U.S. Overland Wagon Road from South Pass to Salt Lake City.[21] This ploy silenced Magraw's campaign against the Mormons. But through an accident of timing, Magraw's call to arms now took on a life of its own.

That March the Supreme Court had delivered its decision in the tortuous Dred Scott case. In the wake of that decision, Buchanan found himself pressed to reassert the federal government's authority in America's western territories. But how could Buchanan make such a test case without inflaming the explosive issue of slavery? Magraw's demand for an invasion of Utah seemed to offer a plausible solution.

A crisis in Utah Territory—real or manufactured—provided the distraction from slavery that Buchanan urgently needed. He would assert federal authority in the territories by dispatching 2,500 troops to Utah under Colonel Albert Sidney Johnston to suppress a "Mormon rebellion" and install a new slate of federal officials.[22] The slavery issue would be avoided altogether.

The task of provisioning Johnston's huge expedition fell, logically, to Russell, Majors & Waddell. But this greatest of Western freighting firms had never handled a job the magnitude of Johnston's Utah expedition. The assignment would demand a huge financial investment, requiring about 350 wagons—enough to make up fourteen trains, an aggregation nine miles long—as well as 350 teamsters to drive them and 3,432 head of oxen to pull them.[23]

The result, for the government and its freighters alike, was a disaster. Soon after Johnston's troops left Fort Leavenworth in July, it became clear that Buchanan had underestimated the Mormons' combativeness, their resourcefulness, and their sense of purpose. When word reached Utah that the U.S. Army was on its way, Brigham Young proclaimed martial law in Utah Territory. He forbade U.S. troops from entering and called up about 5,000 men of the Nauvoo Legion to enforce his order.[24] This Mormon militia was twice as large as Johnston's force and possessed a much clearer idea of its mission.

In September, small Mormon guerrilla forces began setting fire to the government's wagons and stampeding its cattle herds. In October they burned Fort Bridger, the important trading post 115 miles northeast of Salt Lake City. Then they attacked three army supply trains in the Green River valley, running off 1,400 head of cattle and burning seventy-five wagons loaded with three thousand pounds of bacon, coffee, flour, ham, and other foodstuffs that the army desperately needed. In November a mountain blizzard struck the army supply trains along the Sweetwater River with such fury that the animals refused to eat, instead huddling together for protection. Here, at a hastily improvised camp named for the army's commanding general, Winfield Scott, Johnston's army was forced to hunker down for the winter.[25] Lacking the necessary supplies, the troops starved on half-rations, and the Army lost between fifty and two hundred animals each day.[26]

The Mormons' efforts to thwart Johnston's expedition were ironically abetted by William Magraw's incompetence as superintendent of the Overland Wagon Road project, which would have facilitated the movement of all those wagon trains from South Pass to Salt Lake City had the wagons been able to proceed that far. Magraw was discharged from the road project late in 1857.[27] But his aborted road-survey project did produce one valuable side benefit: It apparently introduced the West to a dashing Virginian named Benjamin Franklin Ficklin, then thirty years old.

As a rebellious youth of sixteen Ficklin had been shipped off to the Virginia Military Institute for discipline and taming, only to be expelled for firing a howitzer at the cadet barracks as a prank. Rather than return home and face his father's wrath, Ficklin joined the army, where he subsequently fought in the Mexican War and suffered a wound that earned him readmission to VMI.

After graduating in 1849 at the age of twenty-two, Ficklin briefly tried his hand as a schoolteacher. Lacking the patience for the classroom, Ficklin moved to Alabama, where he got into the overland freighting business. But it was the rowdy West that proved the ideal tonic for Ficklin's independent spirit. He was hired as a surveyor with Magraw's hundred-man U.S. Overland Wagon Road team, and when that work was abandoned because of the Mormon "war," Ficklin served briefly as deputy U.S. marshal in Utah Territory, most likely working out of Camp Scott, the Utah Expedition's winter quarters near Fort Bridger.

In this job, Ficklin probably assisted Magraw's erstwhile partner John Hockaday, who performed his first duties as U.S. attorney for Utah at Camp Scott by presenting a special grand jury with the charges against Mormon militiamen who had been captured while raiding the Utah Expedition's supply trains.[28] Then, early in 1858,

Ficklin joined Colonel Johnston's force as head of a small group of teamster volunteers, making a daring trip into the Flathead Indian country near Fort Bridger to secure cattle and mules for Johnston's army. But Ficklin's volunteers were unable to purchase cattle on suitable terms, and fearing to make the return trip in midwinter, they camped out for weeks, surviving by eating some of their horses.[29] In April, having staggered back to Camp Scott, Ficklin was ordered to ride east to Fort Leavenworth with Colonel Johnston's dispatches.[30]

When the snows finally receded from the overland route to Utah that spring of 1858, Colonel Johnston escorted a new federally appointed governor into Salt Lake City to replace Brigham Young, and federal troops occupied the city, establishing a base on the outskirts called Camp Floyd (for the secretary of war). Buchanan, for his part, issued a pardon to all Mormons who had resisted Johnston's expedition, which the Mormons quickly accepted. Thus the bloodless "Mormon rebellion," surely one of the strangest political and military episodes in U.S. history, dissolved almost as quickly as it had begun.

But for Russell, Majors & Waddell, the damage was fatal. The three partners had lost $500,000 in the Mormon war. Their whole freighting operation, in which they had invested more than $4 million, was for all practical purposes bankrupt.[31] Yet their organization was so huge and so highly regarded that no one else—not even Russell's partners—realized the severity of their problem.

While Russell in Leavenworth City cast about for a way to recoup his partnership's losses, Ben Ficklin—also in Leavenworth City—pondered his future. After his nine-month adventure as surveyor, teamster, and dispatch rider for Johnston's expedition, Ficklin shared something in common with both John Hockaday and William Russell: He was hooked on the challenge of transportation across the Plains.

Where was Slade during this Mormon disaster? A few accounts have placed him in the eye of the storm, leading a Russell, Majors & Waddell train of sixteen wagons in support of Johnston's army. This deduction seems reasonable on the surface: Slade had mastered military freighting during the Mexican War, and he had spent

some of his career leading freight
trains to Salt Lake City. If the pre-
eminent western freighting firm of
the day was desperately searching
for wagonmasters to lead fourteen
trains—and offering a 25 percent
pay premium as an incentive—logic
would seem to dictate that Slade
would have been recruited.[32]

Yet one of the few consistent
threads in Slade's story is its defiance of logic. The supposed evidence that Slade was involved in
the army's Utah expedition crum-
bles upon close examination, especially in light of the possibility that
he may have been some 500 miles
to the south at the time.[33] Indeed,
only the slenderest evidence suggests that Slade ever drove a freight
train for Russell, Majors & Waddell
or for its individual partners.[34]

Ben Ficklin helped survey the U.S.
Overland Wagon Road for the military but
eventually became the general superin-
tendent for Russell, Majors & Waddell's
Central Overland stage line, where he
championed both Jack Slade and the
Pony Express. (*Museum of the
Confederacy*)

If Slade wasn't on the Utah expedition, where was he? That question can be answered only through the broadest sort of speculation.

Bossing wagon trains was seasonal work, involving only four to six
months a year. When a freight train returned to the Missouri River,
Slade was free to seek other work where he found it—perhaps in the
St. Louis area, where some accounts have said he was living in the late
1850s.[35]

The best employment opportunities in that area through much of
that decade lay with the railroads then being extended westward
across southern Illinois to St. Louis. Two of these lines ran through
Slade's native Clinton County, and Slade's relatives were involved with
both of them. His brother's father-in-law, Judge Sidney Breese, was a
leading organizer of the Illinois Central; and Slade's own stepfather,
Elias Dennis, may have been a subcontractor in charge of grading (and

possibly laying the tracks) for a segment of the Ohio & Mississippi Railway.[36] It's possible that Slade, seeking work in his idle time between freighting runs, found a job with one of the railroads through his family connections. If he did, he would have been thrown in with a floating army that the writer Emerson Hough described as "mobs of hard characters . . . wild and lawless."[37]

Judge Alexander Davis, a respected Missouri lawyer and friend of Slade, told the *St. Louis Globe-Democrat* in 1878 that Slade "got into some difficulty with a railroad man out here. He either killed him outright or beat him up so that he died, and after that he went off to Texas and changed his name."[38] This incident surfaced in print as early as 1865, in an account by the Montana journalist Thomas Dimsdale: "Slade was, at the time of his coming West, a fugitive from justice in Illinois, where he killed a man with whom he had been quarreling. Finding his antagonist to be more than his match, he ran away from him, and, in his flight, picking up a stone, he threw it with such deadly aim and violence that it penetrated the skull of his pursuer, over the eye, and killed him."[39]

Slade's much later biographer, Lew Callaway—a Montana chief justice—remarked on the "meager information which has come down" about this alleged rock fight and concluded, "Clearly it was not murder, manslaughter at most. It is probable that had [Slade] stayed at home and stood trial he would have been acquitted."[40]

Even if such a killing never took place, *something* appears to have caused Slade in 1857 or early 1858 to suddenly join the ranks of young men "gone to Texas."[41] And if Slade did go to Texas, he probably took his companion Maria Virginia with him: Judge Davis told the *Globe-Democrat* that Slade was married in Texas, under the name of "John Alfred," and that Davis himself had seen the certificate introduced in court.[42] (Such a surname change, of course, would itself suggest that Slade was a fugitive.) Other evidence—far from conclusive, to be sure—supports the notion that Slade was in Texas in 1857 or early 1858.[43] And if he was in Texas during this time, he could not have been driving a wagon train with Johnston's army expedition to Utah.

How did Slade survive in Texas? Davis, as well as another Slade acquaintance—the Overland stage company telegraph operator James

W. Wilson—said Slade had charge of a stagecoach company there.[44] If so, this interlude represented Slade's transition from a mover of merchandise to a mover of people and mail. Notwithstanding his seeming unwillingness to make long-range plans, when Slade reappeared on the Central Plains in 1858, he was ideally positioned to facilitate a similar transition for either John Hockaday or William Russell. For by this time, mail delivery had succeeded freight hauling as the great passion of western transportation entrepreneurs.

Like every political question in America in the 1850s, mail service to California was eclipsed by the slavery question. Although Americans in California, Oregon, and Utah repeatedly pleaded for better mail service, Congressmen couldn't agree on a transcontinental mail route. Northerners and southerners each insisted on a route through their respective section in anticipation of the very real prospect that the Union would split. Their stalemate, meanwhile, encouraged another prospect: that without reliable mail, California itself would split off from the Union.

In March 1857, after 75,000 Californians signed a petition demanding improved overland mail service, Congress finally authorized a transcontinental mail and passenger service in direct competition with the existing ocean mail and passenger service.[45] This Post Office appropriation bill approved a contract for carrying letter mail and passengers from the Mississippi River to San Francisco.

The contract was for six years' duration—long enough to justify a serious investment by a contractor—at a cost not to exceed $300,000 per year for semimonthly service, $450,000 for weekly service, or $600,000 a year for semiweekly service. This fee schedule was far more lucrative than any prior overland service but also reflected politicians' inability to foresee how the mail business would work in practice. Service of lesser frequency would actually cost *more* to operate, because each individual trip would involve a much larger quantity of mail, so that the contractor would need to invest in extra coaches, mules, and men in order to transport it. But no potential contractor possessed the experience to perceive this conundrum, and the subsidies offered seemed so generous compared to what had been provided before ($32,000 a year to J. B. Mills for a once-a-month mail run to Salt Lake City, and $30,000 to George Chorpenning for once-a-month service from there to California) that no one thought to raise the issue.

The new contract also stipulated that this service was to be performed within a twenty-five-day time frame for each trip, using "good four-horse coaches or spring wagons, suitable for the conveyance of passengers, as well as the safety and security of the mails."[46] Finally, the contract provided land on which to build stations. But the actual route of this mail service wasn't specified—only that the starting point be located on the Mississippi River. Northerners expected that the regular emigrant route by way of Salt Lake City—the route of the Oregon, Mormon, and California trails—would be chosen because it was the shortest and most direct and because the South Pass along that route was one of the few places where wagons could breach the Rockies.[47]

John Hockaday, who submitted a bid for that very route in August 1857, seemed a logical choice: He had already run mail and stagecoach lines, possessed experience as a surveyor, owned a tannery at the midpoint of the route (in Salt Lake City) and a home at the eastern terminus (in Independence), and through his former partner Magraw he enjoyed political connections in Buchanan's administration as well.[48] But the choice was left to Postmaster General Aaron V. Brown, a former Tennessee governor and strong southern sympathizer who had participated in the Nashville convention of 1850, one of the first forums where southern secession was openly discussed. In September 1857, Brown settled on a southern route so roundabout and indirect that none of the nine bidders had dared to suggest it: from St. Louis it curled southward through Arkansas, Texas, and New Mexico to San Diego and then all the way up the California coast to San Francisco. Brown's designated route was nearly 2,800 miles long—more than 800 miles longer than the central overland route. It didn't help Brown's ethical case that the winning bidder, John Butterfield, was a friend of President James Buchanan.[49]

Northerners, midwesterners, and even some Californians were outraged by Brown's choice. "One of the greatest swindles ever perpetrated upon the country by the slave-holders," declared the *Chicago Tribune*. The *New York Press* dubbed Brown's southern course the

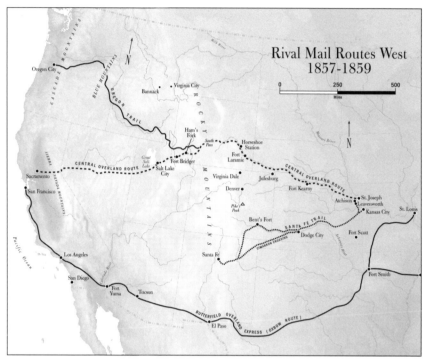

Rival Mail Routes West
1857-1859

While the shorter and more direct route to California was the central overland through Salt Lake City, the postmaster general chose the longer southern "ox-bow" route for the mail contract to California, in part because of concern for the winter weather in the Rockies. Ultimately, both routes obtained contracts to carry U.S. Mail.

"ox-bow route" because it resembled an ox's horns instead of a straight line. Because the route neglected Sacramento (by approaching San Francisco from the south), the *Sacramento Union* also condemned Brown's choice, calling it "a Panama route by land, an overland route to Mexico, a military route to Texas, and an immigrant route to Arizona."[50]

Brown argued that the southern route was more dependable for travel in winter, when the central overland route was often blocked by snow. The government's military expedition to Utah that fall gave him another excuse: if Utah was technically in rebellion, Brown argued, the government couldn't easily control the central route.[51]

But Brown's route failed to address the question of how to provide mail service to Utah, not to mention the political question of how to maintain the North's influence in California. By the spring of 1858 the Utah "rebellion" was over, the need for regular mail service through

Salt Lake seemed more pressing than ever, and the conventional idea that the plains were impassable in winter had been disproven. That January, James Rupe and Charles Morehead, agents for Russell, Majors & Waddell, had delivered receipted bills of lading from Colonel Johnston's frozen camp near Green River to Fort Leavenworth, making the 1,125-mile trip with three mules in thirty days without a change of animals. Johnston himself had organized a monthly military express mail service to Fort Leavenworth.[52] What these men had achieved without too much delay or discomfort, other operators—presumably better organized and financed—could do regularly. All that was necessary was an entrepreneur of sufficient daring and vision, as well as an adequate government subsidy.

Under continued pressure from his northern critics, Postmaster Brown now agreed to award new, more lucrative mail contracts for the central overland route as well; and the two most likely bidders—William H. Russell and John Hockaday—began jockeying for the contract.

Hockaday at this point was serving as Buchanan's designated U.S. attorney for Utah. But in January 1858, while Colonel Johnston's troops were still mired in the snow at Camp Scott en route to Utah, the restless Hockaday left Camp Scott and returned to Washington, where by March he was lobbying for an overland mail contract, possibly in a personal interview with President Buchanan.[53]

Russell, meanwhile, also headed for Washington, where in a February meeting with Secretary of War Floyd he broached for the first time the idea of a relay network of pony express mail couriers between the Missouri River and California.

In this battle of rival dreamers, Hockaday offered the more pragmatic vision. While in Washington he met with George Chorpenning, who was then in the capital to renew his mail contract between Salt Lake and California. Between them Hockaday and Chorpenning agreed to submit their bids in tandem, in effect creating a mail service over a central route all the way to the Pacific. Hockaday would carry the mail from St. Joseph, Missouri—soon to become the western terminus of the Hannibal and St. Joseph Railroad—to Salt Lake City, a distance of 1,140 miles. Chorpenning would carry the mail from there to Placerville, California, eventually shortening his route from 1,000 miles to 660.[54]

On April 1, the Post Office Department—presumably persuaded by this combination—annulled its existing $32,000-a-year contract with S. B. Miles for monthly mail service between Independence and Salt Lake and replaced it with a contract along the same route to Hockaday for "weekly service in four-mule wagons or carriages at $190,000 per annum on a twenty-two day schedule." Chorpenning's contract for the western division was upgraded from a semimonthly schedule paying $34,000 a year to a weekly schedule for $130,000 per year.[55] This de facto joint venture of the Chorpenning and Hockaday lines formed what a Congressional report called the "first Central Overland mail stage, bringing letters and passengers from the East."[56]

In effect the government, which had previously provided only $66,000 for mail on the central overland route between Independence and California, now committed itself to $320,000 a year, a serious investment that would allow Hockaday and Chorpenning to build a network of stations along the route. But the new outlays still paled beside the $600,000 awarded to Butterfield's "ox-bow route" through the Southwest. Moreover, Butterfield's southern contract of September 1857 granted him a full year to launch his operation. Hockaday's contract, by contrast, required him to begin mail service on May 1, 1858, just a month after his contract was awarded. And Hockaday's contract itself lasted only two and a half years, as opposed to six years for Butterfield's.

Clearly, the government was stacking the odds in the competition between regional mail routes to the Pacific. But the exuberant John Hockaday sought to turn these disadvantages to his favor. By seizing a four-month head start on Butterfield, Hockaday reasoned, he and Chorpenning could pre-empt the market for mail and passengers. In the process they would demolish Postmaster General Brown's contention that the southern route was the only viable way to carry mail to California during the winter. They would gamble that their fast mail service to California would embarrass Brown into granting them compensation and conditions equal to Butterfield's.[57]

And so Hockaday rushed his mail operation into service with minimal preparation. His line apparently opened with only seven stations
along the 1,140-mile route from Independence to Salt Lake.[58]
Additional stations would be constructed on an as-needed basis as the
operation proceeded. They would be stocked piecemeal as space for
supplies in the mail coaches permitted. Snowplows to keep the mountain roads open during the harsh winter months would be purchased
eventually, but not right away.

Despite these deficiencies, during most of Hockaday's contract the
mail reached Salt Lake City within the twenty-one-day time limit specified by his Post Office contract. Residents of Sacramento celebrated
the arrival of the first overland mail from St. Joseph on July 20, 1858.[59]
And by then an event in the Rocky Mountains had dramatically
expanded Hockaday's ambitions.

Two parties of gold prospectors had spent that summer industri-
ously panning along creeks in the Pike's Peak region of what was
then western Kansas Territory (present-day central Colorado). In the
first week of July a small party found gold along Cherry Creek, a
branch of the South Platte River. This exciting news was quickly carried eastward across the plains in John Hockaday's own coaches. By
August the news had reached John Cantrell, an experienced miner
from Westport, Missouri, who made a brief visit to Cherry Creek and
returned bearing three ounces of gold that he had panned himself. By
Cantrell's widely publicized estimate, a single man could pan $20 to
$25 worth of gold in a day.[60]

With that news, America's second great gold rush got under way.
The first group of eager gold seekers arrived at Cherry Creek in
October, followed soon by several wagon trains. "Thousands of
adventurers from the western states," the *Missouri Republican* reported, "will soon leave for the west"; by the spring of 1859, the newspaper predicted, "the rush will be immense."[61]

The always excitable William H. Russell, at home in Missouri when
Cantrell returned with his report, was quick to grasp its implications.
"Pike's Peak will rage next year and no mistake," he wrote in a long let-

A miners' camp during the Pike's Peak gold rush in 1860. Anticipation of extra freighting, passenger, and mail opportunities led the irrepressible William H. Russell and his rival John Hockaday to develop competing stage services to the area. (*Denver Public Library*)

ter to his partner William Waddell. A stagecoach line to the gold mines, he argued, offered the possibility of making "enough out of it to cover our extraordinary losses."[62] But Waddell, a much more cautious man, was reluctant to proceed without further assurances that the Cherry Creek strike was not a "flash in the pan." And their third partner, Alexander Majors, preferred to stick to freighting.[63]

John Hockaday too grasped the implications of the gold strike—and once again he beat Russell to the punch. By late summer Hockaday was building more stations on his Salt Lake line, adding more relay teams and orchestrating shorter runs for teams, drivers, and mail conductors. Since the Cherry Creek mines were located some 200 miles south of Hockaday's contracted central overland mail route, in late September he announced that Hockaday & Burr (his Salt Lake mercantile house) would run a line of coaches from Atchison to the mines by the spring of 1859. In October he enlisted a wealthy new partner named William Liggitt to finance this expansion under a separate partnership called Hockaday & Liggitt. By the fall of 1858 the original shoestring Hockaday line to Salt Lake had evolved into a well-organized network of twenty-two stations, spaced roughly 50 miles apart, divided into four divisions, each with a supervising agent and its own staff of drivers and stationmasters. Experienced mountaineers had been hired to conduct the mail through the mountains in the coming winter.

From his warehouse in Atchison, John Hockaday's company sent out three wagon trains in the spring and summer of 1858 to provide construction materials and supplies for mail stations. The first two of these trains consisted of ten wagons each; the third, which departed in June, was a huge train of fifty-seven wagons, sixty men, six horses, 312 mules, and 204,000 pounds of freight.[64]

But Hockaday wasn't finished. Butterfield's ox-bow mail route would begin service on September 15. The gold rush to Pike's Peak, Hockaday anticipated, would produce a demand for new government mail contracts to the gold fields as well as more frequent service along his own central overland route. Now was the moment to maximize his competitive advantage against Butterfield's line. And so Hockaday laid plans for yet another supply train—perhaps the largest commercial wagon train ever assembled.

This mammoth train would be bigger than Hockaday's previous three supply trains combined. It would consist of 105 wagons, 225 men, 200 mules, a thousand head of cattle, fifty horses, and 465,500 pounds of freight. Hockaday's grand vision was not merely to supply his mail stations but to establish them as public trading posts. In effect he would develop these "road ranches," as they came to be called, as branch outlets of Hockaday, Burr & Co., his Salt Lake City dry goods emporium. The company's goal, as the editor of the *Atchison Champion* explained, "is to locate these stores all along the mail route to supply their mail trains as they pass, and also to furnish the people of the plains with merchandise. They will thus avoid the necessity of carrying supplies with each mail train as has heretofore been the custom. Mr. Hockaday, the senior partner of the firm, is now in this place, personally supervising the loading of his goods. The enterprise he has undertaken is a gigantic one, but will be a great promoter of civilization and settlement in the vast territory west of here."[65]

This train's scheduled departure date in late August defied the conventional wisdom that no train leaving the Missouri River after mid-
summer could reach Salt Lake before winter snows blocked bulky
wagons from proceeding. Hockaday doubtless understood that this
huge train couldn't reach Salt Lake until the following spring. His ultimate goal was not to transport goods to Salt Lake, but to establish and
stock as many "station stores" along the route as he possibly could
before winter set in. An undertaking of such unprecedented breadth
and complexity would require a wagonmaster of tremendous experience and skill.

So it came to pass that in July 1858 a twenty-year-old youth named
Hugo Koch, bored with his job as a clerk and bartender at a rough
little hotel in Leavenworth City, conceived the notion of becoming a
bullwhacker on a westbound freight train.[66] Koch gravitated to the
office of Leavenworth's most famous freighting firm, Russell, Majors
& Waddell, which was then outfitting a military supply train to Santa
Fe. Here a clerk cast a disdainful eye upon Koch's smooth hands.

"This is no kindergarten," the clerk informed him, as Koch later
recalled. "We only engage graduate men who have been over the plains
before."

The disheartened Koch confided his disappointment to his
younger brother, who, as steward at a large Leavenworth billiards hall
frequented by "a good class of young and old men," was privy to more
news and gossip than circulated through Koch's small hotel. A day or
two later Koch's brother reported that he had met a wagonmaster who
was short of hands for an ox train to Salt Lake City. Within a few days,
by appointment, Koch recalled,

> I was introduced to Mr. J. A. Slade, a gentleman recently from
> Texas who was engaged as wagonmaster by Hockaday, Burr &
> Co., owners of mail contracts of the Great Central overland mail
> route from St. Joe to San Francisco, who also had a large store at
> Salt Lake City, General Burr being in charge there. Mr. Slade
> seemed pleased with my appearance and upon being informed of

my ignorance of the proposed business, assured me he is proposed to break in and teach willing boys all the intricacies of the
profession of a bull whacker, rather than employ graduates who
professed to more than the boss or wagonmaster, as his title is,
ever knew. So after a few compliments I was duly engaged to make
one of the new crew going to Salt Lake City at a fair compensation, with injunction to be at Atchison, Kansas, by the 24th or
25th of August.[67]

Koch described Slade as a man of "small set features and determined look," who was accompanied—on the journey, if not at the job
interview—"by his wife, who was rather good-looking and about the
same age as her husband; weight, about 160 pounds."[68] The following
month, when Koch reported for work in Atchison, he elaborated on
his new boss: "He was rather a small man with dark hair and eyes,
wore a thin dark moustache, rather swarthy complexion, and appeared
of rather a nervous temperament, as all his motions were quick and his
speech also of rather a high key. He was dressed in good common
clothes, substantial and made for rough wear, and as near as I can
remember he never wore a diamond or ring nor carried a watch but he
did carry a gun."[69]

Slade had been promoted to wagonmaster for this expedition,
according to some accounts, from his previous post as clerk or agent at
Hockaday's Fort Kearny station, which was originally the Hockaday
line's second station west of Independence. In that early seven-station
incarnation of Hockaday's network, Slade's authority may have
extended all the way to the next station at Fort Laramie, 332 miles to
the west.[70]

Thus it seems plausible to conclude that John Hockaday, upon
obtaining his federal mail contract in the spring of 1858, hired Slade
for his knowledge of the central overland route and his freighting background, as well as his stagecoach experience in Texas—although,
given the haste with which Hockaday launched his mail service, his
hiring process was probably less than thorough. Because stagecoaching was a new business in the West, few new drivers were asked for references or credentials.[71]

Once the need to increase and stock stations became evident, Slade was most likely promoted to take charge of that project. It's also possible that Hockaday dispatched Slade to Texas to acquire and bring back the thousand steers needed for the massive freight train that would accomplish the job.[72]

Shortly before Slade left Leavenworth to take charge of the Hockaday train from Atchison to Salt Lake, his friends threw him a small banquet in one of the town's larger restaurants. What happened there was recounted to Koch by an eyewitness:

> There was a regular dining room on the first floor, for the general public, but [for] any special company or club dinner or other close communion affair, they used and prepared and decorated the basement; the owner of the place was a Texas man and great friend of Slade's, and nothing was spared to have this a pleasant affair. The different guests commenced to assemble and were nearly all there, when a big six-foot Texan came into the basement rather heavily loaded up. . . . He very boisterously called for dinner to be served him. The proprietor gently told him to go upstairs and he would be served, but this was a private dinner among friends and they did not wish any strangers there. Whereupon the big Texan whipped out a 12-inch Bowie knife, gave some whoops and swore a blue streak, that he could and would cut any G—d—s— heart out if he interfered or tried to prevent him from having his dinner right here and now.
>
> The guests and Slade were in the rear of this room, but the swearing of the Texan aroused their attention, and as quick as lightning Slade jumped at the big Texan brandishing his big knife and wrested it quickly out of his hand, then taking it and, without cutting the big Texan, drew the knife slowly between his lips the whole length of the knife, saying, "You are pretty s— to talk of cutting anybody's heart out," then turned him and gave him a vigorous kick, saying, "Now you big overgrown son of a—, you get out of here mighty quick and don't you dare show your face to me again or by the eternal you will be another subject for the coroner to sit on."

After this little episode their banquet proceeded and they enjoyed each other's company greatly and at the end wished Slade a successful trip. The big Texan shook the dust of Leavenworth from his boots and he was no more heard from.[73]

"This, then, is the introduction of that notorious character into this country," wrote the Wyoming historian Charles Coutant of Slade years later.[74] And here, on the last and greatest of the Hockaday & Burr mail supply trains from Atchison to Salt Lake City, Slade's legend begins.

PART III

*

Power

A typical freighter wagon train preparing for its journey. (*Denver Public Library*)

Chapter 9

SLADE TAKES CHARGE

*

On the appointed morning in late August 1858, the prospective bullwhacker Hugo Koch left Leavenworth aboard a nine o'clock Missouri River steamer that deposited him seven hours later at Atchison, 25 miles upriver. The Hockaday & Burr office on Commercial Street stood just half a block from the wharf, but Koch—tired, hungry, and almost penniless, having spent nearly all his money on clothes suitable for freighting—failed to notice it.[1] After asking several people for directions to the Hockaday camp, he was finally told to "keep on west and I would strike it."[2] Atchison was (and remains) a town of steep hills sloping down to the river; looking west from the highest elevation, Koch later recalled, "I saw the unlimited prairie as far as the eye could reach."

Yet at the Hockaday camp Koch was initially disappointed to find only a handful of men and just a single discolored wagon—the mess wagon—where he was served a supper of "hard fried rancid bacon, coffee if you can imagine how it would taste from description given as to its browning or roasting, and bread that had burned crust on top, a hardly baked crust on the bottom and half unbaked dough in the center."[3] Koch found himself wondering: "If we live on rancid bacon, outrageous coffee and saleratus dough, right here on the edge of civilization, what will the grub be like when we are 1,000 miles away from every vestige of civilization?"[4]

For his first night, Koch was assigned to keep watch on a thousand steers confined in their corral. "I was surprised to see the size of their horns," he recalled, "and was told they were Texas steers. Texas steers and Missouri drivers and wagonmasters made the best freight locomotion then extant."[5]

The following day after breakfast ("such as it was"), Koch and his fellow teamsters were sent to the levee to assemble the prairie schooners, which had been shipped by boat, "knocked down." Once assembled, each new wagon was pulled to the Hockaday & Burr warehouse for loading. At noon the men returned to camp for dinner, "and sure enough," Koch recalled, "Mr. Slade appeared."

Koch's previously depressed spirits rose when Slade immediately focused on Koch's primary concern: the food.

> When he saw our dinner and mess outfit, he was greatly enraged at the grub and the manner of the tableware. "What!" he said. "No beans, no rice, no syrup! Only one frying pan, no coffee mill, and such bacon not fit for a hog! This will all be changed, and that mighty — quick."
>
> When, after an hour or two, wagonloads of stuff came from town just for our mess, he called the boys together and gathered them into three messes. The mess kit was so arranged that each had two or three frying pans, a Dutch oven for bread, three or four camp kettles of different sizes and a coffee mill and tin plates, spoons, knives and forks and teacups. Then came the provision part. There was plenty of beef, hams, shoulders, new bacon, rice, beans, dried apples, prunes, syrup, baking powder and lots of other things. Of course butter and milk was left off—that was "too expensive." . . . Mr. Slade presided at our mess.
>
> How different it was! . . . Now when the real boss came, why I thought we now can live like kings.[6]

Slade seems to have perceived instinctively an essential truth long grasped by the best military commanders: that men will bear extreme hardship as long as they can look forward to a decent meal at day's end.

Over the next three or four days the wagons were loaded, each with up to ten thousand pounds of merchandise. After loading, Koch recounted, each wagon was pulled by a team of steers up the hill to the camp, where eventually twenty-four loaded wagons were formed into a circular corral barely large enough to contain cattle and drivers overnight—a process that would be repeated each night along the trail, where the cattle slept within the wagon corral and the teamsters slept beneath the wagons themselves.[7]

The next few days were spent branding the initials "J.M." (for J.M. Hockaday) on the left hip of three hundred head of steers, in order to identify steers that night wander off along the trail. "Slade pointed out the steers," Koch recalled, "and one of the Missouri boys would lasso him and I helped jerk him to a big post and another Missouri graduate applied the red hot iron." When all were branded, the cattle were assigned in groups of twelve and hitched to the wagons:

> The yokes and chains were brought to the corral and Slade would sing out: "Brigham, here is your wheeler and this your near-wheeler," and the other boys would help him yoke them. The most of them had never had a yoke on their necks and they struggled hard to get away and it was not all fun, this first yoking. Then came the leaders, then the four swing yokes till he had his team. This operation was repeated 24 times and that made the 25 teams.
>
> What surprised me most was the immense memory of Mr. Slade, for the next time the steers were to be yoked, he knew every steer in every boy's team. Not only that, but he knew the position he had given every individual steer in that team.[8]

When the train finally got moving in September, the sky was clear, the roads were good, the rivers and creeks were neither deep nor wide, and the flat Kansas prairie was rich in feed for the cattle. At first the train made 20 to 25 miles each day. Because the train was organized specifically to stock Hockaday's trading posts as well as his dry goods emporium in Salt Lake, the teamsters found themselves well equipped with most of life's necessities. "As we were loaded with all sorts of merchandise," Koch recalled, "we had a super cargo or clerk, a Mr. Ridgley of St. Louis, and when our shoes gave out we could buy from him, and every 100 miles, fifty cents would be added to the price. It was the same with blankets or underwear or hats or monkey jackets, which was a short coat made to fit tight to the body, reaching a little below the waist. There was no need for overcoats, although they were also to be had, a few of the boys having the abbreviated soldier's overcoats."[9]

As the caravan approached Marysville, Kansas, 118 miles out, the country became "more undulating," pockmarked by huge sinkholes, some as large as an acre, filled with water.

Marysville was the sixth mail station on Hockaday's proposed network but the last white settlement that could be described as a community, although it was just a collection of primitive houses built without the usual sod in the crevices between their logs.[10] Here Slade was approached by the local schoolteacher, who suffered from ague and had concluded that in his condition—a fever marked by periodic intervals of alternating chills and sweating—whacking bulls in the fresh air was preferable to managing a schoolroom. The teacher asked Slade for a place on the line and was accepted.

As the train crossed into Nebraska Territory, the terrain grew rougher, the flat grassy prairie gave way to sandy hills, and firewood became scarce, so that "we had to carry it," Koch wrote. Here Slade's mettle as wagonmaster was first tested. In lieu of firewood, each teamster was given a gunnysack to tie to the side of his wagon, "and whenever he spied a nice buffalo chip he picked it up, as it made good fuel," Koch wrote. The wagons were directed to the creek bottoms, which had an abundance of grass for the cattle. "Slade was certainly a good wagon boss," Koch concluded.[11]

The Platte River and its tributaries were uniformly shallow, but pulling a wagon downhill to a creek was the sort of challenge not easily mastered by a novice. Koch thought he had learned the art of locking a wagon's wheels as it headed downhill. But one day, as he recalled it,

> we had been traveling on the top of a rather high plateau and came
> to the place where a downgrade of perhaps half a mile went down
> to a creek that was rather difficult to cross. When it came my time
> to lock my wheels, I waited a trifle too long and, not watching

closely, I got my fingers caught in the chain and had locked myself to the wheel as the cattle pulled slowly down the hill. In vain I tried to stop the team, and the boys below grew hilarious when they saw my predicament. They called Slade to see the comedy, and at last when they had had enough of the sport came to my rescue and released me from my ludicrous as well as painful position.[12]

Past Fort Kearny (278 miles out) the train came upon an encampment of soldiers returning from Johnston's Utah expedition, now being sent back "to what the boys then termed America, meaning the States." The troops had run short of flour, and Slade's train readily sold them enough to hold them until they reached Fort Kearny.[13]

Beyond the mail station at O'Fallon's Bluffs (400 miles out), the train prepared to cross the South Platte River. Here the banks were shallow and the slope sufficiently gentle that there was no talk about locking of wheels. But "the boys were talking about quicksand," Koch recalled. "I had no idea of quicksands but very soon found out." Although the water did not rise above the hub of a wagon wheel, the river was very wide and took all day to cross. One wagon got stuck in the sand and ultimately required ten teams of cattle"—that is, 120 oxen—to pull it out. Once across, the wagons had to be pulled up "a tremendous hill" to reach the divide between the south and north branches of the Platte. "I presume the number of miles we made that day was not over four or five," Koch wrote, "but it was the hardest day's work so far."[14]

Approaching another mail station at Scott's Bluffs (555 miles out) in mid-October, Slade's ox team overtook a Hockaday & Burr mule team that had started out from Atchison a week earlier. "The boys were worn out," Koch reported. "The mules were tired, they had no more flour and we had to divide grub with them."[15]

Over the campfire one night the teamsters' talk turned to the possibility of building a railroad through this country. "Most of them claimed it would be impossible," according to Koch, "and there was no necessity for one, as they claimed all that could be raised in this country was scalps and papooses." When Koch argued that the topography of the country would offer no impediment to a railroad, someone replied, "Well, generally, only crazy men would think of such an undertaking."

Another night over the campfire, as Koch told it,

> the question of politics came up, and each one had to divulge his political faith. Some were Democrats, some old time Whigs, some Know-nothings, some Squatter sovereigns. Finally my turn came and I avowed I was an abolitionist. Well, all the boys looked at me with blanched faces and in utter silence looked at me and Slade. I saw Slade's muscles of his face twitch with ominous signs of wrath. When he had controlled his welling up passion sufficiently, he said, with eyes dilated and unmistakable gestures, "Fred! If you ever expect to take your scalp back to America, never let me hear you say again you are an abolitionist." I presume the boys expected a shooting, but I now think that Slade considered my youth and innocence and mastered his passion.[16]

On the morning of October 18, 1858, having slept as usual under their wagons, Slade and his crew awoke to find three inches of snow on the ground. Since leaving Atchison they had made remarkable time, covering more than 500 miles in barely a month, and they had supplied twenty-two of the Hockaday line's proposed thirty-six mail stations. But here the first sign of winter had already appeared and they were less than halfway to Salt Lake City.[17] "All emigrants to Utah, California or Oregon for that year had passed before us," Koch noted, "so the only travel besides our own train was the occasional overland mail stages."

Having successfully stared down a hostile band of Indians earlier on the journey, Slade now confronted the second greatest threat to a wagonmaster: pilfering or drunkenness, or both, by his own men. Slade's crew included an alcoholic college boy known as "St. Joe" (for his hometown). The boy's parents, assuming that long weeks on the plains without access to liquor would dry him out, had persuaded Slade to hire the lad. But one late November morning, nearly three months out, following a night in which the men had slept under their wagons rather than in tents because of snow on the ground, "St. Joe" was discovered, as Koch told it, "gloriously drunk and fast asleep under his wagon." He was dumped into his wagon while another bull-whacker was assigned to drive his team.

> Slade raved and was furious, and as we then were not within fifty miles of any place where whiskey was sold or swapped, the question arose: How did "St. Joe" procure the 40 rod, now called by [such] other names as bug juice, benzine and booze?
>
> The next night after Slade gave "St. Joe" a lecture on temperance, he set a detective to work with instructions to watch him. The next morning, however, "St. Joe" was just as drunk as the morning before.... "St. Joe" had somehow ascertained that a barrel of whiskey or brandy was in his wagon and had made a hole in the wagon bed and another in the bottom of the barrel. He was careful at first not to drink too much, but the temptation was too great and he was finally found out.

Slade's retribution in this case was relatively mild: "St. Joe" was switched to another wagon and assessed for the value of the liquor he'd consumed. The punishment apparently sufficed: "So far as I remember that was the last time 'St. Joe' was drunk," Koch wrote.[18] But it was hardly the last time Slade would confront such an issue before the train reached Salt Lake City; and the next time the consequences would be far more serious.

Now the weather grew rougher, the Rockies hovered in the distance—Laramie Peak was already white with snow—and it was too cold and windy to sleep under the wagons. At Fort Laramie (610 miles out), Slade got three large Sibley tents—a new type of tent held up by a single central pole, in the style of an Indian teepee—and quartered each of his three messes there. Here the train camped for a few days. But having given much of their flour to Johnston's soldiers weeks earlier, his men's own supply now ran out. Slade and Ridgley, the train's cargo clerk, negotiated an exchange with the Fort Laramie quartermaster in which they swapped their supply of nails for the quartermaster's flour.

As soon as this transaction was consummated, the train pulled up stakes and started for the North Platte River. It was dark by the time they reached the riverbank. "It was a hard and rather dangerous road to travel in the daytime," Koch wrote, "and of course it was much worse in the dark, but Slade and his assistants managed to get all the train down without mishap."[19]

In the ensuing days, as the wagon train followed the North Platte River in a northwesterly direction, the high country grew rougher and the weather turned colder and stormy. Now the luxury of the Sibley tents proved a godsend. At Horseshoe Creek (37 miles from Fort Laramie and 647 miles out of Atchison), they reached the main mail station of John Hockaday's third division, which stretched westward nearly 250 miles from there to Gilbert's Station at the westerly end of South Pass.[20]

Horseshoe Creek—at that time the next mail station west after Scotts Bluff—was "a roomy log house with several rooms," according to Koch.[21] The Mormons' BYX Express Company (named for Brigham Young) had established a mail station there in 1857, bordered on the north side of the creek by gardens. But later that same year the Mormons had destroyed the Horseshoe station, as well as all their other mail stations, as part of their scorched-earth strategy to impede Colonel Johnston's Utah expedition. By mid-1858 a new division headquarters, surrounded by a stockade enclosing the station buildings and a well, had been constructed, most likely by Hockaday upon launching his mail and stagecoach service that spring.[22] Slade may have been the division superintendent (or "agent") already at this point; there is also some reason to believe that he was then superintendent of both Hockaday's third division as well as the second, which stretched from Fort Kearny to Horseshoe Creek.[23] In any case, from this moment, if not earlier, the Horseshoe Creek station became Slade's headquarters as well as the home he would share with his wife.[24]

Although it was still only November when Slade's freight train arrived at Horseshoe Creek, winter had already begun in earnest, feed was scarce, and Slade decided to halt then and there for the season. The wagons were parked in corrals near the station, and the men who had signed up for a round trip to Salt Lake City and back to Atchison were instead dispatched to Atchison from Horseshoe. Only those few who had agreed to be discharged at Salt Lake (including Hugo Koch) were retained for the duration of the winter.

As their first order of business, Slade and a dozen men took the cattle some 6 miles up Horseshoe Creek, where Koch says good feed and game were plentiful—a comment that suggests Slade was already well familiar with the area. Thereafter the only work involved taking care of the cattle—but, as Koch soon discovered, "That was hard work while it lasted, every day." In freezing temperatures, the ice on the creeks had to be sanded and holes cut so the cattle could drink water. The camp had to be moved every few days to ensure adequate feed for the cattle. On fair days, after the cattle had been taken care of, the men went hunting for their own food.

While Slade's supply train bided its time at Horseshoe Creek, Hockaday & Co.'s coaches continued to carry the mail once a week each way between St. Joseph and Salt Lake City. By December 1858 Hockaday's Salt Lake route numbered some two dozen mail stations. The operation was well on its way to its eventual full complement of thirty-six stations, or an average of one station every 33 miles.[25] Even Postmaster General Brown, in his December annual report to Congress, grudgingly praised the "joint venture" of Hockaday and Chorpenning in delivering cross-country mail over the central route he had earlier rejected:

> The routes between St. Joseph, Missouri, and Salt Lake City, and between Salt Lake and Placerville, California, have been so improved, that the trips through from St. Joseph to Placerville, and back, are performed once a week in thirty-eight days each way. For some months past this service has been performed with remarkable regularity, insomuch as to merit special consideration. It has received from the people of California the warmest applause, and called forth public demonstrations of a most enthusiastic character.[26]

This praise was cold comfort to Hockaday, for it merely reinforced his resentment of the favorable treatment and subsidies that Postmaster Brown had bestowed on Butterfield's Southern "ox-bow" route. Hockaday and Chorpenning had offered to match Butterfield's mail delivery time (twenty days to California) and also to increase their mail runs from weekly to triweekly (compared to Butterfield's semi-weekly service) if they could be assured of compensation equal to the Butterfield line's $600,000 annual subsidy. But Postmaster Brown was unresponsive.

In Congress, northern and western friends of the central overland route had attempted to force Brown's hand. A joint resolution in Congress, passed over stiff southern opposition, directed the postmaster general to speed up the central route service from thirty-eight days to thirty days, with a pro rata increase in compensation. Nevertheless, President Buchanan vetoed the legislation and Brown was off the hook once again.[27]

By late November 1858 Hockaday and Chorpenning resolved to organize a stunt that would seize the public's imagination and, in the process, force Brown to acknowledge that the shorter central route was also faster and better: they would stage a public race against Butterfield to see which line could be first to reach San Francisco with President Buchanan's annual message to Congress.

Even before Buchanan delivered his message to Congress on December 6, a more severe test greeted Hockaday. The great blizzard of December 1–3 struck the Rockies at a moment when Hockaday mails were due from both east and west. This first winter in the new line's existence turned out to be one of the most brutal in memory, with heavy snow, fierce winds, and record low temperatures. Hockaday had hoped to locate enough mountain stations so that, in the event of a storm, passengers could hole up in safety while the mail-bags were sent through on pack mules. Yet at this point, because of his limited government compensation, the Hockaday line operated only some eight stations along the mountainous 476-mile stretch between Horseshoe Creek and Salt Lake City.[28]

The regular westbound mail had left St. Joseph, Missouri, on November 13, and passed Slade's encampment at Horseshoe Creek without incident. It reached Devil's Gate station, 150 miles west of Horseshoe, as scheduled on November 28. The coach then started off for Gilbert's Station at the west end of South Pass, 85 miles farther west. But a threatening snowstorm on November 30 forced the conductor, his assistant and their single passenger to hole up in a willow grove on Rocky Ridge, about 8 miles east of Gilbert's Station. In this camp they were pinned down for three and a half days, while nine of their ten mules froze to death and the men protected their extremities by huddling together for warmth. Abandoning their mail and baggage on December 4, they plowed ahead with their last mule, bucking 8 miles of drifts for five hours to struggle into Gilbert's at 7 P.M.

The eastbound mail, meanwhile, had left Salt Lake City on November 27 with two conductors and two passengers. This party tried to make up the snow delay by traveling both day and night, only to lose their way in the darkness and miss stations, so that they had no choice but to camp out. On November 30, exhausted and already suffering from frostbite, they dragged into Green River station, 167 miles out from Salt Lake.

At this point, the agent for Hockaday's western division, William Ashton, took over, adding two more employees as well as two more passengers to the original four-person eastbound party. During a lull in the storm on December 3, this reconstituted nine-man party started up the trail again, with fresh mules. With Ashton in the lead to clear the trail, they pushed on to reach the summit of South Pass by nightfall. But here a renewed headwind of blowing snow obliterated the trail as well as visibility. Only by luck did the party hit the head of the Sweetwater River, where the exhausted men made a cold camp. Some men's feet were so frozen and swollen that their boots had to be cut off, with no replacements other than spare moccasins.

Early on December 4, as the westbound party abandoned its mail and baggage east of Gilbert's Station, this eastbound party also abandoned its mail, baggage, and mules to plow on afoot, the fit men carrying the disabled. At 8 A.M. they stumbled into Gilbert's Station, where the station agent Henry S. Gilbert and his hands turned their quarters into a makeshift hospital.[29]

Yet such was the crew's dedication to the mail that almost immediately after Ashton's eastbound party arrived at Gilbert's Station on December 4, someone there ventured out to retrieve the mailbags that the group had abandoned that morning at the western summit of South Pass. And when the westbound party struggled in to Gilbert's that evening, Gilbert himself left with a wagon and three men to retrieve the abandoned westbound mail.

Writing from Gilbert's Station at South Pass on December 13, Ashton reported that fourteen or fifteen mules had perished, that seventeen men were badly frozen, and that the thermometer had stood at twenty-eight degrees below zero for four consecutive days. His own hands were so badly frozen, Ashton added, that within a few days he hoped to start for Fort Bridger—118 miles to the west—to have some of his fingers amputated by the surgeon there.[30]

When this storm first struck some 135 miles west of Slade's quarters at Horseshoe Creek, Slade—not yet aware of what had transpired—received word of another crisis: a trailing section of his mammoth freight train that had left Atchison that summer had reached Scott's Bluffs, 92 miles to the east. Its cattle were played out and its crew had mostly returned to Atchison. On December 4 Slade piled some fifteen of his Horseshoe remnant into a four-mule rig for the trip back to Scotts Bluffs, from where they ultimately brought the belated train section to Horseshoe Creek and parked its wagons there with the others.[31]

They had barely returned to Horseshoe Creek when word came through of the disastrous blizzard to the west, and Slade was ordered to take four wagons to Devil's Gate—at the western edge of his division, 150 miles away—to supply that station with provisions. Before embarking, Slade went to Fort Laramie—35 miles in the opposite direction—where he hired several new men. "As this trip was hazardous, owing to the winter," Hugo Koch wrote, "Slade picked out about 65 head of the best steers"—that is, about 17 more than the usual complement—"and four extra men for fear some might freeze to death on the road. This was a cheering proposition, but we started out all right."

The first night out, after making 29 miles, they camped at the LaBonte Creek mail station, a trading post at a high elevation operat-

A supply train makes its way through a blizzard in the Rocky Mountains. (*Library of Congress*)

ed by two Frenchmen—"an ideal place," Koch wrote, "as it was well sheltered against the high winds that seemed to blow incessantly when we were on the road." Here their toughest task was sanding the frozen river so the cattle could walk on the ice, "as generally the Platte river was frozen to the quick sands and the cattle had to be driven to a place where a deep channel could be cut."[32] Along the way Slade's party deposited supplies at the mail stations as they passed. At the Deer Creek Indian agency (70 miles out of Horseshoe) they encountered John Hockaday himself, conducting a personal inspection.[33]

A few days later, approaching the Platte Bridge station (91 miles out of Horseshoe), they found a shivering military detachment, apparently prospecting for gold. Slade sent his train on about 4 miles up the river while he and his assistant, a man named Waters, spent the night at the station, operated by another Frenchman named Richard, "where the wine was red and the company of the officers agreeable," according to Koch. Here it was not Slade but Waters who was done in by imbibing too much wine.

The next morning Slade—without Waters—overtook his crew and selected a spot to cross the frozen river. But he had not tested the strength of the ice, Koch notes, "and as one of these channels of deep water was near the shore, as soon as the wagon was just about its length from the bank the ice broke under the weight of the wagon and it pulled the wheelers into the water also." While Slade and the others were figuring out what to do, Waters belatedly appeared. He was drunk on the red wine from Richard's, and

> when he saw the predicament, he jumped off his mule and called the boys, to take hold of the hind wheels with him and pull the wagon backwards, and he taking hold himself before Slade could prevent him, and then he slipped into the icy Platte river nearly under arms. The boys pulled him out quick as it was very cold [and] he would have frozen to death in a short time. Slade sent the lone Frenchman with him to a little trading post about one and one-half miles from where we were up the river, with the injunction not to let Waters return nor stop until he got to the house and then make him comfortable and dry his clothes.[34]

Meanwhile, Slade shifted the other wagons to a new track where the ice was stronger and doubled up the ox teams, which pulled the remaining three wagons across without incident.

While they were crossing, Slade ordered Koch to unload the partially submerged prairie schooner in order to save the dry part of the load as well as any other damp items that might be salvageable, like flour and corn—a task that required Koch to stand in the freezing water. "I got wet above my knees and had to work in this condition until nearly night," he wrote.

Once Koch emptied the wagon, Slade had it pulled out backward and reloaded. By that time the French station keeper Richard had come from his ranch, bringing, at Slade's request, "a little whiskey for the boys for their extra exertion and cold work." The incident suggests Slade's ambivalent attitude toward liquor. He recognized its destructive influence, but he also perceived its value as a reward and the extent to which men cherished it.[35]

Back on the trail the next day, "the cattle were squirming in their yokes, as the wind blew terribly," Koch wrote, "so much so that the faces of some of the boys looked as if they had been scratched by cats." It took two days just to make the 15 miles from the Platte Bridge to the Red Buttes mail station. Here Slade obtained feed for the cattle and, not knowing what lay ahead, directed the men to fill the vacant places in the wagons with hay. After a day's rest at Red Buttes, they pushed on once more, finally reaching Devil's Gate three days later.[36]

In the face of such brutal weather, any race between the central overland route and Butterfield's southern ox-bow route seemed audacious on its face. But Hockaday and Chorpenning confronted another obstacle for their stunt: Buchanan's administration seemed determined to protect its pet southern route from suffering defeat.

Although Buchanan's message would not be sent to Congress until December 6, under the terms of this "great mail race," a special messenger would leave Washington on the afternoon train of December 3, bearing advance copies to agents of both Hockaday and Butterfield who awaited him in St. Louis. The choice of St. Louis as the starting point in itself favored Butterfield, for he could cover his first 160 miles from there to his eastern terminus at Tipton, Missouri, by rail, whereas Hockaday had to cover twice that distance by horse over wintry roads to reach *his* line's eastern terminus at St. Joseph. Even with this advantage, when the special messenger from Washington arrived in St. Louis on the afternoon of December 5, Buchanan declined to release an advance copy to Hockaday's agent; early the next morning it was given exclusively to Butterfield's agent, who then began his way by rail to Tipton.

Hockaday's frustrated agent, meanwhile, fidgeted in St. Louis until the regular press copy of the president's message arrived on the afternoon of December 8, and he wasn't able to leave until the speech was published in the St. Louis papers the following day. Hockaday's special expressman, waiting impatiently in St. Joseph, didn't receive the president's printed message until December 14, more than a week after Butterfield's expressman left Tipton for California.

Given the brutal state of the weather in the Rockies at the time Buchanan delivered his address, Butterfield might very well have won the race fair and square. In the process, the race would have demonstrated the dangers of relying too heavily on the central route in winter. But by stacking the odds in the race, Buchanan effectively sabotaged his own cause. By the time Hockaday's expressman in St. Joseph headed west on December 14, the worst of the storm in the Rockies had subsided. Hockaday's couriers, benefiting from a large number of well-rested extra horses placed along the route for relays, made the trip from St. Joseph to Salt Lake in just twelve days, and from there Chorpenning's expressman delivered Buchanan's message to Placerville, California, on January 1, seven days from Salt Lake City and nineteen days from St. Joseph. Butterfield, thanks to his head start, delivered the message to San Francisco by December 26 after a trip that took twenty-one days from Tipton. Technically, Butterfield had "won" the race. But Hockaday and Chorpenning had covered the distance in two days' less time.[37]

If the government refused to let John Hockaday compete fairly for mail service, he and the equally optimistic George Chorpenning cherished the hope that they could still make money on their passenger stagecoach service. After "a very pleasant trip" east with Hockaday in January 1859, Chorpenning wrote to a friend from St. Joseph, "There is great excitement in this country about the Cherry Creek gold mines, and there is going to be a '49 [style] stampede from the Western states."[38] But here too the government placed the central route at a disadvantage. While the government diverted all California-bound first-class mail to the Butterfield line, the Hockaday and Chorpenning lines were burdened with newspapers and government reports, often in such bulk that little or no space remained for passengers.[39] Desperate to retain his biggest customer—the U.S. Post Office—Hockaday was ultimately forced to give up his other customers. In mid-February 1859 a small advertising notice began appearing in Salt Lake City newspapers on a weekly basis:

U.S. Mail Line
From St. Joseph to Great Salt Lake City
Notice is hereby given that passengers will not be carried by us on any section of this mail route until further notice, and that the agents and conductors on the route are positively forbidden from taking passengers, on any conditions whatsoever.
J.M. HOCKADAY & Co.[40]

Hockaday's sometime competitor William Russell, meanwhile, remained eager to capitalize on the Pike's Peak gold rush he was sure would occur in the spring. His scheme to launch a stagecoach line to Denver—and perhaps win a mail contract along that route as well—had received only a lukewarm reception from his freighting partners Majors and Waddell. But during a visit to Washington in the winter of 1858–59 (where he tried to persuade Secretary of War Floyd to release Russell, Majors & Waddell from its military freighting contract), Russell ran into his former partner John S. Jones, who had collaborated with Russell to haul military freight to Santa Fe after the Mexican War. Jones's latest firm, Jones & Cartwright, was second in size only to Russell, Majors & Waddell.[41]

By early February Russell and Jones had pooled $40,000 in cash and formed a new partnership to operate a stage line between Leavenworth and Denver, with Russell as its president, Jones as general manager, and Ben Ficklin as route agent.[42] Instead of following the Emigrant Trail across Nebraska Territory, as the Hockaday line did, this new "Leavenworth & Pike's Peak Express" would take a much more direct route to the south, across Kansas Territory. This 687-mile journey would take just seven days, and passengers would pay $125 plus the cost of meals for the privilege.[43]

In his customary sanguine fashion, Russell assumed the line would succeed right from the start and gave no thought to an exit strategy in case it didn't. From their basement office in Leavenworth's most imposing building—the four-story Planter's Hotel—he and Jones equipped their line lavishly, with a thousand Kentucky mules and at least fifteen (and possibly more than fifty) Concord coaches—specially fitted with soft cushions for the rough terrain, insulated for winter warmth, "altogether the finest stages run in the West," according to the Colorado pioneer William Larimer.[44]

Russell and Jones paid nothing in cash for their equipment; instead they signed notes payable in ninety days. But it would take about sixty of those days before the line carried its first paying customers, assuming the snows receded from the Rockies by April. The extent and durability of the anticipated Pike's Peak gold rush was another unknown variable. Failure was a distinct possibility for the new line, but the irrepressible Russell refused to consider it. If this line failed, something else would come up, as it always had in the past. In this manner Russell set in motion a chain of events that would doom him and his partners financially while simultaneously assuring their place in history.

John Hockaday also eagerly anticipated the coming of the spring of 1859 and, with it, the gold rush to Pike's Peak. Even if he couldn't squeeze paying passengers among the bulk mail bundles on his stage-coaches, he cherished the hope that the increased traffic would per-suade the Post Office Department to increase the frequency of his mail service and, presumably, his government subsidy. By the spring he would have thirty-six stations between St. Joseph and Salt Lake City.[45] Hockaday and his partner Liggitt had spent $394,000 to stock and equip the line in its first eleven months, by their later reckoning, although their government subsidy for that period was only $173,250.[46] In the coming warm weather gold rush they saw the prospect of recouping their investment.

But the brutal winter of 1858–59 stubbornly refused to give way to spring. By February Hockaday's loyal deputy William Ashton, who had suffered the amputation of his frozen fingers during the December storm, had been succeeded as agent for the westernmost division by Slade himself. Slade's jurisdiction, which previously covered the Hockaday line's second and third divisions, now shifted westward to the third and fourth divisions, stretching 475 miles from Horseshoe Creek to Salt Lake City.[47] Both men were in Salt Lake City at the time, and on Saturday, February 12, amid a snowstorm, they left with the eastbound mail. We are fortunate to have a first hand account of the extraordinary hardships that faced this particular mail run. An east-bound traveler named S. L. Hubbell left Salt Lake the following day and recounted in a letter written later that month, "I came in sight of the mail party, and stopped two hours to rest."

> . . . arrived at E. Hanks' ranch at nine o'clock at night, and found the mail party eating their supper. They started at ten o'clock, bidding me a final good bye.

I remained all night, and started at six in the morning. At nine o'clock I overtook the mail party at the spring on the Big Mountain; they had traveled all night without sleeping any, and had made 2 miles in eleven hours' travel.

At nine o'clock in the morning, we started again, the mail and my own party, which made seven men. The snow was from six to eight feet deep, and at the spring we could not tell the depth.

We held a consultation about the propriety of turning back; I gave my counsel to turn back, but Agent Slade said, "Go ahead," and we started; and after working from nine in the morning to five in the afternoon, unpacking, dragging and repacking mules, we made in eight hours' travel one half of a mile, and thought we had done big wonders in getting to the top of the Big Mountain. The mail conductor, Mr. Hardin, kept telling us that the worst was to come in going down the Big Mountain.

We started down. I thought that down hill through the snow would be easier, but the snow was at least fifteen or twenty feet deep. We had to drag the mules through the snow, where they sank in deeper than their backs for some 400 yards, where the mules all gave out, and had to lay by to feed and rest.

This was on Sunday. All this time Mr. Slade, Mr. Ashton and Conductor Hardin had not any sleep; all three were snow blind, and did not think it possible to proceed.

Here three discharged teamsters (Mexicans) from Camp Floyd overtook us, and Agent Slade hired them to assist us; and we proceeded to advance slowly, making one mile in about two hours.

At nine in the morning, we came to a camp of the Eastern mail that they made Thursday, the 17th. The mail conductor, A.C. Airs (better known as Texas), had cached the mail and turned back, unable to proceed. He was four days getting back to the Weber station, and two days he was without anything to eat.

We traveled all day Monday, the 21st, and made East Canyon Creek at dark, all hands snow-blind except one Mexican and myself (Slade, Ashton, Hardin and one mail-boy so badly that they could not keep the path without holding on to a mule); the snow was from six to ten feet deep, and not a sign of a trail; and it took two men ahead all the time from the top of the Little Mountain to feel for the trail, which was buried in the snow two or three feet. It was like prospecting for gold—very hard to find.

Tuesday, the 22nd, we traveled down East Canyon, working as hard as ever. Made the Hog's Back, between East Canyon and Weber. No feed for the mules; the poor brutes would chew bridles, ropes, saddles, &c., &c.

Here we discovered the trail that conductor Airs had made. Had it not been that we had found this trail, I do not think that we would have got to the Weber station with more than half of the mules, if any at all.

On Wednesday the 23rd, we arrived at the Weber station at ten o'clock; and the mail left at 11 o'clock with fresh mules.[47]

It had taken Slade's party eleven days to cover the 47 miles. And to what purpose? Their exertions were all part of a grander scheme that few of the individual players fully understood. They must continue to push the mail through the mountains, come hell or high water, not merely because their government contract (and consequently their jobs) required it, but because the nation's needs genuinely demanded it. As the southern states moved toward secession from the Union, as Washington's need to keep California within its orbit grew more urgent, as Utah Territory was reintegrated into the Union, and as the Pike's Peak region was freshly populated with thousands of gold-seekers, eventually the Post Office or Congress or the president would have no choice but to bless the central overland route with larger subsidies. These in turn would enable John Hockaday to build more mountain stations and plow the mountain trails and passes, in which case winter storms would be reduced to minor inconveniences. The coming Pike's Peak gold rush would no doubt attract competing stage lines, like William Russell's, but Hockaday seemed well positioned to withstand them. With his established organization, his network of three dozen stations, and his government mail contract, Hockaday presumed himself the early bird.

As of February 1, Postmaster General Brown had advertised for bids to carry the mail on several new routes to the Pike's Peak gold mines—bids to be submitted in Washington by April 1, decisions to be announced by April 25. A notice of these requests appeared on February 26 in the *Atchison Champion*, where John Hockaday would surely have seen it. One of the proposed new mail lines would connect with Hockaday's existing line at the crossing of the South Platte.[48]

With the coming of spring, Slade and everyone else in John Hockaday's employ had reason to believe that Hockaday's painstaking and costly investment would soon pay off. But Hockaday was about to discover that bad weather was the least of his problems.

Chapter 10

THE FERRIN SHOOTING

∗

The early months of 1859 found Slade and his boss John Hockaday at opposite ends of their mail line, each preoccupied with a different challenge. Along the western half of the line all the way to Salt Lake City, Slade supervised the stagecoach and mail operations while waiting for the spring thaw to deliver him the remains of the freight train he had parked at Horseshoe station in early November. At the eastern end, meanwhile, Hockaday abruptly left Atchison late in February 1859 and headed for Washington.[1] For a man accustomed to riding bumpy stagecoaches to inspect his operations between Atchison and Salt Lake, this much longer journey east was relatively easy. East of St. Louis—thanks in part to the new railroads completed two years earlier in southern Illinois by Slade's relatives Elias Dennis and Sidney Breese—the entire trip could now be made by rail in a few days.

A year earlier, Hockaday's visit to Washington had yielded him a government contract to deliver mail to and from Salt Lake City. Now, having failed to persuade the Post Office Department to increase his inadequate subsidy, Hockaday probably hoped to lobby for a second mail contract to Denver. But once he arrived in the nation's capital, Hockaday found to his dismay that the Congressional mood had shifted in an alarming new direction.

John Hockaday and Postmaster Aaron Brown may have disagreed about the relative merits of the southern and the central mail routes to

California, but Brown at least supported the basic principle that government subsidies for western mail routes were necessary.

Congress had embraced this theory when it subsidized the Butterfield mail line in 1857 and the Hockaday line in 1858. But the notion of using the Post Office for broader public purposes was still widely resisted on philosophical grounds, and not just by Southerners. "The principle has been that the Department should pay its own expenses," argued Senator Jacob Collamer of Vermont, who noted that the Post Office had supported itself from its own revenues when he himself served as postmaster general in 1849 and 1850. Congressional appropriations, according to this theory, were necessary only to meet the temporary losses that might result from occasional changes in postal rates. "If I go to California I must pay my passage," argued Senator Robert A. Toombs of Georgia. "If I send a messenger I pay for him. If I send a message, make me pay for that. This is the rule to which we should adhere."[2] As the postal deficit mounted, the movement to reduce or eliminate subsidized routes gained momentum. After a week of heated debate, Congress adjourned on March 5, 1859, without passing any Post Office appropriations.[3]

In the absence of an appropriations bill, the Post Office Department was reduced to paying its contractors with IOUs that they could cash only at a severe discount. In theory, this problem was temporary, and more than a year and a half remained on Hockaday's mail contract. But in practice it threw Hockaday's increasingly nervous lenders into a panic. In the hope of reassuring them—as well as himself—Hockaday appeared on March 7 at the Post Office Department, where the chief clerk of the Inspection Office obligingly provided him with a written commendation: "The department can safely assure you that you have performed the mail service upon route No. 8911, St. Joseph to Salt Lake City, in a manner highly creditable to yourself as a contractor. . . . The mails have been conveyed with great regularity through the most trying season of the year."[4] Such a letter was critical for John Hockaday's possible future use in any attempt to recover his losses from the government. Under ordinary circumstances it would have mollified his creditors. But the next day Postmaster Brown, the primary champion of the subsidy policy, suddenly dropped dead at the age of sixty-three.

Brown's successor—the former commissioner of patents, Judge Joseph Holt of Kentucky—was a southerner like Brown but Brown's antithesis in terms of policy: Holt believed the Post Office should support itself like any private business. Upon taking office Holt reviewed the department's mail contracts and was flabbergasted by his findings. The Post Office, he discovered, supported six mail lines to the Pacific, none of which brought in even a small fraction of its cost. Butterfield's southern "ox-bow" line cost $600,000 a year but brought in only $27,230. The Hockaday-Chorpenning central overland route cost much less ($320,000 between the two contractors) but brought in far less, too: a minuscule $5,412. Even the relatively well-utilized steamship route from New York and New Orleans via Panama barely brought in one-third of its cost.

To some extent these dismaying figures reflected the large quantity of newspapers and government documents that mail contractors were required to carry free of charge. But Holt saw only the bottom line: All told, the six routes were costing the government nearly $2.2 million but bringing in less than $340,000, a net loss to the department of more than $1.8 million a year.[5]

Armed with these figures, Holt moved swiftly to correct the abuses he perceived. He shut down two lines altogether, negotiated a new steamship service at less than half the previous cost and reduced service and fees on two other lines. All told, Holt's reductions amounted to more than $900,000 in savings. Only the southern service was left untouched, because Butterfield's ironclad contract there permitted no adjustments.[6]

Holt also rejected every one of the numerous bids that his predecessor had solicited for a mail service to Denver. John Hockaday had not even bothered to submit a bid, perhaps because he'd learned that William Russell and John Jones were already organizing a direct line from Leavenworth to Denver—their ambitious Leavenworth & Pike's Peak Express Company.[7] Holt's rejection didn't deter Russell and Jones's plans to proceed, but it did increase their interest in securing some other existing government mail contract—the closest of which, of course, was John Hockaday's line to Salt Lake.

Although Hockaday's mail contract still had more than a year and a half to run, that didn't prevent Holt from trying to renegotiate it. On March 26, Hockaday was summoned to the office of Assistant Postmaster General William H. Dundas. Since Congress had failed to appropriate postal funds, Dundas explained, he was asking Hockaday to voluntarily submit a proposal for reducing his mail service from weekly to semi-monthly, at a corresponding reduction in pay, effective July 1.

As Hockaday readily grasped—but the Post Office Department did not—such a reduction in service would actually *increase* his expenses. Slade himself, in an affidavit filed later that year, attested that "It costs the contractors more to transport the mail semi-monthly than it did when it was carried weekly." On his division, Slade said, the change had required building three additional stations and increasing the number of mules from 181 before July 1 to 349 afterward.[8]

Two days after his meeting with Dundas, Hockaday calmly set down his objections in a letter to Holt, adding that any reduction in compensation would undermine his credit with his lenders, effectively driving him out of business. Nevertheless, in the second week of April, Dundas notified Hockaday that the matter was no longer up for discussion. Holt had already decided to invoke a loophole in Hockaday's contract, enabling the department to reduce Hockaday's service (and Chorpenning's west of Salt Lake City as well) from weekly to semi-monthly as of July 1. Although the contract offered no provision for reducing Hockaday's annual fee in such a case, Holt reduced it anyway, from $190,000 to $125,000.[9]

The stunned John Hockaday was in no condition to challenge the government's arbitrary decision. Instead Hockaday's initial reaction was to continue operating the mail service on a weekly basis, in the hope that ultimately Congress would compensate him for the difference. "This," he replied to Holt three days later, "is the only method I can see of protecting my securities"—that is, his lenders—"and myself from ruin and loss."[10] But Hockaday quickly realized the folly of this wishful thinking. The news of his reduced fee, compounding the news of the delayed Congressional Post Office appropriations bill, would bring a swarm of frightened creditors to Hockaday's door, demanding their money.

The public and his customers knew nothing of this impending debacle. As late as April 12 the weekly *Valley Tan* newspaper in Salt Lake City excitedly informed its readers: "Messrs. Hockaday & Co. are preparing to open early with a splendid lot of coaches; and next summer the problem will be solved to the satisfaction of every one that the shortest route from the Mississippi river, the quickest time can be made, and more comfort had on the Great Central or Salt Lake route than any other overland mail route across the continent."[11]

John Hockaday knew better: He was facing certain ruin. By the time the *Valley Tan* news item appeared, he had sped west to salvage what he could of his stagecoach and mail empire.

By coincidence, Hockaday learned the news of his reduced subsidy at just the time that John Jones and William Russell launched their own stage line across Kansas Territory to Denver. Their first pair of passenger coaches left Leavenworth on April 8, arriving on schedule at Denver twenty days later. Before long the Leavenworth & Pike's Peak Express Co. was making the journey in less than a week. In addition to passengers, who paid $125 for the trip from Leavenworth to Denver (or twenty-five cents per mile for shorter distances), the Leavenworth & Pike's Peak Express Co. also carried private letters at the exorbitant fee of twenty-five cents each or packages for one dollar per pound.[12]

Russell's skeptical freighting partners, Alexander Majors and William B. Waddell, had remained aloof from this venture. Majors believed the Pike's Peak area wasn't sufficiently developed to support a stage line. Both he and Waddell feared that the line's enormous cost would jeopardize not only the Jones & Russell partnership but Russell, Majors & Waddell as well, and they voiced their misgivings publicly.

When the perpetually excitable Russell got wind of these reports—the day before his first coaches left Leavenworth—he wrote Waddell a blistering note, fuming, "I care not who started such reports. I trust you and Mr. M[ajors] did not. I pronounce them calumniators and liars and will on my return hold any man accountable who has falsely slandered me."[13]

With the redemption of the stagecoach line's ninety-day notes bearing down on Russell and Jones, the maiden journey of their line failed to attract the volume of paying passengers and packages that they needed. Thus at the very moment John Hockaday was desperately searching for a way to unload his business, Jones and Russell were searching equally desperately for a government mail contract to supplement their passenger revenues.

Even before Jones and Russell's second westbound trip could be completed, Hockaday appeared in Leavenworth, where on May 11 he agreed to sell them his Salt Lake mail contract. Although Jones and Russell themselves were deeply in debt, the deal seemed too good for them to pass up: For $50,000 in cash, they got a mail contract with seventeen months remaining, worth $177,000 in total compensation.[14]

The deal also required Jones & Russell to buy Hockaday's entire stagecoach operation—all of the stations, equipment, and stock—for an unspecified sum, to be fixed by appraisers. This was clearly a distress sale for Hockaday: the market price of mules had dropped sharply in the year since he had acquired his stock.[15] That summer the appraisal fixed the value of the Hockaday line's property at $94,000, bringing the total sale price to $144,000, much of it to be paid in promissory notes over the next year.[16]

With John Hockaday's stage line came the services of Hockaday's employees, including Joseph Alfred Slade. But neither Slade nor anyone else in Hockaday's employ was aware at first that a new boss had taken charge. Under the agreement, the sale would be kept secret and Hockaday would continue to operate his stagecoach line and mail service until the transition was completed as of July 1. Then John Hockaday, the energetic but undercapitalized young man who had established America's first reliable mail service to Salt Lake City—and who had seemed, just a few months earlier, well situated to develop a first-class stage line as well—would vanish from the central overland to his dry goods store in Salt Lake City, his life's work wiped out in a moment by the arbitrary acts of Washington politicians. "He now remains in a state of medical and physical debility," it was reported a year later, "which disqualifies him from bestowing any attention whatever to his business."[17]

Jones and Russell had no money of their own to acquire John Hockaday's line, of course. But the guaranteed cash flow from Hockaday's mail contract enabled them to pry their first loans from

Russell's reluctant freighting partners, Alexander Majors and William Waddell. And Hockaday's undervalued equipment and mules provided Russell and Jones with the collateral to finance their purchase through the shrewd freighter Ben Holladay, who for the moment was sitting on a cash surplus while harboring hopes of returning to the stagecoach business he had briefly tried to enter in 1856.[18] Ben Holladay was an old friend of William Russell's as well as Russell's partner in a recent venture to supply Camp Floyd in Utah with flour from the Salt Lake valley.[19]

If Jones and Russell's venture failed, these lenders—Majors, Waddell, and Holladay—would be most at risk, and consequently most likely to take it over. But of course the word *failure* could not be found in Russell's dictionary. As in all his ventures, the "Napoleon of the West" simply proceeded with the acquisition of the Hockaday stage line on the assumption that it would succeed.

John Hockaday was out of the mail and coach business, but his Salt Lake emporium remained, and so did his freighting business from Atchison to Salt Lake. And until July 1, as far as anyone knew, he was still operating the stage and mail line to Salt Lake, and his employees were charged above all with demonstrating to Congress and the postmaster general that the mails could go through the central route on schedule.

Yet the brutal winter of 1858–59 refused to cooperate. Even when the first belated hints of spring reached the Plains, the snowy mountains remained impassable, and the rivers below flooded their banks. On March 22—the first full day of what should have been spring—the *Valley Tan* of Salt Lake City reported that the mail from the East "encountered a succession of storms and hard weather, unparalleled in the history of the plains and mountains. Most all the men became snow-blind, and had to lay down frequently in the snow for whole days, with nothing to eat but crackers.... There is no doubt of it, that this has been the hardest winter ever experienced in the mountains."[20] A week later the same paper reported that two more Eastern mails "have been detained for more than nine days at the South Platte, which is breaking up and flooding out, also several days at Rocky Ridge and the South Pass, by snow storms."[21]

By April 19 the snow had finally subsided, but still the Eastern mails were delayed, due to a new weather catastrophe: "The probability is that all the mails, both going and coming from the States, are corralled by the South Platte, which is doubtless flooding out," the *Valley Tan* concluded.[22] Yet another weather-related mail crisis on Slade's division was reported on April 26: The mails "could not come through Weber Valley, as Weber River was very high and altogether impracticable . . . and in the canyons the snow has drifted to an enormous depth, the mules very frequently going clean out of sight, packs and all. In addition to this they soon gave out, and the men became snow blind. . . . Rude sleighs were constructed, and the mail bags drawn to the top of the mountain, and from there *snaked* down with ropes."[23]

While Slade grappled with the line's twice-weekly mail runs through this weather, he also confronted the challenge of reassembling the mammoth supply train that he had parked the previous fall at Horseshoe station. Not until April was the train finally reconstituted and back on the road to Salt Lake, where its arrival was awaited with great anticipation.

"There will be more goods thrown into this market this season than was ever known in any previous year," reported Salt Lake's *Valley Tan* on April 26, writing excitedly of "the immense trains groaning almost under the weight of merchandise that will be in from the East. . . . Among the first trains that will come in from the Eastward will be those of John M. Hockaday & Co. and Livingston, Kinkead & Co., both of which are well up on the road; and if the present pleasant weather continues, these two trains will shortly roll in."[24]

Slade was no longer the wagonmaster for Hockaday's giant westbound train, having succeeded the frostbitten William Ashton as agent for Hockaday's westernmost mail and stagecoach division. But as the Hockaday operation was now organized, Slade was expected to take charge once it entered his division at Green River, more than 300 miles west of Horseshoe Creek.[25] The train finally reached Green River about May 20, but when Slade joined it he found the train in chaos and at least some of the teamsters drunk and rebellious.

What happened next has never been definitely ascertained, since no eyewitness account exists. But the incident ensured for all time

Slade's reputation as either a decisive commander or a trigger-happy drunk, depending on which account the listener chose to believe.

The first report of the incident was provided three days later by Slade's predecessor William Ashton, in a dispatch to the *Valley Tan* from Green River:

> On the 20th inst., a difficulty occurred between Mr. Slade (the agent of J.M. Hockaday & Co.) and some of the men in the trains belonging to that company. In the affray, one Andrew Ferrin was killed. From the best information I can get Mr. Slade was justifiable in shooting him. The train was one that Mr. Slade brought out last fall as far as [Fort] Laramie, and [he] was fully authorized to take charge of it when it reached his division of the road; and on the day of the fatal accident, Mr. Slade meeting the train, found that some of the men had broken into boxes containing liquors, and having helped themselves abundantly, were prepared to resist anything.[26]

Support for this account was later provided by the pioneer James Wilson, who subsequently worked for Slade as a telegraph operator at Horseshoe. The train, Wilson recalled in a 1907 memoir, "was held up near Fort Bridger by the drivers and the wagon-master run off. Slade was sent to quell the trouble, which he did most effectively."[27]

But in another account of the Ferrin shooting, from the memoirs of the frontier trader Granville Stuart, the drunken culprit is not the teamster Ferrin (sometimes called Farrar or Farren)[28] but Slade himself:

> In April [1859] we moved from Henry's Fork to the mouth of Ham's Fork, where we remained a month. . . . While camped here a mule train of sixteen wagons loaded with freight for Salt Lake City camped a short distance above us on the stream. In a few minutes we heard a shot fired and as there seemed to be some excitement we walked up to the wagons, and were shocked to see one of the drivers lying on the ground, shot through the heart. The wagon boss had gotten drunk at Green River, about fifteen miles back, was cussing the driver about some trifle, the driver

had talked back, and the "boss," who was J. A. Slade, drew his revolver and shot the man dead. Later the teamsters dug a grave by the roadside, wrapped the dead man in his blankets and buried him. The train went on to Salt Lake and nothing was done about the murder.[29]

This version too, enjoys support and elaboration from the Wyoming historian C. G. Coutant, whose 1899 account may have relied on the teamster Hugo Koch as its source:

> Soon after arriving in Wyoming he [Slade] killed Andrew Farrar, a man connected with the train. The two were drinking together at some point east of Green River and got into an animated conversation, during which something was said about shooting, Slade remarking that no man must dare him to shoot. Farrar, who was fast reaching a maudlin condition, replied, "I dare you to shoot me." Instantly Slade drew his revolver and fired, inflicting a dangerous wound on the person of Farrar. Horrified at what he had done, he expressed the greatest sorrow to the wounded man and those around him and instantly dispatched a messenger on a fast horse to Fort Bridger to secure a surgeon. The doctor came promptly, but his services were without avail and Farrar died.[30]

The two conflicting versions of the Ferrin shooting—Slade as courageous wagonmaster suppressing a drunken insurrection, and Slade as a drunk accidentally killing one of his own men—agree on one basic point: Slade did indeed fatally shoot one of his teamsters near Ham's Fork along Green River. But in the absence of an eyewitness account, which story is to be believed?

Both versions of the Ferrin shooting are provided by reliable (if not objective) sources. Ashton, as a loyal Hockaday agent, and Wilson, as a Slade colleague, may have sought in their accounts to tone down their colleague's transgression. Conversely, if Slade's teamsters were indeed drunk and rebellious, they would be unlikely to acknowledge as much to a passerby like Granville Stuart.

Both versions, too, are consistent with Slade's behavior at various points in his career. From the day Hockaday's mammoth freight train left Atchison the previous September, Slade's concern about keeping his men away from the train's liquor supply was paramount. So was his determination to keep the train (and, throughout that long winter, the mails) moving in the face of all obstacles, as well as his willingness to draw his gun against superior numbers (as in his confrontation with hostile Indians in Nebraska Territory). And yet, later in his career Slade often lost control of himself while drunk, only to apologize profusely afterward, including one occasion on which he accidentally shot and wounded a personal friend.

Perhaps the best clue to what really happened at Ham's Fork that May day lies in what occurred *after* the shooting. "The teamsters dug a grave by the roadside, wrapped the dead man in his blankets and buried him," Stuart related, after which "the train went on to Salt Lake and nothing was done about the murder." By contrast, the previous summer, in the same vicinity, the mere rumor that a Russell, Majors & Waddell wagonmaster named Dave Wagner had killed a mutinous teamster had nearly caused him to be lynched by a gang from another wagon train. The rumor was unfounded—Wagner had knocked out the teamster with a spade as the man was reaching for his gun—yet a week later the same teamster retaliated by shooting Wagner to death.[31]

Had Slade shot Ferrin without justification, it is difficult to believe that frontier teamsters—a notoriously wild and defiant bunch—would have submitted so passively to his authority from that point on. It's also difficult to believe that Slade wouldn't have fled the scene to escape their certain revenge.

It's likewise difficult to believe that an unjust killing would have attracted no apparent attention or concern either among Slade's employers or among legal authorities, in Salt Lake City or elsewhere. In the wake of the Ferrin shooting, Slade suffered no loss of rank or authority in John Hockaday's organization, nor was he demoted or fired when Jones and Russell took it over. Just six weeks after the shooting, the pioneer Louis R. Maillet rode a stage with "Slade, division agent" from Gilbert's station to Ham's Fork—the very spot where the shooting took place—without mention of the homicide.[32]

"This was a wild, uninhabited area," one Slade biography suggests, by way of explanation for the apparent law-enforcement apathy, "and

shootings like this were not investigated."[33] Yet the overland route to
Salt Lake City was actually well-
traveled—as Ashton's dispatch
from Green River noted, "Trains
loaded with goods are passing here
daily"—and the Ferrin shooting
was sufficiently unusual that the
story soon assumed legendary status. (Ferrin's grave was pointed out
to the English traveler Sir Richard
Burton when his stagecoach passed
it some fifteen months later.)[34]
Someone, somewhere, would have
complained to John Hockaday's
organization or to legal authorities
in Salt Lake City—if Slade's killing
of Ferrin wasn't justified.

For all the killings subsequently
attributed to Slade, the shooting of
the unfortunate Ferrin remains the
only death by Slade's hand that was
confirmed and verified beyond any

Laughed at for His Foolishness and Shot Dead by Slade. Charles M. Russell's sensationalized painting of the death of teamster Andrew Ferrin helped spread Slade's reputation as a callous gunslinger who shot men for sport. The actual facts of the incident were quite different.

doubt. Yet the story, embellished wherever teamsters gathered over
campfires and in saloons, soon took wings along the Overland Trail,
creating a full-blown myth of Slade as a mankiller. By the time it
reached the ears of the master storyteller Mark Twain, Slade's shooting of Ferrin was no longer a matter of either duty or drunkenness but
a sheer diabolical act:

> One day on the plains he had an angry dispute with one of his
> wagon-drivers, and both drew their revolvers. But the driver was
> the quicker artist, and had his weapon cocked first. So Slade said
> it was a pity to waste life on so small a matter, and proposed that
> the pistols be thrown on the ground and the quarrel settled by a
> fistfight. The unsuspecting driver agreed, and threw down his

pistol—whereupon Slade laughed at his simplicity, and shot him dead![35]

Mark Twain never claimed to be a historian, but his was the first widely published report of the Ferrin shooting. And such was the power of Mark Twain's pen that his version eventually was accepted by many historians who should have known better. The Twain account also inspired an equally vivid—and equally fictitious—action painting by the noted Western artist Charles M. Russell, titled *Laughed at for His Foolishness and Shot Dead by Slade.*

Missing from these stories and drawings is any sense of the larger issue at hand that day at Ham's Fork—or, more to the point, what seemed to Slade to be at stake that day. In the telling of Mark Twain, Charles Russell, and Granville Stuart—and, indeed, the teamsters Stuart questioned after the shooting—the Ferrin shooting was merely the pointless result of a battle of egos between two drunken freighters. But Slade had organized that freight train, had captained it across more than 1,000 miles, had nurtured it through the winter, and seen it reconstituted the following spring. His actions throughout those nine months suggest an obsession with delivering the supply train, at long last, to its final destination in Salt Lake City. Having brought it within 150 miles of its goal, would such a man have been likely to jeopardize the whole venture with a frivolous drunken shooting spree?

The ironic piece of this story, of course, is that Slade's shooting of Ferrin took place five days after John Hockaday sold his mail contract as well as his stagecoach line to William Russell and John Jones. The sale would not officially be made public for another six weeks (although word of it leaked out almost immediately). Like the Post Office appropriations bill in Congress, Slade's exertions in behalf of John Hockaday, not to mention the sacrifice of Ferrin's life, had come too late to save Hockaday's mail and stagecoach empire. Now another dreamer would have to pick up and carry that torch.

When John Hockaday sold out on May 15, William Russell and John Jones technically became owners of two stagecoach lines:

their own Leavenworth & Pike's Peak Express Co. across Kansas Territory to Denver, and the former Hockaday line's Platte River route across Nebraska Territory to Salt Lake. But for such a debt-ridden partnership, the notion of operating two parallel lines barely 100 miles apart was out of the question. At about the time of the sale, Jones stepped down as general superintendent, to be replaced by Beverly D. Williams of Denver. As the stage driver Frank Root later described him,

> Socially Williams was one of the best fellows in the world, but as manager of a great stage company's property on the frontier he was not a success. He knew very little about the plains, it was said, and much less of the people residing there. He seemed to look upon everyone he employed as honest, capable and efficient, when in reality some of them were at heart scoundrels and thieves, who systematically stole the company's property. Because a man knew the plains over which the stages ran, Williams would venture to hire him as a station keeper. Thus it was that he had in his employ a number of unprincipled rascals.[36]

To Williams would go the awesome task of merging the two stagecoach lines within a matter of weeks.

To abandon Jones & Russell's Leavenworth & Pike's Peak line across Kansas Territory, which had just been constructed and furnished at great expense, seemed the height of folly. But in the end the route was dictated by the Post Office Department: Jones & Russell were free to operate stagecoaches wherever they chose, but the mail contract between St. Joseph and Salt Lake City required the contractor to stop at both Fort Kearny and Fort Laramie. So Jones & Russell's lavishly prepared Kansas route was abandoned in favor of John Hockaday's old Platte River route; Denver would be served by opening a branch line along the South Platte.

With only a month before the two operations would be merged on July 1, the critical question for Williams was where to locate the junction at which the Denver and Salt Lake routes would diverge, and whom to put in charge of this junction. Between the Missouri and the Rockies the most likely stations were the lonely "road ranches" scattered along the trail at twenty- or thirty-mile intervals. These "ranch-es" were really wayside inns, consisting of a single sod structure that functioned as a combination residence, farmhouse, store, tavern, and restaurant. Most ranches were equipped with large jacks, so that wagon wheels could be pulled and axles retarred. According to one traveler, these ranches were "generally kept by mongrel French or half-breed Indians who divide their time between smoking, sleeping and playing the fiddle. They usually have from one to six squaws and papooses without number."[37]

Such a ranch seemed the logical place for a critical junction of the stage line. But a considerable cultural divide separated the Frenchmen who operated these ranches from the mostly English-speaking officials of the stage line. Although these ranchers subsisted by servicing freighters and passing emigrant trains, they tended to resent the institu-tionalization represented by the stagecoach line. "They belonged to the worst type of Canadian French," wrote one stagecoach driver, "having Indian women, and half-breed families. They had dominated the old immigrant trail in summer, with no one to molest or make them afraid….It soon was apparent that the coming of the stage did not meet with their approval. In fact they looked upon it as a trespass on their domains, and in their unmitigated ignorance, thought to drive it from the road. So they began to molest and harass it in various ways. Stock was chased away from the station, and some mules were shot at night."[38]

The choice of location for the stagecoach junction was equally problematic. On a map, the logical place to split the two stage routes was the spot in western Nebraska Territory where the Platte branched into two forks. From here a stage line could follow the South Platte River to Denver or the North Platte to Fort Laramie and from there on to Salt Lake. But the river was difficult to ford at that point. Through much of the 1850s, westbound wagon trains had experimented with a variety of fords through a process of trial and error.

By 1859 a new ford with a more gradual descent was discovered, about a hundred miles west of the forks of the Platte, along the South Platte at its junction with Lodgepole Creek. Long before, this spot had been a favorite north-south crossing for the Cheyenne and other

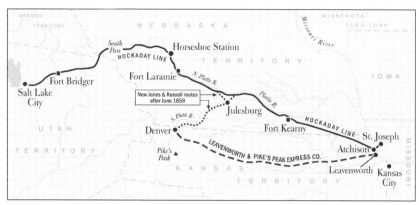

After buying John Hockaday's stage line to Salt Lake City in May 1859, Jones and Russell abandoned their Leavenworth & Pike's Peak Express Company and instead launched a spur line to Denver from Hockaday's old route. Julesburg was chosen as the critical point where the two lines diverged.

Indian tribes during their buffalo hunts.[39] This spot—known variously as Upper California Crossing, Morrell's Crossing, Laramie Crossing, and Goodale's Crossing[40]—soon became the preferred ford for most westbound wagon trains as well as any traffic headed for Denver. On the south bank at this spot in the late 1850s a French-Canadian trader named Jules Beni had opened a small trading post and a large sodhouse that served as saloon, restaurant, hotel, store and anything else that might accommodate travelers' needs.[41] Beni (pronounced be-NAY)[42] was about fifty years old and generally known on the Plains as "Old Jules," in deference to his relatively advanced age. "Nearly all the people scattered along the road," wrote the pioneer Nathaniel Langford in 1890, "regarded him as their leader and adviser, and he was proud of the position. He espoused their quarrels with outsiders, and reconciled all differences occurring among themselves. In this way, he exercised the power of a chief over the class, and maintained a rustic dignity, which commanded respect within the sphere of its influence."[43]

Jules was said to be of mixed French and Indian parentage, born in Ontario, a large, thickset man of dark complexion and dark eyes, who wore his hair down to his shoulders and dressed in buckskin jacket and breeches.[44] He was described as a man of "keen native shrewdness

and peppery disposition, becoming more dangerous as he grew older."
He was said to have taken an Indian woman in marriage.[45]

As traffic increased at the Upper California Crossing, Jules had
added a warehouse, a blacksmith shop, a stable, and a billiard saloon,
all built, in the absence of trees nearby, from cedar logs hauled by oxen
from Cottonwood Springs, some 105 miles to the east.[46] Jules's cluster of squat buildings never numbered more than a dozen and never
housed more than fifty permanent residents, but "Julesburg," as it
came to be known, was the largest settlement between the Missouri
River and the Rockies, as well as the roughest: a wicked little place
where unscrupulous men gravitated to prey on the exhausted travelers
passing through.[47] "Vile whiskey was sold in 'two bits a glass'," wrote
a local historian; "roads being long and transportation high, it was
mixed with water to make it go as far as possible."[48]

Mark Twain, who passed through in 1861 on his way west,
described Julesburg as "the strangest, quaintest, funniest frontier town
that our untraveled eyes had ever stared at and been astonished
with…. It did seem strange enough to see a town again after what
appeared to us such a long acquaintance with deep, still, almost lifeless
and houseless solitude! We tumbled out into the busy street feeling
like meteoric people crumbled off the corner of some other world, and
wakened up suddenly in this."[49]

The village as well as the 25-mile stretch to the northwest along
Lodgepole Creek—where Jules had built another ranch—came to be
called "Jules Stretch."[50] This frontier fiefdom of barely one hundred
souls, seemingly in the middle of nowhere, was actually centrally located within the three civilized outposts of the Great Plains: barely 200
miles west of Fort Kearny, less than 200 miles northeast of Denver, and
175 miles southeast of Fort Laramie.[51] Thus Julesburg seemed to
Beverly Williams the logical junction for Jones & Russell's branch line
to Denver, and Jules its logical stationmaster.[52] The optimistic
Williams overlooked the fact that Jules operated as a law unto himself,
that he had never worked within an organization, and that Julesburg
was a dangerous place, in part because Williams had little alternative.
Jules seemed no less reliable than other ranchers along the line, and

Julesburg, 1865

Julesburg, where Slade confronted Jules Beni in 1859. The South Platte River can be seen at the right and Fort Sedgwick (built 1864) in the background. This drawing was made shortly before Sioux Indians burned down the hamlet in February 1865.

time was of the essence, because Jones & Russell's ninety-day notes were about to come due.

In June a new station was constructed at Julesburg, and Jules was put in charge of it as well as the entire 25-mile "Jules stretch" to the northwest.[53] The four divisions of John Hockaday's old line were now reconstituted as three divisions between St. Joseph and Salt Lake, each run by a division superintendent who remained under the new regime. (Slade apparently remained in charge of the westernmost division between South Pass and Salt Lake City.)[54] The 200-mile branch line from Julesburg to Denver was designated as a fourth division.[55] But Julesburg was the linchpin of this system, and almost from Old Jules's first day, a disturbing pattern developed. Company horses and hay would be run off by thieves, to be returned for a reward arranged by Old Jules and charged to the company. Sometimes Jules used the company's horses and hay on his own ranch. Stagecoach passengers complained about being overcharged by Jules for meals consisting of "bread, beans, meat, dried apples and coffee," as well as for their lodgings.

Jules was not the leader of an outlaw gang, as some observers later charged—he was too much of a one-man gang to work with a group.[56] But he does seem to have been in cahoots with outlaws, and he does seem to have been preoccupied with milking the perquisites of his job at his employer's expense.

Yet these were minor transgressions. What most alarmed the company about Jules's management was not his petty thievery but the delays and schedule disruptions caused by the constant disappearance of horses (and hay with which to feed them), as well as Jules's incompetence. On several occasions, westbound mail intended for Denver had mistakenly been sent on to Salt Lake City instead—foul-ups that suggest that Jules was inattentive to his job or perhaps even illiterate.[57] Whatever the reason, the company's failure to deliver the mail reliably and on time would likely cause the government to cancel the cherished mail contract that Jones & Russell had sunk so deeply into debt to acquire.[58]

Jules's response to the company's complaints was less than reassuring. On one occasion, when Jules was "more than half drunk," he demonstrated to a rapt but incredulous audience a method of making mortar as Jules claimed he had seen it done in Omaha. He brought several sacks of flour (worth a dollar a pound at the time) and a barrel of whiskey (which sold at ten dollars a quart) out of the station onto Julesburg's only street. Here he proceeded to pour the flour into a mortar bed, soak it with the whiskey and stir it to smoothness. When someone suggested that these were expensive ingredients for mortar, Jules seemed unconcerned. An onlooker surmised that the materials had been the stage company's property, and more would be available when they were gone.[59]

William Russell's freighting partners, Alexander Majors and William Waddell, watched these developments with mounting apprehension. They had opposed Russell's stage line from the start and had refused to participate, but now they were being dragged into it in spite of themselves. Russell had optimistically assumed that hordes of easterners would head for the Pike's Peak gold diggings in 1859. And indeed about 150,000 people did make the trek that year. But most of them traveled not by stagecoach but by wagon train, in small parties of their own, on horseback, or on foot. Between Jules Beni's mischief at Julesburg and the failure to generate passenger revenues, Jones & Russell's stage line operated at a deficit from its inception.[60]

Russell had impetuously launched his Denver stagecoach line in order to rescue Russell, Majors & Waddell from the financial crisis caused by its disastrous Utah military expedition, but now the stagecoach line was failing as well, and threatening to pull Russell, Majors & Waddell down with it. By the end of the summer of 1859, Jones & Russell Co. owed more than $525,000, of which well over $100,000 was due to Russell, Majors & Waddell.[61] If the Leavenworth & Pike's Peak Express failed, Russell, Majors & Waddell would fail as well.

To prevent such a catastrophe, on October 28 Russell, Majors & Waddell acquired this bankrupt stage line and reorganized it as a new five-man partnership dominated by Russell.[62] John Hockaday's pioneering mail line to Salt Lake City had lasted all of fifteen months; now its successor, Russell's more ambitious Leavenworth & Pike's Peak Express Co., had failed just six months after its first run. But Russell himself, as president of the as-yet-unnamed new stage company, saw only new opportunities.

The Post Office Department's greatest prize—the $600,000-a-year contract held by John Butterfield's rival California mail operation—still had nearly five years to run. But Russell sensed that opposition to Butterfield's "ox-bow" route was mounting because of its length as well as its southern location. He also sensed that George Chorpenning's mail contract from Salt Lake to California, which paid $130,000 a year, might be vulnerable. Russell further surmised that his existing stagecoach lines to Denver and Salt Lake City, by themselves, wouldn't persuade the Post Office Department to cancel Butterfield's California mail contract and turn it over to Russell. What was needed was some dramatic gesture that would seize the imagination of the public and politicians alike.

Although Russell's newly constituted company operated no stage lines west of Salt Lake City, Russell now formulated an even more ambitious strategy to divert more Post Office funding to the central overland route. In its new incarnation, his existing stagecoach line to

Salt Lake and Denver would also launch a fast-mail service to California carried by lightweight express riders mounted on fast ponies.

Russell was hardly the first dreamer to conceive a horseback relay system for delivering mail across vast distances: Marco Polo had found a similar system in thirteenth-century China, operating with "post-stations twenty-five miles apart, and stations for foot carriers three miles apart, on the chief routes through his dominion."[63] In 1853 President Franklin Pierce's annual message to Congress, which had arrived at San Francisco by steamer, was delivered to Portland, Oregon, by relays of fast-riding horsemen.[64]

The idea of a cross-country pony express appears to have been first conceived by Ben Ficklin, who planted the idea with California's senior U.S. Senator, William M. Gwin, while the two men traveled across the continent on horseback in 1854. The following January Gwin introduced a bill in Congress "looking to the establishment of a weekly letter express between St. Louis and San Francisco, the schedule to be ten days," but his bill was never referred out of the Senate's Committee on Military Affairs.[65] Russell himself came up with a similar idea in the winter of 1857–58 while traveling across the plains to Utah to deliver supplies to Albert Sidney Johnston's army there, and he subsequently broached the idea in Washington to Secretary of War Floyd and various senators and congressmen. But the Virginian Floyd opposed the idea rather than jeopardize the southern "ox-bow" mail contract awarded in 1857 to Butterfield.[66]

By the fall of 1859, though, the "Pony Express" increasingly looked like an idea whose time had come. The opening of the Hannibal & St. Joseph Railroad that February brought the rails across the state of Missouri as far west as the Missouri River.[67] The telegraph, invented just fifteen years earlier by Samuel F. B. Morse, now also reached St. Joseph. But west of St. Joseph there were neither railroads nor telegraph lines. It was understood that both would be extended eventually; but in the meantime the need to speed communication to California was urgent. At the very moment Russell was scrambling to save his reconstituted stagecoach line, his friend Senator Gwin of California was dangling temptation before him. A Pony Express to

California would increase westward migration, boost passenger traffic on Russell's stage line, and possibly cause the closing of Butterfield's southern mail route in favor of another route (like Russell's) that wasn't vulnerable to southern interference.[68]

But the logistics of a mail relay stretching 1,966 miles from the Missouri River to Sacramento were so daunting that only an incurable dreamer like Russell would have considered implementing it. Swift ponies were indeed faster than the mules or draft horses used to pull stagecoaches, but they lacked endurance. The stage line currently maintained stations at 20- to 30-mile intervals where animals could be changed or rested; ponies racing at breakneck speed would need changing every ten miles or less. And west of Salt Lake City, Russell's stage line had no operations at all.

All told, dozens of new stations would be required between the Missouri River and Sacramento. In the absence of forests, lumber to build the stations and corrals would have to be hauled great distances. Hundreds of high-quality ponies, capable of outrunning the Indians' swift ponies, would need to be purchased, probably at three or four times the cost of ordinary range-bred horses.[69] And a new breed of employee—young, skinny riders—would need to be hired and trained.

The enterprise would likely cost Russell, Majors & Waddell more than half a million dollars—for a mail service that was likely to be superseded by the telegraph and the railroads within a few years. And this expense would be piled on top of more than half a million dollars in existing bills that would fall due in the first six months of 1860.[70]

Russell, in his customary wishful thinking mode, saw not the risks but only the opportunities. Because of the difficulty of securing and transporting supplies, only a freighting firm like Russell, Majors & Waddell could attempt a Pony Express. The financial risks were indeed huge, but Russell presumed he could protect the stagecoach line through a legal device. The Pony Express would be operated by the stagecoach line, which in turn would shield its investors and the line itself by reorganizing not as a partnership but as a corporation.

After returning East in November, Russell wrote Waddell from New York that he was preparing a charter for the new corporation, to be organized in New York four days later and then submitted to the

Kansas territorial legislature. Its name, Russell informed Waddell just the day before the organization, would be the Central Overland California & Pike's Peak Express Company. In passing, Russell mentioned that the Rocky Mountain region "is the place to make our money instead of freighting." Neither Majors nor Waddell had been consulted about this new business plan or this grandiloquent title, nor did they receive Russell's letter until the organization was a *fait accompli.*[71] Since Russell had already set the wheels in motion, Majors and Waddell had no choice but to go along; any public appearance of dissension among the partners could jeopardize their credit and consequently the whole partnership, as Russell well knew.

The first order of business in pursuit of Russell's dream was revamping the stagecoach line's existing operations. The trusting general superintendent Beverly Williams was replaced by the energetic Ben Ficklin, who was instructed to "clean up the line." That meant, above all, replacing Jules Beni as stationmaster at Julesburg. But Jules was a proud and volatile man who would not go quietly. The man who dismissed him might be murdered. And even if Jules did accept his dismissal, he essentially owned the town and would remain on the scene as proprietor of his ranch there. He might have to be driven away or even killed.

Ficklin's appointment of Joseph Alfred Slade to take on this task has puzzled many historians, but at the time the choice was obvious. Slade already worked for the stage line as the superintendent of the neighboring division to the west. He seemed immune to peril, or at least inured to it. Against impossible odds and weather he had driven Hockaday's mammoth freight train from Atchison to Salt Lake. He had pushed a mail run through a blizzard. He had faced down hostile Indians on the Overland Trail. Less than six months earlier he had quelled an incipient mutiny at Ham's Fork and shot the apparent ringleader dead in the process. He was said to harbor implacable hatreds, especially for horse thieves; and what was Jules Beni if not a horse thief? What Slade had done to the rebellious teamster Andrew Ferrin, presumably, he could do to Jules Beni as well.

In his choice of Slade, Ficklin perceived what everyone else— including Jules—already sensed: that Slade would clean up the line or

die trying. Shrewdly, Ficklin calculated that Slade's fearsome reputation alone might suffice to drive Jules out. Curiously, neither Ficklin
nor anyone else on the frontier seems to have been aware that Slade
had grown up in a family of lawmen, as the son and stepson of U.S.
marshals. Slade may have been flawed; but rarely had a man and a mission been so ideally suited.[72]

In his days as an obscure wagonmaster, Slade had often let off steam
in Atchison at the end of his freighting runs. Slade's stature had
grown as well over the same period, but Atchison (now a genuine frontier metropolis consisting of hotels, shops, saloons, and some 2,500
permanent residents by 1859) remained the venue where, as the stage
driver Frank Root put it, Slade "would occasionally have a 'high old
time' when in company with some of the wide-awake stage boys."[73] By
the time of one such visit early in December 1859—shortly after
Ficklin appointed him to clean up Julesburg—Slade was one of the
best-known figures on the Plains. It was on that visit that Slade crossed
the path of another rising luminary whose fame in those parts exceeded his own: Abraham Lincoln.

As a freshman Congressman in 1848, Lincoln had sacrificed an
apparently promising political career by his outspoken opposition to
James K. Polk's popular war against Mexico. After he declined to seek
reelection that year, Lincoln returned to Illinois and the private practice of law, "riding circuit"—first by stagecoach and later by railroad—
with his fellow Springfield lawyers to try cases in surrounding counties where lawyers were sparse. Over the next six years, the flickering
candle of Lincoln's political future was sustained only by his ambitious
wife, Mary.[74] To Lincoln, unlike his wife, elected office was never an
end in itself. It would take some larger issue to get him back into politics. The Kansas-Nebraska Act of 1854—created by Lincoln's fellow
Illinoisan, the Democrat Stephen A. Douglas—opened the prospect
that, through the device known as "popular sovereignty," slavery
would spread to one or both of those territories and the rest of the
unorganized West as well, and Lincoln reentered the political ring to
resist that result.

As the Republican candidate for the U.S. Senate in 1858 he failed to defeat Douglas but seized the nation's imagination with the combination of his rhetorical and moral power. By late 1859 Lincoln was widely touted as the likely Republican candidate for president the following year.

Several times during 1859 Lincoln was invited to Kansas Territory, and he finally agreed to visit Kansas in the first week of December 1859, timing his visit to coincide with the territorial elections there to determine whether Kansas would enter the Union as a free or slave state. At Elwood, just over the Missouri River from St. Joseph, Lincoln spoke on November 30 in the dining room of the Great Western Hotel. Here and over the next week he spoke about limiting slavery in the territories, broaching a notion that he would expand in the months to come: that the Kansas-Nebraska Act, in its presumption that "slavery is not wrong," represented a radical departure from the policy of the nation's founders.

When Lincoln reached Atchison on December 2, the news of John Brown's execution that day had just arrived by telegraph from Virginia. Lincoln was taken to the Massasoit House—Atchison's best hotel—where leading citizens flocked to shake hands and chat. Atchison, unlike Leavenworth, remained a center of proslavery activity, but Lincoln's celebrity and charm transcended political differences. Easily he fixed himself near the hotel's great stove to receive his callers, including some of the territory's most prominent men. With Colonel P. T. Abell, head of the local proslavery party, Lincoln tipped up his chair and shared stories about their common Kentucky roots and about Illinoisans they both knew who, like Lincoln, had moved there from Kentucky.[75]

That night at 8 P.M. a brass band escorted Lincoln to Atchison's Methodist Church, a frame building overlooking much of the town. Here Lincoln addressed a packed house as well as hundreds more who stood outside or hung from trees to hear him.

Lincoln drew laughter when he singled out in his audience one of the territory's leading citizens, General Benjamin Stringfellow, a native Virginian who had declared that Kansas could never be a free state because "no white man could break prairie." If that were so, Lincoln replied with a smile, then he himself must be a negro, for he had many times broken prairie.[76]

Alluding to southern threats to secede from the Union, Lincoln declared that any attempt at secession would be treason. Drawing himself up and leaning forward with his arms extended until they seemed to reach across the small auditorium, he added, "If they attempt to put their threats into execution we will hang them as they have hanged old John Brown today."[77]

When someone in the crowd asked, "What about old John Brown?" Lincoln replied that Brown had been hung "and he ought to have been hung." Brown, Lincoln said, had shown "great courage, rare unselfishness," but had gone too far: "Old John Brown has just been executed for treason against the state. We cannot object, even though he agreed with us in thinking slavery wrong. That cannot excuse violence, bloodshed and treason."[78]

After ninety minutes Lincoln looked at his watch and suggested that perhaps he was speaking too long, but the crowd shouted, "Go on! Go on!" So he spoke for another fifty minutes. Even then the fascinated crowd did not disperse, but followed the brass band that escorted him to the Massasoit House. Here in the hotel's parlors a prolonged reception took place, Lincoln swapping yarns with free-state and pro-slavery adherents alike. All were pioneers just as he had once been, and Lincoln felt completely at home with their needs, their problems and their aspirations. John Ingalls, later a U.S. Senator from Kansas, recalled finding Lincoln at the hotel the following morning

> in the bar room by a red hot box stove, engaged in telling jokes and yarns and stories to a crowd of overland stage drivers and other rough characters of the frontier, who received his narrations with the most boisterous and inextinguishable laughter. He exhibited there, as always, an extraordinary facility for forming personal relations with all sorts of men. Think of him sitting there with one rubber shoe on and the other unbuckled on his knee for probably half an hour, the carriage waiting outside to take him about the town, while he entertained the crowd with his inexhaustible fun and bursts of uproarious laughter![79]

Slade was among the "overland stage drivers" regaled by Lincoln. His presence was noted because Slade too was by now a celebrated figure on the Plains, and there was some curiosity, as one observer put it, as to whether Lincoln could work his customary charm on "a hard-boiled individual named Slade who had never been known to laugh."[80] Slade's political leanings, if any, were unknown; but what little evidence exists suggests that he and Lincoln would have been on opposite sides of the slavery issue. Yet here was Slade, like everyone else within riding distance of Atchison, basking in Lincoln's glow. The encounter was reported years later by the Atchison newspaper editor, E. W. Howe: "Lincoln told this story that night: Lincoln's children were about him one evening, and one of them asked Mr. Lincoln what he said when he proposed to Mrs. Lincoln. He hesitated about answering their query, but the children persisted. Finally, in his droll way he informed the children that he said, 'Yes.' Old Joe Slade laughed at that, and it was not long before word went out that Lincoln had made Slade laugh."[81] If Lincoln could make Slade laugh, who knew what else he might achieve?

On that note, the unlikely encounter between the two Illinoisans ended and the two men departed in opposite directions. Less than three months later, at the Cooper Union in New York City, Lincoln unveiled for a sophisticated audience of northeastern Republicans the idea he had first tested in Kansas, eloquently attacking the argument that slavery had been created and approved by the nation's founders. Slade, meanwhile, headed west for his inevitable confrontation with Jules Beni and the outlaws who infested the Central Overland's Sweetwater Division.

Chapter 11

THE LAW WEST
OF KEARNY

★

In a crisis, most people instinctively flee, but a few instinctively flourish. For the first twenty-eight years of his life Slade had attracted little notice. But in the fall of 1859, with both the Central Overland and the Union itself on the brink of dissolution, Slade appears to have accepted the challenge of rescuing both, even if he was unaware that this was what he was doing. Just as his father, a generation earlier, had breathed life into the village of Carlyle by the sheer force of his will, so Slade now set himself single-handedly to the task of imposing order on his beleaguered company's Sweetwater Division.

In the midst of chaos, what struck most observers about Slade at this moment was the clarity he applied to his new mission. Above all else, he concluded, the mails must go through on time, and passengers must be transported in safety and as much comfort as circumstances would permit. To achieve these ends, the line must be purged of outlaws.

Under ordinary circumstances an aggrieved community of miners or settlers would defend itself by forming posses, courts, and juries. But here the only victimized community was the Central Overland and its paying customers, so the company must take matters into its own hands. The appropriate medicine for the company's particular disease was not the courts—for there were none—but fear. In the absence of conventional legal authorities between Atchison and Salt Lake City—

aside from the military, which was authorized to deal only with Indians—Slade must perform the job himself. He must whip his drivers and station keepers into a de facto posse and take on the roles of sheriff, prosecutor, and judge.

From his headquarters at Horseshoe Creek, some 225 miles northwest of Julesburg, Slade moved deliberately to establish his authority over his new domain, which stretched nearly 500 miles from Julesburg to South Pass. Methodically, he rode up and down the route—often in the company's scheduled stagecoaches—surveying every road, inspecting the stations, sizing up the drivers and station keepers, conducting inventories of horses, mules, harnesses, and coaches, replacing missing stock and weeding out unreliable employees.

The first order of business—the replacement of Jules Beni as stationmaster at Julesburg—took place without the expected violent confrontation.[1] Since Jules would continue to operate his trading post and to service Central Overland passengers in his combination barn/hotel/restaurant/saloon, neither he nor the stage company could afford to antagonize the other. In any case, Jules was dismissed as stationmaster and replaced by Slade's appointee, probably Green M. Thompson.[2] Exactly who delivered the news to Jules is unclear.

In retrospect Jules stepped aside peacefully because he was dismissed not for theft but for incompetence, a vaguer and less volatile charge. Since Ficklin and Slade were both new to their jobs as general superintendent and division agent, respectively, they had had scarce opportunity at this point to address the more serious question: whether Jules had stolen from the company, and, if so, how much he owed.

Once Slade had discharged Jules, relations between the two men appeared to be civil, or at least Slade thought so. "Slade and Jules had some difficulty regarding stock," wrote E. W. Whitcomb, a neighbor of Slade's at Horseshoe in 1861, "but had arrived at an understanding which Slade supposed was settled amicably."[3] "Jules and Slade had frequent collisions," wrote Nathaniel Langford, who knew Slade later, "which generally originated in some real or supposed encroachment by the latter upon the dignity or importance of the former. They always arose from trivial causes, and were forgotten by Slade as soon as over; but Jules treasured them up until the account against his rival became too heavy to be borne."[4]

Still, Jules avoided a direct confrontation because Slade's reputation as a gunman—and specifically his killing of the teamster Andrew Ferrin the previous May—had preceded him. The company counted on that reputation to intimidate outlaws and hostile Indians as well. But the first challenge to Slade's authority came from neither Jules Beni nor outlaws and Indians, but within his own ranks.

The stage lines, like the freight lines before them, functioned as a magnet for rough vagabonds who drifted to the frontier as if caught in an inexorable current.[5] "I scarcely ever saw a sober driver," wrote the acerbic English explorer Sir Richard Burton (translator, among his other achievements, of the first unexpurgated version of the *Thousand and One Nights*), who crossed the West by stagecoach in 1860. "As for the profanity, the Western equivalent for hard swearing—they would make the flush of shame crimson the cheek of the old Isis bargee"— that is, an English bargeman, not known for delicate speech.[6] Frank Root, a stage driver himself, suggested that many of his fellow drivers "ought to have been boarding at the penitentiary instead of living at the expense of the stage officials."[7] To manage these wild men, Slade had to be wilder and tougher than they were.

Few stagecoach employees were asked for their credentials or references; it was up to Slade to determine their qualifications and whip them into shape. A Central Overland driver named H. M. (Hank) Inghram recalled that when he first applied to Slade for a job, Slade asked him if he could drive. When Inghram replied affirmatively, Slade said, "Well, damn ye, drive then, and if you don't, I'll kill ye." After a few trips, when Inghram had proved himself to Slade's satisfaction, Slade gave him a sawed-off, double-barreled shotgun loaded with buckshot, and a job—not as a driver, but as a stagecoach guard, with instructions to "shoot to get 'em."[8]

Slade applied one test to all new drivers, a driver named Dave Horn later recounted:

> He would sit on the box with the driver, and when they came to a bad grade he would grab the buffalo laprobe, wave it, and give a series of Comanche yells. Of course, the horses would run away.

> If the driver kept his head and got them stopped at the foot of the
> grade, Slade would make no comment, but if the driver turned
> white or got rattled Slade would throw him off the box, set him
> afoot and drive the stage himself to the next station. That particu-
> lar driver never could get another job on Slade's division.[9]

Slade, Horn recalled, "was hard as granite, and insisted on his
drivers coming in on time. Washouts, holdups and attacks by Indians
were part of the daily routine, and Slade would not accept them as ali-
bis." One day a driver named Charley Norris encountered "a terrific
blizzard,"

> and though he put his horses through for all he was worth, he got
> into Julesburg half an hour late. Slade met him, watch in hand,
> and said, "What excuse have you for being late?" Charley started
> to explain about the heavy drifts in the road, but before he could
> say a dozen words, Slade reached up, caught him by the collar,
> jerked him off the box, and kicked him in the side.... Then, shak-
> ing him as a terrier does a rat, he said, "I won't do anything this
> time to you, but if it ever happens again I'll make you wish you
> were never born."[10]

In an emergency, if a stage driver was killed or injured, Slade himself sometimes jumped into the breach, if only to demonstrate his own
expertise. On one of his inspection trips, an officer from Fort Laramie,
traveling as a passenger, asked Slade if the coach couldn't go faster.
Slade promptly climbed into the driver's seat, took the reins, and raced
the coach across the prairies and through fords at a breakneck pace. At
several turns in the road the coach seemed likely to flip over, only to be
saved by Slade's skill. As the story is told, when the coach rattled into
the next station, its horses foaming at the mouth, "it was a very meek
soldier who climbed out of the doorway."[11]

If Slade drove his employees hard, he also earned their loyalty with
unexpected gestures of appreciation. One stock tender at an isolated
station recalled that "Sometimes he would bring me a box of good
cigars, a bundle of illustrated papers, or a basket of fresh fruit from the
settlements."[12]

Slade at this time was "an untiring worker," the driver Frank Root later recalled, "at first putting in the most of his time day and night for the interest of the company by which he was employed, as well as doing everything he could for the comfort of the passengers."[13] He seemed to work at his job all the time, striving to bring order from the chaos that Old Jules had left. Nothing, he announced wherever he went along his division, must be allowed to interfere with the coaches, passengers, horses, or any other property of the company.[14] His determination and his commanding presence established the Central Overland in most people's minds as a far more formidable organization than it ever really was.

With a few well-chosen examples to make his point, Slade quickly demonstrated that he meant business. When a supply of hay belonging to the Central Overland unaccountably caught fire, Slade bought a stack to replace it from a nearby ranchman. When the new stack was found to contain willows and brush, Slade chained the rancher to a log near the stack and set the log on fire, threatening to throw both log and rancher into the flames. Only upon the ranchman's promise to leave the vicinity did Slade release him; the rancher promptly departed.

When a stagecoach was held up and the passengers robbed, Slade and a few chosen employees gave chase. The robbers—two, three, or four, depending on the account—were captured and hanged from a gatepost, and their bodies were left to hang as warning. Shortly afterward two horse thieves were hanged to the limb of a tree, either by Slade or his men; their bodies too were left hanging to spread Slade's message.[15]

Before Slade's arrival on the Sweetwater Division, the Central Overland stagecoaches had been perceived as vulnerable moving targets for outlaws and Indians; now the coaches were viewed as predators themselves. "Heretofore at the sight of desperadoes, the drivers would whip their horses into a fury of getting away," one account explained, "but now Slade would simply slow down and the first man within range would 'get his.'"[16]

How many people Slade killed personally in this process of spreading terror—or whether he actually killed any—is unknown; the many accounts of these feats in his first months on the Sweetwater Division are skimpy on details or identifications. It was said that Slade, in company with two or three followers, routinely tracked down and executed outlaws; more likely, such executions occurred only once or twice.[17] As with Slade's shooting of Ferrin at Green River earlier that year, a single killing cast a long shadow. "He had the reputation of having killed his three men," reported the English traveler Richard Burton after meeting Slade in August 1860.[18] Mark Twain, who met Slade in the summer of 1861, later wrote that "in order to bring about this wholesome change, Slade had to kill several men—some say three, others say four, and others six."[19] Whether he had killed one, three, or more, in a region where (contrary to popular notions back in the States) killings were relatively rare, that reputation sufficed.

"By this time the outlaws learned that he feared nothing," wrote the driver Frank Root. "Wherever there was trouble on the division the life of the offenders was short. He made friends by killing a half-dozen of the worst characters. After he had done this the company's property was unmolested and the coaches began to run with more regularity. While there were occasional delays [elsewhere] on the line, the stage on Slade's division went through safely and without delay."[20]

Slade's headquarters at Horseshoe station was said to be "the most pretentious" station between Julesburg and Sacramento"—pretentious, that is, in the nineteenth-century sense of well-equipped rather than ostentatious.[21] During Slade's tenure there its supply station, which served most if not all of his division, came to include a blacksmith shop, coach shops, harness shops, warehouses, lodging houses, offices, and corrals.[22] The sophisticated support system included a cistern that piped water from the well to the barn, and a tunnel almost six feet below ground, running from the field to the house, presumably in case of an Indian attack.[23] A traveler who passed through a few years after the station was abandoned recorded her presumption that Slade was "a freebooter, and even a murderer," but added, "This did not prevent his station from being one of the best on the road, his horses always good."[24]

"Best on the road," of course, was a relative term on the Plains, where trees—and consequently log cabins—were in short supply. In the absence of accessible lumber or logs, settlers cut strips of surface dirt and grass from the ground and built houses by piling the sod strips on top of one another. Door and window openings were outlined with poles, and the structure was customarily covered with cow or buffalo hides. Properly constructed, a sod house could keep out wind and rain, but many settlers lived in drafty shacks that leaked whenever it rained. A wood structure like the station at Horseshoe or Julesburg was a relative mansion on the Plains; the necessary lumber was hauled hundreds of miles, from Denver or Cottonwood Springs in western Nebraska Territory.

But the comfort level of such a place was a far cry from the civilized East or the Old World across the Atlantic. After bouncing for weeks in a westbound stagecoach in August 1860, Richard Burton looked forward to a night spent in "superior comfort" in Slade's home station. Upon his arrival at 9:30 P.M. he indeed pronounced himself impressed "by the aspect of the buildings, which were on an extensive scale—in fact, got up regardless of expense." But Burton was dismayed by the absence of a welcoming party—Slade was elsewhere—as well as by everything else he found: "An ominous silence. . . . reigned around. At last, by hard knocking, we were admitted into a house with the Floridian style of verandah . . . and by the pretensions of the room we at once divined our misfortune—we were threatened with a 'lady'. . . . Our mishap was really worse than we expected—we were exposed to two 'ladies,' and one of these was a 'Bloomer.'"[25]

The "Bloomer" whom Burton found in the house—presumably a follower of the early feminist Amelia Bloomer, who refused to wear petticoats—turned out to be a passenger, waiting with her husband (who slept in the barn) to join Burton's stage to travel to California. Burton described her as a "hermaphrodite . . . an uncouth being, her hair, cut level with her eyes, depended with the graceful curl of a drake's tail around a flat Turanian countenance, whose only expression was sullen insolence." The second lady was Slade's wife, Virginia, who, "though more decently attired, was like women in this wild part of the world generally—cold and disagreeable in manner, full of 'proper pride,' with a touch-me not air."[26]

Burton concluded that Horseshoe station was "one of the worst places on the line,"[27] a station conducted upon the principle of the western hotel-keeper of the last generation. . . . That is to say, for his own convenience; the public there was the last thing thought of.

One of our party who had ventured into the kitchen was fiercely ejected by the "ladies." In asking about dormitories we were informed that "lady travelers" were admitted into the house, but that the ruder sex must sleep where it could—or not sleep at all if preferred. We found a barn outside; it was hardly fit for a decently brought-up pig; the floor was damp and knotty; there was not even a door to keep out the night breeze, now becoming raw, and several drunken fellows lay in different parts of it. Two were in one bunk, embracing maudlingly, and freely calling for drinks of water. Into this disreputable hole we were all thrust for the night: amongst us, it must be remembered, was a federal judge, who had officiated for years at a European court. His position, poor man! procured him nothing but a broken-down pallet.[28]

At the end of January 1860, in anticipation of the Pony Express, Slade's jurisdiction was shifted slightly eastward. It now stretched from Fort Kearny on the east to his headquarters at Horseshoe on the west—a domain of nearly 400 miles.[29] By this time most outlaws had paid him the inadvertent compliment of fleeing his division and relocating in the Rocky Ridge region just west of his own. At this moment, as the Montana journalist Thomas Dimsdale observed a few years later, Slade "was feared a great deal more, generally, than the Almighty, from Kearny west."[30]

Slade's thoroughness in cleaning up his division reflected well on his boss, the general superintendent Ben Ficklin. Although Ficklin was merely an employee who held no stock in the Central Overland, he was included as one of its twelve incorporators when William Russell drew up the company's corporate charter for submission to the Kansas Territorial Legislature late in 1859. Ficklin's value to the company is suggested by the fact that his name was listed third among the incorporators, behind only Russell and Jones and ahead of Majors and Waddell.[31]

Although the outlaws had departed from Slade's division, Jules Beni could not be cowed so easily. He remained at his trading post at

Julesburg, requiring Slade to coexist uneasily with him and extracting a measure of retribution—as well as cash—by continuing his practice of stealing the company's horses and tricking Slade into buying them back.

Having taken an Indian woman as his de facto wife, Jules "was in with the Indians around there," one of Slade's stage drivers, Charles Higginbotham, later recalled, "and when the horses were turned out for feed they [the Indians] would run them off and cache them in the gullies. Then Jules would go to Slade and offer to find the horses for a reward, and when he got the money he'd send out and have the Indians bring them in."[32]

Ficklin, after investigating, concluded that Jules had been stealing from the company and forced Jules to a settlement.[33] Jules blamed Slade for some of Ficklin's acts. Slade, for his part, convinced of Jules's rascality, maintained a wary watch on him. He and Ficklin could turn a blind eye to Jules's petty acts of horse thievery as long as the Central Overland was a stagecoach company primarily dependent on mules for transportation. But horses—the best and most costly horses that could be found—were essential to Russell's and Ficklin's new strategy for saving the line: the Pony Express.

William Russell's freighting partners, Alexander Majors and William B. Waddell, were as reluctant to support the Pony Express as they had been to support Russell's Leavenworth & Pike's Peak Express. But once again the incorrigible Russell dragged them into it against their better judgment. He first broached the Pony Express idea to his two partners when they took over the Leavenworth & Pike's Peak in late October 1859. Then he headed for Washington, where Senator Gwin of California urged Russell to launch the Pony Express immediately. Russell, who needed no urging, promised Gwin he would proceed as long as he had the support of Majors and Waddell. Russell immediately returned to Leavenworth and laid out the proposition to his partners, only to hear them object, not unreasonably, that the Pony Express could never pay its expenses.[34]

Russell urged Majors and Waddell to reconsider. Once the Pony Express had convincingly demonstrated that the central route to California was feasible over the winter, he said, Senator Gwin had promised to use his influence to get the line a Congressional subsidy. Outmaneuvered, Majors and Waddell reluctantly "concluded to sustain him in the undertaking," as Majors put it.[35]

Russell lost no time in following up. Although the Central Overland hadn't yet received its corporate charter from the Kansas Territorial Legislature, he and Ficklin returned to Washington, and on January 27, 1860—seventeen days before the corporate charter was granted—Russell telegraphed his son John: "Have determined to establish a Pony Express to Sacramento, California, commencing 3d of April. Time ten days."[36]

His announcement that same day to newspapers in New York, Washington, and the West caused a sensation. Three days later a lengthy article in the *Washington Evening Star* reported: "An independent horse express across the Plains, to California, . . . shall make the trip between the extreme points to which the magnetic telegraph now operates, in eight days; which for the transmission of news will enable parties in New York and San Francisco to communicate with each other in that time. . . . One of the best points in the affair is, that they do not propose to ask Government pecuniary assistance; a new feature, indeed, in any such far western enterprise."[37]

The headlines in the *Leavenworth Times*—which assumed Leavenworth would serve as the line's eastern terminal—were less restrained:

GREAT EXPRESS ENTERPRISE

FROM LEAVENWORTH TO SACRAMENTO IN TEN
DAYS!

Clear the Track and Let the Pony Come Through[38]

Within days of this announcement both Russell and Ficklin hastened back to the West. Russell brought with him the charter for the Central Overland California & Pike's Peak Express Company, which

he presented to the Kansas
Territorial Legislature early in
February. Because of the charter's
broad provisions, the legislators
resisted granting approval, and
only Russell's aggressive lobbying
secured its passage on February 13,
1860. (Waddell later scolded
Russell for "buying the charter.")
Not until June, by which time the
Pony Express had been operating
for more than two months, did
Russell provide his partner
Waddell with an introspective peek
into his smoke-and-mirrors methods: "I was disposed to make her
[the Central Overland California &
Pike's Peak Express Co.] share a
part of our heavy expense, and to
do so most effectively I was compelled to build a world wide repu-

"Orphans preferred": This and similar
advertisements for Pony Express riders
appeared in Western newspapers in 1860.

tation, even at considerable expense (which all things considered is
quite inconsiderate) and also to incur large expenses in many ways, the
details of which I cannot commit to paper."[39]

Ficklin, meanwhile, set about reorganizing the line for the coming
of the Pony Express. The stagecoach route—previously divided into
three stagecoach divisions between St. Joseph and Salt Lake City—
was now reorganized into five divisions between the Missouri River
and Sacramento, each run by a division agent. These five men Ficklin
charged with the awesome task of constructing and supplying 190 stations spaced at intervals of 10 or 12 miles—the distance a horse could
travel at maximum speed without collapsing[40]—building and repairing
the necessary roads, purchasing five hundred of the best horses money
could buy, and hiring eighty riders, as well as station keepers and stock
tenders—all this within sixty-five days, in the dead of winter.[41] The
route and terrain was relatively easy from St. Joseph to Fort Kearny,

but from there—the beginning of Slade's domain—to Salt Lake City the route became increasingly difficult.[42]

Late in January Ficklin traveled to Denver, where he arranged with Robert B. Bradford—a cousin of Waddell who operated a store there in partnership with Russell, Majors & Waddell—to build stage stations as far west as Julesburg and stock them with equipment and provisions. By March 15 all of those stations were under construction.[43] At the eastern and western ends of the line, where trees were more plentiful, these stations were built of logs or lumber. But in Utah and the Sierra Nevada they were constructed of adobe bricks—produced on the spot—or stone laid up without mortar. On Slade's division from Fort Kearny to the Rockies, some Pony Express stations were built with sod, others with adobe bricks, and some amounted to mere holes in a hillside, roofed over with logs, brush, and a dirt roof. Only the more important home stations, such as Julesburg and Slade's headquarters at Horseshoe Creek, were built of lumber hauled at least 100 miles.[44]

During the early spring of 1860, the Central Overland sent out wagon trains with building materials and supplies to construct the needed relay stations along the entire route between Leavenworth and Sacramento. Supply trains originated from Leavenworth, Denver, Salt Lake City, and Sacramento, along with work crews to locate and construct stations along the route.[45] Although the Central Overland was in serious financial trouble from the day of its creation in October 1859, it spared no expense in constructing and equipping stations.[46]

The greatest and most important expense, though, was the purchase of nearly five hundred horses. Russell's dream depended above all on the ability of Pony Express horses to make an average of twelve and a half miles per hour without stopping between relay stations—a tall order even for a Kentucky thoroughbred.[47] The finest Eastern horses failed to meet this standard: They lacked the toughness to withstand the desert sands in summer and the heavy snows of winter.[48] With loans from his fellow freighter and occasional partner Ben Holladay—who accepted the horses as collateral—Russell plunged ahead. On February 10 he advertised in the *Leavenworth Daily Times*:

WANTED

200 grey mares, from four to seven years old, not to exceed fifteen hands high, well broke to the saddle and warranted sound, with black hoofs, and suitable for running the "Overland Poney Express."[49]

Slade and the other two division agents east of Salt Lake City bought some of their horses from the quartermaster at Fort Leavenworth and others on the open market, usually paying $150 to $200 per horse.[50] In Salt Lake City, Russell instructed A. B. Miller, his partner in another venture there, to buy two hundred good horses for the line's central division. Although this was beyond Slade's bailiwick, he and Ficklin and two other men—all chosen specifically for their knowledge of horses—were sent along to assist Miller.[51] Once purchased, many if not most of these horses were kept at the Russell, Majors & Waddell herd camps near Camp Floyd, Utah, before being distributed along the planned route.[52]

"The men who bought the horses knew their business," said William Campbell, a Pony Express rider on Slade's division. "Sometimes we used to say that the company had bought up every mean, bucking, kicking horse that could be found, but they were good stock and could outrun anything along the trail."[53]

Next the five division agents had to hire among them roughly two hundred men for station keepers and stock tenders, as well as more than eighty riders.[54] Each of the newly constructed Pony Express stations housed both a station keeper and a stock tender (the older and larger stations that were also used by the stagecoaches usually had a staff of four to six men).[55] The stock tenders were vital to provide the horses with the best of care and feed. But the riders, who would be asked to put their lives on the line, had to be "young, good horsemen, accustomed to outdoor life, able to endure severe hardship and fatigue, and fearless."[56]

One such rider was Henry Avis, who was born in St. Louis in 1840 and taken by his parents to Kansas City while he was still a boy. In his middle teens Avis found work breaking wild horses around Kansas

City and Fort Leavenworth and soon was considered an expert. At eighteen he was hired to accompany a supply train to a fur trader's post near Fort Laramie. While there, he was hired by John Hockaday's new stage line to drive coaches from Fort Laramie to Salt Lake City, and he was probably still driving stages when the Pony Express opportunity arose. When Avis—only twenty years old—took that job, he was put on Slade's division to ride a 150-mile stretch between Mud Springs (northwest of Julesburg) and Horseshoe Station.[57]

Like Avis, most of the riders hired on Slade's division were either natives of Missouri, Kansas or Nebraska, or Easterners drawn to the frontier. But many of Slade's riders were not all that young: Their ranks included old employees of Russell, Majors & Waddell or other freighting outfits, former stagecoach drivers and a few hardened veterans of the Santa Fe Trail.[58]

Not until the first week of March did the partners choose the eastern terminus of the Pony Express. Although Russell, Majors & Waddell maintained its headquarters as well as its huge freight warehouses and extensive corrals at Leavenworth, Russell picked St. Joseph as the line's eastern terminus because it was the western end of both the railroad and the telegraph line, and also because civic leaders in St. Joseph offered him land, an office building, and other concessions.[59]

Once the final route was laid out, the stations constructed, and the horses, station keepers, and riders hired and in place, the final task prior to the first scheduled run on April 3 was a public announcement. An advertisement in the *San Francisco Bulletin* of March 17 conveyed the first news to astonished Californians—"Pony Express—Nine Days from San Francisco to New York."[60] Barely a week later, similar ads appeared in the *Missouri Republican* and the *New York Daily Tribune*: "To San Francisco in Eight Days by the Central Overland California and Pike's Peak Express Co."[61]

On paper, the scheduled time from St. Joseph to Fort Kearny was to be thirty-four hours; to Salt Lake, 124 hours; to Sacramento, 234 hours. Including a six-hour railroad trip from there to San Francisco, a message telegraphed from New York to St. Joseph could reach San Francisco in 240 hours—that is, exactly ten days later. Barely two months after Russell's first announcement of the Pony Express had

startled the country, his "great race
against time" was almost ready to
begin operating.

In the last month leading up to
the inaugural Pony Express run,
Slade supervised the completion of
stations, distributed stock, assigned
riders to their posts, and appointed
station keepers and stock tenders.[62]
As Slade drove his men relentlessly
to finish by the April 3 deadline,
Jules Beni, unnoticed by Slade,
stewed in Julesburg, his fury stoked
by a combination of petty slights.
"Jules had a boy working for him
around the station, but never paid
him anything," one of Slade's station keepers recalled later, "so the
boy got tired of it and quit, going up

Frank E. Webner, Pony Express rider, in
1861. Not all of Slade's riders were young;
their ranks included former freighters and
stagecoach drivers. (*National Archives*)

to Horseshoe, where he got a job from Slade. This made Jules mad, and
he did a good deal of blowing about how he would fix Slade for coax-
ing the boy away from him."[63]

At roughly the same time, Jules's antagonistic behavior was brought
to Slade's attention. As his subsequent colleague James Wilson
described Slade's reaction, "Slade, in his quick impulsive way,
remarked that if Jules did not quit bothering the stage line and its
employees, he would kill him. This chance remark was at once repeated to Jules while Slade, all unsuspecting, continued slowly arranging
matters along his line."[64]

Shortly thereafter, Slade came into Jules's restaurant one evening,
ordered a plate of oysters, and then pitched the plate in Jules's face.[65]
At the same time, Jules learned that Slade was hunting Central
Overland horses that had last been seen in Jules's corrals farther up
"Jules Stretch." One day Slade rode to those corrals and appropriated
a team of mares he believed Jules had stolen from the company.[66]

To the extent that Slade calculated the likely impact of these acts at all, he may have assumed they would cow Jules into submission or drive him away altogether. Or he may have been trying to goad Jules into a fight—which Jules, well aware of Slade's reputation with a gun, hoped to avoid. "Slade did not fear him, as he thought Jules was too cowardly," one of Slade's Pony Express riders, J. K. Ellis, later explained.[67] But Slade had misjudged the effect of Jules's accumulated humiliations: Jules, both terrified and infuriated by Slade's words and deeds, prepared himself for a showdown with Slade.

On an inspection trip in mid-March, less than three weeks before the launch of the Pony Express, Slade spent the night at Lodge Pole station, about 15 miles west of Julesburg, with the station keepers James Boner and Phil James. "Whenever he was inspecting the stations in his division," Boner explained years later, "he stopped with Phil and me, because most of the stations were kept by Frenchmen of a class that were not very agreeable, as they generally had a lot of Indians hanging around." Slade felt comfortable in these surroundings—apparently so unconcerned by the potential threat posed by Jules that when he boarded the stage to Julesburg the next morning he neglected to take his knife and pistol with him. "After he had been gone a while," Boner recalled, "I happened to notice them on the table, and said to Phil, 'Phil, Slade has gone without his gun, and I'll just bet that Jules shoots him, if he gets a chance.'"[68]

On Slade's arrival at Julesburg, Slade and Jules accosted each other with their customary outward courtesy and, seated on the fence and some wagon hubs fronting the station, fell into conversation with two of Slade's stage drivers, Tom Bryan and Si Shurry.[69] Two houses belonging to Jules stood nearby: an adobe structure where Jules lived, and a frame structure—the combination store, restaurant, bar, and hotel where the stage boys and passengers took their meals.[70] At some point in the conversation, Jules noticed that Slade was unarmed. Shortly he disappeared into his house.

Slade now proposed that he and his comrades go into the restaurant and indulge in their pastime of playing cards for canned fruit, oysters and other frontier delicacies, "it being the only way they had of getting them," Slade's later neighbor E. W. Whitcomb recalled.[71] By another account, Slade simply said, "I will go in and get something to eat."[72] In either case, Slade walked away from his comrades and headed toward the frame building. He had nearly reached the door when Jules emerged from the adobe house with a revolver in his hand.

"Look out!" one of the drivers shouted to Slade. "He's going to shoot!" As Slade turned, Jules fired the contents of his six-shooter—three, five or six bullets, depending upon the account—into Slade's body in rapid succession.[73]

Incredibly, Slade did not fall immediately but staggered around the side of the frame house toward the stage station. Jules, eager to finish what he had started, reached inside the doorway of his house and emerged a moment later with a double-barreled shotgun loaded with buckshot. Its contents too Jules emptied into his adversary.

Now Slade crumpled to the ground, motionless. "I never saw a man so badly riddled as he was," his friend Boner later recalled. "He was like a sieve."[74]

Jules, presuming he had killed his rival, turned coolly to Bryan and Shurry. "There are some blankets and a box," he gestured to them. "You can make him a coffin if you like."[75]

Bryan and Shurry picked up Slade's apparently lifeless body and carried it into the station, where they set him down on a bunk. There seemed little they could do for him. Slade's wife, Maria Virginia, was at Horseshoe Station, nearly 225 miles to the northwest. Slade, his life apparently passing before him in his final moments, made just one request. Someone, he recalled, had once predicted that he would die with his boots on. Could Bryan and Shurry remove his boots? He did not, Slade explained, want the prediction to be fulfilled.[76]

Now, less than three weeks before the scheduled opening of the Pony Express, the new relay system would be put to the test under emergency conditions. Rider J. K. Ellis was saddled up and dispatched to Fort Laramie, 175 miles to the northwest, in the hope that a relay horse would await him at each of the stations planted at ten-mile intervals.[77] Fort Laramie represented the nearest legal authority; more important at this moment, it housed a military surgeon who held the only chance to save Slade's life.

But it seemed like a hopeless errand. Even under the Pony Express's proposed high-speed schedule, Fort Laramie was a hard day's ride from Julesburg. "No one who witnessed the attack," Slade's acquaintance Langford later recounted, "supposed he could survive an hour."[78]

As Ellis sped toward Fort Laramie, an eastbound stagecoach carried the news of the shooting to St. Joseph, where it was reported in a local paper on March 19. From that town—the western terminus of the railroad and the telegraph—the news soon spread to the East. On March 27 the *Constitution* of Washington, D.C., informed its readers: "The *St. Joseph Journal* of the 19th learns that Jule Beni, an old mountaineer, shot Joseph A. Slade, a mail agent, a few days since, at the crossing of the South Platte, putting six shot in him, and killing him instantly."[79]

To those who read this item, its implication seemed clear: The last best hope of the Central Overland was dead even before the Pony Express had made its first run.

Chapter 12

THE PONY EXPRESS

*

"If you shoot at a king you must kill him," said Emerson.[1] Jules had shot Slade at least five times but had failed to kill him, at least not instantly.[2] That Slade continued to breathe was, to everyone present, even more astonishing than the rashness of Jules's action. What Jules had hoped to accomplish by killing Slade, how he expected to escape the Central Overland's certain retribution, and what would become of him or his properties thereafter clearly were questions Jules had not considered when he impulsively grabbed his pistol and shotgun, just as he had apparently failed to check the freshness of his gunpowder.[3]

The triumph implied in Jules's casual burial instructions to Slade's drivers lasted only briefly. Within moments of the shooting, a west-bound stage fortuitously arrived, bearing none other than the Central Overland's general superintendent, Ben Ficklin himself. In the com-motion of the moment, Ficklin had Jules arrested and strung up on a scaffold that the men improvised between two wagons. Because Slade was still breathing, confusion reigned as to an appropriate punish-ment. Twice—three times, by some accounts—Jules was drawn up and strangled until he was black in the face, then lowered while still alive. When he was let down for the last time, Ficklin extracted a promise from Jules to leave the country, whereupon Jules was released.[4] Another account, by a traveler who passed through Julesburg a few weeks later, contends that the rope broke, and Jules, "alighting upon his feet . . . made his escape, being aided by the Indians," who were encamped nearby.[5]

By changing to a fresh horse at every station along the way—usually at intervals of ten miles or so—and by refusing to pause for food, J. K. Ellis made the 175-mile journey to Fort Laramie to fetch a military surgeon in eighteen hours. "I believe," he later remarked, "it breaks the record for a straightaway ride by a single individual."

The post surgeon Ellis found at Fort Laramie was Edward W. Johns, who had been stationed there since April 1858 and had probably never previously treated a gunshot wound.[6] In 1860 the best doctors available in the West were likely to be found in the army, but those doctors—military or civilian—who did practice surgery rarely invaded the body in any significant way. Instead they tended to scrape their scalpels along the surface of the skin or close to it, avoiding deep penetration to major arteries or vessels. They adhered to a long tradition of removing foreign bodies—bullets, arrowheads, slingshot pellets, and other metal fragments—in the belief that they "poisoned" the wound. The basic principle was "Get the lead out"—as long as it wasn't in too deep.[7]

At Fort Laramie the surgeon mostly treated accidental wounds, smashed hands or limbs or illness. Johns occupied much of his time at Fort Laramie by handling nonmedical duties as well, such as acting quartermaster and acting commissary of stores. Still, a military posting appealed to many a young doctor in the late 1850s and early 1860s: It was a regular job that absolved him of the need to establish a practice; it offered an opportunity to learn firsthand about scurvy, trauma, and other maladies; and it provided time to experiment with herbs and medications.[8] Doctors tended to float through Fort Laramie for periods of anywhere from one month to two or three years, after which they would put their experience to use elsewhere. In this respect the military surgeon's position carried greater cachet than that of officers, many of whom simply served time in the same isolated post from one decade to the next.[9]

Within another day or so after Ellis's arrival at Fort Laramie, surgeon Johns was by Slade's bedside to find the patient still clinging to life, tended by his friends from Lodge Pole station, Jim Boner and Phil James.[10]

Johns "picked out nearly a handful of pistol balls from Slade's body," according to Boner, who probably exaggerated.[11] Most of the lead in Slade's body remained, but enough had been removed to improve Slade's chances of survival.[12] A traveler passing through Julesburg on his way to Denver, probably in late March, reported paying a short visit to Slade at Julesburg and described himself "glad to find him in a fair way of recovery."[13]

Now Slade was moved to Lodge Pole station and the care of Boner and James. Here he rested for about two weeks, virtually unable to eat and living mostly on milk from a cow that James and Boner kept at the station. Although the cow customarily wandered away during the day to graze, Slade's dependence on milk required Boner and James to keep the cow close at hand. To this end they built a makeshift corral from wagon beds piled in the form of a square, where they kept the cow's calf, on the theory that the mother would not wander far from her young. Slade, whose bed was by the window in the sodhouse, was sufficiently alert to keep watch for Indians and other potential thieves, some of whom he recognized by name. As Boner later recalled,

> One day Slade said to me. . . . "Jim, there's Dog Belly after the calf." So I took the pistol, and went to the door, and as I raised it, old Dog Belly saw me. He was crawling along behind the wagon beds, and made a jump clear over them just as I shot.
>
> The bullet went right through the wagon bed, right where Mr. Dog Belly had been, and you ought to have seen him streak it across the prairie.[14]

After some two weeks Slade was deemed sufficiently strong to make a journey of several days—accompanied by Boner and James—to Horseshoe station and the care of his wife, some 225 miles to the northwest.[15] By now his chances of recovery seemed better. But whether he would work again—and if so, when—nobody could say. Jules had not killed the king, but he had indeed disabled him.

On April 3, 1860—barely two months after William Russell had announced his proposed Pony Express—the new line was ready to begin operations. In St. Joseph a holiday atmosphere prevailed: Flags and bunting were hung on the downtown business houses. That afternoon adults and children crowded Pattee Park, across from the Pony Express stable, to watch the first rider take off at 5 P.M. To reach Sacramento in ten days was "the greatest enterprise of modern times," as a local newspaper put it.[16] Everyone wanted to be a part of that miracle.[17]

Eventually the *Missouri*'s whistle was heard at the edge of the town, and a few minutes later the little train ground to a halt at the Hannibal & St. Joseph depot. The special messenger surrendered his pouch, which included special tissue-paper editions of the *New York Herald* and *Tribune*. These were quickly transferred to the waiting saddlebag, which already contained letters collected at St. Joseph as well as a congratulatory message telegraphed from President Buchanan in Washington for delivery to the governor of California in Sacramento.[18] While the bay mare and its rider, Johnson William Richardson, waited impatiently, the equally impatient crowd was subjected to political oratory from the incumbent St. Joseph mayor, M. Jeff Thompson. William Russell and Ben Ficklin were both on hand, but neither delivered a speech. It was left to Russell's freighting partner Alexander Majors to capture the meaning of the moment: The crowd that evening, he said, was not witnessing the grand conclusion of human history but merely the beginning; the Pony Express was but the temporary forerunner of "a tireless iron horse" that would soon crown the West with "evidences of civilization and man's irresistible mania for progression."[19]

When Majors was finished, a cannon boomed a salute, and Richardson stepped into the saddle to begin his historic ride. A short gallop took him to the ferry landing, where a boat waited to carry him across the Missouri River to Elwood, in Kansas Territory. There another crowd cheered him on his way, and Richardson galloped westward through the balmy spring night.[20]

Five days later, somewhere on the road west of Salt Lake City, the eastbound and westbound Pony Express riders met. At that moment,

The nearly 2,000-mile route of the Pony Express provided a change of horses at stations located roughly every 10 miles. It delivered letters to California in ten days but lost a fortune for its backers.

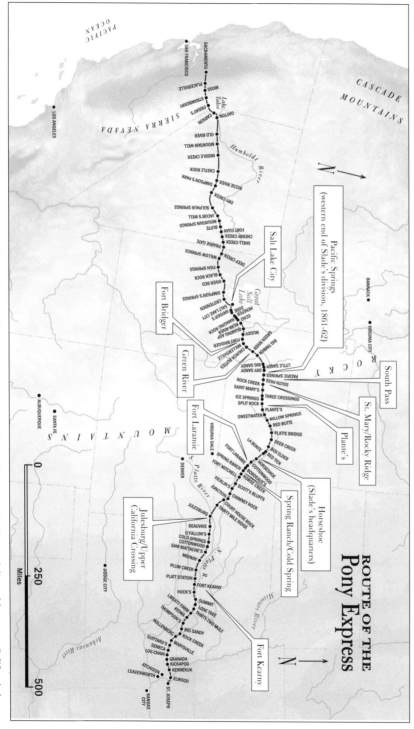

Russell's dream—the bridging of almost 2,000 miles of plains, deserts and mountains—was effectively completed.[21]

At the western end of the line, the *Sacramento Union* learned from the local telegraph office on the morning of April 13 that the final Pony Express relay rider, William Hamilton, had crossed the California state line but had not yet reached Placerville, 45 miles east of Sacramento. When the *Union* advised its readers that Hamilton would arrive late that afternoon, nearly a hundred townspeople spontaneously organized a horseback welcoming committee. Flags were run up on all of Sacramento's public buildings; a cannon was mounted in the square at Tenth Street, and churches and firehouses were warned in advance to ring their bells.

When Hamilton reached Sutter's Fort at 5:25 P.M. he found himself riding though a double line of mounted Sacramentans; when he entered the town to a cheering throng, the cannon fired forty rounds before it quit. At 12:38 the next morning, Hamilton and his mail pouch disembarked from the cutter *Antelope* in San Francisco, where another ceremony took place.[22]

The only near-disaster during the Pony's initial runs occurred on the eastbound trip near the scene of Slade's personal calamity. At Julesburg the South Platte River was swollen from recent rains, but the determined rider plunged in to attempt the crossing anyway. His horse was swept off its feet and downstream into the river's notorious quicksand. Rather than lose time rescuing the animal, the rider stripped off the *mochila*—the saddle cover that held his four small leather mailbags—then waded ashore with it, commandeered another horse from a spectator, and dashed on. The crowd of emigrants and stagecoach passengers who had gathered to watch cheered him until he was beyond earshot, then fished his horse out of the river. On April 13 at 5 P.M., the last eastbound rider—the same Johnson William Richardson who had set out from St. Joseph on April 3—dismounted at the Pattee House on schedule, having covered the last hundred miles in just eight hours.[23]

Neither Slade nor his nemesis Jules Beni witnessed these historic events. While Slade recuperated at Lodge Pole station and then

A Pony Express rider passes a telegraph construction crew near Salt Lake City in 1861. When the telegraph line reached the Pacific that fall, the Pony Express was discontinued. (*Library of Congress*)

at Horseshoe, Jules Beni "disappeared in the farther West, and took to lodge and squaw"—that is, he settled with one of the Indian tribes that (unlike the whites of the West) suffered from a surplus of women and welcomed the spousal companionship of an unattached male, even temporarily.[24] When Sir Richard Burton penned those words in August 1860, his informants—most likely Central Overland drivers who worked for Slade—had little idea where Jules was; they knew only that he was no longer within Slade's division. In fact, if Jules stayed with an Indian tribe he did so only briefly. At some point he went to Denver to consummate another relationship.[25]

Adeline Cayou's father was a boatman of French ancestry who in the early 1850s came up the Missouri from St. Louis to the river ports of Kansas and Nebraska Territories. When his wife developed consumption in the late 1850s, Cayou took his family westward on a wagon train, in the hope that the fresh mountain air of the Rockies might cure her. Somewhere before reaching Denver they met Jules Beni, who shared their French origins and had reestablished himself with a trading post. Jules promptly fell in love with the Cayous' thirteen-year-old daughter Adeline and, although he was nearly forty years her senior, asked for her hand in marriage.[26]

"There were few [white] women in the country in those days," Adeline later recalled, "and Jules said to my parents that he would take good care of me, and so they gave me to him, and they went on to Denver."[27] According to Adeline, Jules took her to a new ranch at Cottonwood Springs, about 100 miles east of Julesburg.[28] "He was very good to me," she added, "and treated me more like a daughter than a wife."[29] The contradictory interviews Adeline gave decades later suggest that she was largely ignorant of Jules's recent history.[30] Jules "had a man and his wife to take care of the place," Adeline recalled, "and I just did whatever I wanted to. We were on the great trail to California and Pike's Peak and trains would come by and purchase supplies from us, so I did not get lonesome."[31]

The reader is left to conclude that Jules and Adeline did not spend much time together.[32] Jules had fled from Slade's division and took care not to return there, but he still maintained a network of friends there, mostly other French ranchers along the stage line. Although Jules apparently sold his Julesburg ranch and trading post to the wagonmaster George Chrisman, who became the Central Overland's station keeper at Julesburg, Jules still retained horses and other property—valued at $10,000 by one estimate—within Slade's division, which he was eager to reclaim.[33] Such a recovery, of course, would involve returning to Slade's domain in violation of his promise to Ficklin (not to mention the likelihood that he would be killed by one of Slade's friends). So for the moment Jules bided his time.

The first east and west runs of the Pony Express seized the nation's attention just as William Russell had hoped.

On the frontier itself, the Pony's success rejuvenated Edward Creighton, the industrious telegraph supervisor (and friend of Alexander Majors) who had extended the first telegraph lines across Illinois and Missouri, only to halt them at Leavenworth after New Year's Day 1859 for lack of financial support.[34] Now Creighton extended his line up the Missouri River to Omaha and laid plans to proceed from there across the rest of the country.

William Russell found himself hailed wherever he went.[35] In Washington congratulations were showered on him from President Buchanan to Congressional cloakrooms to ordinary citizens on the street. The Pony Express instantly put rival mail routes and carriers on the defensive, just as Russell had imagined it would. Russell's magnificent strategy—to spend a fortune in order to magnify his reputation so as to recoup his losses with a lucrative mail contract—seemed to be working just as he had planned.

But as Russell—and perhaps only Russell—well understood, this public relations victory had come at a high financial price. No expense had been spared to assure the Pony's success: it had cost about $100,000 to set up. Yet unlike the Central Overland stage line, the Pony Express had no government mail subsidy; its only revenues came from the $5 fee it charged per letter. This charge brought in only about $500 a day, while the Pony's expenses were at least twice that amount. Above and beyond its exorbitant startup costs, the Pony Express was losing between $15,000 and $20,000 a month.[36]

These losses by themselves neither surprised nor alarmed Russell and his partners: they had conceived the Pony Express as a promotional investment that would put them in a favorable competitive position when Butterfield's southern overland mail contract expired in 1863. Majors, for one, counted on the completion of the transcontinental telegraph line to render the Pony Express obsolete within a year or two.[37]

But Russell's immediate problem was the mountain of debts that threatened to swamp the partnership long before then. Bills that predated the Pony Express—amounting to more than $500,000—were due in the first six months of 1860, and lenders were no longer willing to tolerate Russell's scheme of issuing new notes to pay off old ones. Between April 26 and June 19, 1860, Russell received $695,000 worth of acceptances from the War Department—that is, notes issued by Secretary Floyd stating the amounts due to Russell, Majors & Waddell for work performed—but most creditors either refused to accept them as collateral or discounted them heavily.

In his desperation for ready cash, Russell now turned to the stock of the Central Overland. "Send mine to me at New York," he wrote to Waddell on May 11, "and I will try and see if it can be used as collateral. Think that $50,000 might be borrowed on it for twelve months, and if it can be done had better use yours and Mr. M[ajors's] also."[38] Seemingly against all reason, Russell clung to the unlikely hope that he could keep his head above water until the War Department's reimbursement for the Mormon War losses came through. (Secretary of War Floyd had airily agreed to pay the claim, if the attorney general ruled that it was valid.)[39] Beyond that, Russell staked his hopes on a scheme promoted by Senator Gwin of California to carry mail thrice weekly to the Pacific for an annual government subsidy of $900,000, with the possibility for a future increase to six times a week for $1.2 million.[40] If that came through, his financial worries would be over.

Ficklin, the Central Overland's general superintendent, was ener-gized by the Pony's initial success but unaware of its desperate financial condition. Consequently he was eager to seize the moment by increasing the Pony's service from weekly to semi-weekly. To do so, of course, required Russell's approval, and that required Ficklin to trav-el to Washington for a face-to-face meeting with the company's impetuous and visionary president. Since Russell always played his cards close to the vest, Ficklin was probably unaware that, in Russell's grand scheme, the Pony Express was merely an expensive and tempo-rary promotional stunt that could never hope to make money on its own. As far as Russell was concerned, the Pony had already made its point, and the sooner it could be curtailed or eliminated altogether, the better. But rather than wait to meet Russell, later in April 1860 Ficklin appears to have taken some preliminary steps toward increasing the Pony Express service—steps that he believed would strengthen his hand and overcome any objections Russell might raise.

One such step was the necessity of removing the outlaws now con-gregating in the Rocky Ridge area west of Slade's division, which now stretched from Fort Kearny west to Horseshoe. Many of these outlaws had moved there precisely to escape Slade's reach. So thoroughly had Slade done his work that peace apparently reigned within his division during his long recuperation.[41] But the Central Overland driver Frank Root's description of the Rocky Ridge country at this time is an uncanny echo of descriptions of Julesburg the previous fall:

> This division was now fast gaining the reputation of being one of the worst sections of the stage line. It had become infested by a gang of outlaws and desperadoes who recognized no authority

except violence. Murders were of frequent occurrence, in broad daylight, being committed on the slightest misunderstanding. The revolver and bowie-knife were the principal weapons used in settling a dispute. In a country where there was no law in those days, it was supposed the parties killing one another had their private reasons; hence no one mixed up in such matters. When a murder had taken place all would officiate at the burial, the murderer himself being prominent, and assisting in performing the last sad rites.[42]

Slade had cleared many of these desperadoes out of the Julesburg area, and Ficklin appears to have concluded that Slade, once his health was restored, was the man to drive them away from Rocky Ridge as well. It was probably at this point that Ficklin first contemplated shifting Slade's authority westward. Since late January, Slade's division had stretched more than 400 miles from Fort Kearny to Horseshoe; now Ficklin proposed to shift it from Julesburg on the east all the way to Pacific Springs on the west, a distance of more than 500 miles.[43]

At this moment, of course, Slade was home at Horseshoe station recuperating from his wounds, with no indication of when he would be fully healed, if at all. His condition defied the primitive knowledge of the few physicians in the West. Yet no one else seemed adequately suited for the job. It was apparently in this situation that Ficklin conceived a daring plan: The Central Overland would take the extraordinary step of transporting Slade to St. Louis for further medical care.

At a time when medical education elsewhere generally consisted only of lectures, the two St. Louis medical schools—at St. Louis University and Kemper College—used the city's hospitals for clinical instruction. Jefferson Barracks, the military post south of St. Louis, had employed at least two surgeons as early as 1828 and as many as five by 1860, from which evidence it is safe to assume that the post housed a hospital as well.[44] Clearly, this gateway city to the West harbored an impressive concentration of medical knowledge. There, Ficklin reasoned, Slade would benefit from the best medical care to be found west of the Mississippi. The sooner surgeons there could extract most or all of the lead from Slade's body, the sooner he would recuperate and return to work.

This idea was almost as audacious as the notion of delivering a letter across the continent in ten days. It was a testament both to Ficklin's
boldness and to Slade's value to the company. St. Louis was 1,000
miles from Horseshoe—including 750 by bumpy stagecoach, uncomfortable even to travelers in the full bloom of health. The trip would
take at least ten days or more each way. There was no assurance that
such a journey wouldn't exacerbate Slade's condition or even kill him.
But the impatient Ficklin—apparently assuming that a disabled Slade
was useless to him in any case—was willing to take the chance.

Upon Ficklin's direction, probably late in April Slade was taken to
St. Joseph by stagecoach and from there by railroad to St. Louis.[45] To
ease the journey, by some accounts, Ficklin provided his own personal stagecoach for the trip; it's also possible that Ficklin himself accompanied Slade on the trip.[46]

The patient, who only a few weeks earlier had been in such pain that
he could swallow no food, arrived safely in St. Louis, where in short
order surgeons extracted between five and seven of the thirteen bullets—enough, it was believed, to enable him to resume his normal life.[47]

Yet in retrospect surgery was only part of the solution to Slade's
wounds. The other part—infection—remained unknown to medical
practice. Any soft-lead projectile—whether pistol ball, bullet, or buckshot pellet—fired from a weapon charged with black powder would
have carried bacteria on its surface. If it passed through clothing and
then through skin, it would have transmitted bacteria-laden powder,
cloth, and skin into the bodily tissue. Thus even if a shot struck no
vital organs or blood vessels, the chance that it would cause severe systemic infection was immense. Then it was just a matter of time before
the victim expired.[48]

For several weeks more Slade recuperated, probably with his family in Carlyle, just 50 miles east of St. Louis.[49] Yet in a nation careening
toward civil war Carlyle provided no refuge from the factional passions
sweeping the country. In a speech in Carlyle that year, the civic leader
Benjamin Bond—nephew of the state's first governor and brother of
Thomas Bond, Slade's Mexican War captain and western traveling
companion—articulated the case for the "peace Democrats" who constituted the town's great majority. "Suppose the South, so run mad,

that they would not be wooed and won back to the Union—what then?" Bond asked rhetorically. "Why . . . in God's name, let them go in peace, until they shall have learned from sad experience and a stern necessity, that they cannot keep house without us."[50]

Such passions in even a small and relatively isolated town seemed to confirm Ben Ficklin's case for increasing the frequency of the Pony Express. Ficklin's gamble with Slade's physical health appeared to have paid off, not least thanks to Slade's apparently tenacious will to survive, which medical historians still found astonishing more than a century and a half later.[51] But the likely catalyst for Ficklin's gamble—his proposal to Russell to increase Pony Express service—proved more difficult.

The effect of the Pony Express on Washington was immediate and profound. Five weeks after the Pony was launched, a special Congressional committee recommended building a railroad along the Platte River route to Salt Lake City. On May 11, also just five weeks after the Pony Express got under way, Postmaster General Holt abruptly annulled George Chorpenning's semi-monthly mail contract between California and Salt Lake and awarded the annual $83,241 fee to the Central Overland instead.[52] For the first time, William Russell's company held a monopoly on U.S. mail service over the entire central route, enabling it to compete head-to-head with Butterfield's southern route for the primary transcontinental federal mail contract.[53]

Around this time Ficklin arrived in Washington to urge Russell and various politicians to increase the Pony Express service from weekly to semi-weekly. To Ficklin this seemed a propitious moment. But to Russell, this was the moment when both his financial pressures and the long-smoldering resentments of his partners Waddell and Majors had begun to erupt. It was also the moment to chastise Ficklin for insubordination and to remind him who was boss. On May 11—the day that Chorpenning's mail contract was turned over to the Central Overland—Russell flatly vetoed Ficklin's idea and wrote to Waddell to do nothing about it.[54] The strong-willed Ficklin took this rejection—as well as Russell's implication that Ficklin couldn't be trusted to follow orders—as a personal insult.

Ficklin returned to Leavenworth and resumed his duties as route superintendent, but his quarrel with the equally stubborn Russell continued. Although Ficklin was held in high regard by Majors, Waddell, and most other men involved with the Central Overland, the personality differences between Russell and Ficklin seemed irreconcilable. Russell sent two letters to the St. Joseph office accusing Ficklin of incompetence, and in early June Ficklin telegraphed his resignation, adding, "Send a man for my place damned quick."[55] Since Russell was deeply religious, this use of a blasphemous word over the telegraph lines further infuriated him. On June 6 Russell wired Waddell, Majors, and John S. Jones, quoting from Ficklin's telegram and instructing them to replace him. But Russell's partners, tired of being pushed around, refused. Instead Waddell sent Russell a letter saying that the Central Overland could not get along without Ficklin.

Russell's furious response on June 13 suggests the company's fragile state as well as his own fraying emotional condition. "So far as I am concerned," he wrote, "if he [Ficklin] were the only living man in the world (which I do not believe) that would put it through, and without him the Co. must sink and all would be lost, I would say let him go by all means. . . . If his resignation is not accepted and some other good man put in his place, my resignation is before you and my stock for sale."[56]

Before this letter reached its recipient, Waddell prevailed upon Ficklin to send Russell a conciliatory letter that might have healed their rift. But those letters crossed in the mail, and in the meantime Waddell had had the temerity to suggest that Russell and Ficklin were actually temperamental twins, each demanding the lead role or none at all.[57] To this astute if undiplomatic perception, Russell replied: "If after all my toil and sacrifice I am to be really *abused* for my course, it is high time that some other and more competent man be placed at the head of it... Would rather dig for my bread than work and live as I have for the past six months... I am confident of one thing, however, and that is with all Mr. Ficklin's boasted economy, if allowed to control as you say he must, the Co. will break up in 12 months."[58]

Presumably after heaving a collective sigh, Russell's three partners in Leavenworth, acting in their capacity as the Central Overland's executive committee, held a meeting and accepted Ficklin's resignation, effective July 1.[59] Just three months after the Pony Express was launched, the man most responsible for implementing it—and for advancing Slade's career—was gone.

Ficklin's resignation came scant weeks after Congress passed the Pacific Telegraph Act, which authorized bids to construct a telegraph line to the Pacific, and Ficklin promptly joined with Hiram Sibley and Jeptha Wade to organize the Overland Telegraph Company to string wires from the west as Edward Creighton was doing from the East.[60]

Russell was less fortunate. Sinking further into his desperate delusions, Russell now proposed a thrice-weekly trans-continental mail service to the Post Office Department—not for the $600,000 annual fee that Senator Gwin had advocated, but for $900,000. "Today's cabinet settles the question," he wrote Waddell on July 10. But at that meeting Russell's contract bid was brushed aside, and no action was taken regarding a new mail arrangement over the Central Overland route.[61] Now Russell's last hope for saving the Central Overland—as well as Russell, Majors & Waddell—lay in the War Department and his petition for reimbursement of the freighting concern's losses in the Mormon War. But War Secretary Floyd was preoccupied with the huge new expenses generated by the unprecedented threat of civil war.

The Republican Party, meeting in Chicago on May 25, had bypassed the established presidential favorites—Senator William Seward of New York and Governor Salmon Chase of Ohio—and instead anointed Abraham Lincoln of Illinois, a mere private citizen but the most articulate opponent of extending slavery into the territories, and also the Republican most likely to carry the essential western states. The Democratic split into northern and southern factions, combined with the certain anti-slavery vote of newly arrived German and Scandinavian immigrants, held forth the possibility that Lincoln and his fledgling party might well squeeze out a victory in the electoral college.[62] But Lincoln's arrival in the White House would almost certainly be greeted by the departure of the Southern slave states and, consequently, civil war. Senator Gwin of California, a Tennessean by birth who had later moved to Mississippi, was talking openly of forming a Western federation that would be allied neither with North nor

South.[63] Secretary of War Floyd, the former governor of Virginia, was in the process of transferring 115,000 Army rifles, as well as ammunition and other armaments, from Northern forts to Southern arsenals.[64] When the Southern Democrats opened their convention on June 28 at Baltimore, the full California delegation demonstrated its Southern sympathies by moving in with them.[65]

The federal government's need to maintain timely communication between California and the East seemed more urgent than ever. Over the summer of 1860 the Central Overland was already preparing its route for winter, at considerable expense. The temporary tents and makeshift shacks thrown up during the Pony's opening weeks were replaced with permanent buildings. Station keepers and their helpers spent much of their time building these new quarters and raising hay for the ponies, in the hope of reducing the company's enormous outlay for feed.[66]

Slade returned to his Horseshoe headquarters and his newly constituted division shortly before Ben Ficklin departed, probably early or mid-June 1860.[67] Yet by the time of Slade's return the fragility of the Pony Express had already been exposed. On May 7 a band of Paiute Indians attacked a Pony Express station in the Carson Valley west of Salt Lake City, killing seven men and burning down the station house. The attacks spread over the next few weeks, forcing the closing of numerous stations west of Salt Lake City. On June 1 the Pony Express service was temporarily suspended until the route could be properly protected. In San Francisco, the Pony's division agent W. W. Finney asked the army for a contingent of seventy-five armed men, even though, as he acknowledged, the Pony Express was a private enterprise with no claim to government resources. Eventually, at the request of several Congressmen, Secretary of War Floyd dispatched troops from Camp Floyd in Utah. But only after a bloody month-long struggle—and an additional outlay of more than $75,000 by the Pony Express—were the Paiutes subdued and service restored on June 22.[68]

Along Slade's division the primary threat was not Indians but outlaws. During the summer of 1860 the coaches of the Central Overland carried increasingly large shipments of gold dust eastward from the Pike's Peak region, eventually growing routinely to $12,000 to $15,000 per trip. In late August a coach arrived at Leavenworth with $35,000 in the care of the messenger and $100,000 in the hands of the passengers (many of whom preferred to carry their own treasure rather than entrust it to anyone else).[69] These shipments passed through Julesburg without apparent incident. Still, the outlaws who now clustered in the Rocky Ridge area west of Horseshoe posed a threat to westbound stagecoaches, including the few that might be carrying gold.

It was generally assumed that Slade would clean up the Rocky Ridge area just as he had whipped Julesburg into shape, by making a few terrifying examples and relying on the subsequent word of mouth to drive troublemakers away. His expected terrible vengeance against Jules was awaited with morbid fascination. "The only sentiment of all, except the friends of Jules, was, that this attack upon Slade, as brutal as it was unprovoked, should be avenged," wrote Slade's subsequent friend Nathaniel Langford. "Slade must improve the first opportunity to kill Jules. This was deemed right and just. In no other way could he, in the parlance of the country, get even with him."[70]

When Sir Richard Burton spent a night at Horseshoe on August 14, 1860, what struck him first was the fierceness in Slade's eyes: "Of gougers fierce, the eyes that pierce, the fiercest gouger he," he wrote.[71] Burton acerbically described Slade appearing "for an evening party" wearing "the revolver and bowie-knife here, there and everywhere"— a logical reaction, Burton suggested, to Jules Beni's ambushing of the unarmed Slade. After discussing that shooting and Jules's eventual disappearance, Burton added: "The avenger of blood threatens to follow him up, but as yet he has taken no steps."[72]

Yet the "avenger of blood," as Slade was widely perceived, seemed strangely cautious about pursuing Jules at this point. In the words of Nathaniel Langford, Slade "determined to kill Jules upon sight, but not to go out of his way to meet him. Indeed, he sent him word to that effect"—most likely in Denver—"and warned him against a return to his division."[73]

Meanwhile, Slade turned his attention to the gangs around Rocky Ridge. Frank Root's account of the cleanup is not firsthand—Root didn't join the Central Overland until 1863—and no doubt suffers from hyperbole. But at the very least it provides a vivid sense of how Slade's presence was perceived.

In taking up his abode where the country was so full of horse thieves and desperate characters, Slade came to the conclusion that the only thing to do under the circumstances was to shoot all such offenders as fast as they became known. He immediately began a forward movement on their works, and, one by one, he picked out and killed the leaders of the notorious gang. In a remarkably short space of time all depredations on the stage line ceased, a considerable [amount] of the stolen stock was recovered, and several of the worst outlaws in the district were shot. Something of this kind had to be done before the authorities could operate the line with anything like satisfactory results. His work of cleaning out the cutthroats and desperadoes was commended by the stage-line management. Most of those who had been under the control of the highwaymen now began to respect him and lend him their assistance in future operations. All agreed that he had done a good job, and it was but a short time until it was as quiet on the Rocky Ridge division as he had fixed things during his employment at old Julesburg.[74]

Yet Root's account provides only two specific examples of Slade's law-enforcement exploits at this time. In one, "Two horse-thieves who had stolen overland-stage stock were captured by him and he hung both to the limb of a tree." In the other, "One time while a party of emigrants were going overland, some of their stock had suddenly disappeared. Slade having been apprised of all the facts, he, with another man, made his way to a ranch where he was satisfied, from the character borne by the occupants, that the stock had been taken and secreted, and, opening the door, commenced blazing away at the promiscuous crowds inside, three of whom he killed, while the fourth was badly wounded."[75]

The absence of specific names, dates, and places in this and similar accounts leaves a reader to wonder whether such events actually occurred, or whether they were exaggerated, or whether they were conflated with similar events in the minds of travelers and stage drivers eager to believe them. Whether these tales of Slade's heroics were accurate or groundless, their effect was the same. As at Julesburg the previous fall, within a short time Slade enjoyed a reputation so fearsome that few men dared to antagonize him.

One specific episode from the summer of 1860 suggests not so much Slade's brutality as his concern for the safety of the Central Overland's passengers. Among Richard Burton's westbound party that August was an army officer with his wife and baby daughter. Slade was so solicitous about the baby's safety that he took the couple and their child in his own buckboard some 200 miles over the Rocky Ridge Road to Wind River summit, which the officer later described as "the most Indian infested and bandit frequented on the whole trail across the country." For an outriding escort, the officer said, Slade provided "sixteen of the most villainous cutthroats on the plains."[76]

The Central Overland owed its financial bind largely to the fact that William Russell had staked his hopes on a man who was every bit as desperate as he was. Through most of 1860 Secretary of War John B. Floyd labored under two extraordinary sets of pressures. One was the mounting expense of preparing for civil war, and the other was the pressure from his fellow southerners to transfer arms from the north to the south. One by-product of these pressures was a delay in the War Department's payments to Russell, Majors & Waddell—not only for the firm's Mormon War losses of 1857–58, but even for current contracts. Instead, Floyd issued acceptances—notes stating the amounts owed to the firm—for Russell to use in seeking further loans. To keep Russell off his back—and to keep Russell's firms from folding—Floyd allowed the acceptances to exceed the actual amounts owed to Russell, Majors & Waddell. This practice was not only dishonest; it was also ineffective, because most lenders doubted the credibility of Floyd's acceptances and discounted them accordingly.

"Harried to death about money," Russell wrote to Waddell on June 30. "Know not where to turn or how it will result."[77] In his desperate search for funds, Russell was referred in July to Godard Bailey, a lawyer and clerk in the Interior Department. Bailey, who was related to Secretary Floyd's wife, knew about the false acceptances and was concerned about the disgrace that would befall Floyd if they were made public. To avoid such a scandal, Bailey delivered $150,000 worth of Missouri and Tennessee bonds for Russell's temporary use as collateral for loans, with the stipulation that they be returned within ninety days. Even steeply discounted, these bonds sufficed to spare Russell, Majors & Waddell from bankruptcy in July, but not for long. Soon Bailey was propping up Russell further with a second group of bonds, from Missouri, North Carolina and Florida, worth $387,000. Eventually the total value of the bonds provided to Russell by Bailey came to $870,000.[78]

In normal times Russell might have steered his company through this crisis and returned the bonds, as Bailey had stipulated, without any outsider being the wiser. But this arrangement occurred in the midst of the presidential campaign of 1860, the most contentious in American history. To a large extent North and South had already drifted apart, and the nation's financial foundations were tottering as a consequence. Money was tight, banks were calling in loans, and the value of stocks and other securities was falling.

Russell was especially vulnerable because all the bonds he had borrowed from Bailey had been issued by slave states threatening secession. As a result, the bonds' value declined sharply, and the lenders holding the bonds as collateral demanded more security, with the threat that otherwise the bonds would be sold. When Russell imparted this news to Bailey in September, Bailey in his alarm revealed for the first time the ownership of the bonds. Bailey did not own them, he informed Russell; he was merely their custodian. The bonds were held in trust by the Department of the Interior as part of what was known as the Indian Trust Fund, representing unpaid annuities to various Indian tribes. Bailey had allowed Russell to make use of them, but the bonds had to be returned. William Russell, a frightened and helpless man on the brink of financial ruin, was now technically a criminal.[79]

In October, having exhausted every survival strategy, legal and illegal, Russell, Majors & Waddell finally acknowledged the reality that had existed since the Mormon expedition more than two years earlier: the West's greatest freighting partnership was bankrupt.[80] The Central Overland California & Pike's Peak Express Company, in which the three partners were major stockholders, was also in dire financial straits. Employees' pay was often delayed, causing some wits among them to refer to the company as "Clean Out of Cash & Poor Pay."[81]

But the Central Overland survived by virtue of its unique status as a chartered corporation, and its Pony Express persisted as well.[82]

As Edward Creighton's Pacific Telegraph Company crept westward, the Pony Express readily shortened its route wherever telegraph poles and wires arose to provide a faster alternative. By November 3 Creighton had pushed his line past Omaha and as far west as Fort Kearny, which promptly became the Pony's new eastern terminus. From the West Coast, the telegraph now reached as far east as Carson City, which meant the original Pony Express route of 1,900 miles was reduced by more than 400 miles.[83]

Still, the importance of the Pony Express was heightened by the momentous presidential election campaign of 1860. As November approached, Californians eagerly awaited the arrival of each pony with news of day-to-day events back east. That news, to be sure, was usually eight to ten days old, but it was far more current than any other source and consequently influenced events in California. In October, for example, Pennsylvania held its election a month ahead of the rest of the country, and when the combination of telegraph and Pony Express brought news of Lincoln's Pennsylvania victory to California, it energized jubilant Republicans to redouble their efforts to carry the state for Lincoln in the weeks remaining before the national election—lead time that would not have been available without the Pony and the telegraph.[84]

In late October, as election anticipation mounted, Julesburg and its surroundings were struck by a severe storm of wind, hail, and snow. Emigrant trains were forced to gather around the Central Overland's stage station for protection, and the Pony Express was delayed for five hours.[85] Nevertheless, following the election on November 6, the first eastbound Pony Express relay from California reached the Fort Kearny telegraph station on November 22 with inconclusive reports that Lincoln was leading the northern Democrat Stephen Douglas in California by only a few hundred votes and a recount would be necessary. Not until a month after the election did a Pony rider arrive at Fort Kearny with the news that Lincoln had a safe plurality in California.[86]

Lincoln did not need California's four electoral votes to win the election—he won eighteen of thirty-three states and nearly three-fifths of the electoral college in a four-man race. But he had become president with less than 40 percent of the popular vote. In nine southern states he had not even been listed on the ballot. Out of 996 counties in the slave-holding states, he had won only two, both in Missouri.

But in the coming struggle Lincoln would need California's wealth in the Union camp, and Californians would need Lincoln's support for a railroad to the Pacific, which would do more for the state's economic prospects than anything since the gold rush.[87] In those respects the arrival of California's election returns ended weeks of suspense for easterners and Californians alike.[88]

Nearly four months remained between Lincoln's election and his inauguration the following March—ample time for the Union to disintegrate. South Carolina—accusing Lincoln of excluding the South from the Union's "common territory" in the West—became the first slave state to secede on December 20. By February 1, 1861, six more states, stretching from Georgia to Texas, had seceded as well. In each of these states the governors seized all the federal forts and arsenals that Secretary of War Floyd had replenished over the past year.[89] On February 9 delegates from the seven seceding states gathered in Montgomery, Alabama, to form the Confederate States of America and install Jefferson Davis of Mississippi as the new nation's president.

Amid such an upheaval, California with its vast gold wealth held the balance between North and South. What would California do? Two California Congressmen publicly advocated an independent "Pacific republic" in January 1861, but the California legislature responded by urging Congress to financially support the Pony Express so as to strengthen the state's ties with Washington.[90] A secessionist scheme to seize the Presidio at San Francisco, then commanded by the Texan General Albert Sidney Johnston, was foiled by press reports rushed from coast to coast via Pony Express; Johnston, embarrassed by the subsequent headlines, remained loyally at his post until April 25—weeks after the Civil War began—when he resigned his commission and formally joined the Confederate army.[91]

This demonstration of the power of the Pony Express should have been a triumphant moment for William H. Russell. And indeed, on

December 19 the *Rocky Mountain News* in Denver had paid tribute to him and his Central Overland: "This old pioneer line which made its advent in Denver on the 8th day of May, 1859, still continues the even tenor of its way, winning popularity and steadily growing in public favor.... It stands today, probably, the best fitted, best stocked and best managed route of the same magnitude in the world.... In months the arrivals at Denver do not vary two hours from the regular time.... Its projector and President, William H. Russell, well deserved the name of 'Napoleon of the West.'"[92]

Yet it was precisely at this moment that Russell's financial house of cards collapsed. On December 24—five days after the *Rocky Mountain News* editorial, and four days after South Carolina seceded—Russell was arrested in New York for his role in the Indian Trust bond scandal and taken to a District of Columbia jail, where a judge set his bail at the astronomical sum of $500,000.[93] Five days later, Secretary of War Floyd was forced to resign for his part in the same scandal.[94]

Russell was subsequently bailed out of jail by friends and summoned to testify before Congressional investigations; he escaped prosecution on a technicality, but his credibility and his credit alike were destroyed. On January 30, 1861, Russell signed most of his holdings over to his largest creditor, his old friend and sometime freighting rival Ben Holladay, who fancied *himself* "The Napoleon of the West."[95] From this point Holladay effectively took charge of the Central Overland's operations east of Salt Lake City.[96] In April at Leavenworth, Russell formally resigned as the Central Overland's president, to be succeeded by Ben Holladay's cousin, the St. Joseph lawyer Bela Hughes.[97] In that role Hughes appears to have functioned largely as Holladay's envoy.[98]

Only as Russell departed from the national stage did the government finally acknowledge its dependence on both the Central Overland mail route and the Pony Express.[99] In February 1861, after Texas seceded from the Union and Arkansas state troops seized the U.S. Arsenal at Little Rock, the Post Office Department ordered John Butterfield to move his stagecoaches from the southern "ox-bow" route to the Central Overland's route, and Butterfield's Overland Mail

Company was merged with the Central Overland. (Butterfield was put in charge of the route west of Salt Lake City, and the Central Overland was given the eastern half.) Early in March Congress passed "Hale's Bill," providing for daily stagecoach mail service on the Central Overland route to California as well as a semi-weekly Pony Express, effective July 1, at a total annual compensation of $1 million;[100] the contract specified that the Pony Express was to be continued "until the completion of the transcontinental telegraph." It was the government's first official recognition of the value of Russell's elaborate publicity stunt.[101]

At his inauguration on March 4 Lincoln sought to reassure the eight slave states still remaining in the Union by reaffirming what he had said several times before: "I have no purpose, directly or indirectly, to interfere with the institution of slavery in the States where it exists. I believe I have no lawful right to do so, and I have no inclination to do so."

Yet to the seven Confederate states—as well as to the growing sentiment in the North for "letting the erring sisters depart in peace"— Lincoln was intransigent: "The union of these states is perpetual," he insisted, and "It is safe to assert that no government ever had a provision in its organic law for its own termination. . . . No state upon its own mere motion can lawfully get out of the Union." Therefore, Lincoln said, he would consider that "the Union is unbroken," and as president he would take care "that the laws of the Union be faithfully executed in all the states."

In advance of Lincoln's address, the Pony Express notified its division superintendents that the message must be sped through, regardless of horseflesh; and the division agents in turn notified station keepers to prepare the speediest horses. March was generally a month of heavy snows on the Plains and in the Rockies; deep snows had already blocked the Overland Trail that winter, causing stagecoach mail to pile up at Julesburg for a month. "The closer it got to the mountains, the worse the conditions got," said the rider W. A. (Bill) Cates, who carried Lincoln's message through 75 windswept miles of Slade's division. "We had the best horses available—several of them were killed."

Nevertheless, Lincoln's address reached Salt Lake City on March 12, and five days later it reached the telegraph station at Fort Churchill, where it was wired instantly to the newspapers in San Francisco.[102]

Before dawn on April 12 a Confederate battery opened fire on federal troops stationed at Fort Sumter in Charleston harbor; the next afternoon the fort surrendered and its troops were evacuated. The Union that for eighty-five years had represented the world's best hope for the cause of self-government was split, perhaps forever. An entire set of national assumptions and supporting icons had vanished. Suddenly America's innocent romance with the West was gone.

Yet Slade, who had been given up for dead only a year earlier, soldiered on. His putative assassin, Jules Beni, remained at large, openly boasting that he had put Slade out of action.[103] The outlaw gangs were drifting back to Slade's Rocky Ridge domain, perhaps emboldened by his seeming reluctance to pursue Jules. But these were trifling matters next to a new concern: The fledgling Confederate states, in their desperate pursuit of support, had formed alliances with several powerful Indian nations that, like the South, nursed common and long-standing grievances against the United States. Urged on by the Confederacy, the Sioux and other Indian nations now declared *their* secession from the Union as well. Technically these declarations meant nothing, because Washington had viewed the Indian tribes as foreign nations all along. But by formally joining the Confederacy and raising armies to fight for its cause, these Indian nations posed a new threat to the frontier states of Kansas and Missouri, as well as any other vestiges of Union authority.[104]

On the very day of Lincoln's inauguration, a messenger from Fort Laramie arrived at Horseshoe station with a request for Slade's help in recovering stolen Army horses.[105] Slade's work, like the Union's, was just beginning.

Chapter 13

AVENGING ANGEL

*

When Ben Holladay took charge of the Central Overland's east-ern branch early in 1861, he was forty-one years old and six feet tall, an energetic and ambitious dynamo just entering his prime. Everything about the stage line's flamboyant new de facto boss seemed larger than life. He wore emeralds and diamonds sewn into his vests and handed out twenty-dollar gold pieces as tips. He drank and gam-bled with abandon. He maintained offices in New York and San Francisco, traveling between them in a special stagecoach equipped with appointments fit for a king as well as sleeping accommodations, pulled by scores of special teams—animals often driven to destruction in his quest for speed. His mansion in Washington, D.C., was filled with paintings by European masters, a large classical library of hand-somely bound volumes, marble statuary and two bronze lions at the front door that cost $6,000 each. His Ophir Hall on the Hudson—named for his silver mine in Virginia City, Nevada Territory—was sur-rounded by a thousand acres. As Holladay's brother-in-law put it, "Nothing was too big for him to undertake."[1]

Ben Holladay was Slade's kind of boss, and Slade was Holladay's kind of division superintendent. Like Slade, Holladay was quick-tem-pered but also gregarious and likable. Like Slade he seemed to thrive on immense challenges involving immense risk. Like Slade (and unlike William Russell and Ben Ficklin), he never allowed his considerable ego to undermine the business at hand.

Like the showman P. T. Barnum, Holladay keenly grasped the value of theatrical gestures. He once spent more than $10,000 in order to break the stagecoach speed record from California to the Missouri River, covering 2,000 miles in just twelve days and two hours. To expunge Julesburg's unsavory reputation, he changed its name to Overland City. In any given situation, "he believed results justified means," said his friend, the Missouri legislator John Doniphan.[2]

Like William H. Russell, Ben Holladay was willing to risk his entire fortune when a greater one loomed in view; but unlike Russell, Holladay kept a cool and calculating head beneath his flamboyant facade. (Holladay once donated a vacant lot to a Baptist church with the condition that, should the site ever be used for nonchurch purposes, it would revert to his heirs.)[3]

To the German-born journalist and financier Henry Villard, Holladay was "a genuine specimen of the successful Western pioneer.... illiterate, coarse, pretentious, boastful, false and cunning."[4] To John Doniphan, who knew him better, Holladay resembled Napoleon: He "had faults of disposition and education, but he was brave, strong, aggressive, talented and generous," a man of "wonderful nerve and activity" who could be "haughty and dictatorial" but on balance was "one of God's gifted children."[5]

The Central Overland wasn't Holladay's only stage line—he owned others on less traveled routes—nor did it enjoy a monopoly (several competitors fought it for passenger traffic, especially on the spur line to and from Denver). Still, Holladay aimed to make the Central Overland the leading stage line not only in America but also the world.[6]

To his devoted riders, drivers, and passengers Holladay seemed to be everywhere and abreast of everything. "One single tireless man," wrote a passenger, "with the finest talent for business combinations that exists in America, was forever dropping into cabins under the snow-peaks and adobes sweltering on the sand of the desert; making the master's eye felt by the very horses; creating a belief in his omnipresence."[7]

Under Holladay, men who couldn't deliver speed and consistency were encouraged to leave.[8] A Pony Express rider named Alex Toponce recalled:

Just west of Kearny was a long, sandy hill to climb, and going out
one morning I overtook a lot of soldiers in Government ambu-
lances. They were walking their teams up this hill. I had to turn
out of the road to pass them, and my horse changed from a gallop
to a walk while going up the hill.

Suddenly a man put his head out of the window of a stage and
called to me, "Hey, young man."

I rode over and said, "Yes, sir."

It was Ben Holladay, the boss of the mail line. "Young man," he
said, "the company furnishes the horses. You furnish the spurs."

I took the hint and went up the hill on a lope. Soon after that I
quit the fast mail business.[9]

Like Slade, Holladay was idolized by his men, who circulated and
embellished tales of his exploits in order to bask in his reflected glory.
According to one such story, a youth who had crossed to California in
the Overland stage subsequently encountered a preacher who praised
Moses for guiding the Israelites across 300 miles of desert over forty
years.

"Forty years?" the youth supposedly replied. "Only 300 miles?
Hump! Ben Holladay would have fetched them through in thirty-six
hours."[10]

And like Slade, Holladay seemed to revel in the gossip he inspired.
The challenge of operating a stage line—never mind the world's greatest stage line—in the midst of a civil war would burn out many a lesser man. But with Ben Holladay as both a goad and a source of moral
support, Slade in 1861 seemed energized as never before.

Slade was home at his Horseshoe headquarters on the day of
Lincoln's inauguration when the Army's messenger arrived to
enlist his help. During that winter of 1860–61 the Army had kept a
herd of horses and mules—forty by one account, two or three hundred
by another—in a loosely guarded corral near Fort Laramie.[11] That
same winter three youthful teamster brothers named Davenport had
been stranded at Fort Laramie. They made camp a few miles below the
fort, where they tried their hand as trappers. At first they seemed suc-

cessful and sold mink, otter, and muskrat furs to a French trader named Beauvais who operated five miles below the fort. Occasionally they visited the fort and traded at the store there as well.

But sometime in late February the fort's entire herd was run off, and the Davenport brothers disappeared from the area as well. The presumed thieves enjoyed a good head start because the theft had gone unnoticed for several days.

The Fort Laramie commander dispatched a corporal named George Beatty with a posse of six dragoons and a dozen civilian "squawmen" (the term applied to whites, usually French, who lived with the Indians) to pursue the

The stagecoach king Ben Holladay implored Slade to "Get that fellow Jules, and let everybody know you got him." (*Library of Congress*)

thieves, with orders to "either hang them or shoot them." On their way west, Beatty stopped at Horseshoe station on March 4 with a letter for Slade from the fort quartermaster, asking for his help. Slade promptly gave Beatty a letter to show to all the station keepers along Beatty's westward journey, instructing them to give Beatty anything he needed.

Near Independence Rock, 180 miles west of Fort Laramie, Beatty's detail recovered the stolen animals and hung the only thief they found. The other thief or thieves—who had apparently been out hunting and may have observed the hanging from a distance—escaped. When Beatty returned to Fort Laramie and reported to the commanding colonel, the officer said only, "I wish to God, corporal, you had got the other one."

About this time, a footsore and hungry wayfarer sought shelter at a stage and Pony Express station somewhere east of Fort Laramie. Because the station was not on the route that Beatty's posse had covered, the station keeper was unaware of the theft of the horses. Still, long before that incident Slade had warned his station keepers not to harbor suspicious characters. Anything that bore even the appearance of collusion with horse thieves, Slade had announced, would be punished not merely with dismissal but with death.

In this case, the station keeper explained Slade's strict rules against harboring or feeding of anyone but company employees and passengers. But the weather was so cold that turning the man away would surely have resulted in his freezing to death. Ultimately the station keeper agreed to let his pitiful visitor stay the night. After the drifter had eaten, he crawled under a pile of gunnysacks in one corner and went to sleep.

About midnight the eastbound stage arrived, with Slade aboard. While the horses were being changed, Slade walked into the one-room station for "his usual piece of pie." To the station keeper's relief, Slade left without noticing anything suspicious. The next morning, after eating breakfast, the wayfarer departed, heading east on foot.

Two days later, to this station keeper's dismay, Slade returned on the stage from the east. With him on the seat, shackled hand and foot with a heavy iron bar between his ankles, was the young drifter who had hidden under the gunnysacks. Not by a flicker of an eyelid did the passenger betray the station keeper, who finally mustered up the courage to ask Slade who his prisoner was.

"Why, don't you know who it is?" Slade asked quietly. "This is the last one of the Davenport brothers, the one that got away." The prisoner had been picked up near Scott's Bluff, Slade explained, and a Pony Express rider had brought word to return him to Fort Laramie for hanging.

The stage, with Slade and his prisoner aboard, continued on its way but never reached Fort Laramie. At the bridge over the Laramie River, a delegation—whether military men or Slade's is unclear—halted the coach. Midway across the bridge a rope was adjusted around the prisoner's neck. When the crowd asked him to jump from the bridge railing, he obligingly complied.

Years later, the writer Arthur Chapman asked the unidentified station keeper what he would have done had this last of the Davenports told Slade of the station keeper's inadvertent hospitality. "I would have packed up my blankets and some bacon and hiked for the sagebrush at jackrabbit speed," was the reply. "Slade was in no mood to put up with the slightest infraction of his rules that winter. He would have killed me without waiting for any explanation."[12]

That same winter a Mexican and an American, both working in some capacity for the Central Overland, got into a quarrel at La Bonte's ranch, a Pony Express station 29 miles west of Horseshoe.[13] In the process, the Mexican killed the American and then escaped to the road ranch of John Sarah, located on the Bitter Cottonwood Creek, about 12 miles east of Horseshoe.[14] Slade sent word to Sarah to order the Mexican away. Sarah replied that he was keeping a road ranch and did not propose to send any person away who paid for his entertainment. Again Slade advised Sarah to get rid of the Mexican, but to no purpose.[15]

Slade responded by dispatching some of his men—two by one account, "a coach load," by another—with instructions to "clean out the Sarah place." Whether intentionally or not, this vague order was every bit as careless as Slade's remark a year earlier that Jules Beni would be killed if he continued to steal horses. Slade didn't always calculate the likely effect of his words on his unruly and overzealous employees. Conversely, he may have calculated the effect all too well. Like Henry II asking, "Who will rid me of this priest?" Slade may have hoped that his men would solve the problem while absolving Slade of the messy details.

His men, eager to carry out Slade's orders, appeared at Sarah's saloon a few nights later. They drank heavily and precipitated a fight with Sarah. In the ensuing melee, they killed Sarah as well as his Indian wife and an old ranchman; then they burned the house over them. (Apparently forgotten in the melee was the fugitive killer whose presence had provoked Slade's ire to begin with; he appears to have departed before Slade's men arrived.)

A guest of the ranch named Winters managed to escape and made his way on foot to Fort Laramie, where he reported the massacre to the military authorities.[16] Sarah's four children—two girls aged twelve and eight, a five-year-old boy, and a baby girl a few months old—were less fortunate. The eldest girl, with the baby on her back and the other sister by her side, climbed out of a rear window and escaped in the darkness to the prairie, where a few weeks later the bodies of all three were discovered, frozen from exposure.

The boy, who was separated from his sisters in the darkness, was found after the melee—in one account, by Slade's men that night; in another, by an Indian several days later. In both accounts the boy was taken to Slade's headquarters at Horseshoe station. Because Slade was away at the time, the boy was received by Virginia Slade, whose reaction is described by one of Slade's riders: "She knew nothing of the tragedy at the time, knowing only that the child was in distress, and having no children of her own, her whole heart went out to the little boy. She worked for hours picking prickly pear thorns out of his flesh. It was a week before she got him into a normal condition mentally. He was almost starved, and frightened at any unusual noise, and would hide from strangers."[17]

Slade, by one account, had never intended Sarah's death, much less the destruction of his whole family, and was greatly disturbed by the incident. What happened to the killers is not recorded. "Both outfits"—presumably Slade's and the French ranchers—"were toughs and people paid no attention to what had happened," the Army corporal George Beatty of Fort Laramie shrugged in an interview sixty-two years later.

To make what amends they could, Slade and his wife took the boy into their home and cared for him.[18] Although they never legally adopted the boy, they called him "Jemmy Slade," and he remained with them thereafter. Thus this "gentle, well-behaved child, remarkable for his beautiful, soft black eyes, and for his polite address," became the only child the Slades had, and a further enhancement to Slade's mystique along the Central Overland.[19]

In the wake of the Davenport capture and the Sarah massacre, Slade was soon credited or blamed for every heroic or homicidal exploit within his division. On the plains, fact and fiction alike—indistinguishable because they were unverifiable—were spread by word of mouth along regular lines of travel, and no line was more traveled than the Central Overland route. "Almost everyone who passed across the mountains on the Overland stage line would hear stories about the desperate character of Slade," wrote the historian Emerson Hough in 1908.[20] True or false, the stories were widely believed and consequently affected people's reactions to Slade.

Lesser men latched on to his reputation as a way of inflating their own. One acquaintance named Tom Rivington claimed to have been present when Slade shot a man for stealing a harness. "Slade gave him a running start," Rivington claimed many years later. "The bullet made a bad flesh wound on the fellow's west end. I was just a boy but I can see the fellow running yet. He got well and was a good citizen afterwards."[21]

The outlaw Polk Wells similarly claimed that, as an eleven-year-old runaway working with a freighting train near Julesburg, he was taught to shoot by Slade and his wife, who offered to adopt Wells (presumably before they adopted Jemmy Sarah). As Wells described the encounter in his memoirs (written in prison long after Slade died), he found Virginia Slade even more dazzling than Slade himself. "Mrs. Slade was a tall, sprightly woman, with the most pleasing, or insinuating manner I ever beheld and it was, perhaps, owing to this characteristic that I was led to regard her as handsome and to almost reverence her as a superior being. She read my thoughts or estimation of her as she would the pages of a book and having heard me say I had no relations with the outfit, proposed that I leave it and make my home with her and her husband."

The Slades, Wells said, promised to furnish him with "an abundance of good things to eat, a fine horse to ride, and breech-loading guns with which to hunt buffalo." After sealing the bargain "with a kiss," Wells scampered back to the wagon train to get his things, only to be informed by the foreman of the identity of his putative foster parents. The mere mention of Slade's name, Wells recalled, produced "a sudden and violent revulsion of feeling toward him and his—to me— accomplished wife." So Wells remained with the train—angering Slade, he claimed, by doing so.[22]

Murders and shootings committed by others were often credited to Slade. Deeds he *did* commit were usually exaggerated. In the version of the Sarah tragedy told by "several people" to Mark Twain—himself the best-known distributor and embellisher of Slade stories—Slade "went to the Frenchman's house very late one night, knocked, and when his enemy opened the door, shot him dead—pushed the corpse inside the door with his foot, set the house on fire and burned up the dead man, his widow and three children!" Another legend conveyed to Twain held that one morning at Rocky Ridge, Slade observed at a distance a man who had offended him some days before. "Gentlemen," Slade announced, according to Twain, "it is a good twenty-yard shot— I'll clip the third button on his coat!" Twain added: "Which he did. The bystanders all admired it. And they all attended the funeral, too."

When Mark Twain heard these stories about the ferocious Slade he was not yet a world-famous writer but an impressionable twenty-six-year-old Missouri native named Samuel Clemens, making his first trip out West by stage in company with his brother Orion, who was recently appointed to a position in Nevada's new territorial government. "Really and truly, two-thirds of the talk of drivers and conductors had been about this man Slade," Twain later wrote, "ever since the day before we reached Julesburg."[23]

> There was such magic in that name, SLADE! Day or night, now, I stood always ready to drop any subject in hand, to listen to something new about Slade and his ghastly exploits. Even before we got to Overland City [that is, Julesburg], we had begun to hear about Slade and his "division" (for he was a "division-agent") on the Overland; and from the hour we had left Overland City we had heard drivers and conductors talk about only three things— "Californy," the Nevada silver mines, and this desperado Slade. And a deal the most of the talk was about Slade. We had gradually come to have a realizing sense of the fact that Slade was a man whose heart and hands and soul were steeped in the blood of offenders against his dignity; a man who awfully avenged all injuries, affronts, insults or slights, of whatever kind—on the spot if he could, years afterward if lack of earlier opportunity compelled it; a man whose hate tortured him day and night till vengeance appeased it—and not an ordinary vengeance either, but his enemy's absolute death—nothing less; a man whose face

would light up with a terrible joy when he surprised a foe and had him at a disadvantage. A high and efficient servant of the Overland, an outlaw among outlaws and yet their relentless scourge, Slade was at once the most bloody, the most dangerous and the most valuable citizen that inhabited the savage fastnesses of the mountains.[24]

The real Slade whom Clemens met for perhaps an hour at Rocky Ridge station on August 2, 1861, was but a pale shadow of Twain's overheated imagination.[25]

In due time we rattled up to a stage-station, and sat down to breakfast with a half-savage, half-civilized company of armed and bearded mountaineers, ranchmen and station employees. The most gentlemanly-appearing, quiet and affable officer we had yet found along the road in the Overland Company's service was the person who sat at the head of the table, at my elbow. Never youth stared and shivered as I did when I heard them call him SLADE!

He was so friendly and so gentle-spoken that I warmed to him in spite of his awful history. It was hardly possible to realize that this pleasant person was the pitiless scourge of the outlaws, the raw-head-and-bloody-bones the nursing mothers of the mountains terrified their children with. . . .

The coffee ran out. At least it was reduced to one tin-cupful, and Slade was about to take it when he saw that my cup was empty.

He politely offered to fill it, but although I wanted it, I politely declined. I was afraid he had not killed anybody that morning, and might be needing diversion. But still with firm politeness he insisted on filling my cup, and said I had traveled all night and better deserved it than he—and while he talked he placidly poured the fluid, to the last drop. I thanked him and drank it, but it gave me no comfort, for I could not feel sure that he would not be sorry, presently, that he had given it away, and proceed to kill me to distract his thoughts from the loss. But nothing of the kind occurred. . . . Slade came out to the coach and saw us off, first ordering certain rearrangements of the mail-bags for our comfort,

and then we took leave of him, satisfied that we should hear of him
again, some day, and wondering in what connection.[26]

Another tale passed on to Twain told of a saloonkeeper who somehow antagonized Slade. A day or two later Slade came in and called for
some brandy. In Twain's recounting, "The man reached under the
counter (ostensibly to get a bottle—possibly to get something else), but
Slade smiled upon him that peculiarly bland and satisfied smile of his
which the neighbors had long ago learned to recognize as a death-war-
rant in disguise, and told him to 'none of that!—pass out the high-
priced article.' So the poor barkeeper had to turn his back and get the
high-priced brandy from the shelf; and when he faced around again he
was looking into the muzzle of Slade's pistol. 'And the next instant,'
added my informant, impressively, 'He was one of the deadest men
that ever lived'."[27]

None of these stories was ever verified, and as one observer
remarked, they are "so at variance with Slade's methods as to be
beyond belief."[28] All of them allegedly took place at a time when the
supposedly vengeful and vindictive Slade had yet to take any steps
whatever against his prime nemesis, Jules Beni.

The impatient Ben Holladay himself implored Slade to send a sig-
nal to the outlaw element by eliminating Jules. "Get that fellow Jules,"
Holladay is reliably reported to have told Slade, "and let everybody
know you got him."[29] Still, Slade made no move against Jules, other
than to send word reiterating his pledge not to harm Jules if Jules
avoided Slade's division. Holladay seems to have perceived, as Slade
apparently did not, that Jules remained a menace to the company,
whether or not he trespassed on Slade's division.

One story conveyed by Mark Twain and recounted by others inadvertently portrays a Slade who thoughtlessly let his guard down (as he
had done a year earlier with Jules), with near-tragic consequences.
Slade was allegedly captured by a dozen of his enemies and taken to a
lonely log cabin where he was kept prisoner, awaiting the arrival of the
outlaw chiefs—Jules, perhaps?—who were to determine how to dispose of him. Slade, either in despair or resourcefulness, or both, prevailed on his guards to bring his wife to him so he could say farewell

and instruct her as to how to dispose of his property after he was gone. "She jumped on a horse and rode for life and death," Twain later wrote. "When she arrived, they let her in without searching her, and before the door could be closed she whipped out a couple of revolvers, and she and her lord marched forth defying the party. And then, under a brisk fire, they mounted double and galloped away unharmed!"[30]

Much of Slade's perceived power, of course, was a matter of wishful thinking on the part of Central Overland employees, emigrants, and ranchers who yearned for a strong protecting hand. The occasional miscreant who stood up to Slade often found, to his astonishment, that Slade backed off. A stagecoach driver known as "Rowdy Pete," who was shorter than Slade, got into an argument with him in a barroom at Green

What did Slade look like? This image is probably, but not certainly, reliable. Its provenance can be traced back only to 1941, when it was donated to the Pioneer Museum in Fort Collins, Colorado. But a similar image, said to be "sketched from an old photograph," appeared in the *Kansas City Star* of May 27, 1906. The photograph itself has not surfaced.

River. To the onlookers' astonishment, Rowdy Pete walked up to Slade, snatched his gun, and pulled his nose. Instead of taking serious offense, Slade passed the incident off as a joke, and Rowdy Pete retained his job as a stage driver.[31]

In another incident somewhere along the Central Overland stage route, Slade and one Bob Scott were said to have been drinking heavily while playing poker in a saloon. As drink followed drink, their bets grew larger until Slade's money was exhausted. At this point, according to Nathaniel Langford, Slade pointed to the piles of coin heaped on the table and said, "Bob, that money belongs to me."

"It does if the cards say so," Scott supposedly replied, "not otherwise."

"Perhaps," Slade replied, "my cards are not better than yours, but"—here he drew his revolver—"my *hand* is."

When Slade reached forward to gather in the pile of twenty-dollar gold coins, Scott suddenly pushed Slade's pistol aside with one hand and punched Slade between the eyes with the other. Slade fell, and Scott pounced on top of him, refusing to rise until Slade promised to behave himself.

At this point, the poker game resumed as if the fight had never taken place. After a few more hands, Slade, by now thoroughly sobered, quietly remarked, "Well, Bob, if you'd pounded me about two minutes longer, I'd have got sober sooner."[32]

These and similar Slade stories follow a similar pattern: In each, Slade when drunk turns into an irrational bully, then seems almost grateful when someone sets him straight. Tom Rivington, one of Slade's colleagues, recalled Slade drinking at an Army post, most likely Fort Laramie:

> He and some army officers got drunk. They were in the sutler's store. A major, I do not remember his name, came to me to get Slade out of the store before he wrecked it. The major gave me $2. I went in and got Jack by the hand and said, "Come on Jack, let's go down to the stage station and go to bed."
>
> He said, "All right, Bud." Every time Slade got with a bunch of officers he got full.[33]

A young drifter named John Young Nelson, tending bar at a ranch east of Julesburg, recalled a westbound coach from Fort Kearny driving up with Slade and "half a dozen men out on a 'bust'." Nelson was aware that "Slade had under him a harder set of assistants and helpers generally than any one on the line." Although Nelson didn't recognize them at first, Slade quickly set him straight:

> Stepping right up to the bar, [he] leant his elbows on it, and staring me full in the face, said, in an overbearing and bullying tone: "Do you know me?"

"No, I don't," I replied.

"Well," he said, "I am the man who killed the Saviour."

Since Slade and his companions were all intoxicated, Nelson tried to humor them. But Slade picked up a decanter of whiskey and aimed it at Nelson's head. Nelson dodged and caught the blow on his left elbow, and with his right hand he grabbed an old sawed-off double-barreled shotgun and fired at Slade's head.

"Fortunately for him one of his companions knocked the barrel up, and the charge of twenty-four buckshot went through the roof of the shanty, making a hole the size of the plate and scattering the turf in all directions," Nelson recounted. "This sobered him for an instant, and he backed to the end of the cabin, where he stood and stared at me."

At this moment, according to Nelson, Slade's friends interceded and said: "Hold on, boy! This is all fun; don't let's have any fighting." Finally peace reigned, "and we all had a drink."

Yet moments later, when an English emigrant drove up to the shanty, Slade snatched a four-pound weight from the scale on the counter and heaved it through the window at the traveler, barely missing his head. The Englishman dragged his rifle out of his wagon, stepped into the shanty, and pointing the rifle at Slade's head, said: "You heaved that weight at me. What did you do it for?" Slade, according to Nelson, "said it was only done in fun; and the others, trying to make peace, apologized for him, and begged the Englishman not to notice it."[34]

If Samuel Clemens fancied himself Slade's amanuensis, his timing left a great deal to be desired. The coach bearing the Clemens brothers had barely departed from Rocky Ridge on August 2, 1861, when the curtain rose on two of Slade's most celebrated exploits—genuine heroics, unlike the myths that seized Mark Twain's attention.

Two dangerous men—Charley Bacon, a French Canadian, and Harry Smith, a Canadian of Scotch descent—had for several years kept a trading post at Split Rock, perhaps 15 miles east of Independence Rock, about 160 miles west of Slade's Horseshoe headquarters.[35] By 1861 Split Rock was also operating as a Pony Express relay station under Slade's jurisdiction. About that time several emigrants who had passed Split Rock were said to have disappeared mysteriously. Cattle and horses belonging to neighbors were recognized among Bacon's and Smith's herds.

That year a Dr. Bartholomew was living with his wife and small children near the Sweetwater River, not far from Bacon and Smith. Bartholomew's ranch—which contained about forty head of cattle, thirty horses, and a hundred chickens—was a tempting target for unscrupulous neighbors. According to one account, in July 1861 Bartholomew hired Bacon and Smith to build a chimney. They erected the chimney but demanded more than the agreed-upon price, and when Bartholomew objected, they shot and killed him.[36] (In another version, Bacon and Smith hired Bartholomew, but Smith got drunk, argued with Bartholomew, Bartholomew called Smith a liar, and Smith shot him, saying, "No man could do that and live.")[37] Smith then compounded the crime by propositioning Bartholomew's widow. When she spurned his advances, he apparently drove her out, and she and her children sought refuge at the ranch of Joseph Plante, a wealthy French-Canadian who maintained a sizable store some four miles east of Bacon and Smith. (Plante appears to have been one of the few French-Canadians who enjoyed Slade's favor.)[38]

Plante had no relatives, and about ten days after killing Bartholomew, Bacon and Smith resolved to kill Plante as well and seize his property. When Plante learned of this plot—perhaps from Bartholomew's widow—he wrote to Slade to seek his advice. In the process he informed Slade of Dr. Bartholomew's murder. Slade's reply, written on a Tuesday in August, was brief and succinct: "Sit in your store with a shot-gun loaded with buckshot and shoot the first one that tries to enter. I will be there next Friday and I will fix those fellows. Have two rawhide lariats ready."[39]

That Friday, true to his word, Slade and four men arrived at Plante's in an extra coach. According to the later account of Amede Bessette—the station keeper at Platte Bridge, located about midway between Plante's store and Slade's Horseshoe headquarters—Smith had been in Plante's store for about an hour, trying to provoke a quarrel with Plante in French.

Slade was informed of all this. He went to Smith in the store and approaching close to him said, "Smith, you said lately that no man could call you a liar and live. Pull out your gun, for I am determined to tell [you] what I think of you, and I expect to be shot."

The two men stood about ten inches apart, Slade's left hand on the right shoulder of Smith. Looking at him square in the face, Slade said to Smith, "You are a liar, a thief and a murderer, and the greatest coward on earth, for you killed a man who had two children to support, to get his wife, and you did not succeed, but I shall punish you severely for it."

Saying the last word, he shoved him away. Slade then told his men to go to work. They took Smith, tied his hands behind him, and walked about sixty feet away to the gate beam. Slade threw a rawhide lariat around Smith's neck, threw the end of it over the beam and pulled him up until his feet were elevated three feet above the ground.[40]

At this point Slade sent his men in the coach to fetch Bacon. They returned, stopping the coach so that Bacon would stand close to Smith's hanging body when he stepped off. As he stepped to the ground, according to Bessette's account, Bacon "handed a terrible blow to Smith, striking the body about six inches above the knee and causing it to swing back and forth. . . . With an oath, he said, 'You son of a bitch, I will meet you within an hour from now, and will whip hell out of you.' The same kind of rope was put around his neck, and he was pulled up in the same manner that Smith had been. The ends of both lariats were tied to a post planted in front of the gate. They were left there all night."[41]

After the hangings, Slade and Plante took a buggy to Mrs. Bartholomew's home to tell her what had happened and ascertain her plans. Slade urged her to stay on the ranch, explaining that she could hire someone to care for the cattle and horses and make a good living with the equipment the farm possessed. But the widow said she preferred to return to her parents in Omaha. Slade acquiesced and said he would make all the necessary arrangements. "I don't want you to stay here any longer," he told her, according to Bessette. "Get ready and come down with me to see my wife."

Slade resolved to sell the Bartholomew ranch then and there to one of Plante's workers named Ben Caron, who had about $1,000 in cash and was willing to take the property for that relatively reasonable price. The next morning, when Bacon and Smith were cut down and buried, Slade found $320.75 in Bacon's pockets and $203 in Smith's. Under the laws then in force, a wife didn't automatically inherit her husband's property (as Slade's own mother had discovered nearly thirty years earlier). Nevertheless, Slade gave the proceeds—more than $1,500 all told, most of it in gold coin—to Mrs. Bartholomew, who boarded Slade's coach with the money stuffed into sacks and pillowcases.

This transaction reflected not only Slade's passion to avenge injustice but also his business acumen. On their way to Horseshoe, Slade told Bartholomew's widow, "If you could have had your father and mother with you and stayed on the ranch, you would have made more money, for the ranch and stock are well worth $10,000."

"Oh, Mr. Slade," the widow replied, "the ranch was not mine."

"Oh yes it was," Slade answered. "After those men killed your husband up there, and we had put them out of the way, everything was yours. I am a good deal of an Indian that way. I made those fellows pay for the life of your husband. The money I have given you was not mine, but yours." The thousand dollars Caron paid for the Bartholomew ranch, Slade reasoned, was a tremendous bargain: "He will make money there."

Mrs. Bartholomew and her children spent about a month in the Slades' home at Horseshoe station. Since Mrs. Bartholomew and Virginia Slade were of a similar size, Virginia gave the widow several of her dresses, and from her old clothes Virginia made enough outfits to last the children a year. When the Bartholomews were ready to leave, Slade gave the widow a stagecoach pass good for passage for herself and her children to Omaha.

A few weeks later, according to Bessette, "Mr. and Mrs. Slade were the recipients of a letter from the parents of Mrs. Bartholomew, full of thanks and good wishes. Mrs. Bartholomew kept up a regular correspondence with her inestimable friends. Slade remained upon his mail division, looked upon as a demi-god by everybody."[42]

To be sure, when Slade took Mrs. Bartholomew from Plante's east-ward to Horseshoe, he may have had more on his mind than hospital-ity to a bereaved widow. He may have received word at this time that the greatest threat to his elevated status—the one man who had defied Slade and lived to tell the tale—had broken his pledge and returned to Slade's division.[43]

By the summer of 1861 Jules Beni was rumored to have left Denver—probably with his young bride, Adeline—and surfaced west of Rocky Ridge, where he was said to be buying and selling cattle in collusion with some of the outlaws who had moved there to place themselves, as Jules had, beyond Slade's reach.[44] Henry Gilbert, who had given up his trading post west of South Pass (where Slade and his mail team had found refuge during the frozen winter of 1858–59) and moved 100 miles west, to the Fort Bridger vicinity, reported encoun-tering Jules at this time.[45]

Having shot Slade multiple times in the spring of 1860 without suf-fering retribution, Jules Beni by the summer of 1861 apparently had come to believe himself invulnerable to Slade.[46] (How he reacted to Slade's miraculous survival is unrecorded.) "Jules used to brag to me that Slade was bluffed and would give him no more trouble," Henry Gilbert told a reporter more than forty years later.[47] Other men claimed to have heard Jules boasting that he was "not afraid of any damned driver, express rider or anyone else in the mail company," and that if Slade himself did not kill Jules he would himself be slaughtered by Jules.[48]

Jules could hardly be blamed for his braggadocio. Eighteen months earlier, it was Slade who had tried to provoke a confrontation with Jules; now the shoe seemed to be on the other foot. However much Jules boasted of his hold over Slade, Slade steadfastly refused to accept the challenge, until Jules left him no choice.

Jules had an associate who traded with emigrants at Wagon Hound Creek, only about 20 miles northwest of Slade's headquarters at Horseshoe.[49] Sometime that summer of 1861 Jules sent a man to the Wagon Hound ranch to retrieve his stock. Slade met Jules's hired hand

and informed him that no one could move the stock but Jules himself.[50] Shortly afterward, probably in late August, Jules accepted this
challenge and started for Wagon Creek, ostensibly to retrieve his
herd—armed, according to one account, with a shotgun, a bowie knife,
a revolver and a powerful field glass.[51] Yet when Jules left Wagon
Hound Creek he did not return westward to the Fort Bridger area from
which he had presumably come. Instead, Jules crossed to the north
side of the North Platte River—presumably to avoid Slade's headquarters and other Central Overland stations on the south side—and proceeded in a southwesterly direction along the riverbank opposite the
Central Overland route.[52] He may have been headed for Cottonwood
Springs, about a hundred miles east of Overland City (as Julesburg
was now known), where he kept a ranch with his teenage bride Adeline
Cayou. Whether Jules was driving his herd is unclear.[53] Along his way
he told several people that he was going to kill Slade.[54] By nearly all
accounts he was alone—presuming, apparently, that Slade would meet
him in man-to-man combat and that he, Jules, would prevail.[55]

    As was the case in his impulsive shooting of Slade seventeen months
earlier, Jules seems to have given no thought to the likely consequences
of his actions. That is, if he killed Slade, then what? Slade's men had
nearly lynched Jules the previous year, and doubtless would finish the
job now if he slew their leader. Among young men in the West, rash and
thoughtless acts of bravado were commonplace and even expected. But
Jules was about fifty-two—an old man by Western standards.[56] In this
particular conflict the generational roles were reversed: Jules took the
role of the youthful hothead while Slade, twenty-two years younger,
played the cautious and responsible authority figure.

    Had Slade been home at Horseshoe, the two antagonists might have
collided then and there. But when Slade first heard of Jules's arrival and
threats, he was some 400 miles west at Pacific Springs, the far western
end of his division. At once he started eastward.[57] Thus both men were
heading in the same direction, several days' ride apart.

    Yet even now Slade seemed inclined to avoid violence. Halting at
Horseshoe, he is said to have remained there for a week in order to
allow Jules and his stock to pass out of the country peacefully (and also,
perhaps, to help the widow Bartholomew get settled at his home).[58]

At the end of the week, Slade proceeded on to Fort Laramie, where he learned that Jules had not left the country at all, but had spent the previous night 12 miles south at Bordeaux's ranch, where he had repeated his threats, flaunted his pistol, and declared that he would lie in wait at some point on the road until Slade appeared.[59] At this news, finally, Slade decided to act.

"Slade simply had to get Jules or quit the line," the respected driver (and later Wells Fargo superintendent) E. M. "Gov" Pollinger told a historian. "There was no other way out. Order in the division depended on Slade, and he could not enforce it while Jules was alive and defiant. You may not see it now, but it was plain enough then."[60] The contrast is striking: Where the impressionable Mark Twain perceived Slade as "a man who awfully avenged all injuries, affronts, insults or slights, of whatever kind," Pollinger (and perhaps Ben Holladay as well) saw Slade as a man in danger of losing his job for failure to move decisively against Jules.

Still Slade hesitated. Unlike Bacon and Smith, Jules hadn't actually killed anybody. He had *attempted* to kill Slade seventeen months earlier but had been released on his pledge to leave the region. Now he had broken his pledge and had threatened to kill Slade. The appropriate punishment was not so obvious as it had been in the case of Bacon and Smith. At Fort Laramie, Slade sought out the officers and laid the situation before them.

In theory, the Army to which he turned embodied the federal government's presence in the West, yet in practice it possessed no authority to intervene in civilian crimes. More important, by the end of the 1850s the frontier army consisted of fewer than eight thousand men,[61] more than half of whom were poor and illiterate recent immigrants from Europe, or social outcasts with no better prospects than to sign up for a five-year enlistment at seven dollars a month (eight in the cavalry).[62] "The greater part of the army," one sergeant wrote to his parents, "consist of men who either do not care to work, or who, because of being addicted to drink, cannot find employment."[63]

The quality of the officer corps was little better. Because promotions were based entirely on seniority, the officer ranks were burdened with ancient and worn-out time-servers. Of the U.S. Army's nineteen regimental colonels in 1860, fifteen had more than forty years' service, eleven were veterans of the War of 1812, and two had joined the Army in 1801.[64]

Lacking modern insights into human behavior, the Army relied on harsh physical punishment to keep its troops in line—which, not surprisingly, rarely succeeded. A man might be confined in the bare, unheated guardhouse, or hung by his thumbs, his toes barely touching the floor. He could be shackled to an iron ball weighing anywhere from ten to twenty-five pounds, or spread-eagled on the ground beneath a swarm of buffalo gnats.[65]

This army's greatest enemy was boredom; most soldiers of the West never saw combat or even a hostile Indian, and the Army of the West lost more men to disease and desertion than to enemy action.[66]

That spring of 1861 one of Slade's Central Overland employees, the boisterous Frank McCarty, had turned up drunk at Fort Laramie, fired one or two shots at the flag (calling it "Uncle Sam's handkerchief") and departed without being molested (although the commanding officer came out after McCarty had safely departed and ordered the guard to arrest him if they could find him). "This indicates to a small degree the laxity of the military," wrote Slade's Horseshoe Creek neighbor Elias Whitcomb.[67]

Having served in the Army himself, Slade may well have understood subconsciously that these misfits in military uniforms were no better qualified to maintain order on the frontier than the roughnecks who worked for Slade; that the Army's officers were no more capable or sober than the Central Overland's division agents and station keepers; and that the Army's methods for training, motivating, and disciplining men were probably less effective than Slade's own methods. Still, he sought the Army's advice and approval instead of proceeding on his own.

The officers at Fort Laramie, well aware of Jules's threats, and doubtless also well aware of Slade's value to them as a civilian peacekeeper, gave Slade their blessing to take preemptive action against Jules. Unless he acted promptly, they said, Jules would kill him, and in any case there would be no peace on Slade's division while Jules lived.[68]

Now Slade huddled with some of his men. By one account, Slade offered a $500 reward to any man who would capture Jules and bring him in alive—but no reward if Jules were dead.[69] In the meantime Slade sent four men on horseback to Bordeaux's to capture Jules and disarm him; Slade and a friend followed soon after in a coach.

When the coach reached Bordeaux's, Slade learned that Jules had indeed spent the night there but had since fled south. James Bordeaux, the station keeper, confirmed that Jules had uttered threats against Slade. Bordeaux, like many other French ranch-keepers along the stage line, had coexisted uneasily with Slade. He had come west from St. Louis as a trapper with his family when Slade was still an infant; now he was forty-seven, with a Lakota Indian wife and a large family, and was vulnerable to Slade's prejudices and unpredictable behavior when drunk.[70] On the one hand, his daughter later recalled, "My father and Slade were always good friends; in fact, he stayed at our place many times." On the other, the raid by Slade's men on John Sarah's ranch earlier that year had led Bordeaux to store most of his goods in a tent hidden in the woods. He was likely to face retribution from Slade for having harbored Jules the previous night; but if Jules killed Slade, Bordeaux was likely to suffer at the hands of Jules's men and the other French ranchers along the line.

When Slade's coach departed from Bordeaux's in pursuit of Jules, Bordeaux himself climbed aboard, carrying what was described as "a small armory of guns and pistols." Whether out of genuine loyalty or shrewd calculation, in this instance Bordeaux bet his future on Slade.

The next station, some 13 miles farther southeast, was Sochet's ranch, at Cold Spring. As the coach, with Slade holding the reins, approached Sochet's, Slade saw Nelson Vaughan and John Frey—two of the men he had dispatched to capture Jules—riding toward the coach at top speed. At first Slade and his companions concluded that they had failed to find their quarry. But as they drew closer they realized that Vaughan and Frey were whooping and waving their hats in celebration: Jules had indeed been captured and was being held at Cold Spring.[71]

According to Slade's Horseshoe neighbor Elias Whitcomb, Jules had stopped at Sochet's ranch, where Slade had three men watching for him, all mounted on mules. Jules grew suspicious and mounted his horse to ride away. But when he heard the men ask Sochet if he had seen any mules, he was thrown off his guard, returned, and dismounted. Instantly he was covered with shotguns and ordered to surrender. Jules started to run and was shot in the hip and relieved of his gun; he then crawled into a hole back of the house, where he was followed and compelled to surrender.[72]

At least, this is what Slade was told. According to probably the most reliable informant—the driver (and later Wells Fargo superintendent) Gov Pollinger—Vaughan and Frey had actually captured Jules during a gunfight in which Jules was wounded. They bound him to a packhorse and started for Cold Spring, but to their dismay Jules died before they arrived. Fearful of arousing Slade's wrath—and of losing his posted $500 reward—once at Cold Spring they tied Jules in a sitting position to the snubbing-post in the corral.

What happened next has been the subject of debate ever since, especially since no eyewitness account was ever published. Hastily, Slade drove the coach to the Cold Spring station and dismounted.

"I suppose you had to kill him," Slade remarked, "and if you did, you do not get any reward."

Vaughan and Frey insisted Jules was not yet dead, only wounded: "He's out in the corral."

When Slade walked out back to the corral sand saw Jules's inert body lashed to the fence, he said, "The man is dead."

"He's only playing possum," they replied.

"I'll see whether he's playing possum," Slade said. Here he took out his knife and cut off an ear. When Jules did not flinch, Slade remarked, "That proves it, but I might just as well have the other ear," and took that as well.[73]

The more lurid version of Jules's death—circulated with far greater alacrity precisely because of its garishness—was told by James Boner, who kept the Central Overland station at Lodge Pole, near Julesburg. In this account, Slade found Jules alive and tied to a corral post at Cold Spring and told him: "You made me suffer, now I'll try to pay you for it." He then sadistically proceeded to shoot Jules in nonvital places, taking care to keep him alive and pausing between each shot to go inside Sochet's saloon for a drink until Jules finally expired. At which time Slade—by then drunk—cut off the dead man's ears and put them in his vest pocket.[74]

In one variation to this story, Jules pleaded with Slade for a chance to see his wife, only to be told, "When you shot me you gave me no chance to see my wife . . . so now take your medicine."[75] In still another, between shots and drinks Slade offered Jules the opportunity to write out his last will and testament.[76] As one Wyoming newspaper, in a typical exaggeration of the Slade myth, described the incident, "The inhuman Slade . . . cut off Jules' ears and shot him full of holes."[77]

The death of Jules, and the shocking manner in which it supposedly occurred, solidified Slade's reputation as (in Twain's phrase) "a man whose heart and hands and soul were steeped in the blood of offenders against his dignity." Yet Slade's behavior toward Jules from the moment Jules shot him in March 1860 consistently suggests the opposite conclusion. The primitive code of the West demanded that Slade prove his manhood by extracting an eye for an eye in mortal combat. Yet having already killed or confronted toughs many times over, Slade in this instance turned the other cheek. Instead of seeking violent retribution against Jules, he had sought to enforce some communal notion of legal procedure. The aggravated narratives of the Jules killing, Slade's acquaintance Nathaniel Langford noted in 1890, were "false in every particular. Jules was not only the first, but the most constant aggressor." Even had the worst stories been true, Langford suggested, Slade would have been justified: "In the situation he accepted, an active business man, entrusted with duties which required constant exposure of his person both night and day, what else could he do, to save his own life, than kill the person who threatened and sought an opportunity to take it? . . . It was impossible to avoid a collision with him; and to kill him under such circumstances was a clear act of self-defense."[78]

In the aftermath of Jules's death, Slade again seems to have taken pains to subordinate himself and his ego to traditional moral and legal standards. Bordeaux—presumably the closest thing to a neutral party in a feud between a stage man and a French rancher—was designated to select sufficient stock to reimburse Slade for expenses incurred when he recovered from Jules's attack the previous year. The remainder of Jules's stock and the money on his person were disposed of, according to one account, in accordance with Jules's own directions.[79] (His widow, the teenage Adeline, claimed in one account that Slade and his party appropriated virtually all of Jules's property; in another account she said she took all his money—some $500—to St. Joseph that winter and rejoined her parents in Denver the following spring.)[80] Then Slade surrendered himself to the military authorities at Fort Laramie, inviting the commandant to investigate the incident. Since the officers had advised him to kill Jules only the day before Jules's death, they refused to press any charges.[81]

Perhaps to indulge the fierce image that both he and the rest of the world fancied, Slade carried at least one of Jules's ears with him thereafter. The killing of Jules was the only sadistic act ever attributed to Slade, and he had taken great pains to avoid it; yet to some extent he was bound to live up to the violent image he had helped to create. The Jules episode suggests that Slade may have felt some ambivalence about that image and what might happen as, inevitably, he lost control of it.

Throughout the spring and summer of 1861 the telegraph and Pony Express in tandem sped the news of the shelling of Fort Sumter; the secession of Virginia, North Carolina, and Arkansas; the Confederate seizure of the federal arsenal at Harpers Ferry and the great navy yard near Norfolk; Lincoln's call for volunteers; and the disastrous federal defeats at Bull Run. As the full horror of the Civil War became evident, the West—which since the California gold rush had mostly attracted footloose young bachelors in search of riches and adventure—began to see a new type of emigrant: war refugees, draft dodgers, southern sympathizers fleeing the North, and Union supporters fleeing the South. Now the West beckoned to anyone reluctant to take sides in the Civil War, or whose sympathies were suspect.

Edward Creighton's Pacific Telegraph Company had strung its lines as far west as Fort Kearny in November 1860, and its federal contract gave him two years to reach Salt Lake City. But each new war crisis brought increased pressure to complete the job sooner. In early summer, Creighton's construction crews set out from Fort Kearny.[82] To reach Salt Lake City before winter would require advancing ten to twelve miles a day, seven days a week. Almost a thousand oxen were required to haul the lumber for telegraph poles as well as other supplies for the crews working westward.[83] Nevertheless, by July 2 the telegraph line had reached Julesburg; by July 16 it had reached Chimney Rock; by August 5 it was three miles beyond Fort Laramie; and by late August the line connected Slade's headquarters at Horseshoe station with his division's eastern terminus at Julesburg.[84]

As Creighton's operation made its way westward toward Salt Lake City, Ben Ficklin's Overland Telegraph Company made its way eastward from the Pacific Coast, reaching Salt Lake City in mid-July.[85] The day was fast approaching when messages could be telegraphed instantaneously between Washington and San Francisco and the Pony Express would no longer be needed.

The "singing wires" and the poles that supported them might have been easily destroyed by Indians but for their perceived mystical powers. On one occasion Creighton intimidated a group of curious Cheyenne Indians by telling them that lightning ran along the wires, and he demonstrated his point by giving them a shock from the battery.[86] At Fort Bridger later in August, Creighton invited the Shoshone chief Washakie to "talk" with a Sioux chieftain at Slade's Horseshoe station, 360 miles to the east. The Shoshone chief asked a question, which the Sioux answered. Several questions and answers followed back and forth between the two chieftains. Greatly mystified but suspicious that some trick had been played upon them, the chiefs agreed to meet midway between Fort Bridger and Horseshoe to compare notes. That meeting convinced them—and, consequently, most Indian tribes—that the wire was indeed an instrument of the Indian god Manitou and therefore not to be disturbed.[87]

By September the Civil War, now five months old, had spilled westward into Kentucky and Missouri, two slave states that had remained tenuously within the Union. Confederate encroachments into Kentucky forced the Union's commanding general in Missouri, John C. Frémont, to take his army south along the Mississippi River, leaving

Missourians to engage their rival local militias in a statewide civil war. Because St. Joseph could no longer be relied upon as a Union stronghold, in September the Post Office Department ordered the Central Overland to move its eastern terminus 14 miles westward to Atchison, in Kansas, which was now connected to St. Joseph by a rail line.[88]

The stage line's nominal president, Ben Holladay's cousin Bela Hughes himself, felt the need to demonstrate his loyalty to the Union by leaving St. Joseph and moving to Atchison, and the Central Overland took the precaution of requiring its employees to swear an oath of allegiance to the United States. As of November 2 all but two employees had taken the oath, but that did not prevent bitter St. Joseph civic boosters from denouncing the stage line that had abandoned their town. A St. Joseph correspondent calling himself "Paul Jones," writing to the *St. Louis Missouri Democrat* in October, claimed that four-fifths of Central Overland employees were secessionists and that the company discriminated against Union men. President Hughes, Jones claimed, was a "rascal secessionist," and Jones added gratuitously: "Why is Mr. Slade kept in their employ?—a division agent having charge of the entire route from the crossing of the South Platte to the Pacific Springs. He is a vile-mouth, rabid secessionist."[89]

On October 22 the eastern telegraph reached Salt Lake City, where the Mormon leader Brigham Young sent the first eastbound message to a Western Union official in Cleveland, Ohio. "Utah has not seceded," Young declared, "but is firm for the Constitution and the laws of our once happy country." Two days later California's chief justice, Stephen Field—in the absence of the governor—flashed *his* ringing affirmation of loyalty all the way to President Lincoln in Washington: "The people of California desire to congratulate you upon the completion of the great work. They believe it will be the means of strengthening the attachment which binds both the East and the West to the Union, and they desire in this—the first message across the continent—to express their loyalty to the Union and their determination to stand by its government on this its day of trial."[90]

No longer would Union supporters in the East and West need to wait a week or more to learn what the other side of the country was thinking. Now they could reinforce their mutual loyalty and plan their strategies almost with the speed of a spoken conversation.

The Pony Express, its route drastically shortened and its purpose now virtually eliminated by the telegraph, was quietly discontinued, with none of the fanfare that had launched it, following completion of its run on October 26. In eighteen tumultuous months it had made 308 runs each way, carrying about 34,753 pieces of mail, yet losing only one *mochila* in the process. It had captured the world's imagination and helped keep the West in the Union. But as a business operation the Pony Express had brought in only a tiny fraction of the $500,000 or so that was invested in it.[91]

To Slade and his fellow division superintendents came orders—presumably by telegraph—to sell the horses or add them to the livestock at the stage stations. Pony Express relay stations were to be dismantled or turned over to Western Union, the operating telegraph company. Riders, station keepers, stock tenders, and blacksmiths were told to find new jobs.[92]

As a Central Overland agent whose division stretched 500 miles—more than twice the length of some other Central Overland divisions—Slade had benefited from the ability to send and receive messages quickly via Pony Express and stagecoach. Now, with seven telegraph stations between Julesburg and Rocky Ridge, he possessed an even more effective tool for policing his division and tracking stagecoach arrivals and departures.[93] The advent of the telegraph—as well as the elimination of the threat posed by Jules Beni in the Rocky Ridge country—may have motivated Slade's immediate boss, route superintendent Isaac Eaton, to grant Slade some long-overdue relief. Probably that fall, Eaton created a new division between Sweetwater Bridge and Pacific Springs while reducing Slade's 500-mile jurisdiction to a more manageable stretch of some 390 miles from Julesburg to Sweetwater Bridge—still the longest division on the Central Overland.[94]

In theory the new telegraph operators at Central Overland stations worked for Western Union; in practice Slade supervised them with the same stiff discipline that he meted out to his own employees. At Deer Creek, a trading station about a hundred miles west of Fort Laramie, the appointed telegraph operator was a small, frail nineteen-year-old named Oscar Collister. Like so many other ranches along the Central Overland route, Deer Creek consisted of a cluster of primitive cabins, a stockade used as a corral and an extensive stable, all owned by a Frenchman named Bisonette and operated by several of his employees. Prior to his arrival there, Collister was advised by his Western Union superior of the "very hostile feeling between Slade and the French" and instructed to "keep the friendship of both parties, and show equal regard to all."[95] As Collister later told it, he managed to get on Slade's bad side, but Slade soon rectified the relationship when he discovered that Collister wasn't at fault:

> I was for some time ignored by Slade when passing him on the road, and finally was taken to task by him over the wire, in a misunderstanding over a report of a stage passing the station. I had been erroneously informed of the time the stage passed while I was asleep, and Slade had told the operator at the first crossing of the Sweetwater River that another operator would be required after he had passed his station that night. However, in the conversation between myself and Slade when we met personally, Slade admitted that he was wrong in judging me as he had, and wished to consider the incident closed. He warned me against the French who composed the majority of his associates, and informed the operator at his station [Horseshoe] when he got home that he believed I was all right, and asked why the operator had not told him that I was not a Frenchman. From then on most friendly relations existed between the stage men and myself.[96]

Slade's efforts to maintain order along his division involved controlling not only outlaws and Indians but also the more complicated task of controlling his own men and, ultimately, his own inability to hold his liquor. Day-to-day life in the early West was not merely dull, it was often awesomely dull.[97] The healthiest antidote to boredom for lonely frontier males was hunting, but hunting was a less convenient and less sociable diversion than drinking.

Everywhere on the frontier, the historian Robert Utley observed, "nearly all men drank nearly all the time, which made nearly all men drunk most of the time."[98] A man who would not partake of whiskey or tobacco was "little short of an outlaw," complained a California miner named George McCowen, who said he took up smoking simply to avoid trouble.[99] Some stations along the Central Overland's stagecoach route lacked kitchens, but every road ranch had its saloon. Hamlets like Julesburg supported taverns long before anyone thought to build a dance hall, opera house, or church.

Alcoholic drinks were called "spirits" because they lifted the spirit, at least for the moment. But they impaired a man's judgment, inflated his sense of power, removed his inhibitions, and exaggerated his perceptions of insults and threats. They created the delusion of well-being even as they lowered body temperature and undermined the drinker's immune system.[100] In San Francisco men enfeebled by alcohol died of infectious diseases in shanty bunks while drunkards caroused in the saloon below.[101]

Yet since the eighteenth century, most Americans had associated whiskey with self-sufficiency, robust health, industriousness, and national pride. Laborers digging the Erie Canal in the early 1820s were given a quart of Monongahela whiskey a day, issued in eight four-ounce portions beginning at 6 A.M., on the presumption that the practice was healthy. The frontier Army of the early 1860s offered a similar inducement to soldiers constructing its forts.[102] Nineteenth-century American men commonly drank whiskey at breakfast and on through the day, perceiving the practice as a key to manly strength and good fellowship.[103] But thousands of otherwise productive and good-natured men provided walking evidence to the contrary—none more so than Slade himself.

Like Slade, his wife Virginia keenly perceived the dangers of liquor, but her efforts against it weren't always consistent. In the spring of 1861 a man named Elias W. Whitcomb opened a trading store near Slade's headquarters at Horseshoe Creek, offering groceries, a few articles of clothing, and liquor. "So far as my personal experiences with Slade were concerned," Whitcomb later recalled, "I found him a good neighbor, he being one of those characters who if he took a liking to you would do anything in his power for you, but if he had formed a dislike for you, and should happen to be under the influence of liquor, you were sure to have trouble with him."

Slade often came to Whitcomb's store to play cards. On these occasions he invariably drank, and sometimes he drank too freely. Mrs. Slade, who bore the consequences when Slade got home, concluded that he might not get drunk so often if he had to travel farther for his whiskey. On one occasion in the fall of 1861, when Slade had gone to Julesburg, the men remaining at Horseshoe took the opportunity to "get on a glorious drunk," as Whitcomb put it.[104] With the men in this condition, Mrs. Slade suggested that they clean out Whitcomb's liquor supply, and eight or ten "liquor-crazed men" set off to carry out her wishes. Fortunately for Whitcomb, one of the Overland employees raced to his store ahead of the others and warned him of the danger, whereupon Whitcomb and his lone employee grabbed their overcoats and headed for the brush.

As with the earlier effort to "clean out" John Sarah for harboring a killer, this effort to clean out Whitcomb's liquor supply got out of hand. Slade's men burned Whitcomb's house to the ground, destroying all of his possessions (except for a few horses and cattle grazing miles away) but managing to save two half-barrels of whiskey and a box of tobacco. These they carted to Slade's station, where they consumed one of the half-barrels and emptied the other one into the well. In this inebriated state, one of the men suggested that they burn down the Horseshoe station itself, and another seized a firebrand and started toward the haystacks, which were connected to the stables and other outbuildings.

By this time Mrs. Slade—terrified by the events she had set in motion—hit on the idea of telegraphing her husband at Julesburg to apprise him of the situation and asking him to return as soon as possible. Then she armed herself with a pistol, kicked over the whiskey barrel, announced that her husband was on his way, and threatened to shoot the first man who approached her. "This determined action on her part," Whitcomb said later, "immediately put a damper on the enthusiasm of the men."

Of course Mrs. Slade was bluffing. Slade was not on the way; he was some 225 miles to the southeast, a good two days' ride. But the men were none the wiser. Their leader, Frank McCarty—the same McCarty who the previous spring had brazenly shot holes in the flag at Fort Laramie—threatened to kill Slade. And, indeed, for the next few days McCarty met every arriving coach, armed with a shotgun in order to shoot Slade as he stepped off.

By this time the men, McCarty included, had sobered up and "become extremely penitent," Whitcomb said. "McCarty promised me that thereafter all the money he could scrape together would be paid to me until I recovered my losses," but "as the men were paid only once or twice a year, they forgot their promises."

When Slade returned to Horseshoe, according to Whitcomb, "he was very indignant. He sent for me and talked the matter over." Whitcomb's books and accounts had been destroyed in the fire, but he figured his loss at $4,000—a large amount at a time when Slade's own salary was only $900 a year. As a result, Whitcomb said, "He discharged every man who was implicated in the affair and offered to help me in any way he could. I prevailed upon him to withdraw his order to discharge the men, as I considered their discharge would do me no good and do them much harm. Therefore, he retained them in his employ on condition that in the future they be on their good behavior. Slade never knew of his wife's agency in the affair unless she acknowledged it."[105]

As Slade surely must have known, a pledge of good behavior was worth very little in the face of the temptations posed by liquor. A few months later the same group, led by McCarty, surprised two freighters camping at Mud Springs, northwest of Julesburg, and drove them off. The freighters' wagons were loaded with whiskey to be distributed to the ranches and trading posts along the route. After working themselves up with a few drinks, McCarty and his men proceeded to steal one wagon's entire liquor supply.[106]

These incidents help explain why settlers and travelers were often unable to distinguish between the outlaw gangs and what Whitcomb called "the lawless character" of "the average employee of the stage company."[107] Yet in this world of flawed and fallible men, a single manifestly flawed individual managed to stand out. James Wilson, the telegraph operator at Horseshoe that fall, recalled that "As customary in those days, when the stage pulled up we were greeted by a large portion of the population—ex-Pony Express riders, stage drivers, stock men, express messengers, mule skinners, gamblers and adventurers of every kind, with the usual mixture of half- and quarter-breeds (Sioux and French)." In this crowd, Wilson added, Slade was "easily discernible—a rather short, stoutly built man" who "combined the chin of a desperado with the head of a Napoleon."[108]

Ben Holladay, the supposed "Napoleon of the West," had told Slade to "get that fellow Jules, and let everyone know you got him"—and now, having dispatched his rival, Slade himself was acclaimed as a Napoleon, even as yet another would-be American Napoleon was rising in the East.

Chapter 14

SURVIVAL

*

The news carried by the telegraph as 1861 wore on was increasingly grim. Lincoln's original call for 75,000 volunteer soldiers had seemed sufficient to smother the South's rebellion in its infancy. But the Civil War's first pitched battle—at Manassas, Virginia, on July 21—turned into a rout of Union forces. After several hours' fighting, Federal troops had panicked and fled 30 miles back to the Potomac.

Congress soon authorized the enlistment of 500,000 three-year volunteers. The dashing young general George McClellan, fresh from a minor victory in western Virginia, was summoned to Washington to organize a new army and then, at the tender age of thirty-four, to succeed Winfield Scott as supreme commander.

Within three months McClellan had organized 100,000 unruly civilians into his glittering Army of the Potomac. He had been expected to open an offensive campaign to capture Richmond, the new Confederate capital, before winter, while the Virginia roads were still hard and dry. But by mid-December McClellan had contracted typhoid fever and was absent from duty for several weeks. When Treasury Secretary Salmon P. Chase warned him that month that funds for the war would run out within two months, McClellan told him not to worry; he would take Richmond before then.

Yet even as he returned to duty, McClellan hesitated to send his army into battle and the public confidence that he had enjoyed only months earlier began to fade. McClellan, Lincoln complained, had a bad case of "the slows."[1] With the aid of the telegraph, the capital's disillusionment quickly spread across the country. This war was likely to be longer and harder than anyone on either side had imagined.

While the "Young Napoleon" McClellan sowed dismay on the Potomac, the "Napoleon of the West" sowed bafflement along the Central Overland route. What, the frontier wondered as 1861 gave way to 1862, was Ben Holladay's game?

Even with a new U.S. mail contract worth $475,000 a year, the Central Overland continued to lose money.[2] Yet Ben Holladay had persisted in investing his time, energy, and capital in the stage line of which he remained technically only a very large creditor. Holladay appeared to be maneuvering to gain full legal control of a corporation that no one else wanted. But for what purpose? He was presumed to know what he was doing. What value did Holladay see in the Central Overland that no one else recognized?

One thing: Ben Holladay's farsighted but also calculating mind perceived that the inevitable coming of a transcontinental railroad would constitute a boon, not a death sentence, for the Western stage-coach business. Such a railroad would exponentially increase the volume of cross-country passenger traffic—and those passengers, for decades to come, would need stagecoaches to go from rail depots to points where no tracks reached.

But such a strategy would work only if Holladay enjoyed maximum control to pursue his vision. To that end he shrewdly reckoned that the very disasters that had plagued his predecessors—the blizzards, the floods, the outlaws, Indians, the financial losses—could be turned to his advantage: They could drive away nervous Central Overland stockholders and potential competitors alike.

Where some people see disaster, others see opportunity. Each new war crisis, Ben Holladay speculated, would leverage his own influence with federal officials, who would need him (and his lifeline to the West's gold and silver) more than he needed them.

Under Holladay's management, the winter weather on the Central Overland route was no more cooperative than it had been for the company's previous owners. In the winter of 1861–62, blinding blizzards and deep snows that one writer called "unprecedented" broke up the stage and mail service for days at a stretch. Coaches sometimes ran a week behind schedule. The spring thaws brought no relief, either. Roads became water-filled ruts of mud and sand, and creeks grew into raging torrents, impossible to ford. Coaches that became mired would have to be unloaded and, with assistance from the passengers, pushed out of the bogs. Slade's time was entirely occupied with getting the coaches through on schedule.[3]

But thanks to the war, the Central Overland no longer confronted competition from any southern mail route. And the blizzards represented the opportunity that Holladay had been waiting for. In February 1862 the stage line was advertised for sale at Atchison, and at the auction on March 21 the company was sold to the highest bidder: Ben Holladay. The man who had been the Central Overland's primary lender for the previous three years and its de facto boss for the past year was now its actual owner, free and clear.[4]

Holladay's first test occurred the very month he became the Central Overland's sole owner. At the time, General McClellan and his grandiloquent Army of the Potomac had not even left Washington. McClellan did not launch his ambitious Peninsula campaign in Virginia until late March 1862; and although his force vastly outnumbered the smaller Confederate army of Robert E. Lee, McClellan failed to capture Richmond as the spring wore on.

The Civil War had already mushroomed into the largest land war ever fought in the Western Hemisphere.[5] The federal government, whose expenses in December 1860 had averaged only $172,000 a day, was spending $1.5 million daily on the war by early 1862. Taxes could cover only about one-fourth of these expenditures; the rest would have to be borrowed, and the Treasury Department hadn't yet found an effective way to market its loans.[6]

In the West, the war had depleted the army of its officers, many of them Southerners who resigned their commissions to join the Confederate army. In addition, whole regiments were withdrawn from the West to serve the army's needs in the war's main theater of operations, the East. All but a half-dozen companies of regular troops were drained from the military posts along the Central Overland's route. Small garrisons remained at Fort Kearny and Fort Laramie, but responsibility for protecting settlers and emigrants from hostile Indians was largely turned over to state militias. In the territories west of Kansas, not yet organized into states, citizen militias were haphazard or nonexistent.[7] In practice, as a Central Overland superintendent later testified, this meant that "no military protection was offered whatever between Salt Lake City and Fort Laramie."[8]

Yet the enemy in the West—an enemy of Washington's own making—remained after the soldiers withdrew. Unlike the Confederacy, which fought for the dubious cause of slavery, the Indians had nursed legitimate grievances against white Americans and their government for more than a decade.

Northwest of Fort Laramie, as Ben Holladay noted, the Central Overland's stage line ran "through a mountainous country, with fine grass and water, and full of game, a great hunting region for several tribes of Indians, all refusing to sell or treat with the government."[9] From the north and east, the Sioux regularly sent hunting parties far into Slade's Sweetwater and South Pass country. The Crows, who were otherwise peacefully disposed toward the whites, came down regularly from the north to find horses, whether the owners were white or red. The Shoshones, whose wise chief Washakie had cooperated with the whites, ranged as far south and west as Fort Bridger. The Arapahoes, who had signed no treaty, sent hunting and horse-stealing parties of their own.[10]

As late as 1858 the subsequent Central Overland paymaster David Street had crossed the plains from the Missouri River to Salt Lake City in a party of no more than ten men and sometimes as few as two, without disturbance. "We saw many Indians," he later recalled, "but all were perfectly friendly."[11] But now that the soldiers were withdrawing, resistance to whites was no longer futile; and Southern sympathizers were encouraging the Indians to rise up in revolt. Observant men noticed in the early spring of 1862 that the Plains Indians were acquiring more firearms and horses.[12] The white man, the Indians now believed, was in retreat from the West; here was the moment to hasten his departure. The Central Overland route, Ben Holladay later reflected, had "little open country; Indians could drop on a station or coach without a moment's warning."[13] Thus Slade's division on the Central Overland became the Indians' most visible and logical target.

Between March 15, 1862, and the end of April several bands of Indians repeatedly struck Central Overland stations, driving off stock, wrecking stations, and destroying hay and grain over a broad front that extended for some 250 miles from Horse Creek station in the east to Muddy Creek station, halfway between Pacific Springs and Salt Lake City.

After attacking Dry Sandy, far to the west of Slade's division, on March 15, the Sioux, or possibly the Snake Indians, first struck Slade's division on March 23 at Horse Creek station, some 130 miles west of Horseshoe, where they drove off five horses and eighteen mules. The station keeper, Dwight Fisk, attributed his survival to his being a sound sleeper: when the Indians surrounded his corral, he failed to wake up.[14]

A week later and 40 miles to the east, Indians raided the Platte Bridge station west of Horseshoe, driving off thirteen mules. Red Buttes, the station immediately west of Platte Bridge, was attacked on April 1, with a loss of fifteen mules and horses.

As the Indians had hoped, the attacks disrupted the stagecoach schedule as the division agents scrambled to replace their stolen stock and man their vulnerable stations. In desperation, the division superintendents telegraphed for help to Isaac Eaton, the line's route superintendent from Atchison to Salt Lake. Eaton ordered them to operate double coaches over the line's most exposed stretches, loaded with extra well-armed men. On April 18 Eaton persuaded Brigadier General James Craig to proclaim martial law along the route and mobilize his available troops, which amounted to only half a regiment.[15] But by that date the Indians had inflicted far more serious damage.

On April 16, as Eaton had instructed, a pair of westbound coaches set out from Sweetwater Bridge, the westernmost station in Slade's reconstituted division. Aboard were nine armed men, including the new agent for the adjacent division, Lemuel Flowers; his predecessor,

William A. Reid; and one stranded passenger. With incomplete teams pulling the heavy loads through a blowing snowstorm, the two coaches made only 12 miles to the next stop—Plante's station, the scene of Slade's capture of Bartholomew's killers the previous summer. Here the party put up for the night.

The next morning, despite the storm, they pushed on to Split Rock, to find that Indians had driven off the stock, killed two men, and left the station deserted. Some four miles farther on, a whooping swarm of Indians burst upon the tandem coaches from ambush. The initial volley of fire sent a ball through the breast of the lead driver, Arthur Stephenson. The remaining crewmembers whipped the coaches up to a side-by-side position, cut loose the frantic mules, and threw every movable object between the wheels to create a breastworks. In rapid succession, five more men fell wounded, including agent Flowers, who took two shots through the hips, and former agent Reid, who was shot in the back. Nevertheless, the stage men were able to fight back with the multiple six-shooters they had brought for just such an emergency.

Not until 4 P.M. did the Indians withdraw, after a four-hour battle. All nine of the stage men were still alive, but some were barely able to walk. Without mules to transport them, the survivors limped and carried each other eight more miles to the next station, at Three Crossings of the Sweetwater. Here they learned from the station keeper and his wife that the Three Crossings station had just been raided the previous day, with a loss of twenty-two mules and horses, ten sets of stage harness, and three head of oxen.[16] Plante's station, where the stage crew had stayed the night of April 16, was raided on the eighteenth, with a loss of five mules, four horses, and twenty sets of harness. That same day at Sweetwater Bridge, eight horses and mules were stampeded.

Over the next six days Indian raiders thought to be Sioux struck Central Overland stations at Split Rock, Ice Springs, and Red Buttes, driving off more animals and wrecking the stations. At Green River station on the twenty-third—west of Flowers's division—a raid by twenty-four Snakes or Arapahoes burned the building, drove off five horses, destroyed grain sacks and harnesses, and killed the station keeper, John Maloy.[17] At Red Buttes station, Slade had barely replaced the fifteen horses and mules driven off on April 1 when the Indians returned again on April 24, taking six more mules and horses.

With that attack, travel on the Central Overland was temporarily halted altogether.[18] Nearly three weeks passed before the wounded men from Lemuel Flowers's tandem stage party could be conveyed to Fort Bridger for medical care.[19] Westbound mail was held up at Julesburg, so that by early June the undelivered mail sacks filled a warehouse there.[20]

In a matter of weeks a 300-mile stretch of the Central Overland had effectively been destroyed. Even the telegraph line, once taboo to superstitious Indians, had been severed repeatedly as the emboldened Indians recognized the line as a means of white communication.[21] By Slade's calculation, the total property loss from these five raids exceeded $12,000 on his division alone.[22] Many stations that hadn't been attacked had been abandoned by employees fearful of future raids.[23] Those station keepers between Julesburg and Green River who remained at their posts were ordered to bury all their provisions, including the U.S. Mail, to protect them from further attacks.[24] Some terrified settlers fled in haste without taking or burying any personal belongings as they sought refuge at Fort Laramie or Fort Bridger.[25]

Ben Holladay was fortuitously in Washington that spring and personally appealed to the government for military protection. A meeting with Postmaster General Montgomery Blair led to a meeting with Secretary of War Edwin Stanton, and in due course Holladay found himself at the White House, making his case to Lincoln. The meeting occurred at one of the darkest points of the Civil War: McClellan had finally launched his ambitious Peninsula campaign but still had not captured Richmond.

"Mr. Holladay, you must have protection," the president told him, according to Holladay's later recollection. "The mails must be carried."[26]

Holladay suggested that, since military posts in the West were so scattered and undermanned, Lincoln should ask Brigham Young in Salt Lake City to raise Mormon soldiers to protect the line. This was an audacious request—the federal government had waged war against

Young's Mormon militia barely four years earlier—but these were different times, and Lincoln promised to push the matter. By May 1, Brigham Young had agreed to equip a company of Mormon cavalry for ninety days' service to protect the telegraph and stage lines.[27]

But before leaving Washington, Ben Holladay bargained for a benefit that he probably coveted more than military protection: permission to move his line to a more profitable route hundreds of miles to the south. Here again Holladay sought to turn adversity to his advantage. The Indian depredations had handed him an excuse to do something he had wanted to do long before a single Indian had attacked a station.

The Central Overland, like the Jones & Russell stage line before it, used the old Overland route along the North Platte River only because that route was mandated by the federal mail contract. And the Post Office mandated that route only because the U.S. Overland Wagon Road had been built along that route in 1857 (by William Magraw and Ben Ficklin, among others). That Overland Trail route along the North Platte through South Pass, in turn, had been chosen for the federal road because, in its previous incarnations as the Oregon Trail and the Mormon Trail, it had become the most trafficked road to the far west. But that was no longer the case since gold had been discovered near Pike's Peak, well to the south. Nearly twelve years earlier Holladay had found a shorter and more southerly route to California, sometimes called the Cherokee Trail, that led through the Bridger Pass and Bitter Creek.

"There was no road," Ben Holladay later recalled, "except an Indian lodgepole trail for 250 miles, no grass and bad water; but it was an open country, and I believed there would be less Indian troubles."[28] Even a year before the Indian troubles, Holladay had considered moving his main line south, especially after May 1861, when Captain E. L. Berthoud discovered the Berthoud Pass through a formidable barrier of the Rockies west of Denver.[29] By following the South Platte rather than the North Platte from Julesburg, Holladay could reduce the distance between Julesburg and Salt Lake City by some 150 miles.[30] And doing so would move his main line closer to Denver, now an important destination. If Holladay could relocate his main route south through the newly created territory of Colorado, he might not need to operate his existing spur line to Denver along the South Platte from Julesburg. Instead he could send cross-country stages bound for Salt Lake and California directly through the Pike's Peak gold country.

But this was not the argument Ben Holladay broached to Postmaster General Blair after his meeting with Lincoln. Instead, Holladay couched his case for a new route in terms of the Central Overland's need to avoid rampaging Indians. As Holladay anticipated, Blair was in no position to dictate terms. The mails must go to the Pacific, Blair told Holladay; if not by one road, try another.[31] The government granted him *both* military protection and the right to shift his route.

Following this meeting, Holladay proceeded westward to inspect the damage from the Indian raids personally. At Fort Laramie late in May, he and the line's paymaster, David Street, were joined by General Craig. Farther up the line at Horseshoe station, Slade received word on the last day of May to remain there until Holladay's party arrived. Within a few days Holladay's group arrived, and together the four men proceeded west across what remained of Slade's division, hoping to join a detachment of Craig's soldiers who had been sent out in advance.

It was on this journey that Holladay first informed Slade that he was contemplating relocating the line to a more southern route through the Rockies. Holladay had already dispatched an exploration party under John Kerr, just a few weeks earlier, from Denver via the Cherokee Trail, with instructions to assess the route's possibilities and report to Holladay at the end of their respective tours, in Salt Lake City.[32] In this manner Slade was notified that the extensive fiefdom he had constructed, supervised, and protected over the previous three years, often risking his life as well as those of countless others, was about to be permanently abandoned.

How Slade took this news was not recorded. But as the party proceeded westward, the devastation they encountered suggested that the decision to abandon the line was not Holladay's or Slade's to make; Slade's division had effectively been forsaken already. From Horseshoe to Ham's Fork, only a few stations and road ranches were still occupied. Those that were deserted had been ransacked and, in some cases, burned to the ground.

The persistence of danger was made clear at the upper crossing of the Sweetwater, some 150 miles west of Horseshoe, where the Holladay party found General Craig's soldiers preparing to fight a band of Indians, who retreated only after a standoff of several hours. Near Split Rock, another 22 miles farther west—where Lemuel Flowers and his crew had fought their pitched battle with Indians in April—the party found the Flowers party's two abandoned stage-coaches, riddled with bullets and arrows. Not until they reached South Pass, about 250 miles west of Horseshoe, did the party find horses or mules in any corral along the road.[33]

As Street later recalled the scene they encountered,

> we found the stage line in a disorganized condition; stations and property abandoned. The employees had taken the stock, coach-es and such property as they could haul in them to places which afforded the most security from Indian attacks, or in stage phrase-ology had "bunched the stock." We found mail matter strewn in and about the station, in some places to the depth of a foot or more, where the Indians had emptied it in order to get the mail bags. It was about three or four weeks after the last raid of the Indians on the line. . . . The employees were excited and alarmed, for the Indians were known to be still in the vicinity. . . . The only troops we saw between Fort Laramie and South Pass was a small detachment of cavalry under Lieutenant Wilcox, at the last cross-ing of [the] Sweetwater. General Craig left us at South Pass, and admitted that with the small force of troops at his disposal he could not protect the stage line for such a distance.[34]

At the end of the inspection tour, Ben Holladay continued on to Salt Lake City, where as planned he received Kerr's report on the fea-sibility of operating stages on the Cherokee Trail to the south. "A full interview with him and examination of his notes convinced me I was right," Holladay later recalled, "and unless we moved that portion of the route, with the stock and entire outfit, between Julesburg and Green River, over to the Bridger Pass trail, the overland mail would be a failure."[35]

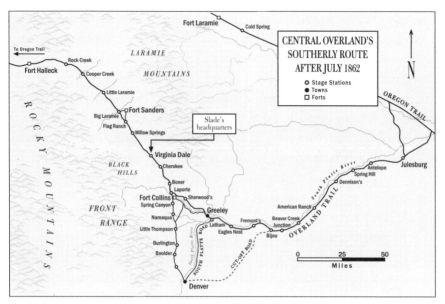

Holladay's new southerly route through Colorado Territory, launched in the summer of 1862.

One problem remained for Holladay: Although Postmaster General Blair had allowed him a free hand in choosing his new mail route, Blair had granted him a lapse of only twenty days' service in which to make the changeover.[36] Thus having decided to change routes, Holladay immediately issued two sets of orders from Salt Lake City.

On the one hand, Slade and the agents of the two other immobilized divisions to his west—Flowers and James E. Bromley—were directed to repair and staff the abandoned stations as quickly as possible in order to resume operations. Slade was told to gather all the mail strewn about the plains and return it to Julesburg until the stage schedule could resume. In effect Slade and his fellow division agents were asked to perform the thankless and seemingly pointless task of reviving a line that faced imminent abandonment. Yet revive it they did, and by the middle of June the stages were operating once again.[37]

On the other hand, Holladay immediately sent the explorer John Kerr and his party back to the Cherokee Trail, this time equipped with tents, stakes, and instructions to locate stations along the way.

Holladay hired mechanics, laborers, and teams of mules; stocked supplies, lumber, and building materials; and directed Kerr's men to begin constructing stations and roads at once.[38]

At the same time that Slade was cleaning up and restoring his division on the North Platte route, he was appointed division agent for the portion of the new line running from Latham, northeast of Denver, to the crossing of the North Platte River just beyond Elk Mountain, 226 miles northwest of Latham. This was the stretch that ran closest to Denver. But the two stations nearest to Denver—Latham and Laporte—were sparsely populated, like much of the country through which Slade's new division ran. At Latham the stage station was the only house for at least two years thereafter—a one-and-a-half-story log building with a large frame addition on the north side, comprising a bedroom, kitchen, dining room, and storehouse. The village of Laporte was more reminiscent of Julesburg, consisting of a handful of homes and several saloons, and even a brewery.[39]

Slade rejected both of these places for his new headquarters and searched instead for a more central location within his division. In the mountains some 100 miles northwest of Denver he came upon a magical little hidden valley—the sort of place capable of stirring visitors into rhapsodic effusions.[40]

Here, near a charming creek and surrounded by breathtaking mountain vistas, Slade hired a contractor to build a station—and not just any station. The long, one-story main building was constructed from hand-hewn logs using an uncommon mortise and tenon technique, brought to the U.S. by French fur trappers who built their cabins along the Rocky Mountain creeks in this manner. The building was divided into three parts, with vertical posts mortised into the end logs to separate each section. The east and center sections were clapboarded and had an open shed-roofed porch on each end. Shingles for the roof were freighted in from St. Joseph, Missouri, some 700 miles away, at the exorbitant cost of $1.50 per pound. A large stone chimney was attached to the east wall, with a six-by-six pane window to one side.[41]

To the east of the station stood a high hill where a man perched on the summit could simultaneously see the plains for miles to the east, the station below to the west, and the approaching stage road to the

In an idyllic hidden valley, Slade built his new division headquarters and named it Virginia Dale, for his wife. The livery barn is in the foreground; the station house to the rear, where the Slades lived, still stands. This photo was taken in 1870, two years after the station was abandoned. (*Denver Public Library*)

northwest; here Slade commissioned a stone lookout where he kept a watchman most of the time to warn against Indians or outlaws.[42]

Clearly, Slade gave great thought to this complex of station house, stage stables, and outbuildings, as if he intended to remain here for a long time. He christened the station Virginia Dale, in honor of his wife.[43] The creek had already been named Dale Creek, whether by Slade or someone else is unclear.[44]

On July 8, barely three weeks after service on the North Platte line was restored, Slade and his fellow superintendents received Ben Holladay's official notification that the North Platte route between Julesburg and Green River—a distance of nearly 700 miles—was to be permanently abandoned in favor of the South Platte and Cherokee Trail to the south (even though the telegraph line remained on the North Platte route).[45] All the livestock and equipment that Slade had been told a month earlier to replenish on the North Platte route— including about 350 horses and mules, as well as some cattle—was now to be removed, as quickly as possible, to the Cherokee Trail. The twenty-six functioning stage stations along the old route, estimated to have cost $25,000 to build, were to be left behind, as well as a large supply of grain also valued at $25,000. Slade's entire complex at Horseshoe station—the blacksmith shop, coach shops, harness shops, warehouses, lodging houses, offices, and corrals—was to be shut down.[46] On the new line, station employees would live and work in temporary huts and tents until permanent stations were built. All this was to be done, Holladay emphasized, "without interfering with the regular schedule time of the mails."[47]

Barely had Slade launched this Herculean task when he and the Central Overland confronted another crisis of an entirely different nature. The *Silver Age,* a newspaper in Carson City, Nevada Territory, published a series of items attacking the Central Overland and its employees, especially Slade. Its report was approvingly summarized by the *Deseret News*, the Mormon organ in Salt Lake City, on July 16:

TELLING TRUTHS

The *Silver Age* has, of late, been commenting upon and giving some historical relations in reference to certain employees and station-keepers of the Overland Mail Company, eastward from Great Salt Lake City, holding them up to public view in no enviable light. Among the prominent characters thus referred to are J.H. [sic] Slade, Division Agent, and Thomas Miles, station-keeper at La Bonte. The former of these notables, as alleged, killed, by shooting and hanging, about twenty persons within the last year, and committed divers other actions and deeds, rendering him the terror of all the settlers between Pacific Springs and Julesburg, and the dislike of all the drivers and employees on that division of the road. Several of his bloody deeds are related, which correspond with the reports circulated here at the time, or shortly after those tragic occurrences. . . .

How much truth there may be in the statements made by our contemporary concerning the attachees in question, and the management of affairs on the eastern end of the Overland route, from the commencement up to recent date, we do not pretend to know, further than that they are in strict accordance with the various reports that have gained publicity, and generally believed to be true. The publishment of the facts, as understood, will not, in our opinion, impair the character of the *Age* for truth and veracity, and when it states that there is more to be feared from the white desperadoes who infest the Overland route than from the natives, no apprehensions need be entertained of successful contradiction.[48]

A reader removed from that time and place may recognize instantly the circularity of the editor's reasoning. The publication by the *Silver Age* of tales that had circulated widely in Salt Lake and were "generally believed to be true" effectively confirmed their accuracy. If a story transmitted orally along the Overland route appeared in print, then its validity was assumed, and its re-publication in the *Deseret News* further ensured its validity.

Ben Holladay, who had always grasped the importance of public confidence to his line, had perceived the danger of such published reports. That was why he took the trouble to visit the editor of the *Silver Age* (and possibly editors in Salt Lake City and Denver who picked up those reports) to deny this portrayal of Slade.[49] His protest to the newspaper surely reflected the high value he placed on Slade's services.

Slade himself did not respond to these articles—perhaps because he was preoccupied with the changeover to his new division; perhaps because courtrooms and newspaper columns were unfamiliar arenas to him. But there may have been another reason as well for Slade's silence. In some corner of his mind he perhaps perceived that the editorials, by reinforcing his terrifying image, enhanced his effectiveness as a peacekeeper.

In any case, the press in mail-starved California took a very different perspective on Slade and the Central Overland. The *San Francisco Bulletin* that year praised the mail service from the East, noting that the mail from Atchison usually went through in seventeen days, much faster than the twenty-three allowed by the U.S. Mail contract.[50] A month after Slade was attacked by the *Deseret News*, a correspondent from Salt Lake who previously had often complained about the eastern mail took the opportunity to set the record straight in a lengthy dispatch that the *Sacramento Daily Union* published on its front page. The trouble, wrote the pseudonymous correspondent "Liberal" on

August 7, lay not with the Central Overland but with outlaws, and Slade was not the problem but the cure.

Although the correspondent hadn't met Slade personally, he provided a second-hand evaluation of "this little terror of the Plains":

> He has friends as well as enemies—considerably of the former, notwithstanding that he has passed a few over Jordan. . . . The Agent is represented unassuming, attentive to his business, of few words, not ungentlemanly or uncourteous to strangers, on hand where he should be and never calculates to be over "crowded." Those under his direction and the other agents speak well of him, acknowledging, however, that he is somewhat fast and fiery, a hard customer when he "takes a twist" [i.e., when he drinks], and not infallible in action under that peculiar mood. He carries a certain amount of powder and lead outside, and has quite a decent dose of the latter beneath the skin.

After recounting Slade's feud with Jules Beni and Jules's subsequent death, the correspondent rendered judgment:

> Some four or five others "went up" on one occasion under Slade's supervision, after making a clean breast of the murders they had committed on the road—murders for money, and horse stealing without number. The partisan feeling growing out of these matters has made a notoriety for the agent, and his friends make him a hero and scourge to thieves and murderers; his enemies paint him in some other colors. . . . But if he never does worse than hang and shoot the crowd of blacklegs who infest the plains, we shall never vote for his dismissal from service, and I think it will be some time before Ben [Holladay] gratifies anybody with his discharge from that division. If there is any virtue in hoping, I should really hope to see half a dozen Slades on the eastern line with carte blanche to treat every thief as a Secessionist.[51]

In one court of public opinion, at least, Slade had been vindicated. The *Deseret News* never retracted its attack on Slade, but neither did it publish any further criticism.

By the end of July 1862, Slade had transferred all the livestock on his division to the new line. He had also placed all of his old division's wagons and coaches on the new line. Daily mail service along the new route began on July 21, even before most stations were ready.[52] By July 27 the new road was stocked.[53]

At the same time, the Army opened Fort Halleck at the base of Elk Mountain and within Slade's division, some 75 miles northwest of Virginia Dale, to furnish protection along Holladay's new route.[54] Two days later a company of cavalry settled in at Laporte, just 30 miles south of Slade's new Virginia Dale headquarters.[55] On July 31 Ben Holladay's agent John Kerr arrived in Salt Lake City after testing the stagecoach journey over the Cherokee Trail and told Holladay that the new line was ready to start.[56] On August 11 the Overland's coaches were carrying passengers regularly.[57]

The new route still required Holladay to service Denver via a tri-weekly branch line. But at roughly this time, the Colorado territorial legislature made a main line through Denver more feasible by granting the Central Overland the right to build toll bridges and operate ferries along its route.[58] By early September, an exuberant Ben Holladay made the trip from Salt Lake City east to Latham in just four days. He proceeded on to Atchison, where he wrote an open letter to the editor of the *Rocky Mountain News* in Denver. In it Holladay thanked the Colorado legislature and the territory's citizens for their support of his new route. Then he announced: "In view of these facts I have instructed my agents to change the route from the present course to one bearing via Denver to Laporte, so that hereafter you will have the great through mails passing direct through your city."[59]

D enver had been an important settlement from the moment gold was discovered on Pike's Peak in 1858, and the town had continued to grow ever since. By 1863 it would claim 5,000 inhabitants, five brick stores, four churches, a school, a U.S. mint, two banks, two theaters, three daily newspapers, and many gambling houses. Next to Salt Lake City it was now the largest town between the Missouri River and California—larger even than St. Joseph or Atchison.[60] The new route announced by Ben Holladay looped southwest from Latham some 40 miles down the South Platte to Denver, then looped northwest some 60 miles to Laporte before proceeding on from there to Virginia Dale and Green River and then intersecting with the old line at Fort Bridger. Even with this diversion, the new route was still some 50 miles shorter to Salt Lake than the old one—and of course it passed through Denver as well. With Holladay's announcement of the route change, this promising community now fell into Slade's domain.

Denver's euphoria over Ben Holladay's new route was exceeded only by local astonishment at the speed with which the change had been effected. After riding the stage from Denver to Salt Lake, a *Rocky Mountain News* editor named Edward Bliss paid tribute to "the admirable condition and excellent management of Ben Holladay's Overland Stage Line," and marveled that within one summer

> an entire new and before untraveled road was opened from this city through Bridger's Pass; stations at intervals of from twelve to fifteen miles [were] erected on a route extending nearly three hundred miles; and an immense amount of stock and material [was] transferred from the old Northern route, without interfering with the regular daily transit of the mail coach. . . . We are now on the direct line of the great Overland Mail Route, and a fresh impetus to our business and enterprise is already manifest. No stage line in the world is more systematically and admirably managed than that between Denver and Salt Lake. The stock is in excellent condition, the stations comfortable and convenient, and the time schedule most punctually adhered to throughout.[61]

How could a division agent like Slade have supervised the scouring of 350 miles of his old line for lost mail and equipment while simultaneously scouring 226 miles of his new division for station sites? How did Slade elicit such a heroic performance from the same group of roughnecks who had burned down Elias Whitcomb's store the previous fall and murdered John Sarah's family eighteen months earlier?

To Holladay's biographer, "The fact that the stage company did not break its regular schedule of mails in making a change of route is further evidence of Holladay's executive ability."[62] To Edward Bliss, at

Denver (shown above in 1860) began as a mining camp in 1858. By 1862, when it fell within Slade's new domain, it was the second largest town between the Missouri River and California. Note the saloon on the left. (*Denver Public Library*)

the *Rocky Mountain News*, it was a reflection of "the enterprise, determination and vigor of the man who planned and prosecuted this great work."63 Holladay did indeed demand the impossible of his men. But the Central Overland driver Frank Root contended that the credit belonged to the men who delivered Holladay the impossible.

> With all the money at the back of the great stage line, and the untiring push and energy of Ben Holladay, it is believed he would not have made a success of the enterprise except for the efficiency and fidelity of the men he drew around him. His managers and superintendents, agents and messengers, with few exceptions, were capable, efficient, and honest. His drivers and stock tenders were the best. No storms nor dangers seemed to daunt them. It appeared marvelous at the time, and many who made the long ride across the continent have often wondered since what it was that inspired them. Their lives were frequently in peril. Apparently they knew no fear. Evidently there was some incentive that induced those men to face so many dangers.64

As the summer of 1862 gave way to fall, both Ben Holladay and his most famous division agent had reason to believe they had turned a corner. Their stage line had survived the Indian raids of the spring and now seemed on a stable footing at last. Holladay had the safer, shorter, and more lucrative main mail route through Denver that he had always coveted. The army was committed to protecting it.

The Union's fortunes in the Civil War had taken a turn for the better as well. At Sharpsburg in western Maryland on September 17, McClellan's Army of the Potomac had finally stood up to Lee's invading Army of Northern Virginia. The battle of Antietam Creek, as it was called, was the bloodiest day of the war and not so much a victory as a stalemate: McClellan failed to pursue Lee's reeling army, instead allowing the exhausted Confederates to slip virtually unmolested across the Potomac into Virginia. But for the first time in the war, an advancing Confederate force had been halted. As a result, European nations dependent on Southern cotton would think twice before recognizing the Confederacy or providing support for the South. It now seemed likely that the Union would survive, and so would the Central Overland.

At Virginia Dale, meanwhile, Slade had added an unexpected asset to the stage line's barren and ugly surroundings: an oasis of natural beauty in the desert. Virginia Dale, once exposed to Central Overland travelers, became a favorite camping place, where freighters and emigrants paused for days to rest their stock. "It was not unusual," wrote the son of one Colorado pioneer, "to see from fifty to a hundred canvas-covered wagons with their loads of merchandise and freight camped at the Dale."[65] Where once travelers passing through Slade's old headquarters had mainly recalled Slade's "eyes that pierce" (as Sir Richard Burton put it in 1860), now they marveled that the superintendent had chosen this idyllic spot. Hard-boiled Overland employees lowered their voices reverently when they mentioned what one of them called this "beautiful and romantic spot on Dale Creek."[66] Within just a few years Virginia Dale's fame was spread across the country and even to Europe by magazine writers and newspaper correspondents who passed through as Overland stage passengers.[67]

In such a tranquil refuge, with no more worlds to conquer, with his operation running smoothly, with idle time on his hands, an outwardly impenetrable man like Slade might rediscover the civilized gentleman hidden beneath his rough façade. But how would a man who thrived on crises respond when there were no more crises to manage?

PART IV

*

Purgatory

A downtown street in Salt Lake City in the late 1860s. From its founding in 1847, this Mormon enclave became a central stopping place for all travelers, if only by virtue of its status as the largest town between the Missouri River and the Pacific. (*Library of Congress*)

Chapter 15

THE BREAKING POINT

✳

By the fall of 1862 the Central Overland California & Pike's Peak
Express Company had a new southern route, a new name—the
Overland Stage Company—and a relatively smooth new operation.[1]
Stages departing daily from Atchison regularly made the journey to
Salt Lake in just eleven days and a few hours.[2] New station buildings
had replaced the summer's makeshift tents. Soldiers based at the new
Fort Halleck patrolled the new route, even though Indians rarely ven-
tured that far south.

All resistance to Slade's authority had crumbled. The previous
spring's Indian raids, the threats from the outlaw gangs beyond Rocky
Ridge, the exhausting pressure of the Pony Express experiment,
Slade's long humiliation at the hands of Jules Beni, the stage line that
was once dubbed "Clean Out of Cash & Poor Pay"—all these travails
now receded into distant memory. With the Union capture of New
Orleans on May 1 and Union forces in control of Missouri and Kansas,
even the war—still raging in the East, but largely quiescent west of the
Mississippi—seemed a thing of the past from Slade's peaceful aerie at
Virginia Dale.

At the age of thirty-one, Slade seemed at last to have put his years
of perpetual risk-taking behind him. All that was required of him now
was to tend to a division agent's customary duties. And therein lay the
problem, for Slade's years on the North Platte line had addicted him
to excitement and inured him to danger.

The very absence of adversity imposed a new and peculiar burden upon Slade. His effectiveness for the stage company relied to some extent on the fearsome legend that had been created around him—a legend that Slade, in some corner of his mind, had come to believe. For the enforcer once known as "the law west of Kearny," it would not do to quietly accept the bland image of a company manager consigned to domestic life in a picturesque valley with his devoted wife and adopted son. The old legend needed to be perpetuated.

In short order some of Slade's routine duties became adventures in themselves. On his inspection trips between Virginia Dale and Denver, when the stage would stop for a change of horses, Slade developed the habit of inviting the passengers inside the station for a drink with him. While the drinks were being prepared, he would regale his guests with stories of his exploits.

On these occasions Slade was usually accompanied and encouraged by one or two of his Overland Stage Company employees, who in these situations functioned as his adoring claque. His most prominent props were his Colt revolver—which he often flourished and occasionally discharged—and Jules Beni's dried ears, which Slade usually carried as a watch-charm or inside his pocket. As a stunt, he developed the practice of buying a drink, reaching into his pocket and offering one of Jules's ears as payment, to the astonishment of his wide-eyed audience.[3] A bullwhacker passing through Virginia Dale that fall remarked that he had seen Slade, "in fine fettle," entertaining an emigrant's daughter by putting a few pebbles in one of Jules's dried ears and giving it to the little girl as a rattle, much to her glee.[4]

In theory these stunts were harmless enough and perhaps even endearing to impressionable travelers from "the States." Slade was a gregarious companion and an engaging storyteller, and alcohol was the common currency among virtually all sociable men in the West. The problem with Slade's new putative role as a celebrity superintendent was the same trouble that had plagued him since the days when his freighting runs ended in the saloons of Atchison and Leavenworth: his inability to hold his liquor.

In the past Slade's periodic drinking binges had remained peripheral to the long, arduous weeks and months he devoted to his work. But now the intervals between sprees grew shorter, while Slade's drunken behavior grew progressively more violent. Previously Slade had been perceived as a fearless and tireless worker who occasionally drank to excess; now, settlers along the Cherokee Trail came to perceive Slade not as the man who cleaned up Julesburg, kept the mails running on time, and discovered Virginia Dale, but as a dangerous drunk who had lost the ability to govern himself. Typical was the first, and lasting, impression Slade made on Frank G. Bartholf, an early settler in the valley of Colorado's Big Thompson Creek and later a Larimer County commissioner:

> I received my first introduction to Slade over on the Little Thompson [creek] at the stage station in the fall of 1862. Slade was coming down over the line from his station at Virginia Dale, and at Laporte he got drunk. Between Laporte and Big Thompson station he began firing down through the top of the coach and the four passengers inside rolled out on the prairie. Slade drove into the Big Thompson station at Mariana's on the dead run, and, going inside, ordered the agent, a man named Boutwell, to make him a cocktail. A loaded shotgun stood in the corner. Slade picked it up and cocking both barrels covered Boutwell with it and ordered the drink mixed in a certain manner. Hardly able to hold anything, his hand shook so, Boutwell did as directed. When he had completed the mixture, Slade ordered him to come from behind the counter and place the glass on the muzzle end of the gun, which he did, the two barrels of the gun staring him in the face all the way.
>
> After pouring the decoction down his throat, Slade mounted the stage and ran the horses over to the Little Thompson station where one of them laid down completely exhausted.
>
> I was keeping the station for my brother-in-law, who had gone up into the hills to bring down his wife. As the stage drove up I went out to unhitch the horses. The driver made some insulting remark to me and I answered him pretty short. Biff! Something struck me across the right eye. I turned quickly and looked straight into the muzzle of two revolvers. I had never seen Slade before but I realized at once that we were introduced.

After I went into the stable he walked over to where a couple of young fellows were camped and threatened to shoot one of their horses and did kill their dog that was quietly lying under the wagon. Then he kicked their coffee pot over, put out their fire and went off. All this time the two fellows with their guns in hand stood and watched him. He had terrorized them and they dared not lift a finger.[5]

As in the past, once Slade had slept off the effects of alcohol he habitually expressed remorse for his boorish behavior and offered to pay the damages. "Usually little attention was paid to Slade and his wild unruly manner," notes a biographer of Mariano Medina, who operated a trading post on the Big Thompson, "because he always paid for any damage he did."[6] After Frank Bartholf's confrontation with Slade at Little Thompson station, Slade wrote him a letter of apology, saying he had mistaken Bartholf for the station agent and that he did not allow any of his agents to "sass him."[7] This capacity, and even eagerness, for remorse and apology set Slade apart from virtually all other men in the West, most of whom considered any expression of regret as a sign of weakness if not outright cowardice.

Also consistent with his past drinking behavior, even when drunk Slade tended to back off when confronted. Although the Colorado pioneer Hal Sayre had founded the saloon settlement of Laporte two years earlier, Sayre himself was "particularly abstemious," as his son later described him: "He never touched alcohol, and even refrained from tea or coffee. He never smoked and ate very little meat. The only vice he seemed to pick up from the early days was profanity." This obsessively temperate man of twenty-seven once spent a night at a small log roadhouse while riding from Laporte to Denver, along Slade's division. Sayre had rolled himself up in his blanket on the floor of the combined office, lobby, and bar when, according to his son, Slade entered with a party and ordered everyone present to take a drink. "Father would have shot it out with him from his recumbent position on the floor," Sayre's son recalled, "had not cooler heads stepped in to urge father to subside, and Slade to let him alone."[8]

On one visit to Mariano Medina's trading post, Slade began acting abusively and destructively. In Medina's absence, his fourteen-year-old son, Antonio, grabbed a rifle and would have pulled the trigger if his mother had not knocked the barrel up toward the ceiling and hastened the boy out of the room.[9]

Slade's posture toward alcohol with his employees was decidedly different. As a stagecoach superintendent, he readily perceived its effects on his stage drivers, some of whom had wrecked their coaches when intoxicated. He prohibited his drivers from drinking on duty, and at least some of his violence when drunk was directed at tavern keepers who persisted in selling liquor to his drivers. For himself, however, he couldn't resist the camaraderie of the Laporte saloons and encouraged his employees to join him. Once he came under liquor's influence he became not the supervisor of his men but their goad.

Of course the carousing opportunities in the settlements along Slade's division were limited. But a larger and more exciting recreational outlet awaited Slade at the southern end of his division in Denver, with some thirty-five saloons and brothels, most of them located within a few blocks of the Overland's stage depot at Fifteenth and Blake Streets.[10] Denver's most essential institution was the saloon: In the town's early years, they doubled as community centers, clubs, hotels, restaurants, bakeries, hospitals, museums, and banks. Denver's first church services and first theater performances were held in drinking halls.[11]

Equally appealing to carousers was Denver's virtual absence of law enforcement. Only three years had passed since the Pike's Peak gold rush of 1859, when the area was still part of Kansas Territory and the nearest organized courts were hundreds of miles to the east. Killings, claim-jumpings, and horse thefts in and around Denver went unpunished until the gold prospectors, farmers, and other settlers created their own impromptu "miners' courts" and "people's courts." These courts benefited from the presence of lawyers who had inevitably joined the hordes of gold-seekers from "the States." But the improvised law dispensed by these courts bore no resemblance to the formal courts back East.

By 1861 the separate Territory of Colorado had been approved by Congress, with territorial district courts and judges appointed by President Lincoln in Washington.[12] Yet in practice these courts still reflected the wild communities they served. As late as 1862 gangs of armed toughs commonly entered Denver restaurants, ate their fill, then walked out without paying, daring the proprietor to challenge them. Stores were robbed in broad daylight; residents were beaten mercilessly by bored hoodlums looking for excitement. In such a place a potential carouser like Slade could get roaring drunk with impunity.[13]

In his days on the Overland Trail and the Central Overland's North Platte route, Slade's behavior had probably been constrained by his distance from other such wide-open towns like Atchison and Salt Lake City. Denver, by contrast, stood less than 100 miles southeast of Virginia Dale and was an important junction within his division, so the temptation to enjoy himself there was no doubt impossible to resist. For his visits to Denver, Slade purchased a beaded and gaudily colored buckskin suit, said to have cost him $750.[14] Here the dimensions of his carousing expanded, and so did the consequences.

One of his favorite entertainments in Denver, according to the Overland Stage official Robert Spotswood, was saloon-wrecking: "He would shatter all the mirrors, drive everybody into the street and then shoot out the lights. Next day he invariably came and apologized, and paid the damages."[15] Slade's outrageous acts further fueled his notoriety and provided another element to the future gunslinger stereotype: shooting up the town.

One night two soldiers on furlough in Denver, holding an impromptu reunion with their former employer, the wagonmaster Alexander Toponce, went out to see the sights. "At one place we met up with Slade, drunk and all dressed up," Toponce later recalled. "When he tried to start some trouble, I, knowing his reputation as a bad man, grabbed him before he could draw his gun, and the three of us threw him out into the street."[16]

On another occasion, the Overland Stage Company's paymaster, David Street, heard that Slade was wrecking a Denver saloon and attempted to intervene. Street was one of the company's senior executives (although he was then only twenty-five) as well as Slade's good friend; he had accompanied Slade and Ben Holladay on their tour of stations raided by Indians that spring, and "there is no doubt that Mr. Street stood highest in Slade's esteem," Robert Spotswood later told an interviewer. Nevertheless, "When Mr. Street arrived, Slade had made a complete wreck of a saloon. Mr. Street tried to induce Slade to leave. Slade, apparently not recognizing him, shot him down, as it happened inflicting a wound that was not dangerous. Next day, when Slade was informed what he had done, he was nearly broken-hearted. He refused to go home until he heard that 'Dave' was on the way to recovery."[17]

Slade's contemporaries and many subsequent historians professed shock or bewilderment over his seemingly sudden degeneration from public protector to pathetic public nuisance, seemingly bent on self-destruction. "Unaccountably, he had by this time become a brawling drunkard," the *Dictionary of American Biography* remarked in 1936.[18] A friend of Slade's offered this explanation: "After years of contention with desperate men, he became so reckless and regardless of human life that his best friends must concede that he was at times a most dangerous character."[19]

Yet Slade was hardly the first man to break under the pressures of the overland transportation business. John Jones, William Russell's partner in the Leavenworth & Pike's Peak Express Company, had resigned as general superintendent of that line after just three months on the job. His successor, Beverly Williams, lasted less than six months. Ben Ficklin, the celebrated man of action who launched the Pony Express, impulsively threw up his hands and quit after less than nine months as the Pony's general superintendent. J. H. Clute, Ficklin's highly regarded successor, lasted twenty-one months at most.[20] William Russell—the "Napoleon of the West" himself—was driven to such financial desperation that he landed in jail for fraud. So distressed was Jerome B. Simpson, the Central Overland's vice president and New York agent on whom Russell had relied heavily for raising money via the tainted bonds, that he stopped eating and suffered such a loss of weight in the summer of 1860 that his physician, fearing he would die, ordered him to the south of France for two or three months' rest.[21] William Magraw similarly cracked after losing both his mail contract in 1856 and his contract to build the government's wagon road to Salt Lake in 1857, irrationally blaming his misfortune on the road project's chief engineer, Frederick West Lander. When the two men subsequently met at Willard's Hotel in Washington, Magraw struck Lander three times with a billy club, and on their next accidental encounter—at the Kirkwood Hotel in the spring of 1860—Magraw drew a pistol, and a violent scuffle ensued.[22]

John Hockaday—whose ambitious empire, as late as April 1859, comprised a stagecoach line with a U.S. Mail contract, an overland freighting concern, and a major dry goods store in Salt Lake City—was observed only a year later at Gilbert's store, near Rocky Ridge, standing "in the doorway of the hut hatless, coatless, and with his hair abroad in a wild, insane manner," swigging whiskey from a two-gallon keg and "challenging then and there to mortal combat the presumed purloiner of his animals," only to collapse into a slumber "with whatever dreams may visit the brain of the sodden inebriate."[23]

In contrast, Slade by the time of his arrival at Virginia Dale had shouldered the burdens of the Central Overland stage line, as well as its predecessor, its successor, and the Pony Express, for nearly four years—an eternity by the standards of that time. He had single-handedly supervised the line's longest and most dangerous divisions, covering distances of up to 500 miles. In the process he had faced down hostile Indians, had been snow-blinded in a blizzard, had suppressed a drunken insurrection by teamsters on his supply train, had been shot and left for dead, had defended the route from numerous outlaws, and had witnessed the destruction and abandonment of his extraordinary network of relay stations.

Far lesser traumas had destroyed Slade's colleagues and employers, either physically or psychologically, in far less time. "That he lived through it all was a miracle," remarked his acquaintance Nathaniel Langford. "A man of weaker resolution, and less fertility of resource, would have been killed before the close of his first year's service."[24] The relevant question, then, is not why Slade cracked in the fall of 1862, but why it didn't happen sooner.

How often Slade's sprees occurred that fall, and the extent to which they interfered with Slade's duties, are difficult questions to answer. Because Slade's drunken binges were his most visible and

THE BREAKING POINT * 271

most talked-about activities, many observers developed the impression that he did little else that season. Where once the overland grapevine had magnified and multiplied Slade's heroic deeds, now it did the same for his rampages. In mid-November the *Weekly Commonwealth and Republican* of Denver reported rumors of "a series of outrages" along the Overland stage route, "committed by parties of men ransacking and burning stations and plundering. . . . Rumor says that these parties are composed of some of the employees of the company. . . . Suspicion had rested on Mr. Slade as instigator of the riots."[25] The newspaper hastened to add, "We only give it as rumor and cannot speak for its truth."

This author has identified five specific Slade drinking incidents in and around Laporte that fall, as well as two such sprees in Denver. There may have been more. Yet clearly Slade's rampages were not everyday occurrences: throughout those months the Overland Stage Company made no effort to replace or even reprimand him, which suggests that the company still valued his services, or that it could find no one else qualified to replace him. On the frontier, steadfastness was always a relative term, and Slade for all his faults remained one of the stage company's most dependable managers. "With the exception of times when he went on his sprees," said Luke Voorhees, a driver who worked for Slade, "he was a very good man to look after the best interests of the stage company at that period of the Wild West."[26] Even after Slade shot his own Overland Stage Company colleague David Street in Denver, Robert Spotswood noted, "No complaint was made against Slade by Mr. Street. Slade kept on in the employ of the company."[27]

At least one of Slade's rampages that fall of 1862 stemmed specifically from his efforts to control the drinking of his own drivers. In October, after a drunken stage driver had lost control of his coach, smashing up the vehicle and injuring some of the passengers, Slade sent word to the station keeper at Laporte not to sell liquor to any of his drivers. The station keeper, a general storekeeper named George R. Sanderson, sent word back that he would sell to whom he pleased, and added gratuitously that he was not at all frightened by Slade's famous killing of Jules Beni.[28] According to one account, Slade warned Sanderson several times, to no purpose; on the contrary, Sanderson "laid in a lot of firearms, until his place became a small arsenal, and he became very boastful and threatened to shoot Slade if the latter attempted to interfere with his business."[29] What happened next was described by the early settler Frank Bartholf to a local historian:

> Two nights later when the stage drove up to the Laporte station Slade and three of his men walked into the store and began to shoot at the bottles on the shelves. Then they caught the agent [Sanderson], tied him with rope, spilled all the flour on the floor and opened all the faucets to the barrels of liquor and molasses and allowed their contents to mix with the flour. Then they went out of doors and taking runs, slid through the mixture on the floor. When they tired of their fun, Slade turned to the agent and said, "Now, when I tell you not to sell liquor to my men, I mean it."[30]

Slade shortly paid Sanderson $800 for the damages, according to one of Slade's drivers, "which did not cover the damage, but Sanderson felt lucky to get this much."[31]

Another potential target of Slade's wrath was the civilian-run supply store at Fort Halleck—and here he was treading on more dangerous ground. Fort Halleck, 75 miles northwest of Virginia Dale, had been garrisoned since July specifically to protect Slade's division from Indians; by mid-October, a passing Overland passenger reported, "This new military post is rapidly advancing toward completion. Extensive quarters have been erected, ample stabling room for several cavalry companies is already provided, and the boys at Fort Halleck will soon be snugly ensconced in comfortable winter quarters."[32]

The Fort Halleck sutler's store, like those at other military posts, supplied travelers with groceries, clothes, and even luxuries like lotion and soap. Its tavern was patronized by passing emigrants and other private citizens, including Overland Stage Company drivers, but was off-limits to enlisted men.[33] Early in November, Slade and several of his men, once again drunk, invaded the sutler's store. In the course of that spree, according to one stage man, Slade amused himself "by shooting holes through the canned goods, such as cove oysters, canned peaches and other luxuries as they were called at that time."[34]

Having effectively destroyed the store, Slade and his men then apparently returned to Virginia Dale by stagecoach.

But this time Slade had gone too far. His rampage at the sutler's store constituted an offense against government property, and no mere apology and reimbursement would suffice to make amends. Within a day or two the Fort Halleck commandant, Captain Hardy, ordered a detachment of his cavalry corps to arrest Slade. When Slade learned of this order, he fled to Denver, a day's stagecoach ride to the southeast. It is a perverse tribute to his division's efficiency that Slade's stage—benefiting from a fresh change of horses at each station along the route—was able to reach Denver while his military pursuers were forced to abandon the chase once their own horses were used up.

Nevertheless, before returning to Fort Halleck the soldiers posted a courier to Denver with instructions to arrest Slade. On November 13, a Denver newspaper reported:

> Immediately on the receipt of the dispatch, the Provost Guard, in company with U.S. Marshal A.C. Hunt, proceeded to a house where they found him in bed. They arrested him and took him to jail on Larimer St., from whence he was taken by a writ of habeas corpus issued by Judge Hall, who admitted him to bail in the sum of $2,000 to appear for hearing on Tuesday morning [Nov. 18] at 9 o'clock.[35]

The bail appears to have been posted by Bela M. Hughes, Ben Holladay's lawyer and the Overland Stage Company's general counsel.[36] Slade returned to Virginia Dale, and the hearing scheduled for November 18 never took place. Captain Hardy at Fort Halleck was less interested in punishing Slade—no sanction could restrain his future behavior when drunk—than in removing him from the vicinity. Rather than see its faithful division superintendent returned to jail, the Overland Stage Company negotiated an agreement. In exchange for the army's promise to drop the charges against Slade, the company promised to dismiss its unruly agent. On November 15, the man once known as "the law west of Kearny" was fired.[37]

The relief of Denver residents is suggested by the announcement that appeared three days later in the *Rocky Mountain News*:

> We are pleased to learn that Lem Flowers, formerly division agent
> on the Overland Stage line between North Platte and Millersville
> (a station east of Fort Bridger), has been transferred to the division
> between Denver and North Platte, formerly in charge of Mr.
> Slade. The numerous friends of Mr. Flowers in this city will
> rejoice to see him oftener. Mr. Flowers is one of the very best
> agents on the line, and we shall look forward to an improved con-
> dition on the division.[38]

Slade's replacement was the same Lem Flowers who had been wounded the previous April in the Indian raid near Sweetwater Bridge. After the Central Overland's old North Platte route was abandoned that summer, Flowers had been moved to a division in the Green River vicinity, where Slade's new southern route intersected with the old North Platte route. By November 17 Flowers had been replaced at Green River by James Stewart and was on his way to Virginia Dale.[39]

There remained the not inconsiderable question of who would break the news to Slade himself. Since no one in the company's Denver office seemed willing to convey bad news to a reputed killer, the chore was assigned to Robert Spotswood, an express messenger who rode shotgun on the company's stages between Atchison and Denver.[40] Spotswood seemed like a logical choice because express coaches carried no passengers but were filled instead with packages, and consequently were favorite targets of highwaymen. The trip from Atchison to Denver took six days, and at night Spotswood usually buckled himself with straps to the rear boot of the coach to avoid being jolted out onto the prairie while he slept.[41] With that sort of experience, Spotswood was presumed to be accustomed to great peril.

On the other hand, Spotswood was only twenty-one and was a relatively new hire by the company. When told he must travel to Virginia Dale and deliver Slade his termination papers, Spotswood later recalled, "My friends in Denver bade me goodbye almost tearfully. It was predicted that I would never return to Denver alive. 'Slade will kill you rather than yield his post,' I was told, but I answered that the killing would have to take place as there was nothing for me to do but go ahead and obey the company's orders."[42]

When Spotswood arrived at Virginia Dale he found not the fire-eating drunk of legend but the quiet gentleman whose courtly manners had once impressed people every bit as much as his drinking binges. "There was no wild outbreak on Slade's part," Spotswood recalled. "He bowed to the will of the company without a word, and he and his wife did everything in their power to make my stay agreeable during the next two or three days. Slade made an accounting and turned over everything in good shape. His own stock he separated from that belonging to the company. He had many horses and mules and wagons"—presumably appropriated from Jules Beni as compensation for his shooting—"and he told me he intended to return to his old business as a freighter."[43]

That remark suggests that Slade had indeed been thinking about leaving. Slade seems to have welcomed Spotswood's news for doing what he could not: liberate himself from his self-destructive behavior so he could get on with his life. With this quiet acceptance of his fate, Slade's tumultuous tenure with the Central Overland reached an unexpected peaceful conclusion that kept his awesome reputation largely intact.

"No more exalted tribute can be paid to his character," wrote his acquaintance Langford, "than to say that he organized, managed and controlled for several years, acceptably to the public and the company, the great central division of the Overland stage route through six hundred miles of territory destitute of inhabitants and law, exposed for the entire distance to hostile Indians and overrun with a wild, reckless class of freebooters who maintained their infamous assumptions with pistol and Bowie knife. No man without a peculiar fitness for such a position could have done this."[44]

Slade had driven the Central Overland beyond its potential; he had pushed himself to his limits; and ultimately he had tried the patience of civilized settlers. Now, as Slade himself readily recognized, it was time to move on and build a new life. But he would have to do that alone, without the quasi-legal authority and the corporate infrastructure he had enjoyed for years.

Chapter 16

GOLD FEVER

∗

Suddenly Slade was out of work, the contract freighting season was over, and winter was approaching. In this limbo he and Virginia headed east to Illinois to visit his family in Carlyle.[1] But if Slade had harbored any thoughts of returning permanently to his hometown, what he found there now must surely have dismayed him.

Carlyle's hopes of becoming anything more than a county seat had died with Charles Slade's death in 1834. Slade's mother, Mary Dennis, now sixty-three, presided over a declining family. Her husband Elias Dennis, still an ambitious and relatively robust man thirteen years her junior, had effectively abandoned her twice: first in March 1857, when he accepted the prestigious but thankless task of serving as U.S. marshal of "bleeding Kansas" for a year; and then after war broke out in the spring of 1861, when Elias had organized a state militia regiment and won election as its colonel.[2] He had left home that August and participated in the Union capture of Fort Donelson, Tennessee, in February 1862. By the time Slade arrived in Carlyle, Elias Dennis had been promoted to brigadier general and was heading south to northern Louisiana with the army of Ulysses S. Grant.[3]

Only two of Slade's full siblings, both unmarried, remained in Carlyle—his eldest brother William, now forty-two and tending the family's mill and ferry, and Maria Virginia, a physically and emotionally frail spinster of thirty, seemingly without prospects of marriage or anything else. Slade's half-brother Elias Dennis, Jr., now twenty-two, was also still unmarried. Only a single member of the next generation—Charles R. Slade, Jr., the sixteen-year-old son of Slade's older brother who died in the Mexican War—had survived. The Dennis household itself, which in 1850 had bustled with seven family members and two servants, was now down to just Mary, her spinster daughter Virginia, and her son Elias Dennis Jr., plus a single servant girl.[4]

Nor could Mary or her children find much consolation in the relative material comforts of their earlier years. Their ferry across the Kaskaskia River had been rendered obsolete by the construction in 1859 of a magnificent suspension bridge at a cost of $40,000.[5] At the same time, the Slade household had become the focal point for seemingly endless inheritance legal battles reminiscent of Dickens's 1853 novel *Bleak House.* Most of the large estate left by Charles Slade in 1834—some 100 acres, including the mill and ferry—had been dissipated by protracted litigation among Charles's creditors and relatives. Not only Charles's estate but also the estate of Charles's brother Richard, who had died in Carlyle in 1835, were still being consumed by legal fees at the end of 1862, both cases exacerbated by the Slades' inability to locate many of their far-flung relatives.[6]

Slade was legally entitled to one-sixtieth of his uncle Richard Slade's estate, but there was clearly no point to waiting around to collect it.[7] His best prospects, now as in 1849 when he had left for the first time, lay in the West.

Yet his options were limited. For all his past value to the Overland Stage Company and its predecessor lines, no employer was likely to hire Slade after his drunken rampages in Colorado Territory. Reenlisting in the military was also out of the question after his rampage at Fort Halleck. And for the first and only time in his life, Slade that winter became, technically, a fugitive from justice.

Although the Fort Halleck commander had dropped the charges for Slade's outburst there in November, in late February 1863 a grand jury in Denver belatedly indicted Slade and three of his stage drivers for assault with intent to kill the Laporte tavern keeper George Sanderson the previous October.[8] No effort appears to have been made to arrest Slade, but clearly a wanted man was best advised to leave "the States" and join the growing numbers of fugitives from both the law and the war in the least organized territories of the West.[9]

By early spring Slade and his wife had located to a ranch near Fort Bridger, Utah Territory, where Slade hooked up with a fellow Illinoisan named John Ely, described as "a magnificent specimen of a frontiersman, standing six foot three inches in his stockings."[10] Although Ely towered over Slade, the two men probably complemented each other well: Slade contributed freighting experience and managerial skills, while Ely was a financial adventurer willing to gamble his fortune on Nevada mines and any other opportunity that might arise. "Slade & Ely," as they styled their partnership, became a small but well-equipped contract freighting outfit.

Slade's choice of this location, like his previous choice of Virginia Dale, demonstrated his commercial acumen. The area between Fort Bridger and Green River, 65 miles to the east, was a logical spot for freighting in and out of Salt Lake City, 115 miles to the southwest. It was accessible to the emigrant trains heading southwest along the Fort Bridger route to Utah and California, as well as to emigrant trains turning northwest toward Oregon and Washington Territory. The mining camps of Bannack, Idaho Territory, where gold had been discovered along Grasshopper Creek in 1862, lay some 400 miles to the northwest. And the area abounded in forage for Slade's oxen.[11]

Fort Bridger itself, unlike the Army's customarily austere forts, had been a privately owned trading post long before the mountain man Jim Bridger leased it to the government during the Utah "rebellion" in 1857, and it remained a convivial meeting place for travelers and settlers.[12] The frontiersman Granville Stuart, who camped there for two weeks in the summer of 1858, said Fort Bridger reminded him of "the good old days in California":

> Money, all in twenty, ten and five dollar gold pieces, was plentiful, and the way everybody drank, gambled and scattered it around was almost equal to the days of forty-nine. A host of gamblers had congregated there and many of them were at the top of their profession. When the outsiders "busted" they preyed upon one another and it was amazing to see the way they stacked up their

coin on their favorite card. I saw them win and lose five thousand dollars on the turn of a single monte card.[13]

Slade still had friends and acquaintances in the Fort Bridger area who held him in high regard. Henry Gilbert, the former storekeeper and station agent on Slade's division near South Pass, now lived at the fort with his wife and child while operating as a military contractor, constructing a bridge at Ham's Fork and furnishing army posts with hay and beef.[14] A writer named Fitz Hugh Ludlow, crossing the country by stagecoach, found Slade at Fort Bridger and thought him "a model of manly beauty." In his subsequent account Ludlow provided what may be the only evidence of Slade's conscious concern for his public reputation:

> I had an interesting talk with him, and asked him for an account of his celebrated fights with Old Jule, as well as the terrible vengeance which he wreaked upon him. Our time being limited, of his own accord he promised to write me what I asked, and forward it to me for use in this or any future work I might write... Without any appearance of self-conceit, he still seemed pleased when I told him what was very true—that his adventures in the wilds would afford materials for an intensely interesting romance of adventure.[15]

Such moments of adulation probably exacerbated Slade's difficulty in accepting his new situation. The nation's eyes were no longer upon him; now he was a player on a peripheral stage while the central struggle for the Union's survival played out 2,000 miles to the east. And on this secondary stage he possessed greatly diminished power. Although legend had it that he had cleaned up his divisions on the Central Overland single-handedly, in fact he had always operated with the support of his armed stage company employees. Slade still carried Jules's ears in his pocket, but now the armed employees were gone, and many of his enemies remained. For years Slade had been accustomed to dominating every situation; now his power was gone. It remained to be seen whether he could adapt to this new reality.

Slade & Ely had barely launched its operations when a new opportunity arose some 400 miles to the north. That May a party of six

Idaho prospectors, disappointed with the gold findings at Bannack, ventured some 60 miles northeastward into the Yellowstone Valley on a prospecting trip.[16] Among the group's leaders was Bill Fairweather, reputedly a friend of Slade's (he may have accompanied Slade on a freighting party in 1858).[17] The prospectors had hoped to join a larger expedition led by Granville Stuart's brother James but were detained by their lack of horses. By the time they came upon a village of Flathead Indians and purchased the necessary horses, they were too late to join James Stuart's group.[18]

On such twists of fate are fortunes made and communities born. As the six miners camped glumly beside a creek overhung by alder bushes on May 26, 1863, Fairweather panned gravel from a streambed and discovered gold.[19] This vein of placer gold—that is, "free" gold found in the form of nuggets and flakes in the sand and gravel of streambeds—was far richer than the shallow gravels that they and thousands of other miners had worked since the previous year on Grasshopper Creek. Fairweather had stumbled upon what was subsequently pronounced the richest placer gold strike in the Rocky Mountains.

Fairweather's partner Henry Edgar promptly named the stream Alder Gulch, after the dense growth of dark green alders and willows on either side.[20] The six men immediately recognized the magnitude of their find and agreed to keep it to themselves. But after a few days they needed to return to Bannack for supplies, and once there the secret proved impossible to keep. When they slipped out of town and started back to Alder Gulch, they were amazed to find hundreds of prospectors following them, strung out for a quarter of a mile.[21] "Some were on foot carrying a blanket and a few pounds of food on their backs," the frontiersman Granville Stuart noted in his journal. "Others were leading pack horses, others [on] horseback leading pack animals. The packs had been hurriedly placed and some had come loose and the frightened animals, running about with blankets flying and pots and pans rattling, had frightened others and the hillside was strewn with camp outfits and grub."[22]

This first stampede reached Alder Gulch on June 6, and within ten days the gulch was staked out for 12 miles, each man allowed a hun-

dred feet along the creek.²³ Some
10,000 prospectors—that is, more
than double the population of
Denver—had settled in a dozen mining camps.²⁴ In the absence of houses, Stuart noted, "every sort of shelter
was resorted to: Some made dug-
outs, some utilized a convenient shel-
tering rock, and by placing brush and
blankets around it constructed a living place; others spread their blankets under a pine tree and had no
shelter other than that furnished by
the green boughs overhead."²⁵

Bill Fairweather's discovery of gold in
May 1863 triggered a stampede to
Alder Gulch. He subsequently became
Jack Slade's drinking companion in
Virginia City. (*Montana Historical
Society*)

The same gold-seekers who had
once flocked to California and Pike's
Peak now deserted those camps for
Alder Gulch. "All classes are leaving
this community and other Western diggings," the *San Francisco
Bulletin* acknowledged that summer. "The bummer and the attorney,
the merchant and the gambler, the miner and the general sport—all go
in, cheek by jowl, on the principle of root hog or die."²⁶

That description of the new arrivals was perhaps too kind. An
observant eleven-year-old girl named Mollie Sheehan later remembered "Rough-clad men with long hair and flowing beards [who]
swarmed everywhere."²⁷ The Alder Gulch discovery attracted "the
greatest aggregation of toughs and criminals that ever got together in
the West," claimed the miner Alexander Toponce, who was among the
first stampede of prospectors from Bannack. "They came up the
Missouri river on the steamboats by the scores, deserters from the
Union and Rebel armies, river pirates and professional gamblers and
sharpers." Many of them, Toponce added,

> came out there to escape the draft in the Northern states. And
> when [the Confederate] General Price was defeated at Pea Ridge
> [Missouri, March 1862], hundreds of stragglers from his army

struck out across the prairies for the mining camps. It was a standing joke in Idaho that "the left wing of Price's army" was located
in Cassia county.

At times there was a good deal of feeling . . . between the men
from the South and the North. The Southerners were in the
majority in some camps. We could tell when they had got news of
a defeat of the Rebel army by their long faces and the way they
stood around in groups whispering. Then when they heard of a
rebel victory they would get loud and hilarious and would shoot
off their pistols and yell "Hurrah for Jeff Davis!"

But when news came of the fall of Vicksburg and then of the
battle of Gettysburg [both on July 4, 1863], the Union men took
heart and from that time on the Secession sentiment was not so
strong.[28]

That this chaotic and rootless instant community belonged to the
United States seemed clear enough. But everything else about its legal
status—including the allegiance of its settlers, many of whom were
Confederates—was mired in confusion. In the two years since the war
started in 1861, Congress had created five new territories in the West,
in some cases carving new territories out of parts of old ones.[29] The
territorial status of Bannack and Alder Gulch hadn't mattered much
before 1862, when nobody lived there; but now some 15,000 people
had settled in an area that had once belonged to Dakota Territory, then
to Washington Territory, then (as of March 1863) to Idaho Territory,
and eventually to Montana Territory. The nearest capitals that had
exercised jurisdiction over Alder Gulch were in Olympia, on Puget
Sound by the Pacific; in Yankton, 1,000 miles to the east; and in
Lewiston, 500 miles to the northwest and across the Bitterroot mountains.[30]

Just two weeks after Fairweather struck gold, the Alder Gulch miners organized a court to stake off claims. A week later, a town site company recorded a claim to 320 acres of land and a town was laid out in
the heart of Alder Gulch. At first the town was named Varina in honor
of the first lady of the Confederacy, Mrs. Jefferson Davis, but it was
changed shortly when the only local legal authority—the miners' elected judge, Dr. G. G. Bissell, formerly of Connecticut—refused to use

Virginia City, Montana, in 1866, with Alder Gulch in the foreground. Within a month after gold was discovered in May 1863, a town of some 10,000 people sprang up. By that fall, Virginia City abounded in saloons, dance halls, restaurants, dry goods stores, a hotel, a theater, and a school—all the basic civic necessities except a church, a courthouse, and a jail. (*Montana Historical Society*)

"Varina" on official documents; "Virginia is Southern enough," Bissell supposedly declared, and so the Idaho boomtown of Virginia City got its name.[31]

Although the closest sawmill was 75 miles away, near Bannack, "the nearby mountains furnished an abundance of house logs," Stuart wrote, "and the ring of the axe was a familiar sound and soon log houses made their appearance on all sides." The first wood building was occupied by a baker—"the first time in the history of founding a mining camp where the bakery got ahead of the saloon," Stuart puckishly remarked. But following the pattern of San Francisco and Denver, Virginia City's tone was set by its second business, a tavern. "Saloons, gambling houses, public dance halls (hurdy gurdies) ran wide open," Stuart reported, "and here, as in California, gold dust flowed in a yellow stream from the buckskin bags of the miners into the coffers of the saloons, dance halls and gambling dens."[32]

The town's inevitable brothels cured at least one twenty-two-year-old stable boy of any illusions he might have had about the mysteries of the sex act, as he described it decades later:

> What I had plenty of chances to view were standard brothel fornications. A primitive low-class house (more a half-converted sta-

ble) butted up against the back of Zeke's livery stable and when tired of shoveling shit, I would sometimes place a bloodshot eye to a convenient knothole and witness the miners' brief and nasty coupling with the half a dozen young ladies who populated the establishment. One was a Siwash Indian, who was the best looking of the lot, one was a skinny Chinese girl with little English and a tubercular cough that sometimes kept me awake late at night, next was a pregnant mulatto girl. I don't think the miners sought out the establishment for sexual variety because the customers were usually drunk and just in from distant claims.[33]

The saloonkeepers and gamblers were soon followed by the merchants, packers, teamsters, stage lines, and express companies, which arrived, not coincidentally, with the speculators and promoters.[34] "Up and down the narrow streets labored bull trains of sixteen- and twenty-horse teams pulling three and four wagons lashed together, and long strings of packhorses, mules or donkeys," recalled young Mollie Sheehan. By that fall of 1863 Virginia City contained general stores, comfortable log cabins, a hotel, several restaurants, a Jesuit priest who conducted open-air Mass for the heavily Irish mining population, and a theater built of logs, with a stage in one end and furnished with pine seats with rude backs. Such was the extent of the migration to Alder Gulch that the first arrivals included a number of families, among whom "all the ladies did their own housework and in case of sickness helped nurse and care for their neighbors," Stuart noted. By the first winter the town even had a private school run by young Englishman named Thomas Dimsdale.[35] At that point, curiously, Virginia City lacked only two basic communal institutions: a church, and a jail.[36]

More than merchants and saloonkeepers, the new mining mecca in its first months needed freighters like Slade. Neither agriculture nor industry existed in Idaho to support Virginia City's booming new population. Miners might be fed by wild game hunters, but everything else eaten, worn, or used had to be imported from afar, and everyone in Alder Gulch paid accordingly: sixty cents a pound for sugar, a dollar a pound for potatoes, $1.50 for a dozen eggs.[37]

Missouri River steamboats could deliver goods from the East to Fort Benton, but at that point the Missouri was navigable only three months a year—and in any case, Fort Benton was more than 150 miles from Virginia City.[38] Most of the trails to Virginia City were accessible only by pack mules and horses, which were limited to carrying goods of small bulk and weight. But from Slade's base near Fort Bridger to Alder Gulch more than 400 miles to the north ran a roundabout wagon trail along the valley of the Malad River through Soda Springs and Fort Hall on the Snake River. It crossed the Continental Divide through the Monida Pass, 6,800 feet above sea level, then took the traveler across the Big Hole Basin into Bannack and then eastward seventy miles to Virginia City.[39] Over such a route, a train of wagons from Fort Bridger could deliver heavy goods—furniture, store fixtures, iron tubs and sinks—within a matter of weeks.

As soon as news of the Alder Gulch strike reached Fort Bridger in June 1863, Henry Gilbert asked Slade to transport a wagon train loaded with freight that Gilbert presumed he could sell in Virginia City at a large profit. In addition he asked Slade to transport some of his own household goods, with an eye toward moving his family there. The Gilbert family would not take much in the way of creature comforts: every available space in the wagons would be packed with freight to be sold at Virginia City. Only by conspiring with a teamster was Margaret Gilbert able to smuggle a precious ingrain carpet onto a wagon.[40]

Gilbert's greatest concern was delivering the goods safely through a route that was likely, before long, to be infested with bandits, not to mention Indians. Slade's name and fearsome reputation alone, Gilbert believed, would deter the most dangerous outlaws.[41]

Slade, who was low on funds, proposed that they combine their wagons and livestock and form a partnership for the venture. Gilbert consented, and Slade left for Virginia City (perhaps with his partner Ely) almost immediately.[42] Gilbert did not go with him because his wife was pregnant and he planned to follow after she delivered later that summer.[43] In later years Gilbert often disparaged Slade, but his willingness to entrust Slade with a huge stock of goods as well as much of his household belongings testifies to Gilbert's belief in Slade's integrity and competence.

The journey that June probably took two or three weeks.[44] Somewhere near Soda Springs, Slade's expedition fell in with another

The taciturn James Williams who tangled with Slade on the way to Alder Gulch later became the vigilantes' executive officer and the real power behind the movement. (*Montana Historical Society*)

wagon train.[45] Its leader, James Williams, was a Pennsylvania native who had been a Free State man in Leavenworth during the Kansas Territory troubles in 1857–58, when Slade's stepfather Elias Dennis was U.S. marshal there. From there Williams had followed the Pike's Peak gold rush to Colorado, where he accumulated a modest stake worth some four thousand dollars and briefly tried his hand at farming. Williams was about to return to Pennsylvania in the spring of 1863 when he learned of the Alder Gulch strike and headed there instead.

At the age of twenty-nine Williams was strongly built and slow moving. Like Slade he had won a name for himself for his coolness and courage during the Kansas border war; like Slade, his eyes were kindly and humorous except when he was angry; then, said one who knew him, "The eyes turned jet black and in anger their menace was deadly—on my word, the glance was terrifying!"[46]

At Soda Springs the Slade and Williams trains camped together. Since both trains were following the same course through a dangerous country, the two groups agreed to proceed together under a single captain, to be elected by majority vote. In a spirit of conviviality, liquor began to flow, and before long Slade had imbibed to excess, with predictable results that terrified Williams's men as well as enough of Slade's to carry the election in Williams's favor. When Slade, now thoroughly drunk, was told of the proposed election, he announced that they could hold an election if they wanted, but regardless of the result, *he* would be the captain.

Williams, at five feet ten inches and 190 pounds, was larger than Slade, and now he sought him out. "Slade," he said, "I understand you say that no matter who is elected you will still be captain of this outfit. I want to say that whoever is elected captain will be captain." In a menacing tone, he added: "Did you hear what I said?"

Williams was not the first man to challenge Slade when drunk, and Slade, once called to account, characteristically acknowledged his own inebriated state and relented. According to the only account of that meeting—apparently provided by Williams—Slade smiled and replied, "All right, Cap, that suits me." In later years Williams remarked that "I appointed Slade my lieutenant and I never had a man work with me that I got along with better."[47] But it would not be the last time Williams and Slade would confront each other.[48]

Slade reached Virginia City in late June or early July to discover that almost everyone of note from his Overland days was already there.[49] Fairweather was reveling in his status as the man whose discovery had spawned the town. George Chrisman, Slade's former station agent at Julesburg who had bought out Jules Beni's ranch, was a prominent storekeeper in Bannack.[50] Amede Bessette, Slade's stationmaster at North Platte Bridge for two years, was in Bannack as well.[51] Also here were several former Pony Express riders, including the well-known "Pony Bob" Haslam. Jim Kiskadden, a good-natured gentleman gambler and speculative entrepreneur whom Slade may have known in Salt Lake City, was here as well, buying gold for his banker brother in Salt Lake and "figuring out ways whereby he might acquire great wealth without too much effort," as one account put it.[52] The trader Granville Stuart, who had stumbled upon the aftermath of Slade's shooting of the teamster Andrew Ferrin at Ham's Fork in 1859, was here. Jim Boner, the station keeper near Julesburg who had nursed Slade after his shooting by Jules, arrived in July.[53] Henry Gilbert was due to arrive as soon as his wife gave birth later that summer. The trader Louis Maillet, who had accompanied Slade on a westbound stagecoach from Gilbert's Station in July 1859, was on his way from Salt Lake with a highly prized cargo of flour.[54]

Slade also found that his past reputation had preceded him. From his very first day in Virginia City he was a figure of curiosity, if not awe.

"No other man could have so aroused the interest of the miners," noted one account, "for Slade at that time was the subject of awed discussion at every camp-fire and every cabin in the West." On the day Slade arrived, this account added hyperbolically, "Miners dropped pick and shovel and went to Virginia City to get a glimpse of the new arrival."[55]

In addition to old acquaintances and celebrity status, Slade found one more attraction: the gold strike was genuine. In the first year, Alder Gulch would yield $10 million from a stretch barely twelve miles long—as much as all of California had produced during the first year of the Gold Rush in '49. Over the next three years Alder Gulch would yield $30 million.[56]

As at other strikes, most of the miners were quickly parted from their newfound wealth: "Like most young men we only wanted money to spend," confessed one Idaho miner. "If I had taken my money and invested it I would have been a millionaire."[57] But Slade was "a man of good business qualifications and possessed a knack of making money in fields where others failed," wrote John Clampitt, later a federal attorney in the Rockies.[58] Whether or not Slade had intended to settle permanently in Virginia City when he left Fort Bridger, he made that decision now. He announced his intention to engage in short-haul freighting.[59] He invested at least some of the proceeds of his freighting expedition in the rich gold mining claims at Nevada City—another camp a mile and a half north of Virginia City—and also possibly at Granite Gulch, about three miles north of Virginia City.[60] But he soon perceived a business opportunity that apparently hadn't occurred to others.

Like all commodities, milk and cheese were in short supply in Virginia City. Although Slade had no experience as a dairy farmer, he ventured some 14 miles to the northeast across the Tobacco Root mountain range that separated Alder Gulch from the Madison River Valley.[61] Here, on a slope of rolling hills dropping down to the Madison River—a spot almost as beautiful and isolated as Virginia Dale had been—he found an enormous pasture. While thousands of miners jostled over narrow hundred-foot claims along Alder Creek, Slade invoked the squatter's privilege of staking a claim to 320 acres and stocked it with a herd of milk cows.[62]

Some 15 miles northeast of Virginia City, Slade staked out a 320-acre pasture and stocked it with a herd of dairy cows. His cabin there was still standing in 1908 when this photo was taken. The man at the left has been identified as either George Ballard or Jim Gunn, who lived in the nearby town of McAllister and often took tourists to the long-abandoned site for pictures like this one. (*Denver Public Library*)

At first that summer the Slades lived with their adopted son Jemmy in a tent on this farm, which Slade christened "Ravenswood"; the miner John X. Beidler later wrote of visiting Slade there "and his wife cooked a good dinner for us."[63] Eventually Slade built a rudimentary house on a windy peak.[64]

Shortly after staking his claim, Slade took a wagon team and several men in to Virginia City to pick up supplies to build a cabin and corral. A lumberyard had been set up there by Nathaniel Langford, a native of upstate New York who had subsequently moved to St. Paul, Minnesota. In 1862 Langford had headed west from there as second assistant to Captain James L. Fisk, with a party assigned to build a wagon road to Fort Benton at the far northwestern bend of the Missouri River. After narrowly escaping death at the hands of the Blackfeet Indians and coming close to starving, Langford had settled in Virginia City at the news of the gold strike there. That summer he was not quite thirty-one—a year and a half younger than Slade—and like Slade he was not a miner but a would-be entrepreneur who saw opportunity in a mining town. But he had not previously met Slade or even heard of him, and consequently was unprepared for Slade's inclination to use his reputation as a bargaining tool.

As Langford later recalled their first encounter, Slade selected "a quantity of long boards" from the piles and directed his teamsters to load them on the wagon and take them away.

After the men had started with the load, Slade asked me, "How long credit will you give me on this purchase?"

"About as long as it will take to weigh the dust," I replied.

He remarked good-humoredly, "That's played out."

"As I can buy for cash only, I must of necessity require immediate payment on all sales," I said, by way of explanation.

Slade immediately called to the teamster to return and unload the lumber, remarking as soon as it was placed upon the piles, "Well, I can't get along without the boards anyhow; load them up again."

The man obeyed and left again with the load, Slade insisting, as before, that he must have time to pay for it, and I as earnest in the demand for immediate payment. The teamster returned and unloaded a second time.

"I must and will have the lumber," said Slade; and the teamster, by his direction, was proceeding to reload it a third time, when I forbade his doing so, until it was paid for.

Our conversation now, without being angry, became very earnest, and I fully explained why I could not sell to any man upon credit.

"Oh, well," said he, with a significant toss of the head: "I guess you'll let me have it."

"Certainly not," I replied. "Why should I let you have it sooner than another?"

"Then I guess you don't know who I am," he quickly rejoined, fixing his keen dark eyes on me.

"No, I don't; but if I did, it could make no difference."

"Well," he continued, in an authoritative tone and manner, "my name is Slade."

It so happened that I had never heard of him, my attention being wholly engrossed with business, so I replied, laughingly, "I don't know now, any better than before."

"You must have heard of Slade of the Overland."

"Never before," I said.

The reply seemed to annoy him. He gave me a look of mingled doubt and wonder, which, had it taken the form of words, would have said, "You are either trying to fool me or are yourself a fool." No doubt he thought it strange that I should never have heard of a man who had been so conspicuous in mountain history.

"Well," he said, "if you do not know me, ask any of the boys who I am, and they will inform you. I'm going to have this lumber; that is dead sure," and with an air of much importance, he moved to a group of eight or ten men that had just come out of Skinner's saloon, all of whom were attaches of his. "Come boys," said he, "load up the wagon."

Several of my friends were standing near, and the matter between us had fully ripened into a conflict. At this moment John Ely, an old friend, elbowed his way through the crowd, and learning the cause of the difficulty, told me to let Slade have the lumber, and he would see that I was paid the next day. Ely then took me aside and informed me of the desperate character of Slade, and advised me to avoid him, as he was drunk, and would certainly shoot me at our next meeting.[65]

This, of course, was the same advice that had been given to Robert Spotswood by his friends in Denver the previous fall, when he was dispatched to bring Slade the news of his dismissal from the Overland. The night of the lumberyard encounter, Slade went on a drinking spree, and Langford lived to provide what is perhaps the most vivid eyewitness description of Slade under the influence. The binge started when Slade picked a fight with Jack Gallagher, a tall, dark, and striking-looking drifter who shared some of Slade's characteristics: courteous and soft-spoken when sober, dangerous and uncontrollable when drunk.[66] Slade's fight with Gallagher, Langford said, "had not bystanders disarmed the combatants, would have had a fatal termination."[67]

Soon after this was over I saw [Slade] enter the California Exchange, accompanied by two friends whom he invited to drink with him. When in the act of raising their glasses, Slade drew back his powerful arm and struck the one nearest him a violent blow on the forehead. He fell heavily to the floor. Slade left immediately, and the man, being raised, recovered consciousness and disappeared.

Slade returned in a few moments with another friend whom he asked to drink, and struck down. Again he went out, and soon came in with another whom he attempted to serve in the same manner, but this man rose immediately to his feet. Slade was foiled by the interference of bystanders, in the attempt to strike him again.

Turning on his heel, his eye caught mine. I was standing a few feet from him by the wall. He advanced rapidly towards me, and, expecting an assault, I assumed a posture of defense.

Greatly to my surprise, he accosted me civilly, and throwing his arm around me, said jocosely, "Old fellow! You didn't think I was going to cheat you out of that lumber, did you?"

He then asked me to drink. I respectfully declined.

"It's all right," said he, and walked away. I met him afterwards several times during the evening, but he said nothing more.[68]

The wife of such an unpredictable and notorious figure had to work hard to establish and maintain her own reputation in new surroundings. Virginia Slade's marriage safely elevated her above the social level of the hurdy-gurdies whence she had come, but she was never entirely accepted by the wives of merchants, lawyers, and Masons who constituted Virginia City's upper crust—apparently a matter of great concern to her. By some accounts Virginia was admired and popular and frequently attended social gatherings; she was "probably the best dancer in town," according to the merchant Charles Cannon.[69] "Mrs. Slade . . . bears an excellent character here and is thought much of by all acquaintants," wrote a correspondent to Denver's *Rocky Mountain News* the following year.[70] But Virginia's presumed dance-hall past, as well as her proficiency with cards, guns, and horses, set her apart from Virginia City's other wives and mothers. On one occasion when Virginia entertained "a young lady, somewhat unsophisticated but of an unblemished character," one local merchant concluded that "Mrs. Slade is an unfit associate for her" and contrived to rescue the innocent girl from Mrs. Slade's company.[71]

Elevating one's social standing was no easy trick in a town where, according to Langford, on Sundays "citizens of acknowledged respectability often walked, more often perhaps rode side by side on horseback, with noted courtesans in open day through the crowded streets, and seemingly suffered no harm in reputation."[72] On Sundays—"always a gala day," in Langford's words, when "thousands of people crowded the thoroughfares, ready to rush in any direction of promised excitement"—the Slades often joined the horse races on the main drag of Wallace Street: Virginia aboard Billy Bay, her gorgeous black stallion from Kentucky, and Slade on his reliable Copperbottom, which unfailingly brought its master home, drunk or sober.[73] But Sunday on Wallace Street, with its prizefights, auctions, and hacks rattling "to and fro between the several towns, freighted with drunken and rowdy humanity of both sexes," was an unreliable venue for aspiring social climbers.[74]

A more promising showcase lay in the frequent dances, social gatherings, and theatrical entertainments that most of the town's families patronized, often bringing their children with them to sleep in an adjoining room. Unlike Sundays on Wallace Street, these parties required a ticket (usually $3 or $5) for admission, which imposed a measure of social control. These parties, the trader Granville Stuart recalled, "were very informal and most enjoyable. Dancing would be kept up until an early hour in the morning. A fine supper was usually served at midnight."

By at least some accounts, Slade often escorted Virginia to these dances, where she was a much-sought-after dancing partner. While other women wore simple cotton dresses, Virginia is said to have appeared in long, flowing silk gowns, which she sewed herself.[75] On the night of one ball later that year, when Slade was away on a freighting expedition, a miner named Charley Brown persuaded another man to go to bed so that Brown might "borrow" the sleeper's clothes in order to lead the grand march with Mrs. Slade.[76] One unverified account claims that Virginia Slade entertained at dinner parties with candles, linen, and silver tableware.[77]

Why would such an outgoing and sociable couple like the Slades have chosen to isolate themselves at Ravenswood, as they had done also at Virginia Dale? No sure answer to this question exists, but we can hazard a guess: it may have been the means by which Virginia—and perhaps Slade himself—hoped to keep him from the increasingly dangerous temptations of liquor.

Whether Slade himself actually milked cows or made cheese at Ravenswood is open to question, but he did own a herd of cows.[78] In any case ranching was not a sufficient outlet for Slade's energies. Although Slade maintained his claim to Ravenswood, within a month or so of his arrival a more lucrative and less labor-intensive business opportunity occurred to him.

After gold had been discovered at Bannack in 1862, gold-seekers from the East had needed a safe shortcut that would take emigrant wagon trains there from the Oregon Trail. In 1863 a gentleman-adventurer from Georgia named John M. Bozeman found a suitable wagon route that branched northward from the old Oregon Trail on the North Platte River some 20 miles north of Slade's former headquarters at Horseshoe Creek. This Bozeman Trail, as it came to be known, stretched north and west for 530 miles; in 1865 it became the focus of Red Cloud's War, the Army's confrontation with the Oglala Lakota chief Red Cloud. But when Slade arrived in the summer of 1863, the last few miles of the Bozeman Trail were largely impassable to wagons, which risked tipping over at that point.[79] A better road was needed. If Slade could provide it, he reasoned, emigrant wagons and muleskinners would readily pay a toll for its use.

Soon the Slades had taken their possessions a few miles westward and squatted on a new piece of ground, consisting of 160 unwanted acres in the midst of precipitous mountains where, in the words of one observer, "a horse could hardly find room to turn." Here, over the rest of the summer, Slade cleared out several miles for a passable wagon road that would bypass the rough section of the Bozeman Trail—a remarkable project that probably involved several men using horse-drawn slips or graders to cut the roadway into the side of the steep hill.[80] Along this road, near a lava formation about eight miles east of Virginia City, he found the ideal spot for his toll gate and house, just west of a swamp and a short distance east of a small spring that emerged, cold and sparkling, from beneath the lava. The tollhouse, which he called Spring Dale, was a substantial, low, stone structure, at

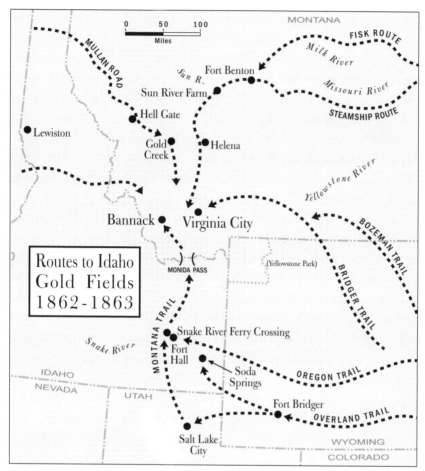

MONTANA

0   50   100
Miles

MULLAN ROAD

Sun R.   Fort Benton

Sun River Farm

Hell Gate

Lewiston

Gold Creek   Helena

FISK ROUTE

Milk River

Missouri River

STEAMSHIP ROUTE

Yellowstone River

Bannack   Virginia City

BOZEMAN TRAIL

Routes to Idaho
Gold Fields
1862-1863

MONIDA PASS

(Yellowstone Park)

BRIDGER TRAIL

MONTANA TRAIL

Snake River

Snake River Ferry Crossing

Fort Hall

Soda Springs

OREGON TRAIL

IDAHO
NEVADA   UTAH

Fort Bridger

OVERLAND TRAIL

Salt Lake City

WYOMING

COLORADO

Early routes to the Montana gold fields.

least sixteen feet square, covered with a pole-and-sod roof and more comfortable than the house at Ravenswood.[81] But it was a lonely place, located in "one of the wildest dells of the mountains overlooking it," according to Nathaniel Langford.[82] Here, while Slade tended the dairy farm, Virginia Slade stayed with an Indian woman for company and collected tolls from passing travelers.[83]

Virginia City was barely three months old in September when news of an impending local crisis arrived. Of all the various supply lines to Alder Gulch, the most important line conveyed goods by

Missouri River steamer from St. Louis to Fort Benton, at the Missouri's headwaters, and from there by wagon for the remaining 150 miles to Alder Gulch.[84] But steamers rarely made it all the way to Fort Benton. In seasons of low water—about nine months of the year— freighters couldn't negotiate the rapids that far.[85] A steamer's cargo in itself could jeopardize its safety: Two years earlier, an American Fur Company steamboat had exploded and lost all of its cargo at the mouth of the Milk River, 200 miles downstream from Fort Benton, when a deckhand trying to steal some alcohol had accidentally caused a fire in the hold.

That summer of 1863 the enterprising merchant brothers J. V. and W. H. Hardie had left St. Joseph, Missouri, having loaded the steamboat *Alone* with enough general merchandise and provisions to see Virginia City through its first winter. But the boat had left too late in the summer and had been forced to unload its cargo at a civilian trading post called Fort Galpin, far to the north and east at the mouth of the Milk River. J. V. Hardie commandeered a stagecoach to Virginia City in the hope of enlisting a freighter willing to retrieve the goods, but it seemed an impossible mission.[86] From Alder Gulch to the mouth of the Milk River was a distance of more than 350 miles. No road of any sort existed for nearly two-thirds of that distance. The territory north of the Missouri was claimed by the Blackfoot Indians; to the south were roving bands of Crows, Sioux, and Gros Ventres. All of these tribes regarded a wagon train as an intrusion on their domain and consequently a justified target for attack. Even without hostile Indians, the lateness of the season meant there would be no feed for the stock along the way, other than dry wild bunch grass. And even with ample feed and without fear of Indians, such an expedition might well be snowed in before it could return.

No man in or around Alder Gulch, Hardie found, was willing to undertake such a perilous trip. With one exception. This was precisely the sort of challenge for which Slade had hungered since he had left the Overland.

His partner John Ely had already taken several thousand dollars in gold from his placer claim in Lower Alder Gulch; now, with funds advanced by Ely, Slade purchased wagons and mules and hired team-

The remains of Slade's stone tollhouse at Spring Dale. From here Virginia Slade saddled up for her desperate attempt to save her husband's life. (*Montana Historical Society*)

sters and packers to accompany him to the Milk River.[87] "The magic name of 'Slade of the Overland'," according to one account, "was sufficient to bring to his corrals every man in the mountains who could pack a horse or pop a bull whip."[88] A loan of $3,460 was advanced to Slade & Ely on September 24, apparently by a consortium of local merchants through Slade's old Julesburg station agent George Chrisman.[89]

Fort Galpin lay almost on the Canadian border. The only roads north from Alder Gulch tended to head in a westerly direction, toward the Deer Lodge Valley. Slade and his crew would be venturing where no wagon wheel had ever rolled before; they would have to build their own roads and bridges and find their own fords.[90]

Slade's expedition left Virginia City in late September.[91] According to some of his men's uncorroborated tales, on their way to the Milk River they twice fought off Indian attacks; they also encountered quicksand at many of the streams they forded. But no record of their journey was kept, nor did Slade or any of his teamsters keep diaries. Precisely how they reached Fort Galpin and returned with their cargo remains largely a mystery. The only contemporaneous account of the journey consisted of two sentences some months later in the *Montana Post*.[92] The ordinarily loquacious Slade himself is not known to have spoken of the journey after it was over.

The only specific evidence of the expedition's challenges was discovered some thirty years later by the young lawyer Lew Callaway:

In the early '90s I went from White Sulphur Springs to the vicinity of Martindale [Mont.]. Sitting with the stage-driver I saw on the right of the road on which we were traveling a cut or notch almost straight down a long hillside. Asking the driver what caused it, he said, "That man Slade had to rough-lock his wheels to get off that high bench when he was on his way to the mouth of the Milk River to get freight the steamboat had unloaded on the south side of the Missouri. He must have got back some different way." About thirty years had passed since Slade had made the journey.[93]

However it was done, in the dead of a Northwest winter Slade brought his train in to Virginia City about December 10, without the loss of a man or an item of goods.[94] "Everybody thought they would be snowed up," the newly arrived Missouri lawyer Alexander Davis later recalled, "but Slade was a man of unequaled resources, and he got in this time as on many other occasions when nobody else would have dared to travel."[95]

Slade's expedition to the Milk River had probably saved Virginia City from starvation. In the process it made him a local hero, and the proceeds left him prosperous and idle as winter approached, bringing a cold so bitter that, as one mother wrote, "I was so afraid that the children would freeze their noses or ears in the night that [I] got up a number of times in the night to see that their heads were covered. Their beds would be covered with frost. I saw their breath freeze."[96]

In their stone tollhouse at Spring Dale, Slade and Virginia settled down for the winter. The pine trees along the mountain slope provided ample firewood. In such circumstances the Slades could look forward to the first peaceful period of their married life.[97]

But of course it was too quiet for Slade. And the Virginia City to which he returned on December 10 was a different place from the town he had left some two and a half months earlier. A new crisis had arisen that no man in Alder Gulch could easily avoid, least of all Slade of the Overland.

Chapter 17

REIGN OF TERROR

*

For four months after Fairweather's party struck gold in late May, settlers had poured into Alder Gulch by the thousands. All were driven there by dreams of wealth, yet the gold mined by prospectors possessed value only if they could use it somewhere else. With the onset of autumn, many prospectors who had spent the summer arduously panning for gold began to think about taking their hard-earned riches back to their wives and families in the civilized States before winter came on. Thus just as Slade's expedition departed for the Milk River in late September, the settlers he left behind began to make a painful discovery: in Alder Gulch it was easier to find gold than to take it away.

Virginia City may have tolerated drunkenness, prostitution, brawling, and gunfights, but robberies were rare, if only because a thief was easily discovered and in any case had no place to hide or spend his ill-gotten gains. A densely populated town or mining camp was an inhospitable place for a robber. But on the roads between the camps, witnesses were few and far between. So robbery became a concern for miners only when they attempted to leave.

They had three ways out, and two of them were impractical. Slade's toll road east to the Bozeman Trail was passable, but the Bozeman Trail itself was little more than a rudimentary shortcut path to the California/Oregon Trail. Or an eastbound miner could head northwest over the mountains to Fort Benton and from there travel in relative safety and comfort down the Missouri River by boat all the way to St. Louis—but this late in the season the river was already too low for boats to reach Fort Benton, which was precisely why Slade's expedition had been sent to the Milk River (an impossible mission for anyone but Slade).

That left just one travel option: by stagecoach from Virginia City west to Bannack and then south to Salt Lake City. By the summer of 1863 two stagecoach lines operated daily runs from Virginia City to Bannack and then to Salt Lake.[1] If a man planned to leave Virginia City or Bannack with gold, word got around.

The first apparent victim was an Idaho trader named Lloyd Magruder, who set up a dry goods shop in Virginia City in early September and sold out his entire inventory for some $12,000 in gold dust within three weeks. Magruder left Bannack on October 5 in the company of a group of freighters and was never heard from again.[2]

On October 26, two hooded men armed with shotguns held up the Peabody & Caldwell stagecoach on its trip from Virginia City to Bannack; the primary target was an Irish miner named "Bummer Dan" McFadden, who was robbed of $2,500 in gold.[3] On November 13, the respected settler Sam Hauser left Virginia City with more than $14,000 in gold dust; two nights later Hauser and his companions claimed to see four spectral figures in masks who rode off after they were spotted.[4] Late in November an A. J. Oliver & Co. stagecoach from Virginia City to Bannack was held up by three masked men; their prime target was a miner named Leroy Southmayd, who gave up $400 in gold dust.[5] In the first week of December a wagon train led by the freighter Milton S. Moody was held up by two masked gunmen, both of whom were shot and stumbled away before they could be identified.[6]

To the terrified settlers of eastern Idaho, these five incidents seemed to suggest the existence of an organized band of road agents who functioned with inside knowledge of departures from the gold camps. "There is certainly an organized band of highway men about here and something will have to be done soon to protect life and property," Granville Stuart of Virginia City noted in his journal of November 30.

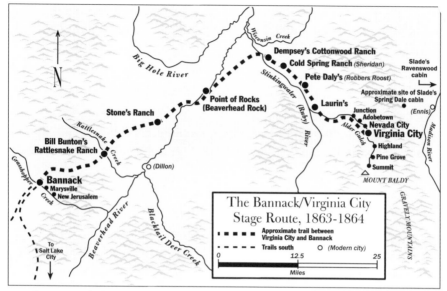

The Bannack/Virginia City
Stage Route, 1863-1864

Stage routes in the Bannack and Virginia City area of eastern Idaho Territory (later Montana), 1863–64.

But if such a band did exist, who was behind it? Astonishingly, many settlers increasingly came to suspect Henry Plummer, the elected sheriff of Bannack district and, by default, of Alder Gulch as well. Plummer, some people claimed, always seemed to be out of town when a holdup took place. Plummer had been a passenger in the stagecoach that took Sam Hauser from Virginia City to Bannack, had been given Hauser's gold sack for safekeeping overnight, and the next day had solicitously pressed upon Hauser a warm coat and a red scarf—which Hauser, in retrospect, believed was a means of identifying him to the holdup men.[7] Plummer's deputies included a killer named Buck Stinson, a mule thief and escaped convict named Ned Ray, and another unsavory tough named Jack Gallagher, with whom Slade had tangled earlier that summer. Two of Plummer's business partners at Bannack—in a mining claim and a saloon—were escapees from San Quentin Prison in California.[8]

These suspicions were entirely circumstantial, of course. There was little in Henry Plummer's California gold rush background to suggest an outlaw or a cunning criminal genius, as many in the east Idaho diggings were beginning to perceive him. More likely he was a lawman/politician who had simply improvised his way out of one scrape after another, benefiting from a combination of luck and other people's gullibility. The five killings he was known to have committed might well have been justified.

In any case, little of Plummer's past was known at Bannack when he arrived there in the fall of 1862. Two months after Idaho Territory was created in March 1863, Plummer campaigned energetically for the newly created position of sheriff and was elected handily in an open election on May 24.[9] He appeared to pursue his duties conscientiously, at least at first. Still, *somebody* was robbing those stagecoaches. If not Plummer, people wondered, then who?

Three of Plummer's appointed deputies—Ray, Stinson, and Gallagher—were unsavory toughs, but his chief deputy, D. H. Dillingham, enjoyed an honest reputation, if not much experience. Plummer's deputies did not know or trust each other well, and soon after being elected sheriff, Plummer compounded the problem by departing for Sun River, more than 200 miles north, to consummate the courtship of his intended bride, Electa Bryan, that he had commenced the previous fall. He was gone for the rest of May and most of June and consequently was totally unaware of Bill Fairweather's gold strike in Alder Gulch on May 26.[10]

While Plummer was away, his honest chief deputy Dillingham learned that travelers from Bannack to Virginia City were going to be robbed by three men and warned the victims.[11] Word got back to the three alleged outlaws—one of whom was Dillingham's fellow deputy sheriff, Buck Stinson—who promptly abandoned the robbery. Shortly afterward, Stinson and his two associates confronted Dillingham on Wallace Street in Virginia City in broad daylight. Rushing up to the chief deputy with their pistols drawn, they cursed him as a liar and opened fire, killing him instantly.[12]

This murder on June 29 occurred barely ten feet from an outdoor court that was meeting under a tree to settle disputes over mining claims.[13] The three killers—Stinson, Haze Lyons, and Charley Forbes—were promptly arrested and the court was pressed into service to try them immediately.[14] Although the killing seemed like an open-and-shut case, Stinson and Lyons contended that it had occurred accidentally, while they were upbraiding Dillingham for falsely accusing them of plotting the stagecoach robbery.[15] Both men were found guilty and sentenced to hang by a seemingly unanimous voice vote, but en route to the gallows weeping sympathizers prevailed on the crowd to take another vote, and then another, until both men as well as the third killer, Forbes, were acquitted and set free.[16]

Although little other criminal activity took place in eastern Idaho that summer of 1863, the failure to punish anyone for Dillingham's murder remained in people's minds three months later when the wave of stagecoach robberies began.

"There was no safety for life or property only so far as each individual could, with his trusty rifle, protect his own," the trader Granville Stuart later insisted. Respectable citizens far outnumbered the desperadoes, Stuart acknowledged, but "having come from all corners of the earth, they were unacquainted and did not know whom to trust. On the other hand, the 'Roughs' were organized....At times it would seem that they had the upper hand and would run affairs to suit themselves."[17]

In such an environment, it seemed, "No man's life was safe in Virginia City at that time if it was thought he had money," recalled Margaret Gilbert, wife of Slade's partner Henry Gilbert, who arrived that fall. "He might be called to his door and shot down or he might be killed on his way to or from his home. It was nothing unusual to see a dead man in the street in the morning."[18] Although eight white settlers had been murdered in eastern Idaho since the first gold strike near Bannack in 1862, the figure of 102 murders was circulated, repeated and—in the absence of newspapers or formal courts—generally accepted.[19] In a community of 10,000, even eight murders was sufficient to spread terror.

Under such circumstances miners did their limited best to take precautions. One day in Virginia City that fall a miner came to Mrs. Gilbert's house and handed her a buckskin bag. Years later she recalled the conversation:

> "There's ten thousand dollars' worth of gold dust in this bag, Mrs. Gilbert. Will you keep it for me till tomorrow?" I asked him

why he did not put it in the bank and he said he was afraid—that there were spies outside the bank and any miner who entered or left the place was a marked man. I said, "I'll keep it at your own risk," and gave the bag a toss under the bed. The next day he came and asked me if I had his dust. "I don't know," I said. "Look under the bed and see if it's still there." He dove under the bed and brought out the bag and left town with it.[20]

Yet even as a sense of helplessness seemed to pervade the Alder Gulch gold camps, the seeds of a countervailing force were being planted. Virginia City's business class included a small but solid core of potential civic leaders bound by their common ties as members of the Freemasons, the worldwide secret fraternity. One was Alexander Davis, a young lawyer and state legislator from St. Joseph, Missouri, who had voluntarily freed his inherited slaves but joined a Confederate state militia at the onset of the war out of his belief in states' rights. Captured, imprisoned, and pardoned six months later, Davis had headed for Virginia City in the fall of 1863 to pick up the pieces of his life at age thirty-one.[21]

The St. Joseph merchant and newspaper publisher Paris Pfouts, whose sister was married to Ben Holladay's brother Andrew, had similarly joined a pro-slavery militia in Missouri when the war broke out but soon fled to Denver for his safety, with the convenient aid of a free stagecoach pass furnished by the Central Overland's president (and Holladay's cousin), Bela Hughes.[22] Soon after he arrived in Colorado, Pfouts was elected master of the Denver Masonic Lodge, but a year later, threatened with military arrest for his Southern sympathies, Pfouts and his partner closed their Denver store and transported their goods to Virginia City. By November Pfouts had established Virginia City's largest general store and soon after organized the territory's first Masonic Lodge.[23]

Another potential community pillar was Wilbur Sanders, an attorney from Akron, Ohio, who in June 1863 set out with his wife and two children for Lewiston, the capital of the newly created Idaho Territory. They were accompanying the family of Sanders's uncle, Sidney Edgerton, the new territory's recently appointed chief justice. By

The respected lawyer Alexander Davis, upper left, refused to join the vigilantes, shamed them into creating a public court, and defended Slade against them. The merchant Paris Pfouts, upper right, a friend of Slade's, was one of the five Virginia City men who formed the Vigilance Committee in December 1863. He served as its president and was later elected mayor. The lawyer Wilbur Sanders, lower left, a founding vigilante, prosecuted the open-air murder trial of George Ives and tried to dissuade Slade from drinking. John S. Lott, lower right, a Nevada City merchant, was elected secretary of the vigilantes. Although he and James Williams were the committee's only members from Nevada City, their camp's influence was disproportionate, with fateful consequences. (*Montana Historical Society*)

September their party had reached Bannack. But Lewiston lay another 700 miles across the Bitterroot mountains, and finding the way impassable, they chose to winter instead in that raw mining camp. The following February, by which time most of Bannack's population (as well as its legal business) had removed to Virginia City, Sanders and his family moved there as well.[24]

Although some people in Bannack and Virginia City harbored suspicions about Henry Plummer, Plummer's ability to charm innocent men—and especially women—allayed most doubts. Plummer especially went out of his way to ingratiate himself with his respected next-door neighbor in Bannack, the lawyer Wilbur Sanders. In November 1863 Plummer invited Sanders and his uncle, Chief Justice Edgerton, and their wives to his home for Thanksgiving. The holiday came at the very time that Slade's expedition was making its way to the Milk River in its daring attempt to save eastern Idaho from starvation, yet Plummer's house evinced no sign of hardship. Harriet Sanders later described the meal:

> Considering the meagerness of delicacies in the market and the extortionate prices charged, even for the necessities of life, that repast was one of the most sumptuous dinners I ever attended....[Plummer] sent to Salt Lake City, a distance of five hundred miles, and everything that money could buy was served, delicately cooked and with all the style that would characterize a banquet at "Sherry's." I now recall to mind that the turkey cost forty dollars in gold.

Plummer, Harriet Sanders added, "was slender, graceful and mild of speech. He had pleasing manners and fine address, a fair complexion, sandy hair and blue eyes—the last person whom one would select as a daring highwayman and murderer."[25]

Ultimately it took the murder of a mere youth in early December—coincidentally, just about the time that Slade returned from his successful expedition to the Milk River—to rouse the Gulch's respectable citizens to action. The young man, Nicholas Tiebalt, had sold his employers a span of mules for $200 in gold. On his way to deliver the mules to Summit, the uppermost camp along Alder Gulch, Tiebalt spent the night at a road ranch where, unbeknownst to him, a charming rogue named George Ives often stayed. Ives was tall, blond, smooth-shaven, and handsome and exuded an aristocratic air; like Plummer he was a New Englander by birth and had headed for California during the gold rush. Eventually he followed the gold-seekers to Bannack, where he arrived in February 1863.[26] He had a strong taste for whiskey and, after a few drinks, often rode his horse into a store or saloon, tossing his buckskin purse on the counter and asking for one or more ounces of gold dust "as a loan," while amusing himself by firing his revolver at the lamps and other furnishings.[27]

In the course of that night at the road ranch, young Tiebalt may have naively mentioned that he had gold on his person. The next morning, when he set out again with the mules, Tiebalt was overtaken and killed by a bandit who took both his gold and the mules.[28]

Ten days later a rancher named William Palmer, crossing the Ruby Valley with his team on his way to Alder Gulch, fired at a grouse flying overhead; the bird fell through the willows upon Nicholas Tiebalt's frozen body. "The marks of a small lariat were on the dead man's wrists and neck," wrote the local schoolmaster and journalist Thomas Dimsdale. "He had been dragged through the brush while living, after being shot, and when found lay on his face, his right arm bent across his chest and his left hand grasping the willows above him."[29]

Palmer, stunned, took the body to a nearby *wickiup*—a brush shelter resembling a teepee—and asked the two occupants, one of whom was later identified as Long John Franck, to help him lift the body into his wagon so he could take it to Virginia City for identification. They seemed unsurprised by Palmer's discovery and refused to help him.[30]

Palmer, shocked by their callousness, loaded the corpse himself and drove it on to Nevada City, the miners' camp a mile below Virginia City. Among the miners who recognized Tiebalt's body was Captain James Williams, the hard-nosed wagonmaster who had confronted Slade on the way to Alder Gulch the previous spring. Williams had been among the frustrated miners who guarded Deputy Dillingham's three killers overnight in June, only to see them set free the next day. Now an agitated miner named William Clark suggested to Williams that they organize a vigilante committee: "This thing," Clark said, "has been running on long enough and has got to be stopped."

Williams offered to provide fifty or sixty saddle horses and twenty-five or thirty saddles and bridles for a posse. By late that afternoon a dozen men had volunteered, and Williams himself—one of the few miners with actual military experience—was prevailed upon to join them. At about ten o'clock on that cold December night, this party started out in search of Long John Franck, whose callousness toward Palmer had made him a prime suspect.

Before daybreak the next morning they came upon the *wickiup*, surrounded it with their guns drawn and seized Long John. Although Williams was not the posse's captain, he seems at this point to have instinctively taken charge, just as he had done in his confrontation with Slade the previous spring. At first Long John vigorously denied his involvement in Tiebalt's murder, but soon he broke down. He did not kill Tiebalt, Long John said, but one of the killers was inside the *wickiup*: George Ives. The posse promptly arrested Ives, Long John, and one other man.

When the posse members reached their own camp at Nevada City, an angry crowd gathered, and the local merchant John Lott argued forcefully that "if they are tried there [in Virginia City], we'll have another Dillingham mess." Upon a vote of the assembled crowd, the prisoners were held at Nevada City.

Although no courtroom—or any sort of assembly hall—existed at Nevada City, the community attempted to provide the semblance of a legal trial. The trial that began on December 19 was held outdoors in the town's main street, with hundreds of miners in attendance. Heat was provided by log fires built in the open. Two judges, two clerks, and twenty-four jurors were chosen. Wilbur Sanders, then in Virginia City to rally support for creating a new territory east of the Bitterroot Mountains (and thereby spare himself and his uncle Sidney Edgerton the need to continue on to Idaho's capital at Lewiston), was persuaded to act as lead prosecutor.[31]

Ives and two co-defendants were represented by four defense attorneys, Alexander Davis among them.[32] Two sheriffs were elected to maintain order, and a protective circle of one hundred armed men, commanded by James Williams, surrounded the participants. The proceedings were delayed by the endless haggling of the defense attorneys, until on the third day the impatient crowd of miners demanded an end by nightfall.[33]

But the most striking thing about this trial could not easily be articulated by the spectators gathered there. Previous trials in the territory usually found the prosecution in a self-protective mode, for fear of the unknown desperadoes who might lurk in the audience. Here the prosecution was emboldened by the support of a sympathetic crowd.[34]

The night before the Ives trial ended, Sanders, the merchant Paris Pfouts, and three other men held a secret meeting in Virginia City. Pfouts had organized a local Masonic lodge only two weeks earlier and became its first master.[35] The Masons of course were a secret society; as a prominent Mason later suggested, "The Masons knew they could trust each other and consequently they took counsel of each other."[36] In those two elements—secrecy and trust—Pfouts perceived the tools for combating a perceived threat. If Ives was found guilty the next day, the five men agreed that they must avoid the sort of emotional pleas and recounts that had undermined the verdicts in the Dillingham murder. Once convicted, the killer must be executed immediately; any hesitation would make a mockery of a public trial and would embolden other killers in the area.

The solution, they agreed, was to create a formal Vigilance Committee, complete with officers, rules, and clearly defined objectives. Its purpose would be to carry out Ives's sentence and then find and root out his accomplices and anyone else who threatened the community, dispensing with the cumbersome and unpredictable burden of holding lengthy public trials.[37] "If every Road Agent cost as much labor, time and money for his conviction," explained the local journalist, Mason and vigilante sympathizer Thomas Dimsdale, "the efforts of the citizens would have, practically, failed altogether. Some shorter, surer, and at least equitable method of procedure was to be found."[38] Pfouts later wrote, "We agreed to hold another meeting the following night, and each one of us was to bring such other gentlemen as were willing to unite with us in the cause, but the utmost caution was to be observed in inviting none but those known to be trustworthy."[39]

The next afternoon, as darkness set in on that shortest day of the year, Sanders delivered an eloquent closing argument at the Ives trial. About six o'clock, after only a half hour's deliberation, the jurors returned a guilty verdict. Sanders, recalling the fiasco in the escape of Dillingham's murderers six months earlier, moved that Ives be hanged immediately.

Until this moment Ives himself had treated the proceedings nonchalantly, apparently presuming that his resourceful friends—perhaps

Sheriff Plummer himself?—would come to his rescue. Now he asked for a postponement until the next day, so that he could make his will and write to his mother and sisters. To this the miner John X. Beidler shouted, "Sanders, ask him how much time he gave the Dutchman!" meaning the young victim Tiebalt.

This drew a laugh from the crowd and an overwhelming vote to proceed with the hanging—although, to be sure, perhaps more than a hundred shouted, "No!" For some of Ives's friends were among the crowd, fully armed, and doing their best to sow doubt and confusion. Some murmured that Sheriff Plummer was probably on his way with a writ of habeas corpus that would free Ives from these extralegal proceedings. Some shouted, "Don't hang him!"; others called, "Let's banish him"; still others cried, "Hang Long John—he's the real murderer."

At this critical moment, Williams asserted command. "Men!" he announced. "'Bout face! Prepare to shoot!" The friends of Ives melted away, and Ives mounted an improvised scaffold on an unfinished frame building. Williams commanded, "Men, do your duty"; the box was jerked from under Ives; and the deed was done.[40]

But the exhilaration of the moment was tempered by apprehension. Ives was dead, but the presumed gang to which he belonged still existed. Having publicly committed themselves, James Williams and his fellow vigilantes believed themselves marked men. Now there was no turning back from the path they had chosen. They must destroy the rest of the road agents before the road agents destroyed them.

Yet in fact there had never been any danger that Sheriff Plummer would interrupt the Ives trial and take custody of the defendant. When word reached Plummer that Ives had been charged with murder, he remarked to friends that he dared not leave Bannack. Instead of interfering with the trial, he would post sentries around Bannack to protect himself from these newly constituted vigilantes.[41] He was as scared of them as they were of him.

That night, at a meeting called by Pfouts and Sanders, a dozen men—all Masons except for James Williams—gathered in the house of Jeremiah M. Fox and took the oath as members of the first formal Vigilance Committee in Alder Gulch.[42] Lacking experience at vigilante justice, the group largely took its cues from a store clerk from

California, where during the gold rush men of property and influence had formed vigilance committees to protect private property and defy corrupt or unfriendly politicians. "The question arose as to how we could organize," wrote one of the vigilantes later, "and this man from California suggested he had the oath, and told us what the particulars were and how the committee was organized in California."[43]

But these vigilantes differed from their California brothers in one important aspect: they would utilize the secret and ceremonial character of Freemasonry against the outlaws.[44] Instead of conducting cumbersome and risky public tribunals like the trial of George Ives, they would conduct trials and executions in secret. Instead of drawing jurors from the general population, as the Ives trial had done, the vigilantes would leave the trial and sentencing of criminals to their executive committee of seventeen members.[45] Instead of polling the general population for guidance, as the miners' courts had done, the vigilantes would take counsel only among themselves.[46] The miners had tried to enforce peace publicly and (so the vigilantes believed) had failed; the vigilantes would act privately, and the only punishment they would inflict would be death. To the argument that "the punishment was severe beyond all proportion to the crime," the trader Granville Stuart later noted that "there was no recognized court in the country and the nearest jail was at Walla Walla, four hundred and twenty-five miles distant, over rugged mountains. . . . Hence it was advisable to inflict such punishment as would strike terror to the minds of the evil doers, and exercise a restraining influence over them."[47]

The following day, a second vigilante committee was formed at Nevada City, just a mile away. Its immediate objective differed from the Virginia City group's. On the scaffold, Ives had blamed young Tiebalt's killing on an associate named Aleck Carter—which suggested that some of Tiebalt's murderers were still at large. John Lott, James Williams, and the others who had organized the posse that captured Ives were determined to arrest his accomplices before the news could reach them.

"We the undersigned," this Nevada group declared, in the first vigilante oath committed to paper, "uniting ourselves in a party for the laudable purpose of arresting thieves & murderers & recover stolen property do pledge ourselves upon our sacred honor each to all others & solemnly swear that we will reveal no secrets, violate no laws of right & not desert each other or our standard of justice so help us God as witness our hand & seal this 23 of December, A.D. 1863."[48]

In theory the Nevada City committee functioned as the Virginia City committee's ally; at least two of its members—John Lott and James Williams—were involved in the Virginia committee as well. In a series of meetings over the next three or four days, the Virginia City vigilantes grew to about fifty in number—"all among the best and most reliable citizens," Pfouts later wrote.[49] But the Nevada committee's adherents grew to about 250. In the rush to organize, no one raised the question of what might happen should these two secretive vigilante committees ever disagree.

S lade at this point had returned from the Milk River less than two weeks earlier. In many respects he was an ideal candidate for the vigilantes. He had famously stamped out criminal gangs for the Central Overland; he had already picked a fight with Plummer's dreaded deputy Jack Gallagher; and his Milk River success had endowed him with the status of a local hero who had saved Alder Gulch from imminent starvation. Slade was friendly with several of the founding vigilantes, including Paris Pfouts, Wilbur Sanders, X. Beidler (who had dined at Slade's Ravenswood ranch that summer), and Jim Kiskadden; and he had worked closely (albeit reluctantly) with James Williams when their wagon trains had joined forces that spring.

The vigilantes' secrecy oath makes it impossible to say with certainty whether Slade joined their ranks, but much evidence suggests that he was probably among that first group of fifty Virginia City recruits. The local schoolmaster and journalist Thomas Dimsdale later identified Slade as a vigilante; so did the vigilante sympathizer Nathaniel Langford as well as the Virginia City lawyer Alexander Davis, who added that Slade "was one of the leading men, and very active in aiding its operations." And Slade is known to have assisted the vigilantes in at least one of their arrests. But if Slade did join the vigilantes, he

The Virginia City lumber merchant Nathaniel Langford, left, rejected Slade's demand for credit and lived to tell the tale. The vigilante X. Beidler warned Slade to go home during one drinking binge, to no avail. (*Montana Historical Society*)

does not appear to have been more than a marginal participant. Nor did he serve on the seventeen-member executive committee, if only because his drinking problems persisted: "He soon commenced getting drunk, going into saloons, slapping men in the face, and committing other insults and outrages," Davis recalled.[50]

During those frantic days at the end of 1863 the Vigilance Committee drew up a formal set of regulations and by-laws. Pfouts was elected president, James Williams executive officer, Wilbur Sanders prosecuting officer, and John Lott—the Nevada City merchant who a week earlier had persuaded the Ives posse to hold the trial there rather than in Virginia City—was elected secretary.[51] In theory, the relationship between Pfouts and Williams was analogous to a civilian president and his commanding general; in practice, while Williams treated Pfouts with due respect, the real power rested with Williams. (Lott later observed that "Williams was really the executive head, but Pfouts was the ornimental [*sic*] one, and a good one, too.")[52]

The founding Virginia City vigilantes were mostly businessmen, not gunfighters. To perform the actual dirty work of apprehending and hanging the road agents they would need to recruit miners from the surrounding camps. This would not be an easy task. The vigilantes tended to be Protestant Masons and predominantly Northern Republicans; the miners were heavily Roman Catholic (whose Pope had condemned Freemasonry as a naturalistic deistic religion in conflict with Church doctrine) and Southern Democrat.[53] Yet the vigilantes proposed to bypass the miners' democratic courts and render their own secret verdicts instead. But in the wake of the Ives trial, the vigilantes were able to exploit the urgency of the moment. Within the next few days at least 300 and possibly as many as 1,500 men enrolled in vigilante companies, not only at Virginia City and Nevada City but also at gold camps up and down Alder Gulch.[54]

One conspicuous exception was the respected Missouri lawyer Alexander Davis, himself a Mason and seemingly a logical choice for the Vigilance Committee. When the vigilantes asked him to join, Davis politely refused, explaining that as a lawyer he could not be party to executions that lacked the sanction of a court and jury. According to his son Walter, Davis was given three choices. He could join the vigilantes, leave the region, or be hanged. Davis replied: "Gentlemen, I cannot join the vigilantes. I will not leave the region, for I have the right to be here. So I suppose you will have to hang me."[55] In his case the vigilantes backed off, but the incident suggests that many men of weaker spines were coerced into joining.

Shortly before New Year's Day, in biting cold weather and deep snow, a group of twenty-five Nevada City vigilantes led by James Williams set out to the west out on horses and mules into the Stinkingwater Valley (so named by prospectors who had found an Indian burial ground there). On the way to the small town of Deer Lodge, a supposed road agent hangout, they passed a red-haired, red-whiskered man riding in the opposite direction. At Deer Lodge they found no outlaws, the road agents apparently having just been warned to leave by the very messenger the posse had passed. But two days later, after resting their animals in the town, Williams's posse proceeded to Rattlesnake Creek, where they found the same red-haired man inside a *wickiup*. His name was Erastus Yeager, better known as "Red," and he was the gang's messenger, as the vigilantes discovered when they searched him and found a written message warning the road agents that the vigilantes were on the way.

Yeager, advised that he was about to hang, broke down and confessed his membership in the gang and much more. Far from being a loyal gang member, it developed, Yeager harbored a fierce hatred toward Bill Bunton, one of his confederates who, he said, had introduced him to a life of crime at Lewiston some years earlier. Yeager begged the vigilantes to seek out and punish all of his fellow desperadoes. He provided the vigilantes with a list of twenty-two gang members and their functions in the organization, down to "secretary," "stool-pigeon," "roadster," "spy," "fence," "horse thief," "telegraph man," and "council-room keeper at Bannack City."[56] At the top of Yeager's list was the name of Henry Plummer, chief. For the first time, the astounded vigilantes confirmed their suspicion that their sheriff was an outlaw leader.

Yeager led the vigilantes to a road agent hangout known as Robbers' Roost, where they found and arrested the gang's secretary, George Brown, who had written the incriminating letter found on Yeager's person.[57] As had been the case for George Ives, the vigilantes intended to take their two captives to Virginia City for trial before the group's executive committee. But as they proceeded, they concluded that they might encounter trouble there, or along the way. On January 4, near a cottonwood grove, both men were tried and hanged. Upon Brown's back the Vigilantes fastened a placard reading "Corresponding Secretary"; on Yeager, the placard read, "Red, Road Agent and Messenger."[58]

This, at least, was the vigilantes' account of their first two executions. Red Yeager's list was never produced in public. Because the vigilantes tried their victims in secret —when they gave them trials at all— and executed them immediately afterward, settlers and later historians alike had only the vigilantes' version of events to go on. Some later commentators argued that Red Yeager was not a road agent at all, but merely a naïve fellow who had unknowingly been given an message to carry (as travelers often did), and that the vigilantes merely exploited public fear of a criminal gang as a pretext to eliminate and intimidate their political enemies, Sheriff Henry Plummer first and foremost among them.[59]

Back in Virginia City three days later, armed now with Red Yeager's information, the Vigilance Committee moved swiftly to capture Plummer and his confederates before they could learn that their cover was blown. John Lott and three men were dispatched to Bannack to enlist the help of known sympathizers. There on January 10 the party arrested Sheriff Plummer's deputies, Ned Ray and Buck Stinson, before either man could get word to Plummer. Plummer himself was surprised at his home, unarmed and with his coat off. Moments later, he and his deputies faced a scaffold that Plummer had erected for the hanging of another man.

Was Henry Plummer the evil mastermind of a criminal gang, as the vigilantes believed? Or was he a victim of circumstances? The vigilante apologist Dimsdale later claimed that Plummer confessed numerous crimes and murders before dying, but the record suggests that he maintained his innocence to the end, nor was he implicated by other road agents hanged by the vigilantes.[60] A public trial might have sorted out the accusations and determined the truth. But the vigilantes, convinced of Plummer's guilt, were equally convinced that he could manipulate any public trial. Under the common-law principle of "innocent until proven guilty," many a criminal had been acquitted by a jury for lack of sufficient evidence.

A public trial might also sow doubts about the vigilantes' own methods. Only Plummer's immediate death would send the clear and unequivocal message that the vigilantes felt was necessary.

At least some evidence exists that this first flurry of executions effectively broke the gang as a threat to communal peace. Some of the lesser members of the gang—those who were warned by Red Yeager before he was captured—laid plans to flee across the Bitterroot mountains toward Lewiston.[61] But within twenty-four hours the vigilantes executed two more alleged road agents at Bannack.

It is easy to understand how laymen who felt their lives or property threatened could believe that a few salutary hangings might enhance their security. The vigilantes failed to perceive that an execution carried out without the sanction of law or even broad public acceptance inevitably breeds resentment, so that the executioners' security is more threatened than before.

In Virginia City, vigilante president Paris Pfouts believed that the executions at Bannack "exasperated the members of the band of cut-throats in Virginia City and they threatened terrible vengeance on the Vigilantes." Pfouts claimed that one man "fired off his pistol and swore he would kill me."[62]

On January 13 the executive committee learned that six of the men on Yeager's list—including Haze Lyons, one of the killers of Deputy Dillingham—were hiding in the saloons and brothels of Virginia City itself. That night James Williams threw a cordon of 250 men around the town with orders to permit no one to leave without written authority. Vigilante companies from six mining camps were summoned the next morning, not only to capture the road agents but also as a show of force. One of the wanted road agents, Bill Hunter, escaped in the freezing cold by climbing down a drain ditch, but the other five were soon captured and hanged simultaneously from a beam that ran across the center of an unfinished building in the heart of the town, in sight of hundreds of armed vigilantes and many more spectators.[63]

"I do not know that I can now recall the exact crime for which each man was hung," the vigilante captain Adriel B. Davis told a reporter years later, "but they were all thorough scoundrels, and might have been tried for any one of a dozen crimes."[64]

This practice of executing men for crimes they might have committed inevitably generated criticism, which the vigilantes found it necessary to suppress. Although the vigilantes' regulations provided no punishment other than death, now they responded by banishing their most articulate critics from the territory.[65] Among these were two of the lawyers who had defended George Ives at Alder Gulch's last public murder trial. Although countless petty criminals and low-lifes were allowed to remain in Alder Gulch, "The administration of justice, and the peace and safety of the people, demanded the banishment of both these men," the vigilante sympathizer Nathaniel Langford later explained.[66]

Slade seems never to have come to terms with the new Alder Gulch he found on his return from the Milk River. Before he had departed, some seventy-five days earlier, Virginia City was a wild place where even the most outrageous behavior was tolerated; yet by mid-January all of Alder Gulch was seemingly cowed by armed and organized vigilante companies that hunted down and summarily executed anyone perceived as a threat to the public peace. In this brave new world where anyone not aligned with the vigilantes fell under suspicion, Slade was a man without a constituency. If he took the vigilante oath, he soon seems to have lost interest in its work; he was neither their enthusiastic partner nor—like Alexander Davis—their critic. Basking in his status as a local hero, he seems not to have grasped the enormity of the change that had come over the community—or, if he did, he assumed that his status had rendered him impervious to it.

Slade had returned from the Milk River on December 10, just nine days before the George Ives trial and less than two weeks before the vigilantes organized. At a moment when everyone else in Alder Gulch seemed preoccupied with the peril posed by the road agents, Slade's own perilous expedition had left him in comfortable financial condition and in a celebratory mood. By January the ground throughout the region was frozen, preventing him from working on his ranches, had he been inclined to do so.[67] At Spring Dale he was safely removed from the turmoil in Virginia City, but he couldn't abide the solitude of a rancher's life. His years on the Central Overland had accustomed him to the companionship of men who followed his orders. In this frozen winter, that sort of companionship could be found only in Virginia City's saloons.

And so at the very moment the vigilantes were imposing civic order on Alder Gulch, Slade resumed his old destructive drinking habits.

Having broken the power of the road agents' gang, the vigilantes were eager to legitimize their actions, especially in the light of Alexander Davis's principled refusal to endorse them. Shortly after the mass hangings at Virginia City on January 14, the vigilantes co-opted Davis by establishing a "people's court" where offenders would be tried openly—not by the vigilantes, but by a judge and jury. At a public meeting, Davis was elected judge of this court, against his will; but since he had advocated its creation, he reluctantly accepted.[68] The miners also elected a sheriff, Major Alvin Brookie, one of the founding vigilantes, who would bear responsibility for arresting suspects and bringing them before the court.[69]

Under Davis's leadership, this court offered the prospect of an orderly evolution from the unwieldy makeshift miners' courts to what Thomas Dimsdale called "the nearest approach to social order that the circumstances permitted."[70] In this people's court, unlike the vigilante tribunals, a defendant had a right to be present at his own trial, defense attorneys were permitted, and in general the spirit of English common law was invoked to provide a check on the blood-lust of angry mobs.[71]

Such a court's effectiveness depended entirely on the people's willingness to recognize its authority. But the vigilantes who had established Davis's court refused to disband, for fear that they might be targeted for revenge once they broke up. This collection of merchants and miners, who a few weeks earlier had trembled at the prospect of taking human life, were reluctant to give up the upper hand against their perceived enemies once they gained it. Nor could the vigilantes control what might occur if any of the surviving road agents had the opportunity to testify in Virginia City before an independent jury in an open court run by a trained and courageous judge like Davis.

Thus instead of terminating the vigilantes' activity, the creation of the people's court inadvertently accelerated it. Instead of putting away their guns and returning to mining gold and peddling dry goods and sundries, the vigilantes now determined to capture and hang the remaining road agents on Red Yeager's list—the men who, around New Year's Day, had fled Deer Lodge to the Bitterroot Mountains after Yeager's message had warned them to leave. Any man who had fled was presumed, by that very act, to have revealed his guilt.

Over the next twelve days, many miles from Alder Gulch and the people's court of Alexander Davis, men were hunted down in lonely cabins or in brush *wickiups* in isolated gulches. By January 26, eight more men had been captured and executed. One of them was Steve

Marshland, who had participated in robberies but by the vigilantes' own acknowledgment had never committed a murder, and at the time of his hanging was dying of frostbite and posed no threat to anyone. Another was George Shears, a twenty-one-year-old horse thief who surrendered quietly and confessed his guilt, saying that he knew he would have to "go up sometime." He was taken to a barn at Frenchtown, where the hangman's rope had been thrown over a beam, and told to climb a ladder to the point where the drop would be sufficient to kill him.

"Gentlemen," he called down to them, "I am not used to this business, never having been hung before. Shall I jump off or slide off?" He was advised that jumping off would hasten his death.

"All right," Shears replied, according to the Vigilantes' accounts, "goodbye!"—and jumped.[72]

The impartial administration of justice was inevitably complicated by the intimate nature of a small town where everyone knew everyone else's personal business. Alexander Davis, the new judge, maintained his office and his court in the two-room stone store building of Paris Pfouts, the president of the vigilantes. Jeremiah M. Fox, the deputy sheriff as well as a founding vigilante, slept with Pfouts in a corner of the store that was partitioned off with canvas. Two brothers, William and Arthur Hunt, also slept in the Pfouts store, on a roll of bedding. In this manner the Hunts and Pfouts—and by extension the rest of the town—became intimately familiar with Fox's embarrassing personal affairs.

Fox's new wife, it seems, had left him upon arriving in Virginia City to set up housekeeping with Henry Edgar, one of the discoverers of Alder Gulch and an old friend of hers. Shortly thereafter she left Edgar and returned to Fox with a long sack containing between $8,000 and $10,000 worth of gold dust belonging to Edgar. Mrs. Fox then left Virginia City for Colorado with the gold sack, abetted by her husband, who accompanied her to Fort Bridger before returning to Virginia City.

This, at least, was the story told by Edgar and elaborated in rumors circulated by the Hunt brothers. Whether fairly or not, Deputy Sheriff Fox became an object of ridicule from the day he took office in mid-

January. Yet this was the man who was often called upon to serve as acting sheriff in Brookie's absence.[73]

By the end of January only five men on the list of road agents supposedly supplied by Red Yeager remained alive and at large.[74] Bill Hunter had escaped from Virginia City on January 13 by climbing down a drain ditch; by late January, lacking friends or any support network, he was surely close to death of frost or starvation. Nevertheless, when Hunter was spotted amid a sudden gold stampede to the Gallatin Valley east of Alder Gulch, James Williams immediately dispatched four men with orders to capture and execute the fugitive, notwithstanding a great snowstorm that had just blown in.[75] The party was led by Captain Adriel B. Davis (not to be confused with Judge Alexander Davis), who with Williams had been among Virginia City's twelve original vigilantes. On the way, the party picked up two more men.

En route to the mouth of the Gallatin River this six-man posse spent the night at Slade's stone tollhouse on what had come to be called Slade Creek. Here they found Slade, his wife Virginia, their adopted son Jemmy, and "Old Jimmy" Boner (then all of forty-eight years old), Slade's former station keeper on the Central Overland, whom Slade had hired as a cook. A. B. Davis later recalled that Boner cooked dinner for the party and then the posse turned to playing cards: "They gambled all night at Slade's and the next morning we were told by the hostler that Mrs. Slade had won $1,200"—further evidence that Virginia Slade had probably worked in gambling halls before meeting her husband.[76]

The next morning, February 2, in freezing cold and snow, the group pushed onward, apparently without Slade.[77] By evening, after proceeding about 20 miles, they found shelter in a cabin also occupied by another traveler: Bill Hunter. After a promise that he would be taken to Virginia City to stand trial, Hunter agreed to go willingly.[78] The promise was not kept. After proceeding homeward for about two miles, the group halted some 20 miles above the Gallatin River, at "the foot of a tree which seemed as if it had been fashioned by nature for a gallows," as the Montana historian M. A. Leeson described it in 1885. By majority vote, Hunter was hanged then and there.[79]

Hunter's execution raised the number of vigilante victims to twenty-one and, perhaps as a result, the stagecoach robberies in east Idaho abruptly ended. No one then in Alder Gulch appears to have calculated the cost of this reign of terror: In a matter of six weeks, the vigilantes had killed far more people than all the road agents and reckless gunmen in east Idaho had killed in the previous eighteen months.[80]

Despite his wife's protests, Slade on his return from the Milk River fell into the habit of making frequent trips to Virginia City, where he joined a band of drinking cronies who included the leader of the Alder Gulch "discovery party" himself, Bill Fairweather. As in his Virginia Dale days, Slade liked to shock bystanders by paying for his drinks with Jules Beni's gruesome ears. "He had always a band of his men around him," Judge Davis recalled, "so if anyone resenting an insult got the better of Slade, there were others behind to shoot them down." A common feat of Slade's when he got on a spree was what he called "taking the town."[81] Precisely what this involved was described by eleven-year-old Mollie Sheehan, who witnessed one of Slade's binges one day while she headed toward the meat market in Virginia City:

> I was alarmed by a clatter past me of horse's hoofs and the crack of pistol shots. A man galloping his horse recklessly down the street was firing a six-shooter in the air and whooping wildly. Suddenly he reared his horse back on its haunches, turned it sharply, and forced it through the swinging door of a saloon. I sidled into the first open doorway that I dared enter. "That's Slade," said the storekeeper, "on one of his sprees, shootin' up the town, scarin' women an' children. That smart aleck orter be strung up." He led me out the back door and warned me to run home quickly and stay out of range of stray bullets. "He'll get his needin's yit," he threatened.[82]

Under the influence of alcohol, Slade seemed to revel in his obnoxiousness. On horseback, he would "stand in the middle of the crowded street until there was no one in sight," the freighter Alexander

Toponce recalled. "Then he would laugh and go into the saloon for more drinks."[83]

Nor did Slade confine these drinking sprees to Virginia City. For want of anything better to do, Slade sometimes rode the twelve-mile length of Alder Gulch, stopping in the towns of Central, Nevada, Adobetown, and Junction, patronizing the saloons and occasionally wrecking one.

Did these binges represent a cry for help from a man who had cracked under the strain of endless ordeals? The residents of Alder Gulch were left to grapple with an impossible conundrum: how could the community's savior also be its greatest troublemaker?

Slade when drunk was not merely a threat to property; he was also an obvious threat to Virginia City's self-appointed guardians of civic order. The miner J. M. Venable described Slade's talent at conflating the vigilante president Pfouts and Deputy Sheriff Fox with a brothel proprietor known as Moll Featherlegs:

> Slade and [Bill] Fairweather had become great cronies. Whenever the former was in town he hunted up his friend Bill.... When the cronies went on a spree they would go from one saloon to another, shouting and singing about Fox, Pfouts, Featherlegs and company!... They would make up songs telling how Edgar was cheated out of his gold dust. This boisterous manner of connecting their names with the Fox-Edgar affair and with a courtesan was very annoying, especially to Pfouts. He and Fox both went to Slade and Fairweather, when they were sober, and ordered them not to use their names again in public. Fox threatened them with arrest if the offense was repeated.[84]

The vigilantes were preoccupied above all with sending the message that they were not to be trifled with. That was precisely what Slade, under the influence, was doing, and very publicly, too.

Once a spree was over, Slade would return to the tollhouse at Spring Dale and, a day or two later—respectful, well-mannered, and aghast at the trouble he had caused—he would ride into Virginia City to apologize and pay for all the damage.[85] When sober, "He was always very pleasant in his dealings with me," said Alexander Toponce—the same Toponce who had watched the drunken Slade scatter a crowd from Wallace Street.[86] But as Slade's rampages continued, local merchants lost patience with his pattern of contrition and reimbursement. "There were not a few who regarded payment as small satisfaction for the outrage," wrote the local journalist Thomas Dimsdale, "and these men were his personal enemies."[87]

During one binge that February, Slade barged into Virginia City's theater and surprised the audience by firing his revolver during the performance, according to Harriet Sanders. Her husband, Wilbur, the attorney, had moved his family from Bannack to Virginia City that month and tended to sympathize with Slade's affliction. "Mr. Sanders had volunteered upon a number of occasions to say to him that he must go home at once and never again be guilty of such misdemeanors, or his safety no one could be responsible for," Harriet wrote in her memoirs.[88]

Later that month the theater scheduled a performance of Shakespeare's *Othello*. In a town starved for uplifting entertainment, this was no minor undertaking. The well-known Dean Haine troupe of Salt Lake City was to travel nearly 500 miles by stagecoach to perform. As Harriet Sanders recalled, Wilbur took the precaution of approaching Slade in advance:

> Mr. Sanders asked him one day if he intended to go the theater when the Dean Haine troupe came. He said, "Why do you ask that question? I know why you ask. Mrs. Sanders wishes to go, and she is afraid of me. Take your wife and tell her to have no fears. I give my word that no one shall be hurt." It is needless to say that I went, and he kept his word.[89]

Precisely when Slade's sprees occurred, and how often, is difficult to pin down. The fact that a vigilante posse spent the night at Slade's tollhouse on February 1 would seem to suggest that he remained in the vigilantes' good graces at that point. On the other hand, the local journalist Thomas Dimsdale remarked, "On returning from Milk River he became more and more addicted to drinking."[90] A code of morals and manners established at a Virginia City miners' meeting on February 7 may have been provoked by Slade's previous binges: it provided fines for cursing, discharging firearms, or threatening or endangering the lives of others.[91]

For all his anti-social behavior when drunk, Slade when sober demonstrated more respect for the people's court in its first month than the vigilantes did. After the new public morals regulations were approved, Slade twice was charged by Brookie, the new sheriff, and voluntarily appeared before Judge Davis, who held court in the store owned by the vigilante president Paris Pfouts. In both instances Slade was cited for misdemeanors and readily paid the fines Davis imposed upon him for a first and second offense.

Even before these episodes, Davis and Slade appear to have developed something of a mutual admiration society, and Davis functioned informally as Slade's legal adviser.[92] Freemason and social pillar though he may have been, Davis seems to have preferred Slade's company to that of the town's merchants and politicians. On the basis of just a few months' acquaintance—for Davis had arrived at Virginia City while Slade was away on the Milk River—Davis concluded that Slade was "a very fearless man, the bravest I think I ever saw, and the finest formed, a man of great power, quick and active, very intelligent, and when sober one of the most pleasant men to talk to that you could find anywhere. He looked as little like a desperado as could be, and if you didn't see him in one of his rages you would take him to be a man of the kindest heart and gentlest disposition."[93]

Davis, along with Brookie and Pfouts, became "apologists for Slade," Davis later recalled, "and whenever the people would threaten to hang him we would plead for him. . . . We made it our business to talk to Slade about the feeling of the people, and tried to get him to do better, but he kept cutting up all the time."[94]

In the tollhouse at Spring Dale, Virginia Slade took to sitting in the winter darkness and awaiting the sound of Slade's faithful "Old Copperbottom," trotting home with her husband in the saddle. Some nights Slade did not return from Virginia City at all, opting to sleep in a stable beneath his horse rather than negotiate the eight-mile ride through the hills. The Slades' boy Jemmy, their cook Jim Boner, and perhaps a few other hands provided Virginia some companionship, but in her husband's absence this fiery woman's life must have been lonely.

A charming tale holds that Slade came home very drunk one night and announced that he was leaving her. In response, Virginia drew two loaded revolvers, pointed them at his head and told him, "You took me for better or for worse and now you're not going to cast me off like an old shoe." To this Slade shrugged, patted her affectionately and replied, "Oh, forget it. I was only joking." The story is impossible to verify—perhaps it was witnessed by Boner?—but it is consistent with Slade's tendency, when drunk, to back down if confronted. And it reflects the genuinely affectionate, if strangely fierce, devotion that existed between the Slades.[95]

Virginia had hoped to control her husband's drinking by removing him from Virginia City's saloons, but clearly that strategy had failed: Instead it had removed him from Spring Dale. In bleak February there was little else to do in Alder Gulch but drink in Virginia City's saloons; and once there, a man was hard put to attempt the long trek home. The central fact of Slade's behavior hadn't changed since the late 1850s: when drunk, he couldn't control himself. In the past, someone—Virginia, or a friend, or a rival, or his superiors on the Central Overland, or the commandant at Fort Halleck—had usually intervened when liquor took him too far, for which intervention he was usually grateful. But now both Slade and the world around him had changed with dizzying speed. The public hero of December had become the public nuisance of February, in a place that no longer tolerated nuisances.

Slade was helpless to curb his addiction, as was his wife. Nor, apparently, could the influential Virginia City citizens who sympathized with his plight: Judge Davis, prosecutor Sanders, Sheriff Brookie, and the vigilante president Pfouts. The vigilantes were hanging anyone who violated their notions of order and safety. They were banishing anyone who challenged their authority, even respectable lawyers. How, then, would they handle the man who had saved the town?

Chapter 18

JUDGMENT DAY

*

About the first of March 1864 the newly elected Sheriff Alvin
Brookie was called away to Argenta, a camp near Bannack, where
he was negotiating to buy a mining property. In Brookie's extended
absence, as had happened often over the previous six weeks, he was
replaced as acting sheriff by his deputy. Jeremiah M. Fox was a founding vigilante like Brookie but a figure of lesser stature, violent-tem-
pered and insecure, whose past misadventures had already been targeted for ridicule by Slade during his alcoholic binges.[1]

Meanwhile, Slade's drinking sprees continued. "Slade and
Fairweather on a drunk today," Granville Stuart recorded matter-of-
factly in his journal on Wednesday, February 24.[2] The following
Tuesday, March 1, just about the time Fox became acting sheriff, Slade
and his drunken entourage invaded Virginia City again, carousing and
wrecking saloons and stores. On this occasion, according to one
account, "Some Missourians had just arrived in town. Their mules
were resting in the little poplar grove down by the Chinese joss house.
To win a brutal bet, Slade whipped out a knife and cut off a mule's ear."[3]

After two rampages in February Slade had appeared before Judge
Davis and humbly paid the fines stipulated by the miners at their
February 7 meeting.[4] He had also apologized to storekeepers and reim-
bursed them for the damages he had caused. But the miners' regulation
made no provision for a third offense. Clearly, the first two fines had

failed to improve his behavior; on the contrary, the penalties and warnings "seemed only to encourage him the more," one miner observed.[5] Slade had not killed or injured anyone, but he had caused extensive damage and terrified many people, and now he had mutilated a defenseless animal.

The logical solution—a jail in which to confine drunks and troublemakers—seems not to have occurred to anyone; as Granville Stuart had put it, these communities were "too small and too poor" to build one.[6] In its absence, a newly constituted court had few resources to deal with such a situation.

After his mule-ear-cutting escapade of March 1 Slade did not wait to learn what penalty Judge Davis might impose for a third offense. This time he retreated to his Spring Dale ranch and remained there.[7] But a week later, on March 8, Slade and his hangers-on returned. This time the group included Bill Fairweather and at least three of Slade's apparent employees: Dan Harding, Charley Edwards, and Naylor Thompson.[8]

That evening they disrupted business at two Virginia City brothels. At the Chebang, they wrecked furniture and fixtures, effectively bankrupting the madam, Annie Skeggs, according to her estimate.[9] The second victimized madam was the woman known as Moll Featherlegs, whom Slade had previously slandered in song. This time Featherlegs brought a suit then and there before Judge Davis's court.[10] Slade and his comrades responded by walking the streets for the rest of the night, loudly repeating their ditty about "Pfouts, Fox and Featherlegs" and "using the most abusive language to any with whom he happened to come in contact."[11] They were not merely disturbing the peace; they were also exhausting whatever good will remained from two of the town's most powerful men, one of whom, at least, was inclined to treat Slade kindly.

The following morning—having apparently stayed up all night[12]— Slade was still drunk and belligerent. He rode his horse, Old Copperbottom, into Dorris's store; when asked to leave, he drew his revolver and threatened to kill the speaker. Then he led his horse into a saloon, bought a bottle of wine and attempted to force it down his horse's mouth.[13]

From there, Slade and at least six of his chums walked into the Washington Billiards Hall, a bustling place even in daytime, where a drink or a game of billiards could be had for fifty cents. Here he found Jim Kiskadden and the vigilante "X." Beidler. Beidler's account of that encounter is self-serving but the most vivid portrait of Slade's state of mind that day as well as the reaction he provoked among those who crossed his path.

> Kiskadden was a friend of Slade's and they got into a conversation and not being interested, I got up to go out when Slade shouted: "God damn you, where are you going? Are you afraid?"
>
> I told him I was not interested in the conversation and that I had the privilege to go where I wanted to and that I did not have to go.
>
> When the people in the saloon heard Slade and I having these words everybody rushed out of the saloon, thinking our guns would go off and someone would get hurt sure and were afraid of any stray balls catching them.
>
> Slade saw the consternation of the people in the saloon but did not see me move and he said, "X, come back," which I did and he then asked me to take a drink. I said I would sooner do that than fight.
>
> We went to the bar—Johnny Tomlinson was bartender—and we all took whiskey straight—Kiskadden, Slade and myself. After we got our glasses filled and were going to drink, Slade, still mad, said: "You do not have to drink unless you want to"—meaning that I could fight instead.
>
> I said, "Mr. Slade that is another privilege and I will not drink."
>
> By this time people who had stampeded out at our first growl were getting in again when they saw us going to drink, but when they again heard our talk they again rushed out like a flock of sheep in a great hurry with a band of wolves behind them. During this stampede Slade had insulted the bartender, Tomlinson, and he [Tomlinson] raised a big Colt's Navy revolver in front of Slade and declared himself to take a hand in the fight and Slade then weakened and said: "Let us quit."

I told him I was glad, knowing well that right behind me stood at least six of Slade's pals and fighters and anyone that hurt Slade was going to be killed instantly.

When Slade had quit and left, I turned to Kiskadden and asked him if he had brought me into the saloon to get into a fuss with Slade. He denied having done so, which I believed, and we left.[14]

At some point during this day, word of Slade's antics appears to have reached Captain James Williams, the vigilantes' executive officer, at his camp at Nevada City, a mile and a half to the south. Williams dispatched Slade's old acquaintance Alexander Toponce to tell Slade to go home. Toponce—whose recollections, like Beidler's, must be somewhat discounted for their self-serving nature—later described his effort:

Slade's horse was in the livery barn, so I got it and led it up to the corner saloon, where I tied it outside to the rack. I could hear shots inside the saloon.

I opened the door of the saloon, keeping one hand on my pistol. I saw that Slade had chased the bar-keeper under the bar and with both elbows resting on the bar he was amusing himself with shooting off the necks of the bottles on the back bar. There was no one else left in the saloon.

I had my six-shooter in my hand and I spoke to him. "Slade, put down them guns," and he whirled with both guns leveled but when he saw me, he said, "Hello, Alex! Come, have a drink."

I stepped up to the bar and said, "If I drink with you, you'll have to lay down them guns."

He laid them on the bar in front of him and I reached over and took them and shoved them along the bar so that I stood between the bar and him.

Then the bar-keeper popped his head up and asked what we would have.

"I brought up your horse, Slade," I told him. "It's hitched outside. And I have a message for you."

"What is it, Alex?" he asked.

"The message is that you must get over the hill at once, and if you will take my advice you will go, right away," I told him.

Then he bristled up, "Who sends this message to me?" he demanded.

"That's the message, Slade," I said. "Get over the hill as quick as you can."

"All right," he said finally, "I'll go after I have had one more drink."

But after he had one more drink he got meaner and more defiant and said he was not afraid of the "stranglers," and I had to give up and go back and report to Captain Williams.[15]

That evening a traveling show was scheduled to entertain at Virginia City's theater. The featured attraction was the actress Kate Harper, who was said to enjoy a great reputation in the mining camps.[16] The theater was crowded with men and families, who had paid $2.50 a ticket for the privilege. Slade and an unidentified companion were in the audience as well. When Kate Harper came on stage dressed in a ballerina's tutu and began to dance, Slade "ordered her in a loud and vulgar voice to take off the balance of her dress," Beidler later recalled, "which disgusted the audience and they commenced leaving. Men with their wives and daughters could not stay. The show ended right there and I avoided Slade that evening as well as I could and I did not see him after the Theater."[17]

Yet still Slade did not go home. He spent much of the night carousing with Fairweather and the others. By he time he finally retired— apparently to sleep in the livery stable beneath his horse—Slade had managed, in the course of two nights and one day, to offend, insult, disgust, alienate, or frighten virtually every man, woman, and child in Virginia City.

The morning of Thursday, March 10 arrived cold and windy in Virginia City.[18]

As morning dawned, Slade was still intoxicated, but his mood now was prankish rather than belligerent. While he and his tipsy comrades loitered outside a saloon, they spied a milk wagon coming up the street. Slade beckoned to the driver and said he was thirsty. The driver handed him a gallon can and Slade, perched astride the wagon wheel, attempted to maintain his balance while simultaneously drinking from the can. When he spilled the milk on his shirtfront, his companions laughed, and so did the driver. Slade promptly emptied the rest of the can's contents over the milkman's head, gleefully joining his companions' laughter, then turned over the wagon.[19] This was no laughing matter: As Slade himself had astutely perceived the previous summer, milk was a precious commodity in a community with some three hundred young children.[20]

Slade and his entourage now entered the small saloon, where on some perceived insult, and seemingly for want of anything better to do, Slade picked fights with two of his own companions, Dan Harding and Charley Edwards. His confused state of mind is suggested by an observer's account of these whippings. After Slade punched Harding in the mouth, the sight of the blood gushing from Harding's face caused Slade to pull out his own handkerchief and repair the damage. The door to the saloon was open, the passing miner J. M. Venable later recalled, "and we could see Slade wiping blood off Dan Harding's mouth."[21]

Nevertheless, that scuffle among friends triggered the arrival of Jeremiah M. Fox, the acting sheriff. Fox was already angry at Slade and Fairweather because they had been singing about him again the previous night. The saloon was just three or four doors below Judge Davis's office in the Pfouts & Russell store, and a few minutes later Fox entered that office and asked Davis for a warrant for disturbing the peace—not for Slade, but for Slade's friend Fairweather.[22] While the judge made out the warrant, Fox turned to Venable and three other men who happened to be in the store and deputized them to help him make the arrest, which would not be easy. "We all tried to argue him out of such a course," Venable later recalled.

Before Davis had completed the forms, word of the warrant leaked out to Slade's group. Davis was still making out the warrant when the drunken Fairweather and three friends burst into the office. As Sheriff Fox turned to read the warrant, according to Venable, Fairweather snatched it from his hands and tore it to shreds, shouting, "To hell

Jackson Street, Virginia City, looking south. As a crowd gathered here on March 10, 1864, the lawyer Wilbur Sanders pleaded with Slade to climb on his horse and ride home. (*Montana Historical Society*)

with you and your warrants!" At roughly this time, Slade, equally drunk, entered the office and egged his friend on, shouting, "Go in, Bill! I'm with you!" Fairweather, shaking himself free of Fox's grip, drew his Navy revolver with his right hand. Fox made a move as if to draw his gun but thought better of it. Fairweather's friend George Oer and two other companions drew their guns.

At this point, according to Davis, "I got down off the bench and told Slade I had done a great deal for him, but that if this thing was to go on he might just as well make the issue then and there. At this Slade quieted down, said he was my friend, that he had always liked me but didn't like this fellow Fox, the sheriff. I told him that Fairweather would have to submit to the law which the people had made, whereupon Slade and his crowd marched out."[23]

Unlike the remarkably stoic and patient Judge Davis, the humiliated Sheriff Fox seems at this moment to have abandoned faith in the people's court. "Being at least as prudent as he was valiant," as the vigilantes' scribe Dimsdale put it, Fox did not pursue Fairweather or Slade; instead, "he succumbed, leaving Slade the master of the situation and the conqueror and ruler of the courts, law and law-makers.

This was a declaration of war, and was so accepted."[24] Fox and his instant deputies were incapable of waging such a war, but of course Fox knew of another organization that could. Left alone in the courtroom with Judge Davis and the four recalcitrant deputies, Fox, as Venable recalled, "turned to us with a faint smile and said, 'We will do nothing more about the warrants just now.' Then he dismissed us as a sheriff's posse."[25]

It was not yet noon. Fox left the courtroom to assemble an impromptu meeting of the vigilantes' executive committee. In the process he climbed on his horse and rode the mile and half down the gulch to Nevada City, the most active nest of vigilante volunteers, to fetch the committee's most important member, its executive officer James Williams. At Nevada he failed to find Williams—who at that moment was three and a half miles farther down the gulch, at German Bar—but Fox did find the merchant John S. Lott, the vigilantes' secretary-treasurer.[26]

About noon, as Venable and his three cabin-mates left the courtroom to go home for dinner, they met Fox coming back up the gulch on horseback. "Hurry back, boys!" Fox called to them, according to Venable's recollection. "You'll see some fun!" Mulling this exhortation over their noon dinner, Venable and his companions decided to leave their guns home, "so as to have an excuse if Fox called us again to act as a posse."[27]

Behind a wagon at the rear of a store on Main Street, a small cluster of men conducted a hasty meeting of the Vigilance Committee.[28] John Lott was there; so was the lawyer Wilbur Sanders, and so, presumably were Paris Pfouts, X. Beidler, and Sheriff Fox. "The meeting," Lott wrote many years later, "was peculiar and hasty. . . . In five minutes, they settled the question."[29]

Precisely what Fox told his fellow Vigilantes about that morning's courtroom confrontation is unknown. According to the later accounts of both Venable and Judge Davis himself, Slade's only offense (in the courtroom, at least) was to verbally encourage Fairweather's defiance of Sheriff Fox and Judge Davis. But somehow, as the story was transmitted to the vigilantes and then spread through the town, it took on a very different cast. Now—as the vigilantes' apologist Dimsdale dutifully reported the "facts" a year later—it was Slade, not Fairweather, who had been served with a warrant; Slade, not Fairweather, who had gleefully torn the warrant to shreds; and Slade who was the beneficiary of the guns pulled on Fox by Fairweather, George Oer, and two of their other drinking companions.[30]

Within five minutes the committee members had agreed to arrest Slade, but they lacked any consensus as to what they should do with him. Most of the committee members were friends or acquaintances of Slade's and reluctant to take drastic measures, feeling, as one writer put it, that "the town was indebted to him for past favors."[31] Dimsdale, whose account is the closest thing to an official vigilante version of events, notes, "His execution had not been agreed upon, and, at that time, would have been negatived, most assuredly."[32]

Yet vacillation was the one posture the vigilantes could not afford. Any public display of indecision or weakness would undermine the vigilantes' effectiveness. "It was desirable to show that there was a feeling of unanimity on the subject, all along the gulch," Dimsdale explained.[33] It would not do merely to impose another fine on Slade. And the only other options were banishment or death.

Rather than decide Slade's fate, the committee members deferred that responsibility—not to Judge Davis and the people's court that Slade was accused of defying, but to the miners' community at Nevada City, which James Williams had whipped into the most effective vigilante militia in Alder Gulch. Lott was dispatched to Nevada City to advise the miners there of Slade's likely arrest and to determine their attitude as to his punishment.[34] But on what basis would the miners at Nevada render their decision? Who would present the facts to them? Who would argue the case for the defense? In the rush to take decisive action, these questions were ignored.[35]

While Lott rode to Nevada to assemble and poll the miners there, Sheriff Fox—perhaps without informing his fellow committee members—rode off to German Bar, 5 miles down the gulch, to fetch Captain Williams.[36] By Venable's account, Williams promptly rode to Nevada City and assembled a large force of miners to march into Virginia City "to carry out Fox's orders."[37] According to Dimsdale, when Lott arrived at Nevada "to inform the leading men of what was on hand…. the miners turned out almost *en masse,* leaving their work and forming in solid column, about six hundred strong, armed to the teeth."[38]

By this time Williams had returned to Nevada City from German Bar and presumably took the lead in forming the armed column. Whether the miners ever took a vote as to how to proceed is a question on which Dimsdale's account is silent; instead, Dimsdale wrote only that Williams "well knew the temper of his men, on the subject"— which seems to imply that no vote was taken.

As the armed column assembled and the miners cleaned and loaded their rifles and revolvers, Williams rode ahead to Virginia City and hastily reassembled the vigilantes' executive committee behind the wagon where they had gathered earlier. "The meeting was small," Dimsdale reported, "as the Virginia men were loath to act at all."

Williams—a man who, whatever his other faults, possessed a uniquely forceful and uncluttered mind—told the few committee members what they seem not to have wanted to hear: "He told them plainly that the miners meant 'business'," Dimsdale wrote. If the miners at Nevada City marched up to Virginia City to arrest Slade, "they would not stand in the street to be shot down by Slade's friends; but they would take him and hang him."

Neither Slade nor his friends had shot anyone, but the committee members, worn down by the situation and seemingly grateful to be relieved of it, agreed to accept the miners' decision, so long as "the whole body of the miners were of the opinion that he should be hanged," according to Dimsdale. Williams promptly rode off "at hot speed" to rejoin his command at Nevada City.[39]

By now it was about 3 P.M. In Virginia City merchants and miners, sensing that something was afoot, gathered in small groups on Wallace Street for the latest intelligence about that morning's courtroom dust-up, the vigilante meeting, and the militia assembling at Nevada. Only Slade, still drunk, seemed oblivious to these developments.

After the second vigilante committee disbanded with Williams's threat to hang Slade, Beidler attempted—to the extent that a man ostensibly sworn to secrecy was able—to warn Slade that he was in danger. Beidler understood that the miners from Nevada would march to Virginia on foot; if Slade could mount his horse and ride to his home 8 miles in the opposite direction, the Nevada City miners would not pursue him.

Beidler sought out Slade's friend Jerry Sullivan and beseeched him to persuade Slade to go home. "Jerry said he couldn't touch him," Beidler later recalled. Beidler next went into Jim Kiskadden's store and made the same request of Kiskadden. As they were talking, Slade himself entered the store.

"X," Slade said to Beidler, "I guess the Vigilante Committee is played out."

"It looks so," Beidler replied, in the peculiar enigmatic argot of a man sworn to keep a secret that was rapidly becoming common knowledge, "but you will change your mind in three hours." As Beidler described the moment: "He looked at me very enquiringly with those eyes of his and asked how I knew. I told him he would see, and I again asked Kiskadden to try to coax him to go, and Slade said he would if Kiskadden would give him his Derringer, which he did, and I then told Slade to get on his favorite horse, old 'Copperbottom,' and cross the hill, which he did."[40]

As Dimsdale described the conversation, "a leading member of the committee [presumably Beidler] told him, 'Slade, get your horse at once, and go home, or there will be - - - - to pay'."

> Slade started and took a long look with his dark and piercing eyes, at the gentleman—"What do you mean?" said he.
>
> "You have no right to ask me what I mean," was the quiet reply, "get your horse at once, and remember what I tell you."[41]

However much this message may have startled Slade, he did not go very far once he had mounted his horse. The sight of his friends on the street apparently dispelled his fears and reinforced his false sense of security, and he dismounted to join them in another drink. It may have registered on Slade that his crony Fairweather was no longer among this group. Some of Fairweather's friends, fearing that he too was in danger, had seized him, locked him in Kiskadden's store, and refused to let him out in order to spare him from the miners' wrath.[42]

Sensing that he was in danger but unable to think clearly, Slade ducked into a store where Judge Davis was talking with the proprietor, who had reported some goods stolen. As Davis recalled, Slade came in with a cocked Derringer, caught Davis by the collar, and announced, "You are my prisoner."

Davis, ever the stoic, treated this outburst as a harmless prank. "All right, Slade," Davis replied, continuing to talk to Locke, the shopkeeper.

"By God, I mean what I say," Slade insisted, jostling Davis. "You are my prisoner. They are going to hang me, and I am going to hold you as a hostage."

As Davis put his hand on Slade's arm to try to pacify him, Bill Hunt stepped forward—the same Bill Hunt who, with his brother, had developed an animus toward Sheriff Fox while rooming with Fox on the floor of Pfouts & Russell's store. Hunt held a revolver in each hand and told Slade: "You let him go." Then, turning to Davis, he added, "Go where you please; if he touches you, I'll kill him."

Judge Davis replied that he didn't think Slade meant any harm, and Slade said to Hunt, "What have you got to do with it?" Hunt replied that Davis was "a representative of the people there" as well as Hunt's friend, and he didn't intend to see Davis hurt. With that civil response, Slade calmed down, and he and Hunt, notwithstanding the imminent threat to Slade's life, engaged in a polite conversation.

"Slade," Hunt said finally, according to Davis, "if I had been sheriff this morning, the first thing I'd have done when I got up would have been to arrest you, and if I'd done it, I should, perhaps, have saved your life. The way you are going on now, you will be hanged before sunset."

"By God," Slade replied jovially, "we'll elect you sheriff." Then Slade began apologizing to Davis and Hunt alike. "He was just that kind of man," Davis later recalled, "saying he was only joking with me; didn't intend harming me, but that he liked me very much."

Hunt and Slade left the store together to reaffirm their friendship in the only way possible in Virginia City: over a drink. Outside, they ran into Slade's friend Jerry Sullivan, whom Beidler had earlier unsuccessfully importuned to persuade Slade to go home. Sullivan, learning what had just happened, took Slade into his office and disarmed him to prevent him from causing any more trouble. That done, Slade immediately returned to Locke's store to apologize to Judge Davis yet again. According to Davis, this time Slade

> apologized for what he had done, said he didn't intend anything by it, and asked my pardon. I told him that was all right, it was granted, and commenced pleading with him to get on his horse and go home. He promised to do it. I told him there would be trouble if he didn't; that the people were very much excited; that the couriers had gone to Nevada City and the Summit, and the town would be full of people in a little while, and I asked him, for God's sake, to get on his horse and go home. He said he would do it, if I forgave him for what he had done. I told him that was all right, and again urged him to go. He started out like he was going home.
>
> In a short time he was again in front of the store on horseback, and called me out. He wanted to shake hands with me before he started, and to know if I forgave him for his wild freak. I told him I did, and again pleaded with him to go home. He spurred his horse and went away.[43]

By this time a large crowd of armed men had been sighted coming up the gulch from Nevada City. The miners, with James Williams and John Lott leading the way on horseback, had begun their march from Nevada City at about 3:40.[44] At the corner of Wallace and Jackson Streets a Virginia City resident named A. M. Hart found Slade standing and talking with Colonel Wilbur Sanders, the prosecutor and vigilante.

"Get on your horse and go home, and I will see that the mob does not follow you," Sanders was saying, according to Hart.

"I have not done anything," Slade replied. "What should I go home for?"

Sanders repeated his imprecation four or five times without success. "I ain't going to be run out of town," Slade insisted. Finally Sanders walked away.[45]

At about 4 P.M. Harriet Sanders was surprised to see her husband come in the door of their house on Jackson Street.[46] "It was an unusual hour," Harriet Sanders later recalled, "and I asked the cause, to which he replied that Mr. Slade was again in town and behaving in such a manner that he expected there would be a hanging and he did not wish to be present, thinking he would be called upon and unwilling to use his influence in his behalf."[47]

Judge Davis, on the other hand, seemed more than willing to intervene to save Slade. Three times he had urged Slade to get on his horse and go home, only to find Slade seeking him out again to beg the forgiveness that Davis had readily granted. Now, believing Slade was finally headed home, Davis left Locke's store and returned to his office in the Pfouts & Russell store. To his astonishment, a few minutes later Slade returned again, dismounted and entered the store—this time to apologize not only to Davis (for the fourth time) but also to the vigilante president Paris Pfouts, whom Slade had mocked in his late-night songs.[48] With that conciliatory gesture he inadvertently sealed his fate.

Slade "begged my pardon once more and had me search him to see he wasn't armed," Davis recalled. "He made the same explanations as before, and I used every argument I could to induce him to go, for God's sake to get on his horse and go, that the people would surely hang him if he didn't. He said he was going, but that he couldn't go without coming to see me again, and then the first thing I knew there were poked into the doorway enough guns to fill it, and I saw 300 or 400 armed men in regular military style."[49]

It was now about 4:30 P.M. Upon their arrival at Virginia City, the Nevada City vigilantes had thrown a guard around the town, just as they had done before the five road agents were hanged there in January. A second guard had surrounded the Pfouts & Russell store where Slade, oblivious to what was happening, was rendering his apologies inside. "Business was suspended, crowds gathered; the streets were full; old muskets and rifles glistened, and still no excitement prevailed," wrote one observer just a few hours later. "Gangs of men could be seen in every direction, but hardly a word was spoken. Nine-tenths of the people knew nothing of this affair or what the men were about to do. The question would be asked in every group: 'What is the fuss?' 'Who is dead?' and etc."[50]

Captain James Williams stepped into the store and announced: "Slade you are my prisoner."

"All right," Slade replied, and submitted quietly. Williams searched him for arms but found none, Slade's friend Jerry Sullivan already having disarmed him less than an hour before. Then Williams informed Slade of his fate: "The Committee have decided upon your execution. If you have any business to settle, you must attend to it immediately."[51]

This statement was less than forthright. The vigilantes' executive committee had not decreed Slade's execution; it had deferred that decision to the whole body of miners at Nevada City, with the stipulation that the vote must be unanimous. But the Nevada City miners had never voted; they had simply followed the lead of Williams, who in turn had followed the lead of Deputy Sheriff Fox. "Men who took part in the execution were told that an investigating committee had ordered the lynching," the miner J. M. Venable recalled years later. "Many did not know who had been sentenced or why." One member of Williams's armed execution party later told Venable that "they had been called together hurriedly and few of them knew what was going on in Virginia City."[52] Everyone involved in the decision to execute Slade had shifted the responsibility to someone else; yet once made, the decision had to be carried out swiftly and forcefully. And in carrying it out, Williams had neglected to provide Slade with any recitation of his alleged capital crimes.[53]

The news sobered Slade immediately, as Nathaniel Langford later reconstructed the scene.

> "My execution! My death! My God! Gentlemen, you will not proceed to such extremities! The Committee cannot have decreed this."
>
> "It is even so, and you had better at once give the little time left you to arrange your business."
>
> This appalling repetition of the sentence of the Committee seemed to deprive him of every vestige of manliness and courage.
>
> He fell upon his knees, and with clasped hands shuffled over the floor from one to another of those who had been his friends,

begging for his life. Clasping the hands of Judge Davis and Captain Williams, he implored them for mercy, mingling with his appeals prayers and promises, and requests that his wife might be sent for.[54]

Slade was advised that he had only an hour to live, and was taken into a back room of the Pfouts store to settle his affairs. Instead, he continued to expend all his energy on appealing his sentence.

Judge Davis alone stood by Slade at this moment. When Slade begged the judge to save him, Davis replied, "I would do anything in God's world to save him," and appealed to Williams to reconsider. Slade had committed no crime in Idaho worse than a misdemeanor, Davis argued, and other men had been merely banished for greater offenses. "I . . . offered to go with him out of the country, right down to Salt Lake, if they would but spare his life," Davis later recalled.

Williams refused to budge. According to Davis, "Williams said the people had passed on his case, and determined he should be hanged."[55] Although the ostensible reason for Slade's arrest was his alleged defiance of the people's court, Williams never acknowledged Davis's standing as judge of that court, nor did Williams mention the court at all. Nor, needless to add, did he acknowledge the moment's greatest paradox: that the man pleading most passionately on Slade's behalf was himself the judge of that very court.

Davis asked Williams if he could go outside and make a speech to the people. A wagon stood outside the store, and Davis proposed to climb on the wagon and argue the case for taking Slade out of the country.

"You have my consent to go," Williams replied, according to Davis, "but you won't more than get straightened in the wagon before you'll be full of bullets; you might go out and talk among the crowd and see what the feeling is." As Davis recalled,

> I said I would do anything I could to spare Slade's life. So I went out, and among the crowd, and talked to the leading men and to my friends. They all said about what Williams did. They wouldn't see me hurt for anything, but represented what Williams was,

and that I would be riddled with bullets if I attempted to make a speech for Slade; that Brookie and Pfouts and myself had kept them from hanging him for two or three months, and that after all Slade was no better than he was before. They said, too, that if Slade were [sent] away, I knew he would come back and kill a lot more men, and that the best thing would be to hang him.[56]

Here, most likely, was the unspoken root of the impetus to hang Slade. Although he had committed no serious crime in Alder Gulch, "his record in other places seemed to be against him," Margaret Gilbert, the wife of Slade's former partner Henry Gilbert, told an interviewer many years later. "The fact of the matter is that those responsible for Slade's arrest were afraid to let him go. They feared that he would kill them if he was released."[57] The man who had taken no action for seventeen months after being ambushed by Jules Beni, and who even then had pursued Jules only when prodded to do so by Ben Holladay, was now to be condemned for his supposedly vindictive nature.

At last Davis realized the futility of his efforts: "I saw it wasn't worth while to talk any further about making a speech to the people. I went back and told Slade I could do nothing for him and told him what had occurred, and he just kept begging and begging me, and got so wrought up that I shed tears as freely as a child. They took him out and left me in there, for I didn't want to see him hanged."[58]

Even viewed from a distance of more than 140 years, Davis's impassioned defense of Slade remains extraordinary, and not only for its courage. More remarkable is the extent of Davis's devotion. Judge Davis had arrived in Virginia City only the previous fall; he was well respected there and presumably hoped to maintain his stature; and he had known Slade only since Slade's return from the Milk River in December—a three-month period during which, in the eyes of most Alder Gulch residents, Slade had caused nothing but trouble. Yet Davis was willing to accompany Slade into exile rather than see him die. In so many words, this highly respected community leader implied that, if forced to choose between Alder Gulch and Joseph Alfred Slade, he would choose Slade.

Perhaps most ironic of all, Davis may have misread the temper of the crowd. The Nevada City armed miners seemed intent on hanging Slade, but the Virginia City spectators were not. Men who for weeks had wished Slade gone were suddenly appalled by the nightmare unfolding before them. "There was not a man from Virginia City in the band intent on lynching Slade," recalled J. M. Venable, who was there. "I don't believe there was one, outside of the actual instigators, who knew what was going to happen."59 The crowd in fact included many Slade sympathizers who felt as helpless as Judge Davis to prevent the hanging.

But as Judge Davis abandoned his efforts, one Slade friend climbed into the saddle and galloped away at full speed to fetch the sole remaining person who, at this extreme moment, seemed capable of saving Slade's life: his wife, Virginia. She had, after all, saved it before.

The toll house at Spring Dale in the canyon on the Madison, where Virginia had waited in vain for her husband the past two nights, stood some 8 hilly miles from Virginia City.60 On a fast horse a rider might have reached it in a half-hour. Whoever that rider was—he has never been identified—he immediately impressed upon Virginia the urgency of the situation.61 She had no time to devise a plan of action. As the story has come down, she strapped on Slade's Navy pistol.62 From Slade's corral she picked out Billy Bay, the Kentucky thoroughbred that Slade had purchased from Major Malcolm Clarke, a trader for the American Fur Company. Billy Bay's reputation for speed and endurance were legendary, as was his remarkable history. He was said to have been stolen by Piegan Indians in a raid near the Great Salt Lake and had been the pride of the tribe for several years before his recapture. The Piegans were said to have staked large sums of money, pelts, and other valuables on Billy Bay in intertribal races.63

The image of Virginia Slade astride Billy Bay as she rode at breakneck speed to rescue her husband—her black tresses blowing in the March wind, his mouth foaming from exhaustion—subsequently became the stuff of Western legend. From Spring Dale, the first half-mile was uphill, but the rest of the road to Virginia City was almost all downhill.[64] The romanticized description by the historian Lew Callaway captured the urgency, if not the factual detail, of a ride that would thrill all who later heard of it: "With all the skill of a perfect equestrienne she urged the great horse up the heavy grade to the mountain top. From there she could see the city 2 miles below. Could she arrive in time? The road was steep and rocky, dangerous at high speed. But she did not hesitate. Down the declivity she plunged regardless of danger to herself or horse, risking the loss of all if she should fall."[65]

M eanwhile, as Slade begged for his life inside the Pfouts store and Judge Davis begged for Slade's life in front of it, a party was sent to arrange a place for the execution. There were no trees in Virginia City, all of them having been cut down for winter firewood. But in a ravine a hundred yards down the gulch the hanging party found the Elephant Corral, an auction and slaughter pen whose eastern gateposts stood just barely high enough to accommodate a hanging. Across the top the executioners laid a beam, to which they suspended a rope with a seven-looped knot. A dry goods box (or, by another account, an empty beef scaffold) was pressed into service as the platform.[66] While a crowd gathered, Slade—still begging for his life—was conducted to the spot by a large armed guard. "The hills and streets, housetops and every vacant spot in sight was covered with men, women and children," wrote one observer.[67] Molly Sheehan, then eleven, recalled the scene more than sixty years later:

> I recognized Slade, dressed in fringed buckskin, hatless, with a man on either side of him, who forced him to walk under the corral gate. His arms were pinioned, the elbows were bent so as to bring his hands up to his breast. He kept moving his hands back and forth, palms upward, and opening and closing them as he cried, "For God's sake, let me see my dear, beloved wife!" I distinctly heard him say this three times in a piercing, anguished voice.[68]

The doomed man was made to mount the stand and given ten minutes to say what he pleased.[69] But according to Dimsdale, by this time Slade "had so exhausted himself by tears, prayers and lamentations, that he had scarcely strength left to stand under the fatal beam."[70] He pleaded not only for his wife, but also for Judge Davis and Wilbur Sanders, persisting in the belief that these two respected figures possessed the power to save him.

X. Beidler later maintained that Sanders couldn't be found.[71] In fact, two of Slade's friends rushed over to Sanders's house and did find the prosecutor there. According to Harriet Sanders, they "begged Mr. Sanders to return with them and save their friend, saying that Mr. Slade was calling for him and saying that he must have time to settle his business and he wanted Mr. Sanders to be his lawyer. Mr. Sanders replied, 'I can do nothing. It is too late,' and further told them how many times he had persuaded Mr. Slade to go home and warned him that such conduct would occur once too often and then he could not help him."[72]

Slade's repeated cries for Judge Davis did succeed in moving Captain Williams to send for Davis, who came down to the gallows to speak to Slade on Williams's promise that, as Davis put it, "They would not hang him until I was out of sight."[73] By this time Slade's arms had been pinioned behind him and the rope had been tied around Slade's neck. Slade, according to one observer, begged Davis "in the most entreating language . . . to plead with the people for an innocent man. The prisoner said if they would allow him to leave the country he would immediately do so and go anywhere directed."[74] Davis, by his own recollection, "told him I had done everything I could, but that the people refused to allow anything I would have to say to affect their judgment."[75]

As Davis forlornly made his way back to his office, Slade's "legs now trembled, his face was pale, and his whole frame was nervous," wrote one observer. "He was now certain his time had come." Again he begged to see his wife. He had important business matters to explain to her, he said.[76]

This plea elicited widespread sympathy among the spectators. Many of Slade's friends wept bitterly. "Several of us who were spectators began shouting, 'Let him see his wife!'," recalled the Virginia City miner A. M. Hart.[77] These shouts grew into a rhythmic chant: "Give him time to see his wife! Give him time to see his wife!"

As the chant grew louder, Slade's friends in the crowd were emboldened by word that Virginia Slade had indeed been sent for and was likely on her way. "The whisper went around," said the Virginia City miner J. M. Venable, "that if this time were granted, his friends could muster enough guns to rescue him."[78] "Excitement now prevailed," wrote another observer, "and a general fight was anticipated."[79]

But the Nevada City miners who comprised Slade's execution force maintained the military discipline that Williams had imposed on them since December. If anything, Slade's pathetic pleadings and his complete loss of composure—in contrast to the wisecracking nonchalance that many of the road agents had displayed at *their* executions—merely stiffened the miners' resolve to hang him. "The miners believed that a man who had not hesitated to inflict death upon so many of his fellows ought to at least meet his fate with manliness," Slade's partner Henry Gilbert later reflected.[80] As the vigilante X. Beidler described the temper of the squad, "The two hundred miners were getting impatient and shouted: 'Time's up!' These men were running mines on their own account and wanted to get back and clean up and attend to their business as they did not come on any child's play."[81]

At this point, according to the young Molly Sheehan, "The stir among the men [in the crowd of spectators] increased; voices rose louder, gesturing arms pointed to the long winding road down the hill from the east. Down that long hill-road a woman was racing on horseback. Someone shouted, 'There she comes!'"

Other witnesses suggest Virginia arrived perhaps a half-hour later. In either case, from the time Virginia Slade crossed the ridge where the town first came into view, it took her about ten minutes to reach Virginia City. As she rode down the incline, she could see the town in the distance, and any man in the hanging crowd with a good eye for game could see *her*—sitting "straight as an Indian in her sidesaddle," as the miner Venable described her.[82]

Williams and his lieutenants were well aware of Virginia Slade's skill with horse and gun, her fearlessness and passion, and her local popularity. No doubt they had heard of previous occasions on which Virginia had supposedly rescued her husband. They believed that, in the heat of her fury, Mrs. Slade was quite capable of inciting a bloody revolt among Slade's armed friends as well as others whose resentment of the vigilantes had simmered for weeks. Whether they actually saw her approaching or heard that she was on her way, their fear of her arrival merely reinforced their haste to finish the job.[83]

"The mob [from Nevada City] turned their guns upon us and commanded us to shut up," A. M. Hart recalled.[84] Wrote another observer: "Three hundred guns were leveled on the crowd, and in an instant more everything was as still as the hush of midnight."[85]

Now Williams gave his well-known final order: "Men, do your duty!" While Slade was still asking for a few moments longer, and without his being blindfolded, the box was kicked from beneath his feet. He died almost instantly with the fall of the drop.

In the emotional silence that followed, Slade's friend Naylor Thompson, standing a bit farther down the gulch, swore vengeance against the perpetrators; by one account, Thompson pulled out his rifle and knelt down as if to fire. He was immediately pursued by more than a dozen of the guards, who tried to march him to the gallows as well until some Vigilance Committee members interceded.[86]

The vigilantes had customarily hanged their victims from prominent places—high trees or, in the case of the five road agents executed on January 14, from the top of an unfinished building—and then left the bodies to hang for anywhere from an hour to a day as a warning. But Slade's scaffold was such a low and makeshift affair that his body fell thirty inches, so that the toes of his boots touched the ground. For thirty-one minutes his body remained in that wretched position.[87] Then, about six o'clock, Slade's friend Jim Kiskadden approached X. Beidler and asked, "Can't I get men enough to cut Slade down before Mrs. Slade gets here?" Beidler recalled: "I got some friends of mine and I cut him down and we packed him to the Virginia City Hotel and took the ropes off his legs, arms and feet, and just as I was through, someone said: 'Mrs. Slade is coming!' I threw a blanket over the things to hide them from her."[88]

By one account Virginia Slade arrived just ten minutes after her husband's body was cut down and laid out.[89] According to one eyewitness, "Just as they were carrying the body from the gallows to the hotel she was seen coming across the hill as fast as her horse could carry her."[90] Galloping wildly into Wallace Street, Mrs. Slade was conducted to the parlor of the Virginia Hotel before anyone dared to tell her what had happened.[91] Her first reaction was described by one of the men standing there: "She stood silently looking at the corpse for a few minutes, and then turning to the crowd that was standing around, said, 'Will some one tell me who did this?' No one answering her, she repeated the question, and finally the third time she repeated the question at the top of her voice."[92]

Throwing herself across the corpse, Virginia wept bitterly for her husband while screaming her contempt for the assembled crowd—not only for those who had deprived her of her partner but above all for Slade's friends who had stood passively by. Why, she asked one of Slade's friends, had he not pulled out his pistol and shot him like a man rather than see him hanged like an animal? "I would have done it had I been here," she exclaimed. "He should never have died by the rope of a hangman. No dog's death should have come to such a man."[93]

She seemed to have sensed throughout their marriage that something like this would happen—that the greater tragedy was not his dying but the manner of his death, which would overshadow everything else he had achieved. This apprehension would prove prescient: by 1899 the first of a long line of frontier historians, Charles Coutant, would confidently inform his readers, "Like most men of his class, Slade was a coward at heart, as his conduct at the time of his death proved."[94]

Of course, there was a better explanation for Slade's incredulous tears on the gallows. As he had remarked to Wilbur Sanders that very afternoon, "I have not done anything"—or at least not anything that would justify hanging. That was the crucial point that somehow got lost in the rush to his execution—a point that only Slade, even in the depths of his drunken stupor, had the clarity of mind to perceive. Right up to the very end, he simply couldn't believe what was happening.

Hours elapsed before Virginia Slade was sufficiently composed to direct the disposition of her husband's body.[95] He would be buried the next day on the mountain opposite the town, but she would not suffer him to remain in this place, among his enemies. Nor would she see him buried with the road agents on Boot Hill, lest posterity confuse him with them. "As soon as a metallic case can be brought here," a correspondent noted later that very night, "the body will be taken to Illinois."[96]

Already that evening the Vigilante X. Beidler claimed to discern a positive change in Virginia City as a result of the hanging. "The miners returned to their work and the town quieted down and peace reigned," Beidler later maintained. "The Slade men dispersed as their leader was gone and they had seen a lesson."[97] But another observer of the hanging derived a very different lesson.

"Of the propriety or justice of this dreadful tragedy I have nothing to say," wrote the pseudonymous "Valley Tan" that night in a dispatch to the *Rocky Mountain News*. "Thus endeth the life of one who might have been a useful member of society, and who might have been beloved by this and other communities."

Slade's life was over. The struggle over his legacy had begun.

PART V

*

Posterity

After her husband's death, Virginia Slade moved into this two-room house on Van Buren Street in Virginia City. Here she kept his body—preserved in a tin-lined casket—in the front room until the spring thaw enabled her to transport it for burial in Salt Lake City. The house still stands; as recently as the 1990s it was the home of a vigilante's great-grandson. (*Roy O'Dell*)

Chapter 19

THE WIDOW AND
THE TOWN

∗

In the days immediately following her husband's death, Virginia
Slade did not retreat to Spring Dale to mourn in seclusion. Instead
she rented a two-room house on Van Buren Street in Virginia City and
moved there, the better to defy Slade's executioners and prevent them
from looting his assets. Above all she was determined to salvage her
husband's reputation; by word and deed she would dissuade anyone
inclined to lump her husband with the other vigilante victims.

"She then was a good woman, a general favorite," the merchant
Charles W. Cannon later recalled, "but she became a tigress after Slade
was hanged."[1] Those who knew her earlier might have phrased it differently: she had always been a tigress, but now she was more so.

As her first order of business, Mrs. Slade requested a funeral service—something no other vigilante victim had been granted. In order to
dress for the funeral entirely in black, she dispatched a friend to
Harriet Sanders with a request to lend her a pair of black stockings, to
which Mrs. Sanders readily complied. And Mrs. Slade specifically
asked that a sermon be preached at the funeral.[2]

This last request presented a challenge for the Reverend A. M.
Torbett, Virginia City's only Protestant minister. At funerals it was
customary to overlook the vices of the deceased and focus on his
virtues. And this funeral was likely to be well attended, if only because
sermons, eulogies, and other speeches served as a primary source of

public entertainment in isolated communities. Abraham Lincoln had demonstrated as much during his Kansas visit four years earlier. Oratorical skill was an important tool for any minister hoping to attract a flock and raise donations.

But Torbett had arrived in Virginia City only a month or two earlier. He was the first Protestant minister in all of east Idaho (a Jesuit priest had arrived the previous summer), and consequently Torbett's small Baptist church on Idaho Street was attended and supported by Protestants of all denominations.[3] He could not afford to take sides in denominational squabbles, much less political ones. Nor could he afford to offend the vigilantes by praising one of their victims.

The Slade funeral may have been Torbett's first in Virginia City; surely it was his most controversial during his subsequent three years there.[4] Many settlers attended Slade's funeral merely to see how Torbett would handle it—among them Wilbur Sanders and his wife, Harriet, who later wrote, "I confess to have had a little curiosity to know what would be said upon such an occasion." She subsequently pronounced Torbett's eulogy one that "I will never forget."

"It has been my practice for the past thirty years, when preaching funeral sermons," Torbett announced in his introductory remarks, "to make little or no reference to the dead, and I will not digress from my usual habit." He proceeded to deliver his sermon without any further allusion to the deceased.[5]

Virginia Slade's ambitions for her husband's body posed a stickier issue. In isolated mining camps, out of necessity, a local carpenter ordinarily built a simple wood coffin and doubled as the undertaker. The body was buried almost immediately to avoid decay. Virginia Slade, in contrast, was determined to remove her husband's body from east Idaho. Yet transporting his remains to his family home in Illinois, as she desired, would require preserving it for weeks or months. The science of embalming was as yet unknown, as were the preservative properties of formaldehyde.[6] Arsenic was serviceable but highly toxic. But Virginia Slade was every bit as daring and resourceful as her husband. From the Central Overland to the Milk River, her husband had repeatedly achieved the impossible; she would do no less for him.

Two commodities were necessary to remove the body: a preservative, and a leakproof coffin in which to fill it. Pure alcohol or whiskey would suffice—and in Virginia City, whiskey was the most likely available liquid. Whether Virginia Slade ordered a metallic coffin from Salt Lake City or prevailed upon a local tinsmith named Merk is unclear.[7] In either case, some carpenter or tinsmith lined the coffin with tin and zinc, rendering it leakproof by soldering overlapping joints. Once the coffin was sealed and filled with whiskey, the fumes from the liquor would preserve the remains for perhaps a few months.

After the job was completed, Virginia placed the coffin in the front room of the small house on Van Buren Street.[8] For more than three months she lived there with her husband's body, oblivious to the chortlings of neighbors who snickered that Slade had been pickled in death as in life. The previous summer Virginia had hungered for this community's respect; now she was preoccupied not with what Alder Gulch thought of her, but with what posterity would think of her husband. Patiently, she waited for the day when the roads would thaw and she would be emotionally and financially ready to manage such an ambitious journey. Then she could attempt to transport her delicate and unwieldy cargo, and her husband could receive an honorable burial among his friends and family.[9]

In the meantime Virginia turned her attention to Slade's killers. The vigilantes had hoped by their actions to intimidate their perceived enemies; now she would return the compliment. "Somehow she got the idea that I was a Vigilante, and was active in carrying out the sentence on her husband," the merchant Charles Cannon later recalled. "She threatened to kill me and several others on sight."

Cannon's clothing store was a long, narrow log building, with tables placed end to end down the center, piled high with all sorts of coats, pants, and shirts. As Cannon later recalled, a few days after Slade's hanging,

> Some fellow came running into the store yelling, "Charlie look out! Mrs. Slade is coming!" Just as she came in the front door flourishing one of those big powder and ball six shooters . . . I dived under one of the tables . . . near the back door. She did not see me. She went up and down the aisles of the store swearing she would kill me, but as she was unable to find me, she went away. In the meantime I had escaped.

The next day I had to go to Salt Lake on business for the firm.
I was so busy I neglected to arrange for a seat on the stage. I got
to the coach in time, but there were two fellows sitting with the
driver, so I had to crawl inside. All the seats were taken except one
in the middle. I took it and the coach started. I looked around and
to my horror Mrs. Slade was in the back seat directly behind me.

The stage didn't stop for twenty miles. Mrs. Slade had on that
six-shooter, and I did not know when she might shoot me. When
we stopped to change horses I got out and gave one of the passengers who had been sitting with the driver twenty dollars for his
seat. As I look back I suppose I wasn't in any danger that day, but
certainly I wasn't comfortable.[10]

Because Slade had spent his last hour begging for his life, he had
devoted no attention to his estate. That estate, it developed soon
after his death, was considerable. Slade owned two ranches, freighting
equipment and horses, as well as a herd of dairy cows valued at
$3,000. He was a substantial investor in Virginia City's mining indus-
try, with claims valued at $3,250. He held a note for a personal loan of
$1,250 that would soon fall due to his estate. He also owned—precise-
ly how, nobody knew—134 shares of stock in Wells Fargo, the
California stagecoach company, conservatively valued at $100 per
share, or $13,400 in the aggregate.[11] Here was a further reminder that
Slade was no ordinary vigilante target.

Yet his creditors, many of them represented by Wilbur Sanders,
claimed that Slade owed them more than $4,000 in debts. The dozens
of claims filed and approved in the ensuing months covered everything
from labor on Slade's stone house ($216) to stable care ($123) to
boots ($67.80) to appraisals of Slade's ranches ($57) to seventy-seven
pounds of pork ($57.75). The Idaho Billiard Room submitted a claim
for $201.25 for liquor and breakage. Slade's probate file also included
several claims for bar bills and liquor up to and including the day of
his death—grim documentary corroboration that Slade was, in the
words of Wilbur Sanders, "still drunk" when he was hanged.[12]

The task of sorting out the estate's assets and liabilities fell to the probate court created by Virginia City's founders the previous June. Here on April 14 Mrs. Slade filed a petition seeking authority to take charge of the estate. She asserted that her husband had written a will leaving everything to her and naming her as executrix, and that his property was worth $5,000. But in her fury at the creditors now seemingly hungering to carve up his estate, Mrs. Slade refused to produce his will—if indeed such a will existed.

On the same day, Sanders, representing two creditors, filed a petition asking the probate judge to order Mrs. Slade into court, on the ground that she was committing "waste" and disposing of Slade's property without authority.[13] Sanders or his clients may have had reliable information that Mrs. Slade was liquidating Slade's personal property with the intention of leaving east Idaho. She had already traveled to Salt Lake in March—on the journey that made Charles Cannon so nervous—and would do so again in April and June, possibly with Slade's friend Jim Kiskadden, who had a brother and friends there.[14] They may also have feared that, in her anger, Mrs. Slade intended to stiff her husband's creditors, especially those belonging to the two groups she blamed for his death: vigilantes and saloon keepers.[15]

The court scheduled a hearing for April 29 to prove the will, but neither side showed up that day. Three days later the probate judge, T. C. Jones, declared that Mrs. Slade "has departed from said County taking with her property belonging to said estate." A prominent and reputable merchant named George B. Parker, who also served as Virginia City's first postmaster, was appointed as the Slade estate's administrator.[16] Yet the following day a new mortgage on Slade's receivables was created that somehow gave Judge Jones himself a financial interest in Slade's estate. Like many another widow, Virginia Slade may have mistrusted the lawyers and judges who took charge of her husband's assets; but Judge Jones's maneuverings suggest that her mistrust may have been justified.[17]

In theory, all of Slade's real and personal property was turned over to Parker as the estate's administrator, but not so in practice, as Parker discovered one day when confronted by Mrs. Slade, who had apparently returned from Salt Lake. The encounter was later described by

Mrs. Granville Stuart:

> Among the personal effects was a pair of ivory-handled silver
> mounted Colt revolvers. These Mrs. Slade claimed as her person-
> al property and called at Parker's store to claim them.
>
> Mr. Parker politely explained that the revolvers in question had
> been turned over to him as part of the Slade estate and that he
> would be held responsible for them and that he could not give
> them to her.
>
> Mrs. Slade walked out of the store without comment but
> returned soon after and walking up to Mr. Parker said, "You say
> you cannot give me my revolvers, perhaps I can persuade you to
> change your mind." At this she presented the muzzle of a .45 Colt
> in his face. George took no time to reason with the lady but
> promptly handed her the revolvers which she coolly took posses-
> sion of and left the store.[18]

Mrs. Slade's refusal to cooperate and her frequent removals to Salt
Lake City emboldened would-be creditors to file claims of dubious
merit. After all, in the absence of both Slade and his wife, and in a town
without roots, who could really say whether a claim was valid or not?
Perhaps the most blatant was an affidavit prepared by Wilbur Sanders
for Slade's executioner, James Williams. In it Williams swore that he
had worked as Slade's personal employee from October 1, 1862, to
January 1, 1863, at $30 per month, and for the first seven and a half
months of 1863 at $40 per month, for a total of $390 that Williams
said was due him from Slade's estate.

Had Slade or his widow been available, no doubt they would have
pointed out the salient facts: In October 1862 Slade was still an
employee of the Overland Stage Company, headquartered at Virginia
Dale in Colorado, while Williams and his brother were raising corn on
a large range south of Pueblo, Colorado Territory. Even if Williams
had somehow managed to journey more than 200 miles north to work
for Slade, he would have done so as an employee not of Slade but of
the Overland. After the stage line fired Slade that November, he had
spent the winter visiting his family in Illinois while Williams remained
with his brother on their Colorado farm until they sold it in the spring

of 1863. Williams and Slade could not have known each other until that spring, when their wagon trains combined en route to the east Idaho gold diggings. In effect, Williams's claim ludicrously implied that, at the very moment when the two men competed against each other to be captain of that wagon train, Williams was Slade's personal employee.

Although Williams's original claim was accidentally lost or destroyed, Williams solemnly resubmitted the same claim again in January 1865. To administrator Parker's credit, the claim was apparently never approved.[19] Among his admirers Williams was celebrated as a self-effacing man of considerable courage and integrity; but his filing of a fraudulent claim against his own deceased victim must give an observer pause.

In June, Virginia (possibly with assistance from her husband's friend Jim Kiskadden) loaded Slade's coffin aboard the Peabody & Caldwell Company stage bound for Salt Lake. The long coffin was wedged on the roof between the coach's "boots" and lashed there with ropes. The sound of the liquid inside the coffin, sloshing back and forth, was plainly audible to Virginia and her fellow passengers. As she had no doubt intended, the bizarre sight of the coffin bumping its way past settlements, mining camps, and way-stations left an indelible impression on those it passed, forcing them to inquire as to the identity of its occupant and why he was being transported such an extraordinary distance. When the coach crossed the Snake River ferry at Fort Hall, a ferry worker named Ben Arnold preserved a mental picture of the grim vision. "Mrs. Slade was a beautiful woman, and bore all the marks of an energetic and forceful one, too," Arnold later recalled. "Here she was bringing the body of her husband four hundred fifty miles for burial as a protest against what she called an outrage."[20]

On July 20 Slade was temporarily buried in the pauper's section of Salt Lake City Cemetery.[21] One account suggests that Mrs. Slade was not present for the actual interment, and no stone marked his grave. Salt Lake was intended, after all, only as an interim resting place.[22] "Killed by Vigilance Committee," the cemetery's sexton noted in his ledger. "To be removed to Illinois in the fall."[23]

How and when was word of Slade's death received in Illinois? No telegraph wires connected east Idaho to the outside world. Newspapers usually took three or four weeks to reach Virginia City from California, and weeks longer from the States in the East. The previous December 10—the day Slade returned from his Milk River expedition—the Carlyle *Weekly Union Banner* had published an erroneous report that "Alfred Slade, an old citizen of our town, was killed a short time since near Brunswick City, Idaho Territory."[24] Two weeks later, in correcting its error, the *Union Banner* provided a hint of how news of Slade's hanging would have been received in his hometown: "We are glad to be able to correct a report which we published last week of the death of Alfred Slade. We are informed by his friends that he is alive and well. This welcome intelligence will dispell the gloom which the unfortunate report cast over his friends."[25]

Certainly by the summer of 1864 the second, unhappily accurate, report of Slade's death had reached Carlyle. That August a Carlyle woman named Elizabeth Ruble penned a letter to her uncle in California filled with local chitchat. Midway through the letter these lines appeared: "Annie saw William Slade the other day and he told her to send his respects to you and tell you that he had not forgotten you. I suppose you have heard that Alfred was hung at Idaho for disorderly conduct."[26]

In a single succinct line of gossip, this Illinois woman who lived more than 1,500 miles from Virginia City had furnished what Captain James Williams and his fellow vigilantes, in their haste, had neglected to provide: the only reason ever given for Slade's execution.

In May 1864, thanks to prodding from Wilbur Sanders's uncle Sidney Edgerton, the U.S. Congress recognized the futility of governing east Idaho from Lewiston, beyond the Bitterroot Mountains— the lawless situation that had given rise to the vigilantes in the first place. Now the entire vast area east of the Bitterroot Mountains was broken off into a new territory called Montana. Since virtually the whole population of the new Montana Territory was located between Alder Gulch and Bannack, this once-isolated region would now be blessed with its own duly appointed territorial government as well as courts and a U.S. marshal. In theory, the vigilantes would no longer be needed.

But in June an Irish miner named Murphy was shot twice through the window and doorway of his tiny cabin in Nevada City. Although he was badly hurt, Murphy identified his assailant as a saloonkeeper named James Brady, with whom he had feuded. Once again James Williams reactivated his vigilante posse and captured Brady that night. The next afternoon—following an examination by Paris Pfouts and some fifty Vigilante leaders—Brady was hanged from a gallows fashioned out of a butcher's hoist.

This execution provoked as much dissension as Slade's, albeit for a different reason: Thanks to his strong constitution, Murphy recovered from his wounds, thereafter to become embarrassing living evidence of the pitfalls of vigilante justice.[27] The vigilantes' apologist Thomas Dimsdale later took his stab at rationalizing the Brady hanging: "What the state of a man's health has to do with the crime of the villain who shoots him," he argued limply, "will to us forever remain an enigma."[28]

Although the vigilantes had supposedly extinguished the last of the road agents with Bill Hunter's hanging in early February, on August 21 a stagecoach headed from Virginia City to Salt Lake was ambushed by a pack of robbers who made off with some $27,000 in gold. Two weeks week later James Williams and his men captured a "rough" named Jem Kelly and hanged him for the crime.[29]

In September a Virginia City miner named John Dolan was accused of robbing $700 in gold dust from his cabin mate; Dolan convincingly denied his guilt but then bolted in the direction of Salt Lake City, in the process persuading the Vigilance Committee that he was guilty after all. Although Dolan's alleged offense was neither murder nor highway robbery nor assault with a deadly weapon, the committee dispatched to Utah a private detective, who with a few allies seized Dolan over the objections of a local marshal and returned him to Nevada City. There he was hanged on September 17, despite a near-riot by a crowd of several thousand objecting settlers. To their growing list of unorthodox crime prevention methods, the vigilantes had now added kidnapping and defiance of territorial officials not only in Montana Territory but in Utah Territory as well.[30]

The rising chorus of objections to their methods merely heightened the vigilantes' sensitivity to criticism. In Bannack on October 31 they hanged a harmless drunk named R. C. Rawley, whom they had banished the previous winter. His "crime" was to have written a letter complaining about his treatment.[31]

The feeding frenzy on her husband's estate was apparently more than even the combative Virginia Slade could stomach. Through most of the probate process "she was in Utah," a lawyer representing her later contended, "and was so disgusted with the outcome, that she refused to have anything to do with it or to send for the money."[32]

Slade's remaining personal property—whatever Virginia hadn't spirited away—was sold by the estate's administrator, George Parker, at a public auction in Virginia City on December 19, 1864. The 320-acre Ravenswood dairy ranch, appraised at $2,000, went to one John R. Rockfellow on a bid of $500; Spring Dale, with its toll road and stone house but half the size of Ravenswood, was appraised at $250 and went to a Benjamin F. Christenot for $105. All told, Parker appears to have raised nearly $8,500 in assets and paid out nearly $4,140 in claims, including $1,004 for administrative expenses. Yet in the administrator's final account, filed on November 7, 1865, only $359.41 was left for Virginia Slade.

This paltry proceed reflected in part the fact that Parker had earlier advanced Mrs. Slade $400 against her share of the estate.[33] It also reflected the likelihood that Mrs. Slade had already liquidated some of the assets and taken them away, probably to Salt Lake City. (Slade's Wells Fargo shares, worth some $13,400, never came to light in Parker's report.)[34] It may also have reflected honest carelessness and sloppiness in a makeshift frontier court unprepared to deal with an estate of such size and complexity.

Nevertheless, Parker himself, in his final report, denounced Virginia City's probate court and Judge Jones for "gross negligence."[35] A Montana probate judge who investigated Slade's estate more than a

century later suggested that some creditors had received double payments from Slade's estate—once in advances at administrator Parker's
store, and again on the final settlement of the estate.[36] "We can rest
assured that not all frontier robberies were confined to stagecoaches or
gambling dens," concluded the judge, John B. McClernan.[37]

If Mrs. Slade had remained in Virginia City to contest the proceedings, McClernan speculated, the final result would have been very different: "At least half of the creditors would never have filed a claim
against her; and the other half would have hesitated considerably
before attempting to enforce collection... The early miners of Virginia
City were quick to rise up in anger and hang a man but they would
have been equally quick to rise up in sympathy to protect his widow in
the full enjoyment of all her husband's property."[38] But of course the
world of courts and lawyers was as alien to Mrs. Slade as it had been
to her husband.

Virginia Slade actually did remain in Virginia City long enough to
develop a relationship with Slade's friend Kiskadden, a big, brawny
fellow who had much to recommend himself to a woman beyond his
dashing good looks and careful attention to his attire. Like Slade,
Kiskadden exuded a determined air that seemed to insist, "Things
must go my way." More important, he was a prosperous hardware merchant, with a brother in Salt Lake City who had made a fortune freighting gold and supplies during the Pike's Peak gold rush.[39]

On March 22, 1865, barely a year after Slade's death, Virginia and
Kiskadden were married at her Virginia City home in a ceremony performed by Montana Territory's new chief justice, Hezekiah Hosmer.
The *Montana Post*, recently launched by the schoolmaster Thomas
Dimsdale, reported the reception and described two wedding cakes
inscribed with the letter "V" in gold. "May you and your amiable bride
enjoy many long years of happiness and content," the newspaper edi-
torialized. "May the pathway in life's journey be smooth and the end
far-off."[40]

Two weeks later, the Ravenswood ranch that Rockfellow had
bought at auction for $500 was deeded back to the new Mrs.
Kiskadden for $850.[41] Yet the newlyweds left immediately for Salt

Lake City. Like so much else that Virginia failed to grasp in this bewildering new world of courts and lawyers, she seems not to have understood that ranch claims, like mining claims, were merely temporary; they depended for their validity on continuous occupancy and improvement over certain time periods before they could ripen into permanent legal titles. When the gold ran out on a good mining claim, the miner simply abandoned the claim without bothering further about the legal title; but a woman who abandoned a 320-acre ranch effectively gave up a potentially valuable investment.[42]

Within six months of the wedding Virginia had left her new husband, never to return to him. In Virginia City it was theorized that, in her overriding devotion to Slade, Virginia had romanced and married Kiskadden primarily for his access to the stagecoaches and ancillary services that enabled her to remove Slade's body to Salt Lake City, and that subsequently she had lost interest in him.[43] By one account, Virginia was too high-strung for the easygoing Kiskadden: "Virginia is a very desperate woman," he is said to have told friends just before they parted.[44] In 1866 Virginia was seen with her ward Jemmy in Denver.[45] By October 1868, when Kiskadden obtained a divorce in Salt Lake City, Virginia had moved on to St. Louis. "At this time they have not lived together for three years," the decree noted. "It is impossible for them to live again in peace and union and their welfare requires their separation."[46]

The final settlement of $359.41 approved for Virginia from Slade's estate in late 1865 turned out not to be final after all; certain closing administrative expenses remained to be deducted. On October 27, 1866, a check for the net proceeds—$305.91—was paid to Word & Spratt, a Virginia City law partnership recorded as representing J. H. Kiskadden and M. V. Kiskadden. The firm likely turned this money over to Kiskadden, unaware that Virginia had already left him. If that is the case, Virginia received nothing from the final settlement of her first husband's estate.[47]

On September 24, 1864—exactly one year after Slade left Virginia City to recover the town's supplies from the mouth of the Milk River—Dimsdale's *Montana Post* published a "Warning to

Housekeepers": "There is not such a quantity of flour in town as will suffice to meet the winter's consumption." The *Post* reminded its readers that the roads to Salt Lake City were likely to be impassable to freight wagons come winter. "We therefore consider it only a matter of common prudence, to lay in stock of necessary articles before the supply is diminished or suspended by winter."[48]

Before the winter was over, there was no bread in Alder Gulch. A group of supply trains had corralled for the winter on the Snake River barely 100 miles away but on the wrong side of the Continental Divide. This time there was no Jack Slade to volunteer to undertake the perilous journey for the necessary supplies.

Borrowing the same tactic they had employed against Slade, on April 18, 1865, some 480 miners from Nevada City, armed with rifles and shotguns, marched into Virginia City. As they had done for Slade's arrest, the force was divided into six companies, each commanded by a captain and moving forward in military fashion. At their head rode an unidentified commander holding aloft as his banner an empty flour sack nailed to a staff. This time the miners' purpose was not to arrest a drunk who was tearing up the town but to tear up the town themselves, in search of precious flour they believed was being hoarded in Virginia City's stores, warehouses, and restaurants.

Among the victims of this looting was Wilbur Sanders, a founding vigilante, whose home was ransacked when a rumor spread that he had flour. Mrs. Sanders invited the men to come in and try to find some; but later, when she went downtown in search of flour herself, her house was invaded again.

Eventually the searchers took 82 sacks of flour to Leviathan Hall, where the supply was rationed out and sold to anyone who could prove he had no flour. The "flour committee," as the raiders styled themselves, subsequently repaid the cost of the flour they had seized, but only at the much lower prices that had prevailed before the winter. In the aftermath, the town's first mayor—the vigilante president Paris Pfouts—published a notice in the *Montana Post* to the effect that if there were any more such disturbances he would proclaim martial law.[49]

Captain James Williams does not appear to have been involved in this "flour riot," as it came to be known. Following the widely criticized vigilante hangings of the unproven petty thief John Dolan and the harmless drunk R. C. Rawley in the fall of 1864, Williams "quit his gruesome work with a sigh of great relief, and retired as quietly as he could," in the words of his admiring biographer.[50] When Montana's first district court convened in December 1864—in the dining room of the Planters Hotel in Virginia City—the territory's new chief justice, Hezekiah Hosmer, employed a combination of flattery and reprimand in an attempt to persuade the vigilantes to disband. With Captain Williams and other vigilantes seated before him as members of the first grand jury, Hosmer tactfully praised the vigilantes for assuming, in the absence of the law, "the delicate and responsible office of purging society of all offenders against its peace, happiness and safety"; but he also argued that the vigilantes were no longer needed, and that if their activity persisted, it would corrupt the vigilantes themselves. "Let us erect no more impromptu scaffolds," Hosmer exhorted. "Let us inflict no more midnight executions."[51]

His inspirational plea fell on deaf ears. Another gold discovery, this one at the Last Chance Gulch in the summer of 1864, had triggered a new stampede to what became the town of Helena, 125 miles to the north. Once again the vigilantes felt compelled to impose order at the new diggings. But this time they encountered serious resistance from settlers whose credentials were perhaps even more respectable than those claimed by the vigilantes. "In times past you did do some glorious work," wrote a "sworn band of law-abiding citizens" to the vigilantes in a notice published in the *Montana Post*, "but the time has come when law should be enforced. . . . We are American citizens and you shall not drive and hang whom you please."[52]

Their plea too fell on deaf ears. Between the spring of 1865 and the spring of 1870—when vigilantes seized two prisoners from a Helena jail by force and hanged them in defiance of a territorial judge—thirty more men were lynched by Montana vigilantes, bringing to fifty-seven the total executed by vigilantes since Red Yeager and George Brown were hanged in the first days of 1864.[53]

Only a handful of this second wave of lynchings occurred in Alder

Gulch. But then, by 1865 some two-thirds of the Gulch's population had moved on to the Last Chance diggings around Helena. By the middle of 1865 only about 7,500 people remained in Alder Gulch; within another decade only a few hundred would be left.[54] Having yielded more than $70 million in gold, and having served for ten years as the territorial capital of Montana, this community that the vigilantes had saved from the road agents at the cost of two dozen lives was fast on its way to becoming a ghost town.[55]

Chapter 20

VICTIMS AND SURVIVORS

*

The news of Robert E. Lee's surrender to Ulysses S. Grant at Appomattox in April 1865 reached Virginia City in the record time of thirteen days.[1] In Texas and other places where news traveled even more slowly, sporadic skirmishes continued. But for all practical purposes the Civil War ended with this defeat of the Confederacy's largest army.

Four years earlier the South had gone to war with seemingly impressive advantages: a fighting military tradition, an array of brilliant generals led by Lee himself, and arsenals amply stocked with guns and ammunition by the outgoing U.S. Secretary of War, the Virginian John B. Floyd. Yet ultimately the key to victory lay elsewhere. "The Yankees did not whip us in the field," a Confederate leader observed after Lee surrendered. "We were whipped in the Treasury Department."[2] And not until years after Appomattox did it become clear that the U.S. Treasury Department could not have financed the Civil War without the West.

The $150 million borrowed by the Treasury Department from banks in New York, Boston, and Philadelphia during the summer and fall of 1861 had virtually depleted the Union's gold supply then and there. By December 1861 Northern banks were in danger of suspending specie payments—that is, payments in gold or silver rather than notes. Those banks, and the Union as well, were rescued between 1862 and 1865 only by a stream of raw gold and silver that flowed steadily eastward from California, Nevada and Colorado. The same Central Overland stagecoach and mail service that had kept California in the Union on the eve of the Civil War also became the Union's lifeline to the wealth of the West once the war began.

Despite the North's awesome final war debt of more than $2.5 billion, the value of the Union's dollar—and consequently the Union's ability to borrow—never fell below a specie value of fifty cents throughout the war. The Confederate dollar, meanwhile, dropped to a twenty-cent specie value in 1862 and then slid to near worthlessness. The South had the guns and the dedicated fighting men but no borrowing power; the North, by holding on to the West and its treasures, exercised the power of the purse. That had made all the difference, as Lincoln himself acknowledged. "I would rather have Nevada in the Union than another million men," the president remarked when that sparsely populated territory applied for statehood in 1864.[3]

In the process of sustaining the Central Overland California & Pike's Peak Express Company, Slade and his scruffy band of drivers, riders, and station keepers had unwittingly saved the Union. But by the time the House Ways and Means Committee reached that implied conclusion in 1869, Slade had been dead for five years.

The completion of the transcontinental railroad in 1869 and the Santa Fe Railroad in 1880 finished the job of connecting East and West that the traders, freighters, stagecoaches, and telegraph lines had begun. The "Great American Desert" was rapidly vanishing. The age of the ox-drawn wagon and the horse-drawn stagecoach was drawing to a close. So was the era of the Plains Indian that stretched back well before Columbus. Soon the prairie schooners and Concord stagecoaches would be broken up for scrap or consigned to museums; the Indians would be driven onto reservations; the oxen would be sold for beef; and the trappers, traders, bullwhackers, wagonmasters, riverboat men, and stagecoach drivers would recede into the pages of history.

The first published account of Slade's life appeared as a by-product within the first published defense of the vigilantes. The weekly *Montana Post* was launched in Virginia City in the fall of 1864, and after a single issue Thomas Dimsdale, the town's English-born school-master, took charge as its editor. Dimsdale was not a vigilante himself, but he was a Mason with close ties to the vigilantes. To Granville Stuart, Dimsdale was "a man of culture and refinement"[4]; to the eleven-year-old Molly Sheehan, he was "small, delicate-looking and gentle"[5]; by other accounts he was a weakling and a sycophant, eager to curry favor with the local establishment.[6] After an anonymous book criticizing the vigilantes appeared in the summer of 1865, Dimsdale undertook the awesome task of researching and publishing his own serialized history of the vigilantes over twenty-nine weeks beginning that August.[7] Dimsdale's apologia convincingly portrayed Henry Plummer as the leader and mastermind of a highly coordinated gang of road agents who had committed, Dimsdale maintained, 102 murders before the vigilantes brought them to justice.

Dimsdale never claimed to write as an unbiased observer; more-over, in a practice common at the time, he solicited financial support from the vigilantes he proposed to glorify. James Williams, for example, refused Dimsdale's request for $200 and consequently was referred to by Dimsdale only obliquely as "the leader," never by name.[8] Nevertheless, Dimsdale's detail and reportage was so extensive that when his articles were assembled in book form as *Vigilantes of Montana* in 1866—just months before Dimsdale died of consumption—his account became, if only by default, the definitive source on the subject for the next 140 years. Charles Dickens, on a visit to the U.S., borrowed a friend's copy and pronounced *Vigilantes of Montana* one of the best books he had read.

Dimsdale's chapter on Slade was in many respects subtle and per-ceptive. The editor readily acknowledged that Slade was no road agent and "was never accused, or even suspected, of either murder or rob-bery committed in this Territory."[9] Those who saw Slade "in his natu-ral state only," Dimsdale wrote, "would pronounce him to be a kind husband, a most hospitable host and a courteous gentleman."[10] Dimsdale wrote admiringly of Slade's capacities for making money and attracting loyal friends (although Dimsdale astutely added that "anoth-er, and less desirable class of friends were attracted by his very reckless-ness").[11] When Slade was arrested, Dimsdale duly reported, "scarcely a leading man in Virginia could be found" to serve in the guard, and "all lamented the stern necessity which dictated the execution."[12]

Yet Dimsdale's primary purpose was not to analyze the execution but to justify it. To this end he recounted Slade's drunken binges as well as his alleged past crimes, from his supposed youthful murder in Carlyle to his mutilation of Jules Beni.

Dimsdale also addressed the questions raised by the crowd at Slade's execution and thereafter: Why were other men banished by the vigilantes for lesser offenses rather than executed? Why were Fairweather and Slade's other carousing friends permitted to go scot-free? "The answer is very sim-

Thomas Dimsdale, the English-born Virginia City schoolmaster and editor, wrote the ultimate vigilante apology but discussed Slade with surprising subtlety and perception. (*Montana Historical Society*)

ple," Dimsdale explained. "The Vigilantes deplored the sad but imperative necessity for the making of one example. That, they knew, would be sufficient."[13] Here, by implication, was the first acknowledgement that Slade was targeted by the vigilantes not for any specific offense but simply because he was perceived as the ringleader of a group of troublemakers. Had he been less influential, they might have executed Fairweather or another of his drinking cronies.

The hanging of the road agents, Dimsdale concluded, was "the result of the popular verdict and judgment against robbers and murderers." Slade's death, on the other hand, was "the protest of society on behalf of social order and the rights of man."[14] That notion was repeated and reinforced by other writers for years thereafter. "Slade was to learn what society means, and what the social compact means," wrote the journalist Emerson Hough in a 1908 paean to vigilantism. "He had had his fair frontier chance and had misused it."[15]

In subsequent years vigilante defenders contended that Slade's execution had been the one mistake in the vigilantes' otherwise blameless record. "Save for this execution the Vigilantes of Montana have been well nigh universally commended," wrote the Montana Supreme Court Chief Justice Llewellyn Callaway. "For this act they have been fiercely condemned and as vigorously commended."[16]

Just as vigilante justice had failed to eliminate crime by executing alleged criminals, so the vigilantes' published arguments failed to silence their critics. Twenty-five years after Dimsdale, the Alder Gulch merchant and Freemason Nathaniel Langford wrote his memoir, *Vigilante Days and Ways,* for much the same reason that had motivated Dimsdale: to explain to a new generation of doubters why the vigilantes took the law into their own hands. Yet Langford too reinforced the notion that the Slade hanging was an unfortunate exception. Langford closed his chapter on Slade by quoting from a personal letter by a friend of Slade's:

> Slade was unquestionably a most useful man in his time to the stage line, and to the cause of progress in the Far West, and he never was a robber, as some have represented; but after years of contention with desperate men, he became so reckless and regardless of human life that his best friends must concede that he was at times a most dangerous character, and no doubt, by his defiance of the authority and wholesome discipline of the Vigilantes, brought upon himself the calamity which he suffered.[17]

By the time these reflections appeared, though, anyone hoping to examine Slade's career seriously had long since been overshadowed by a writer of vastly greater stature, if less fidelity to historical truth. The young journalist Samuel Clemens had met Slade for an hour over breakfast while traveling the Central Overland route to Nevada in August 1861. During the next decade, two of his collections of sketches—*The Celebrated Jumping Frog of Calaveras County* and *Innocents Abroad*—had established Clemens as a great humorist and storyteller. In his new persona as Mark Twain, he set out to reinforce his growing celebrity with yet another collection based on his travels through the

West. As a first step toward this project, in the fall of 1870 Twain dispatched a letter from his home in Buffalo, New York, to the postmaster in Virginia City.

> Dear Sir:
> Four or five years ago a righteous Vigilance Committee in your city hanged a casual acquaintance of mine named Slade.... Now I am writing a book.... I thought I would just rescue my late friend Slade from oblivion & set a sympathetic public to weeping for him.... & the object of this letter is to beg of you to ask some one connected with your city papers to send me a Virginia City newspaper of that day if it can be done without mutilating a file.[18]

Whether Twain received a reply isn't known, but he subsequently obtained a copy of Dimsdale's book and drew heavily on it for details about Slade's life and death.

There remained the challenge of re-creating Twain's meeting with Slade, about which Twain recalled practically nothing. To his older brother (and former traveling companion) Orion Clemens, Twain wrote: "Please sit down right away & torture your memory & write down in minute detail every fact & exploit in the desperado Slade's life that we heard on the Overland—& also describe his appearance & conversation as we saw him at Rocky Ridge station at breakfast. I want to make up a telling chapter from it for the book."[19] Orion Clemens, who apparently had recorded little or nothing about Slade in his journal during that 1861 trip, compliantly provided his brother with "all I can remember and more than I recollect distinctly or feel entirely certain of trusting that it would be practically near enough correct."[20] Orion's reply included an extensive description of Slade's appearance ("about your size, if any difference rather shorter and more slender") and some details about their meeting with Slade at Rocky Ridge.

It is a mark of Twain's talent as a raconteur that from these slim fragments he managed to cobble together three highly readable chapters about Slade, including a description of his execution lifted verbatim from Dimsdale's book. A close reading of Twain's account makes clear that the Slade portrayed there—the Slade "steeped in the blood of offenders against his dignity," the Slade who had shot the teamster

Andrew Ferrin for sport, the Slade who "had taken the lives of twenty-six human beings, or all men lied about him!"—was a figure of myth rather than history. Twain's dual purpose was to preserve Western folklore while simultaneously promoting himself as a young man who had looked into the eyes of a killer and lived to tell the tale.

Upon its publication in 1872, *Roughing It* signaled Mark Twain's arrival as a great native writer who, in the process of collecting and inflating tall tales in manic, hilarious, and sometimes painterly detail, had somehow captured the flavor of America's fading stagecoach era more vividly than any historian had done. Twain's special gift lay in his instinctive understanding of the romantic appeal of evil—that most people, including Twain himself, found outlaws more exciting than saints.

Such was the success and power of Twain's pen that, in years to come, most historians who wrote about Slade—even the *Dictionary of American Biography*— cited *Roughing It* as their authority, and sometimes their sole authority. The incisive literary critic George Orwell, in a 1944 essay, chastised Twain—not for misrepresenting Slade, but for writing so admiringly about "the disgusting bandit Slade, hero of twenty-eight murders."[21] And thanks to Twain's example, Slade became fair game for anyone equipped with a literary license. "You remember Falstaff because he was fat and because he lied so beautifully," suggested one typical entry. "You remember Slade because he was bad and because he shot so beautifully."[22]

Instead of rescuing Slade from oblivion, Mark Twain did to Slade what Shakespeare did to Richard III. Just as each new generation of historians discovered a noble Richard III, only to be overwhelmed in the popular mind by Shakespeare's paranoid hunchback, so historians examining Slade were similarly helpless to erase the desperado Slade painted by Mark Twain. By citing Dimsdale as his authority, Twain effectively endorsed and promoted Dimsdale's narrative, just as Dimsdale's account reinforced the vigilantes' narrative.

The vigilantes subsequently claimed a place in Montana history comparable to that of the Minutemen in Massachusetts and the Green Mountain Boys in Vermont. In 1907 the Montana legislature placed a bronze plaque in the capitol's main hall honoring Captain James

Williams, "through whose untiring efforts and intrepid daring, law and order were established in Montana, and who. . . brought to justice the most desperate criminals in the Northwest." In 1920 Montana officials, hoping to attract automobile tourists from Yellowstone National Park, renamed the connecting route "The Vigilante Trail" and marked it with distinctive disks bearing the vigilantes' secret numbers, 3-7-77. In 1956 those same mysterious numbers were added to the Montana Highway Patrol's shoulder patches and car door shields.[23] Not until 1958 did a serious historian challenge the gospel according to Dimsdale; and not until 2004 did any historian produce an account capable of displacing Dimsdale as the definitive source on the vigilante era.[24] Yet even in the year 2003, in a book about the Pony Express with serious historical pretensions, that author's five-page portrait of Slade relied almost entirely on *Roughing It* as well as a book by another celebrated conjurer of Western fantasy, William F. Cody.[25]

As an eleven-year-old in Kansas Territory in 1857, Cody had worked briefly for Russell, Majors & Waddell, carrying messages on horseback from their office in Leavenworth City to the telegraph office at Fort Leavenworth, three miles to the north.[26] On this slender basis he subsequently attached himself to the great tradition of the Pony Express. Beginning in 1879, Cody wrote a series of autobiographies claiming that he had twice been hired as a Pony Express rider—first in 1859, and the second time in the summer of 1860, when Slade supposedly hired him at Horseshoe station. In one such self-promotional account, published in 1908, Slade singles out the fourteen-year-old Will Cody for a special assignment, saying, "Billy, I want you to come down to my headquarters, and I'll make you a sort of supernumerary rider, and send you out only when it is necessary."[27]

These claims were demonstrably false: the Pony Express did not begin operating until April 1860, and in the summer of 1860 Cody was in Denver with his uncle. But what Will Cody lacked in frontier experience he more than made up for in public relations acumen. The "Buffalo Bill" persona that Cody shrewdly conjured for himself in his wildly popular Wild West Show delivered not the historical West but the fantasy that Easterners yearned to experience. By attaching himself (as Mark Twain had also done) to legendary figures like Slade and

Wild Bill Hickok, Cody established himself as the personification of the West. Thanks to his skill as a publicist and self-promoter, Cody (like Twain) ultimately became much more famous than Slade. Cody's supposed cowboy companions and mentors were conveniently unavailable to debunk his stories because, by the time his tracts appeared, all of them were dead.[28]

Another who seized the new opportunities of the war and its after-math was Slade's stepfather, the Union Brigadier General Elias S. Dennis. For his service in the capture of Mobile, Alabama, Dennis was mustered out in 1865 with the honorary rank of brevet major general. But instead of returning to his wife and family in Carlyle after the war, Dennis created a new life for himself in Madison Parish, Louisiana, which he had formerly governed as a conqueror. Here he became a cotton farmer and politician. At first Dennis was distrusted by the locals, who presumed him a Republican carpetbagger, but eventually he won the trust of prominent whites, who recognized his value as a rare fellow Democrat capable of winning black votes while simultane-ously treating whites fairly. He was elected parish judge in 1874 and sheriff in 1880, and unlike most rapacious Northern opportunists in the postwar South was generally admired for his fairness, wisdom, and moderation in office.[29]

Reinventing himself in this manner, of course, required abandoning his wife in Illinois: Slade's mother, Mary Dark Kain Slade Dennis. When the war ended Dennis was still a healthy and rugged man of fifty-two, Mary was a declining and impoverished woman of sixty-five, and Dennis seems to have left her with the same alacrity with which, three decades earlier, he had married her as the heiress to Carlyle's property and prestige. When Mary's divorce petition was granted in August 1871, she testified that Elias had left her four years earlier and had lived apart from her ever since, "without so much as seeing her or writing a letter, or even furnishing her with the common necessaries of life," despite his knowledge of "her destitute circumstances."[30]

At some point during his new life in Louisiana, Dennis became much admired by a wealthy widow who ultimately willed him her plantation. Unfortunately, the will proved to be defective and Dennis received nothing from it when she died. Undeterred, in 1875 he married Mary A. McFarland, another landed Madison Parish widow, who owned a 757-acre plantation called "McFarland Place." Although his treatment of Slade's mother had rendered him a pariah in Carlyle, Illinois, in 1887 Dennis inexplicably moved back there with his son, Slade's half-brother Elias Dennis, Jr. His Louisiana wife did not join him, although she did visit him in Carlyle from time to time until his death there, in December 1894, at the age of eighty-two.[31] His gravestone bears no epitaph. But in consideration of his service as a U.S. marshal in "bleeding Kansas," as a Civil War general and as a force for reconciliation in postwar Louisiana, it might fairly be said: He put his country before his family.

The genuine heroes of the early West—those who survived—had either burned out by the end of the Civil War or were incapable of adjusting to the new rules of the game. William H. Russell, head of the great freighting firm of Russell, Majors & Waddell, sought bankruptcy protection in New York in 1868 and subsequently eked out a modest living as a notary public and a peddler of a neuralgia cure until his death in Missouri in 1872 at age sixty; his passing was barely mentioned in the newspapers.[32] After the collapse of their freighting partnership, William Waddell apparently never engaged in business again. The loss of his fortune, prestige, property and his son—killed defending a slave during the Civil War—bore so heavily upon Waddell that his health failed and he died at his son-in-law's Missouri farm in 1872, at the age of sixty-five.[33]

Their third partner, Alexander Majors, remained in the freighting business into the mid-1860s despite his lack of financial resources, relying instead on his reputation to attract equipment, livestock, and men. In 1867 he moved his family to Salt Lake City and engaged in grading the roadbed and furnishing ties and telegraph poles for the Union Pacific Railroad. He also prospected for silver in the Utah mountains. In the early 1890s, by which time Majors was eighty, William F. Cody found him living alone in near-poverty in Chicago; at

Cody's suggestion, Majors wrote, and Cody published, his memoirs as a way of restoring his finances. *Seventy Years On the Frontier,* published in both paperback and hardcover form in 1893, was the first book ever to summarize the story of the Pony Express. Yet its sparsity of detail puzzled later chroniclers. Upon investigation they found that Cody's editor, preoccupied with creating a book that would attract a popular audience, had eviscerated much of the original Majors manuscript. In the end Majors was no writer, just as Cody was no cowboy.

Ben Ficklin, Russell's dashing first general superintendent of the Pony Express, returned to Virginia when the Civil War broke out and was commissioned a major in the Virginia volunteers. After the war he established stage lines in the southwestern states and the Indian Territory north of Texas.[34] Over dinner at the Willard Hotel in Washington in 1871, this bold survivor of the Pony Express and the Civil War choked on a jagged fish bone and died, at the age of forty-four.[35]

Ben Holladay, the self-styled stagecoach king, managed his survival more adeptly than his predecessors at the Central Overland. In 1866, presciently sensing that the days of stagecoaching were numbered, he sold his renamed Holladay Overland Mail line to Wells Fargo for $1.8 million in cash and Wells Fargo stock. The consolidation was approved that November at a meeting in Denver, where the votes cast in favor included a block of 134 shares of Wells Fargo stock voted "in person" for a "J. Slode"—almost certainly the same block of 134 shares that turned up in Slade's estate, and most likely voted at the meeting by Slade's wife Virginia (who was seen in Denver at that time) or by someone representing her.[36] Without knowing it, Holladay had sold his stage line to a company that was partly owned by his former employee, Jack Slade.

Ben Holladay lost most of his fortune in the Panic of 1873 and never recouped his losses from the Indian raids on his old Central Overland route that began in the spring of 1862. In 1877 Congress offered him $100,000—less than a fifth of his claim—to settle the account. Holladay characteristically refused the offer, saying that if the United States was not able to pay its debts he could give it his claim. He left Washington and apparently never returned. Years after his death in 1887,

Holladay's heirs sued for the full amount, and a reimbursement bill was submitted in Congress in 1907. But the bill failed to pass, and the claim of Holladay's heirs was dismissed by a court in 1912.[37]

Dame Fortune, which had twice smiled on Slade's crony Bill Fairweather—first when he struck gold at Alder Gulch and then when he was spared Slade's fate at the hands of the vigilantes—was less kind to him thereafter. Fairweather sold his Alder Gulch claim for $40,000 and sought new adventures in Canada and Alaska, where he was unable to repeat his previous success; returning to Montana, he dropped dead in a roadhouse in 1875 at the age of thirty-nine.[38] Slade's freighting partner John Ely gained and lost several mining fortunes and founded the town of Ely, Nevada; his investing career took him as far as Paris, France, in the early 1870s before he too died in poverty in Montana.[39] Alexander Davis, Slade's friend and the judge of Virginia City's People's Court, returned to Missouri in 1869, practiced law in St. Louis and died there in 1896.[40]

Whether out of modesty, shame, or fear of retribution, few of the leading vigilantes discussed their work publicly after they disbanded. The self-effacing merchant Paris Pfouts, the vigilantes' president and later mayor of Virginia City, wrote his memoirs in 1868 but devoted just three of its 109 pages to the vigilantes. One exception, X. Beidler, dictated his memoirs in the 1880s and was widely chastised for claiming more credit for the vigilantes' success than he deserved. He worked as a stagecoach guard and a deputy U.S. marshal up to his death in Helena in 1890.[41] Wilbur Sanders, one of the few vigilantes to benefit from the association, prospered as an attorney in Helena and was chosen a U.S. Senator by the legislature shortly after Montana achieved statehood in 1889.[42] Adriel B. Davis, who captained the Nevada City force that arrested Slade, did not speak publicly about his vigilante experience until thirty-five years later, and then he gave most of the credit to his superior, Captain James Williams, who he said "put in more time, more money, more horses, and lost more, and made greater personal sacrifices than any other one member of the Vigilance Committee."[43]

James Williams, Slade's taciturn executioner, retired from the vigilantes without ceremony and thereafter seldom spoke of his connection to them. He turned from gold mining to cattle farming, got married in 1866 and fathered seven children, but neither the farm nor the marriage seems to have brought him much satisfaction. The ranch failed to prosper, and Elizabeth Williams developed what a neighbor described as a "shrewish turn of mind," often nagging her husband about his shortcomings.[44] Although Williams had avoided strong liquor when important work was at hand, as he grew older he tended to imbibe freely, until—like his old adversary Slade—it became difficult for him to stay sober when he visited Virginia City. On these occasions, wrote Lew Callaway, who knew Williams in the 1880s, "He could not resist the temptation to drink with his old friends."[45]

After creditors liquidated his ranch and sold off his herd, Williams regrouped with a new farm, only to face fresh disaster when the deadly winter of 1886–87 killed thousands of head of cattle across Montana. In mid-February, following a futile meeting with his banker in Virginia City, Williams purchased an ounce of laudanum, a popular opium-based painkiller. A few days later, on the second day of a new snowstorm, he trudged across his lower field, past the humped-up bodies of his starving cattle. Beneath a dense clump of willows he sat down, removed his mittens, drank the laudanum, pulled his cap over his eyes and went to sleep. He was fifty-two.[46]

After Virginia Slade left Jim Kiskadden, he remained in Salt Lake City as the cashier at the Miners National Bank, which his brother William co-founded in 1866.[47] Jim was still an eligible match: he drew a good salary, dressed well, always wore immaculate linen with a large diamond on his shirtfront, and was recognized as the town's champion billiard player. After his divorce was finalized in 1868 Kiskadden began courting a local actress named Annie Asenith Adams. But several obstacles stood in his way: "Senith," as she was known, was a Mormon and Kiskadden was a gentile, as the Mormons called nonbelievers; at age twenty, she was more than twelve years his junior;[48] she was being courted by a more handsome rival; and she refused to marry a previously married man. She had seen enough of that to make her dread it, she said.

To discourage the match, Senith's parents sent her to visit her grandparents in Clark County, Missouri. Kiskadden seized the opportunity, followed her, and married her there in August 1869. Three years later their daughter Maude was born within a stone's throw of the Salt Lake Theatre where Senith often performed.

In 1874 the Kiskaddens spent a season in Virginia City, where Senith was engaged with a stock theater troupe, and the following year they moved to San Francisco, where Kiskadden took a job as a bookkeeper. Here their daughter followed her mother into the theater, opting for the sake of brevity to adopt her mother's maiden name for the stage. Kiskadden died there, apparently of a drinking problem, in 1883 at the age of forty-seven. But his elfin daughter Maude Adams flourished on stages throughout the world into the mid-twentieth century. When J. M. Barrie adapted his novel *Peter Pan* for the stage in 1904, he created the central role with Maude Adams in mind.[49]

Most of Slade's old domain along the Central Overland Line— which in his day had belonged variously to the territories of Nebraska, Dakota, Utah and Idaho—fell under the jurisdiction of the newly created territory of Wyoming in 1869. Twenty years later, workmen taking out an irrigation ditch at a farm along the North Platte, 18 miles below Fort Laramie, unearthed a human skeleton. The bones of course lacked identification, but in the days that followed local old-timers concluded they must belong to the only man ever buried in that vicinity: Slade's nemesis Jules Beni, executed by Slade's men more than twenty-seven years earlier.[50]

Jules Beni's widowed child bride, Adeline Cayou, returned to Nebraska after Jules's death in 1861 and married a man named Billy Beckstead and, after he died, his brother Elton. She had eleven children all told, one of whom may have been fathered by Jules. (In any case, Jules left other descendants through an earlier wife, an Arapaho woman named Mahon, or Snakewoman. In 1937 an Oklahoman named Albert Keith provided an extensive family tree to the Oklahoma Historical Society.)[51]

In the 1890s Addie Beckstead gave several contradictory interviews about Jules Beni's feud with Slade. In her telling, it was not the
unarmed Slade who was shot by Jules but Slade who drew his gun
first, only to be wounded because "Jules was quicker with his shotgun." Moreover, after this shooting Slade was sent by stagecoach to
Denver (not St. Louis) for surgical treatment, at Jules's generous
expense.[52] When Addie Beckstead died in 1921, officially at the age of
seventy-two but probably a few years older, a Nebraska historian gently suggested, "It would seem when Jules was killed that his friends did
not correctly relate to the widow all the details of the tragedy."[53]

B
y the time Slade's mother, Mary Dennis, died in Carlyle in January
1873, she had lost two husbands, three children, and virtually all
of her property. "The life of the deceased," wrote the *Carlyle
Constitution and Union*, with much the same circumspection that the
Reverend Torbett had displayed at Jack Slade's own funeral nine years
earlier, "has been altogether an eventful one, one full of pleasures in
her early years, and crowded with sorrows ere the close, and we will,
therefore, draw a vail [*sic*] over that which is past."[54] Her final estate
listed assets of only $131 and debts of $254.64; to pay those debts, her
meager household goods were sold at a public auction the following
year.[55]

Mary's progeny had been dispersed, as were her assets. The five
children she had borne to Charles Slade produced just two grandchil-
dren, only one of whom lived to adulthood; and that grandchild—
Richard Slade, the son of Charles Richard Slade, who had died during the occupation of Santa Fe—left Carlyle for the West at age fifteen
and died violently in California in 1880 at the age of thirty-five. Like
his famous uncle Jack Slade, Richard was said to be "well liked; only
under the influence of liquor was he at all disagreeable."[56] The blood-
line of Mary Dark Kain Slade Dennis would survive only through Elias
Dennis, Jr., her son by her second husband.

Mary's oldest son, William Slade, remained in Carlyle throughout
his life (except for his brief diversions to Mexico in 1847 and to
California in 1849), where he tended his mother and the family's

declining fortunes as best he could. William did not marry until 1877, when he was fifty-seven.[57] In 1880, in an attempt to sort out his uncle Richard Slade's estate—still unresolved after forty-five years—William filed a petition indicating that the families of Charles Slade's brothers and sisters from Alexandria had lost touch with each other.[58]

William's death in 1884 at the age of sixty-four left his fragile spinster sister Virginia as the sole remaining Slade in Carlyle. After being duped into an abortive three-week marriage to a Montana minister in 1887, when she was fifty-five, Virginia returned to Carlyle in humiliation and poverty, seemingly destined for the county poorhouse. Only because her parents had donated twenty acres for the courthouse in 1825—most of which the county had subsequently sold for working cash—did the county commissioners spare her that disgrace; instead they paid for her board in various private homes. Until her death in 1911 at the age of seventy-nine she maintained the punctilious English ritual of taking tea and toast each afternoon at 4 P.M. Virginia liked to reminisce about her girlhood, when, as she told it, she was the belle of Carlyle. She never mentioned her poverty, nor did she ever mention her tragic brother Jack. If anyone else did, recalled a Carlyle woman whose grandparents boarded Virginia, "Her lips quivered pitifully, her frail body trembled, her face turned gray, but she spoke not a word."[59]

But what of the other Virginia Slade—Jack Slade's widow? When her marriage to Kiskadden broke up in late 1865 Virginia had already moved to Denver and then to St. Louis, and she appears to have remained there, at least for a while. After divorcing Kiskadden in 1868, Virginia was married for a third time, in St. Louis, to a James Reed in June 1870.[60] Of Reed nothing is known; and Virginia's marriage to him, like her union with Kiskadden, appears to have endured only briefly.

Thereafter her trail grows cold. By one account Virginia was still living in St. Louis in 1883.[61] By another she was "keeping a house of ill fame in Omaha."[62] Old-timers claimed to have seen her in, of all places, Julesburg.[63] Her common-law adopted son Jemmy Slade, who followed her to Denver in 1866, was reported to be living in Boulder

County, Colorado, in 1910, by which time he would have been close to sixty.[64]

A consistent and dismaying thread runs through these sketchy reports of Virginia's whereabouts: Without her first life partner, this resourceful and magnetic woman seems to have been rendered helpless to take charge of her own life. Although St. Louis was just 50 miles west of Carlyle, Virginia apparently made no effort to contact Slade's family there. The petition that William Slade filed in 1880 in connection with his uncle Richard Slade's estate duly noted that Maria V. Kiskadden, as Jack Slade's widow, was entitled to one-sixtieth of the family's real estate but that "diligent inquiry" had failed to locate her.[65] As Slade's widow, Virginia was also entitled to a Mexican War widow's pension, but no evidence exists that she ever applied for one.[66] What became of Slade's 134 shares of Wells Fargo Company stock, or of the Ravenswood claim in Montana that she bought back from Rockfellow in 1865 for $850, is unknown, but one can hazard a guess that both probably slipped from her hands for her failure to exercise her ownership rights. Nor did Virginia further pursue her ambitious plan to remove Slade's body from its temporary resting place in Salt Lake City.

Virginia was last heard from in 1890, when she engaged a Chicago lawyer in a desperate attempt to recover any remnant of Slade's estate from Madison County, Montana. By this time the hell-raising woman who had once whipped Billy Bay up Raspberry Hill from Spring Dale in a wild dash to save her husband was close to sixty; she was also, her lawyer's correspondence makes clear, destitute.[67] After writing a letter of inquiry to the Madison County clerk on February 10, 1890, and receiving by reply a request for more particulars, the lawyer, J. O'Brien Scobey, set down the essence of Mrs. Slade's complaint. It constitutes the only written record of Virginia Slade's view of her husband and his demise. "I find upon inquiry," wrote Scobey from his Loop office on March 12,

> that the Slade you refer to whom the old settlers remember as having been hanged by a vigilante committee in 1864…. is the same man whose estate I am looking after for his widow. The manner of

Mr. Slade's death is hardly a fair index to the character of the man. My understanding is that the man was a prominent and with all a respected, influential and quite wealthy citizen, but on the day of his death unfortunately got into bad company, got drunk and with his companions cut up some capers that did not satisfy the community, and in the heat of the excitement a committee seized them all and strung them up, but of course that has nothing to do with his estate. It seems according to the story of Mrs. Slade that although he was quite wealthy there was a general rush by every body to get a share of the property, and when it was finally wound up there were only two or three hundred dollars left for her of which she was formally notified by the Court at that time. She was then in Utah, and was so disgusted with the outcome that she refused to have anything more to do with it or to send for the money, but circumstances with her have changed and $250 or $300 would now appear to her to be quite a snug fortune. If the money was in the hands of the Court at that time, and has never been drawn it must still be in the custody of somebody.[68]

The lawyer's words make clear that, nearly twenty-four years after Slade's estate was closed, his widow remained unaware that her final share of $305.91 had been sent by the court to Jim Kiskadden's lawyers, who in turn had sent the check to Kiskadden, not realizing that Virginia was no longer living with him. There was of course no money left for Virginia at the Madison County District Court as of 1890.

With that last pathetic gesture, this inscrutable woman—so commanding in Slade's company—vanishes from history's stage. "She came from a bordello and went back to one," argues Anne Seagraves, author of a book about Western prostitutes, citing no supporting evidence other than her own woman's intuition. "The love of her life was Jack Slade."[69]

One of the last survivors of Slade's Virginia City sojourn was interviewed in 1935 as part of an oral history project conducted by the federal government's Works Progress Administration. S. B. B. Willson had been twenty-two when he arrived in Virginia City from Wisconsin in 1863; when a researcher found him living out his days in the Montana Old Soldiers Home, he was ninety-four. Willson's chatty and self-deprecating account suggests a man who was grateful for a visitor's attention; but it also bears the ring of truth, if only because, unlike most survivors of the Old West, Willson cheerfully painted himself as neither heroic nor demonic but merely mediocre.

Willson confessed to having committed worse crimes than Slade did. Once, for example, he relieved a drunk of his gold. And Willson's judgment of the vigilantes and their defenders was unequivocal.

> If Professor Dimsdale had included me in his little book, that non-sequential nightmare of misinformation, I would have been [as] famous as he made Henry Plummer famous.... The good professor's book was written to justify the murdering the Vigilantes did in the name of law and order. He got most of the details wrong, but he probably did so deliberately to protect those who hanged those they thought needed hanging. Others felt it was those being hanged who should have hanged those doing the hanging. There's something to be said for both sides....
>
> Perhaps one reason I had no stomach for celebration after the Vigilance Committee hanged wrongdoers was that my rich imagination, combined with certain intimate knowledge of my own considerable sins, made it too easy for me to visualize the rope around my own neck.... The Vigilance Committee hanged several men for less than the crimes I committed. Captain Joseph Slade is just one who leaps to mind. It is said he had killed men, but he was not hanged for that crime.[70]

In August 1899, the State Association of Montana Pioneers gathered at Virginia City. For whatever reason, it turned out to be the largest meeting the association ever held. Men and women, vigilantes and miners, friends and foes journeyed even from distant states to reconnect and share memories of their youth. Wilbur Sanders, the vigilante founder-turned U.S. Senator, was there; so was Adriel B. Davis, the vigilante captain; so were Jim Boner, who had cared for Slade after he was shot by Jules Beni; and Charles Cannon, the Virginia City merchant whom Virginia Slade had chased through his store; and Henry Edgar, who had struck gold with Bill Fairweather and subsequently cuckolded Sheriff Fox's wife; and A. M. Hart, who had witnessed the street conversation between Sanders and Slade hours before Slade was hanged.[71] "There was, of course, much talk of the Vigilantes, of the leaders of that sterling band, of the road agents, of Slade and Maria Virginia Slade, his wife," wrote Lew Callaway.[72]

By this time some plausible explanations for Slade's enigmatic behavior had surfaced. In his 1886 novella, *The Strange Case of Dr. Jekyll and Mr. Hyde*, Robert Louis Stevenson had painted the first vivid portrayal of the psychopathology of a "split personality." In 1889 a federal attorney named John Clampitt, after investigating Slade's career, exonerated him of any guilt and blamed his wildness instead on "the fiery compounds he poured into his system" which "clouded his mind [and] dethroned his reason."[73]

These ostensibly scientific explanations failed to prevent the assembled pioneers from mulling yet again the riddle of Slade's life and especially the incomprehensible chain of events on his last day that led to his death. "Never," wrote Callaway, "did man tempt fate more recklessly."[74]

And even a century and a half later it's tempting to wonder what Slade might have accomplished subsequently if only he had climbed on his horse and trotted home instead of returning one last time to apologize to Judge Davis inside the Pfouts & Russell store. Would he have survived to swap stories at reunions like this one? To appear in Wild West shows with Buffalo Bill? To sustain his wife in her old age? To write his own story for posterity instead of allowing his executioners to write it?

But of course such speculation is useless. If Slade hadn't tempted fate so recklessly on March 10, 1864, he would have returned to Virginia City a week or a month later to tempt it again. Sober or otherwise, tempting fate recklessly was what Slade was all about. It was what the opening of the West was all about.

Slade's zinc-lined coffin rests today with some 360 other unidentified bodies in a pauper's field, perhaps a third the size of a football field, near the southwest corner of Salt Lake City Cemetery.[75] In the center of this manicured grassy lawn stands a single military headstone bearing a small cross above this inscription:

JOSEPH A SLADE

ILLINOIS

CO A 1 REGT ILL FOOT VOLS

MEXICAN WAR

MARCH 9 1864

But who is really buried beneath that stone, and who placed the stone there—not to mention who supplied the erroneous death date—is unclear. Even Slade's gravestone, it seems, remains a mystery.[76] In death as in life, the real Slade continues to elude us.

NOTES

PREFACE

1 Langford, *Vigilante Days and Ways*, pp. 361–362.

2 Private letter from Settle cited by Dabney Otis Collins, "On the Trail of Jack Slade," p. 1.

3 Root and Connelley, *The Overland Stage to California*, p. 146.

CHAPTER 1

1 The visit described took place March 13, 1995. I have also taken some information from a second visit to Julesburg in March 2007.

2 *Trails West*, p. 46, 53; *Kearney Hub*, March 24, 2007.

3 Exhibit at Scotts Bluff National Monument, Gering, Nebraska. Also the artist, William H. Jackson, in description of his crossing there, July 27, 1866, in *Julesburg Grit-Advocate*, on file at Fort Sedgwick Historical Society, Julesburg, Colo.; also in Ruth (Mrs. Guy) Dunn, "History of California Crossing."

4 For this insight I am grateful to David Courtwright, whose 1996 book *Violent Land* explores the similarities between violence in the Old West and in modern inner-city neighborhoods.

5 California's population in 1860 was 379,994; see U.S. Census.

6 Howard, *Hoofbeats of Destiny*, p. 119.

7 The earliest published use of the name "Jack Slade" that I have found appeared as the headline of an article in the *Omaha Daily Herald*, Aug. 24, 1871, p. 2, col. 4.

CHAPTER 2

1 Judith Joy, "The Alexandria Connection," *Centralia* (Ill.) *Sentinel*, Sept. 28, 1980.

2 My discussion of the family of Charles Slade, Sr., relies heavily on the pioneering research done in the 1980s by Roy Paul O'Dell of Cambridge, England. See O'Dell and Jessen, *An Ear in His Pocket*, pp. 96–104.

3 Bailyn, *The Peopling of British North America*, p. 15.

4 The connection between the Slades and the interrelated Carlyle and Fairfax families of Alexandria is slender and circumstantial but strikes me as persuasive nevertheless. A reminiscence about Charles Slade, Jr., published in 1865 said he called his Illinois town Carlyle "because it was a family name. He [Charles] told me it was the name of his grandmother." See Rev. Thomas Lippincott, "Early Days in Madison County #20," *Alton (Ill.) Weekly Telegraph*, Feb. 17, 1865. Whether this referred to Charles's grandmother Slade or his grandmother Otis is not specified.

5 See Carlyle House biography of John Carlyle at http://www.carlylehouse.org/history/jc.html.

6 "Alexandria Archaeology Looks Back at 250 Years of Alexandria History: Discovering the 1750s." Alexandria Archaeology Museum. See http://oha.ci/.alexandria.va.us/archaeology/decades/ar-decades-1750.html.

7 See, among other sources, Thomas Fairfax biography in "Virtual American Biographies" at http://famousamericans.net/thomasfairfax.

8 Thomas Fairfax biography in "Virtual American Biographies."

9 See Miller, *Portrait of a Town: Alexandria, 1820–1830*, p. 325, which contains references to his estate gleaned from the *Alexandria Gazette*. Also see Miller, *Artisans and Merchants of Alexandria, Va., 1780–1820*, vol. 2, p. 127, which contains references to his businesses as early as 1804.

10 The 1800 census of Fourth Ward of Alexandria, published in *Virginia Genealogist*, Jan.–Mar. 1960, pp. 51–59.

11 Miller, *Artisans and Merchants of Alexandria, Va., 1780–1820*, vol. 2, p. 127.

12 Rev. Mason L. Weems (1759–1825) had at least three daughters and at least one son. His daughter Susana married Charles Slade's oldest son Richard Slade in 1820 and died in child-birth in 1821; see her obituary in *Alexandria Gazette*, Oct. 25, 1821, p. 3. Her younger sister (Weems's third daughter) Charlotte (1801–1841) married Charles Slade's second son, Henry C. Slade; see her obituary in *Alexandria Gazette*, April 26, 1841, p. 3. In 1829, after Rev. Weems died, his son, also the Rev. Mason L. Weems, married Ascenath O. Slade, youngest daughter of Charles Slade; see *Alexandria Gazette*, July 11, 1829, p. 3.

13 Alexandria Will Book 2, p. 394; written Dec. 25, 1810; probated Nov. 18, 1820. Charles left the house and furniture to his wife along with one-third of his other real property, with the rest to his children; but Mary predeceased him in 1818. Richard and Henry subsequently took over their father's properties; see listings in Miller, *Artisans and Merchants of Alexandria, Virginia, 1780–1820*, vol. 2, pp. 127–128.

14 Most biographies, including his Congressional biography, say Charles Slade the younger was born in England. See, for example, Snyder, "Charles Slade," p. 207; Carlyle *Calumet of Peace*, July 15, 1855 (*Annals of Carlyle*, a compendium of Carlyle newspaper clips, p. 561). One exception is Charles Slade's obituary in the *Alexandria* (Va.) *Gazette*, July 26, 1834, which describes him as "a native of Alexandria"; see O'Dell and Jessen, *An Ear in His Pocket*, p. 101. No source gives a date of birth for Charles. I surmise 1797 as his birth year because his older brothers Richard and Henry were most likely born in 1794 and 1796.

15 *Calumet of Peace*, Carlyle, July 15, 1855, cited in *Annals of Carlyle*, p. 562, is the only reference I have found to his work as a ropemaker. His apprenticeship is presumed, because he was under twenty-one at this time.

16 Miller, *Artisans and Merchants of Alexandria, Va., 1780–1820*, vol. 2, p. 128.

17 See, for example, Courtwright, *Violent Land*, p. 48.

18 Catherine Goodwin, interview with author, March 3, 1995.

19 Brands. *The Age of Gold*, p. 136.

20 Charles sold "a quantity of merchandise and furniture" to Henry, and Henry agreed to cover other debts of Charles. The agreement is attached to their father's probate file; see Prince William County Va. Will Book M, p. 198. The best argument for the Carlyle family's

patronage lies in the fact that the Slades named their new town in Illinois Carlyle and named one of its principal streets Fairfax.

21 *History of Marion and Clinton Counties,* p. 52, says Charles and Thomas Slade arrived "with an extensive stock of goods." This entry does not list their older brother Richard, although he is mentioned on p. 172 as one of three Slade brothers who arrived in 1816. Richard apparently returned to Virginia soon after their arrival in Illinois; *Alexandria Gazette* of March 5 and 14, 1818, refers to his store and his plan to move to Europe, and an April 8, 1818, item refers to his former store.

22 Charles Slade Sr.'s will was proved Nov. 18, 1820, according to his probate file. See *Index to Alexandria Wills, Administrations and Guardianships,* p. 113. His wife Mary died in 1818, according to an unverified source.

CHAPTER 3

1 See, for example, Snyder, "Charles Slade," p. 207.

2 This is speculation. Ducomb, in "A Silent Drum Beside the Okaw," p. 3, says the Slade brothers made their journey on horseback. In *History of Marion and Clinton Counties,* p. 52, the Slades arrived "with an extensive stock of goods," presumably carted in a wagon.

3 Display case at General Dean Suspension Bridge, Carlyle, Ill.

4 Ducomb, "A Silent Drum Beside the Okaw," p. 3.

5 Dearinger, "Sketches from Carlyle," p. 11.

6 Display case at General Dean Suspension Bridge, Carlyle, Ill.

7 The earliest available source refers to Hill as Isaac, not John; see *Calumet of Peace,* Carlyle, July 15, 1855, in *Annals of Carlyle,* p. 561. Others sources refer to him as John, including Snyder, "Charles Slade," p. 207. John Hill seems the more likely name, since it appears in the list of early land claims filed; see *History of Marion and Clinton Counties,* p. 174.

8 Snyder, "Charles Slade," p. 207; also *History of Marion and Clinton Counties,* p. 172.

9 *History of Marion and Clinton Counties,* p. 174.

10 Author's interview with Mary Meyer, Carlyle, March 1995.

11 *History of Marion and Clinton Counties,* p. 174. By 1818 many citizens were in debt for their newly acquired lands and fending off squatters on their property. Congress, hoping to ease the debt load and make land elsewhere more affordable for squatters, reduced the price of land from $2 to $1.25 an acre. See *Encyclopedia Britannica* (1964), vol. 12, p. 86.

12 *History of Marion and Clinton Counties,* p. 172: "Whence Hill came, or where he went after selling out his possessions, we have been unable to ascertain." Snyder, "Charles Slade," p. 207, suggests that after Hill sold his claim to the Slades he "entered land nearby under the $2 an acre act of Congress." But I have found no record of such a purchase (other than Hill's original purchase of 160 acres in April 1815; see *History of Marion and Clinton Counties,* p. 174). In any case Hill appears to have left soon after the sale to the Slades.

13 The death of his wife Susanna, age twenty-two, daughter of Rev. Mason Weems, in childbirth, Oct. 7, 1821, at Dumfries, Va., south of Alexandria, is recorded *in Alexandria Gazette,* Oct. 25, 1821.

14 *Economist,* Oct. 1, 2005, p. 16, citing a figure as of 1820.

15 Snyder, "Charles Slade," p. 207; also *History of Marion and Clinton Counties*, p. 173, and *Annals of Carlyle*, p. 4.

16 Lippincott, "Early Days in Madison County, #20," says Charles Slade told him that Carlyle was the name of his grandmother, although which grandmother isn't specified. The Carlyle *Calumet of Peace*, July 15, 1855 (*Annals of Carlyle*, p. 561), says Slade laid out Carlyle "together with a man named Thomas F. Herbert." This Herbert may have been a friend from Alexandria and was perhaps a relative of the Carlyle family there: John Carlyle's daughter Sarah married William Herbert, president of the Bank of Alexandria. Sarah and William did not have a son named Thomas, but Thomas Herbert may have been a collateral relative. An Alexandria directory refers to a merchant named Thomas F. Herbert who dissolved his business there in 1818. Thomas Herbert of Carlyle, Ill., became Carlyle's first postmaster in 1819; when he died in 1822, Charles Slade was named his executor.

17 Snyder, "Charles Slade," p. 207.

18 *Calumet of Peace*, Carlyle, July 15, 1855, quoted in *Annals of Carlyle*, p. 561.

19 *History of Marion and Clinton Counties*, p. 52.

20 The $500 lot is mentioned by Ducomb in "A Silent Drum Beside the Okaw," p. 3; also *Annals of Carlyle*, p. 5.

21 *Melchor Engle Family History and Genealogy 1730–1940*, cited in Maria Eugenia DeGroat, *The Kith and Kin of the Darke-Dark Clan in America, 1680–1973*, pp. 39–40.

22 *History of Marion and Clinton Counties*, p. 174, lists a purchase by Kain on Jan. 28, 1818, and a second purchase of 200 acres on June 27, 1818.

23 The date was June 23, 1819; see obituary of Mary Dark Kain Slade Dennis, *Constitution and Union*, Carlyle, Ill., Jan. 23, 1873. This wedding date is consistent with the birth date of their first son, William, on April 21, 1820. O'Dell and Jessen, in *An Ear in His Pocket*, p. 10, say the first wedding of a white couple in that territory occurred on Nov. 2, 1820, but Charles and Mary Slade were married more than a year earlier.

24 For the children's birth dates, see Mary D. Slade's petition for appointment as guardian of her late husband's heirs, Clinton County probate records, Aug. 12, 1836. Although Mary's maiden name was Mary Darke Kain, after her marriage to Charles Slade she took to calling herself "Mary Dark Slade"—dropping the "e" from Darke—and indeed many of her relatives subsequently used the name Dark rather than Darke.

25 "Life Story of Jack Slade, Carlyle Native," *Carlyle Union-Banner*, Historical Progress Edition, 1954. Herbert misspelled the town's name as "Carlisle," but Charles Slade as his successor corrected it back to "Carlyle," although not until 1828. Herbert died in 1822 (Charles Slade is mentioned as the administrator of Thomas F. Herbert's estate in a filing on Dec. 19, 1822).

26 See Illinois General Assembly *House Journal* for 1819: pp. 121, 123, 139, 151, 152, 154, 155. The bank is mentioned in an entry of March 22, 1819, cited in Virginia Wilson, "Genealogical Abstracts from Early Laws for Illinois," *Illinois State Genealogical Quarterly* 9 (1977), p. 2, cited in Wickliffe, "Elias Smith Dennis, Forgotten Hero of Carlyle," p. 13.

27 *History of Marion and Clinton Counties*, p. 175. On March 6, 1819, the legislature passed a resolution "to receive proposals for gifts to the state of land and money in return for the location of the capital 'on the Kaskaskia river, at some point at or above Carlyle'." See Solon Justus Buck, *Illinois in 1818*, p. 310.

28 *History of Marion and Clinton Counties*, p. 174. Ironically, the decisive vote against Carlyle was cast by Andrew Bankson, himself a resident of what subsequently became Carlyle's home county.

29 Snyder, "Charles Slade," p. 208, says Charles Slade was elected to the General Assembly in 1820 "and was then chiefly instrumental in securing the organization of Clinton County."

30 Washington County was created in 1818 and then included most of the present-day Clinton County, including the town of Carlyle. See White, *Origin and Evolution of Illinois Counties*, pp. 34-39.

31 Snyder, "Charles Slade," p. 208; also White, *Origin and Evolution of Illinois Counties*, p. 35.

32 *History of Marion and Clinton Counties*, p. 174.

33 The full deed of May 17, 1825, is reprinted in *History of Marion and Clinton Counties*, pp. 80-81.

34 *History of Marion and Clinton Counties*, p. 80.

35 "Life Story of Jack Slade," *Carlyle Union-Banner*, Historical Progress Edition, 1954.

36 1825 Carlyle County census. http://www.rootsweb.com/~ilclint2/census/ 1825clinton.htm. The census is also transcribed in *History of Marion and Clinton Counties*, pp. 78-79.

37 See Virginia Wilson, "Genealogical Abstracts from Early Laws for Illinois," in Illinois State Genealogical Quarterly, 9 (1977), p. 61, cited in Wickliffe, "Elias Smith Dennis, Forgotten Hero of Carlyle," p. 14. Neither Herbert nor Hubbard appears in the 1825 Clinton County census.

38 O'Dell and Jessen, *An Ear in His Pocket*, p. 100, cites 1820 as the year the house was built. When the house was torn down in the 1940s, "much walnut lumber was found inside," I was told by a local historian, Mary Meyer, in an interview in March 1995.

39 *Centralia* (Ill.) *Sentinel*, March 15, 1937.

40 *History of Marion and Clinton Counties*, pp. 173-174.

41 "Suspension Bridge, Carlyle, Clinton County, Illinois," typed ms. ILL-225, undated (after 1932), at Abraham Lincoln Presidential Library, Springfield, Ill. The bridge he ingeniously constructed there was actually more of a mud bridge supported by logs: first Charles found a spot on the stream where the banks were firm and not too steep. Then he cut down tall, well-proportioned trees with which to make mudsills, many of them fifty to seventy-five feet long. The ends of these sills were set into the banks down to the water level; then heavy oak planks were laid and securely fastened upon the sills. Then the banks were graded so a team could easily ascend and descend. Whenever the water rose above the bridge's level, the weight of the water tended to hold the bridge down instead of make it float away. "All that was needed to construct such a bridge," noted one observer, "were axmen, scorers, hewers and whip-saw men."

42 O'Dell, first draft of *An Ear in His Pocket*, p. 10.

43 *History of Marion and Clinton Counties*, pp. 78-79, contains all the names of householders listed in the 1825 Clinton County census. A transcribed version can also be accessed at http://www.rootsweb.com/~ilclint2/census/1825clinton.htm.

44 The 1830 federal census finds ten or eleven (the number is not clear) in Charles Slade's household—six or seven males and four females—but does not indicate whether any were slaves. Charles, his wife, and three young children accounted for five household members. Of the others, one was a male in his forties, two were males between age fifteen and twenty, and one was a female between fifteen and twenty. These may have been the five slaves listed in the 1825 Carlyle census. The 1840 federal census counts ten in the household, of whom nine are listed as employed "in agriculture." For more on Coles, see Gordon, *The Man Who Freed His Slaves.*

45 David Turk, historian, U.S. Marshals Service, correspondence with the author, Jan. 23, 2007, confirmed that Jackson appointed Charles Slade on April 20, 1829, when Congress was recessed; the Senate confirmed him in 1830. The appointment is also mentioned in Snyder, "Charles Slade," p. 208; and Callaway, *Two True Tales of the Wild West*, p. 98.

46 Snyder, "Charles Slade," p. 208.

47 *History of Marion and Clinton Counties*, p. 173; also "Suspension Bridge," p. 3.

48 *History of Marion and Clinton Counties*, p. 176.

49 The full text of this anonymous and undated letter, probably written in 1833 or 1834, is found in *History of Marion and Clinton Counties*, pp. 82–83. The book suggests that the letter may actually have been written not by a Virginian but by a local Carlyle man. Much of the letter constitutes a complaint about self-appointed enforcers of local morality.

50 No birth certificate for Joseph Alfred Slade has ever been found. The best record is his mother's application to become guardian of her children following her husband's death, which lists her five children and their dates of birth. See Clinton County probate records, Aug. 12, 1836; also on file at the Clinton County Historical Society.

51 See, for example, *Sangamo Journal*, Springfield, Ill., Aug. 18, 1832, p. 3, col. 2.

52 Charles E. Rosenberg, *The Cholera Years* (1962), quoted in Stephen Shapin, "Sick City," *New Yorker*, Nov. 6, 2006, p. 112. Not until 1883 would the German physician Robert Koch conclude that cholera is caused by a comma-shaped bacterium—*vibrio cholerae*—most commonly transmitted by contaminated drinking water.

53 Charles Slade's Congressional biography says he ran as a Jacksonian.

54 Snyder, "Charles Slade," pp. 208–209. Slade received 2,470 votes to 2,078 for Edwards, 1,670 for Breese, 1,020 for Dunn, and 551 for Webb. The election was held August 13, 1832.

55 Charles Slade's Congressional biography says he "served from March 4, 1833." Snyder, "Charles Slade," says Charles took his seat in Washington on the first Monday in December 1833. *Biographical Dictionary of U.S. Congress*, Bicentennial edition (1989), p. 114, says the Twenty-Third Congress came into being March 4, 1833, but the first session of Congress sat from Dec. 2, 1833, to June 30, 1834.

56 South Carolina rescinded its nullification ordinance on March 15, 1833.

57 James, *The Life of Andrew Jackson*, vol. 2, p. 358. Also, House History, Office of the Clerk, U.S. House of Representatives, http://clerk.house.gov/art_history/house_history/index.html.

58 *Sangamo Journal*, Springfield, Ill., Aug. 30, 1834, p. 3, col. 1.

59 "The Late Charles Slade," *Alexandria* (Va.) *Gazette*, July 25, 1834, reprinted in full in O'Dell and Jessen, *An Ear in His Pocket*, pp. 101–103.

60 See Snyder, "Charles Slade," p. 209, and "The Late Charles Slade." His road improvement bill is mentioned in *History of Marion and Clinton Counties*, p. 82. *Sangamo Journal*, Jan. 18, 1834, reporting Charles Slade's two motions of Dec. 18, 1833, describes the proposed national road as leading from Vandalia to the Mississippi River, presumably picking up the Goshen Road at Carlyle.

61 Charles Slade's candidacy for reelection is reported in the *Sangamo Journal*, March 8, 1834, p. 3, col. 1.

62 O'Dell and Jessen, *An Ear in His Pocket*, pp. 103, 108. Also records in the Alexandria Public Library.

63 Mary C. Slade married David English of Georgetown, Dec. 8, 1816; see *Alexandria Gazette*, Dec. 7, 1816, p. 3. Maria Catherine Slade married Capt. John Heath of Richmond, Va., Nov. 30, 1832; see *Alexandria Gazette*, Dec. 3, 1832, p. 3. She died Sept. 8, 1834, at her residence in Richmond, Va.; see *Alexandria Gazette*, Sept. 19, 1834, p. 3. Ascenath married Mason L. Weems, son of the author of the same name, at Dumfries, Va.; see *Alexandria Gazette*, July 11, 1829, p. 3.

64 The best account of Charles's final journey and death is found in Snyder, "Charles Slade," p. 209. Charles's obituary in the *Vincennes* (Ind.) *Western Sun and General Advertiser*, July 12, 1834, p. 3, col. 4, says he died at the house of Captain James Steen. This is repeated in the *Alexandria Gazette*, July 25, 1834, p. 3.

CHAPTER 4

1 U.S. census for Carlyle, 1830, lists only Charles by name as head of the household but enumerates each resident by gender and age—a total of seven males and four females.

2 In the probate proceedings for the estate of Charles Slade, Sr., Henry sought to hold Charles Jr.'s heirs responsible for Charles Jr.'s debts. The will of Charles Slade, Sr. (1810), and the ensuing probate file (beginning 1820) can be found in Prince William Co., Va., Will Book L, pp. 405–407; also on film 633122 of the Mormon Family History Library.

3 Carlyle's articles of incorporation of January 10, 1837, contain an enumeration of the town's inhabitants; it lists Mary D. Slade as head of a household of six souls, presumably Mary and her five children. See *History of Marion and Clinton Counties*, p. 174.

4 Presumed from the fact that Richard died at Charles Slade's residence soon thereafter and had no listed permanent residence of his own at the time. See *Alexandria Gazette*, Sept. 22, 1835, p. 3.

5 *Alexandria Gazette* obituary notice for Thomas Slade, May 26, 1835, p. 3. Carlyle's articles of incorporation of Jan. 10, 1837, contain an enumeration of the town's inhabitants; it lists Caroline Slade as the head of a household of three souls and Mary D. Slade as head of a household of six souls. See *History of Marion and Clinton Counties*, p. 174.

6 The surviving records on Thomas are confusing and contradictory. He is listed as head of a Carlyle household in the Illinois census of 1825 and also in the U.S. census of 1830 for Carlyle. The latter lists four people in his household, who appear to include his wife, a son under the age of five, and a female servant. But a Thomas Slade is also listed as a hackman in the Washington city directory for 1827; he also appears in the 1830 census for the District of Columbia. But Thomas died in Carlyle on March 10, 1835; see *Alexandria Gazette*, May 26, 1835, p. 3.

7 Richard Slade died Sept. 6, 1835, "after a short illness, in the 42nd year of his age"; see *Alexandria Gazette* obituary, Sept. 22, 1835, p. 3. The account says he died at his late brother Charles's home in Carlyle. It is not clear whether Richard lived there, but it seems likely, given the size of the house.

8 Clinton County Probate Record C, 1836–1839, p. 1, Aug. 12, 1836; also available at Clinton County Historical Society, Carlyle.

9 Carlyle's articles of incorporation of Jan. 10, 1837, list twenty-three households. See *History of Marion and Clinton Counties*, p. 174.

10 In 1836, as the Second Bank of the United States expired due to Jackson's veto four years earlier, Jackson issued an executive order requiring that all public lands be paid for in gold or silver. His purpose was to bolster the soundness of currency at a time when the widespread circulation of paper banknotes was blamed for the nation's alternating cycles of inflation and depression. But Jackson's "Specie Circular," as his order was called, produced the opposite effect: Suddenly gold and silver virtually vanished from circulation, to be replaced by paper notes of dubious value. Banks in western states like Illinois, unable to meet the sudden demand for gold and silver, began to fail, one after the other.

11 Rottenberg, *The Man Who Made Wall Street*, p. 28.

12 Elias Dennis obituary, Dec. 20, 1894, unidentified Carlyle newspaper, cited in *Carlyle Newspaper Excerpts,* Clinton Co. Historical Society, p. 104.

13 Charles Richard Slade (known as Richard) married Eloise Breese in Carlyle, Feb. 24, 1843. Her father, Sidney Breese, was appointed circuit judge of the second district and moved to Carlyle in 1835. See his Congressional biography.

14 *Clinton County Historical Society Quarterly,* 14, p. 2.

15 *Centralia* (Ill.) *Evening Sentinel*, March 15, 1937.

16 The film is *Jack Slade* (1953), directed by Harold Schuster, with Mark Stevens in the title role and Dorothy Malone as his wife. For samples of the film's publicity, see "Tag lines for *Jack Slade*" at http://www.imdb.com/title/tt0045925/taglines.

17 Coutant, *History of Wyoming*, p. 401.

18 An alternative variation of this tale—in which an older Alfred Slade, aged twenty-two or twenty-six, kills a man with a rock during a fight sometime in the 1850s—is also unlikely but at least more plausible. For an analysis of these stories and the relevant evidence, see Chapter 8.

19 Callaway, *Two True Tales of the Wild West*, p. 99.

20 The school, located at Jefferson and Fourth streets, is described in *Annals of Carlyle*, p. 10. Written communications and account books were an important part of Slade's later duties with the Central Overland stage company and the Pony Express. The earliest existing specimen of Alfred Slade's signature can be found in the "Oath of Identity" he signed upon his discharge from the Army on Oct. 31, 1848. The signature was acknowledged by a justice of the peace at Carlyle on Nov. 3, 1848—proof that Alfred Slade could read and write at the age of seventeen, if not earlier. Among other evidence that Slade was literate: Post office lists of Nov. 11 and Nov. 18, 1858 include his name on a list of unclaimed mail at Salt Lake City post office; see *Valley Tan*, Nov. 12, 1858, or http://udn.lib.utah.edu/valleytan/image/519.pdf. Also, the Bartholomew incident in 1861 concerns a letter written by Slade; and following the affair Slade and his wife were said to have corresponded with Bartholomew's widow (see Chapter 13).

CHAPTER 5

1 McCartney, Samuel Bigger, *Illinois in the Mexican War*, p. 10.

2 John Justin Smith, *The War With Mexico* (1919), Vol. I, p. 124.

3 Ibid.

4 Winders, *Mr. Polk's Army*, p. 8.

5 Winders, *Mr. Polk's Army*, p. 8. Polk's war message of May 11, 1846, said "some 16 were killed and wounded."

6 Polk's war message to Congress, May 11, 1846.

7 Winders, *Mr. Polk's Army*, p. 9.

8 See Haven and Belden, *A History of the Colt Revolver*; also Hadley, *Colt: The Making of an American Legend*.

9 Singletary, *The Mexican War*, p. 24.

10 Winders, *Mr. Polk's Army*, p. 10.

11 Winders, *Mr. Polk's Army*, p. 69; Singletary, *The Mexican War*, p. 26.

12 *Illinois State Register*, May 29, 1846, cited in McCartney, *Illinois in the Mexican War*, p. 21.

13 Winders, *Mr. Polk's Army*, pp. 66–67, gives the minimum age of enlistment as eighteen.

14 McCartney, *Illinois in the Mexican War*, pp. 19, 21.

15 Winders, *Mr. Polk's Army*, p. 70.

16 *Record of Illinois Soldiers in the Black Hawk War and the Mexican War*, p. xxviii, says 6,000 more volunteers were sought, Of this call, one regiment (about 1,000 men) was assigned to Illinois. Myers, "Illinois Volunteers in New Mexico," p. 6, says all the new volunteer units were requisitioned from Illinois and Missouri.

17 Winders, *Mr. Polk's Army*, pp. 71–72.

18 Thomas Bond's obituary mentions his relationship to Shadrach Bond; see *Carlyle* (Ill.) *Constitution and Union*, Sept. 30, 1875. The 1850 U.S. census for Carlyle lists Thomas Bond as a carpenter.

19 *Record of the Services of Illinois Soldiers in the Black Hawk War and the Mexican War*, p. xxviii.

20 Details about William's war record are sketchy. As a "Polk man," he was appointed a second lieutenant "in the new regiments"; see *Sangamo Journal*, Springfield, Ill., March 18, 1847, p. 3, col. 1. Other sources say he was a lieutenant in the 16th U.S. Infantry during the Mexican War; see O'Dell and Jessen, *An Ear in His Pocket*, pp. 11–12, citing Carlyle Cemetery records; Ducomb, "A Silent Drum Beside the Okaw," p. 6; and Collins, "On the Trail of Jack Slade," p. 19. *Annals of Carlyle*, p. 18, mentions him on the volunteer muster roll of May 18, 1847. But William's name does not appear with Bond's Company A in the adjutant general's report (*Record of Illinois Soldiers in the Black Hawk War and the Mexican War*, pp. 208–209) nor in the list of volunteers in *History of Marion and Clinton Counties*, pp. 121–122.

21 *Record of Illinois Soldiers in the Black Hawk War and the Mexican War*, pp. 208–209; *History of Marion and Clinton Counties,*), pp. 121–122. This fifth regiment of Illinois volun-

teers, having replaced the original First Regiment called up for one year in 1846, was officially called the First Regiment of Illinois Infantry, thus confusing the historical record: the regiment was referred to as both the First and Fifth Illinois Volunteers. See Myers, "Illinois
Volunteers in New Mexico, 1847–48," p. 6.

22 McClernan, *Slade's Wells Fargo Colt*, p. 37, drawing on records in the National Archives.
The minimum enlistment age of eighteen was rarely enforced; the army took the word of anyone willing to enlist, and also accepted a parent's or relative's waiver for recruits between the
age of seventeen and eighteen. Author's interview with John Richley, April 2, 2007.

23 Winders, *Mr. Polk's Army*, pp. 12–13, 73.

24 Winders, *Mr. Polk's Army*, p. 73.

25 Bond obituary, *Carlyle* (Ill.) *Constitution and Union*, Sept. 30, 1875.

26 Address by John Rodgers quoted in *Carlyle* (Ill.) *Constitution and Union*, Sept. 13, 1894,
cited in *Carlyle Newspaper Excerpts*, p. 98.

27 McClernan, *Slade's Wells Fargo Colt*, p. 38.

28 Myers, "Illinois Volunteers in New Mexico, 1847–48," p. 7.

29 *Record of Illinois Soldiers in the Black Hawk War and the Mexican War*, p. 208.

30 McClernan, *Slade's Wells Fargo Colt*, p. 38, says Company A left Alton on June 19 and
arrived at Leavenworth on June 24, and the last company arrived at Leavenworth from Alton
on June 29. *Record of Illinois Soldiers in the Black Hawk War and the Mexican War*, p. xxviii,
says the regiment left Alton by steamer for Fort Leavenworth on June 14.

31 Myers, "Illinois Volunteers in New Mexico, 1847–48," p. 6. A regimental return of June
1846 refers to it, apparently incorrectly, as "Fort Leavenworth in the Missouri Territory." See
McClernan, *Slade's Wells Fargo Colt*, p. 38.

32 Myers, "Illinois Volunteers in New Mexico, 1847–48," p. 7.

33 Myers, "Illinois Volunteers in New Mexico, 1847–48," p. 7. The West End still exists at
Fort Leavenworth, although today it is called the Parade Grounds.

34 Myers, "Illinois Volunteers in New Mexico, 1847–48," p. 12.

35 *History of Marion and Clinton Counties*, p. 122.

36 Singletary, *The Mexican War*, p. 25.

37 Myers, "Illinois Volunteers in New Mexico, 1847–48," pp. 7–8.

38 Myers, "Illinois Volunteers in New Mexico, 1847–48," pp. 9–10.

39 Myers, "Illinois Volunteers in New Mexico, 1847–48," p. 9. Also see Hylton, *Citizen
Soldiers*; also O'Dell and Jessen, *An Ear in His Pocket*, p. 9.

40 Myers, "Illinois Volunteers in New Mexico, 1847–48," p. 10.

41 Walker, *The Wagonmasters*, p. 228.

42 Settle, *War Drums and Wagon Wheels*, p. 28.

43 Frederick, *Ben Holladay*, pp. 26–27.

44 McClernan, *Slade's Wells Fargo Colt*, p. 38.

45 Military records, precise about most dates, are vague about just when the First Illinois
arrived in Santa Fe, apparently because so many detachments arrived on different days. The
most precise source, Myers, "Illinois Volunteers in New Mexico, 1847–48," p. 11, says Newby

arrived on either September 11 or 13; other contingents presumably arrived earlier. *History of Marion and Clinton Counties,* p. 122, says the expedition arrived in Santa Fe Sept. 12. Cottingham, in *General John A. Logan,* p. 4, says the march from Fort Leavenworth (presumably for Logan's Company H) took twenty-seven days. If the march began on July 9, that suggests an arrival about August 5. McClernan, *Slade's Wells Fargo Colt,* p. 38, says his review of all muster rolls indicates that the main body of the regiment reached Santa Fe in late August or early September.

46 Myers, "Illinois Volunteers in New Mexico, 1847–48," p. 13.

47 Duffus, *Santa Fe Trail,* pp. 217–218.

48 Duffus, *Santa Fe Trail,* p. 217.

49 Mark Neely, Jr., *The Civil War and the Limits of Destruction,* cited in McPherson, "Was It More Restrained Than You Think?" *New York Review of Books,* Feb. 14, 2008, pp. 42–43.

50 Duffus, *Santa Fe Trail,* p. 214.

51 Singletary, *The Mexican War,* p. 106.

52 Myers, "Illinois Volunteers in New Mexico, 1847–48," p. 15.

53 Winders, *Mr. Polk's Army,* pp. 85–86.

54 Courtwright, *Violent Land,* p. 45.

55 Only 1,548 officers and men died of wounds suffered in battle; 10,970 fell to illness. See Winders, *Mr. Polk's Army,* p. 140.

56 Winders, *Mr. Polk's Army,* p. 146. Also see Singletary, *The Mexican War,* p. 144.

57 Courtwright, *Violent Land,* p. 45.

58 Joseph A. Slade's discharge form, Alton, Ill., Oct. 16, 1848. Available at National Archives and at Clinton County Historical Society, Carlyle, Ill.; also see full text in McClernan, *Slade's Wells Fargo Colt,* pp. 39–40; O'Dell and Jessen, *An Ear in His Pocket,* p. 9.

59 Death notice for Charles R. Slade, *Alexandria* (Va.) *Gazette and Virginia Advertiser,* April 29, 1848, p. 2.

60 In February 1848, Companies A and C met Company I at Albuquerque. Slade's Company A remained at Albuquerque until after June 1848, when the regiment headed for home. See McClernan, *Slade's Wells Fargo Colt,* pp. 38–39. *History of Marion and Clinton Counties,* p. 122, says a detachment started for Albuquerque on Feb. 9, 1848; also, pp. 121–122 list war fatalities for Company A; the first in Albuquerque occurred on Feb. 14, 1848, from which I deduce that the company must have arrived in Albuquerque on or before that date.

61 The muster roll of Company A lists 115 names, all from Clinton County or "not listed" but presumably also from Clinton County. Myers, "Illinois Volunteers in New Mexico, 1847–48," p. 12, says Company A lost thirteen men to death; five were discharged; and two were left sick at Fort Leavenworth. *History of Marion and Clinton Counties,* p. 122, lists fifteen men from Company A who died in the war.

62 Yenne, *Indian Wars,* pp. 39–40.

63 Myers, "Illinois Volunteers in New Mexico, 1847–48," p. 24; Slade's discharge form at National Archives or Clinton Co. Historical Society, Carlyle (also see McClernan, *Slade's Wells Fargo Colt,* pp. 39–40).

64 *James K. Polk's Diary*, entry of March 5, 1949, vol. IV, pp. 375–376.

65 Charles B. Gillespie, "Marshall's own account of the gold discovery," *Century* Magazine, Feb. 1891, cited in Emilie Davie, ed., *Profile of America*, pp. 151–152.

66 *Encyclopedia Britannica*, vol. 10 (1964), p. 535.

67 "Oath of Identity," National Archives, Washington, D.C.; also McClernan, *Slade's Wells Fargo Colt*, p. 41.

68 McClernan, *Slade's Wells Fargo Colt*, p. 41. McClernan erroneously records the name of Elias S. Dennis as "Elias P. Deming," presumably due to difficulty reading Dennis's handwriting in the original letter on file at the National Archives.

69 McClernan, p. 41. McClernan erroneously records the name of Elias S. Dennis as "Elias P. Deming," presumably due to difficulty reading Dennis's handwriting in the original letter on file at the National Archives.

70 McClernan, *Slade's Wells Fargo Colt*, p. 42.

71 McClernan, *Slade's Wells Fargo Colt*, p. 43, citing correspondence from the Bureau of Land Management in Sacramento, Aug. 21, 1973.

72 Suggested to the author by Nelson Ober, letter of April 20, 1999.

CHAPTER 6

1 "The First Wagon Train into California, 1849," excerpts from the journal of William G. Johnston, quoted in Davies, ed., *Profile of America*, pp. 152–155.

2 *U.S. Immigration and Naturalization*, p. 334, says about 40,000 to 50,000 gold seekers arrived in 1849. Courtwright, in *Violent Land*, p. 67, says the number of arrivals in 1849 was 89,000.

3 Brands, *The Age of Gold* (2005).

4 Howard, *Hoofbeats of Destiny*, p. 25.

5 To most historians, the eleven years from the day Alfred Slade left the Army in 1848 to the day he was hired to clean up Julesburg in 1859 comprise his "lost years," a time when Slade merely "disappeared into the West." Much of Slade's whereabouts during that time do indeed remain a mystery, but enough clues exist to permit, if not solid conclusions, at least reasonable speculations. Two slender clues suggest that Alfred Slade did indeed reach California that summer. One is the letter sent by his stepfather Elias Dennis to his Congressman in February 1849, suggesting that Alfred would depart for California "some time in the month of April"; see Chapter 5. The other is the California-bound departure that May of Alfred's less adventurous older brother William—perhaps to visit Alfred, possibly even to fetch him back home to Illinois.

6 *Sangamo Journal*, May 23, 1849, p. 2, col. 6. It says the "Pioneer Line" of carriages, and train, had 125 passengers bound for San Francisco. The passenger list included one other Carlyle resident, H. Wilcox. If Alfred Slade left Carlyle sometime in April, it's conceivable that he might have been with this train as well—not as a passenger (because his name isn't mentioned on the passenger list) but as a freighter. But this is simply speculation.

7 For estimates of California gold production see, for example, *U.S. Immigration and Migration*, p. 334; Clampitt, *Echoes from the Rocky Mountains*, p. 624; Hough, *The Story of the Outlaw*, p. 82.

8 *U.S. Immigration and Migration,* p. 336.

9 *U.S. Immigration and Migration,* p. 337. If the pioneer lacked his own farm wagon, he might wind up spending between $300 and $600 to buy a prairie schooner, and a team of oxen or mules might cost between $300 and $600.

10 *U.S. Immigration and Migration,* pp. 334-335, says the journey via Cape Horn took about five months. Other sources say six.

11 Rev. Samuel Parker, *Journal of an Exploring Tour Beyond the Rocky Mountains* (1844), cited in "Historic South Pass," p. 9.

12 *U.S. Immigration and Migration,* pp. 330-332.

13 *U.S. Immigration and Migration,* p. 331.

14 Walker, *The Wagonmasters,* p. 44, says there were 11,000 Mormons in Utah by 1850; Denton, *American Massacre,* p. 165, says the population of Salt Lake City was 20,000 in 1857.

15 Fradkin, *Stagecoach,* p. 52; Denton, *American Massacre,* p. 102.

16 Settle and Settle, *Empire on Wheels,* p. 70.

17 Johnston, "The First Wagon Train into California, 1849," pp. 152-155.

18 Johnston, "The First Wagon Train into California, 1849," p. 155.

19 Courtwright, *Violent Land,* p. 62.

20 Courtwright, *Violent Land,* p. 70.

21 Courtwright, *Violent Land,* p. 68.

22 *U.S. Immigration and Migration,* p. 335.

23 This is possible but seems unlikely. The journey from Independence to California took three months or more. If Alfred Slade left Carlyle in April 1849, he would not have arrived in California before mid-July. Yet his brother William left Independence for California on May 9, presumably before Alfred had even arrived in the gold country. It does seem likely that William went to join Alfred; and it is remotely possible that he went to fetch Alfred home, having heard accounts of disease and death in California even before Alfred arrived there.

24 U.S. census, Clinton County, Ill., Oct. 29, 1850.

25 See biography of Thomas Maddux in *History of Marion and Clinton Counties,* p. 179.

26 U.S. census, Clinton County, Ill., 1850.

27 See biography of Thomas Maddux in *History of Marion and Clinton Counties,* p. 179.

28 Loomis, *Wells Fargo,* p. 41.

29 John B. McClernan searched the index to the 1850 California Census and found thirteen Slades in the gold country at that time, including a J. Slade, a J. B. Slade and a Jas. B. Slade in Calaveras County; a John M. Slade and a William Slade in El Dorado County; and a Jon. W. Slade in Sacramento County. See McClernan, *Slade's Wells Fargo Colt,* p. 42. Given the unreliability of early censuses, any of these might be Joseph A. Slade of Illinois or his brother William—or none: Joseph A. Slade and William too, remember, are included in the 1850 census for Carlyle, Illinois. Obviously they could not have been in two places at once, although they could have been listed in two different censuses. It seems most likely to me that Alfred Slade left for California in the spring or summer of 1850 but was listed by his family on his

hometown census in Illinois that fall; by that time he might have arrived in California for his second visit and been recorded in the census there. But this is purely speculation.

30 *History of Marion and Clinton Counties,* p. 179.

31 Hough, *The Story of the Outlaw,* pp. 76–77.

32 Hough, *The Story of the Outlaw,* pp. 32–33.

33 Slade's Congressional affidavits of 1859 and 1862 identify him only as "J. A. Slade." Root, in *The Overland Stage to California,* routinely refers to Slade as "Jack." Root was a clerk in the Atchison, Kan., post office pre-1863, appointed an Overland messenger in January 1863. His knowledge of Slade appears to have been contemporaneous but secondhand. Chapman writes, in *The Pony Express,* p. 184: "When Slade was not within earshot, the men on the frontier called him 'Jack.' When he was around, they never forgot the 'Captain.'" Slade was usually referred to as "Jack" in twentieth-century literature, but I have found no references to him by that name when he was alive; the earliest appeared Aug. 24, 1871, in the *Omaha Daily Herald,* p. 2, col. 4. A Slade employee, Charles Higganbotham, interviewed in the *Anaconda* (Mont.) *Standard,* June 20, 1920 (when he was eighty years old), said, "I notice the newspapers, when they mention Slade in telling of the early days, always call him A.J. [*sic*] Slade, but everybody knew him as Charley in the old days."

34 Slade's estate was found to contain 134 shares of Wells Fargo stock upon his death in 1864. How he obtained this stock is unknown. The most likely explanation is that he drove stagecoaches for Wells Fargo in its earliest years and was paid in stock in lieu of cash. The company says its earliest existing stock ledger begins in 1866. There is no mention of a Joseph A. Slade in the ledger for 1866 to 1870; the 1870 stock ledger does list a John Slade as owning 150 shares. Letter from Robert G. Pacini, History Dept., Wells Fargo Bank, to Dabney Otis Collins, March 19, 1976.

35 Callaway, *Two True Tales of the Wild West,* p. 100.

36 E. W. Whitcomb memoirs (1906), cited in O'Dell's first draft manuscript for *An Ear in His Pocket,* p. 62, note 2.

37 Nelson Ober letter to author, April 20, 1999, p. 1, says documents show that Slade was in Arlington, Va., in August and September 1853.

38 William C. Phillips vs. Joseph A. Slade, State of Illinois, Clinton Co., term of the Clinton Circuit Court, A.D. 1853. See Carlyle *Age of Progress,* Sept. 6, 1853.

39 Dabney O. Collins, "On the Trail of Jack Slade" (manuscript), p. 3, citing Illinois probate deed record, Nov. 23, 1854, found in Clinton Co. Courthouse, Ill.

40 There is no evidence of Slade's having run his own business earlier than the spring of 1863, when he formed the contract freighting partnership of Slade & Ely. In Virginia City, Mont., that summer he also set up a toll road and a dairy farm. But his contemporaries often referred to his skill as a businessman, and so it is possible he did engage in contract freighting in the mid-1850s as well. Upon leaving the Overland Stage Co. in the fall of 1862 Slade remarked to Robert Spotswood that "he intended to return to his old business as a freighter." See Spotswood obituary in "Dead Pioneer Told Stories of Early Days," *Denver Republican,* April 19, 1910.

41 See, for example, David Luban, "The Defense of Torture," *New York Review of Books,* March 15, 2007, p. 38.

42 Brands, *The Age of Gold*, pp. 140-141.

43 Settle and Settle, *Empire on Wheels*, p. 4. Yenne, *Indian Wars*, p. 41, says there were eight forts in the West in 1848, and the number grew to 52 by 1854, which seems highly unlikely.

44 Walker, *The Wagonmasters*, pp. 3, 6, 8.

45 Walker, *The Wagonmasters*, p. 17.

46 Walker, *The Wagonmasters*, p. 3.

47 Root and Connelley, *The Overland Stage to California*, p. 420.

48 Walker, *The Wagonmasters*, pp. 74-75; Howard, *Hoofbeats of Destiny*, pp. 36-37.

49 See, for example, Settle and Settle, *Empire on Wheels*, p. 478; Root and Connelley, *The Overland Stage to California*, pp. 22-23.

50 Walker, *The Wagonmasters*, p. 56.

51 Root and Connelley, *The Overland Stage to California*, pp. 301, 409.

52 Thomas Forsyth to Lewis Cass, Oct. 24, 1831, cited in Walker, *The Wagonmasters*, p. 106.

53 Root and Connelley, *The Overland Stage to California*, p. 420.

54 Walker, *The Wagonmasters*, p. 51; Howard, *Hoofbeats of Destiny*, p. 36.

55 Walker, *The Wagonmasters*, p. 97.

56 Walker, *The Wagonmasters*, p. 95.

57 See, among others, Monahan, *Destination: Denver City*, pp. 43-44.

58 Settle and Settle, *Saddles and Spurs*, pp. 1-4.

59 Moody, *Stagecoach West*, p. 141.

60 Moody, *Stagecoach West*, pp. 139-140; Settle and Settle, *War Drums and Wagon Wheels*, pp. 34-35, 254.

61 Settle and Settle, *War Drums and Wagon Wheels*, p. 38.

62 Settle and Settle, *War Drums and Wagon Wheels*, pp. 31-32, 37; Moody, *Stagecoach West*, p. 142.

63 Moody, *Stagecoach West*, p. 143; Settle and Settle, *War Drums and Wagon Wheels*, pp. 31-32; Settle and Settle, *Saddles and Spurs*, pp. 6-10.

64 Settle and Settle, *War Drums and Wagon Wheels*, pp. 179-180.

65 Settle and Settle, *War Drums and Wagon Wheels*, pp. 87-88.

66 Settle and Settle, *War Drums and Wagon Wheels*, p. 40; Moody, *Stagecoach West*, pp. 142-143.

67 Settle and Settle, *War Drums and Wagon Wheels*, pp. 40-43, 45-46; Moody, *Stagecoach West*, p. 144; Settle and Settle, *Saddles and Spurs*, pp. 13-15.

68 The two-year contract was awarded March 27, 1855. Settle and Settle, *War Drums and Wagon Wheels*, pp. 40-43, 45-46; Moody, *Stagecoach West*, p. 144; Settle and Settle, *Saddles and Spurs*, pp. 13-15.

69 Settle and Settle, *War Drums and Wagon Wheels*, pp. 45-46.

70 Percival G. Lowe, 1858, quoted in Walker, *The Wagonmasters*, p. 248.

71 The definitive book on freighting—Walker, *The Wagonmasters*—refers to Slade as "the most highly publicized and infamous wagonmaster" (p. 81).

72 A list of "Fort Leavenworth freight contractors, 1848–54" is posted at the Fort Leavenworth Military Museum. It lists freighting contracts by year without giving specific dates. For 1854 the only two listed are "Majors & Waddell: Government stores to Albuquerque for $10.83 per 100 lbs." and "William McKnight: Government stores to Fort Fillmore for $13.75 per 100 lbs. and to El Paso for $17.60 per 100 lbs." Both these trains would have used the Santa Fe Trail. If the list is in chronological order, it would seem likely that Slade was in the latter train to Fort Fillmore and El Paso, if indeed he was on any of these trains. John Richley, a military historian formerly posted at Fort Leavenworth, suggests there may have been more than two trains contracted from Fort Leavenworth that year, if only because Fort Leavenworth's sole function between 1854 and 1881 was to serve as an arsenal and supply base; author's interview with John Richley, April 25, 2007.

73 The fact that Slade in the summer of 1858 was leading a freight train for a lesser operation like Hockaday & Burr suggests to me that he hadn't previously worked for Russell, Majors & Waddell, the gold standard of freighting concerns. Either that, or—equally likely—something untoward had occurred in Slade's life prior to that summer that rendered him unacceptable to Russell, Majors & Waddell.

74 Hugo Koch, "Early Days in Wyoming," Part 2, *Lander* (Wyo.) *Wind River Mountaineer*, March 13, 1908.

75 Hugo Koch, "Early Days in Wyoming," Part 4, *Lander* (Wyo.) *Wind River Mountaineer*, March 27, 1908.

76 Hugo Koch, "Early Days in Wyoming," Part 6, *Lander* (Wyo.) *Wind River Mountaineer*, April 10, 1908.

77 Walker, *The Wagonmasters*, p. 87; Colyer, "Freighting Across the Plains," p. 7.

78 Frederick, *Ben Holladay*, p. 33.

79 Howard, *Hoofbeats of Destiny*, p. 36.

80 Callaway, *Two True Tales of the Wild West*, pp. 100–101.

81 McClernan, *Slade's Wells Fargo Colt*, pp. 20 and 30, identifies eight different weapons Slade used at one time or another. These included five pistols, a Deringer, a long gun—a .56 caliber Joslyn rifle—and a sawed-off ten-gauge shotgun. The reference to Slade as "a walking arsenal" is taken from the 1940 Works Progress Administration booklet *Utah: A Guide to the State*, p. 357, cited in McClernan, p. 30.

82 Root and Connelley, *The Overland Stage to California*, p. 481.

83 *Life and Adventures of Polk Wells, The Notorious Outlaw*, p. 42.

84 There are many holes in this account. Wells was born June 5, 1851, and claimed to have met Slade at age eleven at Julesburg. If he was eleven at this time, as he claims, this encounter would have occurred sometime after June 1862. Yet Slade's division was shifted away from Julesburg in July 1862. Nevertheless, the encounter is conceivable; it's possible that Wells's memory of specific dates and places is confused.

85 Schlesinger, *The Age of Jackson*, p. 448.

86 Callaway, *Two True Tales of the Wild West*, p. 101.

87 Walker, *The Wagonmasters*, p. 78; Colyer, "Freighting Across the Plains," p. 7.

88 Walker, *The Wagonmasters*, pp. 77–78.

89 Walker, *The Wagonmasters*, p. 77.

90 Callaway, *Two True Tales of the Wild West*, p. 103; Parkhill, *Law Goes West*, p. 123.

91 Alderson, "Some New Slade Stories: Beatty and Horse Thieves."

92 Ware, *The Indian War of 1864*, p. 264.

93 Walker, *The Wagonmasters*, pp. 81–82.

94 Dimsdale, *Vigilantes of Montana*, pp. 8–9.

95 Beehrer, "Freighting Across the Plains," p. 16.

96 Seagraves, *Soiled Doves*, p. x.

97 Courtwright, *Violent Land*, p. 51.

98 Courtwright, *Violent Land*, p. 70.

99 Seagraves, *Soiled Doves*, p. x.

100 Seagraves, *Soiled Doves*, p. xi.

101 Dee Brown, *The Gentle Tamers*, cited in Seagraves, *Soiled Doves*, p. xi.

102 Loomis, *Wells Fargo*, p. 56.

103 Courtwright, *Violent Land*, pp. 70–71.

104 Courtwright, *Violent Land*, p. 68.

105 *Trails West*, p. 138.

106 Robert Spotswood, quoted in Chapman, "Jack Slade, Man-killer."

107 Chapman, *The Pony Express*, p. 191.

CHAPTER 7

1 Langford, *Vigilante Days and Ways*, p. 371.

2 Towle, *Vigilante Woman*, p. 124.

3 Mrs. Henry S. Gilbert, quoted in Chapman, "Vigilante Vengeance," p. 8.

4 *Frontier Times*, December 1932, p. 129. The Bishop quote is also cited in *Jackson County Star*, March 6, 1930, which reprinted its story from *Colorado Highways* magazine.

5 O'Dell manuscript for *An Ear in His Pocket*, p. 128, citing Dick Baker, "The Notorious Mrs. Jack Slade," *Triangle Review*, Oct. 20, 1973; O'Dell also cites Watrous, *History of Larimer County, Colo.*, p. 75.

6 Ludlow, *Heart of the Continent*, p. 296.

7 Interview with George Beatty, undated interview in *Bynum* (Mont.) *Herald*, July 1923.

8 Coutant, *History of Wyoming*, p. 401.

9 Lilley, "The Settlement and Early History of Virginia Dale," pp. 12 ff. Lilley's father, Harry H. Lilley, owned Table Mountain Ranch, a mile north of Virginia Dale, when Slade was division superintendent headquartered there.

10 Since Slade married Virginia in Texas, some accounts presume she was a Texan and that Slade met her there. Jenkins, "Kiskadden-Slade," p. 88: "Here (in Texas) he met and married Virginia Marie [*sic*], a beautiful and attractive young lady. In 1859 they were living in Missouri." Dabney O. Collins, "On the Trail of Jack Slade" (typed manuscript): "No one who ever saw her sit a horse doubted that Virginia Dale was born to the saddle. A Texan? It's pos-

sible, even probable. At this time, trail herds on longhorns were being driven from Texas into Missouri and Kansas. Virginia could have accompanied a herd driven by her family to Independence or Westport. Slade could have met her here, or in another border town." Such speculations are of course highly speculative. O'Dell and Jessen, *An Ear in His Pocket*, p. 21, suggests Maria Virginia was from Georgia, but this assertion is based entirely on secondary sources.

11 The monograph is Silvey, "The Mysterious Maria Virginia Slade." Several points argue against Silvey's thesis that the two Maria Virginia Slades were the same woman. First, the physical and temperamental descriptions of the two women are very different. Mrs. Slade was almost universally described as large, striking, tough, active, gutsy, and rambunctious. Slade's sister Virginia is described as tall but slender, elegant, dainty, cautious, and passive. A very credible source—Judge Alexander Davis, a native Missourian, who practiced law in St. Joseph, knew the Slades in Virginia City, and returned to Missouri to practice law in St. Louis—told the *St. Louis Globe-Democrat* in 1878 that Mrs. Slade was a native Missourian, raised in Carthage; that Slade had fled to Texas with her after killing a "railroad man" with a rock near St. Louis (perhaps about 1857); that the Slades were married in Texas; and that he (Davis) had seen the marriage certificate. Davis was an understated fellow, trained in the law, not given to exaggeration. See *Helena Weekly Herald*, July 25, 1878. Silvey also contends that in no accounts do the two Maria Virginia Slades appear at the same place at the same time. Perhaps not, but both women's names do appear together on at least one legal document. In 1880 Slade's older brother William filed a document in Carlyle concerning the real estate holdings of Slade's uncle Richard Slade, who had died in 1835 without a will. Among other things, this petition lists all the "heirs at law" to Richard's estate, many of whose whereabouts were unknown. The list includes William's sister, identified as "Maria V. Slade." It also includes Slade's "widow Maria Slade, since intermarried with one Kiscadden [*sic*]."

12 Alexander Davis interview in *Helena Weekly Herald*, July 25, 1878 (reprinted from *St. Louis Globe-Democrat*): "She was raised down here in Carthage, Missouri, a native Missourian. He married her in Texas." The town of Carthage was platted in 1842, so Virginia could not have been born there. The bullwhacker Hugo Koch said Virginia was "about the same age as her husband," who was born in 1831; see Coutant, *History of Wyoming*, p. 401. The 1850 U.S. census for Jasper County, Missouri, where Carthage is located, lists no Maria Virginia Dale, nor anyone else named Maria Virginia (but as a rule, the U.S. Census did not list middle names). It does list five Marias, one Virginia, and four families named Dale. The closest possible fit in the Jasper County census is a Mary A. Dale, age twenty, born in Missouri, daughter of Elijah and Frances Dale. Censuses then were notoriously careless about names and ages, so this could be Slade's future wife, but there's no certainty. It's also possible that Maria Virginia left Jasper County before 1850 and/or changed her first or last name to work in a dance hall, as many such women did. The 1850 U.S. Census for Missouri does list a Maria Dale in Platte County, Carrol Township, a logical location for the future Mrs. Slade— just across the Missouri River from the freighting towns subsequently frequented by Slade. But her age is listed as only eight years. And Judge Davis said Mrs. Slade came from Jasper County, not Platte County.

13 Watrous in his *History of Larimer County, Colo.*, among others, says Slade "named the station Virginia Dale in honor of his wife's maiden name" (p. 189). Later historians have

pointed to the fallacious logic here: A "dale" is another word for valley; Slade's station there was most certainly located in a dale; and the creek flowing nearby was named Dale Creek, so "Virginia Dale" refers to the valley and the creek, not Mrs. Slade's maiden name. Dale as Maria Virginia's maiden name is not documented in any known civil records, marriage or otherwise; letter to author from Nan and Georgia Weber, Nov. 11, 2006. Still, I wonder if we aren't being too hasty in dismissing Watrous's original conclusion. Ball, in *Go West Young Man*, p. 30, says Slade was the first white man to locate (in 1862) at Virginia Dale; as of 1860, according to local historian and Slade biographer Kenneth Jessen, the town of Colona (now Laporte) was the only settlement in all of Larimer County. If Slade himself named Dale Creek, it's worth noting that when he settled outside Virginia City, Montana, a year later (1863), the creek running through his property was called Slade Creek, not some generic creek name. If Slade named his creek in Montana for his own surname, it is possible that he named the creek and the station in Colorado for his wife's maiden name.

14 Seagraves, *Soiled Doves*, pp. 119 ff. Also see Towle, *Vigilante Woman*, p. 124.

15 In all the contemporaneous accounts of Virginia Slade that I have perused, only one provides even a hint that she was not considered a respectable woman. In an interview in the Virginia City (Mont.) *Alder Gulch Times*, Sept. 15, 1899, p. 1 ff, the Virginia City merchant Charles Cannon describes Virginia as a "disreputable character" and "an unfit associate" for a naïve younger woman who had been visiting her. The interview largely concerns Cannon's efforts to retrieve the girl from Mrs. Slade's home without insulting Mrs. Slade.

16 Towle, *Vigilante Woman*, p. 124.

17 "Jim Slade's Help-meet," p. 1.

18 Robert Spotswood, of Denver, quoted in interview, Arthur Chapman, "Jack Slade, Mankiller."

19 Clampitt, *Echoes from the Rocky Mountains*, p. 502.

20 Callaway, *Two True Tales of the Wild West*, p. 14.

21 Bettelyoun, *With My Own Eyes*, p. 8. Bettelyoun's memory is certainly subject to question: because she was born in 1857, she could not have known Slade herself past the age of five and must have heard these stories secondhand, probably from her parents. The "white wife in Denver" is presumably a reference to Maria Virginia, who in 1862 actually lived about 100 miles north of Denver, at Virginia Dale. Bettelyoun's memoir is hardly a work of scrupulous scholarship—for example, in a note (note 15, p. 131) apparently written after her oral memoir was transcribed, she apologizes for some mistakes in her discussion of Slade. Still, Bettelyoun's book is the only known account of Slade from an Indian perspective.

22 The best definitive source on John Hockaday's background is Gray, "The Salt Lake Hockaday Mail," part I, pp. 12 ff. Also see Mackinnon, "Buchanan's Spoils System and the Utah Expedition," pp. 143-144. Nelson Ober, in letter to author, Oct. 9, 2006, said Hockaday had dropped out of West point "a week or so" before graduation—a common ploy then used by young men to gain an education while avoiding military service. Some sources say Hockaday was as young as twenty-one in 1858; but Hockaday himself stated in 1859 that he had "an acquaintance of seven years" with the Overland route, which suggests he first traveled part of it in 1852; see Mackinnon, p. 143.

23 Gray, "The Salt Lake Hockaday Mail," Part I, p. 15.

24 Mackinnon, "Buchanan's Spoils System and the Utah Expedition," pp. 133, 144. Like many entrepreneurs of his time (including Slade), Hockaday seems to have been a peripatetic figure: Root and Hickman, "Pike's Peak Express Companies, Part II," p. 486, say Hockaday lived in Independence, Mo.

25 Walker, *The Wagonmasters,* p. 72.

26 Frederick, *Ben Holladay,* p. 29.

27 Walker, *The Wagonmasters,* p. 72.

28 For Ben Holladay's background, see Frederick, *Ben Holladay,* pp. 23–37.

29 For a good discussion of this point, see George Frederickson, "The Long Trek to Freedom," *New York Review of Books,* July 14, 2005, p. 40.

30 Settle and Settle, *Empire on Wheels,* p. 17 ff.

31 *New York Times,* Aug. 3, 1857, cited in Mackinnon, "The Buchanan Spoils System and the Utah Expedition," p. 144. Gray, "The Salt Lake Hockaday Mail," Part I, p. 15, notes that Hockaday was identified as U.S. attorney for Utah as early as May 22, 1857, but was not officially retained by Buchanan until August 3, leading Gray to speculate that Hockaday might have been appointed by President Franklin Pierce early in 1857.

32 Frederick, *Ben Holladay,* pp. 39–41.

33 Hafen, *The Overland Mail, 1849–1869,* p. 37.

34 Hafen, *The Overland Mail, 1849–1869,* pp. 45–46.

35 Corbett, *Orphans Preferred,* p. 33.

36 Banning, *Six Horses,* p. 173.

37 When Joseph Holt succeeded Aaron Brown as postmaster general in March of 1859, he found six mail lines in operation to the Pacific Coast, costing the government annual gross disbursements of $2,184,697 but bringing in only $339,747 in receipts, a net annual loss of $1,844.949. The semi-weekly Butterfield route from St. Louis cost $600,000 and brought in only $27,230; the Hockaday-Chorpenning weekly central overland route cost $320,000 and brought in the minuscule sum of $5,412. See Hafen, *The Overland Mail, 1849–1869,* pp. 134–135.

38 Hafen, *The Overland Mail, 1849–1869,* pp. 56–60.

39 Hafen, *The Overland Mail, 1849–1869,* pp. 63–64. The Woodward-Chorpenning service started in May 1851.

40 Banning, *Six Horses,* p. 173.

41 Mackinnon, "The Buchanan Spoils System and the Utah Expedition,"), pp. 137–138. One or two of Magraw's brothers were among James Buchanan's close advisers; in 1853, when Buchanan was U.S. minister to Britain, Buchanan had recommended Magraw for a minor federal appointment, vouching for Magraw's faithful support of the Democratic Party, and later that year Magraw's older brother had courted Buchanan's niece.

42 Mackinnon, "Buchanan's Spoils System and the Utah Expedition," p. 134. Gray, in "The Salt Lake Hockaday Mail," Part I, p. 12, says "the arrangement between the Hockadays and Magraw was probably a limited one, for no record of a full partnership has been found."

43 Monahan, *Destination: Denver City,* p. 49, quotes freighter John J. Thomas to the effect that Ike Hockaday was a cousin of John. (Other writers speculate that Isaac was either John's brother or cousin.)

44 Mackinnon, "The Buchanan Spoils System and the Utah Expedition," p. 133. Other sources say the contracted amount was even less: $13,500.

45 Majors, *Seventy Years on the Frontier*, p. 165, says this trip took place in the fall of 1858, but the 1858 Hockaday operation he describes here actually sounds more like the Magraw-Hockaday mail and stagecoach line of 1854–56, which had only six stations along the 1,200-mile route; see Gray, "The Salt Lake Hockaday Mail," Part I, p. 12. Majors's book was published some thirty-five years later, when Majors was seventy-nine and reluctantly writing his memoirs, at the urging of the promotion-minded William F. Cody, to make money. With the passage of time, Majors may have been confused. Nevertheless, this paragraph became the basis for subsequent erroneous assertions that the Hockaday & Co. line of 1858–59 was poorly equipped and had hardly any stations.

46 Mackinnon, "Buchanan's Spoils System and the Utah Expedition," p. 134. Gray, in "The Salt Lake Hockaday Mail," Part I, p. 12, says Magraw requested release from his mail contract after the Indian raid of 1854, but this seems unlikely, given Magraw's subsequent bitterness against the Mormon contractor who succeeded him; see Mackinnon.

47 Walker, *The Wagonmasters*, p. 65; Brands, *The Age of Gold*, pp. 410–411.

48 Brands, *The Age of Gold*, pp. 410–411.

CHAPTER 8

1 Fradkin, *Stagecoach*, pp. 44–45; also Ware, *The Indian War of 1864*, p. 69.

2 *Trails West*, p. 61.

3 Stewart, "Travelers by Overland," *American West*, July 1968, p. 4; Frederick, *Ben Holladay*, pp. 86–87.

4 Frederick, *Ben Holladay*, p. 111.

5 Frederick, *Ben Holladay*, pp. 84–85, 113.

6 Root and Connelley, *The Overland Stage to California*, p. 65.

7 Frederick, *Ben Holladay*, p. 110.

8 Regular government postage for a half-ounce letter through most of the late 1850s was ten cents. When the Pony Express was launched in April 1860, an additional charge of $5 per half-ounce was levied, subsequently reduced to $1 per half-ounce. See Hafen, *The Overland Mail, 1849–1869*, p. 180.

9 Chapman, *The Pony Express*, p. 264.

10 Stewart, "Travelers by Overland," p. 6.

11 Root and Connelley, *The Overland Stage to California*, p. 66.

12 Myers, *Deaths of the Bravos*, p. 380.

13 Brands, *The Age of Gold*, pp. 411–412.

14 Frederick, *Ben Holladay*, p. 111. These fares are for 1862.

15 These figures are drawn from Frederick, *Ben Holladay*, pp. 71–72; Root and Connelley, *The Overland Stage to California*, p. 72; also Root and Hickman, "Pike's Peak Express Companies," Part III, p. 35.

16 Gray, "The Salt Lake Hockaday Mail," Part I, p. 13.

17 Magraw to Franklin Pierce, Oct. 3, 1856, cited in Mackinnon, "The Buchanan Spoils System and the Utah Expedition," p. 130.

18 Denton, *American Massacre*, p. 108.

19 Gray, "The Salt Lake Hockaday Mail," Part I, p. 14.

20 Mackinnon, "The Buchanan Spoils System and the Utah Expedition," p. 136.

21 Settle and Settle, *War Drums and Wagon Wheels,* p. 66; Mackinnon, "The Buchanan Spoils System and the Utah Expedition," p. 137.

22 Settle and Settle, *War Drums and Wagon Wheels,* p. 55.

23 Settle and Settle, *War Drums and Wagon Wheels,* pp. 54–55, 69.

24 O'Dell and Jessen, *An Ear in His Pocket,* p. 15.

25 Settle and Settle, *War Drums and Wagon Wheels,* pp. 74–75; Denton, *American Massacre,* p. 168.

26 Denton, *American Massacre,* p. 178.

27 Mackinnon, "The Buchanan Spoils System and the Utah Expedition," pp. 139–141; Settle and Settle, *War Drums and Wagon Wheels,* p. 66.

28 W. N. Davis, Jr., "Western Justice: The Court at Fort Bridger, Utah Territory," *Utah Historical Quarterly,* 22 (April 1955), p. 102, cited in Mackinnon, "The Buchanan Spoils System and the Utah Expedition," p. 144.

29 Settle and Settle, *War Drums and Wagon Wheels,* p. 247; Stuart, *Forty Years on the Frontier,* pp. 129–130, mentions meeting ten men under Ficklin's command, stationed at Fort Bridger, "who had been teamsters in the employ of Johnston's army," about Jan. 1, 1858.

30 Settle and Settle, *War Drums and Wagon Wheels,* p. 247.

31 Howard, *Hoofbeats of Destiny,* pp. 22, 25.

32 The pay premium is mentioned in Settle and Settle, *War Drums and Wagon Wheels,* p. 55.

33 O'Dell and Jessen, *An Ear in His Pocket,* p. 15: "In 1857, Slade was hired to lead sixteen wagons loaded with supplies from Westport, Mo., to a spot near Fort Bridger, Wyoming. Slade worked for the famous freighting firm of Russell, Majors & Waddell, who had the government contract to supply General Johnston's Utah expedition." But the authors provide no source for this assertion, and in correspondence with the author acknowledged that it could be mistaken (the book's original manuscript, p. 38, says Slade "may have been hired"). The number of wagons in the train cited by O'Dell and Jessen (16) is inconsistent with the figure of twenty-five for each of fourteen trains cited by Settle and Settle in *War Drums and Wagon Wheels,* p. 55. A Slade employee on the Central Overland stage line, James W. Wilson, in "Reminiscences of Overland Days," p. 4, wrote, that Slade "remained in California but a short time, returning to the Missouri River and bringing a train of government freight to Camp Floyd, Utah." Walker, *The Wagonmasters,* p. 81, says, "In 1858 Slade was a wagonmaster of a train of army supplies to Camp Floyd; outside Salt Lake City, Frank A. Root told of a quarrel between Slade and one of his teamsters. Both men drew their revolvers; the driver's gun was cocked, Slade's was not." This clearly refers to the shooting of Andrew Ferrin, which unquestionably occurred on a Hockaday & Burr freight train in May 1859, not a military train in 1858. The Root account (in *The Overland Stage to California,* p. 478) cited above by Walker makes no mention of a military train, saying only that Slade "joined a California-bound wagon train, and was given the position of train-master." An undated clip from the *Centralia* (Ill.)

Sentinel, by Mark Hodapp, on file at the Clinton County (Ill.) Historical Society, quotes a local historian, George Ross, to the effect that "in 1857 Slade was hired to lead a military train of supplies for the army for an attack on the Mormons." I believe that Wilson, Walker, Ross, and those who cite them all committed the same error, confusing Slade's Salt Lake expedition for Hockaday in 1858 with the army's expedition to Utah in 1857–58, and confusing the army's Camp Floyd and Camp Scott (outside Salt Lake City) with Hockaday & Burr's dry goods emporium (in Salt Lake City). Also, had Slade worked for Russell, Majors & Waddell in the 1857–58 Utah expedition, it seems likely he would have driven a train for that same firm in the summer of 1858, instead of hiring on with an upstart rival outfit like Hockaday & Burr.

34 Slade was contacted at Leavenworth, Kansas, by his family in Illinois concerning a legal estate matter, dated Nov. 23, 1854. At that point the town of Leavenworth was only a few months old, although Fort Leavenworth nearby had existed since 1827. This would seem to suggest that Slade's only reason to be in Leavenworth was a military freighting job. But Russell, Majors & Waddell did not yet exist at that point; that partnership was formed a month later, on Dec. 28, 1854, and wasn't awarded its monopoly military freighting contract until March 27, 1855; see Settle and Settle, *War Drums and Wagon Wheels*, p. 40. Thus Slade probably worked for some other private freighting contractor operating out of Fort Leavenworth. Fort Leavenworth itself didn't become a military freighting center until its quartermaster depot was established in 1854 (author's interview with Fort Leavenworth historian John Richley, April 25, 2007). A list of freighting contracts, 1848–54, posted at the Fort Leavenworth Museum (dated by year only, but in chronological order), lists only fourteen such expeditions during that seven-year period and only two in 1854: one to Majors & Waddell (Russell had not yet joined the partnership) to transport government stores to Albuquerque; and the other to William McKnight to transport supplies to Fort Fillmore (in southern New Mexico) as well as to El Paso.

35 See, for example, the 1906 memoirs of Slade's Wyoming neighbor E. W. Whitcomb, cited in O'Dell manuscript for *An Ear in His Pocket*, p. 62, note 2.

36 The journalist Nelson Ober, in a letter to the author dated Jan. 10, 2001, said he had once seen a reference to Dennis as a subcontractor on the Ohio & Mississippi but couldn't retrieve the citation on further checking.

37 Hough, *Story of the Outlaw*, pp. 32–33.

38 *St. Louis Globe Democrat*, reprinted in *Helena Weekly Herald*, July 25, 1878.

39 Dimsdale, *Vigilantes of Montana*, pp. 175–176. To be sure, Dimsdale wrote as an apologist for Slade's Montana enemies, and he functioned at a time when journalists didn't hesitate to concoct missing information to flesh out a story. Dimsdale remarks, for example, that "Johnson, the sheriff, who pursued him for nearly four hundred miles, was in Virginia City not long since, as we have been informed by persons who knew him well." Yet at the time Dimsdale wrote, there had never been a sheriff named Johnson in Slade's native Clinton County or the adjacent Marion County. *History of Marion and Clinton Counties* provides a list of all sheriffs up to 1881. See pages 76 (Marion) and 92 (Clinton).

40 Callaway, *Two True Tales of the Wild West*, p. 99. Yet even Callaway's benign construction of the story is difficult to support in light of the total absence of any contemporaneous record or account of such a death in southern Illinois, a place where murders were rare and consequently extensively reported. The striking thing about this story is the failure of any observer

close to the scene to mention it. In his late twenties and early thirties Slade returned to Carlyle for visits at least twice without being arrested for the supposed murder; and on at least two occasions after his departure he was mentioned warmly in the Carlyle newspapers, without any indication that he had ever been involved in a crime there or elsewhere. Indeed, one account of this supposed murder attributes the story to Slade himself, which suggests that Slade may have invented the tale to enhance his own fearsome reputation. Thus it is conceivable that Slade, during the off-season from freighting, took a job laying the railroad, got into a fight with a fellow worker, killed his rival and fled. But such an incident, if it happened at all, couldn't have occurred in or near Carlyle, and probably couldn't have occurred later than 1857 (when both the Illinois Central and the Ohio & Mississippi were completed).

41 Katherine Goodwin of Carlyle, who as a girl knew Slade's younger sister, offered the theory that Slade fled to Texas in the mistaken belief that he had killed a man, and that the sheriff in Illinois pursued him to tell him that the victim had survived and Slade could come home. Goodwin, interview with the author in March 1995, when she was ninety-six.

42 Such a certificate has never been found by historians. O'Dell, in his first draft of *An Ear in His Pocket*, said he searched for Slade's marriage certificate in Texas as well as California, Utah, Missouri, Wyoming, Montana, Illinois, and Georgia, without success (manuscript p. 132, note 5). But O'Dell was unaware of Davis's remark that Slade was married under the surname of "Alfred."

43 Hugo Koch, "Early Days in Wyoming," Part 1, *Wind River Mountaineer*, Lander, Wyo., March 6, 1908, describes Slade in July 1858 as "recently from Texas." Koch also describes an Atchison restaurant owned by "a Texas man and great friend of Slade's"; see Part 4, March 27, 1908. Under an alternative scenario, Slade might have been hired by the Hockaday mail line in the spring of 1858 and then dispatched to Texas to acquire steers for Hockaday's mail supply train; Koch refers to Slade's great familiarity with the train's 1,000 Texas steers. It's also worth noting that Slade had relatives in Texas: his uncle Henry Slade had moved there from Washington about 1840 and died near Matagorda in 1843, and Henry's daughter Charlotte Hanson was married at Bay Prairie, Texas, in 1843. Whether Slade was in touch with them is unknown.

44 Wilson, "Reminiscences of Overland Days," *Sons of Colorado*, May 1907, p. 4.

45 Hafen, *The Overland Mail, 1849–1869*, pp. 80–87; Bloss, *Pony Express: The Great Gamble*, p. 10.

46 Hafen, *The Overland Mail, 1849–1869*, pp. 87–88.

47 *Trails West*, pp. 58, 69.

48 Hockaday submitted a formal bid for monthly or semimonthly service on Aug. 1, 1857. See U.S. Senate Report No. 259, 36th Cong., 1st sess. (1860), p. 21.

49 Bartlett, *A Social History of the American Frontier, 1776–1890*, pp. 302–303; and Frederick, *Ben Holladay*, p. 52.

50 Hafen, *The Overland Mail, 1849–1869*, pp. 91–92.

51 The Butterfield Overland Mail Company began operating a year later, in September 1858, with an initial run that took just under twenty-four days. By the winter of 1859–60 the average run was reduced to twenty-two days. See "Pony Express: Historic Resource Study," Chapter 2 (National Park Service, 1995–2002), at www.nps.gov/poex/hrs/hrs2a.htm.

52 Settle and Settle, *War Drums and Wagon Wheels*, pp. 77–79.

53 Such a meeting was planned, but it's unclear whether it actually took place. See Mackinnon, "The Buchanan Spoils System and the Utah Expedition," p. 127.

54 Gray, "The Salt Lake Hockaday Mail," Part I, p. 15.

55 Hafen, *The Overland Mail, 1849–1869*, pp. 110–111.

56 U.S. Congress, Senate, *Report of the Postmaster General*, 35th Cong., 2nd sess., S. Ex. Doc. 1, 722.

57 Thompson and West, *History of Nevada*, pp. 102–105; and Bancroft, *History of Nevada, Colorado and Wyoming*, pp. 226–227; and Taylor, *First Mail West*, p. 48; and Hafen, *The Overland Mail, 1849–1869*, pp. 114–115.

58 "Pony Express: Historic Resource Study," Chapter 2 (National Park Service, 1995–2002), an Internet document, says "apparently only seven stations existed along the route," but none of the sources cited supports this statement. The seven original Hockaday stations, according to the NPS, were at Independence (later St. Joseph), Big Blue, Fort Kearny, Fort Laramie, Independence Rock, Black's Fork, and Salt Lake City. See www.nps.gov/poex/hrs/hrs2a.htm.

59 Hafen, *The Overland Mail, 1849–1869*, pp. 110–111; and Moody, *Stagecoach West*, p. 126.

60 Settle and Settle, *War Drums and Wagon Wheels*, pp. 92–93.

61 Root and Hickman, "The Pike's Peak Express Companies," pp. 164–165.

62 Settle and Settle, *War Drums and Wagon Wheels*, pp. 93–94.

63 Settle, *War Drums and Wagon Wheels*, pp. 93–94; also Frederick, *Ben Holladay*, p. 54; Chapman, *The Pony Express*, p. 77.

64 *Atchison Champion*, Aug. 14, 1858, cited in Ingalls, *History of Atchison County, Kansas*, p. 173; also Gray, "The Salt Lake Hockaday Mail," Part I, pp. 17–18. Gray says the third train consisted of 69 men, not 60, but this is probably an error in transcription.

65 *Atchison Champion*, Aug. 14, 1858, cited in Gray, "The Salt Lake Hockaday Mail," Part I, p. 18.

66 Koch was about seventy when he dictated these memoirs in 1908; see Nelson Ober, letter to author, April 20, 1999. If born in 1838, he would have been twenty in 1858.

67 Hugo Koch, "Early Days in Wyoming," Part 1, *Wind River Mountaineer*, Lander, Wyo., March 6, 1908. This paragraph actually refers to "Mr. J. H. Slade" and to "Huckabay & Burr," but these appear to be errors in transcription or typographical errors, as the names appear correctly later in the narrative.

68 Coutant, *History of Wyoming*, p. 401.

69 Koch, "Early Days in Wyoming," Part 4.

70 Colonel John Doniphan, an attorney for the St. Joseph and Grand Island Railroad and amateur historian, writing in the *St. Joseph Argus*, July 8, 1893, said Slade was "promoted from clerk to a supply train to division agent." The article is reprinted in Root and Connelley, *The Overland Stage to California*, pp. 446–447. Callaway, *Two True Tales of the Wild West*, pp. 101–102, says Slade began his career in the central overland stagecoach business as station agent at Kearny with "supervision over considerable territory" but doesn't identify Slade's employer: "At whose special direction he was given the agency at Kearney [sic] remains obscure." Callaway clearly meant to refer here to Fort Kearny (built in 1848) rather than the town of Kearney, which wasn't laid out (and accidentally misspelled with an extra *e*) until 1871.

71 According to one account, Slade was asked if he had ever been to St. Louis or New Orleans. He replied: "No, I hain't never been at Horleans, but I'll tell you where I have been. I've been mighty nigh all over three counties in Illinois." Shumway, *History of Western Nebraska*, p. 56, attributes this anecdote to Mark Twain, who rarely verified stories he heard.

72 Koch describes Slade in July 1858 as "a gentleman recently from Texas"; "Early Days in Wyoming," Part 1. Later in his serialized memoir Koch remarks that the thousand head of cattle were "Texas steers" because "Texas steers and Missouri drivers and wagonmasters made the best freight locomotion then extant" (Part 3, March 20, 1908). Still later, Koch remarks on Slade's "immense memory" concerning these Texas steers (Part 4, March 27, 1908). From these snippets it's possible to surmise that Slade may have brought the steers from Texas to Kansas himself.

73 Koch, "Early Days in Wyoming," Part 4.

74 Coutant, *History of Wyoming*, p. 401.

CHAPTER 9

1 Atchison City Directory, 1859, p. 40, lists J. M. Hockaday & Co., "Salt Lake freighters, and merchants' warehouse, on Levee, office S. side Commercial, between Levee and Second."

2 Koch, "Early Days in Wyoming," Part 1.

3 Koch, "Early Days in Wyoming," Part 2.

4 Koch, "Early Days in Wyoming," Part 4.

5 Koch, "Early Days in Wyoming," Part 3.

6 Koch, "Early Days in Wyoming," Part 4.

7 Koch, "Early Days in Wyoming," Part 4; also Walker, *The Wagonmasters*, p. 116.

8 Koch, "Early Days in Wyoming," Part 4. Koch appears to be describing a train of only 25 wagons pulled by 300 oxen. Yet Koch's chronology is consistent with John S. Gray's chronology for the much larger Hockaday & Burr train of 105 wagons (80 pulled by oxen, 25 by mules), 1,000 oxen and 200 mules; see Gray, "The Salt Lake Hockaday Mail," Part I, p. 18. Also, Koch's memoir twice mentions the figure of 1,000 steers, the same figure provided for the "mammoth" Hockaday & Burr train in the table of freight trains published in the Atchison *Freedom's Champion* of Oct. 30, 1858. I surmise from these inconsistencies that this huge train was organized in three or four sections, of which Koch was familiar with only one. This surmisal is reinforced by Koch's comment that, shortly before reaching Scott's Bluffs mail station, "Our ox team overtook a mule team starting a week before from Atchison"; see Koch, "Early Days in Wyoming," Part 7.

9 Koch, "Early Days in Wyoming," Part 6.

10 Koch, "Early Days in Wyoming," Part 5. The mileage and number of mail stations is taken from O. Allen, *Guide to the Gold Fields*, Washington, 1859, cited in Gray, "The Salt Lake Hockaday Mail," Part I, p. 5.

11 Koch, "Early Days in Wyoming," Part 6.

12 Koch, "Early Days in Wyoming," Part 6.

13 Koch, "Early Days in Wyoming," Part 6.

14 Koch, "Early Days in Wyoming," Part 7.

15 Koch, "Early Days in Wyoming," Part 7.

16 Koch, "Early Days in Wyoming," Part 10.

17 Koch, "Early Days in Wyoming," Part 7, says they awoke on Oct. 18, 1858, "in Wyoming" for the first time, but then he says they continued on to Scotts Bluffs mail station, which is in Nebraska (but which Koch describes as "the first in Wyoming"). Koch's confusion is understandable: Wyoming did not then exist as a separate entity; it was part of Nebraska Territory, which until 1861 included much of present-day Wyoming, Montana, and South Dakota.

18 Koch, "Early Days in Wyoming," Part 8.

19 Koch, "Early Days in Wyoming," Part 9.

20 The earliest known description of Hockaday's four divisions appears in a *New York Tribune* article by Albert G. Browne, Nov. 19, 1858; see Gray, "The Salt Lake Hockaday Mail," Part I, p. 19. The same four divisions are confirmed in O. Allen's *Guide to the Gold Fields*, published in the spring of 1859. Callaway, in *Two True Tales of the Wild West*, p. 100, locates Gilbert's Station at "the westly end of South Pass."

21 Koch, "Early Days in Wyoming," Part 10.

22 Shay, "Horseshoe Creek Crossing and Stage Station," 260-261. Shay says the second station was established in 1859 by the Central Overland Stage Line, but Koch's memoir clearly indicates that the Horseshoe Creek station was operating when his wagon train reached there in the fall of 1858. George W. Beehrer's memoir, "Freighting Across the Plains," p. 14, mentions passing "Horseshoe Bend, a Company station," in the summer of 1858. But the "company" he refers to is Russell, Majors & Waddell, and he seems to be describing a station east of Fort Laramie. Either Beehrer's details are confused or Horseshoe Bend and Horseshoe Creek are two different places. (A place called Horseshoe Bend does exist in southwestern Wyoming, west of Fort Bridger and nowhere near Fort Laramie.)

23 Koch, in "Early Days in Wyoming," Part 10, says Horseshoe "was the central station of the division from O'Fallon's Bluffs in Nebraska to the Devil's Gate in Wyoming," a distance of almost 400 miles. It seems likely to me that Koch was referring to Hockaday's second and third divisions combined (from Fort Kearny in the east to the Sweetwater River in the west), both of which may have been under Slade's supervision at that point. This supervision of two divisions by a single agent is certainly possible: Gray, describing the Hockaday line's supervisory titles in "The Salt Lake Hockaday Mail," Part I, p. 19, distinguishes between the title of "division agent (of one division)" and "division superintendent (of two or more divisions)." This would be consistent with Callaway's remark that Slade began his central overland stagecoach career as agent at (Fort) Kearny, with "supervision over considerable territory." See *Two True Tales of the Wild West*, pp. 101-102. It's also consistent with Perry Jenkins's comment that from Horseshoe Station, as "superintendent of this division," Slade "worked east and west along the route, overseeing the movement of the stages and the shipment and storage of supplies"; see Jenkins, "Kiskadden-Slade," p. 69. Jenkins, who was born in 1872 and taught at several universities, says Slade built the Horseshoe station as well as his home there.

24 That Slade was ultimately expected at Salt Lake City is suggested by the inclusion of his name ("J. A. Slade") on lists of unclaimed mail at the Salt Lake Post Office as of Nov. 11 and Nov. 18, 1858. See *Valley Tan*, Salt Lake City, Nov. 12 and 19, 1858.

25 Gray, "The Salt Lake Hockaday Mail," Part I, p. 17.

26 U.S. Congress, Senate, *Report of the Postmaster General*, 35th Cong., 2nd sess., S. Ex. Doc. 1, 722.

27 Hafen, *The Overland Mail*, pp. 122–123.

28 Koch, "Early Days in Wyoming," Parts 10 and 11, mentions stations west of Horseshoe at LaBonte Creek, Box Elder, Platte Bridge (now Casper), Red Buttes, and Devil's Gate. Gray, in "The Salt Lake Hockaday Mail," Part II, p. 2, says the next station west of Devil's Gate as of December 1858 was Gilbert's station, 85 miles away, and the next west of that was Green River (also known as Big Sandy), another 75 miles to the west. By spring 1859 Hockaday had four stations between Green River and Salt Lake, and eleven stations all told between Horseshoe and Salt Lake; see O. Allen, *Guide to the Gold Fields*, 1859, cited in Gray, Part II, p. 5.

29 Gray, "The Salt Lake Hockaday Mail," Part II, pp. 2–3. The stationmaster Gilbert, then not yet twenty-five, was a Pennsylvania native who had moved to Kansas and Missouri in the mid-1850s with the intention of farming but turned instead to trading with Crow and Sioux Indians and furnishing supplies to emigrants. That spring of 1858 he had headed westward to furnish rations to Colonel Johnston's Utah expedition, only to settle at the west end of South Pass, where he established a trading post and general store that soon became a key station on the Hockaday line. See Gilbert's biography in *Progressive Men of Montana*, p. 174.

30 "Frosty—Very," *Valley Tan*, Salt Lake City, Dec. 17, 1858.

31 Koch, "Early Days in Wyoming," Part 10.

32 Koch, "Early Days in Wyoming," Part 10.

33 Koch, "Early Days in Wyoming," Part 11. Hockaday appears to have been very much a hands-on owner. Gray, "The Salt Lake Hockaday Mail," Part I, p. 19, says, "Hockaday was undoubtedly the general superintendent of his line." Chorpenning, in a letter written Jan. 31, 1859, describes an eastbound stage trip with Hockaday, remarking, "If he had not been along, I would have made it in less than fourteen days, but he had business at every station, which detained him from two to three hours in every instance." See *Valley Tan*, Salt Lake City, March 15, 1859.

34 Koch, "Early Days in Wyoming," Part 11.

35 Koch, "Early Days in Wyoming," Part 11.

36 Koch, "Early Days in Wyoming," Part 11. Koch says it took two days from Red Buttes to the Sweetwater River, a distance of 37 miles. Since Devil's Gate was another 7 miles farther, I presume they reached Devil's Gate on the third day.

37 Gray, "The Salt Lake Hockaday Mail," Part II, pp. 3–4.

38 Chorpenning to Frank D. Gilbert, Jan. 31, 1859, in *Valley Tan*, Salt Lake City, March 15, 1859.

39 Albert G. Browne in *New York Tribune*, Nov. 19, 1858, cited in Gray, "The Salt Lake Hockaday Mail," Part I, p. 19.

40 *Valley Tan*, Salt Lake City, weekly from February 1859 through May 1859. The notice is dated February 14, 1859.

41 Walker, *The Wagonmasters*, pp. 70–71.

42 Settle and Settle, *Empire on Wheels*, p. 35. The Settles say forty shares were issued at $5,000 each, apparently a total initial capitalization of $200,000. Russell contributed $20,000 in cash, and "Jones probably invested a like amount."

43 Frederick, *Ben Holladay*, p. 54; Settle and Settle, *Empire on Wheels*, p. 44.

44 Hafen, *The Overland Mail*, pp. 146–147; Frederick, *Ben Holladay*, p. 54; Settle and Settle,

War Drums and Wagon Wheels, p. 96; Root, *The Overland Stage to California*, p. 157. Root says there were 800 mules and more than fifty coaches; Root says he saw the coaches land at the levee at Leavenworth and that they were the first Concord coaches brought to Kansas; see pp. 153–154. The quote from Larimer's *Reminiscences* is cited in Chapman, *The Pony Express*, pp. 77–78.

45 Gray, "The Salt Lake Hockaday Mail," Part I, p. 17. Allen, *Guide to the Gold Fields*, cited in Gray, "The Salt Lake Hockaday Mail," Part II, p. 5, shows thirty stations over a span of 1,123 miles, which works out to one every 31 miles.

46 U.S. Senate Report No. 259, 36th Cong., 1st sess., June 6, 1860, p. 1. Also see Gray, "The Salt Lake Hockaday Mail," Part II, p. 7.

47 S. L. Hubbell at Weber Station, just east of Salt Lake, to Kirk Anderson, Feb. 23, 1859, in *Valley Tan*, Salt Lake City, March 15, 1859. The letter describes an eastbound mail party that left Salt Lake the previous Saturday with "agent Slade and ex-agent Ashton in company with it." This is the earliest specific contemporaneous reference to Slade as a division agent. See *Valley Tan*, Salt Lake City, March 15, 1859. A letter from Ashton dated May 23, 1859, describing an incident at Green River on May 20, mentions that Slade, "the agent for Hockaday & Co.," was authorized to take charge of a freight train "when it reached his division of the road"; see *Valley Tan*, Salt Lake City, June 1, 1859, p. 2, col. 4–5. Memoirs of Louis R. Maillet refer to the writer boarding a westbound stage on July 2, 1859 at Gilbert's station "with Slade, Division Agent," and riding to Ham's Fork of Green River; see Wheeler, "Historical Sketch of Louis R. Maillet," p. 215. Gilbert's station was the westernmost post on Hockaday's third division; Ham's Fork, Green River, Weber, and of course Salt Lake City were all located along Division 4. For a complete breakdown of Hockaday's divisions and stations, see Gray, "The Salt Lake Hockaday Mail," Part II, p. 5.

48 Gray, "The Salt Lake Hockaday Mail," Part II, p. 4.

CHAPTER 10

1 Gray, "The Salt Lake Hockaday Mail," Part II, p. 5, says Hockaday left Atchison for Washington "about the end of February." (Gray says "February, 1868," but the year is clearly a typographical error.)

2 Hafen, *The Overland Mail*, pp. 129–130.

3 *U.S. Congressional Globe*, 36th Congress, 1st session, p. 2374, cited in Hafen, *The Overland Mail*, p. 140.

4 "Petition for relief of John M. Hockaday and William Liggitt," U.S. Senate Report. No. 259, 36th Congress, 1st session, June 6, 1860, p. 2. Also see Gray, "The Salt Lake Hockaday Mail," Part II, p. 6.

5 Postmaster-general's report, 1859, p. 1408, in U.S. Senate Executive Documents, 36th Congress, 1st session, no. 2 (Serial No. 1025); also see Hafen, *The Overland Mail*, pp. 134–135.

6 Hafen, *The Overland Mail*, pp. 135–136; Gray, "The Salt Lake Hockaday Mail," Part II, p. 6.

7 Gray, "The Salt Lake Hockaday Mail," Part II, p. 6.

8 "Petition for relief of John M. Hockaday and William Liggitt," p. 22. Slade's affidavit is dated Nov. 15, 1859.

9 "Petition for relief of John M. Hockaday and William Liggitt," p. 4. See also Gray, "The Salt Lake Hockaday Mail," Part II, p. 8. Hafen, *The Overland Mail*, p. 150, says the reduced fee was $130,000, not $125,000.

10 Gray, "The Salt Lake Hockaday Mail," Part II, p. 7.

11 *Valley Tan*, Salt Lake City, April 12, 1859.

12 Settle and Settle, *War Drums and Wagon Wheels*, p. 98; also see Root and Hickman, "Pike's Peak Express Companies, Part III: The Platte Route," p. 494.

13 Russell to Waddell, April 17, 1859, cited in Settle and Settle, *War Drums and Wagon Wheels*, p. 98.

14 Gray, "The Salt Lake Hockaday Mail," Part II, pp. 8–9. Gray says the payments came to $175,000; but at an annual rate of $125,000, 17 months would equal $177,083.

15 "Petition for relief of John M. Hockaday and William Liggitt," p. 10.

16 Gray, "The Salt Lake Hockaday Mail," Part II, p. 8; also "Petition for relief of John M. Hockaday and William Liggitt," p. 34. Mackinnon, in "The Buchanan Spoils System and the Utah Expedition," p. 146, inexplicably claims that "Hockaday and his partner sold out for a total of $405,847.51." Mackinnon appears to be counting not only the purchase price ($144,000) but also a later $40,000 government award to Hockaday and Liggitt for their losses, and perhaps also the $221,667 in monthly government payments that Hockaday & Co. received during its 14 months of mail service. But this last figure ($221,667) represents revenues, and should not be confused with the value of the Hockaday operation or the price of the sale.

17 "Petition for relief of John M. Hockaday and William Liggitt," p. 5.

18 Most accounts describe Ben Holladay and Russell as old friends. But Walker, in *The Wagonmasters*, p. 72, says, "Because of pique at what he considered personal slights at the hands of both Russell and Majors, [Ben Holladay] nursed a long-standing grudge against both....When the big firm began to get into financial trouble, he loaned them large sums until they were deeply in his debt and then called for payment of his notes."

19 Settle and Settle, *Empire on Wheels*, pp. 48–49.

20 *Valley Tan*, March 22, 1859.

21 *Valley Tan*, March 29, 1859.

22 *Valley Tan*, April 19, 1859.

23 *Valley Tan*, April 26, 1859.

24 "Large Stocks," *Valley Tan*, April 26, 1859. See udn.lib.utah.edu/valleytan/image/753.pdf.

25 Green River was the easternmost terminus of the Hockaday line's Division 4, which Slade appears to have been in charge of at this point. For a complete breakdown of Hockaday's divisions and stations, see Gray, "The Salt Lake Hockaday Mail," Part II, p. 5. Memoirs of Louis R. Maillet refer to the writer boarding a westbound stage on July 2, 1859 at Gilbert's station "with Slade, Division Agent," and riding to Ham's Fork of Green River; see "Historical Sketch of Louis R. Maillet," *Historical Society of Montana*, 4 (1903), p. 215. Gilbert's station was the westernmost post on Hockaday's third division. This suggests that by July 2 Slade was in charge of both the third division (from Horseshoe Creek to Gilbert's at South Pass) and the fourth division (from Green River to Salt Lake).

26 William Ashton, dispatch dated May 23, 1859, *Valley Tan*, June 1, 1859, p. 2, cols. 4–5.

27 Wilson, "Reminiscences of Overland Days," p. 4. Wilson erroneously referred to the Hockaday train as "one of the government trains."

28 The British traveler Burton, in August 1860, called the victim "Farren"; his source presumably was a stagecoach driver not necessarily attentive to spelling. See Burton, *City of the Saints*, p. 214. Coutant's *History of Wyoming* spelled the name Farrar, as most subsequent accounts have done; see pp. 401–402. My hunch is that the victim's name was transmitted orally in all cases and the listener merely concocted his own spelling.

29 Stuart, *Forty Years on the Frontier*, pp. 150–151. Unlike many Western memoirists, Stuart kept a daily journal, so his memories are probably more reliable than most.

30 Coutant, *History of Wyoming*, pp. 401–402. Coutant implies that his source is Hugo Koch. Koch's own memoir of this wagon train, published in 1908, does not mention the shooting of Ferrin at all; the memoir ends the previous December, when the train wintered at Horseshoe. Although Koch was contracted in July 1858 to remain with the train to its terminus in Salt Lake City, it's unclear whether he was still involved when the train reassembled at Horseshoe in April 1859.

31 Beehrer, "Freighting Across the Plains," p. 2.

32 "Historical Sketch of Louis R. Maillet," p. 215.

33 O'Dell and Jessen, *An Ear in His Pocket*, p. 17.

34 Burton, *The City of the Saints*, p. 114.

35 Twain, *Roughing It*, chapter 10.

36 Root and Connelley, *The Overland Stage to California*, p. 216.

37 Journal of Egbert Railly, cited in Walker, *The Wagonmasters*, pp. 37–38.

38 J. K. Ellis, quoted in manuscript by Jesse Brown, Ms. 122C, Wyoming State Historical library, pp. 2–3.

39 Mrs. Guy Dunn, "History of California Crossing" (Fort Sedgwick Historical Society); "Upper California Crossing," *Overland News*, August 1957, p. 7.

40 Root and Hickman, "Pike's Peak Express Companies, Part III: The Platte Route," note 310.

41 The term "ranch" is defined in Wieler, *Old Julesburg*, pp. 5–6.

42 Interview by Mrs. Clarence Paine with Jules Beni's widow, about 1905, in *Morton's History of Nebraska*, vol. 2, pp. 180–181.

43 Langford, *Vigilante Days and Ways*, pp. 362–363.

44 For descriptions of Jules, see O'Dell, original manuscript for *An Ear in His Pocket*, pp. 81–82, citing MacMurphy, "Some Squatters with a History," p. 4; letters from Joe Rosa to Roy O'Dell, April 4, 1987 and May 30, 1987; Public Archives of Canada, Ottawa; University of Western Ontario, London, Canada. A putative descendant of Jules, M. H. Keith of Livingston, Tex., in 1995 provided the author with a family tree that listed 1809 as the year of Jules's birth; M. H. Keith to Dan Rottenberg, March 30, 1995.

45 Mrs. J. G. Cavender, "Sedgwick County," from *Who's Who in Colorado*, Colorado Press Assn., 1938.

46 Root and Connelley, *The Overland Stage to California*, p. 65. Root says Cottonwood Springs, in present-day southwest Nebraska, was 105 miles from Julesburg.

47 Root and Connelley, *The Overland Stage to California*, p. 213; also C. M. Rolfson, "Historic Julesburg," c. 1943; also Walker, *The Wagonmasters*, p. 38.

48 Mrs. C. F. Parker, "Old Julesburg and Fort Sedgwick," typescript draft for article that appeared in *Colorado* Magazine, July 1930 (collection of Fort Sedgwick Historical Society).

49 Twain, *Roughing It*, chapters 6–7.

50 Parker, "Old Julesburg and Fort Sedgwick," p. 139.

51 The first federal census taken of Nebraska Territory (which included the "Sterling Quadrangle" area north of the 40th parallel in present-day Colorado) in 1860 (after Jules was gone) reported only 173 residents in the "Platte River Settlement" area in and around Julesburg, including fewer than ten families with children. The total also included seven station keepers, ten traders, five stage drivers and two express riders. See Glenn R. Scott, "Geologic map of the Sterling 1 X 2 quadrangle, north-eastern Colorado" (U.S. Geol. Survey Misc. Inv. Series Map I-1092, 1979, pp. 7–8.)

52 Parker, "Old Julesburg and Fort Sedgwick," p. 139, identifies Williams as the man who hired Jules. So do Settle and Settle, *Story of the Pony Express*, p. 103.

53 Parker, "Old Julesburg and Fort Sedgwick," p. 139.

54 Maillet, "Historical Sketch of Louis R. Maillet," p. 215, refers to getting on a westbound stage with "Slade, Division Agent" at Gilbert's station on July 2, 1859.

55 Gray, "The Salt Lake Hockaday Mail," Part II, p. 9. In November 1859, after Slade had been transferred to the central division, he and his two fellow division agents gave affidavits comparing costs and number of mules on their respective divisions before and after July 1, 1859; on this basis the Settles and other historians mistakenly assumed that the three division agents remained in the same divisions throughout the year 1859.

56 Byron Hooper, Jr., suggested that the difficulties caused by Jules were greatly exaggerated: "No robberies were reported, outside of Indian depredations, in the Denver papers of that era while lesser incidences of Overland travel made their way into print. In fact, it was the policy of these very papers to list the amount of gold sent after the coach departed from Denver. All departures carried thousands in gold dust, but there is no record today of any of these coaches being waylaid before or during Slade's tenure in office." See Hooper, "Slade Is No More," p. 2. To be sure, the Central Overland's mail problems at Julesburg before Slade's arrival had more to do with westbound stages headed north to Salt Lake City and California rather than south to Denver.

57 *Overland News*, March 1958, p. 5.

58 O'Dell, manuscript for *An Ear in His Pocket*, pp. 74, 82–83; Callaway, *Two True Tales of the Wild West*, pp. 102–103.

59 This story was recounted by Lt. Eugene Ware, as told to him by an old-timer who claimed to have witnessed the incident; cited in Monahan, *Destination: Denver City*, p. 57.

60 Settle and Settle, *War Drums and Wagon Wheels*, pp. 98, 101.

61 Settle and Settle, *War Drums and Wagon Wheels*, pp. 101, 114–115.

62 The capital stock was fixed at $200,000 and divided into 40 shares, as follows: William H. Russell, 30; John S. Jones, 4; William B. Waddell, Alexander Majors, and Russell's son John, 2 each. Russell may have been expected to distribute most of his shares to other prospective partners in order to raise capital. Contract between Russell, Majors & Waddell and John S. Jones et al., Oct. 28, 1859, cited in Settle and Settle, *Empire on Wheels*, pp. 57–58. By the time

the corporate charter was granted by the Kansas Territorial Legislature on Feb. 13, 1860, its capital stock had been expanded to $500,000, divided into 5,000 shares valued at $100 each. See Settle and Settle, *War Drums and Wagon Wheels*, p. 102.

63 Settle and Settle, *Story of the Pony Express*, p. 24.

64 Settle and Settle, *War Drums and Wagon Wheels*, p. 110, describes the message only as "an important message by President Franklin Pierce" and sets the time as December 1853. Since the president's annual message to Congress was delivered then in the first week of December, I surmise that this is the message to which the Settles refer.

65 Hafen, *The Overland Mail, 1849–1869*, pp. 165–166.

66 Root and Hickman, "The Platte Route, Part IV: The Pony Express and Pacific Telegraph," p. 39. Also Howard, *Hoofbeats of Destiny*, pp. 80–81.

67 The Hannibal & St. Joseph Railroad opened Feb. 23, 1859; see Root and Connelley, *The Overland Stage to California*, p. 413.

68 Bailey, "The Pony Express," pp. 882–883.

69 Chapman, *The Pony Express*, p. 89, says ordinary horses in the West could be had at that time for $50, but the type demanded for Pony Express use brought $150 to $200.

70 Settle and Settle, *War Drums and Wagon Wheels*, pp. 114–115. The Leavenworth & Pike's Peak Express Co. owed $525,532 at the end of October 1859 (including $190,269 owed to Russell, Majors & Waddell). Jones, Russell & Co. balance sheet, Nov. 18, 1859, cited in Settle and Settle, *Empire on Wheels*, p. 57. As to the cost of the Pony Express, in *The Story of the Pony Express*, the Settles remark: "Nobody knows what it cost the Central Overland California & Pike's Peak Express Company to equip, maintain, and operate the Pony Express, but it must have been at least $500,000"; see p. 162.

71 Settle and Settle, *War Drums and Wagon Wheels*, pp. 102, 110. Russell wrote Waddell that he was preparing a charter on November 19, 1859, noting that the new company would be reorganized the following Wednesday, November 23. On the 22nd Russell again wrote Waddell to advise him of the new concern's name.

72 The question of whom Slade replaced as division agent at this point has never been answered to my satisfaction. The most likely candidate was Charles W. Wiley, who testified on Nov. 26, 1859, that his division extended from St. Joseph west to "the crossing of the Platte," i.e., Julesburg. (Although by that point Slade was already in charge of Julesburg.) When the Pony Express was organized in January 1860, Slade's division was extended eastward to Fort Kearny, and Wiley's division (now St. Joseph to Fort Kearny) was turned over to A. E. Lewis. In the absence of other evidence, it seems likely that Wiley was the superintendent of record for Julesburg before Slade was brought in, but since Wiley was domiciled at St. Joseph, Jules Beni probably operated largely autonomously at the division's western end. It's also possible that the 25-mile "Jules Stretch" from Julesburg functioned as a de facto division unto itself before Slade was brought in. What remains unclear is which division agent was in charge of the section from Julesburg to Horseshoe Creek before Slade took charge of it in October 1859.

73 Root and Connelley, *The Overland Stage to California*, p. 218.

74 Baker, *Mary Todd Lincoln*, p. 144, notes: "The record is full of those who remembered Lincoln's saying that his wife expected him to be president, to which idea he responded with bemused astonishment, at least until November 6, 1860."

75 Rufus Rockwell Wilson, *Intimate Memories of Lincoln, Franklin G. Adams, Proceedings of the Kansas Historical Society* 7, pp. 213–214.

76 Frank Root, quoted in Ayers, *Lincoln and Kansas,* p. 90.

77 Ayers, *Lincoln and Kansas,* p. 94, citing an account by Senator John Ingalls in the *Kansas City Star*, 1890. I have not been able to find the original account.

78 The text of Lincoln's Atchison talk does not seem to have survived. I have pieced it together from several sources, including Ayers, *Lincoln and Kansas,* p. 89; also "The Honorable Abe Lincoln . . . on Kansas Soil," Kansas State Historical Society, February 1998; and Alan Farley, "When Lincoln Came to Kansas Territory," address to Fort Leavenworth Historical Society, November 17, 1959.

79 Ayers, *Lincoln and Kansas,* p. 95, citing an article by Ingalls in the *Kansas City Star,* 1890. I haven't found the original article.

80 "New Hotel Opens in Blaze of Glory," *Atchison Globe*, May 26, 1927 (report of speech by E. W. Howe).

81 *Atchison Globe,* May 26, 1927, reporting a speech by its editor, E. W. Howe. Howe mistakenly referred to Slade as "Bill," but Slade is correctly identified in an account in the *Pony Express Courier*, March 1936, p. 12. Howe had been editor of the *Atchison Globe* since 1877; where he heard this story is unknown. Senator John Ingalls, writing in the *Kansas City Star* in 1890, also referred to Lincoln swapping stories with Overland drivers but said the encounter occurred the following morning— Saturday, Dec. 3; see Ayers, *Lincoln and Kansas*, pp. 94–95.

CHAPTER 11

1 Did Slade decide to fire Jules as stationmaster, or was he merely carrying out Ficklin's instructions? I am inclined to the latter view, but definitive evidence is lacking. The stage driver Frank Root, in *The Overland Stage to California* (1901), says, "The discoveries made by Ficklin showed Jules to be a thief and a scoundrel of the worst kind. Jules was at once made to settle with the company" (p. 217). Callaway, in *Two True Tales of the Wild West,* says, "One of the first acts of Ficklin was to remove Jules as station agent at Julesburg and to install Slade as superintendent of the Sweetwater Division" (p. 102), suggesting Jules was removed before Slade even took charge. O'Dell and Jessen, in *An Ear in His Pocket* (1996), say, "To prevent further loss of stock, Ben Ficklin sent Jack Slade out to replace Jules Beni" (p. 50), and "One of Slade's first acts as the new division agent was to relieve Jules Beni of his position as station agent at Julesburg" (p. 23), although no source is cited. Raymond and Mary Settle, the leading scholars of the Russell, Majors & Waddell partnership, have tried to have it both ways. In *Empire on Wheels* (1949), they write: "Ficklin's first step toward remedying this situation was to instruct Joseph A. Slade to discharge Old Jules" (p. 46), but in *The Story of the Pony Express* (1955), they credit the decision to Slade: "Having known all the time that Jules' ranch was headquarters for the outlaws and riff-raff of the frontier, and suspecting that Reni [Beni] himself was the leader of the gang, Slade's first act was to discharge him" (p. 105). It seems most likely to me that Slade discharged Jules on Ficklin's orders, if only because the disruptions at Julesburg were perceived to be the company's greatest problem when Ficklin became general superintendent. It seems most logical that Ficklin concluded Jules must go—and, having made that decision, hired Slade to implement it. But Slade, left to his own devices, no doubt would have reached the same conclusion.

2 O'Dell, draft for *An Ear in His Pocket*, p. 84, note 13; O'Dell and Jessen, *An Ear in His Pocket*, p. 23 (refers only to "another man named Thompson"). Thompson was also appointed U.S. postmaster at Julesburg on May 29, 1860; see *Overland News*, March 1958, p. 5. Cunningham, in "Slade: A Hard Case Study," says "Slade replaced Jules with Green M. Thompson as Julesburg postmaster, May 29, 1860," but he too provides no source; see p. 5. In contrast, Monahan, *Destination: Denver City*, p. 81, says that after Jules fled in the spring of 1860, his ranch was bought by George Chrisman, who also became the Julesburg station-master at that time.

3 Whitcomb, "Alfred Slade at Close Range," p. 14.

4 Langford, *Vigilante Days and Ways*, p. 363.

5 Courtwright, *Violent Land*, p. 47.

6 Burton, *City of the Saints*, cited in Chapman, *The Pony Express*, pp. 98-99.

7 Root and Connelley, *The Overland Stage to California*, p. 216.

8 Shumway, *History of Western Nebraska*, p. 56.

9 *Julesburg Grit-Advocate*, Oct. 7, 1926, cited in *Sedgwick County* (Colo.) *History*, 2, pp. 193-194. The article—an interview with Horn by Fred Lockley—apparently appeared originally in the *Pendleton* (Ore.) *Journal*, where Horn lived. The events he described may have occurred sometime after Slade took over the Sweetwater Division. Horn specifically refers to Julesburg "at the time Slade was division superintendent, under Ben Holladay," which could not be earlier than 1861, but of course Horn's chronology could be mistaken. The article, written in 1926, says that Horn "reached his three score and ten more than ten years ago," which would make Horn a teenager when Slade took over the Sweetwater Division in 1859.

10 *Julesburg Grit-Advocate*, Oct. 7, 1926, cited in *Sedgwick County* (Colo.) *History*, p. 193.

11 Chapman, "Jack Slade, Man-Killer."

12 "Jack Slade's Last Bum." Neither the speaker nor the writer who interviewed him is identified.

13 Root and Connelley, *The Overland Stage to California*, pp. 216-217.

14 Callaway, *Two True Tales of the Wild West*, p. 105.

15 Callaway, *Two True Tales of the Wild West*, p. 105. The customarily judicious and scrupulous Callaway cites no sources for these three incidents, nor could I find mention of any specific robberies of Central Overland stagecoaches during this period, in either Denver newspapers or other sources.

16 Shumway, *History of Western Nebraska*, p. 56.

17 Callaway, *Two True Tales of the Wild West*, p. 105.

18 Burton, *City of the Saints*, p. 114. Burton's presumed source was one or more of Slade's stagecoach drivers.

19 Twain, *Roughing It*, chapter 10. Later in the same chapter, Twain, describing his meeting with Slade at Rocky Ridge station on Aug. 2, 1861, says Slade, "in fights and brawls and various ways, had taken the lives of twenty-six human beings." Twain, of course, functioned more as a storyteller than as a historian.

20 Root and Connelley, *The Overland Stage to California*, p. 479. To be sure, Root's account is secondhand: He did not go to work for the Central Overland until 1863, some six months after Slade left.

21 Settle and Settle, *The Story of the Pony Express*, pp. 109–110.

22 Frederick, *Ben Holladay*, p. 177. This evaluation is as of July 1862, when the station was abandoned.

23 These were discovered by Betty Lancaster, who owned the property after 1945. Author's interview with Betty Lancaster, Glendo, Wyo., March 14, 1995.

24 Johnson, "Eight Hundred Miles in an Ambulance," p. 696.

25 Burton, *City of the Saints*, pp. 113–114. The time of arrival is recorded on p. 508.

26 Burton, *City of the Saints*, p. 114.

27 Burton, *City of the Saints*, p. 508 (day-by-day summary of the journey in the appendix).

28 Burton, *City of the Saints*, p. 115. Burton spent the night at Horseshoe station on Aug. 14, 1860. The identity of the other woman in the Slade home is unknown; as Burton describes, she was presumably a passenger taking advantage of the hospitality extended to women while her husband slept in the barn.

29 Settle and Settle, *War Drums and Wagon Wheels*, p. 112; also Settle and Settle, *The Story of the Pony Express*, p. 34. Both books break down the five divisions by boundaries, headquarters, and superintendents, but neither book attributes the source of this information.

30 Dimsdale, *Vigilantes of Montana*, p. 175.

31 Settle and Settle, in *The Story of the Pony Express*, pp. 136–137, suggest that Ficklin was listed as an incorporator because of his success in cleaning up the line. But Russell organized the company on Nov. 23, 1859, less than four weeks after Ficklin took charge. (The corporate charter wasn't technically granted until Feb. 13, 1860.) It's also likely, of course, that Ficklin's role in organizing the Pony Express was a factor. But the Pony Express organization had barely begun at this point. Of the twelve incorporators, only five (Russell, Jones, Majors, Waddell, and Russell's son John) were stockholders; the rest were valued for other past or potential contributions or connections. Jerome B. Simpson, for example, was the New York agent for Russell, Majors & Waddell; Luther R. Smoot was a banker (in partnership with Russell) in Leavenworth; and Webster M. Samuel was Russell's son-in-law as well as a St. Louis broker. For the full act of incorporation, see Root and Hickman, "Part IV—The Platte Route, Concluded," pp. 44–45.

32 "Drove stage which brought first mail into camp of Butte," interview with Charles Higganbotham, *Anaconda Standard*, Butte, Mont., June 20, 1920, section II, p. 1. Jules's penchant for kidnapping other people's horses and returning them for ransom is mentioned in several sources; see, for example, Captain Eugene F. Ware, *The Indian Wars of 1864*; and Montana pioneer George A. Bruffey, *Eighty-One Years in the West*, p. 27, cited in McClernan, *Slade's Wells Fargo Colt*, p. 24. Both Ware and Bruffey passed through Julesburg in the early 1860s but neither had firsthand knowledge of Slade or Jules.

33 Callaway, *Two True Tales of the Wild West*, p. 106. "Jules was at once made to settle with the stage company for the losses that occurred on his watch," wrote the stage driver Frank Root. "He made a vigorous protest, but had to liquidate, knowing there was no escape"; Root and Connelley, *The Overland Stage to California*, p. 217. Root's use of the word "liquidate" suggests that Jules sold all his properties, but clearly this wasn't so, as he continued to operate his trading post and ranch. Most likely Root means Jules had to liquidate some of his property in order to reimburse the company for its losses.

34 Majors, *Seventy Years on the Frontier*, pp. 182–183, 195.

35 Majors, *Seventy Years on the Frontier*, p. 184; Settle and Settle, *War Drums and Wagon Wheels*, p. 111.

36 Settle and Settle, *Empire on Wheels*, p. 74. For Ficklin's involvement in the origins of the Pony Express, see Hafen, *The Overland Mail, 1849–1869*, p. 165, It points out that Gwin, in his memoirs, refers to Ficklin as the man "who originated the scheme [of the Pony Express] and carried it into operation."

37 *Washington Evening Star*, Jan. 30, 1860, cited in Root and Hickman, "Part IV—The Platte Route, Concluded," p. 43.

38 *Leavenworth Daily Times*, Jan. 31, 1860, cited in Root and Hickman, "Part IV—The Platte Route, Concluded," p. 44.

39 Russell to Waddell, June 19, 1860, cited in Settle and Settle, *Empire on Wheels*, p. 76. This book says the charter was granted on February 20, 1860, but its passage is reported in the *Leavenworth Daily Times* of Feb. 13, 1860, and the charter itself indicates it was approved on Feb. 13. See Root and Hickman, "Part IV—The Platte Route, Concluded," p. 45.

40 Settle and Settle, *The Story of the Pony Express*, p. 39.

41 Settle and Settle, *War Drums and Wagon Wheels*, p. 113.

42 Majors, *Seventy Years on the Frontier*, p. 184; Settle and Settle, *Saddles and Spurs*, 40.

43 Settle and Settle, *Empire on Wheels*, p. 78. But the later Settle work, *Story of the Pony Express*, p. 40, says Bradford built stations only between Julesburg and Denver, which were used for stagecoaches but were not on the Pony Express line. Bradford's connection to Russell, Majors & Waddell is discussed in *Empire on Wheels*, p. 50.

44 Settle and Settle, *The Story of the Pony Express*, p. 39.

45 It is not known with certainty how many stations were in place by April 1860, when the Pony Express made its first run. Settle and Settle, *The Story of the Pony Express*, p. 37, state that there were about 119 stations, with a "home" station every 75 to 100 miles, so a rider could rest before returning in the other direction. But the same authors, in *Empire on Wheels*, p. 78, say the Pony Express system had a total of 153 stations. Others say the system ultimately had 190 stations, or an average of one nearly every ten miles. Whichever number is correct, stations were added and subtracted during the lifetime of the operation. See, among others, Moody, *Stagecoach West*, p. 183; Settle and Settle, *Empire on Wheels*, p. 79; and Settle and Settle, *Saddles and Spurs*, p. 41.

46 Settle and Settle, *Empire on Wheels*, p. 78.

47 Settle and Settle, *The Story of the Pony Express*, p. 39.

48 For a good discussion of Pony Express ponies, see "Expressly About Ponies," by Frank C. Robertson, in Howard, *Hoofbeats of Destiny*, pp. 148–150.

49 Root and Hickman, "Pike's Peak Express Companies, Part IV: The Platte Route Concluded," p. 47.

50 Settle and Settle, *The Story of the Pony Express*, p. 39.

51 John Scudder, "The Pony Express," *Lexington* (Mo.) *News*, Aug. 22, 1888; Majors, *Seventy Years on the Frontier*, p. 106; both cited in Settle and Settle, *Empire on Wheels*, p. 75, and Settle and Settle, *The Story of the Pony Express*, p. 27.

52 Root and Connelley, *The Overland Stage to California*, pp. 106–108.

53 Chapman, *The Pony Express*, pp. 227–228. Campbell, who was ninety-four when Chapman interviewed him in 1932, said he first rode in December 1860 between Fort Kearny and Cottonwood Springs, by which time the telegraph extended to Fort Kearny. (The Settles, in *The Story of the Pony Express*, p. 68, err when they say Campbell was ninety when he died in 1932.)

54 Majors, *Seventy Years on the Frontier*, pp. 184–185, 187. Howard, *Hoofbeats of Destiny*, pp. 62–63, says between eighty and a hundred riders were hired.

55 Settle and Settle, *Story of the Pony Express*, p. 39.

56 Settle and Settle, *Story of the Pony Express*, p. 37.

57 Settle and Settle, *Story of the Pony Express*, pp. 65–66. Mud Springs station was probably located about 12 miles southeast of the current site of Bridgeport, Neb.

58 Settle and Settle, *The Story of the Pony Express*, pp. 37–38; also p. 45. By contrast, young Mormons from Utah comprised the majority of riders and station keepers west of Horseshoe Creek and well beyond Salt Lake City.

59 Settle and Settle, *War Drums and Wagon Wheels*, p. 112; Settle and Settle, *Empire on Wheels*, p. 77; Settle and Settle, *Saddles and Spurs*, pp. 36–37. For a copy of the contract, see "Contract between Citizens of St. Joseph and the Central Overland California & Pike's Peak Express Company, March 2, 1860," Folder 1, *Central Overland Contract, 1860 Collection* (No. 1869), Western Historical Manuscript Collection, University of Missouri, Columbia.

60 Hafen, *The Overland Mail, 1849–1869*, p. 170.

61 *New York Daily Tribune*, March 23, 1860, cited in Root and Hickman, "Pike's Peak Express Companies, Part IV: The Platte Route Concluded," pp. 48–49.

62 Settle and Settle, *The Story of the Pony Express*, p. 35.

63 James Boner, interview in "He Nursed Jim Slade." Dimsdale, *Vigilantes of Montana*. Root and Connelley, *The Overland Stage to California*, p. 479.

64 Wilson, "Reminiscences of Overland Days," p. 5.

65 In a 1902 interview, Henry Gilbert, who operated Gilbert's station at South Pass on the Hockaday stage line and later hired Slade to move his goods to Virginia City, Mont., claimed to have personally witnessed this incident. See "Echoes in Alder Gulch," *Kansas City Star*, May 27, 1906 (published nearly four years after the interview, and four years after Gilbert's death). Gilbert's recitation is so self-serving, contradictory and full of errors that I would dismiss it out of hand, were it not for the fact that Burton's account of August 1860 more or less corroborates Gilbert: Burton, like Gilbert, says Jules shot Slade "after a quarrel which took place at dinner." See Burton, *City of the Saints*, p. 114.

66 Dimsdale, *Vigilantes of Montana*, p. 174. Root and Connelley, *The Overland Stage to California*, p. 479. See also Muir, "The Man Who Was Hanged for a Song," p. 45.

67 J. K. Ellis, memoir, typescript by Jesse Brown, ms. 12C, Wyoming State Historical Library.

68 Boner, interview in "He Nursed Jim Slade." Dimsdale, in *Vigilantes of Montana* (1866), p. 174, says Slade arrived at Julesburg as a stagecoach passenger; that Jules tried to recover the stage team then and there; that a quarrel ensued and Jules, finding Slade unarmed, "fired his gun, loaded with buckshot."

69 Bryan is identified by Jim Boner in "He Nursed Jim Slade," and by Ellis, memoir. Ellis spells Bryan's name "O'Brien," perhaps because Ellis dictated his account. Two secondary sources also identify Bryan, although without attribution: Callaway, *Two True Tales of the Wild West*, p. 106, and O'Dell and Jessen, *An Ear in His Pocket*, p. 50. Ellis's is the only account to identify Shurry or, for that matter, Ellis himself as having been present.

70 Clampitt, *Echoes from the Rocky Mountains*, pp. 503–504.

71 Whitcomb, "Alfred Slade at Close Range," p. 14.

72 Clampitt, *Echoes from the Rocky Mountains*, pp. 503–504.

73 Accounts differ as to how many times Slade was shot by Jules. Boner says Jules "put all six balls" from his pistol into Slade, then emptied both barrels of a double-barreled shotgun; see "He Nursed Jim Slade." Coutant, *History of Wyoming*, p. 403, says Slade was shot thirteen times in all; Emerson Hough, *Story of the Outlaw*, pp. 147–149, says Slade was left lying with "13 bullets and buckshot." Langford, in *Vigilante Days and Ways*, p. 363, says Jules fired five shots from his pistol and that Slade ultimately had "bullets and buckshot to the number of 13 lodged in his person." The rider J. K. Ellis says Jules shot Slade only three times, but Ellis was presumably already on his way to fetch the surgeon at Fort Laramie when the wounds were counted; see Ellis, memoir. The generally reliable John W. Clampitt, a federal attorney in the Western territories, also said Jules fired only three shots from his revolver; see Clampitt, *Echoes from the Rocky Mountains*, pp. 503–504. It's safe to conclude that Jules emptied his revolver of however many balls it contained at that moment; this supports the conclusion that Jules did not plan the shooting in advance but acted spontaneously when he saw Slade was unarmed.

74 Boner, interview in "He Nursed Jim Slade."

75 Whitcomb, "Alfred Slade at Close Range," p. 14. Langford quotes Jules slightly differently: "When he is dead, you can put him in one of these dry-goods boxes and bury him"; see *Vigilante Days and Ways*, p. 363. Langford as well as others after him have added: "Slade rose in his bunk, and glaring out upon Jules, who was standing in front of the station, exclaimed with an oath, 'I shall live long enough to wear one of your ears on my watch-guard. You needn't trouble yourself about my burial'." This melodramatic morsel—apparently first published 29 years later in Clampitt, *Echoes from the Rocky Mountains*, pp. 503–504—enhances the drama of the story, since it foretells what actually came to pass. But it isn't mentioned in the accounts of Ellis or Boner, and it strikes me as too convenient to be credible.

76 Ellis, memoir.

77 Ellis, memoir. The identity of the rider is rarely mentioned. Ellis has claimed the honor for himself, and in the absence of other claimants I accept his version.

78 Langford, *Vigilante Days and Ways*, p. 363. After Ellis, the Pony Express rider who was inside the Julesburg station at the time and was dispatched to ride to Fort Laramie for a surgeon, the next closest person to the events was James Boner, who hosted Slade the night before and also nursed Slade for two weeks after the shooting; see "He Nursed Jim Slade." My account is pieced together from these and other accounts by people most likely to have spoken to witnesses (such as Langford and Frank Root). These are generally consistent with an early published account of the shooting, by Richard Burton, who spent a night at Slade's Horseshoe headquarters in August 1860, some four and half months after the shooting; see

Burton, *City of the Saints,* pp. 114–115. Burton's account of the shooting was most likely obtained from stage drivers or station keepers in the course of his journey. Decades after the shooting Jules's widow, Adeline Cayou (later Beckstead), told interviewers that Slade stopped at Julesburg and ordered drinks for him and his companions, "bent on picking a quarrel with Jules. . . . In due time, Slade drew his pistols, but Jules was quicker with his shotgun and wounded Slade seriously." In Adeline's account, when Slade fell, Jules "told him he would take him to Denver and pay all his doctor bills and expenses if he would shake hands. Slade agreed, and Jules hitched up a team and hauled him clear to Denver." See MacMurphy, "Some Squatters with a History," p. 5; also MacMurphy, "The Heroine of the Jules-Slade Tragedy," in *Nebraska Pioneer Reminiscences,* p. 324. But Adeline was not in Julesburg at the time of the shooting; she may not even yet have been married to Jules; she was only thirteen when she married him; and her stories are rife with contradictions. It seems likely that her source was Jules himself and, later, his friends, all of whom were eager not to upset a very young widow. Adeline's suggestion that Jules was quicker with his gun than Slade is especially ludicrous; Slade's reputation as a gunman was precisely the reason Jules avoided a confrontation with him until the day he observed that Slade was unarmed.

79 "Summary of News," *Constitution,* Washington, D.C., March 27, 1860.

CHAPTER 12

1 The origins of this quote and when it was uttered are obscure. In some versions it is: "If you strike at a king you must kill him." In one version, Emerson said it to Thoreau, quoting the Buddha; Thoreau died in 1862, so the quote presumably precedes that date. Another perhaps more scrupulous source—H. Drinker, Legal *Ethics* (1953), p. 60—claims Emerson said it to Oliver Wendell Holmes when Holmes was a student; Holmes got his law degree in 1866.

2 See note 73 in Chapter 11.

3 Callaway, *Two True Tales of the Wild West,* p. 107, discussing why Jules's guns failed to kill Slade, speculated, "Jules' powder must have been weak." Similarly, *Overland News,* March 1958, p. 5: "Perhaps Jules's powder was old."

4 The *faux* hanging of Jules by Ficklin and his men is described more or less identically in Clampitt, *Echoes from the Rocky Mountains,* pp. 503–504; Langford, *Vigilante Days and Ways,* pp. 363–364; and Coutant, *History of Wyoming,* pp. 402–403. All three say Ficklin arrived shortly after the shooting; Langford knew Slade personally. Clampitt says Ficklin arrived after Jules was strung up and ordered him cut down. Frank Root, who joined the Central Overland as a driver some three years after this incident, wrote that "The next stage that passed over the road had Ficklin aboard and his first duty was to hang Jules, after which he drove on. Jules, however, was not ready to die just yet. Before he had quite ceased to breathe, someone came along and cut the rope." See Root and Connelley, *The Overland Stage to California,* p. 217. The earliest account of the "hanging," albeit by an anonymous traveler who was only passing through, is "Interesting from Kansas: Our Denver City Correspondence, April 10, 1860," in *New York Herald,* May 3, 1860. It makes no reference to Ficklin, noting only that "the few whites at the station, adopting the code of Judge Lynch, hung the Frenchman." The next account, by Burton—presumably recording conversations with Central Overland stage drivers in August 1860—is silent as to the timing of the hanging but says of Jules: "Twice he was hung between wagons, and as often he was cut down. At last he disappeared in the farther West." See *City of the Saints,* p. 115. Roy O'Dell, in his original draft for *An Ear in His Pocket,*

says Ficklin's passing through Julesburg is plausible: During January–March 1860, Ficklin made several business trips to Denver; he was also in St. Joseph, Missouri in late March and early April, presumably preparing for the opening run of the Pony Express. See note 19, page 84. Other versions suggest, less plausibly, that Ficklin was summoned and arrived some time after the shooting. Mrs. C. F. Parker says, "Ficklin was on the telegraph line and got the news. The next stage brought him to the scene to hang Jules, which he promptly did. Fortunately, or unfortunately, for Jules, someone came along and cut the rope before he had quite passed out." But the telegraph line didn't reach Julesburg until more than a year later, on May 24, 1861. See "Old Julesburg and Fort Sedgwick," p. 140.

5 "Interesting from Kansas: Our Denver City Correspondence, April 10, 1860," in *New York Herald,* May 3, 1860.

6 Johns's identity as the surgeon who tended Slade is deduced from Fort Laramie records, which show him as the post's acting assistant surgeon there from April 1858 to August 1860; author's interview with Baird Todd, museum specialist at Fort Laramie, April 9, 2008. A second acting assistant surgeon—Samuel Wilie Crawford—was also assigned to Fort Laramie at this time but seems a less likely candidate: Crawford left the post on a seven-day leave on February 28, 1860, and there is no record of when he returned; moreover, he was transferred to New York City on March 29, 1860. It seems highly unlikely that a surgeon in the process of being transferred back East would have been dispatched to Julesburg at such a time. Officially, both Johns and Crawford held the rank of "acting assistant surgeon."

7 Robert J. T. Joy, M.D., emeritus professor at the Uniformed Services University of the Health Sciences, letter to author, Aug. 29, 2007.

8 This experience proved especially useful to Johns. In 1861 he left the U.S. Army to become a surgeon in the Confederate army. As chief medical purveyor for Richmond during the Union blockade, he was charged with developing indigenous supplies with which to make medicines in army laboratories. He died in 1892. Author's interview with Baird Todd, museum specialist, Fort Laramie, April 9, 2008.

9 For these insights and the identification of Surgeon Johns I am grateful to Baird Todd, museum specialist at Fort Laramie, interview, April 9, 2008.

10 Brown Jesse, reminiscences of J.K. Ellis extracted from *San Francisco Examiner* (undated). Manuscript #122C, Wyoming State Historical Library, Cheyenne.

11 "He Nursed Jim Slade," *Alder Gulch* (Mont.) *Times,* Sept. 22, 1899.

12 This is presumed from Slade's subsequent need for further surgery, which wasn't completely successful either. In *An Ear in His Pocket,* p. 51, O'Dell and Jessen say the Fort Laramie surgeon removed "half a handful of lead" but cite no source.

13 "Interesting from Kansas." The article describes the shooting as having occurred "a few weeks previous."

14 "He Nursed Jim Slade."

15 Boner, in "He Nursed Jim Slade," says "After Slade was moved up to Horseshoe, Phil and I went back to Lodge Pole."

16 *St. Joseph Weekly West,* April 7, 1860, cited in Root and Hickman, "Part IV—The Platte Route Concluded," pp. 51–52.

17 See Settle and Settle, *Story of the Pony Express,* pp. 46–50; also Settle and Settle, *Empire on Wheels,* p. 81.

18 The reference to Buchanan's message is from Root and Connelley, *The Overland Stage to California*, p. 112.

19 Settle and Settle, *Story of the Pony Express*, p. 49.

20 Settle and Settle, *Story of the Pony Express*, p. 49.

21 Settle and Settle, *Empire on Wheels*, p. 83.

22 Settle and Settle, *Story of the Pony Express*, pp. 56–58.

23 Settle and Settle, *Story of the Pony Express*, pp. 54–55. For a description of the *mochila*, see Hafen, *The Overland Mail*, p. 180.

24 Burton, *City of the Saints*, p. 115. For a discussion of the shortage of men in Indian communities, see Courtwright, *Violent Land*, pp. 63–65.

25 Some accounts say Jules fled to Denver after shooting Slade, others say he went to the Rocky Ridge country. I surmise that he went first to live among Indians, then to Denver and later to Rocky Ridge, but this sequence is by no means certain. Sterling (Colo.) paper, about 1943, by C. M. Rolfson (at Fort Sedgwick Historical Society), says Jules "was down in Denver, 175 miles away." The subsequent Central Overland driver Frank Root said, "Jules packed his things on the backs of two mules and pushed west to the Rockies, where he could recuperate, and once more return and meet his deadly enemy," but Root leaves unclear whether by "the Rockies" he means the Pike's Peak–Denver region or the Rocky Ridge region far to the north; see Root and Connelley, *The Overland Stage to California*, pp. 479–480. Clampitt, in *Echoes from the Rocky Mountains* (1889), pp. 503–504, says Jules "quickly departed for Denver" after shooting Slade. Slade's subsequent employee James Wilson said, "Jules went down the Platte river [presumably the South Platte, toward Denver], and remained until the excitement had blown over"; see Wilson, "Reminiscences of Overland Days," p. 5. But these accounts all conflict with Burton's report as of August 1860.

26 I pieced together the credible parts of Adeline Cayou Beckstead's often contradictory story from several publications, most based on one or two interviews by Harriet S. MacMurphy. These include, in chronological order: MacMurphy, "Some Squatters with a History," pp. 4–6; Morton, *Illustrated History of Nebraska*, Vol. II, pp. 180–181; MacMurphy, "Heroine of Jules-Slade Tragedy," in *Nebraska Pioneer Reminiscences*, pp. 322–325; and MacMurphy, "Death of Bellevue Woman Removes Last Figure in Jules-Slade Tragedy," unnamed Bellevue (Neb.) newspaper, late July 1921. Adeline Beckstead died July 22, 1921, according to the *Bellevue* (Neb.) *Press,* Sept. 1, 1961; see O'Dell and Jessen, *An Ear in His Pocket*, p. 57.

27 MacMurphy, "Heroine of Jules-Slade Tragedy," in *Nebraska Pioneer Reminiscences*, p. 324.

28 MacMurphy, "Some Squatters with a History," p. 5.

29 MacMurphy, "Death of Bellevue Woman Removes Last Figure in Jules-Slade Tragedy."

30 As Adeline Cayou Beckstead was quoted in 1916, "Jules had had some trouble with a man named Slade a few years before and had shot Slade, but had taken him to Denver and put him in a hospital and paid to have him cared for and Slade and he had made it all up, my husband thought." She described Slade not as a stagecoach superintendent but as a rancher whose property had been adjacent to Jules's. She was clearly not in command of the facts, but her recollection does establish that she met and married Jules after Jules shot Slade. See MacMurphy, "Heroine of Jules-Slade Tragedy," p. 324.

31 MacMurphy, "Heroine of Jules-Slade Tragedy," p. 324.

32 MacMurphy, "Heroine of Jules-Slade Tragedy," pp. 322–325. *Illustrated History of Nebraska*, p. 181, says Jules married Adeline after shooting Slade (that is, after spring 1860). Other accounts say her parents brought her to Jules's trading post, presumably before the spring of 1860. Other sources say Adeline was betrothed to Jules at age thirteen, after which her parents took her to a place outside Denver.

33 The very young (and not very credible) William F. Cody said that when the Pony Express was "just being started . . . at Julesburg I met Mr. George Chrisman, the leading wagonmaster of Russell, Majors and Waddell, who had always been a good friend to me. He had bought out 'Old Jules,' and was then the owner of Julesburg Ranch, and the agent of the Pony Express line." See Visscher, *The Pony Express*, p. 44. Settle and Settle, *The Story of the Pony Express*, p. 95, also refers to Chrisman as the station keeper at Julesburg, but no dates are given. Slade's subsequent employee James Wilson said, "Jules had about $10,000 worth of stock near Horseshoe, the headquarters of Slade's division." See "Reminiscences of Overland Days," p. 5. More likely Jules's stock was mostly closer to Julesburg.

34 Moore, *Early History of Leavenworth City and County*, p. 223, says Leavenworth became the western terminus of the telegraph on Jan. 1, 1859.

35 Settle and Settle, *Story of the Pony Express*, p. 60.

36 Majors later remarked that "As anticipated, the amount of business transacted over this line was not sufficient to pay one-tenth of its expenses, to say nothing of the capital invested." See Root and Hickman, "Part IV—The Platte Route Concluded," p. 70. Clampitt, *Echoes from the Rocky Mountains*, p. 47, and Root and Hickman, p. 49, say letters were initially carried for $5. The fee on letters was reduced in July 1860 (Root and Hickman, p. 75).

37 Settle and Settle, *War Drums and Wagon Wheels*, p. 115.

38 Settle and Settle, *War Drums and Wagon Wheels*, p. 116.

39 Settle and Settle, *War Drums and Wagon Wheels*, p. 126.

40 Settle and Settle, *Empire on Wheels*, p. 91.

41 Callaway, *Two True Tales of the Wild West*, p. 107. This is the only attempt I've found to explain why Slade's division didn't lapse back into lawlessness during his recovery.

42 Root and Connelley, *The Overland Stage to California*, p. 480. Root was not in the area at the time; he joined the Central Overland as a driver in 1863, so his account is secondhand and perhaps inclined to hyperbole. But his sources presumably were his fellow Central Overland drivers who were indeed firsthand witnesses. I should note that this paragraph bears a striking similarity to a paragraph in Mark Twain's *Roughing It* (1872). Presumably Root, having read *Roughing It*, borrowed Twain's words as a more articulate description.

43 Upon Slade's recovery, probably in June 1860, Ficklin shifted Slade's division to the west; Callaway, for example, says, "As soon as he thought Slade fit Ficklin made him division-agent of Rocky Ridge. There is some indication that Slade also retained his sway over the Sweetwater"; see *Two True Tales of the Wild West*, p. 107. I speculate that the idea first occurred to Ficklin in April, when the Pony Express was just launched and Slade was recently invalided. Ficklin, in a feud with Russell, submitted his resignation on June 7, 1860; and by July 1, 1860, he was gone from the Central Overland. Given Ficklin's preoccupation with his feud with Russell at the time of Slade's return, it seems likely to me that Ficklin formulated the

idea to move Slade's division westward past Rocky Ridge in April. The exact western limit of Slade's division seems to have varied thereafter. Wilson, Slade's telegraph operator at Horseshoe from the fall of 1861, said Pacific Springs was the west end of Slade's division; see "Reminiscences of Overland Days," p. 5. Other accounts also identify him as performing company tasks at Pacific Springs in 1861. An anonymous letter to the *Missouri Democrat* in October 1861—not the most reliable source, to be sure—identifies Slade as "a division agent having charge of the entire route from the crossing of the South Platte [that is, Julesburg] to the Pacific Springs"; see "Paul Jones," letter to *Missouri Democrat*, Oct. 22, 1861, cited in Root and Hickman, "Part IV—The Platte Route, Concluded,"p. 80. An editorial in the Salt Lake *Deseret News*, July 16, 1862, citing an earlier article in the *Silver Age* of Carson City, Nevada Terr., discussing Slade's activities over the previous year, calls Slade "the terror of all the settlers between Pacific Springs and Julesburg." Clearly, Slade was active at the Pacific Springs end of the division: For example, he was said to be at Pacific Springs when he learned of Jules Beni's return in August of 1861; and the murder of Dr. Bartholomew in August 1861, which Slade avenged, took place around Split Rock, about 165 miles west of Horseshoe. On the other hand, in an affidavit given in June 1862, Slade said his division extended only from Julesburg to "Sweetwater Bridge, near the Devil's Gate" (that is, east of Split Rock), a distance of only 346 miles (and extending only about 100 miles west of Horseshoe, not even to the Rocky Ridge area that Slade was instructed to clean up in mid-1860); see *Claim of Benjamin Holladay,* p. 5. (By my calculation, the distance from Julesburg to Sweetwater Bridge was about 390 miles, not 346 as Slade testified.) I surmise that Slade's division extended to Pacific Springs in June 1860 but was shortened to Sweetwater Bridge sometime prior to June 1862. Lemuel Flowers, agent for the adjoining decision to the west, testified in November 1865 that he succeeded William A. Reid as agent for the division between Pacific Springs and Sweetwater Bridge on April 15, 1862; see *Claim of Benjamin Holladay*, pp. 3–4. This would have been a relatively short division (less than 150 miles) and I surmise that it must have been carved out of Slade's much longer division created in the summer of 1860.

44 In 1860 there was only one surgeon at Jefferson Barracks; e-mail message to author from Marc Kollbaum, Jefferson Barracks historian, March 5, 2008.

45 Langford, *Vigilante Days and Ways*, p. 363: "Slade lingered for several weeks at the [unidentified] station, and finally went to St. Louis for treatment." Coutant, *History of Wyoming*, p. 403: "Slade suffered from his wounds for several weeks and finally made a journey to St. Louis to procure surgical assistance." Clampitt's 1889 account, on the other hand, makes no mention of St. Louis or surgery there but comes close: "In a few weeks [after the shooting] he was enabled to be removed to his old home at Carlisle [sic], Illinois, where he rapidly recovered." See *Echoes from the Rocky Mountains*, p. 504. These accounts don't specifically mention Ficklin as the instigator of this journey, but Callaway does: "It is said, how credibly the writer does not avouch, that as soon as he was able to be transported Ficklin had him sent to St. Louis for treatment. . . . As soon as he thought Slade fit Ficklin made him division-agent of Rocky Ridge." See Callaway, *Two True Tales of the Wild West*, p. 107. Conversely, Ducomb says Slade's journey to St. Louis was instigated by his wife, who "stressed the necessity for surgical aid and suggested that he would be near his family [in Carlyle] once again." Ducomb also says Slade's sister Virginia joined him in St. Louis and returned with him to the western plains after a recuperation of "a month or six weeks"; see Ducomb, "A Silent Drum Beside the Okaw," p. 6. Ducomb was an amateur historian with Carlyle roots who worked in

the Clinton County title office; like several other writers who investigated Slade, he appears to have unearthed some useful findings and used his imagination to fill out his story without distinguishing between the fact and invention. He cites no sources for these assertions, and there is no evidence that Slade's sister went West at this time (although she did travel to Wyoming in the 1880s for a brief and disastrous marriage). But Ducomb's suggested timing for Slade's recuperation (a month to six weeks in Carlyle) is consistent with Slade's return to the West by June. Also, the desire to recuperate with Slade's family in Carlyle may explain why Slade was sent to St. Louis for surgery rather than Fort Leavenworth, which in 1860 had a forty-bed military hospital and was about 250 miles closer to Horseshoe than St. Louis was; see e-mail message of Aug. 2, 2007 to the author from Dr. Herschel L. Stroud of the Society of Civil War Surgeons. I surmise from these conflicting strands that the impetus for Slade's journey to St. Louis probably came both from Ficklin and from Slade's relatives.

46 Ficklin's riding the stage is speculation on my part, based on the fact that Ficklin himself journeyed eastward about this time to meet Russell in Washington. The Settles, in *Empire on Wheels* (1949), say, "Ficklin appeared in Washington about the middle of May"; see p. 86. In *The Story of the Pony Express*, the Settles place Ficklin in Washington "some five weeks after the start" of the Pony Express, which would be May 7. These dates would be consistent with Slade's arrival in St. Louis in early May.

47 Langford, *Vigilante Days and Ways* (1890), p. 363, says Slade had eight bullets remaining in his body when he returned from St. Louis. Coutant, *History of Wyoming*, (1899), p. 403: "Seven [of the 13] buckshot were cut out and the balance remained in his person to remind him of vengeance." The St. Louis surgeon who operated on Slade has never been identified, but if Ficklin was willing to send Slade 1,000 miles for surgery, I presume he must have had a specific and highly regarded surgeon in mind. Two likely candidates are the two most prominent surgeons then in St. Louis: Charles Alexander Pope (1818-1870), dean and professor of surgery at St. Louis Medical College, and Joseph Nash McDowell, dean of Missouri Medical College. E-mail message to author from Paul Anderson, associate professor and archivist, Becker Memorial Library, Washington U. Medical School, St. Louis, Feb. 22, 2008.

48 See e-mail message to the author from Dr. Herschel L. Stroud of the Society of Civil War Surgeons, of Aug. 1, 2007.

49 Ducomb, "A Silent Drum Beside the Okaw," p. 6, says Slade recuperated for a month to six weeks before returning west, but cites no source. This timing is consistent with Slade's presumed return to the Central Overland in June 1860. If indeed Slade was wanted for a murder committed in southern Illinois three or four years earlier, as his enemies later claimed, this visit to Carlyle was the sheriff's opportunity to arrest him. But no such arrest took place.

50 "Speech of Hon. Ben. Bond," Feb. 21, 1863, *Carlyle Weekly Reveille,* March 26, 1863, p. 1. The speech refers to, quotes and paraphrases another speech that Bond made in Carlyle, before the war, apparently in 1860. Thomas Bond's obituary, *Carlyle Constitution and Union,* Sept. 30, 1875, in pp. 227-228 of Carlyle newspaper excerpts at Clinton County Historical Society, describes him as "Nephew of Shadrach Bond, first governor of Illinois after it became a state."

51 Even if no vital organs or blood vessels had been hit, "the potential of severe systemic infection seems a certainty," said Dr. Herschel L. Stroud of the Society of Civil War Surgeons.

52 The contract amount appears in U.S. Senate, Executive documents, 36th Congress, 2nd session, III, part 3, no. 1, 436. Cited in Frederick, *Ben Holladay*, pp. 62–63.

53 Settle and Settle, *Empire on Wheels*, pp. 83–84.

54 Settle and Settle, *War Drums and Wagon Wheels*, p. 117.

55 Settle and Settle, *Empire on Wheels*, pp. 86–87; Settle and Settle, *War Drums and Wagon Wheels*, p. 117.

56 Russell to Waddell, June 13, 1860, cited in Settle and Settle, *Empire on Wheels*, p. 87.

57 Settle and Settle, *Empire on Wheels*, p. 87, says only that Waddell wrote a letter on June 11 that "was like salt in the wound." But a subsequent letter from Russell to Waddell refers more specifically to Waddell's comments; see p. 89.

58 Russell to Waddell, cited in Settle and Settle, *Empire on Wheels*, pp. 87–88.

59 Settle and Settle, *Empire on Wheels*, p. 118.

60 The Pacific Telegraph Act became law on June 16, 1860. See Thompson, *Wiring a Continent*, p. 354. There is some reason to believe that Ficklin enticed Alexander Majors into this venture as well—surely an indication that Majors didn't share Russell's low opinion of Ficklin. See Settle and Settle, *War Drums and Wagon Wheels*, p. 247; Settle and Settle, *The Story of the Pony Express*, p. 137. Howard, in *Hoofbeats of Destiny*, p. 129, mentioned Majors as a possible partner with Ficklin in his telegraph venture. Nor was Ficklin's departure from the Central Overland quite the disaster that Majors and Waddell anticipated. Ficklin's less flamboyant successor, J. H. Clute, proved a highly efficient replacement; see Root and Hickman, "Part IV—The Platte Route, Concluded," note 458. (Clute was one of the five men, including Ficklin and Slade, who had bought two hundred horses for the Pony Express in Salt Lake City earlier that year; see Settle and Settle, *Empire on Wheels,* p. 75.)

61 Settle and Settle, *Empire on Wheels*, pp. 91–92.

62 Howard, *Hoofbeats of Destiny*, p. 108.

63 Howard, *Hoofbeats of Destiny*, p. 110.

64 Howard, *Hoofbeats of Destiny*, p. 117.

65 Howard, *Hoofbeats of Destiny*, p. 115.

66 Chapman, *The Pony Express*, p. 159.

67 Precisely when Slade returned to work is unrecorded. My estimate of early or mid-June 1860 is an educated guess based on a few other known dates. Slade obviously was back at work well before Aug. 14, 1860, when Burton found him at Horseshoe; see *City of the Saints*, pp. 114–115. Ficklin was said to have changed Slade's jurisdiction upon Slade's return; yet Ficklin submitted his resignation on June 6 and was gone from the Central Overland by July 1. One source says Slade appointed Green M. Thompson as postmaster at Julesburg on May 29, 1860, which suggests that Slade was back by that date; see "Slade Is No More," p. 5. But this article cites no source and is ambiguous as to who appointed Thompson on May 29: It says, "One of Slade's first acts as division agents [in the fall of 1859] was to relieve Jules…as station agent at Julesburg and replace him with a man by the name of Green M. Thompson, who was appointed postmaster May 29, 1860."

68 Root and Hickman, "Part IV—The Platte Route, Concluded," pp. 58–60.

69 Root and Hickman, "Part IV—The Platte Route, Concluded," p. 74.

70 Langford, *Vigilante Days and Ways*, p. 364.

71 Burton, *City of the Saints*, p. 114. Burton appropriated this line from a poem about rustic American legislators by the Scottish humorist William Edmonstoune Aytoun, which appeared in *Putnam's Magazine of American Literature*, February 1855.

72 Burton, *City of the Saints*, pp. 114–115.

73 Langford, *Vigilante Days and Ways*, p. 364. Also see Clampitt, *Echoes from the Rocky Mountains*, pp. 504–505: "When Slade recovered from his severe wounds and returned again to his field of labor he was disposed to avoid his assailant and went so far as to send word to Jules that he would never 'hurt' him, but warned him at the same time never to come into his immediate neighborhood. . . . Jules was in Denver." Coutant, *History of Wyoming*, p. 403: "When he returned to the road he took occasion to send word to his antagonist that he was determined to kill him on sight, but he would not go out of his way to meet him." C. M. Rolfson, Sterling (Colo.) paper, about 1943 (at a Julesburg museum): "Slade recovered and sent word to Jules that he would not hurt him unless Jules came into his neighborhood. (Jules was down in Denver, 175 miles away.)"

74 Root and Connelley, *The Overland Stage to California*, p. 480.

75 Root and Connelley, *The Overland Stage to California*, pp. 480–481.

76 *Sir Richard F. Burton at Salt Lake City*, privately printed for Richard Walden Hale, Boston, 1932; cited in Chapman, *The Pony Express*, p. 192.

77 Settle and Settle, *War Drums and Wagon Wheels*, p. 131.

78 Settle and Settle, *War Drums and Wagon Wheels*, p. 151.

79 The best discussion of the Indian Trust scandal can be found in Settle and Settle, *War Drums and Wagon Wheels*, pp. 131–152.

80 Howard, *Hoofbeats of Destiny*, p. 120, says bankruptcy proceedings began in October 1860. Strangely, the definitive works by the Settles on Russell, Majors & Waddell—*Empire on Wheels* (1949) and *War Drums and Wagon Wheels* (1966)—allude in passing to the firm's bankruptcy but never indicate when such proceedings began or when the firm ceased operations.

81 Root and Connelley, *The Overland Stage to California*, p. 584; also Hafen, *The Overland Mail*, p. 161. Some Pony Express riders, such as Calvin Downs and the legendary "Pony Bob" Haslam, later accused Slade of holding up their pay and keeping their money for himself. The writer Arthur Chapman, who interviewed numerous former riders and Central Overland officials for his book about the Pony Express, noted that "This is the only claim I have ever heard, reflecting on Slade's honesty, which seemed to be more than hearsay. On the contrary, I have had the assurances of Overland officials that no division was better run than Slade's." See Chapman, *The Pony Express*, pp. 196–197.

82 Settle and Settle, *The Story of the Pony Express*, p. 147.

83 Howard, *Hoofbeats of Destiny*, pp. 129, 133.

84 Root and Hickman, "Part IV—The Platte Route, Concluded," p. 61. Also see Settle and Settle, *The Story of the Pony Express*, p. 163.

85 *Leavenworth Times*, Nov. 1, 1860, cited in Root and Hickman, "Part IV—The Platte Route, Concluded," p. 62.

86 Root and Hickman, "Part IV—The Platte Route, Concluded," p. 61.

87 Brands, *The Age of Gold*, p. 397.

88 In a field of four candidates, Lincoln won 180 electoral votes out of 303 but won only 39.8 percent of the popular vote. Douglas, the runner-up in the popular vote with 29.5 percent, carried just one state and received only 12 electoral votes. The Southern Democrat candidate, John C. Breckinridge of Kentucky, won 18.1 percent of the popular vote and carried 11 states with 72 electoral votes. John C. Bell of the Constitutional Union Party won 12.6 percent of the popular vote and three states with 39 electoral votes.

89 The only exception was Fort Pickens in Pensacola Harbor, Florida.

90 Root and Hickman, "Part IV—The Platte Route, Concluded," p. 763, also note 403.

91 Howard, *Hoofbeats of Destiny*, pp. 125–127.

92 *Rocky Mountain News*, Dec. 19, 1860, cited in Hafen, *The Overland Mail*, pp. 161–162.

93 Settle and Settle, *War Drums and Wagon Wheels*, p. 148; Howard, *Hoofbeats of Destiny*, p. 118.

94 Howard, *Hoofbeats of Destiny*, p. 119.

95 Settle and Settle, *Empire on Wheels*, p. 115.

96 Technically, Ben Holladay didn't buy the Central Overland until an auction in March 1862. Many historians have mistakenly assumed that he did not take charge until then. But under the Postal Appropriation Bill, effective March 2, 1861, Holladay was to operate the stages and the Pony Express east of Salt Lake City (the Butterfield and Wells Fargo interests controlled the line west of Salt Lake); see Chapman, *The Pony Express*, p. 268. Holladay's own petition to Congress for reimbursement of his losses as a mail contractor, dated March 6, 1872, describes himself as "contractor for the transportation of the United States mails on what has heretofore been known as the Overland Mail-Route, between the Missouri River and Salt Lake City" from "the year A.D. 1860, until the 13th day of November 1866"; see "Claim of Ben Holladay," U.S. Senate, 46th Congress, 2nd session, Misc. Doc. 19, Dec. 17, 1879, p. 1. Other anecdotal evidence supports the notion that Holladay was effectively running the Central Overland through most of 1861. For example, Hiram Kelly said he was employed in the fall of 1861 by Ben Holladay of the Overland Stage line, and "his boss Alf Slade put him in charge of the bull teams, placed at various stations for hauling hay and wood"; see Hiram B. Kelly, recollections in letter of March 22, 1915, cited in Trenholm, *Footprints on the Frontier*, p. 247.

97 Settle and Settle, *War Drums and Wagon Wheels*, p. 165. Root and Hickman add: "Hughes was a cousin of Benjamin Holladay and his presidency apparently inaugurated a transitional period in the history of the company, in which Holladay's large loans made him virtually a silent partner"; see "Part IV—The Platte Route, Concluded," p. 37.

98 In testimony years later Hughes described himself in 1861 not as the Central Overland's president but as Holladay's attorney and "general agent for the Overland Stage Line." See Hughes testimony in "Claim of Ben Holliday," Dec. 17, 1879, p. 87. Further evidence that Hughes was not really in charge was provided in 1892 when Hughes, in a letter, said he was unaware that the Central Overland was so heavily in debt when he became its president. See Hughes to John M. Doniphan, May 2, 1892, cited in Hafen, *The Overland Mail*, p. 227.

99 Settle and Settle, *Story of the Pony Express*, p. 147.

100 Root and Hickman, "Part IV—The Platte Route, Concluded," p. 65.

101 Chapman, *The Pony Express*, pp. 267, 268, 287.

102 Chapman, *The Pony Express*, pp. 220-223.

103 Henry Gilbert, who ran the Central Overland station and trading post just west of South Pass, recalled that "Jules used to brag to me that Slade was bluffed and would give him no more trouble." See "Echoes of Alder Gulch." To be sure, Gilbert is not a terribly reliable source—his interview several times implies his foreknowledge of events that subsequently came to pass—and the interview (conducted in 1902) was not published until four years after he died.

104 Ware, *The Indian War of 1864*, pp. 1-3, also 408, discusses the alliance between the Confederacy and several Indian nations.

105 Alderson, "Some New Slade Stories: Beatty and Horse Thieves." George Beatty said that as an army corporal he sought Slade's assistance at Slade's Horseshoe headquarters on March 4, 1861.

CHAPTER 13

1 R. M. Johnson, Holladay's brother-in-law, quoted in Frederick, *Ben Holladay*, p. 277.

2 Doniphan article in *St. Joseph Catholic Tribune*, June 22, 1895, cited in Root and Connelley, *The Overland Stage to California*, p. 450.

3 Frederick, *Ben Holladay, The Stagecoach King*, pp. 24-25. Chapman, *The Pony Express*, pp. 270-271; Banning, *Six Horses*, pp. 239-240.

4 Villard, *Memoirs*, Vol. II, p. 273, cited in Walker, *The Wagonmasters*, pp. 72-73; also Banning, *Six Horses*, p. 240; Root and Connelley, *The Overland Stage to California*, p. 440.

5 Doniphan article in St. Joseph *Catholic Tribune*, June 22, 1895, cited in Root and Connelley, *The Overland Stage to California*, pp. 448-450.

6 Root and Connelley, *The Overland Stage to California*, p. 48.

7 Ludlow, *Heart of the Continent*, p. 249, describing a cross-country stage journey in the spring of 1863.

8 See Chapman, *The Pony Express*, p. 270.

9 Alexander Toponce, *Reminiscences*, cited in Chapman, *The Pony Express*, p. 272.

10 Twain, *Roughing It*, p. 42 (1913 edition), cited in Hafen, *The Overland Mail*, p. 299.

11 There are three sources for this story, two by Arthur Chapman. Chapman, in *The Pony Express*, pp. 188-190, says the thieves took "two or three hundred horses, the property of military officers, the stage company and private citizens." He cites no source. Chapman's magazine article, "Jack Slade, Man-Killer," differs in some details but implies that Chapman interviewed one source, a former Pony Express station keeper. George Beatty, who led the Army detail that recovered the stock, described the herd as "40 head of horse and mules [stolen] from 25 miles west of the fort." Beatty was interviewed in 1923, when he was eighty-six. See Alderson, "Some New Slade Stories: Beatty and Horse Thieves." It's possible that these two accounts concern two different incidents— Chapman mentions the Davenports and Beatty does not; Chapman says there were three horse thieves, Beatty says two— but there's enough similarity between the two to safely assume they both deal with the same incident.

12 I have cobbled together the credible parts of this "station keeper" story from two works by Arthur Chapman— *The Pony Express*, pp. 188-190, and "Jack Slade, Man-Killer." The latter

seems to imply that Chapman interviewed the station keeper, although neither the station keeper nor his station is identified.

13 The location is cited by the army corporal George Beatty in an interview in the *Bynum* (Mont.) *Herald*, July 1923 (undated). Beatty says La Bonte's was "about 20 miles west of Fort Laramie"; it was actually the second Pony Express stop west of Horseshoe— that is, 29 miles west of Horseshoe and about 70 miles west of Fort Laramie. Whitcomb, the best source for this story, says the two men were "in the employ of the U.S. mail service," but he most likely means the Central Overland, which was delivering the mail. See "Alfred Slade at Close Range," p. 11. Both articles erroneously spell La Bonte as "La Bonta."

14 The location of Sarah's ranch is a bit of conjecture on my part. A Cottonwood station of the Pony Express stood about 12 miles east of Horseshoe and about 25 miles northwest of Fort Laramie; Whitcomb said the Sarah ranch was 25 miles from Fort Laramie. See Whitcomb, "Alfred Slade at Close Range," p. 11.

15 Several versions of the Sarah story exist. I have extracted pieces of this story primarily from three sources that strike me as most credible. The primary and probably most reliable source is Elias Whitcomb, who arrived in the area in the spring of 1861, shortly after this incident; see "Alfred Slade at Close Range," 11. Whitcomb described the incident as having occurred "that winter," which I presume, from the chronological order of his account, to be 1860–61. Other writers have interpreted this to mean winter of 1861–62, but that seems less likely to me. The Pony Express rider J. K. Ellis, in his memoir, suggests it occurred even earlier— before Jules Beni shot Slade in April 1860— but this too seems unlikely. A third source is the Army corporal George Beatty, interviewed in Alderson, "Some New Slade Stories: Beatty and Horse Thieves." The usually judicious and knowledgeable Callaway, in *Two True Tales of the Wild West*, p. 114, appears to have relied heavily on Whitcomb and Beatty but cites no sources. Another less credible variation of the Sarah story can be found in Bettelyoun, *With My Own Eyes*, p. 8. John Sarah has also been described as "Jules Savoie" (by Callaway) and "John Savaugh" (by Beatty). As with other stories about the French, accuracy with surnames is minimal. O'Dell, in the notes to his first draft for *An Ear in His Pocket* (p. 64, note 16), argues that Sarah is the correct name (as used by Whitcomb), and I concur.

16 Whitcomb mentions the guest named Winters who reached Fort Laramie. Beatty, who was stationed at Fort Laramie, says the survivor who reached Fort Laramie was a blacksmith. See Alderson, "Some New Slade Stories: Beatty and Horse Thieves."

17 Ellis, memoir.

18 Ellis, in his memoir, says he saw Mrs. Slade with Jemmy in Salt Lake City in 1866, when the boy was "about 13 years old." That would suggest that Jemmy was eight when the Slades adopted him, not five as Whitcomb reported. The Slades' adoption of Jemmy is mentioned in print as early as 1866, in Dimsdale's *Vigilantes of Montana*, p. 175.

19 The description of Jemmy is from Dimsdale, *Vigilantes of Montana*, p. 175.

20 Hough, *The Story of the Outlaw*, p. 146.

21 "Old Timer Traveled the Old Oregon Train with Jack Slade," interview with Tom Rivington in *Guernsey* (Wyo.) *Gazette*, April 8, 1932.

22 *Life and Adventures of Polk Wells, The Notorious Outlaw*, pp. 42–43. There are many holes in this account. Wells was born June 5, 1851; if he was eleven at this time, as he claims, this

encounter at Julesburg would have occurred sometime after June 1862. Slade's division was shifted away from Julesburg in July 1862; and the Slades already had one adopted child (Jemmy) by the spring of 1861. Also, I've found no mention of Mrs. Slade's presence at Julesburg; she lived at Horseshoe station, 225 miles to the northwest. Nevertheless, the encounter is conceivable; it's possible that Wells's memory of dates and places is confused.

23 Twain, *Roughing It,* chapter 10.

24 Twain, *Roughing It,* chapter 9. Actually, Twain didn't hear stage drivers talking this way about Slade until after he met him; presumably he changed the sequence to heighten his book's dramatic anticipation. Orion Clemens to Twain, March 11, 1871, cited in Patterson, "Mark Twain Meets J. Slade," p. 18.

25 The date and place of the meeting have been pinpointed by Stewart in *The American West,* July 1968, p. 11. Good analyses of Twain's meeting with Slade are found in Patterson, "Mark Twain Meets J. Slade," pp. 17–18; also O'Dell and Jessen, *An Ear in His Pocket*, pp. 63–72.

26 Twain, *Roughing It,* chapter 10.

27 Twain, *Roughing It,* chapter 10. Similar versions of this story can be found in Callaway, *Two True Tales of the Wild West,* pp. 108–109; and Root and Connelley, *The Overland Stage to California*, p. 481.

28 Callaway, *Two True Tales of the Wild West*, p. 113.

29 Callaway, *Two True Tales of the Wild West*, p. 108; also see p. 110. This is one of the few points that Callaway specifically attributes in his unfootnoted book. Callaway says his source was E. M. ("Gov") Pollinger, an Overland stage driver and later a Wells Fargo stage superintendent in Montana, who Callaway says "was in a position to learn the facts, and he was a reliable man."

30 Twain, *Roughing It*, chapter 10. Callaway, in *Two True Tales of the Wild West*, pp. 108–109, says this story was "repeated again and again as a fact" without passing judgment himself. This story seems incredible on its face— for one thing, who could have been the source of this story, other than Slade himself, his wife, or his flummoxed captors? Yet this story, more so than some of the other Slade myths, bears a ring of truth. It was not the last time that Slade recklessly exposed himself to risk, or begged pitifully for his life, nor was it the last time that his wife rode boldly to his rescue. Callaway suggests that this capture and escape roused Slade to issue orders to capture Jules and to post a $500 reward for his arrest; see Callaway, *Two True Tales of the Wild West*, p. 109. The $500 reward is mentioned by the relatively reliable E. M. Pollinger, in Callaway, *Two True Tales of the Wild West*, p. 110. But precisely when or how Slade offered such a reward is unclear.

31 Chapman, "Jack Slade, Man-Killer."

32 Langford, *Vigilante Days and Ways*, pp. 370–371. Langford describes the coins on the card table as "double eagles"— that is, twenty-dollar gold coins— but these were not issued until 1877.

33 "Old Timer Traveled the Old Oregon Trail with Jack Slade." Rivington doesn't specifically mention his relationship to Slade; he says only, "A number of times in '62 and '63 I rode with Jack Slade from Fort Bridger to Fort Sedgwick," i.e., Julesburg. Rivington was probably about ninety when this letter was written, some seventy years after the events he describes; his dates are no doubt mistaken, for Slade was gone from the original Overland Trail by the

summer of 1862 and from the Central Overland's employ by November 1862. Rivington identifies the post as "Fort Sanders" but probably means Fort Laramie: Fort Sanders, located near Fort Laramie, was not built until 1866 (it was closed in 1882).

34 Nelson, *Fifty Years on the Trail*, pp. 236 ff. Nelson says this encounter took place about two and a half miles west of Cottonwood Springs, Nebraska Territory— that is, 100 miles east of Julesburg and beyond Slade's division after January 1860. But of course that doesn't preclude Slade's having ventured east to Fort Kearny or even Atchison, as he occasionally did. Nelson implies that the scene occurred in the spring of 1862, when "the Indians at this time were very peaceably disposed." In fact the Sioux were conducting major raids along Slade's division from March 23, 1862, to the end of April, leading to the route's dismantlement. This leads me to suspect that this incident described by Nelson occurred earlier, probably in 1861. Nelson's self-serving details of his confrontation may be questioned, as well as his description of Slade: Nelson calls him "a tall, heavy-looking fellow, with small deep-set eyes and the look of a wolf," which is accurate except that Slade was short. But the terrified Nelson can be excused for perceiving Slade, many years later, as larger than he was. At the very least, Nelson's description of Slade's behavior when drunk is consistent with those of others.

35 Bessette, "A Story of Joseph A. Slade," is the original source of this story. Bessette says it took place in the summer of 1861; Callaway (*Two True Tales of the Wild West*, p. 114) and other secondary sources (probably relying on Callaway) place it in the summer of 1860. Bessette says Smith and Bacon lived "about 15 miles below Independence Rock, Wyoming . . . on the Sweetwater River"; Boner says Smith and Bacon lived at Split Rock station, one station below Boner's at the Three Crossings of the Sweetwater, and two stations below Gilbert's. A route chart shows Split Rock as 22 miles west of (that is, above) Independence Rock, 12 miles east of the Three Crossings of the Sweetwater and 69 miles east of Gilbert's. See Gray, "The Salt Lake Hockaday Mail," Part II, p. 5. Callaway, p. 114, refers to Bacon as Becom. But Jim Boner, interviewed in 1899, also refers to "Bacon" rather than "Becom," and he said there were three men: "Pete and Charley Bacon and a man named Smith." See "He Nursed Jim Slade."

36 Callaway, *Two True Tales of the Wild West*, p. 114.

37 Bessette, "A Story of Joseph A. Slade," p. 3.

38 Bessette, "A Story of Joseph A. Slade," p. 3, says Plante lived "four miles above Bacon and Smith"— that is— four miles west. But on Pony Express maps, Plante's station is east of (below) Split Rock, where Smith and Bacon lived. The latter is probably correct; even Bessette (pp. 5–6) describes Slade and Mrs. Bartholomew gathering her things at the Bartholomew ranch, riding from there (eastward) to Plante's store, and then continuing on eastward from there to Horseshoe.

39 Bessette, "A Story of Joseph A. Slade," p. 3. Bessette said he saw the actual letter "about one year later."

40 Bessette, "A Story of Joseph A. Slade," p. 4. Bessette writes as if he witnessed this whole scene but doesn't specifically say that he did; he does say, though, "Let me here tell you what I have seen, heard and know" (p. 2).

41 Bessette, "A Story of Joseph A. Slade," p. 4.

42 Bessette, "A Story of Joseph A. Slade," p. 6.

43 The timing is conjecture on my part. Both the Bartholomew murder and the return of Jules Beni are said to have occurred in August 1861. When Slade learned of Jules's return, he was at Pacific Springs, by one account (Coutant, *History of Wyoming*, p. 403), and at "Rocky Ridge/Sweetwater" by another (Clampitt, *Echoes from the Rocky Mountains*, pp. 503–504). Both accounts say Slade promptly headed east until he reached Horseshoe, where he paused for a week. On this journey Slade would have passed Split Rock and Plante's, both of which were not far east of Rocky Ridge and the Three Crossings of the Sweetwater.

44 See, for example, Langford, *Vigilante Days and Ways*, p. 364.

45 See "Echoes of Alder Gulch." Gilbert does not specify where he met Jules. But based on other accounts that place Jules west of the Rocky Ridge country in late 1860 and 1861, it seems likely that he would have encountered Gilbert at Gilbert's station at Millersville, or at Fort Bridger itself, 20 miles west of Millersville and about 360 miles west of Slade's Horseshoe Creek headquarters. Gilbert's biography in *Progressive Men of Montana*, p. 174, says he opened a trading post and general store at South Pass— that is, the last crossing of the Sweetwater, about 235 miles west of Horseshoe station— in the spring of 1858, sold it late in 1859, and established a trading post at "the foot of the Rocky Ridge" (east of his first store), then moved westward in the fall of 1860 to Fort Bridger and "soon after established a store for Indian trade at Millersville." Gilbert was married in November 1860 and sometime in 1861 relocated to a ranch south of Fort Bridger, so this may be where he encountered Jules. Gilbert's chronology is consistent with the memoir of Louis Maillet, who recalled stopping at Gilbert's station "at the last crossing of the Sweetwater" on July 2, 1859; see Wheeler, "Historical Sketch of Louis R. Maillet," p. 215.

46 The dates of Jules's foray into Slade's division and his eventual death are hard to pin down, but late August or perhaps early September 1861 seem most logical to me. The Pony Express rider J. K. Ellis, says that after the first shooting Slade and Jules didn't meet "at least until July 1861"; see Jesse Brown, reminiscences of J. K. Ellis extracted from *San Francisco Examiner* (undated), manuscript #122C, Wyoming State Historical Library, Cheyenne, p. 4. C. M. Rolfson says Jules was killed in August 1861; see "Historic Julesburg," *Sterling* (Col.) newspaper, undated clip, about 1943. Banning, in *Six Horses*, p. 261, says Jules was killed in September 1861. Slade's neighbor Whitcomb, who settled at Horseshoe in the spring of 1861, says the capture of Jules occurred "the next summer" after the original shooting, presumably the summer of 1861 (Burton, in *City of the Saints*, reported Slade as not yet avenged on Aug. 14, 1860, and Slade and the Central Overland were gone from the Horseshoe area by the summer of 1862); see "Alfred Slade at Close Range," p. 14.

47 "Echoes of Alder Gulch." Gilbert is not a terribly reliable source; his interview seems too eager to claim familiarity with critical events and several times implies his foreknowledge of events that subsequently came to pass. Also, the interview (conducted in 1902) was not published until four years after he died, so he had no opportunity to review and correct it.

48 Coutant, *History of Wyoming*, p. 403.

49 Whitcomb, "Alfred Slade at Close Range," p. 14. Whitcomb lived near Horseshoe at the time of these events.

50 Wilson, "Reminiscences of Overland Days," p. 5. Wilson went to work at Horseshoe station in the fall of 1861, shortly after these events.

51 James Wilson, "Reminiscences of Overland Days," p. 5. Wilson went to work at Horseshoe station in the fall of 1861, shortly after these events.

52 Whitcomb, "Alfred Slade at Close Range," p. 14. Whitcomb lived near Horseshoe at the time of these events.

53 Most accounts suggest that Jules had no herd with him. The exception is Clampitt, *Echoes from the Rocky Mountains*, pp. 503–504: "On the line he [Slade] heard that Jules was nearby, driving some stock along the regular stage road he [Slade] was obliged to pass over in the regular performance of his duties." Also, Jules's widow, Adeline Cayou Beckstead, claimed that Jules and his men were driving cattle when they were attacked by Slade's men; see MacMurphy, "Some Squatters with a History," p. 5.

54 Coutant, *History of Wyoming*, p. 403.

55 The exception is one account of Adeline Cayou Beckstead, who said that Jules entered Slade's division not from the west but from their ranch at Cottonwood Springs, east of Julesburg. She said Jules took along "a Frenchman we had with us, Pete Kozzoo, and an American named Smith, and they were all armed with rifles and pistols and knives. He had a light wagon and a pair of horses, and he thought he was well prepared to defend himself." See MacMurphy, "Some Squatters with a History," p. 5. It is difficult to reconcile Adeline's account with that of Gilbert, who encountered Jules more than 500 miles to the west at Fort Bridger, or with the account of Wilson, who says Jules had stock at Wagon Hound Creek that he came to retrieve. (The latter is at least conceivable if unlikely: Jules might have traveled 350 miles west from Cottonwood Springs to Wagon Hound Creek, then started on his eastward return trip of another 350 miles before Slade at Pacific Springs learned of his presence.) But most accounts presume Jules was harbored west of Slade's division; and in any case Adeline's recollections are contradictory on many points.

56 A family tree assembled by one of his purported descendants, M. H. Keith of Livingston, Tex., said Jules was born in 1809.

57 Langford, *Vigilante Days and Ways*, p. 364; also Coutant, *History of Wyoming*, p. 403. Clampitt, *Echoes from the Rocky Mountains*, pp. 503–504, says Slade was at "Rocky Ridge, Sweetwater" [*sic*], perhaps 30 miles east of Pacific Springs, when he learned of Jules's presence. Either way, Slade was more than 200 miles west of Horseshoe.

58 Slade's rescue of Bartholomew's widow and his pursuit of Bartholomew's killers may have had as much to do with his heading east from Pacific Springs as the news that Jules Beni had returned, but this is pure speculation on my part.

59 Clampitt, *Echoes from the Rocky Mountains*, pp. 503–504.

60 Callaway, *Two True Tales of the Wild West*, p. 110. Callaway says he personally interviewed Pollinger, whom Callaway describes as "in a position to learn the facts, and he was a reliable man."

61 Utley, *Frontiersmen in Blue*, pp. 12, 108.

62 Utley, *Frontiersmen in Blue*, p. 36.

63 Eugene Bandel, *Frontier Life in the Army*, p. 114, cited in Utley, *Frontiersmen in Blue*, p. 35.

64 Utley, *Frontiersmen in Blue*, p. 32.

65 Connell, *Son of the Morning Star*, pp. 152-153; "Fort Laramie: Official Map and Guide," National Park Service, Department of the Interior.

66 Yenne, *Indian Wars*, p. 45.

67 Whitcomb, "Alfred Slade at Close Range," p. 12.

68 The meeting at Fort Laramie is reported in Langford, *Vigilante Days and Ways*, p. 364; Coutant, *History of Wyoming*, p. 403; Hough, *Story of the Outlaw*, pp. 147-149. The latter two may have used Langford as their source.

69 Callaway, citing the "veracious" E. M. Pollinger, in *Two True Tales of the Wild West*, p. 110.

70 Bettelyoun, *With My Own Eyes,* pp. 8, 24-25.

71 Langford, *Vigilante Days and Ways*, pp. 364-365. Langford calls the ranch at Cold Spring "Chansau's"; Boner calls its proprietor Sochet ("He Nursed Jim Slade"); Whitcomb calls him Shosaix (Whitcomb, "Alfred Slade at Close Range," p. 14). It seems clear to me that all three men heard and repeated the Frenchman's name orally; "Sochet" seems the most likely spelling. The identities of Jules's captors remain uncertain. Pollinger says several of Slade's men pursued Jules but he was ultimately caught by Nelson Vaughan and John Frey; see Callaway, *Two True Tales of the Wild West*, p. 110. The *Colorado Gazette* in 1882 identified the captors as "Nelson Vaughn [*sic*], John Fry [*sic*] and another man, who is now a resident of Montana"; see reprint in "Slade the Outlaw." Boner says Jules was captured by Bob Scott and a man named Hodges. James Wilson says Johnny Burnett captured Jules by shooting him through the thigh; see Wilson, "Reminiscences of Overland Days," p. 5. Another less likely account, from the Pony Express rider Calvin Downs, claims that Slade himself captured Jules after a chase "with a single bullet through the hips"— not at Cold Spring, but at Pacific Springs, more than 300 miles to the west; see Chapman, *The Pony Express*, p. 186. Whitcomb, Langford, and Clampitt mention no names of Jules's captors.

72 Whitcomb, "Alfred Slade at Close Range," p. 14. Another version of the capture— less credible, to my mind— holds that Jules was captured not by Frey and Vaughan but by the other two men Slade had dispatched to Cold Spring, Bob Scott and another man named Hodges. Jules was inside Sochet's station house— a combined station, trading post, and saloon— when he saw the stage approaching with Slade at the reins. He ran outside, hid behind a corner of the house and commenced firing at Slade. Scott and Hodges surrounded him from two sides of the house, captured him and tied him to a corral post. See Jim Boner interview in "He Nursed Jim Slade."

73 Callaway, *Two True Tales of the Wild West*, pp. 110-111. Callaway adds that in another variation of this story, Vaughan cut off the ears and gave them to Slade as souvenirs.

74 Boner interview in "He Nursed Jim Slade."

75 Whitcomb, "Alfred Slade at Close Range," p. 14. Another version suggests Slade left Jules tied up overnight before commencing the shooting, with Jules begging him all the while to put an end to his misery. Mark Twain, *Roughing It*, cited in Callaway, *Two True Tales of the Wild West*, p. 109.

76 Hough, *Story of the Outlaw*, pp. 147-149.

77 *Cheyenne Daily Leader*, April 21, 1889, p. 3.

78 Langford, *Vigilante Days and Ways*, p. 366.

79 Clampitt, *Echoes from the Rocky Mountains*, pp. 503–504.

80 Adeline Cayou Beckstead gave one or more interviews decades later to the writer Harriet S. MacMurphy. Her accounts of the Jules-Slade affair are contradictory and totally at odds with other accounts. She describes Slade as a neighboring rancher; says Jules shot Slade after Slade, drunk, reached for his gun; and that Jules then took Slade to Denver and paid all of his doctor bills. In Adeline's account, after shooting Slade, Jules came to Denver, where he met her. He subsequently took her to his new ranch and trading post at Cottonwood Springs, in western Nebraska, about 100 miles east of Julesburg; years later, when Jules and his men returned to Julesburg to retrieve his horses and cattle from his old ranch, "Slade and his gang" drove Jules's men away, and carried Jules to "Slade's ranch," where Slade methodically shot Jules to death. In one account she says Slade and his men took "a lot of the stuff we had in the trading post," that she and some employees fled to Denver; that Jules had money in a bank there but she never found it. In another account, she says Slade's men took about $3,000 worth of goods and stock and left Adeline with about $600. Her story varies with each telling; she seems unaware that Jules had sold his Julesburg ranch to George Chrisman after shooting Slade. "I was just a child and did not know what to do," she adds. It seems likely that her facts are secondhand and colored by a natural desire among her sources to spare her feelings. See MacMurphy, "Some Squatters with a History," pp. 4–5; MacMurphy, "The Heroine of the Jules-Slade Tragedy," in *Nebraska Pioneer Reminiscences*, pp. 324–325; Morton, *Illustrated History of Nebraska*, p. 181.

81 Coutant, *History of Wyoming*, p. 403; Hough, *Story of the Outlaw*, pp. 147–149.

82 Coe, *The Telegraph*, p. 39. Thompson, *Wiring a Continent*, p. 363, says the work started at Omaha on July 4, 1861, but this is surely mistaken: The telegraph had reached Fort Kearny by November 1860.

83 Settle and Settle, *Story of the Pony Express*, p. 160.

84 Corbett, *Orphans Preferred*, p. 119; his source for these dates appears to be the journal of Charles Brown. O'Dell and Jessen, in *An Ear in His Pocket*, pp. 26–27, say supplies for the westward telegraph line reached Julesburg in late July and the line was operating at Horseshoe "within a month's time." Settle and Settle, *The Pony Express*, p. 160, says the line reached Julesburg "by the end of August." Neither O'Dell and Jessen nor the Settles cite their sources. Hafen, in *The Overland Mail*, p. 187, provides somewhat later dates for the westernmost telegraph stations on Creighton's line: Aug. 9, 50 miles west of Fort Kearny; Aug. 27, 60 miles farther west; Sept. 14, 55 miles more (that is, almost to Julesburg); and Oct. 8, 368 miles additional— that is, more than 100 miles west of Horseshoe. The discrepancy in these dates may lie in the difference between the first stringing of wire and the opening of permanent telegraph stations. I am inclined to accept the earlier dates, since Coe, in *The Telegraph*, p. 40, says; "Temporary telegraph offices were set up at the head of the line after each day's run." In any case it seems likely that Horseshoe had telegraph access to points east no later than mid-September 1861 and more likely by late August.

85 The Salt Lake City *Deseret News* of July 10, 1861, reported that the first telegraph pole would be planted "not far from our office" that evening; see Chapman, *The Pony Express*, p. 284.

86 Journal of Charles A. Brown, cited in Corbett, *Orphans Preferred*, pp. 118–119.

87 Chapman, *The Pony Express*, pp. 282–283.

88 A rail line from St. Joseph to Atchison was completed on February 22, 1860, making Atchison the westernmost rail terminus at that point. See Ingalls, *History of Atchison County, Kansas*, p. 174.

89 "Paul Jones," letter to *Missouri Democrat*, Oct. 22, 1861, cited in Root and Hickman, "Part IV: The Platte Route, Concluded." *Kansas Historical Quarterly*, February 1946, p. 80; also see footnote 481. Hughes eventually moved to Denver in the later 1860s; see Root and Connelley, *The Overland Stage to California*, p. 460.

90 Howard, *Hoofbeats of Destiny*, p. 131.

91 Settle and Settle, *War Drums and Wagon Wheels*, p. 114; also appendix, pp. 208–212. The Settles, with their rare access to papers of Russell, Majors & Waddell, are surely the best source on the Pony Express's finances. Chapman, in *The Pony Express*, p. 304, concluded that the Pony's operating expenses alone (excluding initial capital investment in stock, property and equipment) came to $475,000 ($25,000 per month multiplied by 19 months). Receipts from 30,000 letters at an average of $3 per letter (the fee ranged from $1 to $5) he figured at only $90,000. But Chapman overlooked the Pony's share of the U.S. Mail contract for the almost four months between July 1 and Oct. 26, 1861. That contract totaled $1 million a year, of which nearly half was allotted to Holladay's operation east of Salt Lake. The Pony's share of that for four months might have amounted to $100,000. It's unclear whether any such allotment was assigned or calculated. In any case, it's safe to conclude that the Pony was a huge money-loser, as its backers— who conceived it as a "loss leader"— readily understood from the start.

92 Chapman, *The Pony Express,* p. 291.

93 The telegraph stations on Slade's division were located at Julesburg, Mud Springs, Fort Laramie, Horseshoe, Deer Creek, Three Crossings of the Sweetwater, and Rocky Ridge. See Chapman, *The Pony Express*, p. 290.

94 Slade's division, which previously stretched some 500 miles from Julesburg to Pacific Springs, was reduced by about 125 miles sometime between August 1861 and April 1862 at the very latest. In an affidavit given on June 29, 1862, Slade described himself as division agent between Julesburg and Sweetwater Bridge, "a distance of 346 miles" (the distance is closer to 390 by my calculation). August 1861 found him engaged west of Sweetwater Bridge, in dealing with the Bartholomew murder, and he was at Pacific Springs when he learned of Jules Beni's presence; from this evidence I conclude that his division was shortened after August. Lemuel Flowers, agent of the new division created between Sweetwater Bridge and Pacific Springs, said he began in that job on April 15, 1862, having succeeded William A. Reid in that position. Presumably Reid served in that position for at least a few months, which leads me to surmise that the new division was probably created in the fall of 1861. See Slade and Flowers affidavits in "Claim of Ben Holladay," 46th Congress, 2nd session, Misc. Doc. No. 19, Dec. 17, 1879, pp. 3–6. The likely reasons for dividing Slade's old division into two— the arrival of the telegraph (which made it easier to delegate supervisory duties) and the elimination of Jules Beni and the outlaw threat from Slade's western end— are merely a logical deduction on my part. Another possible explanation— management's impatience over Slade's reluctance to pursue Jules— seems less likely: Had that been the case, Slade would have been removed from the Rocky Ridge area before Jules was killed, not after. In any case, Slade was long overdue for some relief: Even at its 346-mile length (390 by my calculation), Slade's new abbreviated division was still much longer than other Central Overland divisions. Flowers's new division to

Slade's west ran only about 125 miles, for example, and the division west of that, from Pacific Springs to Salt Lake City, covered 233 miles. See J. E. Bromley testimony in "Claim of Ben Holladay," p. 7.

95 "Life of Oscar Collister," *Annals of Wyoming*, July 1930, pp. 345–346. Collister says (p. 343) he was born Nov. 14, 1841, so presumably this incident occurred shortly before he turned 20. The superior to whom he refers is Western Union's "assistant superintendent Ellsworth" (p. 344).

96 "Life of Oscar Collister," p. 352. Curiously, in the second installment of this memoir, Collister inexplicably conveys an entirely different impression of Slade to his interviewer: "You asked me about Joseph Slade, but I do not care to discuss him at any length. I cannot say much good of him, and I know a great deal about him otherwise." See *Annals of Wyoming*, October 1930, p. 375. Collister was eighty-eight when these interviews were conducted.

97 Connell, cited in Courtwright, *Violent Land*, p. 126.

98 Courtwright, *Violent Land*, pp. 32–33.

99 Courtwright, *Violent Land*, p. 73.

100 Courtwright, *Violent Land*, p. 70.

101 Courtwright, *Violent Land,* p. 70.

102 Ware, *The Indian War of 1864*, pp. 92–93.

103 "It became routine to drink whiskey at breakfast and to go on drinking all day": Daniel Patrick Moynihan, cited in Seymour Martin Lipset, *American Exceptionalism: A Double-Edged Sword*, p. 271.

104 The time of this incident— fall of 1861— is my deduction. It must have occurred after the telegraph line reached Horseshoe— that is, after September 1 or thereabouts. And Whitcomb's reference to grabbing his overcoat suggests cool weather. Whitcomb himself says in his account, "The telegraph lines had been erected that fall." See Whitcomb, "Alfred Slade at Close Range," pp. 12–13. Whitcomb's account of this incident is corroborated by an undated letter to Whitcomb, written years later by George Cockrell, apparently one of the Overland employees involved in the incident. See "George Cockrell's letter to E.W. Whitcomb," Wyoming State Library, Ms. 432.

105 Whitcomb, "Alfred Slade at Close Range," p. 13.

106 Whitcomb, "Alfred Slade at Close Range," p. 13. This incident occurred sometime in the winter of 1861–62.

107 Whitcomb, "Alfred Slade at Close Range," p. 12.

108 Wilson, "Reminiscences of Overland Days," p. 4. Wilson mistakenly refers to Slade as "James A. Slade," perhaps because Slade was sometimes called Jim.

CHAPTER 14

1 Sears, *George B. McClellan: The Young Napoleon.*

2 The government's California mail contract totaled $1 million, of which $475,000 was the Central Overland's share for the Atchison-to-Salt Lake portion.

3 Harlow, *Old Waybills*, p. 244, cited in Root and Hickman, "Part IV—The Platte Route, Concluded," p. 83, also note 488. Also see Hafen, *The Overland Mail*, p. 227; also O'Dell and Jessen, *An Ear in His Pocket*, p. 31.

4 Settle and Settle, *War Drums and Wagon Wheels*, pp. 166-167; Settle and Settle, *Empire on Wheels*, pp. 128-129; Root and Hickman, "Part IV—The Platte Route, Concluded," p. 89; Hafen, *The Overland Mail*, p. 227; Frederick, *Ben Holladay*, p. 282. John Russell is identified as William Russell's son in Settle and Settle, *The Story of the Pony Express*, p. 22.

5 Yenne, *Indian Wars*, p. 79.

6 Rottenberg, *The Man Who Made Wall Street,* p. 60.

7 Yenne, *Indian Wars*, p. 79; O'Dell and Jessen, *An Ear in His Pocket*, p. 35.

8 Affidavit of Lemuel Flowers, division superintendent between Pacific Springs and Sweetwater Bridge, Nov. 15, 1865; see "Claim of Ben Holladay," 46th Congress, 2nd session, Misc. Doc. No. 19, Dec. 17, 1879, p. 4.

9 Ben Holladay testimony, "Claim of Ben Holladay," p. 61.

10 Chapman, *The Pony Express*, pp. 199-200. Also testimony of David Street; see "Claim of Ben Holladay," p. 51.

11 Testimony of David Street, "Claim of Ben Holladay," p. 53.

12 Hafen, *The Overland Mail*, p. 254.

13 Ben Holladay testimony, "Claim of Ben Holladay," p. 61.

14 "Dwight Fisk: Early Freighter," p. 306.

15 The actual proclamation of martial law may have come weeks later. Hafen, *The Overland Mail*, p. 247, citing the *Rocky Mountain News* of May 28, 1862, says General Craig did not declare martial law until May 15.

16 The attack of April 17 is described by one of the party, T. S. Boardman, in *Alta California*, May 26, 1862, cited in Hafen, *The Overland Mail*, pp. 245-246.

17 Affidavit of J. E. Bromley; see "Claim of Ben Holladay," p. 7; also Frederick, *Ben Holladay*, pp. 170-171.

18 O'Dell and Jessen, *An Ear in His Pocket,* p. 57.

19 O'Dell and Jessen, *An Ear in His Pocket*, pp. 35-37; "Claim of Ben Holladay": affidavit of Lemuel Flowers, pp. 3-4; affidavit of J. A. Slade, pp. 5-6; affidavit of J. E. Bromley, p. 7.

20 Frederick, *Ben Holladay*, p. 175.

21 Harlow, *Old Wires and New Waves*, p. 316.

22 Affidavit of J. A. Slade, June 29, 1862; see "Claim of Ben Holladay," p. 51.

23 Ben Holladay testimony, "Claim of Ben Holladay," p. 61.

24 "Dwight Fisk: Early Freighter," p. 306.

25 O'Dell and Jessen, *An Ear in His Pocket*, p. 37.

26 Ben Holladay testimony, "Claim of Ben Holladay," p. 61.

27 Frederick, *Ben Holladay,* p. 172.

28 Ben Holladay testimony, "Claim of Ben Holladay," p. 61. Holladay said he traversed the Cherokee Trail in August 1850. Also see David Street testimony, p. 51.

29 Hafen, *The Overland Mail*, pp. 222-223. Hafen also notes that even before Holladay considered the Denver route, John Jones, William Russell and Bela Hughes of the Central Overland were in Denver to explore that possibility in April and May 1861; see pp. 219-220. Ultimately the Berthoud Pass proved impractical for stagecoaches, due to its overly steep

grades and the necessity of a tunnel, so from mid-1862 the Overland Stage Co. used the Cherokee Trail northwest from Denver to a point on the North Platte River, near Green River, where it hooked up with the old Emigrant or Oregon Trail. See Hafen, *The Overland Mail*, pp. 230–231.

30 *Rocky Mountain News*, July 29, 1862, estimated the saving at 150 miles; see Hafen, *The Overland Mail*, p. 231.

31 Holladay recalled this conversation in his testimony in "Claim of Ben Holladay," p. 61. Also see Frederick, *Ben Holladay*, p. 177.

32 O'Dell and Jessen, *An Ear in His Pocket*, pp. 37–38; also testimony of David Street, "Claim of Ben Holladay," p. 51; testimony of Holladay, p. 62.

33 Holladay testimony in "Claim of Ben Holladay," p. 62; O'Dell and Jessen, *An Ear in His Pocket*, p. 38.

34 Testimony of David Street, "Claim of Ben Holladay," pp. 51–52.

35 Testimony of Ben Holladay, "Claim of Ben Holladay," p. 62.

36 Frederick. *Ben Holladay*, p. 94.

37 O'Dell and Jessen, *An Ear in His Pocket*, pp. 38–39.

38 Holladay testimony in "Claim of Ben Holladay," p. 62.

39 Frederick. *Ben Holladay*, p. 96. Frederick describes Latham and Laporte as of 1864. He says Laporte in 1864 "had about six dwellings and many saloons." I presume the numbers were somewhat less in 1862, when Slade took charge. Laporte was originally spelled "La Porte" from 1862 to 1894; Kenneth Jessen, e-mail message to author, Jan. 2, 2008. The brewery is mentioned in Bauer, *Colorado Post Offices, 1859–1989*, p. 85.

40 Ball, *Go West Young Man*, p. 30: "Joseph A. Slade was the first white man to locate in what is now known as Virginia Dale." "Nature, with her artistic pencil," wrote a visitor a few months later, "has here been most extravagant with her limnings. Even in the dim starlight, its beauties were most striking and apparent. The dark evergreens dotted the hillsides, and occasionally a giant pine towered upward far above its dwarfy companions, like a sentinel on the outposts of a sleeping encampment." Edward Bliss, "Denver to Salt Lake by Overland Stage"; reprinted in *Colorado*, Sept. 1931, pp. 190–197.

41 Overland Trail website, http://www.over-land.com/vdots.html; also author's interview with local historian Kenneth Jessen, March 27, 2007.

42 Ball, *Go West Young Man*, p. 27.

43 Most sources say Slade named Virginia Dale for his wife. Watrous, for example, says, Slade "named the station Virginia Dale in honor of his wife's maiden name"; see Watrous, *History of Larimer County, Colorado*, p. 189. Robert Spotswood, who relieved Slade at Virginia Dale in 1862, said "Slade named it for his wife," in an interview in 1910; see "Dead pioneer told stories of early days," *Denver Republican*, April 19, 1910. Whether "Dale" was Mrs. Slade's maiden name or a reference to the valley remains unresolved.

44 Who named Dale Creek and what it was named for remain mysteries of some importance to Slade's story. Because the station was named "Virginia Dale," some writers have assumed that Dale was Mrs. Slade's maiden name. Others have argued that the use of "Dale" in the station's name is synonymous with *valley*, as in "Virginia Valley," or that the use of Dale refers to

Dale Creek. But who other than Slade would have named Dale Creek, if indeed Slade was the first white resident of the valley? According to local historian Kenneth Jessen, Colona (later Laporte) was the only settlement in all of Larimer County as of 1860. Slade's arrival in 1862 predates the Union Pacific Railroad's entry into the area, when many geographic features were named. Union Pacific surveyors were responsible for many local names, Jessen suggests; it is possible that one of them gave Dale Creek its name before he arrived, or Slade could have named it. Jessen e-mail message to author, Nov. 4, 2006.

45 Curiously, the telegraph line was not moved south when the stagecoach line moved; it still ran via the North Platte–South Pass route, requiring troops to guard that route as well. On this northern route Indians attacked the Pacific Springs telegraph station on Nov. 24, 1862, killing one man and driving off the stock before troops—summoned by telegraph—arrived; see Hafen, *The Overland Mail*, p. 249, citing *Deseret News*, Salt Lake City, Nov. 26, 1862.

46 Frederick, *Ben Holladay*, pp. 94, 177; O'Dell and Jessen, *An Ear in His Pocket*, p. 39.

47 Holladay's testimony in "Claim of Ben Holladay," p. 62. At the height of the Pony Express this stretch actually contained forty-five stations, but many served only the Pony Express and were discontinued when the Pony Express stopped running in October 1861. Thus twenty-six stage stations remained when the route was moved in July 1862.

48 *Deseret News*, Salt Lake City, July 16, 1862.

49 Callaway, in *Two True Tales of the Wild West*, p. 118, says, "When a Denver newspaper severely criticized Slade's actions editorially, it is said that Ben Holladay himself called upon the editor and took him to task for his aspersions upon his favorite division-agent." I have found no such editorial in a Denver paper; it's possible that such an editorial appeared, but it seems more likely that Callaway confused the *Deseret News* with a Denver paper.

50 Muir, "The Man Who Was Hanged for a Song," p. 46. The article mentions the *San Francisco Bulletin* article but gives no date other than the year 1862.

51 "Letter from Salt Lake," by "Liberal," *Sacramento Daily Union*, Aug. 15, 1862, p. 1.

52 The usually reliable Hafen, in *The Overland Mail*, p. 231, says the new daily mail service started on July 21; so does the Denver magazine *Municipal Facts*; see Lilley, "The Settlement and Early History of Virginia Dale," p. 12.

53 Frederick, *Ben Holladay*, p. 95.

54 A historical marker at the spot, as well as the state of Wyoming's website, say Fort Halleck opened on July 20, 1862; see http://wyoshpo.state.wy.us/halleck.htm. Frederick says the fort was built "in August"; see *Ben Holladay*, p. 178,

55 Hafen, *The Overland Mail*, p. 248; Frederick, *Ben Holladay*, p. 178

56 Frederick, *Ben Holladay*, p. 178.

57 Frederick, *Ben Holladay*, 95.

58 Hafen, *The Overland Mail*, p. 232.

59 *Rocky Mountain News*, Sept. 3, 1862, cited in Frederick, *Ben Holladay*, pp. 95–96.

60 Frederick, *Ben Holladay*, p. 108.

61 Bliss, "Denver to Salt Lake by Overland Stage," p. 197.

62 Frederick, *Ben Holladay*, p. 178.

63 Bliss, "Denver to Salt Lake by Overland Stage," p. 197.

64 Root and Connelley, *The Overland Stage to California*, p. 488.

65 Lilley, "The Settlement and Early History of Virginia Dale," p. 12.

66 Spotswood, quoted in "Dead Pioneer Told Stories of Early Days."

67 Watrous, *History of Larimer County, Colorado*, p. 189. Samuel Bowles, editor of the *Springfield Republican*, described it in 1865: "A pearly, lively-looking stream runs through a beautiful basin, of perhaps one hundred acres, among the mountains, . . . stretching away in smooth and rising pasture to nooks and crannies of the wooded range; fronted by rock embattlement, and flanked by the snowy peaks themselves; warm with a June sun and rare and pure with an air into which no fetid breath has poured itself—it is difficult to imagine a more loveable spot in nature's kingdom." Quoted in "Virginia Dale Stage Station on the Overland Route," p. 78. Slade's original station house still stands, a mini-museum in excellent condition, about a mile off U.S. 287. The log building—nineteen feet wide, and about fifty-six feet long—owes its survival to two factors: the diligent preservation efforts of the Virginia Dale Community Club and the difficulties involved in visiting it. Although the community club owns it, the building is surrounded by private property and is open to the public only twice a year. On these occasions, club members raise funds as well as public awareness by peddling booklets, souvenir mugs, and T-shirts. At all other times, casual visitors and potential vandals must pass through several gates to reach it, and consequently most of them intrude no farther than a historic marker along the highway.

CHAPTER 15

1 Moody, *Stagecoach West*, p. 229, says Holladay changed the name because the line no longer ran to California, and also because he coveted the Overland Mail contract from Salt Lake to California.

2 Root and Connelley, *The Overland Stage to California*, p. 98.

3 Callaway, *Two True Tales of the Wild West*, p. 118.

4 Thomas B. Bishop, a bullwhacker on the old Mormon Trail through Virginia Dale, told this story to his son. See *Rocky Mountain News*, Aug. 19, 1932; also cited in O'Dell and Jessen, *An Ear in His Pocket*, p. 53.

5 Watrous, *History of Larimer County, Colorado*, p. 75. "Mariana's" station referred to the trading post of Mariano Medina, a mountain man who was widely known as "Marianne." James L. Boutwell was the Overland Stage Company agent there. See Gates, *Mariano Medina*, pp. 60–61.

6 Gates, *Mariano Medina*, p. 68.

7 Watrous, *History of Larimer County, Colorado*, p. 75.

8 Sayre, "Hal Sayre—Fifty-Niner," p. 166. Hal Sayre was born in 1835 and died in 1926. The specific location of this incident isn't identified, other than "between Laporte and Denver."

9 Gates, *Mariano Medina*, pp. 67–68.

10 Noel, *The City and the Saloon*, p. 8.

11 Noel, *The City and the Saloon*, p. 12.

12 Parkhill, *Law Goes West*, pp. 17–18.

13 Dorsett, *The Queen City*, p. 30.

14 Callaway, *Two True Tales of The Wild West*, p. 118. Callaway provides no source. That $750 price tag strikes me as unlikely: Slade was making $75 a month at the time, plus his room and board. But Toponce, in his *Reminiscences*, p. 123, also refers to Slade in Denver as "all dressed up." The fact that Slade bought a special suit for his trips to Denver suggests that such trips may have been frequent.

15 Chapman, *The Pony Express*, p. 191.

16 Toponce, *Reminiscence of Alexander Toponce*, p. 123.

17 Chapman, *The Pony Express*, p. 191.

18 *Dictionary of American Biography* (1936), Slade entry by W. J. Ghent, p. 203.

19 Langford, *Vigilante Days and Ways*, p. 376, quoting a letter from an unidentified friend of Slade.

20 Clute succeeded Ficklin on July 1, 1860. Isaac Eaton is referred to as the line's route superintendent as of April 1862 (see chapter 14), so Clute's tenure could not have lasted more than twenty-one months and was probably a good deal shorter.

21 Settle and Settle, *War Drums and Wagon Wheels,* pp. 140, 145. Simpson was a partner in the Central Overland from the fall of 1859; when the company was incorporated in February 1860, he was elected vice president and installed in the company's New York office. See Settle and Settle, *Empire on Wheels*, pp. 61, 76–77.

22 Mackinnon, "The Buchanan Spoils System and the Utah Expedition," pp. 142–143.

23 Captain Tracy's journal, entries for April 13 and 14, 1860, cited in Mackinnon, "The Buchanan Spoils System and the Utah Expedition," p. 147.

24 Langford, *Vigilante Days and Ways*, p. 362.

25 *Weekly Commonwealth and Republican*, Denver, Nov. 13, 1862, p. 3; cited in O'Dell and Jessen, *An Ear in His Pocket*, p. 43.

26 Voorhees, "Reminiscences of an Old Timer" (1920?), ms. #195A, Wyoming Historical Society.

27 Chapman, *The Pony Express*, p. 191.

28 Frank Bartholf's account in Watrous, *History of Larimer County, Colorado*, p. 75.

29 "Jack Slade and His Ancient Stamping Ground," unidentified, undated newspaper clip at Denver Public Library, Western History and Genealogy Department.

30 Frank Bartholf's account in Watrous, *History of Larimer County, Colorado*, p. 75. This incident took place on Oct. 15, 1862, according to the subsequent Denver grand jury indictment of Feb. 23, 1863; see *War of the Rebellion, Official Records,* vol. 13, p. 777, cited in Gray, *Cavalry and Coaches*, p. 22. C. W. Ramer, an Overland stage driver who claimed to have been sleeping at Sanderson's store that night, said he was awakened after midnight by "the reports of pistols and much noise on the outside. The bullets flew so thick and fast that I made a hasty retreat out the back door." Ramer made no mention of Slade's party arriving by stagecoach; in his telling, "Slade and his party had been drinking heavily at the saloon across the river and were shooting up the town." See Ramer, "Experiences in Early Days," pp. 14 ff.

31 Ramer, "Experiences in Early Days," pp. 14 ff.

32 Bliss, "Denver to Salt Lake by Overland Stage in 1862," p. 192.

33 I have found no specific description of the sutler's store at Fort Halleck. For a good general description of a sutler's store at this time, see Mattes, "The Sutler's Store at Fort Laramie,"

pp. 93–125. Fort Halleck formally opened on July 20, 1862, according to Marmor, "The Overland and Cherokee Trails Through the Fort Collins Urban Growth Area," p. 46. But Hafen, in *The Overland Mail*, p. 248, says it opened in the fall; and Alexander Majors, who passed through Fort Halleck in October 1862, noted that it was not yet completed. See Bliss, "Denver to Salt Lake by Overland Stage in 1862," p. 192.

34 Voorhees, "Reminiscences of an Old-Timer."

35 *Weekly Commonwealth and Republican,* Nov. 13, 1862, p. 3, cited in O'Dell and Jessen, *An Ear in His Pocket*, p. 43. Langford, *Vigilante Days and Ways*, p. 367, says Slade and his men "took possession of the sutler's quarters at Fort Halleck" and referred to the soldiers as "following him in the coach to Denver." I suspect that Slade's rampage at Fort Halleck, like his rampage at Sanderson's in Laporte, was in retaliation for the sutler's sale of liquor to his men, but there is no evidence to support this speculation.

36 See biographical note for Bela Hughes in Root and Connelley, *The Overland Stage to California*, p. 458.

37 Gray, *Cavalry and Coaches*, p. 23, cited in O'Dell and Jessen, *An Ear in His Pocket*, p. 43.

38 *Rocky Mountain News,* Nov. 18, 1862, cited in O'Dell and Jessen, *An Ear in His Pocket*, p. 44.

39 This is inferred from James Stewart's testimony in "Claim of Ben Holladay," p. 30. Stewart testified in November 1865 that he had been the Overland's Division Agent "from North Platte River to Green River" since Nov. 17, 1862. Flowers apparently did not remain long after succeeding Slade at Virginia Dale. Ball, in *Go West, Young Man*, p. 30, says Slade was succeeded at Virginia Dale by William S. Taylor, and he in turn by S. C. Leach. Robert Spotswood, testifying in 1879, said he had worked for Holladay's Overland company from November 1862, and said he was put in charge of "the first division out of Denver, from Denver to North Platte, 226 miles" in 1864; see "Claim of Ben Holladay," p. 43.

40 Spotswood's testimony in "Claim of Ben Holladay" in 1879 gave his age as thirty-eight, which would make him about twenty-one in 1862.

41 Spotswood obituary, "Dead Pioneer Told Stories of Early Days," *Denver Republican,* April 19, 1910.

42 Spotswood obituary in "Dead Pioneer Told Stories of Early Days."

43 Ibid.

44 Callaway, *Two True Tales of the Wild West*, p. 119. Langford is mistaken about the length of Slade's division, which never exceeded 500 miles.

CHAPTER 16

1 Langford, *Vigilante Days and Ways*, p. 367, says Slade went immediately to Carlyle. Jenkins, in "Kiskadden-Slade," p. 90, says, "After losing his job the Slades went east to Carlyle but only for a short time." Callaway, in *Two True Tales of the Wild West*, p. 121, says Slade visited Carlyle "in the spring or early summer of 1863," but this is almost certainly mistaken: By that time Slade was operating a contract freighting business around Fort Bridger and then moved on to Virginia City, in what was then Idaho Territory. I presume Slade sold his wagons and stock before returning to Carlyle; when he led a freighting expedition from Fort Bridger to Virginia City the following spring, the wagons and oxen were provided by his client, Henry Gilbert. See Gilbert's biography in *Progressive Men of Montana*, pp. 174–175.

2 Dennis was appointed U.S. marshal for Kansas by President Buchanan in March 1857 and was replaced in March 1858; while there he was domiciled at Leavenworth. His wife Mary apparently did not accompany him. For more information, see "Petition of E.S. Dennis, former Marshal of the Territory of Kansas, Feb. 18, 1861," Petitions and memorials of the House Committee on Territories, 36th Congress (HR 36A-G21.1) in Record Group 233, records of the U.S. House of Representatives. For Dennis's Civil War military career, see *Carlyle Newspaper Excerpts, 1844–1890,* at Clinton County Historical Society, May 11, 1861 (p. 36): Dennis was elected colonel in charge of the 42nd Regiment of Illinois militia. Aug. 17, 1861 (p. 409): Col. E. S. Dennis raising a company for the war.

3 For Elias Dennis material the author is grateful for Dennis's distant relative, Carolyn Dennis Kress, who provided Dennis's papers from the Adjutant General's Office. Dennis was mustered into the service on Aug. 28, 1861, promoted to colonel on May 1, 1862, and to brigadier general on Nov. 29, 1862. Also see "Elias S. Dennis—A Yankee General in King Cotton's Court," at http://www.rootsweb.com/~lamadiso/articles/elias.htm.

4 U.S. Census, 1850, Clinton County, house #767/773. U.S. Census 1860, Clinton County, house #1365.

5 Historic marker erected by Carlyle Junior Woman's Club and Illinois State Historical Society, 1976.

6 See Snyder, "Charles Slade," p. 209. A court filing by William Slade in November 1880 suggests that the estate still hadn't been settled by that date, 45 years after Richard Slade's death. The filing, which lists every conceivable heir of J. A. Slade's grandfather, is available at the Clinton County Historical Society.

7 The November 1880 court filing by William Slade breaks down the interest of all the heirs, assigning 12 shares of 720—that is, one-sixtieth—to Slade's widow, Maria V. Kiscadden [*sic*].

8 Denver grand jury indictment of Feb. 23, 1863; see *War of the Rebellion, Official Records,* vol. 13, p. 777, cited in Gray, *Cavalry and Coaches,* p. 22; also Parkhill, *Law Goes West,* pp. 55–57. (Parkhill dates the indictment as March 2, 1863.) The indictment identifies Slade as William Slade; his three indicted companions were Hiram Kelly, Naylor Thompson, and Robert Scott.

9 One account suggests that during this period Slade "spent months loitering in the gambling halls trying to earn a living at cards"; see O'Dell and Jessen, *An Ear in His Pocket,* p. 44. This account is unsubstantiated and certainly seems out of character for Slade.

10 June Shaputis, "How Ely, Nevada, Got Its Name" (1996), at http://www.webpanda.com/white_pine_county/historical_society/ely_name.htm. Shaputis attributes the quote to Dan McDonald in Sam P. Davis's 1913 *A History of Nevada,* but I found no reference to Ely in that book.

11 McClernan, *Slade's Wells Fargo Colt,* note 36, p. 32.

12 Fort Bridger was leased to the government on Nov. 18, 1857.

13 Stuart, *Forty Years on the Frontier,* pp. 147–148.

14 Gilbert biography in *Progressive Men of Montana,* p. 174.

15 Ludlow, *The Heart of the Continent,* pp. 295–296.

16 The party consisted of Bill Fairweather, Henry Edgar, Bill Sweeny, Tom Cover, Henry Rogers, and Bainey Hughes. See Stuart, *Forty Years on the Frontier,* p. 247.

17 O'Dell, draft manuscript for *An Ear in His Pocket*, p. 40; also note 13 on p. 44.

18 Stuart, *Forty Years on the Frontier,* p. 247.

19 Most accounts say the group struck gold on May 26, 1863. Walter Davis, in his manuscript "Hung for Contempt of Court," p. 2, says the date was May 16.

20 Stuart, *Forty Years on the Frontier,* p. 262.

21 Wolle, *The Bonanza Trail,* p. 181. Stuart, in *Forty Years on the Frontier*, p. 247, said the stampede numbered 70 men; Toponce, who was one of the stampeders from Bannack, said "at least 700 men were in that stampede." See Toponce, *Reminiscences*, p. 41.

22 Stuart, *Forty Years on the Frontier,* p. 247. This journal entry was written July 3, 1863, but probably refers to events in June, since Stuart had been away from his ranch since May 31, when the previous entry was recorded. On page 262 Stuart says the first stampede reached Alder Gulch on June 6, 1863.

23 Stuart, *Forty Years on the Frontier,* pp. 262–263, provided this date and noted that Virginia City was laid out on June 16. Hough, *The Story of the Outlaw,* p. 115, said the gulch was staked out for 12 miles within ten days. The 100-foot limit is mentioned in Toponce, *Reminiscences*, p. 41.

24 Population estimates for Alder Gulch in 1863 vary widely, from as few as 10,000 to as many as 35,000. Local historian John Ellingsen, in *If These Walls Could Talk*, p. 1, says 35,000 people were living in the Alder Gulch district by the fall of 1863, of whom 10,000 resided in Virginia City, the main town. But the first Montana census in 1864 showed 11,493 people living in Madison County; see Johnson, "Flour Famine in Alder Gulch, 1864," *Montana*, Jan. 1957, p. 19. Toponce, in *Reminiscences*, p. 41, said each man was allowed a claim of 100 feet along Alder Creek; assuming claims on both side of the creek, that would allow for fewer than 1,300 claims along a 12-mile stretch.

25 Stuart, *Forty Years on the Frontier,* p. 263.

26 *San Francisco Bulletin*, cited in Muir, "The Man Who Was Hanged for a Song," p. 47. The article provides no specific date other than "that summer [1863]."

27 Ronan, *Frontier Woman,* p. 17. (Mary Ronan, the author, was known as a girl as Mollie Sheehan.)

28 Toponce, *Reminiscences*, pp. 44–45.

29 The new territories were North Dakota and South Dakota (1861), Nevada (1861), Colorado (1861), and Idaho (1863).

30 Langford, *Vigilante Days and Ways*, p. 174.

31 Brantly. "Judicial Department," says the court in Alder Gulch was organized June 9, 1863, with Dr. G. G. Bissell elected judge. Stuart, *Forty Years on the Frontier*, p. 263, sets the date of the town site company's claim as June 16, 1863. Pfouts, *Four Firsts for a Modest Hero*, pp. 95–96, spells the judge's name Bissel and identifies him as being from Connecticut.

32 Stuart, *Forty Years on the Frontier,* p. 266. "A dance at one of the hurdy gurdies cost one dollar and as each dance wound up with an invitation to visit the bar where drinks for self and partner were expected, the cost of a waltz, schottische or quadrille was usually $1.50. Dances kept up all night but were usually orderly…. Every sort of gambling game was indulged in and it was no uncommon thing to see one thousand dollars staked on the turn of a monte card."

33 Willson, *Tough Trip Through Hell*, p. 30. This appears to be an oral history dictated in 1935, when the author was ninety-four.

34 Rodman Paul, *Mining Frontiers*, p. 2, cited in Walker, *The Wagonmasters*, pp. 205-206.

35 Stuart, *Forty Years on the Frontier*, pp. 266-267; Sanders, *Biscuits and Badmen*, p. 28. Hough, *Story of the Outlaw*, p. 117, says Alder Gulch yielded $10 million in gold dust in its first year. A Virginia City history pamphlet says $30 million in gold was produced in the first three seasons. The Jesuit priest, Fr. Joseph Giorda, is mentioned in Ronan, *Frontier Woman*, p. 20. She says the first mass was held in Virginia City on Nov. 1, 1863.

36 Stuart, *Forty Years on the Frontier*, p. 268, says Rev. A. M. Torbett arrived early in 1864, the first Protestant minister in what subsequently became Montana. He opened a small Baptist church on Idaho Street.

37 Walker, *The Wagonmasters*, p. 201; Johnson, *Some Went West*, p. 66.

38 Walker, *The Wagonmasters*, p. 201, says the distance was 150 miles "as the crow files."

39 Walker, *The Wagonmasters*, p. 202; also McClernan, *Slade's Wells Fargo Colt*, note 24, p. 28.

40 Chapman, "Vigilante Vengeance," p. 17.

41 Chapman, "Vigilante Vengeance," p. 17.

42 See Gilbert's biography in *Progressive Men of Montana*, pp. 174-175; also Chapman, "Vigilante Vengeance," pp. 16-17, which includes an interview with Gilbert's widow, Margaret. Precisely how Slade's partner John Ely figured in this deal is unclear; presumably Ely was involved as well, because he arrived at Virginia City about the same time Slade did. Langford, *Vigilante Days and Ways*, p. 369, mentions that Ely guaranteed a lumber purchase for Slade in Virginia City in July. From this reference I presume Ely accompanied Slade from Fort Bridger to Virginia City.

43 Gilbert's son William was born at Fort Bridger, on Aug. 12, 1863; see McClernan, *Slade's Wells Fargo Colt*, p. 28. That very day Gilbert started for Virginia City, where he arrived on Sept. 1; see *Progressive Men of Montana*, pp. 174-175.

44 By comparison, Gilbert later that summer left Fort Bridger on Aug. 12 and arrived at Virginia City on Sept. 1; see *Progressive Men of Montana*, pp. 174-175. James Boner traveled twice as far and still reached Virginia City in July 1863; see *Society of Montana Pioneers*, vol. I (1899), "Madison County Members," cited in McClernan, *Slade's Wells Fargo Colt*, note 24, p. 28.

45 McClernan, in *Slade's Wells Fargo Colt*, concludes that the meeting took place near Soda Springs. See p. 61.

46 Callaway, *Two True Tales of the Wild West*, pp. 11, 13, 120.

47 Callaway, *Two True Tales of the Wild West*, pp. 120-121; also 14-15. Callaway, subsequently chief justice of Montana, knew Williams as a teenager and appears to have heard this story directly from Williams. He appears to be the only person Williams ever spoke to about his tumultuous days as a Virginia City vigilante leader.

48 Where and when this encounter took place, if it took place at all, is a matter of some speculation. Two sources for the story exist. *Alder Gulch Times,* Sept. 15, 1899, p. 1, says Williams and Slade "first met at some point in Idaho on the old wagon road from Denver to this country, where a train had formed to come north." But the ordinarily more reliable Callaway, in *Two True Tales of the Wild West,* pp. 14-15, says Williams was traveling from Denver to Bannack,

and that after the caravan passed through hostile Indian territory without trouble, "the two parties separated at Soda Springs, as the Slade party was headed for Salt Lake"—that is, in the opposite direction from Williams's party. Callaway also says that Slade reached Virginia City in September, not June or July; see p. 27. Both these assertions by Callaway conflict with the known facts as well as with logic. Had Slade been running freight from Fort Bridger to Salt Lake, he would not have gone by way of Soda Springs, but would have taken the much more direct and more traveled Mormon Trail, the same route used by the Central Overland and the Pony Express. Slade's arrival in Virginia City in June or early July is more consistent with all of his activities in Virginia City that summer, also with the biographies of Williams (Slade's reputed traveling companion), who arrived at Bannack on June 20, 1863, according to Callaway (p. 15) and Birney, *Vigilantes,* pp. 224–225, and proceeded to Virginia City about July 1 (Callaway, p. 16). A strict reading of Langford, *Vigilante Days and Ways,* places the time of Langford's encounter with Slade in Virginia City (p. 368) as July 1863. Callaway was a respected lawyer and chief justice of Montana who portrayed Williams as a figure of great integrity as well, but Callaway was only a teenager, and perhaps an impressionable one, when he knew Williams (who died in 1887, when Callaway was nineteen). Since Williams was almost certainly Callaway's source for the story of his first encounter with Slade, these discrepancies call into question whether such an encounter took place at all. Although Williams was generally held in high repute by his peers, he falsified his relationship with Slade on at least one other occasion, when he filed a claim against Slade's estate, saying he had been Slade's employee at the very time the supposed first encounter took place; see Chapter 19.

49 Most accounts have Slade arriving in Virginia City in June, but this seems highly unlikely. Gold was discovered in Alder Gulch on May 26; the first stampede of prospectors from Bannack reached Alder Gulch on June 6. Even if word of the strike had reached Fort Bridger by this time and Slade had left for Virginia City immediately, he would have needed some three weeks to bring a freight train there. Henry Gilbert took twenty days to make the same trip in August, leaving Fort Bridger on Aug. 12 and arriving at Virginia City on Sept. 1; see *Progressive Men of Montana*, pp. 174–175. Slade's roundabout route surely exceeded 400 miles, and Walker, in *The Wagonmasters,* says a mule pack train could average 25 miles a day over this route; see p. 204. But a wagon train loaded with bulkier freight might have taken longer. Slade would have been hard put to arrive in Virginia City with his wagons before July 1.

50 On behalf of local merchants, Chrisman negotiated a loan for Slade & Ely in September 1863; see McClernan, *Slade's Wells Fargo Colt,* pp. 59–60.

51 Quoted in Conway, "The Dr. Jekyll and Mr. Hyde of the Old West."

52 Conway, "The Dr. Jekyll and Mr. Hyde of the Old West," part III. Towle, *Vigilante Woman,* p. 146, said that in Virginia City "Kiskadden and Slade renewed their old friendship," without attribution. Lindsay, *in The Mormons and the Theatre,* p. 58, says in the late 1860s Kiskadden was working as a cashier in his brother William's bank in Salt Lake City. Clark, "The Story Maude Adams Never Told," p. 33, says Kiskadden had known Slade and Virginia "for some time"; on page 34 he says Kiskadden worked in his uncle's bank, but this surely refers to his brother, who co-founded the Miners National Bank in Salt Lake in 1866.

53 *Society of Montana Pioneers*, vol. I (1899), "Madison County Members," cited in McClernan, *Slade's Wells Fargo Colt,* note 24, p. 28.

54 Stuart, *Forty Years on the Frontier,* p. 262, records that Maillet arrived on Nov. 30, 1863.

55 Chapman, "Vigilante Vengeance," p. 14.

56 Virginia City history pamphlet, p. 1. Clampitt, in *Echoes from the Rocky Mountains*, p. 636, placed the figure at $60 million over the first four years.

57 Courtwright, *Violent Land*, p. 67.

58 Clampitt, *Echoes from the Rocky Mountains*, p. 502.

59 Chapman, "Vigilante Vengeance," p. 17.

60 Since Henry Gilbert didn't arrive in Virginia City until Sept. 1, it's unclear who supervised the sale of his freighted goods that summer, which presumably financed Slade's business activities in July and August. McClernan, *Slade's Wells Fargo Colt*, pp. 51–53, notes evidence in Slade's estate that Slade and a partner named Thomas Jones each put up $2,750 to develop the Nevada City claims, "which were certainly rich ones if the moneys involved mean anything." An "A. J. Slade" also staked out at least two mining claims in the Granite Gulch mining district as of Nov. 17, 1863. See Granite Gulch records, index of claims on Mill Bar under A. J. Slade; Granite Gulch records, page 16, entry of Nov. 17, 1863; unlabeled book with pencil entry on inside front cover, "2nd Index to Ter. Records of Madison Co. to pre-emptions," p. 315, entry dated Feb. 4, 1865. Unlike the Nevada City claims, these Granite Gulch claims are not listed in Slade's estate. See McClernan, p. 53, for further discussion. Granite Gulch, also known as Granite Creek, identified by John Ellingsen, e-mail to author, March 4, 2008.

61 Callaway, *Two True Tales of the Wild West*, p. 123. Ravenswood was located in the Madison Valley between the present-day towns of Ennis and McAllister, which are respectively about 15 miles and 20 miles northeast of Virginia City. This is the conclusion of McClernan, who found the ranch on an old survey plat in the U.S. Bureau of Land Management at Billings; see McClernan, *Slade's Wells Fargo Colt*, p. 50. The best description of the two Slade ranches is found in Lowman, "Old Toll House Where Slade Lived…. Still Stands" (although many details, including Slade's name, are incorrect).

62 Slade's estate included a herd of dairy cows; see administrator Parker's petition of Sept. 7, 1864, cited in McClernan, *Slade's Wells Fargo Colt*, p. 53. The dairy farm is also mentioned in O'Dell and Jessen, *An Ear in His Pocket*, p. 73; also in Collins, *The Hanging of "Bad" Jack Slade*, p. 42.

63 Beidler, *X. Beidler, Vigilante*, p. 97.

64 Callaway, *Two True Tales of the Wild West*, p. 123.

65 Langford, *Vigilante Days and Ways*, pp. 368–369. McClernan says "a strict and literal reading of Langford" places the time of this encounter as July 1863; see Slade's *Wells Fargo Colt*, p. 27. It is unclear whether Slade and Ely were still partners at this point. I suspect that, as was often the case in those days, they were partners in specific projects but not on any continuing basis.

66 Gallagher is described by eleven-year-old Mollie Sheehan in Ronan, *Frontier Woman*, pp. 13, 19.

67 Gallagher was hanged by vigilantes as a member of the alleged Henry Plummer gang on Jan. 14, 1864.

68 Langford, *Vigilante Days and Ways*, p. 369.

69 Callaway, *Two True Tales of the Wild West*, p. 128; also Callaway, *Montana's Righteous Hangmen*, p. 110, quotes Cannon re Mrs. Slade's proficiency as a dancer.

70 O'Dell, draft manuscript for *An Ear in His Pocket*, p. 129.

71 "Jim Slade's Help-Meet."

72 Langford, *Vigilante Days and Ways*, p. 173.

73 Towle, *Vigilante Woman*, p. 125. She erroneously calls Virginia Slade's horse Billy Boy. For more background on Billy Bay, see Sanders, *A History of Montana*, p. 229; Conway, "The Dr. Jekyl and Mr. Hyde of the Old West, Part 3"; Birney, *Vigilantes*, p. 334.

74 Langford, *Vigilante Days and Ways*, p. 173.

75 Towle, *Vigilante Woman*, p. 127; Seagraves, *Soiled Doves*, p. 121. Neither author provides supporting evidence.

76 Birney, *Vigilantes*, p. 326.

77 Towle, *Vigilante Woman*, p. 125. No supporting evidence is provided.

78 Slade probate record, Administrator Parker's petition, Sept. 7, 1864, cited in McClernan, *Slade's Wells Fargo Colt,* p. 53.

79 *Trails West*, p. 176; author's interview with Virginia City historian John Ellingsen, March 17, 1995; also historic marker on U.S. 287 north of McAllister, Montana.

80 This is the judgment of John Ellingsen, history curator of the Montana Heritage Commission, based in Virginia City. Such a project, he reasons, must have been undertaken in the summer or fall of 1863, "before the ground froze"; interview with the author, Nov. 19, 2007; e-mail message, Nov. 26, 2007.

81 Lowman, "Old Toll House Where Slade Lived.... Still Stands." The acreage of Ravenswood and Spring Dale are provided in Slade's probate papers; see McClernan, *Slade's Wells Fargo Colt,* p. 55. Callaway, *Two True Tales of the Wild West,* p. 123, says the house at Spring Dale was more comfortable than the one at Ravenswood; Callaway also says Slade set up both ranches after late December 1863, but this is highly unlikely. McClernan, pp. 27-28, argues persuasively that both ranches were set up over the summer of 1863, which surely makes more sense. John Ellingsen told the author he had found the ruins of the Spring Dale structure; its corners, measuring 16 by 16 or perhaps 16 by 20, are still there; author's interview with John Ellingsen, Nov. 19, 2007; e-mail from John Ellingsen, Nov. 28, 2007.

82 Langford, *Vigilante Days and Ways*, p. 371. Langford says the Spring Dale ranch was 12 miles out of Virginia City and makes no mention of the dairy farm Ravenswood. Dimsdale, in *Vigilantes of Montana,* also says the distance was 12 miles, presumably from Spring Dale, but he doesn't say which ranch. Birney, in *Vigilantes*, p. 328, says eight miles; so does Alexander Davis, interviewed in the *Helena Weekly Herald,* July 25, 1878, p. 1. "Valley Tan," in a dispatch from Virginia City to the *Rocky Mountain News,* April 15, 1864, said Slade's ranch was "about ten miles from here." If Spring Dale encompassed several miles of road, that might account for these discrepancies. The miner J. M. Venable, interviewed in 1928, said Slade "bought a ranch on a small creek" eight miles from Virginia City after returning from his Milk River expedition (Dec. 10, 1863), where he wintered his weary stock and built "a small dwelling, a small stable and other buildings." This sounds like Spring Dale, but it seems unlikely the ranch, toll road, and buildings could all have been developed after Dec. 10. Venable makes no mention of the toll road through Spring Dale or the dairy ranch at Ravenswood. See Muir, "The Man Who Was Hanged for a Song," p. 48. That Slade set up both Ravenswood and Spring Dale is beyond dispute: Both ranches were listed in his estate and sold by the estate on Dec. 19, 1864; see Slade estate papers at Montana Historical Society, also McClernan, *Slade's Wells Fargo Colt,* p. 55.

83 Johnson, *Some Went West*, p. 82. She cites no source. Callaway, *Two True Tales of the Wild West*, p. 53, says the stone house "was intended as a toll house" and "was afterwards used for that purpose," implying that Slade never collected tolls there.

84 Walker, *The Wagonmasters*, p. 226.

85 Walker, *The Wagonmasters*, p. 213.

86 *Contributions to the Historical Society of Montana*, Vol. II, p. 320, identifies the steamer as the *Alone*. Other details regarding the Milk River expedition can be found in Vol. I, p. 62; Vol. II, pp. 292, 298, 302, 320, 348; Vol. III, pp. 205, 258, 269–272; Vol. IV, pp. 135; Vol. VII, pp. 259–260; Vol. VIII, pp. 142–144; Vol. IX, p. 346; Vol. X, pp. 4, 5, 92, 139, 163–164, 262, 292–293, 298. For these citations I am indebted to the late Judge John B. McClernan. Another good source is Muir, "The Man Who Was Hanged For a Song," p. 48, which provides an account of the Milk River expedition based on an interview with J. M. Venable. Langford, *Vigilante Days and Ways*, p. 367, says the freighter was loaded with goods from St. Louis (not St. Joseph). It certainly seems possible that the goods were ordered from St. Louis by the Hardie brothers of St. Joseph.

87 Muir, "The Man Who Was Hanged for a Song," p. 48. Muir's account is based on an interview with J. M. Venable.

88 Birney, *Vigilantes*, p. 327.

89 The note is in the Slade file at Montana Historical Society, discussed in McClernan, *Slade's Wells Fargo Colt*, pp. 59–60. The loan was to be repaid on December 1 but was not repaid until May 17, 1864. Whether this loan was in addition to funds provided by Ely is unclear.

90 Muir, "The Man Who Was Hanged for a Song," p. 48. Muir quotes the miner J. M. Venable: "Prior to this [expedition] all the teams' travel had been over the old Mullen military road, which crosses the range from east to west into Deer Lodge Valley, thence back again over the Deer Lodge Pass on to the Big Hole and Beaver Head Rivers, and up to the Stinking Water to Virginia City. I am telling you this to show the resourcefulness and determination of Slade."

91 A loan for $3,460 to Ely & Slade was advanced by George Chrisman, presumably on behalf of local merchants, on Sept. 24, 1863. Slade's expedition probably left after that date. See McClernan, *Slade's Wells Fargo Colt*, pp. 59–60.

92 Collins, "On the Trail of Jack Slade," p. 10, refers to the *Montana Post* article.

93 Callaway, *Two True Tales of the Wild West*, p. 122.

94 Muir, "The Man Who Was Hanged for a Song," p. 48. Also, "Jack Slade Couldn't Hold His 'Likker'," p. 130.

95 "J. A. Slade," p. 1.

96 Mary Edgerton to her sister Martha, Jan. 1864, cited in Allen, *A Decent Orderly Lynching*, p. 258.

97 Callaway, *Two True Tales of the Wild West*, p. 123.

CHAPTER 17

1 Callaway, *Two True Tales of the Wild West*, p. 21.

2 Allen, *A Decent, Orderly Lynching*, pp. 133, 135–136.

3 Allen, *A Decent, Orderly Lynching*, pp. 139–141.

4 Allen, *A Decent, Orderly Lynching*, pp. 140–142.

5 Allen, *A Decent, Orderly Lynching*, pp. 155–157.

6 Allen, *A Decent, Orderly Lynching*, pp. 161–162.

7 Allen, *A Decent, Orderly Lynching*, p. 142.

8 Allen, *A Decent, Orderly Lynching*, p. 90, identifies them as Cyrus Skinner and Charles Ridgley.

9 Allen, *A Decent, Orderly Lynching*, p. 88.

10 Callaway, *Two True Tales of the Wild West*, pp. 19–20. The Alder Gulch miners had elected Richard Todd as their sheriff on June 9; what became of him is unclear. Brantly, "Judicial Department," p. 111, says Todd was succeeded as sheriff in September by J. B. Craven, who soon resigned in favor of Plummer.

11 Allen, *A Decent, Orderly Lynching*, pp. 101–102. Callaway, *Two True Tales of the Wild West*, p. 21, dates this incident in early September and says it involved a prospective stagecoach robbery, but Callaway cites no source.

12 Allen, *A Decent, Orderly Lynching*, p. 102, fixes the date of Dillingham's murder as June 29, 1863.

13 Davis, "Hung for Contempt of Court," ms. p. 5.

14 Langford, *Vigilante Days and Ways*, p. 307, spells Lyons's first name "Hayes"; so does Allen, in *A Decent, Orderly Lynching*. But other references, as well as his gravestone at Virginia City, spell it "Haze."

15 Mather and Boswell, *Vigilante Victims*, accessible at http://www.yanoun.org/mont_vigi/victims/kill_law.html;

16 The best summary of the Dillingham murder and trial appears in Allen, *A Decent, Orderly Lynching*, pp. 102–108. Also see Callaway, *Two True Tales of the Wild West*, pp. 21–22; Sanders, *Biscuits and Badmen*, p. 23; Chapman, "Vigilante Vengeance," p. 61.

17 Stuart, describing Bannack in April 1863, cited in Callaway, *Two True Tales of the Wild West*, p. 20.

18 Chapman, "Vigilante Vengeance," p. 61.

19 Allen, *A Decent, Orderly Lynching*, p. 9. Allen arrived at his figure of eight murders by counting all known killings of white men in the early days of Alder Gulch and Bannack settlement. Allen, e-mail to the author, Dec. 2, 2007.

20 Chapman, "Vigilante Vengeance," p. 61.

21 Walter Davis, "Hung for Contempt of Court," pp. 12–13.

22 Pfouts, *Four Firsts for a Modest Hero* (1868), pp. 87–88. Pfouts's sister was married to Dr. Andrew S. Holladay, brother of Ben Holladay; see Pfouts, p. 79.

23 Pfouts, *Four Firsts for a Modest Hero*, pp. 91–97.

24 Sanders, *Biscuits and Badmen*, pp. ix, 25.

25 Sanders, *Biscuits and Badmen*, pp. 25–26.

26 Allen, *A Decent, Orderly Lynching*, pp. 11–12. Also see description of Ives in Ronan, *Frontier Woman*, pp. 19–20.

27 Langford, *Vigilante Days and Ways*, pp. 224–225.

28 Callaway, *Two True Tales of the Wild West*, pp. 23–24; Langford, *Vigilante Days and Ways*, pp. 227–228. Callaway spells the victim's name "Tbalt."

29 Dimsdale, *Vigilantes of Montana*, cited in Callaway, *Two True Tales of the Wild West*, p. 24.

30 Langford, *Vigilante Days and Ways*, pp. 227–228.

31 Allen, *A Decent, Orderly Lynching*, p. 164.

32 Davis's participation is mentioned in Langford, *Vigilante Days and Ways*, p. 235. Dimsdale, *Vigilantes of Montana*, p. 91, describes Sanders as "at that time residing in Bannack City, but temporarily sojourning at Virginia."

33 "A. B. Davis Talks," *Alder Gulch Times*, Sept. 29, 1899, p. 1.

34 Dimsdale, *Vigilantes of Montana*, p. 97.

35 "Vigilante Code Written by Masons," p. 12. The Virginia City lodge was organized on Dec. 7, 1863.

36 Judge Lew L. Callaway, in *Gould's History of Freemasonry Throughout the World*, ed. Dudley Wright, vol. V, p. 396, cited in Smurr, "Afterthoughts on the Vigilantes," p. 8.

37 Allen, *A Decent, Orderly Lynching*, p. 183.

38 Dimsdale, *Vigilantes of Montana*, p. 102.

39 Pfouts, *Four First for a Modest Hero*, p. 98. The three other men at that first meeting, according to Pfouts, were Captain Nick Wall of St. Louis, Major Alvin V. Brookie, and John Nye.

40 The best accounts of the capture, trial, and execution of Ives are in Langford, *Vigilante Days and Ways*, pp. 224–241; and Callaway, *Two True Tales of the Wild West*, pp. 22–34. Also see Sanders, *Biscuits and Badmen*, p. 74.

41 Allen, *A Decent, Orderly Lynching*, p. 184.

42 Callaway, writing in *Gould's History of Freemasonry*, vol. V, p. 395, identifies Williams as the one non-Mason in the group. Other works, including those by Callaway, say eleven of the twelve original vigilantes were Masons but don't identify the non-Mason. Callaway, in *Two True Tales of the Wild West*, p. 33, quoting A. B. Davis, identifies seven of the men present as Wilbur Sanders, Paris Pfouts, James Williams, J. M. Fox, A. B. Davis, John S. Lott, and Elkanah Morse. Allen, in *A Decent, Orderly Lynching*, p. 184, contends that two other men present—Nicholas Wall and Alvin Brookie—were not Masons, but Callaway and other sources disagree.

43 A. B. Davis, quoted in Callaway, *Two True Tales of the Wild West*, pp. 33–34.

44 Davis, "Hung for Contempt of Court," ms. p. 9.

45 Smurr, "Afterthoughts on the Vigilantes," p. 15.

46 Smurr, "Afterthoughts on the Vigilantes," p. 11.

47 Stuart, *Forty Years on the Frontier*, vol. I, p. 221.

48 Callaway, *Two True Tales of the Wild West*, p. 36.

49 Pfouts, *Four Firsts for a Modest Hero*, p. 98.

50 Dimsdale, *Vigilantes of Montana*, p. 168; Davis interview in "J. A. Slade," p. 1. But it should be noted that Dimsdale and Davis were not vigilantes themselves, and so were not in a position to say definitively. Dimsdale phrases his assertion this way: "J. A. Slade was himself, we have been informed, a Vigilante; he openly boasted of it, and said he knew all that they knew." Langford, in *Vigilante Days and Ways*, p. 373, refers to Slade as "himself a member of

the Vigilantes." Art Pauley, in *Henry Plummer: Lawman and Outlaw*, p. 250, said Slade and his cronies joined en masse when the vigilantes were formed, and that Slade, due to his influence over his rowdy companions, was made a captain, but "in a matter of days Slade's membership in the vigilantes was seen as a mistake" because of Slade's drunken conduct. This scenario sounds plausible, but Pauley provides no attribution for his assertions.

51 Pauley, *Henry Plummer: Lawman and Outlaw*, p. 250; Callaway, *Two True Tales of the Wild West*, p. 39. Sanders at this point was still a resident of Bannack, 70 miles west; but by February he had moved his wife and family to Virginia City; see Sanders, *Biscuits and Badmen*, p. 25.

52 Letter from John Lott to Llewellyn Callaway, cited in Callaway, *Two True Tales of the Wild West*, p. 65.

53 Smurr, "Afterthoughts on the Vigilantes," pp. 19–20; and Mather and Boswell, *Vigilante Victims*. As these sources point out, most of the alleged Idaho outlaws (Plummer excepted) were Southerners; the principal vigilantes (Pfouts excepted) seem to have been mostly Unionists. The first of several papal pronouncements against Freemasonry was Pope Clement XII's *In Eminenti*, April 28, 1738.

54 Callaway, *Two True Tales of the Wild West*, p. 36, says the number was "probably 1,500." Vigilante companies were limited to 50 men each; Callaway mentions ten companies, which would be 500 men. Whatever the number, how so many men could be enlisted in such a short time in secrecy has never been explained.

55 Davis, "Hung for Contempt of Court," p. 12.

56 Allen, *A Decent, Orderly Lynching*, p. 215.

57 For accounts of the capture of Yeager, see Davis, "Hung for Contempt of Court," pp. 10–11; Hough, *The Story of the Outlaw*, p. 122; Chapman, "Vigilante Vengeance," p. 62; Callaway, *Two True Tales of the Wild West*, pp. 39–47.

58 Callaway, *Two True Tales of the Wild West*, pp. 45–46; Chapman, "Vigilante Vengeance," p. 62.

59 This argument is presented in detail in Mather and Boswell, *Vigilante Victims*.

60 For further discussion, see Allen, *A Decent, Orderly Lynching*, p. 229.

61 Smurr, "Afterthoughts on the Vigilantes," p. 12.

62 Pfouts, *Four Firsts for a Modest Hero*, p. 100. Pfouts claimed this threat occurred on Sunday, Jan. 10, but if so, it had nothing to do with Plummer's execution, which didn't take place until that night. The man who allegedly threatened Pfouts, one Harrison, was not among the five road agents executed by the vigilantes at Virginia City on Jan. 14 or any time thereafter.

63 Callaway, *Two True Tales of the Wild West*, p. 49; author's interview with Lewis Headrick, Virginia City, March 18, 1995. Pfouts, in *Four Firsts for a Modest Hero*, p. 100, says the vigilantes arrested seven men but discharged two "because no positive proof implicated them in any of the depredations committed in the territory."

64 "A. B. Davis Talks," p. 1.

65 Callaway, *Two True Tales of the Wild West*, pp. 56–57.

66 Langford, *Vigilante Days and Ways*, pp. 330–331.

67 Toponce, *Reminiscences*, p. 63, says, "After January and February of 1864, people in Montana could not mine. The country was frozen up."

68 See Davis, "Hung for Contempt of Court," p. 12; Smurr, "Afterthoughts on the Vigilantes," p. 14; Dimsdale, *Vigilantes of Montana*, pp. 167–168. Smurr and Dimsdale say the court was set up after the execution of the five road agents on Jan. 14; Helen Sanders, *History of Montana*, p. 226, says the court was set up after the last of the road agents was hanged, on Feb. 3—timing that conveniently supports her thesis that the vigilantes deferred to the court once it was set up. (Helen Sanders was the daughter-in-law of Wilbur Sanders.)

69 Major Brookie is identified by his first name in Pfouts, *Four Firsts for a Modest Hero*, p. 98. Alexander Davis, interviewed in 1878, refers to him as "Mater Brookie," but I suspect this is a reportorial or typographical error. See "J. A. Slade," p. 1. The miner J. M. Venable, who briefly shared a cabin between Virginia City and Nevada City with Brookie and three other men, called him "Major A. V. Brookie," a partner of Dr. J. M. McCann. Venable said Brookie was appointed sheriff after the hanging of Plummer and accepted on an interim basis because the territorial capital at Lewiston was far distant and "it would have taken weeks to get another man appointed." Venable says Brookie was often out of the district on business and let his deputy, J. M. Fox, carry on in his place. See Muir, "The Man Who Was Hanged for a Song," pp. 47–48.

70 Dimsdale, *Vigilantes of Montana*, p. 168.

71 Smurr, "Afterthoughts On the Vigilantes," p. 17; Callaway, in *Gould's History of Freemasonry*, vol. V, p. 395, notes that vigilante trials "were always in secret and the man on trial wasn't there."

72 Callaway, *Two True Tales of the Wild West*, p. 51; Chapman, "Vigilante Vengeance," p. 62.

73 Muir, "The Man Who Was Hanged for a Song," pp. 48–50. The miner J. M. Venable, the source of this story, also notes that Judge Davis was "a good friend of my father's."

74 The complete list of twenty-one alleged road agents executed in 1864 by the vigilantes is as follows: Jan. 4, Erastus "Red" Yeager (or Yager) and George W. Brown, at Stinking Water Valley; Jan. 10, Henry Plummer, Ned Ray, and Buck Stinson, at Bannack; Jan. 11, "Dutch John" Wagoner (or Wagner) and José Pizanthia, at Bannack; Jan. 14, "Clubfoot George" Lane, Frank Parish, Haze Lyons, Jack Gallagher, and Boone Helm, at Virginia City; Jan. 16, Steve Marshland, at Big Hole Ranch; Jan. 19, William Bunton (or Burton) at Deer Lodge Valley; Jan. 24, George Shears, at Frenchtown; Jan. 25, Alexander Carter, Cyrus Skinner, John Cooper, and Robert Zachary, at Hell Gate; Jan. 26, "Whiskey Bill" Graves, at Fort Owens; Feb. 3, Bill Hunter, in the Gallatin Valley. See Sanders, *Biscuits and Badmen*, p. 74. Four of these—Pizanthia, Lyons, Gallagher, and Marshland—did not appear on Yeager's list of road agents. Conversely, four of the men on Yeager's list apparently escaped vigilante justice: Sam Bunton, Billy Terwilliger, Gad Moore, and "Mexican Frank" (whom the vigilantes probably mistakenly identified as Joe Pizanthia, to Pizanthia's misfortune).

75 Callaway, *Two True Tales of the Wild West*, pp. 52–53.

76 Callaway, *Two True Tales of the Wild West*, p. 52. Callaway quotes Davis but cites no source. Davis was alive as late as 1899 and Callaway (born in 1868) might have known him personally. This stay at Slade's probably occurred on the night of Feb. 1–2, 1864.

77 Dimsdale, *Vigilantes of Montana*, p. 161, describes the group that captured Hunter as "six individuals," the same number that had arrived at Slade's house the previous night. Art Pauley, in *Henry Plummer: Lawman and Outlaw*, p. 251, says Slade was a vigilante captain

and left Virginia City with four companions in search of Hunter on Jan. 31. But he cites no support for this assertion, which conflicts with the specific list provided by Callaway. (Dimsdale, in keeping with his practice, does not identify the vigilantes.)

78 *Montana Post,* cited in Pauley, *Henry Plummer: Lawman and Outlaw,* p. 251.

79 Leeson, *History of Montana,* p. 300. Leeson drew on Dimsdale as well as other sources.

80 For a discussion, see Allen, *A Decent, Orderly Lynching,* p. 9.

81 "J. A. Slade," p. 1. Davis's reference to "shoot them down" must be figurative; although Slade and his pals, when drunk, often shot at lampposts and the sky, no one has suggested that they shot any people.

82 Molly Sheehan Ronan, cited in Ronan, *Frontier Woman,* p. 24; also; Allen, *A Decent, Orderly Lynching,* p. 274.

83 Toponce, *Reminiscences,* p. 123.

84 Muir, "The Man Who Was Hanged for a Song," p. 48.

85 Callaway, *Two True Tales of the Wild West,* pp. 123–124.

86 Toponce, *Reminiscences,* p. 123.

87 Dimsdale, *Vigilantes of Montana,* p. 169.

88 Sanders, *Biscuits and Badmen,* p. 28. Mrs. Sanders and her three children moved to Virginia City on Feb. 6, 1864; her husband had moved earlier to purchase and prepare a log cabin for them; see p. 26. Considering Sanders's active involvement in the Ives trial and the vigilantes in December and January, it seems likely that he was already spending most of his time in Virginia City at that point.

89 Sanders, *Biscuits and Badmen,* p. 28.

90 Dimsdale, *Vigilantes of Montana,* p. 168.

91 Bruffey, *Eighty-One Years in the West,* pp. 44–45, mentions this regulation; Allen, *A Decent, Orderly Lynching,* p. 271, notes the date of the meeting, from Granville Stuart's journal.

92 Bruffey, *Eighty-One Years in the West,* pp. 44–45. Bruffey also mentions that Slade was advised by "Thorman & Davis," presumably Davis's firm of Thoroughman & Davis, "not to come to town again, and if he did come to behave himself."

93 Davis, interviewed in "J. A. Slade," p. 1.

94 "J. A. Slade," p. 1. Davis adds that he, Brookie, and Pfouts spoke to Slade several times, "and for three months they didn't hang [him]," which suggests that Slade's binges had begun shortly after his return from the Milk River on Dec. 10.

95 Alderson, "Some New Slade Stories," citing interview with George Beatty, who attributed the story to a couple named Myles, who lived along the stage line from Helena to Diamond City and had formerly worked for Slade on the Central Overland stage route. This anecdote is also mentioned in Towle, *Vigilante Woman,* pp. 126–127, but without attribution.

CHAPTER 18

1 J. M. Venable, interviewed in Muir, "The Man Who Was Hanged for a Song," p. 49. Venable says Brookie subsequently built the first smelter in Montana Territory at Argenta, although Brookie is not mentioned in histories of Argenta that I have seen. According to the Montana

official state website, placer activity took place near Argenta as early as 1862, but the first lode mines were discovered there on June 25, 1864, and the town of Argenta was chartered on Jan. 6, 1865. See www.deq.state.mt.us/abandonedmines/linkdocs/techdocs/2tech.as.

2 Stuart, diary entry, Feb. 24, 1864, cited in Allen, *A Decent, Orderly Lynching*, p. 272.

3 Henry S. Gilbert, quoted in "Echoes in Alder Gulch."

4 Bruffey, *Eighty-One Years in the West,* pp. 44–45, mentions these regulations.

5 Bruffey, *Eighty-One Years in the West,* pp. 44–45,

6 Stuart, *Forty Years on the Frontier,* vol. I, p. 221.

7 Bruffey, *Eighty-One Years in the West,* pp. 44–45.

8 Muir, "The Man Who Was Hanged for a Song," p. 45, identifies Harding; *X. Beidler, Vigilante,* p. 99, identifies Harding and Edwards; Bancroft, *Popular Tribunals,* vol. I, p. 689, says the carousing group consisted of "Naylor Thompson, Harden [*sic*], Slade and others."

9 O'Dell and Jessen, *An Ear in His Pocket,* pp. 77–78. It says the Chebang was owned by "Annie Skeggs, Lib Cunningham and others."

10 Bancroft, *Popular Tribunals,* vol. I, p. 689, says, "A jury of twelve miners formed, who feared not to act upon the testimony," implying that the suit was heard immediately. It seems more likely that the suit was adjudicated sometime later.

11 Bancroft, *Popular Tribunals,* vol. I, p. 689.

12 Callaway, *Two True Tales of the Wild West,* p. 125, says Slade had been up all night as of the morning of March 9. But Callaway confuses many events of March 9 with those of March 10, so he may in fact have been referring to the night of March 9.

13 Dimsdale, *Vigilantes of Montana,* p. 170.

14 Beidler, *X. Beidler: Vigilante,* pp. 97–98. Beidler (like some others) spells Kiskadden's name Kiscadden.

15 Toponce, *Reminiscences,* pp. 123–124. Toponce is unreliable as to time and place—he says Williams was in Virginia City, and that this encounter immediately preceded Slade's arrest, both of which are unlikely. Toponce says the encounter took place "about March 8, 1865," which is off by a year minus (probably) one day. But the conversation as he reports it may well have taken place.

16 Towle, *Vigilante Woman,* p. 140, spells Harper's name Harpe. Beidler, *X. Beidler, Vigilante,* p. 98, spells it Harper. I have found nothing else about Ms. Harper/Harpe.

17 Beidler, *X. Beidler, Vigilante,* p. 98.

18 Muir, "The Man Who Was Hanged for a Song," p. 45, describes the day as "cold and windy," perhaps based on an interview with the miner J. M. Venable. Some accounts, as well as his own gravestone, erroneously place Slade's hanging on March 9, 1864. I have no doubt the hanging took place on March 10. The probate petition filed by Mrs. Slade on April 14, 1864, attests that Slade died on March 10. The best contemporary evidence is the dispatch written by "Valley Tan" for the *Rocky Mountain News,* dated the night of March 10. It relates the events of that day and leaves no question that the events and the day the letter was written were one and the same (e.g., "Early this morning Slade and company were drunk"). See "How Slade Met His Fate," *Rocky Mountain News,* April 15, 1864. Callaway, in *Two True Tales of the Wild West,* also places the date as March 10, although his discussion on pp.

125–126 seems inconclusive. Callaway describes most events of March 10 as happening on March 9; a single line reading, "The night [of March 9] passed" appears to have been inserted in the middle of the narrative, but makes no sense where it is. The same insertion has been made in an earlier version of the same work: see Callaway, "Joseph Alfred Slade: Killer or Victim?" p. 31. I surmise that just before going to press, Callaway (or someone else) realized his mistake and hurriedly inserted this line so as to make Slade's execution fall (correctly) on March 10 in his narrative.

19 Callaway, *Two True Tales of the Wild West*, p. 125. Beidler, *X. Beidler, Vigilante*, p. 99, says Slade ran the milk wagon off the grade and spilled all of its contents.

20 Towle, *Vigilante Woman*, p, 141, says there were only three milk cows in Alder Gulch that spring. She provides no source for these statistics about cows and children. Slade's own probate file indicates that he owned a herd of dairy cows valued at $3,000. In any case, it seems safe to say that milk was a scarce and valued commodity in Alder Gulch.

21 J. M. Venable, interviewed in Muir, "The Man Who Was Hanged for a Song," pp. 45, 49, describes the fight with Harding. Beidler, *X. Beidler, Vigilante*, p. 99, says Slade "whipped Dan Harding and Charley Edwards, his own men."

22 There are two first-person accounts of the scene in Judge Davis's court that morning: one by Judge Davis himself, interviewed in 1878, and one by the miner J. M. Venable, interviewed in 1928. These accounts, given fifty years apart, are sufficiently similar to lend credibility to both. One inconsistency: Venable said Fox sought warrants for both Fairweather and Slade; see Muir, "The Man Who Was Hanged for a Song," p. 49. But Judge Davis himself said Fox sought only a warrant for Fairweather; see "J. A. Slade." Since Davis was the issuing judge and the events were relatively recent when he recalled them, his version seems more likely.

23 Davis, interviewed in "J. A. Slade." Venable's account is slightly different: Slade "derided the court. He told Judge Davis he was too good a fellow to be mixed up with any such petty business. 'This court doesn't amount to anything,' he said. 'Why don't you quit it? No court can keep peace in this district.' Judge Davis smiled and refused to argue." See Muir, "The Man Who Was Hanged for a Song," p. 49. Dimsdale, *Vigilantes of Montana*, p. 169, says Fox arrested Slade—not Fairweather—and that Slade seized the writ and tore it up. This jibes conveniently with the vigilante narrative, but Davis and Venable strike me as more reliable, as both were eyewitnesses.

24 Dimsdale, *Vigilantes of Montana*, p. 169.

25 See Muir, "The Man Who Was Hanged for a Song," p. 49.

26 This is inferred from Lott's letter reporting on the subsequent meeting and Lott's subsequent return to Nevada City to assemble the miners there (see Birney, *Vigilantes*, p. 331); and from J. M. Venable, who reported seeing Fox riding up the gulch from Nevada after Venable's midday meal, and reported that Fox later rode to German Bar to enlist James Williams. See Muir, "The Man Who Was Hanged for a Song," pp. 49–50.

27 Muir, "The Man Who Was Hanged for a Song," pp. 49–50.

28 Dimsdale, *Vigilantes of Montana*, p. 171, describes a second meeting perhaps an hour or so later at this location. I surmise that the first meeting probably occurred at this location as well.

29 Lott letter to Llewellyn L. Callaway, cited in Birney, *Vigilantes*, p. 331. The letter mentions incidentally that Sanders was present. Dimsdale, *Vigilantes of Montana*, p. 171, describes the

location of the meeting. Beidler's memoirs enigmatically fudge the issue of his participation in the meeting, but he notes that "I was well aware of the approach of the Committee [i.e., the armed force of miners from Nevada City] and was informed long before." See *X. Beidler, Vigilante*, pp. 99–100.

30 Dimsdale, *Vigilantes of Montana*, p. 169.

31 Pauley, *Henry Plummer, Lawman and Outlaw*, p. 256.

32 Dimsdale, *Vigilantes of Montana*, p. 170.

33 Dimsdale, *Vigilantes of Montana*, pp. 170–171.

34 Birney, *Vigilantes*, p. 331.

35 Accounts differ as to some minor details. J. M. Venable said Fox initially enlisted Captain Williams's help before he told anyone else in Virginia City. Venable also says Fox found Williams not at Nevada City, a mile and half down Alder Gulch, but at German Bar, five miles down the gulch. This is possible, but precisely how Venable would have known this is unclear. See Muir, "The Man Who Was Hanged for a Song," p. 50. Lott's letter to Callaway says Lott was sent to Nevada City to sound out the miners there on Slade's fate. Since James Williams subsequently led the march of miners from Nevada City to Virginia City, presumably Williams had returned to Nevada City with Lott as well. But Lott's account suggests another possibility: That Williams was not involved in the first meeting of the Virginia City vigilantes. This scenario, though, would contradict Venable's account of having seen Fox coming up the gulch from Nevada after seeking Williams's help. See Birney, *Vigilantes*, p. 331.

36 Venable, interviewed in Muir, "The Man Who Was Hanged for a Song," p. 50. Describing the scene at Slade's hanging, Venable remarked, "There was not a man from Virginia City in the band intent on lynching Slade. I don't believe there was one, outside of the actual instigators, who knew what was going to happen. We, as the sheriff's posse, had not been told—and it is likely that if Fox had told anyone in Virginia City, he would have told us." This is possible but not necessarily logical: Venable said Fox had dismissed him and his cabinmates as deputies earlier in the day.

37 Muir, "The Man Who Was Hanged for a Song," p. 50.

38 Dimsdale reported the size of the force at Nevada City as 600 men. Judge Alexander Davis put it at "300 to 400 armed men"; see "J. A. Slade," p. 1. "Valley Tan," a Virginia City correspondent writing on the night of March 10, estimated the force as "about 300 men"; see "How Slade Met His Fate." The vigilante X. Beidler described the force as 200 miners "with rifles and revolvers in abundance." Callaway, in *Two True Tales of the Wild West*, pp. 55–56 and 126, also says the force was 200 men. Callaway cites no source, but this low figure seems more likely. Most accounts say that the arresting force surrounded the block in which Slade was found, so he could not escape. An intrepid local history researcher, Matt Stiles, measured the distance around that block and concluded that a force of 600 men "would be packed so tightly, they'd be shoulder to shoulder—they couldn't even raise their rifles." Author's interview with Matt Stiles, March 18, 1995. On the other hand, another observer reported that "a guard was put up around the town and also the building that Slade was in"; such a double guard might indeed have required 300 or 400 or even 600 men. See "How Slade Met His Fate."

39 Dimsdale, *Vigilantes of Montana*, pp. 170–171. Dimsdale does not mention Williams or Lott by name—or indeed, most other vigilantes, out of respect (or fear) of their demand for

secrecy. But he consistently refers to Williams as "the leader" or "the leader of the Nevada men." In this case he refers to Lott as "the messenger."

40 Beidler, *X. Beidler, Vigilante*, p. 99.

41 Dimsdale, *Vigilantes of Montana*, p. 170.

42 Addison Wolfe recollections, interview by A. J. Noyes, Corvallis, Ore., Dec. 12, 1915 (typescript).

43 "J. A. Slade," p. 1.

44 "How Slade Met His Fate."

45 Hart, "The Hanging of Slade."

46 Sanders moved in 1867 to a house that was the most luxurious in Virginia City, consisting as it did of three separate rooms, a carpeted floor, muslin-covered ceilings and walls, a cast-iron cookstove, and the territory's first cane-seated rocking chair. The Sanders home still stands, beautifully preserved, on the south side of East Idaho Street, between Broadway and Hamilton. John Ellingsen, e-mail to author, March 10, 2008.

47 Sanders, *Biscuits and Badmen*, p. 28.

48 Callaway, *Two True Tales of the Wild West*, pp. 56, 127, says Slade apologized to Pfouts. Davis, in his 1878 interview, didn't mention Pfouts at this point. Venable, who claimed to be in the store at the time, said Pfouts was present but didn't mention Slade's apologizing to him.

49 "J. A. Slade," p. 1.

50 "How Slade Met His Fate."

51 Langford, *Vigilante Days and Ways*, p. 374.

52 Muir, "The Man Who Was Hanged for a Song," p. 50.

53 Two other motives for hanging Slade have been suggested. The amateur historian Art Pauley, as a teenager, interviewed Felix White, an aged veteran of Virginia City's early days. White implied that "many good men" were friends of Bill Hunter's and held Slade responsible for Hunter's lynching six weeks earlier. "On that day in Daylight Gulch, the friends of Bill Hunter were there and would accept nothing less for Jack Slade than what he had decreed for others." See Pauley, *Henry Plummer: Outlaw and Lawman*, pp. 257–258. Also among those in the crowd at Slade's execution were two former Pony Express riders—Calvin Downs and "Pony Bob" Haslam"—who blamed Slade for holding up their pay when he was a Central Overland division agent. See Settle and Settle, *Story of the Pony Express*, p. 107. Slade was guilty of neither offense (he hosted the vigilante party that captured Hunter but was not involved in Hunter's arrest or execution), and in any case the men who bore these resentments were not instrumental in the decision to hang Slade.

54 Langford, *Vigilante Days and Ways*, p. 374. Davis similarly described Slade: He "commenced to plead with Williams and me, walked around the room praying and beseeching in the most piteous manner." See "J. A. Slade," p. 1.

55 "J. A. Slade," p. 1.

56 "J. A. Slade," p. 1. The reference to "Brookie, Pfouts and myself" actually reads "Bronson, Pfouts and myself," but I presume this is a transcription error on the reporter's part, for Davis earlier refers to Brookie in the same threesome, and I know of no one named Bronson then in Virginia City.

57 Chapman, "Vigilante Vengeance," p. 64.

58 "J. A. Slade," p. 1.

59 Muir, "The Man Who Was Hanged for a Song," p. 50.

60 Estimates of the distance from Spring Dale to Virginia City vary. Davis, in his 1878 interview, said it was "eight miles out on the Madison"; so does Birney in *Vigilantes*, p. 328. Langford, *Vigilante Days and Ways*, p. 371, said it was "on Meadow Creek, 12 miles distant." The eyewitness account of "Valley Tan" in "How Slade Met His Fate" says the ranch was "about ten miles from here." Current residents suggest the distance could be as little as 4 or 5 miles. See author's interviews with John Ellingsen, John Senarius, and Matt Stiles, March 17–18, 1995; the latter rode more or less the same route on horseback regularly as a schoolboy.

61 An unsigned 1892 Montana newspaper article purports to be an interview with the man who rode to fetch Virginia Slade before her famous ride. The rider refers to himself as Jack but is otherwise unidentified. I suspect the whole piece is spurious. See "Jack Slade's Last Bum."

62 McClernan, *Slade's Wells Fargo Colt*, p. 14.

63 On "Billy Bay," see Sanders, *A History of Montana*, p. 229; Conway, "The Dr. Jekyl and Mr. Hyde of the Old West, Part 3"; Birney, *Vigilantes*, p. 334.

64 Author's interview with historian John Senarius, Nevada City, March 17, 1995.

65 Callaway, *Two True Tales of the Wild West*, p. 127.

66 Dimsdale, *Vigilantes of Montana*, p. 172. Callaway, *Two True Tales of the Wild West*, p. 57, identifies the location as "the Elephant Corral, situated in Daylight Gulch, in the very center of the city"; also see Beidler, *X. Beidler, Vigilante*, p. 100. An eyewitness account in "How Slade Met His Fate," describes the location as "a ravine at the edge of the street." Venable described the location as "the old slaughter pen about a hundred yards up the gulch that runs parallel with Main Street"; see Muir, "The Man Who Was Hanged for a Song," p. 50.

67 "How Slade Met His Fate." Also see Callaway, *Two True Tales of the Wild West*, p. 129.

68 Ronan, *Frontier Woman*, p. 24.

69 "How Slade Met His Fate."

70 Dimsdale, *Vigilantes of Montana*, p. 172.

71 Beidler, *X. Beidler, Vigilante*, p. 100.

72 Sanders, *Biscuits and Badmen*, p. 28.

73 "J. A. Slade," p. 1.

74 "How Slade Met His Fate."

75 "J. A. Slade," p. 1.

76 "How Slade Met His Fate."

77 A. M. Hart, "The Hanging of Slade" (manuscript), Sept. 16, 1908.

78 Muir, "The Man Who Was Hanged for a Song," p. 50.

79 "How Slade Met His Fate."

80 "Echoes in Alder Gulch," p. 9.

81 Beidler, *X. Beidler, Vigilante*, pp. 100–101.

82 Muir, "The Man Who Was Hanged for a Song," p. 50. For discussion of the ride from Spring Dale to Virginia City I am grateful to Matt Stiles, John Senarius, and John Ellingsen, all interviewed on March 17 and 18, 1995. Stiles in particular said he had ridden "essentially that ride" many times on his way to school. He said it took him 45 minutes, but of course he wasn't in as much of a hurry as Virginia Slade.

83 The executioners' fears of Virginia Slade are discussed in Callaway, *Two True Tales of the Wild West*, pp. 57, 128.

84 Hart, "The Hanging of Slade."

85 "How Slade Met His Fate."

86 "How Slade Met His Fate"; also Beidler, *X. Beidler, Vigilante*, p. 101. Beidler identifies the man only as "N.T."

87 "How Slade Met His Fate."

88 Beidler, *X. Beidler, Vigilante*, p. 101. Mrs. Slade's time of arrival is recorded as six o'clock by an observer, "Valley Tan," in "How Slade Met His Fate."

89 Davis in "J. A. Slade," says Mrs. Slade arrived "not more than ten minutes after his body was laid out in the Virginia Hotel." Venable, interviewed in Muir, "The Man Who Was Hanged for a Song," p. 50, says Mrs. Slade "was in time to see them cut Slade's body down and lay him out." "Valley Tan," writing that night in "How Slade Met His Fate," says Mrs. Slade arrived "at six o'clock and before the corpse was laid out." Another observer, Captain William Drannan, said, "Just as they were carrying the body from the gallows to the hotel she was seen coming across the hill as fast as her horse could carry her"; see Drannan, *Thirty-One Years on the Plains and in the Mountains*, p. 392. On the other hand, Slade's partner Henry Gilbert said Virginia arrived two hours after the hanging; see "Echoes in Alder Gulch."

90 Drannan, *Thirty-One Years on the Plains and in the Mountains*, p. 392.

91 The Virginia Hotel was located at the southwest corner of Wallace and Van Buren Streets. John Ellingsen, e-mail to the author, March 10, 2008.

92 Drannan, *Thirty-One Years on the Plains and in the Mountains*, p. 392.

93 Langford, *Vigilante Days and Ways*, p. 375.

94 Coutant, *History of Wyoming*, p. 406.

95 Langford, *Vigilante Days and Ways*, p. 375.

96 "How Slade Met His Fate."

97 Beidler, *X. Beidler, Vigilante*, pp. 101–102.

CHAPTER 19

1 Callaway, *Montana's Righteous Hangmen*, p. 110.

2 Sanders, *Biscuits and Badmen*, p. 28.

3 Stuart, *Forty Years on the Frontier*, vol. I, p. 268. Stuart says Torbett "arrived early in 1864." Some sources spell his name Torbet; see, for example, Sanders, *Biscuits and Badmen*, p. 28, which also mentions his Baptist affiliation.

4 Torbett had left Virginia City by July 18, 1867. See Daniel Tuttle, *Reminiscences of a Missionary Bishop*, p. 125, cited in Stuart, *Forty Years on the Frontier*, vol. I, p. 268.

5 Sanders, *Biscuits and Badmen*, p. 28.

6 Formaldehyde was discovered in 1867 by the German chemist August Wilhelm von Hofmann.

7 The dispatch by "Valley Tan" written the night of Slade's death implied that "a metallic case" would be brought to Virginia City from elsewhere; see "How Slade Met His Fate." Also, Charles Cannon's account of seeing Virginia Slade on a stage to Salt Lake a few days after the hanging suggests that perhaps she was going there for the purpose of ordering a metallic casket; see Callaway, *Montana's Righteous Hangmen*, pp. 110–111. The name of the tinsmith Merk was provided to the author by the local historian John Ellingsen. Interview, March 17, 1995.

8 Boren, "Jack Slade's Grave Located," p. 57; also author's interview with John Ellingsen, March 17, 1995. This is the generally accepted version in Virginia City folklore. I should note that Callaway, *Two True Tales of the Wild West*, p. 129, and Langford, *Vigilante Days and Ways*, p. 375, say Slade's body was temporarily buried at Spring Dale, across the road from the tollhouse, but this seems less likely, and certainly logistically far more difficult.

9 The author is grateful to the late Dabney Otis Collins, who researched this subject; see his research manuscript, "On the Trail of Jack Slade," p. 11. Also see "The Man in the Whiskey-Filled Coffin," *The American Funeral Director*, March 1987. Although standard accounts suggest that Virginia was waiting for the roads to open before moving the coffin, in fact the road to Salt Lake City was never closed. Charles Cannon wrote of taking a stage from Virginia City to Salt Lake City a few days after the hanging; indeed, he claimed Mrs. Slade was aboard (see Callaway, *Montana's Righteous Hangmen*, p. 110). Mrs. Slade's presence on that stagecoach seems unlikely—Cannon may have confused it with another stagecoach trip he shared with Mrs. Slade—but by May 2 her creditors claimed she had left the region, presumably for Salt Lake City. See Slade probate papers at Montana Historical Society; also McClernan, *Slade's Wells Fargo Colt*, pp. 31–32. Nevertheless, Slade wasn't buried at Salt Lake City until July 20. I can only conclude that Mrs. Slade wasn't emotionally or financially ready until then to deal with the task of moving her husband's body.

10 Callaway, *Montana's Righteous Hangmen*, pp. 110–111.

11 Loomis, Wells Fargo, says the stock's par value was $100 in 1863 and also 1867–69; see pp. 167 and 197. The market value could have been much higher. Wells Fargo says it has no record of share ownership prior to 1866 and is unable to explain how Slade came to possess 134 shares; letter from Robert G. Pacini, Wells Fargo History Department, to Dabney Otis Collins, March 19, 1976.

12 Slade probate file, Montana Historical Society. The best discussion of this file can be found in McClernan, *Slade's Wells Fargo Colt*, pp. 45–63; also p. 14. The Sanders quote appears in Strahorn, *Fifteen Thousand Miles by Stage*, p. 108.

13 McClernan, *Slade's Wells Fargo Colt*, p. 47.

14 My sense is that Mrs. Slade made the trip to Salt Lake City more than once after her husband's death and perhaps as many as three times. George Cannon said she was in a stagecoach with him to Salt Lake a few days after Slade's hanging, presumably mid-March; see Callaway, *Montana's Righteous Hangmen*, pp. 110–111. She was back in Virginia City to file a petition before the probate court on April 14; see McClernan, *Slade's Wells Fargo Colt*, p. 47; but the judge determined on May 2 that she had left the region. She was back in Virginia City again

in May, if her confrontation with the estate administrator George Parker (appointed May 2) is to be believed (see McClernan, p. 31). Then she left yet again to take her husband's body to Salt Lake, probably in June.

15 McClernan, *Slade's Wells Fargo Colt,* p. 47.

16 McClernan, *Slade's Wells Fargo Colt,* p. 48.

17 McClernan, *Slade's Wells Fargo Colt,* pp. 51–52.

18 Anecdote written by Mrs. Granville Stuart, perhaps from her husband's reminiscences, cited in McClernan, *Slade's Wells Fargo Colt,* p. 31; also in typescript at Montana Historical Society.

19 The Williams claim is discussed in McClernan, *Slade's Wells Fargo Colt,* pp. 60–62. The claimant is identified as James H. Williams; most biographies of Williams make no reference to the middle initial. Nevertheless, it seems very likely that the claimant James Williams and the vigilante James Williams are one and the same, especially since the claim was submitted by Williams's fellow vigilante Wilbur Sanders.

20 Crawford, *Rekindling Camp Fires,* pp. 48–49.

21 Salt Lake City Cemetery Records; O'Dell and Jessen, *An Ear in His Pocket,* p. 85. O'Dell and Jessen say the stagecoach left Virginia City in June; Crawford, in *Rekindling Camp Fires,* says Mrs. Slade left east Idaho less than sixty days after her husband's death; see also McClernan, *Slade's Wells Fargo Colt,* p. 49.

22 Chapman, "Slade of the Overland."

23 *Transcript of Record of the Dead,* Book A, Great Salt Lake City Cemetery, p. 73, Burial #2067.

24 *Carlyle Weekly Union Banner,* Dec. 10, 1863, p. 2. No such place as Brunswick City existed then or later. Perhaps the intended reference was "Bannack," misread or garbled in transmission.

25 *Carlyle Weekly Union Banner,* Dec. 24, 1863, p. 2.

26 Letter from Elizabeth Ruble to "Uncle," Carlyle, Aug. 11, 1864, at Clinton County Historical Society, Carlyle, Ill.

27 Allen, *A Decent, Orderly Lynching,* pp. 292–295.

28 Dimsdale, *Vigilantes of Montana,* p. 178.

29 Allen, *A Decent, Orderly Lynching,* pp. 298–299.

30 Allen, *A Decent, Orderly Lynching,* pp. 301–303.

31 Allen, *A Decent, Orderly Lynching,* pp. 305–307.

32 Letter from J. O'Brien Scobey, Chicago, to Madison County Clerk, March 12, 1890, Montana Historical Society. Also cited in McClernan, *Slade's Wells Fargo Colt,* p. 57; quoted extensively in Collins, *The Hanging of "Bad" Jack Slade,* p. 50.

33 McClernan, *Slade's Wells Fargo Colt,* p. 55.

34 McClernan, *Slade's Wells Fargo Colt,* p. 57.

35 McClernan, *Slade's Wells Fargo Colt,* pp. 52, 56.

36 McClernan, *Slade's Wells Fargo Colt,* p. 55.

37 McClernan, *Slade's Wells Fargo Colt,* p. 52.

38 McClernan, *Slade's Wells Fargo Colt,* pp. 62–63.

39 Lindsay, *The Mormons and the Theatre*, p. 58. Alexander Davis, among others, described Kiskadden as a "well-to-do merchant in Virginia City." See "J. A. Slade," p. 1. Collins, in *The Hanging of "Bad" Jack Slade*, describes Kiskadden as a hardware merchant.

40 *Montana Post*, cited in Towle, *Vigilante Woman*, p. 148.

41 Madison County records, Book F of Deeds, p. 430, cited in McClernan, *Slade's Wells Fargo Colt*, p. 56,

42 Judge Henry McClernan to Professor Stanley Davison, letter, Aug. 31, 1874, Western Montana College, Dillon.

43 This theory was advanced by two Virginia City old-timers that I know of: Dick Pace and Zena Hoff. The latter, an actress who died in the mid-1970s, actually lived in the house where Virginia Slade kept Slade's body immediately after his death. Author's interview with John Ellingsen, Virginia City, March 17, 1995.

44 Towle, *Vigilante Woman*, pp. 148–149. The author provides no source, but support for this theory is provided in a July 1923 interview with George Beatty, then 85 years old: "After Slade was hanged she married Kiskadden at Virginia City, but she was so tough he had to turn her out." See *Bynum Herald*, undated clip, July 1923.

45 McClernan, *Slade's Wells Fargo Colt*, p. 14. Trenholm, "Save Sibley," p. 51, says Virginia and Jemmy were seen together in Denver. Also see Collins, *The Hanging of "Bad" Jack Slade*, p. 50.

46 Salt Lake County records, Oct. 29, 1868, cited in Muir, "The Man Who Was Hanged for a Song," p. 50.

47 McClernan, *Slade's Wells Fargo Colt*, p. 57. The firm of Word & Spratt is mentioned in *Reports of Cases Argued and Determined in the Supreme Court of Montana;* since virtually all legal business in Montana was then conducted in Virginia City, I presume the firm was located there.

48 Johnson, "Flour Famine in Alder Gulch, 1864," *Montana*, Jan. 1957, p. 18.

49 Johnson, "Flour Famine in Alder Gulch, 1864," pp. 18–27; also Stuart, *Forty Years on the Frontier*, vol. II, pp. 28–31.

50 Callaway, *Two True Tales of the Wild West*, p. 63.

51 Callaway, *Two True Tales of the Wild West*, pp. 67–68; Smurr, "Afterthoughts On the Vigilantes," p. 13; Allen, *A Decent, Orderly Lynching*, p. 309.

52 *Montana Post*, August 1867, cited in Smurr, "Afterthoughts on the Vigilantes," p. 10; also Bancroft, *Popular Tribunals*, vol. I, p. 704.

53 Allen, *A Decent, Orderly Lynching*, pp. 365–366, furnishes a complete list of vigilante executions.

54 Author's interview with John Ellingsen, Virginia City, March 17, 1995.

55 *Trails West*, p. 185, says Alder Gulch produced more than $100 million in gold. Wolle, *Bonanza Trail*, p. 179, says the figure is $70 million. John Ellingsen, history curator of the Montana Heritage Commission, notes that there were no good figures for the amount of gold produced by Alder Gulch in the 1860s, but "a good guess as to 1860s gold (before records were kept) was $30 to $50 million in gold at $20.00 per ounce (the official price from the 1860s to 1932)," and perhaps $100 million all told. The equivalent in 2008 dollars would be about $4 to $5 billion. John Ellingsen, e-mail message to author, Dec. 10, 2007.

Thanks to a unique combination of factors—dry weather, civic apathy, and plain luck— nearly all of Virginia City's original 1863 buildings have survived to the present day, when the resident population hovers around 130. Any visitor today can easily retrace Slade's steps on his last fateful two-day drunk in March 1864. For many years the hanging of Slade was reenacted annually by local residents, complete with a local equestrienne performing Virginia Slade's wild ride. Tourists continue to visit the cemetery, where notable pioneers like Thomas Dimsdale and Justice Callaway's parents sleep not all that far from the five road agents who were lynched together in January 1864 by the vigilantes.

Slade's toll road to the Bozeman Trail and his tollhouse overlooking the Madison Valley survived into the mid-1950s, when a rancher fed up with trespassing tourists tore up the road and dynamited the house; all that remain today are the corners of the foundation and some of its timbers. The Virginia Hotel where Slade's body was laid out was destroyed by fire in 1937. But the tiny clapboard house on Van Buren Street where Virginia Slade kept her husband's pickled remains still stands.

CHAPTER 20

1 Lee surrendered April 9, 1865; the news was published in the *Montana Post* on April 22.

2 Oberholtzer, *Jay Cooke,* vol. 1, p. 574.

3 Howard, *Hoofbeats of Destiny,* p. 162, citing E. G. Spaulding, chairman of the House Ways and Means Committee, in his 1869 report on the financial history of the war.

4 Stuart, *Forty Years on the Frontier,* vol. II, pp. 30–31.

5 Ronan, *Frontier Woman,* p. 23.

6 Author's interview with Virginia City historian John Ellingsen, March 17, 1995.

7 The series appeared from August 26, 1865, through May 24, 1866. See Housman, "The Vigilante Movement and Its Press in Montana."

8 See "A. B. Davis Talks"; also Callaway, *Two True Tales of the Wild West,* pp. 11–12.

9 Dimsdale, *Vigilantes of Montana,* p. 168.

10 Dimsdale, *Vigilantes of Montana,* p. 167.

11 Dimsdale, *Vigilantes of Montana,* p. 167.

12 Dimsdale, *Vigilantes of Montana,* p. 173.

13 Dimsdale, *Vigilantes of Montana,* pp. 176–177.

14 Dimsdale, *Vigilantes of Montana,* pp. 176–177.

15 Hough, *The Story of the Outlaw,* pp. 151–152.

16 Callaway, *Two True Tales of the Wild West,* p. 129.

17 Langford, *Vigilante Days and Ways,* p. 376. The author of this letter is not identified.

18 Mark Twain to Hezekiah L. Hosmer, Sept. 15, 1870, cited in O'Dell and Jessen, *An Ear in His Pocket,* pp. 64–65.

19 Samuel Clemens (Mark Twain) to Orion Clemens, March 10, 1871, cited in O'Dell and Jessen, *An Ear in His Pocket,* p. 65.

20 Orion Clemens to Mark Twain, March 11, 1871, cited in O'Dell and Jessen, *An Ear in His Pocket,* p. 65.

21 See Slade's biography by W. J. Ghent in *Dictionary of American Biography*, pp. 202-203. Orwell, "Raffles and Miss Blandish," *Horizon*, August 28, 1944.

22 "Schoolboys Know of Madman Slade," *Julesburg* (Colo.) *Grit-Advocate*, May 23, 1929.

23 Allen, *A Decent, Orderly Lynching*, pp. 359-360.

24 The two works referred to are Smurr, "Afterthoughts on the Vigilantes," *Montana*, Spring 1958, pp. 8-20; and Allen, *A Decent, Orderly Lynching*.

25 See Corbett, *Orphans Preferred*, pp. 135-139, which cites Twain's *Roughing it* as well as *The Great Salt Lake Trail*, an 1898 collaboration of Henry Inman and William F. Cody.

26 The distance is given in Walker, *The Wagonmasters*, p. 56.

27 Visscher, *The Pony Express*, p. 49.

28 The best analysis of Cody's legend appears in Warren, *Buffalo Bill's America*, pp. 17-21.

29 The author is grateful to Carolyn Dennis Kress, a collateral relative of General Dennis, for this information. Also see Dennis's biography at http://www.rootsweb.com/~lamadiso/articles/elias.htm.

30 *Bill in chancery for divorce #44, Mary D. Dennis v. Elias S. Dennis*, Clinton County Court, Aug. 17, 1871.

31 Wickliffe, "Elias Smith Dennis, Forgotten Hero of Carlyle," pp. 11 ff. Also see Dennis obituary in *Carlyle* (Ill.) *Constitution and Union*, Dec. 20, 1894. Also see http://www.rootsweb.com/~lamadiso/articles/elias.htm.

32 Settle and Settle, *War Drums and Wagon Wheels*, p. 169.

33 Settle and Settle, *War Drums and Wagon Wheels*, p. 169.

34 Settle and Settle, *Story of the Pony Express*, pp. 137-138.

35 Maurer, "Pony Express Pioneer Left His Mark on VMI," p. 7.

36 Frederick, *Ben Holladay*, p. 260. The Wells Fargo meeting in Denver took place Nov. 12, 1866; see Loomis, *Wells Fargo*, p. 181. Trenholm, in "Save Sibley!" *Montana*, Autumn 1962, p. 51, says Virginia and Jemmy were seen together in Denver.

37 Frederick, *Ben Holladay*, pp. 238-239. The actual amount of the claim was $526,739. P. 272 mentions Holladay's failure in the panic of 1873.

38 O'Dell and Jessen, *An Ear in His Pocket*, pp. 16-17.

39 Shaputis, "How Ely, Nevada Got Its Name . . . Maybe." See http://www.webpanda.com/white_pine_county/historical_society/ely_name.htm. The author cites Davis, *History of Nevada* (1913) as her source, but I did not find John Ely mentioned in that book.

40 See "J. A. Slade."

41 A. B. Davis suggested that Beidler's efforts were exaggerated; see "A. B. Davis Talks."

42 Johnson, *Some Went West*, p. 75.

43 "A. B. Davis Talks."

44 Allen, *A Decent, Orderly Lynching*, p. 361.

45 Callaway, *Two True Tales of the Wild West*, p. 83.

46 Callaway, *Two True Tales of the Wild West*, pp. 83, 91-92; Allen, *A Decent, Orderly Lynching*, pp. 361-362.

47 Lindsay, *The Mormons and the Theatre*, p. 58, identifies William as Kiskadden's brother.

This is supported by *Reminiscences of Alexander Toponce,* cited in Jenkins, "Kiskadden-Slade," p. 91. Clark, in "The Story Maude Adams Never Told," p. 34, is probably mistaken when he identifies William as Jim Kiskadden's uncle. For William's background, see http://www.media.utah.edu/UHE/b/BANKING.html.

48 Kiskadden was born May 24, 1836, according to his gravestone in Mount Olivet Cemetery, Salt Lake City. Asenith, buried beside him, was born Nov. 9, 1848.

49 See Clark, "The Story Maude Adams Never Told"; also Lindsay, *The Mormons and the Theatre*, pp. 58–63.

50 "Old Jule's Bones," p. 3. It describes the location as the "PF ranch," formerly the old "Rock ranch," where Slade had supposedly mutilated Jules.

51 Anna Barry, "An Interview with Albert W. Keith," July 13, 1937, #4946; also "Interview with Henry Meagher," June 18, 1937, #4632, Oklahoma Historical Society.

52 MacMurphy, "Some Squatters with a History," p. 4.

53 Shumway, *History of Western Nebraska*, p. 58.

54 *Constitution and Union*, Carlyle, Ill., Jan. 23, 1873.

55 See Clinton County court filing re Estate of Mary D. Dennis, April 22, 1874; also sale bill of the deceased, July 22, 1874.

56 *Constitution and Union*, Carlyle, Ill., March 4, 1880. Charles R. Slade died at Bodie, Calif. on Feb. 1, 1880.

57 William married Elmira St. Clair at Carlyle on Sept. 16, 1877. *Carlyle* (Ill.) *Union-Banner,* Sept. 20, 1877.

58 Clinton County Circuit Court document, November term, 1880, at Clinton County Historical Society.

59 Goodwin, "Miss Virginia Slade," manuscript, p. 5; also author's interview with Katherine Goodwin, Carlyle, Ill., March 3, 1995.

60 Marriage certificate, James Reed and Maria V. Kiskadden, St. Louis County, June 8, 1870; filed July 7, 1870.

61 O'Dell, draft manuscript for *An Ear in His Pocket*, p. 130. It cites no source.

62 George Beatty, quoted in *Bynum Herald*, undated clip, July 1923: "The last I heard of her, she was keeping a house of ill fame in Omaha."

63 Author's interview with Lee Kizer, March 13, 1995. Kizer also referred to an unidentified book that made the same claim.

64 Ramer, "Experiences in Early Days."

65 Clinton County Circuit Court document, filed by William Slade, Sept. 29, 1880.

66 Judge John McClernan searched the National Archives for such a pension application, without success. See McClernan, *Slade's Wells Fargo Colt,* p. 57.

67 Virginia City historian John Ellingsen identified the hill northeast of Virginia City, where the Slade toll road was located, as "Raspberry Hill." Ellingsen e-mail to the author, March 10, 2008.

68 J. O'B. Scobey to William Marr, March 12, 1890, at Historical Society of Montana.

69 Author's interview with Anne Seagraves, author of *Soiled Doves,* August 30, 2006.

70 Willson, "Tough Trip Through Hell: The Virginia City Memoirs of S. B. B. Willson" (manuscript, 1935).

71 The presence of Davis, Boner and Cannon is presumed from interviews with them that appeared shortly afterward in the *Alder Gulch Times* issues of Sept. 15, 22, and 29, 1899. Sanders, Edgar, and Hart are mentioned in an account of the meeting in the Virginia City *Madisonian*, Sept. 1, 1899, pp. 1–2.

72 Callaway, *Two True Tales of the Wild West*, p. 93.

73 Clampitt, *Echoes from the Rocky Mountains*, p. 509.

74 Callaway, *Two True Tales of the Wild West*, p. 126.

75 The specific location is Section B4, #23. The number of burials was provided to the author by the cemetery sexton, Mark Edwin Smith, e-mail of March 12, 2008.

76 According to Richard H. Cracroft, a professor at Brigham Young University, the stone was placed there about 1958 by the late Don D. Walker, a professor of English and American studies at the University of Utah (as well as the adviser on Cracroft's master's thesis). Cracroft says Walker became intrigued by Slade's story when he assigned Mark Twain's *Roughing It* to his Western literature class. When Walker subsequently learned that Slade was buried in Salt Lake City, he perceived a teachable moment. Walker wrote to the Department of the Army, pointing out that a Mexican War veteran was entitled to a gravestone, courtesy of the government. Six weeks later a chiseled granite military headstone arrived at Walker's home. Armed with a supply of ready-mix cement, Walker and a half-dozen students set the stone in place and performed a makeshift ceremony that consisted largely of passages read from *Roughing It*.

Cracroft told me he lived across the street from Salt Lake City Cemetery in the early 1960s and visited the Slade gravestone several times during that period. Yet a 1976 article in *Frontier Times* magazine claimed to have found a remnant of Slade's original gravestone in an adjoining section of marked graves. Kerry Ross Boren's article made no mention of the military marker placed by Professor Walker; indeed, Boren wrote, "Efforts are underway... to place a proper marker at Jack Slade's grave with appropriate ceremonies."

To further confuse matters, Jim Stretesky, the county commissioner from Julesburg, told me in 1995 that he had visited the cemetery in his capacity as a Pony Express Centennial vice-president in 1960–61. At Stretesky's request, the caretaker examined his books, then walked Stretesky to what should have been the correct location. The gravesite claimed by *Frontier Times* was mistaken, Stretesky said; but neither was there a marker for Slade then anywhere else. At his urging, Stretesky said, a stone was erected in 1980 by the National Association and Center for Outlaw and Lawman History. Stretesky showed me a photo of the headstone that he snapped on a subsequent visit. It's the same headstone that Cracroft insists was placed there by Don Walker in 1958.

Stretesky has since died. The Center for Outlaw and Lawman History says it has no record of the stone. When I mentioned these conflicting accounts to Professor Cracroft, he professed mystification. "Certainly the stone was in place and those 'ceremonies' had already been performed some years before the 1976 article in *Frontier Times*," he wrote me via e-mail. Then he added cheerfully, "Hurrah for literary historical mysteries." Richard Cracroft e-mail, July 30, 2007. Also see Cracroft, "A Footnote (or Headstone) on Jack Slade of *Roughing It* Infamy," at www.twainquotes.com/Slade.html.

Whoever placed the stone, the actual location of Slade's coffin remains in doubt. Although the cemetery's burial books routinely list each grave by plot, block and lot number, Slade's original entry says only, "Plot B, Single," perhaps because the burial wasn't intended to be permanent. See *Transcript of Record of the Dead, GSL City Cemetery*, Book A, p. 73, burial No. 2067. A subsequent entry in the cemetery's records provides a more precise location— it works out to twenty feet east and fifteen feet south of the marker— although the sexton is uncertain where that entry came from; Mark Edwin Smith, sexton of Salt Lake City Cemetery, e-mail message to the author, March 12, 2008. He says the exact site of Slade's grave is Plot B, Block 4, Lot 2, Grave 3, east tier. He adds, "I don't know why or how it was come by, but it has been written in the records." Smith adds that Slade's official interment number is now 2043, not 2067 as originally entered in Book A of the cemetery's burial records in 1864.

BIBLIOGRAPHY

Suggestions for Further Reading

The following books are the definitive sources on their respective subjects. (For full publishing details, see each book's listing under "Books" below.) I have also added comments about the subject covered and/or historical reliability of the source to many of the bibliography entries.

California Gold Rush: Brands, *The Age of Gold*.

Freighting: Walker, *The Wagonmasters*.

Frontier medicine: Valencius, *The Health of the Country*.

Indians: Yenne, *Indian Wars;* also Michno, *Encyclopedia of Indian Wars*.

Mail service: Hafen, *The Overland Mail, 1849–1869*.

Military in the Mexican War: Winders, *Mr. Polk's Army*.

Military in the West: Utley, *Frontiersmen in Blue*.

Montana vigilantes: Allen, *A Decent, Orderly Lynching*.

Mormons: Denton, *American Massacre*.

Pony Express: Settle and Settle, *The Story of the Pony Express*; also Chapman, *The Pony Express*.

Russell, Majors & Waddell: Settle and Settle, *War Drums and Wagon Wheels*; also Settle and Settle, *Empire on Wheels*.

Stagecoaching: Banning, *Six Horses*; also Root and Connelley, *The Overland Stage to California*.

Telegraph: Thompson, *Wiring a Continent*.

Women in the West: Johnson, *Some Went West*.

Books

Abbott, Carl, Stephen K. Leonard, and Thomas J. Noel, *Colorado: A History of the Centennial State* (Boulder: University Press of Colorado, 2005).

Adams, Ramon, *Six Guns and Saddle Leather: A Bibliography of Books and Pamphlets on Western Outlaws and Gunmen* (Norman: University of Oklahoma Press, 1969). Contains citations of dozens of books referring to Slade. Author is a stickler for factual accuracy who frequently cites errors in books he lists.

Allen, Frederick, *A Decent Orderly Lynching: The Montana Vigilantes* (Norman: University of Oklahoma Press, 2004.) The first truly definitive work on the Montana vigilantes: readable, well researched, and scrupulously fair.

Annals of Carlyle, Illinois 1809–1956. Carlyle (Ill.) Community Development program, 1956.

Ayres, Carol Dark, *Lincoln and Kansas: Partnership for Freedom* (Manhattan, Kan.: Sunflower University Press, 2001). Definitive work on Lincoln's visit to Kansas, 1859.

Bailyn, Bernard, *The Peopling of British North America: An Introduction* (New York: Knopf, 1986). Summary of British emigration to America.

_____, *Voyagers to the West* (New York: Knopf, 1986). Definitive work on British emigration to America.

Ball, George S., *Go West Young Man: Stories of the Pioneers.* (Published by the author, 1970). Pp. 26–31 discusses Virginia Dale, Colo.

Bancroft, Hubert Howe, *Popular Tribunals, vol. I* (San Francisco: History Co., 1887). Pp. 688–692 deals with Slade hanging.

Banning, William, and G. H. Banning, *Six Horses* (New York: Century Co., 1928). Definitive book on stagecoach era, with some discussion of Slade.

Bartlett, I. S., ed., *History of Wyoming, 3* vols. (Chicago: S.J. Clarke Publishing Co., 1918).

Beebe, Lucius, and Charles Clegg, *U.S. West: The Saga of Wells Fargo* (New York: Bonanza Books, 1949).

Beidler, John X., *X. Beidler, Vigilante*. Ed. Helen Fitzgerald Sanders with Wm. H. Bertsche, Jr. (Norman: University of Oklahoma Press, 1957). Memoir of a leading Montana vigilante, dictated in the 1880s.

Berthoff, Rowland, *British Immigrants in Industrial America, 1790–1950* (New York, Russell & Russell, 1953; reprint, 1968).

Bettelyoun, Susan Bordeaux, and Josephine Waggoner, *With My Own Eyes* (Lincoln: University of Nebraska Press, 1998). Author, born 1857, was half-French, half-Indian daughter of one of Slade's station keepers.

Biographical Dictionary of U.S. Congress, Bicentennial Edition (1989).

Birney, Hoffman, *Vigilantes* (Philadelphia: Penn Publishing Co., 1929). A good read, but more style than substance.

Bloss, Roy S., *Pony Express: The Great Gamble* (Berkeley, Calif.: Howell-North, 1959). Deals with Pony Express finances.

Bodnar, John, *The Transplanted*: *A History of Immigrants in Urban America* (Bloomington: Indiana University Press, 1985).

Brands, H. W., *The Age of Gold: The California Gold Rush and the New American Dream* (New York: Doubleday, 2005). Definitive work on the California Gold Rush, and a good read as well.

Brasler, Roy, ed., *Collected Works of Abraham Lincoln,* vol. 3 (New Brunswick: Rutgers University Press, 1953).

Bruffey, George A., *Eighty-One Years in the West* (Butte, Mont.: Butte Miner Co., 1925). Memoir of a pioneer, with some references to Slade in Virginia City.

Burns, Eric, *Spirits of America: A Social History of Alcohol* (Philadelphia: Temple University Press, 2004).

Burton, Sir Richard F., *The City of the Saints, and Across the Rocky Mountains to California* (London: Longman, Green, Longman, and Roberts, 1862). The British traveler's account of his journey across the West, 1860, including his meeting with Slade.

Calhoun, Frederick S., *The Lawmen: United States Marshals and Their Deputies: 1789–1989* (Washington, D.C.: Smithsonian Institution Press, 1990).

Callaway, Lew L., *Montana's Righteous Hangmen: The Vigilantes in Action* (Norman: University of Oklahoma Press, 1982). Largely an update of Callaway's *Two True Tales of the Wild West.*

———, *Two True Tales of the Wild West* (Oakland, Calif.: Maud Gonne Press, 1973). Brief dual biography of Slade and his executioner, James Williams. The author (1868–1951), a Montana Supreme Court justice, knew Williams as a youth and empathizes with both of his subjects; he writes judiciously and perceptively but provides no notes or index.

Chapman, Arthur. *The Pony Express: The Record of a Romantic Adventure in Business* (New York: G. P. Putnam's Sons, 1932). Readable first history of the Pony Express.

Clampitt, John W., *Echoes from the Rocky Mountains* (Chicago: Belford, Clarke & Co., 1889). Author, a former federal attorney, offers a broad take on the West, including a chapter defending Slade.

Cody, William F., *The Life of Buffalo Bill* (Hartford: Frank E. Bliss, 1879). Includes Cody's original spurious claim to having been hired by Slade.

Coe, Lewis, *The Telegraph: A History of Morse's Invention and Its Predecessors in the United States* (Jefferson, N.C.: McFarland, 2003).

Collins, Dabney Otis, *The Hanging of 'Bad' Jack Slade* (Denver: Golden Bell Press, 1963). Fictionalized life of Slade by an author who nevertheless researched his subject extensively.

Connell, Evan S., *Son of the Morning Star* (San Francisco: North Point Press, 1984).

Corbett, Christopher, *Orphans Preferred* (New York: Broadway Books, 2003). Historiography of the Pony Express.

Cottingham, Carl D., *Life and Times of General John A. Logan* (Carbondale, Ill.: Kestrel Press, 1989).

Courtwright, David, *Violent Land: Single Men and Social Disorder from the Frontier to the Inner City* (Cambridge, Mass.: Harvard University Press, 1996). Perceptive, valuable work discusses roots of violence on the frontier as well as in the modern inner city.

Coutant, Charles G., *History of Wyoming* (Laramie: Chaplin, Spafford & Mathison, 1899). Early negative view of Slade.

Crawford, Lewis F., *Rekindling Camp Fires: The Exploits of Ben Arnold (Connor)* (Bismarck, N.D.: Capital Book Co., 1926). A pioneer memoir, with some references to Slade.

Davidson, L., *Rocky Mountain Tales* (Norman: University of Oklahoma Press, 1947). Includes section on "Slade's Revenge."

Davis, Rev. Henry T., *Solitary Places Made Glad* (Cincinnati: Cranston & Stowe, 1890).

Davis, Sam P., *History of Nevada* (Reno: Elms Publishing Co., 1913).

DeGroat, Mary Eugenia, *The Kith and Kin of the Darke-Dark Clan in America, 1680–1973* (Birmingham, Ala.: Privately printed, 1974). Includes Slade's maternal family line.

Denton, Sally, *American Massacre: The Tragedy at Mountain Meadows, September 1857* (New York: Vintage Books, 2004). Definitive, well-written work on the famous Mormon massacre.

DeVoto, Bernard, *Across the Wide Missouri* (New York: Bonanza Books, 1947).

Dickson, Arthur Jerome, *Covered Wagon Days* (Cleveland: Arthur H. Clark Co., 1929).

Dictionary of American Biography. 1935 ed. (New York: Charles Scribner's Sons, 1935). Biography of Slade appears on pp. 202–203.

Dimsdale, Thomas J., *Vigilantes of Montana* (1866). 12th ed. (Butte, Mont.: McKee Printing Co., 1950.) The original detailed vigilante history by the organization's leading apologist.

Dorsett, Lyle W., *The Queen City: A History of Denver* (Boulder, Colo.: Pruett Publishing Co., 1977).

Drannan, Capt. Wm. F., *Thirty-One Years on the Plains and in the Mountains* (Boise, Idaho: D&D Book Co., 1899; Chicago: Rhodes & McClure, 1900). Pioneer memoir; mentions Maria Virginia at Slade hanging.

Duffus, R. L., *The Santa Fe Trail* (1930; Albuquerque: University of New Mexico Press, 1972). Classic, definitive work.

Dunn, Susan, *Dominion of Memories: Jefferson, Madison and the Decline of Virginia* (New York: Basic Books, 2007).

Ellingsen, John, with John DeHaas, Tony Dalich, and Ken Sievert, *If These Walls Could Talk* (1977). History of Virginia City (Mont.) buildings.

Erickson, Charlotte, *Invisible Immigrants: The Adaptation of English and Scottish Immigrants in Nineteenth-Century America* (Coral Gables, Fla.: University of Miami Press, 1972).

Farrington, Dora *They Saw America Born* (Privately printed, 1941), Available online at at http://homepages.rootsweb.com/~davidca/america/america.htm.

Fearon, Henry Bradshaw, *Sketches of America: A Narrative of a Journey of 5,000 Miles Through the Eastern and Western States of America* (London: Longman, Hurst, Rees, Orme and Brown, 1818). Some good contemporaneous descriptions of Illinois c. 1816–18.

Ficklin, William H., *A Genealogical History of the Ficklin Family* (Denver: W. H. Kistler Press, 1912). Ben Ficklin's family tree, with biographies.

Floyd, William H. 3rd, *Phantom Riders of the Pony Express* (Philadelphia: Dorrance & Co., 1958).

Fradkin, Philip L. *Stagecoach: Wells Fargo and the American West* (New York: Simon & Schuster, 2002). Company history.

Frederick, James V. *Ben Holladay, The Stagecoach King: A Chapter in the Development of Transcontinental Transportation* (1940) (Lincoln: University of Nebraska Press, 1968, 1989). Biography and study of Holladay, originally written as a dissertation.

Gard, Wayne, *Frontier Justice* (Norman: University of Oklahoma Press, 1949).

Gates, Zethyl, *Mariano Medina: Colorado Mountain Man* (Boulder, Colo.: Johnson Publishing Co., 1981). Some references to Slade's Virginia Dale period.

Gray, Arthur Amos, *Men Who Built the West* (1945) (Freeport, N.Y.: Books for Libraries Press, 1972).

Gray, John S., *Cavalry and Coaches* (Fort Collins, Colo.: Fort Collins Corral of Westerners, Publication no. 1, Old Army Press, 1978). Early history of Fort Collins, Colo.

Hafen, Le Roy, *The Overland Mail, 1849–1869* (Cleveland: Arthur H. Clark Co., 1926). Definitive scholarly study of early overland mail service.

Haines, Aubrey L., *Historic Sites Along the Oregon Trail* (Denver: Denver Service Center, National Park Service, 1973).

Hall, Thomas B., *Medicine on the Santa Fe Trail*. (Dayton, Ohio: Morningside Bookshop, 1971).

Harlow, Alvin F., *Old Wires and New Waves: The History of the Telegraph, Telephone and Wireless* (New York: D. Appleton-Century, 1936).

Haven, Charles Tower, and Frank A. Belden, *A History of the Colt Revolver* (New York: William Morrow, 1940).

Helvey, Frank, "Experiences on the Frontier," pp. 152–154 in *Nebraska Pioneer Reminiscences* (Nebraska Society of the DAR, 1916). Author, born 1841, recounts his experiences as a freighter.

History of Marion and Clinton Counties, Illinois (Philadelphia: Brink, McDonough & Co., 1881). Contains many references to Slade family.

Hosley, William, *Colt: The Making of an American Legend* (Amherst: University of Massachusetts Press, 1996).

Hough, Emerson, *The Story of the Outlaw* (New York: Outing Publishing Co., 1906). An early attempt to write seriously about the West; includes a section on Slade.

Howard, Robert West, *Hoofbeats of Destiny: The Story of the Pony Express* (New York: Signet Books, 1960). A well-written and perceptive history, especially strong on efforts of Buchanan cabinet members to undermine the Union, pre-Civil War. Drawbacks: Lacks index and footnotes; mixes fictitious characters in with real ones.

Hungerford, Edward, *Wells Fargo: Advancing the American Frontier* (New York: Random House, 1949).

Illinois Adjutant General's Office, *Record of the Services of Illinois Soldiers in the Black Hawk War (1831–32) and in the Mexican War (1846–48)*. (1882).

Ingalls, Sheffield, *History of Atchison County, Kansas* (Lawrence: Standard Publishing Co., 1916).

Inman, Colonel Henry, and William F. Cody, *The Great Salt Lake Trail* (New York: Macmillan Co., 1898*)*. Includes Cody's fictitious recollections of working for Slade.

James, Marquis, *The Life of Andrew Jackson*, 2 vols. (Indianapolis: Bobbs-Merrill, 1938).

Johnson, Dorothy M., *Some Went West* (New York: Dodd, Mead, 1965; Lincoln: University of Nebraska Press, 1997). Book about women of the West, including Slade's wife.

_____, *Western Badmen* (New York: Dodd, Mead, 1970).

Langford, Nathaniel, *Vigilante Days and Ways* (1890; Missoula: Montana State University Press, 1957). Classic memoir by a vigilante sympathizer who knew Slade personally; includes a chapter on Slade.

Leeson, Michael A., *A History of Montana, 1739–1885* (Chicago: Warner, Beers & Co., 1885).

Lewin, Jacqueline, and Marilyn Taylor, *On the Winds of Destiny* (St. Joseph, Mo.: Platte Publishers, 2002).

Lindsay, John S., *The Mormons and the Theatre: The History of Theatricals in Utah* (Salt Lake City: Century Printing, 1905). Discusses Jim Kiskadden and Annie Adams.

Livingston, Joel T., *A History of Jasper County Missouri and Its People*, 2 vols. (Chicago: Lewis Publishing Co., 1912).

Loomis, Noel M., *Wells Fargo* (New York: Clarkson Potter, 1968).

Ludlow, Fitz Hugh, *The Heart of the Continent: A Record of Travel Across the Plains and in Oregon* (New York: Hurd and Houghton, 1870). Perceptive memoir; author met Slade at Fort Bridger, spring 1863.

MacMurphy, Harriet S., "The Heroine of the Jules-Slade Tragedy," pp. 322–325 in *Nebraska Pioneer Reminiscences* (Nebraska Society of the Daughters of the American Revolution, 1916). About Jules Beni's widow, Adeline Beckstead.

Madison County (Mont.) Historical Association, *Pioneer Trails and Trials* (1976).

Majors, Alexander, *Seventy Years on the Frontier* (1893) (Lincoln: University of Nebraska Press, 1989). Memoir of freighting titan, unfortunately heavily cut to appeal to mass audience.

Mandat-Grancey, Edmond, *Cow-Boys and Colonels: Narrative of a Journey Across the Prairie and over the Black Hills of Dakota* (1887; Philadelphia: J. B. Lippincott, 1963). Includes discussion of Slade.

Marsh, Charles W., *Recollections, 1837–1910* (Chicago: Farm Implement News Co., 1910). Memoir; its references to Slade are all secondhand.

Mather, R. E., and F. E. Boswell, *Vigilante Victims* (San Jose, Calif.: History West Publishing Co., 1991). Available online at http://montana-vigilantes.org. Revisionist history of Montana vigilantes argues that 1864 turmoil was no simple combat between good and evil, but a power struggle.

Mattes, Merrill J., *Platte River Road Narratives* (Chicago: University of Illinois Press, 1988). Descriptive bibliography of travel over Central Overland route to Oregon and California.

Mattes, Merrill J., and Paul Henderson, *The Pony Express from St. Joseph to Fort Laramie* (St. Louis: Patrice Press, 1989).

McCartney, Samuel Bigger, *Illinois in the Mexican War* (Evanston, Ill.: Northwestern University, 1939). Probably the best source on this arcane subject.

McClernan, John B., *Slade's Wells Fargo Colt: Historical Notes* (Hicksville, N.Y.:

Exposition Press, 1977). A self-published gem of a book. The author, a Montana probate judge, found and scoured Slade's estate papers. Also includes astute analyses of other materials on Slade.

McCormick, Anita Louise, *The Pony Express in American History* (Berkeley Heights, N.J.: Enslow Publishers, 2001).

Michno, Gregory, *Encyclopedia of Indian Wars: Western Battles and Skirmishes, 1850-1890* (Missoula, Mont.: Mountain Press, 2003).

Miller, T. Michael, *Artisans and Merchants of Alexandria, Virginia, 1780-1820* (Bowie, Md.: Heritage Books, 1991–92). Historical catalogue; entries mention Charles Slade, Sr., and family.

_____, *Portrait of a Town: Alexandria, 1820-1830* (Bowie, Md.: Heritage Books, 1995).

Monahan, Doris, *Destination: Denver City* (Athens: Ohio University Press, 1985).

Moody, Ralph, *Stagecoach West* (New York: T. Y. Crowell Co. [1967]).

Moore, H. Miles, *Early History of Leavenworth City and County* (Leavenworth, Kan.: Dodsworth Book Co., 1906).

Morton, J. Sterling, *Illustrated History of Nebraska* (Lincoln: Jacob North & Co., 1907). Vol. II, pp. 180–181, deals with Slade-Jules feud.

Myers, John, *Deaths of the Bravos* (Lincoln: University of Nebraska Press, 1995). Readable Western narrative; chapters 67 and 70 deal with Slade.

National Geographic Society, *Trails West* (Washington, D.C.: National Geographic Society, 1979).

Nelson, John Young, *Fifty Years on the Trail: A True Story of Western Life* (New York: Frederick Warne & Co., 1889). Memoir; author encountered Slade about 1861–62.

Noel, Thomas J., *The City and the Saloon: Denver, 1858-1916* (Boulder: University Press of Colorado, 1996).

O'Dell, Roy P., and Kenneth C. Jessen, *An Ear in His Pocket: The Life of Jack Slade* (Loveland, Colo.: J. V. Publications, 1996). The authors— historians rather than storytellers—have assembled extensive facts about Slade's life within a compact book. They also break new ground with research into Slade's genealogy.

Parkhill, Forbes, *The Law Goes West* (Denver: Sage Books, 1956). Collection of early Western law cases, including Slade's indictment in Denver.

Pauley, Art, *Henry Plummer, Lawman and Outlaw* (White Sulphur Springs, Mont.: Meagher County News, 1980). Only known biography of the Bannack sheriff lynched by Montana vigilantes; author is an intrepid amateur historian.

Peltier, Jerome, ed. and comp., *Banditti of the Rocky Mountains* (Minneapolis: Ross & Haines, 1964).

Pfouts, Paris Swazy, *Four Firsts for a Modest Hero: The Autobiography of Paris Swazy Pfouts* (1868). Edited by Harold Axford (Helena: Grand Lodge, Ancient Free & Accepted Masons of Montana, 1968). Memoir of vigilante president and Virginia City's first mayor devotes only three pages to the vigilante episode.

Pippenger, Wesley E., *Husbands and Wives Associated with Early Alexandria, Virginia* (Westminster, Md.: Willow Bend Book, 2001).

_____, *Marriage and Death Notices from Alexandria, Virginia Newspapers, vol. I: 1784–1838.*

_____, *Marriage and Death Notices from Alexandria, Virginia Newspapers, vol. II: 1838–1852.*

_____, *Tombstone Inscriptions of Alexandria, Virginia, vol. 3.* (Westminster, Md.: Family Line Publications, 1992).

Polk, James K., *The Diary of James K. Polk During His Presidency, 1845–1849,* 4 vols. (Chicago: A. C. McClurg & Co., 1910).

Progressive Men of the State of Montana (Chicago: A. W. Bowen & Co., ca. 1902). Includes biographies of Henry S. Gilbert, Llewellyn L. Callaway.

Prophet, Don, *The Saga of Slade* (New York: Pageant Press, 1958). Fictionalized life of Slade.

Raymer, Robert G., *Montana: The Land and the People* (Chicago: Lewis Publishing Co., 1930). Discusses Slade's hanging.

Reavis, L. U., *Saint Louis: The Future Great City of the World* (St. Louis: C. R. Barns, 1876).

Rhys, Isaac, *Transformation of Virginia, 1740–1790* (Chapel Hill: University of North Carolina Press, 1982).

Richards, Leonard L., *The California Gold Rush and the Coming of the Civil War* (New York: Knopf, 2007).

Ridley, Jasper, *The Freemasons* (New York: Arcade Publishing, 2001). Good definitive history.

Ronan, Margaret, *Frontier Woman: The Story of Mary Ronan, As Told to Margaret Ronan,* Edited by H. G. Merriam (Missoula: University of Montana, 1973). Originally master's thesis, "Memoirs of a Frontier Woman: Mary C. Ronan," Montana State University, 1932. Memoir dictated about 1929 by Mary Ronan (1852–1940), née Molly Sheehan, who witnessed Slade's hanging at age eleven.

Root, Frank A., with William E. Connelley, *The Overland Stage to California* (Topeka, Kan., 1901; reprint: Glorieta, N.M.: Rio Grande Press, 1970). Formidable combination of stagecoach history and memoir, not always accurate but worth mining; author Root was both a Central Overland driver and a journalist. Much on Slade, although the author missed meeting him on the Central Overland by a few months.

Rottenberg, Dan, *The Man Who Made Wall Street: Anthony J. Drexel and the Rise of Modern Finance* (Philadelphia: University of Pennsylvania Press, 2001).

Russell, Don, *Lives and Legends of Buffalo Bill* (Norman: University of Oklahoma Press, 1960).

Rutkow, Ira M., *Bleeding Blue and Gray: Civil War Surgery and the Evolution of American Medicine* (New York: Random House, 2005).

Sabin, Edwin L., *Wild Men of the Wild West* (New York: Thomas Y. Crowell, 1929).

Sanders, Helen Fitzgerald, *A History of Montana* (Chicago: Lewis Publishing Co., 1913. Describes Slade hanging.

Sanders, James W., *Society of Montana Pioneers,* vol. I (Akron, Ohio: Werner Co., 1899).

Sanders, W. F., and Robert T. Taylor, *Biscuits and Badmen: The Sanders' Story in Their Own Words* (Butte, Mont.: Editorial Review Press, 1982). A kind of Sanders family scrapbook; Harriet Sanders's memories of Bannack and Virginia City are especially useful.

Schlesinger, Arthur M., Jr., *The Age of Jackson* (Boston: Little, Brown, 1953).

Scott, Bob, *Slade! The True Story of the Notorious Badman* (Glendo, Wyo.: High Plains Press, 2004). Its misleading title notwithstanding, this is a fictionalized biography. One compensation: It's the only book I've found that attempts to reflect Slade's agony after he was shot by Jules Beni.

Seagraves, Anne, *Soiled Doves: Prostitution in the Early West* (Hayden, Idaho: Wesanne Publications, 1994). Some good insights into Western prostitutes; includes section on Maria Virginia Slade.

Sears, Stephen W., *George B. McClellan: The Young Napoleon* (New York: Ticknor & Fields, 1988).

Sedgwick County (Colo.) History (Privately printed, 1982). Includes section by Esta Fetzer: "Jack Slade— Judge, Jury & Executioner."

Settle, Raymond W., and Mary L. Settle, *Empire on Wheels* (Stanford: Stanford University Press, 1949). First definitive history of Russell, Majors & Waddell by a first-rate scholarly team; worth perusing even though subsequently superseded by the authors' *War Drums and Wagon Wheels.*

———, *Saddles and Spurs: The Pony Express Saga* (Harrisburg, Pa.: Stackpole Co., 1955; University of Nevada Press, 1972). Originally one of the most complete histories of the Pony Express, albeit somewhat dry (the authors' don't seem to have their hearts in their subject as they did for Russell, Majors & Waddell).

———, *War Drums and Wagon Wheels: The Story of Russell, Majors, and Waddell* (Lincoln: University of Nebraska Press, 1966). An updating of the authors' *Empire on Wheels* based on new material they uncovered; very useful, but overlooks some material from the first book.

Shumway, Grant L., *History of Western Nebraska* (Lincoln: Western Publishing & Engraving Co., 1921).

Singletary, Otis A., *The Mexican War* (Chicago: University of Chicago Press, 1960).

Smith, Justin H., *The War with Mexico*, 2 vols. (New York: Macmillan, 1919).

Sommer, Robin L., *History of the U.S. Marshals: The Proud Story of America's Legendary Lawmen* (Philadelphia: Courage Books, 1993).

Standage, Tom, *A History of the World in Six Glasses* (New York: Walker & Co., 2005). Breezy history of beverages.

Strahorn, Carrie Adell, *Fifteen Thousand Miles by Stage* (New York: G. P. Putnam's Sons, 1911, 1915).

Stuart, Granville, *Forty Years on the Frontier*, 2 vols. (Cleveland: Arthur H. Clark Co., 1925). Classic combination of journal and memoir. Author encountered Slade both on Overland Trail and at Virginia City.

Tabbert, Mark A., *American Freemasons: Three Centuries of Building Communities* (New York: New York University Press, 2005).

Thane, Eric *High Border Country* (New York: Duell, Sloan & Pearce, 1942).

Thomas, D. K., *Wild Life in the Rocky Mountains* (C. E. Thomas Publishing Co., 1917). Discuses Slade sympathetically.

Thompson, Robert L., *Wiring a Continent: The History of the Telegraph Industry in the United States, 1832–1866* (Princeton, N.J.: Princeton University Press, 1947).

Toponce, Alexander, *Reminiscences of Alexander Toponce* (Norman: University of Oklahoma Press, 1971). Memoir of a freighter who knew Slade in Denver and Virginia City.

Towle, Virginia Rowe, *Vigilante Woman* (New York: A. S. Barnes & Co., 1966). Book on female companions of outlaws, well written but historically unreliable. Includes a chapter on Slade's wife.

Trenholm, Virginia, *Footprints on the Frontier* (Douglas, Wyo.: Douglas Enterprise Co., 1945. Classic compilation of folk tales, really more a work of folklore than history. Highly critical of Slade.

Trenholm, Virginia, and Maurice Carley, *Wyoming Pageant* (Casper, Wyo.: Prairie Publishing Co., 1946).

Turner, Frederick Jackson, *The Significance of Sections in American History* (1893) (New York: Henry Holt, 1932).

Twain, Mark, *Roughing It* (1872) (New York: Harper & Bros., 1913). Classic of

American folklore; includes three chapters on Slade. Highly readable but unreliable as history.

Urbanek, Mae Bobb, *Ghost Trails of Wyoming* (Boulder, Colo.: Johnson Publishing Co., 1978). Attributes a stagecoach robbery (with seven killings) to Slade at Point of Rocks in 1863. (Unfounded report first circulated in 1880s.)

Utley, Robert M. *Frontiersmen in Blue: The United States Army and the Indian, 1848–1865* (Lincoln: University of Nebraska Press, 1981). Definitive history of U.S. military in the West.

Valencius, Conevery Bolton, *The Health of the Country: How American Settlers Understood Themselves and Their Land* (New York: Basic Books, 2002). Valuable for its discussion of frontier medicine and surgery, especially in St. Louis.

Visscher, William Lightfoot, *The Pony Express: A Thrilling and Truthful History* (1908) (Golden, Colo.: Outbooks, 1980). First book on the Pony Express, but more entertainment than history.

Voorhees, Luke, *Personal Recollections of Pioneer Life,* published by the author, Cheyenne, 1920. Section discusses Slade.

Walker, Henry P., *The Wagonmasters: High Plains Freighting from the Earliest Days of the Santa Fe Trail to 1880* (Norman: University of Oklahoma Press, 1966). Definitive scholarly history of frontier freighting, very well organized and written.

War of the Rebellion: Official Records of the Union and Confederate Armies (Washington, D.C.: Government Printing Office, 1899). Vol. 13, p. 777, contains record of Slade's indictment (1863) for Laporte, Colo., spree, Oct. 1862.

Ware, Capt. Eugene F., *The Indian War of 1864* (New York: St. Martin's Press, 1960). Perceptive first-person account, but written in 1911, when author's memory may have been hazy.

Warren, Louis S., *Buffalo Bill's America: William Cody and the Wild West Show* (New York: Knopf, 2005). Definitive book on Cody carefully exposes his fictitious tales of his youth.

Watrous, Ansel, *History of Larimer County, Colorado* (Fort Collins, Colo.: Courier Printing & Publishing Co., 1911; reprint, MM Publications, 1976). Much material about Slade, Virginia Dale and Laporte, but not always accurate.

Wells, Polk, *Life and Adventures of Polk Wells, the Notorious Outlaw* (Halls, Mo.: G. A. Warnica, 1907). Memoir of an outlaw (1851–1896) who claimed to have met Slade as a boy.

Whitcomb, Elias W., "Reminiscences of a Pioneer, 1857–1869," as told to his daughter Mrs. E. I. Rivenburg, in 1906, *Wyoming Historical Society Collections*, 1920, pp. 84–95. Discusses Slade on pp. 88–92. Memoir of Slade's neighbor at Horseshoe Creek, Wyoming.

White, Jesse, *Origin and Evolution of Illinois Counties.* (Springfield: State of Illinois, 2003).

Winders, Richard Bruce, *Mr. Polk's Army: The American Military Experience in the Mexican War* (College Station: Texas A&M University Press, 1997). Valuable study of U.S. soldiers in Mexican War.

Wolle, M. S., *The Bonanza Trail: Ghost Towns and Mining Camps of the West* (Chicago: Swallow Press, 1953). Includes section on Slade.

Writers Program, Works Progress Administration, *Wyoming* (Oxford University Press, 1941).

Yenne, Bill, *Indian Wars: The Campaign for the American West* (Yardley, Pa.: Westholme Publishing, 2005). Thorough summary of America's Indian wars.

Articles

"A. B. Davis Talks." *Alder Gulch Times,* Sept. 29, 1899. Interview with Vigilante Captain Adriel B. Davis, not to be confused with Judge Alexander Davis.

"Abe Lincoln Made Jack Slade Laugh." *Pony Express Courier*, March 1936, p. 12. Encounter in Atchison in 1859.

Alderson, Mat W., "Some New Slade Stories: Beatty and Horse Thieves." *Bynum* (Mont.) *Herald,* undated, July 1923. In Slade file at Historical Society of Montana.

"Austin, Pioneer, Says Slade Was Innocent Victim." Unidentified newspaper in Slade file at Historical Society of Montana, Sept. 11, 1924. Interview with Jimmy Austin, an employee of Slade.

"Badman from Carlyle Winds up as Funeral Directors' Item, Naturally." *Carlyle* (Ill.) *Banner*, March 18, 1987.

Bailey, W. F., "The Pony Express." *Century Magazine* (1898), p. 882–883.

Beehrer, George W., with Julie Beehrer Colyer, "Freighting Across the Plains." *Montana: The Magazine of Western History* 12, no. 4, 1962, p. 2. Very good description of a westbound Russell, Majors & Waddell freighting expedition, 1858.

Bessette, Amede, "A Story of Joseph A. Slade." *Dillon* (Mont.) *Examiner,* undated, 1914. Contains account of Bartholomew murder. In Slade file at Historical Society of Montana.

Bliss, Edward, "Denver to Salt Lake by Overland Stage in 1862." *Colorado Magazine,* Vol. 8, no. 5, Sept. 1931, pp. 190–91.

Boren, Kerry Ross, "Jack Slade's Grave Located." *Frontier Times* magazine, April–May 1976, pp. 24 ff.

Boulder County (Colo.) *Miner and Farmer,* Feb. 1, 1940. Article re Slade-Jules feud.

Boyack, Hazel, "Old Fort Bridger: Famous Western Outpost." *Annals of Wyoming*

31, no. 2, Oct. 1959.

Brantly, Theodore, "Judicial Department," in *Contributions to the Historical Society of Montana,* vol. IV, 1903 (Helena: Independent Publishing Co.), pp. 109–112. Discusses creation of Montana courts.

Breihan, Carl, "Joe Slade: Gunfighter." *Westerner,* March–April 1972, p. 38.

Brininstool, E.A., "Jack Slade: The 'Good-Bad' Man." *Pony Express Courier* 2, no. 6, Nov. 1935, p. 12.

Brooks, Edwin, "The Bad Man from Bitter Creek." *Pony Express Courier* 1, no. 6, Nov. 1934, pp. 8–9.

Callaway, Lew L., "J. A. Slade: Killer or Victim?" *Montana: The Magazine of Western History,* Jan. 1953, p. 5. Similar to the Slade section of Callaway's book, *Two True Tales of the Wild West.*

"Captained Vigilantes," *Alder Gulch Times,* Sept. 15, 1899, p. 1. About James Williams.

Chapman, Arthur, "Jack Slade, Man-Killer." *Frontier* 1, no. 2, Nov. 1924.

_____, "Slade of the Overland." *Union Pacific,* Jan. 1931.

_____, "Vigilante Vengeance." *Elks,* Aug. 1927. One of the best and most reliable of the earlier Slade biographies.

Clark, A. L., "The Story Maude Adams Never Told." *True West,* May–June 1967, p. 32.

Cody, Col. William F., "The Great West That Was." *Hearst's,* Oct. 1916.

Collins, Dabney Otis, "Vigilante Justice." *Denver Post* magazine, May 14, 1951.

Collister, Oscar, "Life of Oscar Collister," *Annals of Wyoming* 7, no. 1, July 1930, p. 343; also 7, no. 2, Oct. 1930, p. 375. As told to Mrs. Charles Ellis.

Conway, Dan R., "Captain J. A. Slade." *National Motorist,* Sept. 1935, pp. 4 ff.

_____. "The Dr. Jekyl [*sic*] and Mr. Hyde of the Old West," *Rocky Mountain Husbandman,* three parts beginning June 10, 1927. Refers to Slade as "Jack Albert Slade." Extensive three-part series on Slade. In Slade file at Historical Society of Montana.

Coutant, Charles G., "Dwight Fisk, early freighter." *Annals of Wyoming* 4, no. 1, July 1926, pp. 305–307.

Cunningham, Bob, "Slade: A Hard Case Study." *Journal of the West* 30, no. 4, Oct. 1991, pp. 3–8.

Curtis, Olga, "The Killing of Jules: A Deathless Legend." *Denver Post Empire Magazine,* Aug. 12, 1979, p. 28.

Darwin, Wayne, "Who Really Condemned Slade to Hang?" *Western Frontier*, May 1985, pp. 38–60.

"Dead Pioneer Told Stories of Early Days," *Denver Republican*, April 19, 1910. Remembrance of Robert J. Spotswood.

Dearinger, Lowell A., "Sketches from Carlyle." *Outdoor Illinois*, Dec. 1968, pp. 11–14.

Driggs, Howard R., "Wyoming's Wealth of History." *Annals of Wyoming* 23, no. 2, July 1951, p. 57. Reprinted from Casper *Tribune-Herald*, Feb. 18, 1951.

"Drove Stage Which Brought First Mail into Camp of Butte." *Anaconda Standard*, Butte, Mont., June 20, 1920, sec. II, p. 1. Interview with Charles Higganbotham.

Ducomb, Dean, "A Silent Drum Beside the Okaw." In *The Westerners*, New York Posse Brand Book, vol. 4, no. 1, 1957, p. 1.

"Echoes in Alder Gulch," *Kansas City Star,* May 27, 1906, sec. 3, p. 9. Includes 1902 interview with Henry S. Gilbert, also drawing of Slade "sketched from an old photograph."

"Gold Rush Town Tries to Survive on History," *New York Times,* Jan. 11, 1996, p. A20. About Virginia City.

Gray, John S., "The Salt Lake Hockaday Mail." *Annals of Wyoming*: Part I, vol. 56, no. 2, Fall 1984, p. 12 ff; Part II: vol. 57, no. 1, Spring 1985, p. 2 ff. Best definitive summary of John Hockaday and his operations.

Hart, George, "Some Notes on the Early Life of Joseph A. Slade." *Quarterly of the National Association and Center for Outlaw and Lawman History* 5, no. 1, Oct. 1979.

"He Nursed Jim Slade." *Alder Gulch* (Mont.) *Times,* Sept. 22, 1899. Interview with Jim Boner.

"Historic South Pass." *Wind River Mountaineer* 8 no. 4 (Oct.–Dec. 1991), pp. 4 ff.

Hooper, Byron G., Jr., "Slade Is No More." *Overland News*, Denver. Part 1: March 1958 (vol. 1, no. 8). Part II: vol. 1, no. 9, April 1958. Half fiction, unreliable as history.

_____, "Slade of the Overland." *Overland News*, Denver, 1, no. 9, April 1958.

_____, "Upper California Crossing." *Overland News*, Denver, 1, no. 1, Aug. 1957, p. 1.

Housman, R. L., "The Vigilante Movement and Its Press in Montana." *Americana* 35, no. 1, Jan. 1941.

Hughes, Robert D., "The Hanging of 'Captain' Jack Slade." *Wild West*, Aug. 1998, p. 48.

"J. A. Slade: Montana's Early Day Boss Desperado." Helena *Weekly Herald,* July 25,

1878; reprinted from *St. Louis Globe-Democrat*. Interview with Judge Alexander Davis.

"Jack Slade." *Omaha Daily Herald,* Aug. 24, 1871, p. 2, col. 4. Earliest known published use of "Jack" as Slade's first name.

"Jack Slade Couldn't Hold His 'Likker'." *Frontier Times* 10, no. 3, Dec. 1932, pp. 128–131.

"Jack Slade's Last Bum," *Anaconda* (Mont.) *Standard,* May 1, 1892. Anonymous account of Slade's hanging, ostensibly an interview with unnamed rider who fetched Virginia Slade the day of Slade's hanging.

Jenkins, P. W., "Kiskadden-Slade." *Annals of Wyoming* 21, no. 1, Jan. 1949, pp. 88–92.

Jessen, Kenneth, "Our Local Desperado: Jack Slade," *Fort Collins* (Colo.) *Triangle Review,* Part I, Sept. 28, 1994, p. 6; part II, Oct. 5, 1994, p. 3.

"Jim Slade's Help-meet," *Alder Gulch Times,* Virginia City, Mont., Sept. 15, 1899. Interview with C. W. Cannon. Contains good material on Mrs. Slade.

"John S. Jones: Farmer, Freighter, Frontier Promoter." *Missouri Historical Review,* July 1979.

"Joseph Alfred (Jack) Slade." *Montana: The Magazine of Western History* 10, no. 3, Summer 1960, p. 55.

Johnson, Dorothy M., "Flour Famine in Alder Gulch, 1864." *Montana: The Magazine of Western History* 7, no. 1, Jan. 1957, pp. 18–27.

Johnson, Laura Winthrop, "Eight Hundred Miles in an Ambulance." *Lippincott's* 15, June 1875, p. 696. Discusses author's stop at Slade's Horseshoe station.

Joy, Judith, "The Alexandria Connection Suggests a New Theory on How Carlyle Received Its Name." *Centralia* (Ill.) *Sentinel,* Sept. 28, 1980.

"Julesburg Headquarters of Feud in '60s." *Julesburg* (Colo.) *Grit-Advocate,* June 22, 1911. Interview with Lee Cayou, Jules Beni's brother-in-law.

Koch, Hugo, "Early Days in Wyoming." *Lander* (Wyo.) *Wind River Mountaineer,* published in 11 installments from March 6 to May 22, 1908 (except May 15). Valuable description of wagon train led by Slade in 1858.

Legg, John, "Bordeaux's Trading Post." *Old West,* Spring 1989, pp. 46–49.

"Liberal" (pseudonym), "Letter from Salt Lake," *Sacramento Daily Union,* Aug. 15, 1862, p. 1. A defense of Slade's tactics on the Central Overland.

"Life Story of Jack Slade, Carlyle Native." *Carlyle* (Ill.) *Union Banner,* Historical Progress Edition, undated (c. 1954).

Lilley, Charles W., "The Settlement and Early History of Virginia Dale." *Municipal Facts,* Denver, July–Aug. 1929, pp. 12ff.

Lippincott, Rev. Thomas, "Early Days in Madison County #20." *Alton* (Ill.) *Weekly Telegraph*, Feb. 17, 1865. Refers to Charles Slade's family and naming of Carlyle, Ill.

Long, James A., "Old Julesburg: Wickedest City on the Plains." *Frontier Times*, Feb.–March 1964, p. 24.

Lowman, T. J. "Old Toll House Where Slade Lived Before Vigilantes Hanged Him in the Wild Days of the '60s Still Stands." *Bynum* (Mont.) *Herald*, Sept. 25, 1922. In Slade file at Historical Society of Montana.

Mackinnon, William P., "The Buchanan Spoils System and the Utah Expedition: Careers of W. M. F. Magraw and John M. Hockaday." *Utah Historical Quarterly* 31 (1963): 127–150. Critical scholarly article on Magraw and Hockaday.

MacMurphy, Harriet, "Death of Bellevue Woman Removes Last Figure in Jules-Slade Tragedy," Bellevue (Neb.) untitled newspaper, late July 1921. Obituary of Adeline Cayou Beckstead, widow of Jules Beni.

_____, "Some Squatters with a History." *Trans-Mississippian*, Nov. 1897, pp. 4–6. About Jules Beni's widow, Adeline Beckstead, and her family.

McClelland, Frank, "Name of Joseph Slade Figures Prominently in Early History." *Scottsbluff* (Neb.) *Daily Star-Herald*, Nov. 13, 1938, p. 8.

Matson, Simon E., "Leavenworth & Pike's Peak Express." Cheyenne Co. (Kan.) Historical Society, 1984, p. 21.

Mattes, Merrill J., "The Sutlers Store at Fort Laramie." *Annals of Wyoming* 18, no. 2, 1946, pp. 93–125.

Maurer, David A., "Pony Express Pioneer Left His Mark on VMI." *VMI Alumni Review,* Spring 1993, pp. 2–7. Profile of Ben Ficklin.

McMechen, Edgar C., "Slade's Virginia Dale Days." *Union Pacific*, March 1931.

Menefee, Robert P. Interviewed in *The Madisonian*, Virginia City, Mont., Sept. 1, 1899.

Milner, Clyde A. II, "The Shared Memory of Montana Pioneers." *Montana: The Magazine of Western History* 37, no. 1, Winter 1987, pp. 10ff.

Miners Register, Denver, Nov. 14, 1862. Report of Slade's arrest in Denver.

Muir, Florabel, "The Man Who Was Hanged for a Song." *Liberty,* June 30, 1928, pp. 45 ff. Thorough, well-written account of Slade's demise; includes interview with eyewitness J. M. Venable.

Myers, Lee, "Illinois Volunteers in New Mexico, 1847–48." *New Mexico Historical Review* 47, Jan. 1972, pp. 5–31. Valuable study of a rarely investigated subject.

"News from Bannack—Another Man Hung by the Vigilantes." *Union Vedette,* Fort Douglas, Utah, March 25, 1864. Earliest published account of Slade's hanging.

Nickens, Eddie, "Closed But Not Forgotten." *Historic Preservation,* Nov.–Dec. 1995, pp. 14–15. About Virginia City, Mont.

Norcross, Henry C., "121 Years' History of Carlyle and Clinton Co." *Centralia* (Ill.) *Sentinel,* March 15, 1937.

"Old Jule's [*sic*] Bones," *Cheyenne* (Wyo.) *Daily Leader,* April 21, 1889. About discovery of Jules Beni's bones.

"Old Timer Traveled the Old Oregon Trail with Jack Slade" (Tom Rivington), *Guernsey* (Wyo.) *Gazette,* April 8, 1932.

Pace, Dick, "Tuesday Marks 100th Anniversary of Slade Hanging." *Centralia* (Ill.) *Sentinel,* March 10, 1964.

Parker, Mrs. C. F., "Old Julesburg and Fort Sedgwick." *Colorado* 7, no. 4, July 1930, 139–146.

Patterson, Richard, "Did 'Jack' Slade Really Have Four Ears?" *Quarterly of the National Association and Center for Outlaw and Lawman History* 9, Spring 1985, pp. 16–17.

_____, "Mark Twain Meets J. Slade." *Quarterly of the National Association and Center for Outlaw and Lawman History* 11, no. 3, Winter 1987, pp. 17–18.

_____, 'Was 'Jack' Slade an Outlaw?" *Quarterly of the National Association and Center for Outlaw and Lawman History* 9, Spring 1985, pp. 14–15.

Peterson, H., "Notorious Characters of the Pony Express." *Pony Express Courier* 1, no. 3, Aug. 1934, 6–7. Discussion of Slade, "a bad man hired to kill bad men."

Price, Will, "A Pair of Dried Ears." *True West,* March–April 1960, p. 19.

Ramer, C. W. "Experiences in Early Days." *The Trail,* Denver, Nov. 1910, pp. 14 ff.

Reichman, Warren N., "Ninety Years of Controversy Started with Hanging of Joseph A. Slade." *Madisonian,* Virginia City, Mont., May 29, 1953. Extensive piece about Slade that mixes fact and fiction but is often cited as a historical source.

Robbins, Jim, "Virginia City Mines History." *New York Times,* June 1, 1986.

Rolfson, C. M., "Historic Julesburg," *Sterling* (Colo.) newspaper, undated clip, about 1943. At Fort Sedgwick Historical Society, Julesburg, Colo.

Root, George, and Russell K. Hickman, "Pike's Peak Express Companies, Part III: The Platte Route." *Kansas Historical Quarterly* 13, no. 8, Nov. 1945. Definitive scholarly study of overland mail services. Also available online at www.kancoll.org/khq/1945/45_8_roothickman.htm.

_____, "Part IV— The Platte Route, Concluded: The Pony Express and Pacific Telegraph." *Kansas Historical Quarterly* 14, no. 1, Feb. 1946. Definitive scholarly study of overland mail services. Also available online at /www.kancoll.org/khq/1946/46_1_roothickman.htm.

Rosenberg, Robert G., "The Dempsey-Hockaday Trail." *Annals of Wyoming* 54, no. 1 (Spring 1982): 58 ff.

Sayre, Robert H. "Hal Sayre— Fifty-Niner." *Colorado* Magazine, July 1962.

Schindler, Harold, "Here Lies Joseph Slade." *Salt Lake Tribune,* June 19, 1994, p. D1.

"Schoolboys Know of Madman Slade." *Julesburg* (Colo.) *Grit-Advocate,* May 23, 1929.

Shay, Bill, "Horseshoe Creek Crossing and Stage Station." *Annals of Wyoming* 42, no. 2 (Oct. 1970): 259–263.

"Slade the Outlaw." *Helena* (Mont.) *Weekly Herald,* Oct. 19, 1882, p. 1. (Reprinted from *Colorado Gazette.*)

Smurr, J. W. "Afterthoughts on the Vigilantes." *Montana: The Magazine of Western History* 8, no. 2 (Spring 1958): 8–20. Courageous, incisive, groundbreaking academic analysis of Montana vigilantes.

Snyder, J. F. "Charles Slade." *Illinois State Historical Society Journal,* 1903, pp. 207–210. Useful details about life of Slade's father.

Stewart, George R., "Travelers by 'Overland'." *The American West* 5, no. 4, July 1968.

"Telling truths." *Deseret News,* Salt Lake City, July 16, 1862. Refers to critical editorial about Slade in Carson City (Nev.) *Silver Age.*

Trenholm, Virginia, "Save Sibley." *Montana: The Magazine of Western History* 12, no. 4, Autumn 1962, pp. 47–52.

Tresner, Charlene, "Pioneer Remembers Slade." *Fort Collins Review,* undated article.

"Valley Tan" (pseudonym), "How Slade Met His Fate." *Rocky Mountain News,* April 15, 1864. Good account of Slade hanging, written just hours afterward.

"Vigilante Code Written by Masons." *Montana Standard* (Butte), March 16, 1975. Masonic involvement in Montana vigilantes.

Ward, Josiah M., "Slade, the Man with a Dual Personality." *Denver Post,* March 7, 1920.

Whall, Les, "Captain Jack Slade: Central Overland's Violent Enforcer." Magazine title and date unknown (possibly *Frontier Times*), pp. 66–68.

Wheeler, W. F., "Historical Sketch of Louis R. Maillet" (dictated by Maillet). In *Montana Historical Society Contributions,* vol. IV (Helena: Independent Publishing Co., 1903), p. 215.

Whitcomb, E. W., "Alfred Slade at Close Range" (written in 1906). *The Trail,* Nov. 1921, p. 11–15. Recollections of Slade's neighbor at Horseshoe Creek.

White, Owen P., "Slade the Terrible." *Collier's* 98, no. 19, Nov. 7, 1936, p. 42 ff. A quite complete story of the life of Slade.

Wickliffe, Helen Sharp, "Elias Smith Dennis, Forgotten Hero of Carlyle." *Clinton County* (Ill.) *Historical Quarterly* 4, no. 1, Jan.–March 1981, pp. 11 ff.

Williams, Edith R., "Virginia Dale Stage Station on the Overland Route." *Annals of Wyoming* 33, no. 1, 1961, pp. 74–80.

Wilson, James W., "Reminiscences of Overland Days." *Sons of Colorado* 1, no. 12, May 1907, pp. 3–6. Reminiscences of Slade are virtually all secondhand.

Young, Rowland L., "Where the Deer and the Antelope Play." *American Bar Association Journal* 57, June 1971, pp. 577–579.

Manuscripts and Documents

Barry, Anna R., "An Interview with Albert W. Keith." July 13, 1937. From *Indian Pioneer History*, Indian Archives Division, Oklahoma Historical Society, Oklahoma City. Subject claimed descent from Jules Beni.

Chambers, Janette M., "Entering the LaRamie Region." Unpublished paper at Colorado Women's College, March 10, 1958.

"Claim of Ben Holladay." 46th Congress, Second session, U.S. Senate, Miscellaneous Document no. 19, Dec. 17, 1879. Deals with Holladay's claim for losses suffered in Indian raids, 1862–66. Includes affidavits and testimony from Slade, Holladay, Hughes, Spotswood, Street, many more. U.S. Congressional Serial Set.

Cockrell, George, former Slade employee, undated letter to E. W. Whitcomb, referring to Slade's crew burning down Whitcomb's house at Horseshoe. Wyoming Historical Library, Mss. 432B. Also see excerpt in Trenholm, *Footprints on the Frontier*, pp. 70–72,

Davis, Walter N., "Hung for Contempt of Court" (14 leaves). Includes scant mention of Slade but much about vigilantes, the People's Court and the writer's father, Judge Alexander Davis. At Montana Historical Society, Helena, Ms. 978.6 D28.

Dunn, Ruth (Mrs. Guy), "History of California Crossing Shows Its Part in Early Western Travels." Fort Sedgwick (Colo.) Historical Society document.

Ellis, J. K., Memoir of reminiscences, extracted by Jesse Brown, from *San Francisco Examiner* (undated). Manuscript #122C, Wyoming State Historical Library, Cheyenne.

Ford, Aaron T., *Reminiscence* (1903). 108-page manuscript at Montana Historical Society Archives; describes Mrs. Slade galloping in to save Slade from hanging.

Goodwin, Catherine, "Miss Virginia Slade." Six-page manuscript at Clinton County (Ill.) Historical Society by a woman who knew Slade's sister personally.

Hart, A. M., "The Hanging of Slade," manuscript. Sept. 16, 1908. First-person account.

Hockaday, John. M., to George W. Maypenny, Commissioner of Indian Affairs, June 17, 1854. *Annals of Wyoming* 26, no. 2, July 1954, p. 159.

Mangelsdorf, Philip, "The Pony Express." Unpublished source guide and discussion, on file at Atchison (Kan.) Public Library.

"Mark Twain and Jack Slade Entertain at Weber Station in 1862." Typescript of account by Dick Clayton, Coalville, Utah, retelling narrative of Twain–Slade meeting by Tom Riverton. U.S. Works Progress Administration, Series A, Group 3. Both the year and the location are wrong: Twain and Slade met at Rocky Ridge in Aug. 1861.

Marmor, Jason, *An Historical and Archaeological Survey of the Overland/Cherokee Trails,* City of Fort Collins Planning Dept., 1995. Valuable history of Central Overland's shift to its Colorado route in 1862.

McGrath, Maria Davies, *The Real Pioneers of Colorado.* Vol. 3, p. 266 deals with Slade. Denver Museum, Document Division, CWA Project no. 551.

Noyes, A. J., "Recollections of Addison Wolfe," interviewed Corvallis, Ore., Dec. 12, 1915. Manuscript.

Olsen, Barton Clark, "The Vigilantes of Montana: A Second Look." Master's thesis, University of Utah, 1966.

Parker, Mrs. C. F., "A History of Julesburg and Surrounding Country," manuscript, 1927.

Scott, Glenn R., "Geologic map of the Sterling 1 X 2 quadrangle, north–eastern Colorado." U.S. Geol. Survey Misc. Inv. Series Map I–1092, 1979, pp. 7–8.

Tanner, Daniel, "What's in a Name?" unpublished manuscript on origins of Carlyle (Ill.) town name, 1956. Southern Illinois University community development project at Carlyle. On file at Abraham Lincoln Presidential Library, Springfield, Ill.

Trenholm, Virginia Cole, "Historic Glendo (Wyo.)." Travel folder.

U.S. Senate Report, 36th Congress., First session, Report 259 (June 6, 1860). Committee on Post Offices and Post Roads, report regarding House bill no. 513, for the relief of John M. Hockaday and William Liggitt. U.S. Congressional serials set, 1817–1890, Roll 1040. Includes affidavits by Slade and others.

Willson, S. B. B., "Tough Trip Through Hell: The Virginia City Memoirs of S. B. B. Willson," manuscript, 1935. Historical Society of Montana.

Wolfenbarger, Deon K. "A Brief History of Atchison, Kansas." *Atchison Historic Resources Survey Analysis: Summary Report,* Sept. 1998.

LIBRARY COLLECTIONS

Atchison Public Library, Atchison, Kan.

Case–Halstead Library, Carlyle, Ill. Holdings include censuses on microfilm, some scrapbooks.

Clinton County Historical Society, Carlyle, Ill.

Colorado History Museum, Denver.

Fort Collins (Colo.) Public Library. John S. Gray collection includes three volumes of historical notes.

Fort Sedgwick Historical Society, Julesburg, Colo.

Historical Society of Montana, Helena. Slade file includes the probate records of his estate.

Huntington Library, San Marino, California. William B. Waddell Collection contains papers of a partner of Russell, Majors & Waddell, which operated the Pony Express.

Abraham Lincoln Presidential Library, Springfield, Ill. State historical library of Illinois.

Nebraska State Historical Society, Lincoln.

St. Joseph (Mo.) Museum. Materials on Pony Express.

St. Joseph (Mo.) Public Library. Materials on Pony Express.

Thompson–Hickman Memorial Library, Virginia City, Mont.

Western History Center, Denver Public Library. Extensive collection of newspapers, manuscripts, and other materials.

Western Montana College, Dillon, Mont. Papers of late Professor Davidson.

Wyoming State Historical Library, Cheyenne.

INTERNET RESOURCES

Crews, Tom, *Pony Express Home Station Bunkhouse.* June 1997. *http://www.exphomestation.com.*

Pony Express Historical Association. March 14, 1997. http://stjoseph.net/ponyexpress.

Pony Express: Historic Research Study. National Park Service, 1995–2002. At www.nps.gov/poex/hrs/hrs0.htm.

"Pony Express Information," American West, 1996. http://www.americanwest.com/trails/pages/ponyexp1.htm.

Pony Express Museum, St. Joseph, Mo. http://www.ponyexpress.org.

INDEX

POSTSCRIPT

Huntsville, Alabama
October 7, 2009

Dear Dan:

A brief summary of my personal background includes service as a captain in the U.S. Air Force, assigned to the 659th Tactical Hospital from 1968 to 1970 as the unit's dental officer. The 659th was a small air mobile hospital unit in the casualty chain from Vietnam to the United States.

From what I read in *Death of a Gunfighter*, I suspect that Jack Slade suffered permanent physical effects from his gunshot wounds, as well as mental.

Anyone who has known people who were shot will say that virtually all of them are mentally changed by the experience, even if they recover. Physically and mentally, getting shot is not a minor experience. Those of us in the military who know soldiers personally who have been shot will tell you a wounded soldier is a changed soldier.

It takes longer to recover mentally than it does to heal physically. Slade undoubtedly suffered from this effect. An explanation for his erratic behavior may be that he recovered physically but bore mental scars that were not properly treated.

In military medicine, we have learned how to help wounded soldiers recover physically as well as mentally, but in Slade's day only a little was understood about the physical effects of a bullet wound, and nothing about the mental. He was left to his own devices— perhaps only his whiskey— to deal with it. There were no fellow wounded soldiers to tell him, "I know what it is to be shot and you are acting like someone who needs some time to come back. So, stay here with me Buddy, and let's help each other get well." On the other hand, pouring salt into his wounded mental state, Ben Holladay was pushing Slade to get into another gunfight, which is probably the last thing anyone wants to do who has been shot.

Based on the behavior you described, I am pretty sure Slade suffered from post-traumatic stress.

Sincerely,
John DeShazo, D.M.D.

ACKNOWLEDGMENTS

More than fifty years have passed since I first set out to find the real Jack Slade. But time alone would not have sufficed to capture such an elusive figure. This mission couldn't have succeeded without the expertise and moral support of many dozens of knowledgeable people who generously contributed their time and advice. It is a measure of how much time has passed that some of these people have died in the interim and others (including my original literary agent on this project, Julie Fallowfield) have retired. To all who have participated in this project, my appreciation is long overdue.

Foremost among these is a small circle of Slade aficionados who for the past few years have functioned as my de facto advisory board. This group consists of Nelson Ober of Chico, California; Nan Weber Boruff and her sister Georgia Weber of Salt Lake City; Ken Jessen of Loveland, Colorado; and Carolyn Dennis Kress (herself a collateral relative of Slade's stepfather, Elias Dennis) of Sterling, Nebraska. All of these individuals are devoted Slade researchers who selflessly shared their discoveries, documents, and insights with me. Their love of our mutual subject and of the pursuit of knowledge trumped any selfish proprietary concerns they might justifiably have harbored. Ken Jessen went so far as to provide me with digital images of all the illustrations in his book on Slade, saving me huge amounts of time; and Ken, the Weber sisters and Carolyn Kress also reviewed my book manuscript and provided valuable critiques.

A special tribute must be paid to the one member of this group whom I've never met. Nelson Ober, a retired newspaperman, first wrote to me in 1996 after reading my article about Slade that year in *Civilization* magazine. Subsequently we exchanged long and detailed letters analyzing and debating pieces of the Slade puzzle. With the arrival of the Internet in the late 1990s we continued our exchanges by e-mail as well as telephone. Above all, Nelson prodded me to continue my research and to adhere to the most rigorous intellectual standards. Unlike many Western writers, who accept as fact anything found in print, Nelson took the opposite approach: He accepted nothing unless it could be conclusively proven.

In the summer of 2007 Nelson was diagnosed with a melanoma and told he had six months to live. I urged him to emulate our hero and refuse to accept this prognosis. I am happy to report that, at this writing, Nelson is still very much with us, and I hope he'll still be around to enjoy this book— the fruit of our mutual labors.

Three other equally helpful and knowledgeable individuals came on board somewhat later than the others. Ken Jessen's co-author, Roy O'Dell of Cambridge, England, frequently made himself available for e-mail consultations. Two of the leading authorities on the Montana vigilantes, the author Frederick L. Allen, of Atlanta and Bozeman, Mont., and John Ellingsen, history curator of the Montana Heritage Commission in Virginia City, were unstinting in their willingness to respond to my frequent queries, and both men provided valuable critiques of my chapters dealing with Slade's Virginia City period.

In many places I visited, local history buffs and civic leaders generously interrupted their busy schedules to function as my hosts and guides. These included Mary Meyer, Mary Ellen Hughes, and Catherine Goodwin in Carlyle, Ill.; Lee Kizer, Betsy Marquardt, Doris Heath, and Jim Stretesky in Julesburg, Colo.; Margaret Wilson, Betty Amick, and Betty Lancaster in Glendo, Wyo.; Ken Jessen at Virginia Dale, Colo.; John Ellingsen, John Senarius, Lewis Headrick, Roger Williams, Grace Quilici, Matt Stiles, and Jim Edwards in Virginia City, Mont.; and Nan Weber Boruff and Georgia Weber in Salt Lake City.

Librarians and archivists at virtually every institution I contacted went out of their way to be helpful. Rita Holtz, a researcher at the Alexandria Public Library, saved me a trip by personally conducting extensive research into the Slade, Carlyle, and Fairfax families and sending me her findings. Gwenith Podeschi of the Abraham Lincoln Presidential Library in Springfield, Ill., similarly responded to my queries with extensive research and lengthy replies and analyses. Claudia Bosshamer-Bilimek of the Atchison (Kan.) Public Library assembled copies of many items for me even before I arrived there. Mary McKinstry, the dedicated and knowledgeable director of the Fort Sedgwick Museum, in Julesburg, Colo., opened the museum on a Sunday to accommodate my travel schedule and spent much of the day making copies of items I needed. Harold Gentz of the Clinton County Historical Society in Carlyle, Ill., stayed an hour after closing time to allow me to make copies. A relatively obscure question I directed to John Maurath, director of library services at the Missouri Civil War Museum, elicited not only an answer from him but also two contemporaneous news reports about Slade's shooting by Jules Beni in 1860 that had somehow escaped my notice in fifty years of research.

Other librarians and archivists to whom I am indebted for their personal services include Joan Parker Harms and J. Wendel Cox of the Western History Department at the Denver Public Library; Emily Howie of the Library of Congress; Robert Clark, Brian Shovers, Lory Morrow, and Zoe Ann Stoltz of the Montana Historical Society; Vanessa Martin of the Indiana State Library; Jane Ehrenhart, Jan

Perone, and Mary Michals of the Abraham Lincoln Presidential Library in Springfield, Ill.; Dennie Williamson and Wanda Adams of the Leavenworth (Kan.) Public Library; Derald Linn of the Leavenworth County Historical Society; Vicki Thornton of the St. Joseph (Mo.) Public Library; Jacqueline Lewin of the St. Joseph Museum; Matt Piersol, Linda Hein, and Andrea Failing of the Nebraska State Historical Society's library in Lincoln; Curtis Greubel, Suzi Taylor, Jean Brainerd and Natalya Lenz of the Wyoming State Archives in Cheyenne; Tony Castro of the Utah History Research Center in Salt Lake City; Dorothy Minkhaus, Miriam Hiltsman, and Edith Gehrs of the Clinton County Historical Society in Carlyle, Ill.; Jim Roeckeman and Juanita Evans of the Case-Halstead Library in Carlyle; JoAnn Erdall and Faye Rutherford of the Thompson-Hickman Memorial Library in Virginia City, Mont.; Jim Bartlinski of Carlyle House in Alexandria, Va.; Chris Taylor of the Atchison County (Kan.) Historical Society; Dennis Northcutt of the Missouri Historical Society Library in St. Louis; Marc Kollbaum, historian of Jefferson Barracks in St. Louis; Paul Anderson of the Becker Medical Library at Washington U. in St. Louis; Stephen J. Allie of the Frontier Army Museum at Fort Leavenworth; Baird Todd, museum specialist at Fort Laramie National Historic Site, Wyo.; and Robert Manasek of the Scotts Bluff National Monument in Nebraska.

I'm grateful to similarly selfless scholars and experts elsewhere who permitted me to pick their brains in their specialized fields: Professor Michael Zuckerman of the University of Pennsylvania (American history); T. Michael Miller, the city historian of Alexandria (Va.); James Munson (Alexandria history); medical/military historians Robert J. T. Joy, M.D., of the Uniformed Services University, Bethesda, Md., Tom Sweeney, M.D., and Herschel L. Stroud, D.D.S., of the Society of Civil War Surgeons, Conevery Bolton Valencius of Harvard U., and Russell Maulitz, M.D., of Philadelphia; Ronald Bayer, Esq., of Philadelphia, who helped me decipher Charles Slade Sr.'s will and probate file; Larry Silvey of Cheyenne, Wyo. (the two Virginia Slades); John Richley of Leavenworth, Kan., unofficial historian of Fort Leavenworth (military history); David S. Turk, historian of the U.S. Marshals Service (appointments of Charles Slade and Elias Dennis); Professor Richard H. Cracroft of Brigham Young U. (Slade's tombstone); Richard Sevier of Jackson, Miss. (Elias Dennis); Anne Seagraves of Coeur d'Alene, Idaho (Western prostitutes); and Carol DeChant of Chicago (funeral eulogies).

Others who went out of their way to share their knowledge included Mark Edwin Smith, sexton of Salt Lake City Cemetery; Jack French of Fort Collins, Colo.; Agnes Dix and Rheba Massey of the Fort Collins (Colo.) Museum; Rebecca Lintz of the Colorado History Museum in Denver; Chuck Parsons of the National Association and Center for Outlaw and Lawman History; the photograph collector Timothy Gordon of Missoula, Montana; Sally Webb of the Atchison Area Chamber of Commerce; Roberta Cheney of Cameron, Mont.; Carol Dark Ayres of Leavenworth, Kan.; Wayne Sundberg, of Larimer County, Colo.; Harmon Dennis of Horseshoe Bend, Ark., and his son Larry Dennis of Carrollton, Tex.; and Loren Pospisil and Colleen Maser at the Chimney Rock Visitors Center in Wyoming.

My ability to pursue this project over so many years was sustained by moral and financial support from several sources. A magazine assignment in 1995 from Stephen Smith, editor of *Civilization*, enabled me for the first time to travel extensively along Slade's trail. The cost of my travel on several journeys has been defrayed by the hospitality of such friends as Ronald and Jane Gibbs of Denver, Bea Greenberg Montross of Cheyenne, and Karen Kalish of St. Louis. Julie Fallowfield, my first literary agent, championed this project for many years before her retirement in 1996. In the early 1990s Hilary Hinzmann, then my editor at W.W. Norton, provided a useful critique of my initial proposal for a book about Slade. More recently, David Halpern— the literary agent for my friend Alan Richman— perceived the possibilities in a book on Slade and encouraged me to pursue it.

Above all, this book would not have come to pass without the enthusiasm, editorial skill and marketing savvy of Bruce Franklin, who believed in this project even before he launched Westholme Publishing in 2003, and whose astute critiques helped me sharpen and focus a far-flung manuscript. I am also grateful to Westholme's copy editor, Noreen O'Connor-Abel, and Westholme's skilful cartographer, Tracy Dungan. And for the essential service of nailing down the details of my relationship with Westholme I am grateful to my present literary agent, Linda Langton of Langtons International in New York.

Finally, let me express my unbounded gratitude to my wife, who patiently and cheerfully tolerated my frequent absences, not to mention my even more frequent mental absences when I was physically at home in Philadelphia but emotionally back on the Great Plains of the 1850s and 1860s. Little did Barbara realize when she married me forty-four years ago that she would be marrying Jack Slade as well. And little did I realize that I would find the rare spouse who would understand that my passion for my work would reinforce my passion for her. Every writer should be so lucky.

ABOUT THE AUTHOR

DAN ROTTENBERG is the author of ten nonfiction books, most recently *In the Kingdom of Coal*, a narrative history of the U.S. coal industry, and *The Man Who Made Wall Street*, a biography of the nineteenth-century banker Anthony Drexel. His other books include *Revolution On Wall Street*, a chronicle of the securities industry since World War II; *The Inheritor's Handbook*, the first book on inheritance for those on the receiving end; and *Finding Our Fathers*, the first English-language guide to tracing Jewish ancestors.

He has been the chief editor of seven publications, most recently the *Broad Street Review* (broadstreetreview.com), an arts and culture Web site he launched in 2005. He has also written more than 300 articles for such magazines as *Town & Country, Reader's Digest, The New York Times Magazine* and many others. He served as a consultant in 1981 when *Forbes* magazine launched its annual "Forbes 400" list of wealthiest Americans. His syndicated film commentaries appeared in monthly city magazines around the U.S. from 1971 to 1983. Dan Rottenberg is a native of New York City and a 1964 graduate of the University of Pennsylvania. He lives in Philadelphia with his wife.